Florida

Other Travellers' Wildlife Guides

Alaska
Australia: The East
Belize and Northern Guatemala
Brazil: Amazon and Pantanal
Costa Rica
Ecuador and the Galápagos Islands
Hawaii
Peru
Southern Africa
Southern Mexico

Florida

Fiona Sunquist, Mel Sunquist, Les Beletsky

Illustrated by:
Colin Newman (Plates 1–19, 69–106)
Diane Pierce (birds)
H. Douglas Pratt (birds, mammals)

with additional animal art by:
Priscilla Barrett (mammals)
David Beadle (birds)
David Dennis (amphibians and reptiles)
John Sill (birds)

Photographs by:
Kerry Dressler (plants)
Kerry Dressler, Walter Judd, and Brad Stith (habitats)

Contributors:
Richard Francis
Holly Freifeld
Erin Kennedy
Dennis Paulson
Taylor Stein

CHASTLETON TRAVEL
An imprint of Arris Publishing Ltd
Gloucestershire

First published in Great Britain 2008 by

Chastleton Travel
An imprint of Arris Publishing Ltd
12 Main Street
Adlestrop
Moreton-in-Marsh
Gloucestershire GL56 0YN
www.arrisbooks.com

CONTENTS

Preface   ix

Chapter 1. Ecotourism   1
    What Ecotourism Is and Why It's Important   1
    How Ecotourism Helps   2
    History of Ecotourism in Florida (*by Erin Kennedy and Taylor Stein*)   3

Chapter 2. Florida: Geography and Habitats   6
    A Brief Eco-history of Florida   6
    Geography   8
    Geology   10
    Climate and Best Times to Visit   11
    Vegetation: General Characteristics   12
        Florida's Trees   12
        Palms   12
        Citrus   13
        Epiphytes   13
    Major Habitats and Common Plant Species   13
        Upland Ecosystems   14
        Freshwater Ecosystems   18
        Coastal Ecosystems   21

Chapter 3. Parks and Reserves   24
    Introduction   24
    Getting Around   25
    The Great Florida Birding Trail   26
    Fishing   27
    Canoeing   27
    Manatees   27
    Panhandle (PAN)   29
    North Florida (NFL)   31
    Central Florida (CFL)   33
    South Florida (SFL)   37
    Keys and Other Islands (KEY)   40

Chapter 4. Environmental Threats and Conservation Programs
    (by Holly Freifeld)   44
    Major Environmental Threats   44
    Conservation Programs   45
        Return of the Whooping Crane   45
        The Florida Panther: Teetering on the Brink?   46
        Bald Eagle Recovery   46
        Save the Florida Manatee!   47
        Sea Turtles   48
        Florida Forever   48
        Battle For the Everglades   49
        Environmental Close-up 1. Alien Nation: Non-native Species in Florida   50

Chapter 5. How to Use This Book   54

Some Definitions 54
Information in the Family Profiles 55
Information in the Color Plate Sections 60

Chapter 6. **Amphibians** **62**
General Characteristics and Natural History 62
Seeing Amphibians in Florida 64
Family Profiles 65
1. Salamanders 65
2. Toads and Toad-like Frogs 67
3. Treefrogs 69
4. True Frogs 71
Environmental Close-up 2. Frog Population Declines 72

Chapter 7. **Reptiles** **75**
General Characteristics and Natural History 75
Seeing Reptiles in Florida 78
Family Profiles 79
1. Crocodilians 79
2. Turtles 81
3. Colubrid Snakes 86
4. Venomous Snakes – Elapids 89
5. Venomous Snakes – Viperids 90
6. Geckos 93
7. Iguanids – Anoles and Spiny Lizards 94
8. Skinks and Whiptails 95
9. Glass Lizards 97
Environmental Close-up 3. Living with Alligators 98

Chapter 8. **Birds (by Dennis Paulson)** **100**
Birds: Animals to Watch 101
General Characteristics and Natural History 102
Seeing Birds in Florida 103
Family Profiles 104
1. Loons and Grebes 104
2. Pelicans and Their Relatives 106
3. Long-legged Waders 110
4. Waterfowl 114
5. Raptors 117
6. Chickenlike Birds 123
7. Cranes, Limpkin, and Rails 125
8. Shorebirds 129
9. Gulls, Terns, and Skimmers 133
10. Pigeons and Doves 136
11. Parrots 139
12. Cuckoos 142
13. Owls 144
14. Nightjars 146
15. Hummingbirds 147
16. Kingfishers 150
17. Woodpeckers 152
18. Flycatchers 154
19. Swallows and Swifts 156
20. Crows and Jays 159
21. Titmice and Nuthatches 161
22. Wrens 163
23. Kinglets and Gnatcatchers 165

24. Thrushes — 166
25. Mockingbirds and Thrashers — 168
26. Miscellaneous Perching Birds — 169
27. Vireos — 172
28. Warblers — 173
29. Blackbirds and Starlings — 176
30. Tanagers and Cardinal Grosbeaks — 179
31. Sparrows and Finches — 182
Environmental Close-up 4. Why Is Florida So Full of Exotic Birds? — 187
Environmental Close-up 5. The Advantages of Colonial Nesting — 188

Chapter 9. Mammals — **190**
Introduction — 190
General Characteristics of Mammals — 191
Classification of Mammals — 191
Seeing Mammals in Florida — 192
Family Profiles — 193
1. Opossum — 193
2. Armadillo — 195
3. Bats — 197
Carnivores — 201
4. Raccoon — 202
5. Coyote and Foxes — 204
6. Bear — 205
7. Skunks and Otters — 207
8. Cats — 209
9. Marine Mammals — 212
10. Pigs and Deer — 213
11. Rodents – Mice, Rats, and Pocket Gopher — 215
12. Rodents – Squirrels — 217
13. Rabbits and Hares — 219
Environmental Close-up 6. Reducing Roadkill — 221

Chapter 10. Insects and Other Arthropods (by Dennis Paulson) — **223**
General Characteristics and Natural History — 223
Seeing Insects in Florida — 224

Chapter 11. Coral Reef Wildlife (by Richard Francis) — **226**

References and Additional Reading — **231**

Habitat Photos — **233**

Identification Plates — **247**

Species Index — **489**

General Index — **508**

PREFACE

This book is one of a series intended for the ecotravellers of the world – travellers who are interested in their environment, the sort of people for whom the best part of any trip is 'the day we saw those monkeys' or 'that time we saw the snake eating a frog.' The purpose of the book is to enhance enjoyment of a trip to Florida by helping the visitor to identify the wildlife and plants that he or she is likely to encounter, and to learn a little about wildlife ecology and behavior. The book includes color illustrations of 85 species of amphibians and reptiles, 60 insects, 35 mammals and about 200 birds, in addition to information on the many aquatic inhabitants of Florida's rivers, lakes and coasts (and 175 color illustrations of common reef fish and other marine species).

The idea for these books grew out of our own travel experiences and our perceived need to have a single guidebook to all the wildlife of a region. There are lots of excellent field-guides to birds or mammals or plants, etc., which are fine for the committed birdwatcher or the specialist in lizards, say, or orchids. But the traveller who is interested in birds, lizards, orchids and more can end up dragging a whole library around in a suitcase. What we wanted was one volume to carry with us that would cover everything we were likely to see on our travels, as thorough yet concise as possible, with an indication, when available, of the conservation status of each species or animal group. This book fulfills these needs.

We hope that you will find this guide to Florida's wildlife useful and interesting. Please let us know of any errors you may find, as well as suggestions for future editions. Write to us care of the publisher or e-mail us at ECOTRAVEL8@aol.com (there is also a website for this series of books. www.harcourt-international.com/ecotraveller). However, before you write to us about scientific classifications in the book, we should make one point in our defense. With modern molecular methods being used to compare species, the whole subject of classification is undergoing radical change. Even common species are being reclassified nowadays, after comparative studies of their DNA, and the research is so new that biologists are still arguing about the results. We cannot guarantee that the classifications we have used are absolutely the last word on the subject, or that we have been wholly consistent. But future editions of the book will keep up with developments.

Before we proceed we must acknowledge the help of many people. First, most of the information here comes from published sources, so we owe the authors of those scientific papers and books a great deal of credit (see References and Additional Reading, p. 231). Special thanks to Erin Kennedy and Taylor Stein (University of Florida) for writing the Chapter 1 section on Florida ecotourism, Holly Freifeld for writing Chapter 4 on environmental threats and conservation and the close-up essay on alien species, Dick Franz (Florida Museum of Natural History) for lending his expertise to Chapters 6 and 7 on amphibians and reptiles, Dennis Paulson (Slater Museum of Natural History, University of Puget Sound) for writing Chapters 8 and 10 on birds and insects and providing other information and advice, Richard Francis (California Academy of Sciences) for writing Chapter 11 on coral reef wildlife and the fish plate captions, and Martha Crump for help with the close-up essay on frog population declines. We are also grateful to Mike Manetz, Ellen Thoms, and Felicity Trueblood for their help and expertise. Also thanks to Bob and Kerry Dressler for providing habitat and plant photographs and for writing the plant plate captions. Also thanks to the artists who produced the wonderful illustrations, mainly Colin Newman (amphibians, reptiles, insects, and marine species), Diane Pierce (birds), Douglas Pratt (birds, mammals), and Jeff Parker (habitat illustrations in Chapter 2). Judith Hayter's editorial advice and expertise was very much appreciated, as was the assistance of our editor at Academic Press, Andrew Richford, and his assistant editor, Samantha Fallon.

Finally a word for you, the reader: have a great trip to Florida!

Chapter 1

ECOTOURISM

- *What Ecotourism Is and Why It's Important*
- *How Ecotourism Helps*
- *History of Ecotourism in Florida (by Erin Kennedy and Taylor Stein)*

What Ecotourism Is and Why It's Important

Ecotourism is a subspecies of tourism undertaken by the environmentally concerned. It is a manifestation of our growing interest in the environment around us, and our wish to know more. Specifically, *ecotourism*, or *ecotravel*, is travel to destinations to admire and enjoy wildlife and relatively undisturbed natural areas, as well as indigenous cultures. Aside from pleasure and learning opportunities, a major goal of ecotourism is that travellers want to help conserve the very places – habitats and wildlife – that they visit. That is, through a portion of their tour cost and spending into the local economy of destinations – paying for park admissions, engaging local guides, staying at local hotels, eating at local restaurants, using local transportation services, etc. – ecotourists help to preserve natural areas. Travel for pleasure, once the preserve of a privileged elite, is now within reach of nearly everyone in developed nations; and this new mobility, coupled with an escalating concern for the natural world, has given rise to the sort of travel that allows us to satisfy our curiosity and our conscience at the same time.

There can be few people in the developed world who are not aware of the alarming deterioration in our planet's health. We learn about it in school and through the news media. Species are disappearing, wild habitats are shrinking, and the ice caps are melting – all thanks to the actions of our own species. If there is any ray of light it is that now, at the eleventh hour, we are waking up to the threat. We are becoming conscious of the value and beauty of so much that is on the verge of extinction, and beginning to understand that it is important to conserve *biodiversity* (the different types of animals, plants, and other life forms found within a region) – for our own sake, as well as for the sake of those vanishing species. We have all heard those announcements on the news: botanists and pharmaceutical researchers have developed a new wonder drug that derives from a rare plant found only in the tropical forest. A quarter of all drugs sold in the USA come from natural sources – plants and animals – and if we destroy those sources we are in effect denying important medical help to our children and grandchildren. Ecotourism can help protect natural areas and provide incentives to conserve habitats and species.

Ecotourism also enables us to demonstrate our personal concern towards the conservation of wildlife and their habitats. For instance, not everyone will have the time to volunteer active participation in a river conservation and park program, but we can all contribute by supporting the program with park admission fees. Moreover, the ecotourist is by definition a more thoughtful tourist. By choosing not only where to go but how to go, and how to behave when we get there, we can involve ourselves in an area's conservation. Instead of packing Florida's beaches, we can visit state parks. We can opt occasionally to leave the sports utility vehicle behind while we walk along a forest trail, or canoe or float down the river in an inner-tube. By simply visiting the wild places, and showing our respect for the wildness, we also endorse the work of those who are endeavoring to fight against others who wish to exploit wild places for short-term commercial gain.

How Ecotourism Helps

The economic benefits of ecotourism to a local community are clear. By paying admission fees to enter a park, or by hiring a local guide, the visitor makes a financial contribution to the local economy. That contribution might be used directly, to manage and protect wild areas; or, less directly but just as important, it might provide employment, and thereby encourage local participation and support for sites in need of ecological protection. Also, ecotourism sites tend to be in rural areas, which ordinarily do not warrant much attention, still less development funding, from a central government. But a central government knows a valuable commodity when it sees one, and a popular tourist site is worth supporting. Ecotourism 'works' because local people benefit economically as much or more by preserving habitats and wildlife for continuing use by eco-travellers than they could by 'harvesting' the habitats for short-term gain. Put another way, local people often can sustain themselves better economically by participating in ecotourism than by, for instance, cutting down forests for lumber or hunting animals for meat or the pet trade.

The investment costs involved in developing and maintaining an ecotourist site are minor compared with those for a traditional tourist site because eco-tourists do not require the same infrastructure – paved streets, luxury hotels, and fast-food outlets on every other corner. The profits from ecotourism can be less immediate, it is true, but no one can deny the benefits to education and conservation. As people, local and foreign, visit wild areas they learn more about the sites – from books, from guides, from exhibits, and from their own observations. They come away with an enhanced appreciation of nature and ecology, an increased understanding of the need for preservation, and almost certainly a greater inclination to support conservation measures.

The conscientious visitor will maximize his or her positive contribution to an area, and reduce the negative impact, by keeping alert to the needs of wildlife and habitat preservation. Whether travelling independently or with a tour group, an ecotourist needs to be selective. In this context it might be useful to quote the basic ecotourism guidelines established by international conservation organizations. The United Nations Environmental Programme (UNEP), the International Union for Conservation of Nature (IUCN), and the World Resources Institute (WRI) advise that tours and tour operators should:

- provide significant benefits for local residents; involve local communities in tour planning and implementation;
- contribute to the sustainable management of natural resources;
- incorporate environmental education for tourists and residents;
- manage tours to minimize negative impacts on the environment and local culture.

For example, tour companies could:

- make contributions to the parks or areas visited; support or sponsor small, local environmental projects;
- employ local residents as tour assistants, guides or naturalists;
- wherever possible use local products, transportation, food and locally owned lodging and other services;
- keep tour groups small to minimize negative impact on visited sites; educate ecotourists about local cultures as well as habitat and wildlife;
- co-operate with researchers;

No committed ecotourist will need to be told to disturb wildlife and habitats as little as possible, to stay on the trails and pick up any litter, and to respect local cultures and rules.

The History of Ecotourism in Florida

by Erin Kennedy
Department of Anthropology, University of Florida

and Taylor Stein
School of Forest Resources and Conservation, University of Florida

Florida lures millions of tourists every year with the promise of abundant sunshine, world-famous theme parks, and beautiful, natural scenery. Whether trips are intended as relaxing escapes to the beach or as exciting outdoor adventures, Florida remains one of the top tourist destinations in the United States. In 1999, the Sunshine State hosted approximately 59 million tourists, making it the third most visited state behind Texas and California. These visits contributed $46.7 billion to the Florida economy in 1999, and from the mid–20th century to the present, tourism has generated more money each year than any other industry in the state.

Walt Disney World and its associated attractions, Busch Gardens, Sea World and Universal Studios, remain Florida's primary tourist enticements. The world-wide popularity of these theme parks has brought huge amounts of money to the state, but their fame has also come to overshadow the diversity of Florida's vacation possibilities. In reality, Florida has an immense supply of unique natural wonders just waiting to be discovered. With millions of acres of protected natural areas, the Florida visitor does not have to go far to experience some of the most amazing natural environments in the USA. Travellers can view Roseate Spoonbills and Crested Caracaras in Florida's state parks, or swim with endangered manatees in one of several estuaries along the Florida coast. In fact, recent tourism studies suggest that visitors are beginning to discover these hidden treasures and there is a growing desire among many tourists to incorporate Florida's parks and wildlife into their travel itineraries.

Marketing Florida's natural ecology to tourists, however, is not a novel idea. Almost 100 years before Disney, the state's early tourists came in search of Florida's mild winters, and 1900 km (1200 miles) of sandy beaches. Northerners had been travelling to Florida for health reasons since before the Civil War, but leisure-based travel to the state truly burgeoned during the last two decades of the 19th century. Popular activities for these early travellers included stays at seacoast hotels and strolling, bicycling, or riding in horse-drawn carriages along the coastal beaches. Florida's scenic springs and rivers were an additional draw. Paddlewheel steamboats cruised visitors down the St. John's, Suwannee and Apalachicola Rivers for a glimpse of Florida's wildlife and lush interior wilderness, and glass-bottom boats, invented on site in 1878, allowed visitors to view Silver Spring's underwater wonders.

The opening of Florida's frontier at this time was largely due to the rapid expansion of railroads throughout the state. Innovative industrialists, such as Henry M. Flagler, worked to increase the total rail system from 880 km (550 miles) in 1881 to 5600 km (3500 miles) in 1900. Flagler, a former partner of John D. Rockefeller, constructed the Florida East Coast Railroad, which extended all the way from Jacksonville to Key West. This ambitious endeavor brought new tourist and development opportunities to eastern and southern Florida with the start of the 20th century.

Fifty years later, during what is known as the '1950 boom,' 4.5 million tourists entered the state by car, bus, airplane or train, and almost one million automobiles entered Florida for recreational purposes. This trend showed no signs of slowing, and with the opening of Walt Disney World in 1971, and Epcot Center in 1982, Florida began drawing more tourists each year than it had residents.

While the commercial aspect of Florida's tourist industry is well established, the past decade has seen an increase in the number of visitors who want to experience Florida's 'more natural' recreation activities. Research by the National Parks Service shows that between 1989 and 1993 the number of visitors to Florida's national parks and monuments rose 12%, compared with a 5.9% rise in the total number of visitors to the state.

Florida is an excellent choice for year-round hiking, biking, swimming and snorkeling, but its superb wildlife viewing is a main attraction. Although there is little topographic variation throughout the state, subtle changes in elevation, water drainage and climate produce a great variety of vegetation habitats, and hence a huge diversity of wildlife. An estimated 179 bird species breed in Florida and an additional 300 species arrive each year as seasonal migrants. In addition, Florida is home to the largest population of Bald Eagles outside of Alaska, and is the only place in North America where one can view the Snail Kite, Short-tailed Hawk, Smooth-billed Ani, Mangrove Cuckoo, Black-whiskered Vireo, and White-crowned Pigeon. These statistics bode well for Florida's eco-tourism industry, as birdwatching, or 'birding,' has become the nation's fastest-growing recreational activity.

For those visitors who aren't avid birders, there are plenty of other wildlife attractions to experience. A trip to any one of Florida's more than 7800 lakes and rivers is almost certain to include a sighting of the Florida alligator, which is only one of the state's 141 known species of reptiles and amphibians. A watchful and adventurous ecotraveller may also come in search of Florida's charismatic mammals, which include Black Bear, Bobcat, River Otter, West Indian Manatee, and if one is exceptionally lucky, the Florida Panther.

Statistics emphasizing the growing demand for Florida's watchable wildlife activities have not been lost on the state government and conservation agencies. Almost one half of the state's wetlands and one quarter of its forests have been lost to the needs of Florida's ever-growing population, which gains 700 new residents per day. The key to protecting Florida's wildlife is the preservation of suitable habitat, and Florida has responded to this environmental degradation with the largest and most ambitious land acquisition program in the USA. Passed by the state legislature in 1990, the Preservation 2000 Act provided up to $300 million per year for the acquisition of ecologically valuable land during the 1990s. Florida residents acknowledged the program's success by passing an extension of its funding (The Florida Forever Program; p. 48) with over 70% support.

The protection of Florida's wildlife is also advantageous to the state's economy because wildlife-watching represents a significant and growing part of Florida's tourism market. For instance, in 1996, individuals enjoying the state's watchable wildlife activities spent a total of $1.7 billion. To put this figure in perspective, wildlife recreation in Florida generated nearly twice as much money as the worldwide box office sales from the film Titanic. Many Floridians also gain their personal livelihood from Florida's rich ecological diversity; in fact, wildlife watching activities employ six times more people than the combined number employed by the cities of Tampa and Miami. Even state agencies with non-recreation missions, such as the Florida Division of Forestry and the Fish and Wildlife Conservation Commission, are venturing into nature-based recreation programs with the cooperation of public and private landowners. These initiatives are leading to ambitious projects such as the Great Florida Birding Trail, a 3200-km (2000-mile) route intended for hiking and driving through the state's prime bird habitat (p. 26).

As every ecotraveller would hope, ecotourism is now exhibiting a much greater influence on Florida policy and land management decision-making. More land management agencies, as well as private landowners, are beginning to understand the value of protecting Florida's natural areas, as well as developing and marketing nature-based recreation opportunities. As this trend continues, Florida will move beyond its best-known but limited image as the home of Mickey Mouse and sun-soaked beaches and garner a reputation for what it actually is – an ecotravel gem. Be prepared and enjoy!

Chapter 2

FLORIDA:
GEOGRAPHY AND HABITATS

- *A Brief Eco-history of Southern Mexico*
- *Geography*
- *Geology*
- *Climate and Best Times to Visit*
- *Vegetation: General Characteristics*
  Florida's Trees
  Palms
  Citrus
  Epiphytes
- *Major Habitats and Common Plant Species*
  Upland Ecosystems
  Freshwater Ecosystems
  Coastal Ecosystems

A Brief Eco-history of Florida

The mammal section of the Pleistocene edition of the Ecotravellers' Wildlife Guide to Florida would have looked somewhat different from its counterpart in this book. Though the landscape and vegetation were much the same as today, Pleistocene (12,000 years to 2 million years ago) Florida had many more large mammals. Mammoths, Capybara, tapir and huge, tortoise-like glyptodonts grazed along the riverbanks. Giant armadillos, llamas, and giant ground sloths lived in the forested uplands. Predators such as the cave bear, Jaguar, Puma, and Ocelot prowled the forests and prairies. Surprisingly, the bird section would have looked fairly similar. As well as many of the mammal species mentioned, a 120,000-year-old Pleistocene site in Reddick, near Ocala, has produced fossils of more than 50 species of birds, including ibis, grebes, ducks, raptors, turkeys, owls and woodpeckers. Apart from the many introduced exotics (non-native species), Florida's reptile fauna has also remained relatively unchanged. The same fossil site near Ocala yielded 20 species of snakes and five lizards, as well as Box Turtles, soft-shelled turtles, and Gopher Tortoises, all species still found in Florida today.

By the end of the Pleistocene, some 12,000 years ago, most of the large mammals were extinct. Early hunter-gatherers known as Paleoindians entered Florida around 10,000 BC, overlapping for a short time with some of the larger mammals. Mammoths, mastodons, camels, and horses became extinct shortly after the end of the Pleistocene, perhaps in part because of human exploitation. By 3000 BC there were human settlements in coastal wetland regions throughout Florida. Most of these settlements were dependent on shellfish, and you can still find extensive shell middens (piles of shells discarded by Paleoindians) along the coast, especially in southwest Florida.

The first encounter between the indigenous people of Florida and Europeans took place about 500 years ago. Though others may have reached the peninsula before him, Juan Ponce de Leon is generally credited with being the person to 'discover' Florida. The landing occurred on April 2, 1513, and Ponce de Leon named the place 'La Florida' because, as historian Antonio de Herrera later wrote, 'it was very pretty to behold with many and refreshing trees. And it was flat, and even: and also because they discovered it at the time of Flowery Easter.' A recent resailing of the route suggests that the landing site was near Melbourne Beach, south of Cape Canaveral (Map 1, p. 9).

In 1819, after several alternating periods of Spanish, French and British rule, Spain and the USA signed a treaty of cession by which, in return for Florida, the USA would assume five million dollars worth of Spanish debt. At the time, Florida's population numbered fewer than 8000 people. In 1845, Florida became the 27th State of the American Union and rapid economic growth followed. The population grew from 70,000 in 1845 to more than 140,000 by 1860. After the Civil War ended in 1865, thousands of small-time farmers from Georgia, Alabama, and the Carolinas moved south. Most settled in the northern and central portions of the state; south Florida remained almost uninhabited, with fewer than two inhabitants per square mile.

Beginning in the 1880s, railroads opened up the state to all comers. A railroad magnate, Henry Flagler, built magnificent tourist hotels in St. Augustine and later at Palm Beach, to accommodate people who wished to spend the winter in Florida. Northerners came by the thousands, attracted to the warm climate and sunshine. By 1950, tourism had taken the lead over agriculture as the state's leading revenue producer.

But the long growing season and frost-free climate ensured that agriculture would continue to shape the landscape and play a major role in the state's economy. In the 1940s Florida established itself as a major producer of vegetables. The rich dark soil of the now-drained northern Everglades produced tomatoes, cucumbers, celery, and beans – by 1943 vegetables were being shipped to northern states in refrigerated railroad cars. Sugar cane fields covered the once-flooded land around Lake Okeechobee, and the citrus industry discovered how to turn oranges (Plate C) into frozen concentrate. Growers planted oranges over thousands of hectares of central Florida.

The post-World War II era experienced dramatic growth in urban areas, spurred on by the increasing availability of residential air-conditioning. Florida invested heavily in a state-wide road system, to accommodate the growing tourism business and to unify a diverse population of over 2.7 million people. Vast areas of native forests were logged and replaced with pine plantations to meet the increased demand for wood products. Urbanization continued its expansion in the 1960s and 1970s, and by 1980 the state's population had reached 9 million. During the 1980s, new residents poured into Florida at the rate of 950 a day. Half of them were senior citizens looking for affordable retirement homes in a warm climate. Shopping malls, retirement communities, rest homes, and golf courses mushroomed across the State and the uncontrolled growth caused major problems. Urban sprawl marred once-pristine landscapes, producing what University of Florida historian Michael Gannon calls 'a descent into terminal tackiness.'

Visitors travelling around Florida cannot fail to notice this blight. Get off the beaten path and you will surely encounter faded billboards, garish signs, worn roadside 'attractions,' dilapidated trailers and crackerbox architecture. But, sandwiched somewhere between the tackiness and the theme parks, there is another Florida. In this Florida, Magnificent Frigatebirds soar over tropical mangrove islands. Manatees and otters swim in crystal-clear rivers lined with moss-draped oaks. Rafts of wintering ducks crowd the marshes of the Gulf coast barrier islands. In this Florida, within a two-hour drive of Orlando, you can spend the day collecting shells and sharks' teeth on a tropical Gulf coast beach or watch Sandhill Cranes bugle and dance on a native prairie. If you are lucky, you might even find a fossilized tooth of a mammoth, or the bones of a giant ground sloth in one of the springs.

Geography

Florida is a 725-km (450-mile) long, thumb-shaped peninsula that projects southwards from the southeastern USA (Map 1, p. 9). Beyond the peninsula lies the Florida Keys, a string of more than 100 coral reef and limestone islands that run southwest some 290 km (180 miles) from Biscayne Bay to the Dry Tortugas. From Key Largo to Key West, the islands are connected by a highway (U.S. 1). Though the road ends at Key West, the islands continue, and a further 112 km (70 miles) to the west lies a cluster of remote islands known as the Dry Tortugas.

About 151,670 sq km (58,560 sq miles) in size, Florida is larger than England and Wales or Greece. Florida is bounded by the states Georgia and Alabama to the north, the Atlantic Ocean to the east and the Gulf of Mexico to the west. With about 14 million people, Florida is the fourth most populous state in the USA, trailing California, New York, and Texas. Jacksonville is the largest city, with 700,000+ people, but the Miami-Ft. Lauderdale region is the most populous metropolitan area, with more than 3 million people. Florida is without a doubt one of the fastest-growing states in the USA. Between 1980 and 1990 the state's population increased by 32.8%. By 2025, it is projected to be the third most populous state, with 20.7 million people. Florida's famous sandy beaches account for about 1200 km (750 miles) of the state's 1900 km (1200 miles) of coastline. However, when the Keys and other numerous offshore islands (4500+) are included, the state has more than 12,800 km (8000 miles) of shoreline, second among states only to Alaska.

No part of Florida is more than 96 km (60 miles) from one of its famous beaches, which are consistently rated among the nation's best. University of

Map 1   Florida, showing main cities and towns, rivers, lakes, highways, and the current extent of the Everglades marsh habitat of South Florida.

Maryland coastal geologist Stephen Leatherman rated the nation's beaches on everything from water quality and temperature to scenic beauty. Five Florida beaches – Bahia Honda, Grayton Beach, St. Georges Island, Caladesi Island and Crandon Park – were listed among the USA's top 10.

In the text, we divide Florida into five major geographical regions: *Panhandle, North Florida, Central Florida, South Florida,* and *Keys and Other Islands* (Map 2, p. 28). The Panhandle extends from west Florida eastward to about the Suwannee River. North Florida extends from the Georgia border south to a line that runs from Cedar Key across to Daytona Beach. Central Florida is the next block and extends from coast to coast south to a line north of Lake Okeechobee. South Florida extends from north of the lake to the southern tip of the mainland. The Keys (see Map 3, p. 41) includes the chain of islands from Biscayne Bay to Key West and the Dry Tortugas.

Geology

Ancient rocks deep beneath the surface show that Florida is a fragment of northwest Africa, left attached to North America as, eons ago, the great super-continents split apart, collided and split again. Above this fragment lies a layer of limestone bedrock, formed from the shells and skeletons of marine organisms. As sea levels rose and fell the limestone was eroded by wind, water, and waves, then submerged under new sediments. If you look closely, Florida's marine origins are everywhere. The low central ridge that forms the backbone of north and central Florida was once a coastal dune and just about every piece of rock in the state contains marine fossils.

Florida's current shape is quite recent: the state's general outline has looked like this for only a few thousand years. Some 20,000 years ago, when sea levels were approximately 90 m (300 ft) lower than they are today, the state was nearly double its present size.

As you fly or drive across Florida one of the first things you notice is that it is extremely flat. The highest point in peninsular Florida is not much more than 60 m (200 ft) above sea level. A backbone of sorts, the Trail Ridge and Lake Wales Ridge form a spine down the middle of the state almost as far south as Lake Okeechobee. South of this lake, the entire peninsula is generally less than 8 m (26 ft) above sea level.

As anyone who farms or gardens in Florida will tell you, the state does not have soil, it has sand. Where the sand has been washed away you can see the underlying limestone. In many places the limestone has been dissolved, creating sinkholes and streams that vanish underground and reappear somewhere else as springs. Many of north Florida's lakes have formed in basins that were sinkholes. The state has about 7800 lakes, which range from half-hectare (one-acre) ponds to Lake Okeechobee, which covers an area of 181,000 hectares (448,000 acres).

Florida is a fossil hunter's paradise. You don't need a pick and shovel, just a good eye. Unlike the fossils of the American Northwest, few Florida fossils are encased in rock. They are more likely to be found lying loose on the beach or among the gravel of a small stream. The fossilized remains of large mammals such as saber-toothed tigers, giant ground sloths, and cave bears are abundant in Florida's caves, sinkholes and rivers. It used to be quite common to come across a 2-kg (4.4-lb) tooth of Ice Age mammoths in the Ichnetucknee or Withlacoochee rivers; one can still find smaller teeth, bones and the occasional whale vertebra in the cold, clear waters of these waterways.

Fossil sea shells are common in the banks of rivers, and much of the state's limestone bedrock is made up of the shells of animals that lived in the shallow seas that once covered Florida. Different types of limestone are found in different parts of the state. Limestone in the Florida Keys consists mainly of fossilized corals. Along the east coast, early Floridians quarried great quantities of a limestone rock called 'coquina.' The Castillo de San Marcos in St. Augustine is built entirely of coquina. If you look closely at the walls of this fort you can see millions of fossilized shells.

Fossil shark teeth are also fairly easy to find in streams and rivers and enormous numbers of them turn up on the beaches of southwestern Florida. After a storm, the bones and teeth of ancient horses and ground sloths often wash up on Atlantic coast beaches.

Climate and Best Times to Visit

Florida's official nickname is the 'Sunshine State,' and for good reason – it has the sunniest winter climate in the eastern USA, and the highest average January temperature in the nation. Surrounded by the warm waters of the Gulf of Mexico and the Atlantic Ocean, the climate ranges from temperate in the north to tropical in the extreme south.

Florida winters (December to March) are mild and dry. In northern Florida, winter consists of cool nights and sunny days. Daytime temperatures are usually 10 to 15 °C (50 to 60 °F). Every few weeks a cold front sweeps in from the north, bringing with it a few days of cold cloudy weather, a brief rainy spell, followed by bright clear skies and cooler temperatures. North Florida's famous freezes, when oranges are photographed covered with ice, usually arrive after a front has moved through. Southern Florida is sub-tropical, with daytime winter temperatures of 15 to 24 °C (60 to 75 °F).

Summers (June to September) are hot and humid. Guide books will tell you that the average annual summer temperature is 26.9 °C (80.5 °F) in North Florida but don't be fooled. This average includes the high and low temperature for the 24-hr period. Daytime temperatures across the state in June, July, and August typically hover around 32 °C (90 °F) and the humidity is high. Coastal breezes provide some relief from the humidity, and thus the beaches are popular summer places. Many visitors from north temperate climates acquire a sudden, deep appreciation for the 'Apparatus for Treating Air' (now known as the air conditioner), invented by Willis H. Carrier in 1902.

Summer is also Florida's wet season: about 135 cm (53 in) of rain falls in Florida each year, most of it between June and September. In addition to being one of the sunniest states, Florida is also one of the wettest, second only to Louisiana. Ironically, the state is located at the same latitude as some of the world's great deserts. Average annual rainfall varies from about 101 cm (40 in) in Key West to 157 cm (62 in) in Palm Beach and 137 cm (54 in) in Gainesville. Most of the rain comes in the form of summer thunderstorms, and on most summer days there is a 40 to 50% chance of rain. White puffy clouds build to thunderheads during the day and by afternoon you can usually hear thunder rumbling somewhere nearby. Florida rain is often localized and intense, but mercifully brief. We once measured almost 10 cm (4 in) of rain in our rain gauge after a 35-minute summer rainstorm, while a small town 11 km (7 miles) away stayed bone dry.

Besides being the Sunshine State, southwest Florida is also known as 'the lightning capital of the world.' Meteorologists estimate that there are about 104 lightning strikes a year in each square kilometer of land (40 per sq mile) in central Florida, which is about three times the national average. Lightning kills about ten people per year in Florida and damages millions of dollars' worth of telephones, transformers and electronic equipment. Nearly 30% of lightning victims were in open fields, golf courses, or ballparks. A quarter of the deaths occurred among people who were boating, fishing, or swimming in open water when the thunderstorm passed over.

The hurricane season begins in June and extends through November. The peak hurricane months are September and October, when ocean temperatures are warmest. However, the chances of hurricane-force winds striking Florida in any year are not as great as you might think. Historical records show that Florida is no more vulnerable to hurricanes than the entire Atlantic coast of the USA as far north as Boston. In spite of the great damage they can cause, much of south Florida's plant diversity is thought to be due to hurricanes – they are believed to have blown many of Florida's tropical plants over from the West Indies. The best time to visit Florida depends on your interests and tolerance for heat, humidity, and insects. Reptiles and amphibians are easiest to see in the summer months. However, alligators can usually be seen year round. If birding is high on your list, late September and early October is ideal for fall migrants; January and February are excellent for wintering birds, and spring migration peaks in mid-April to mid-May. Winter is a good time to see colonial wading birds nesting in south Florida, and cold weather attracts manatees to central Florida's freshwater springs.

Vegetation: General Characteristics

Florida's Trees

Florida supports more tree species than any other state in the continental USA. About 275 of the approximately 625 native tree species in North America are found in Florida. A surprising number of these trees do not lose their leaves in winter, even during north Florida's occasional freezes. Palms, magnolia, live oaks, bays, wax myrtle and many others are evergreen, so that in winter the landscape never looks as bare and brown as it does in northern temperate areas.

Palms

Seeing palm trees as you disembark from an aircraft is a sure sign you have arrived in the tropics. Worldwide, the palm family is composed of about 3000 species, only a few of which are indigenous to continental USA. Eight tree-sized palms are native to Florida. All are of tropical origin and all except two are found in south Florida. Florida's native palms include the paurotis palm (*Acoelorrhaphe wrightii*), silver palm (*Coccothrinax argentata*), sabal palm (*Sabal palmetto*; Plate A), saw palmetto (*Serenoa repens*; Plate E), Key thatch palm (*Thrinax morrisii*), Florida thatch palm (*Thrinax radiata*), royal palm (*Roystonea elata*; Plate D), and buccaneer palm (*Pseudophoenix sargentii*).

In addition to these, a large number of non-native palm species are commonly used as ornamental plants and several have now become naturalized. The Washington palm, or petticoat palm (*Washingtonia robusta*), coconut palm (*Cocos nucifera*; Plate A), and date palm (*Phoenix dactylifera*) are the most commonly seen naturalized species.

Sabal palm and saw palmetto are the most widely distributed of Florida's palms; both are common in north Florida, where they survive periodic hard freezes. The sabal palm, also known as the cabbage palm (Plate A), is the state tree. This palm got its common name from the fact that its center, or heart, became survival food for many of the early settlers – when cooked, it supposedly tasted like cabbage. Today sabal palms are disappearing from the wild because they are much in demand by developers for landscaping. The silver palm, the Key thatch palm and the Florida thatch palm are commercially exploited and are included on the state's list of protected flora.

Citrus

In the south and central portions of the state much of the landscape is dominated by rows and rows of well tended, dark green citrus fruit trees. Citrus is big business in Florida. It is the state's leading agricultural crop; more than 300 million boxes of citrus worth more than $1.5 billion were harvested in 1997–1998.

Spanish settlers brought the first oranges (Plate C) to Florida, probably for medicinal reasons. Spanish law required each sailor to carry 100 orange seeds with him and plant them when he reached land. At that time citrus was used to prevent scurvy, a disease caused by lack of vitamin C. (British sailors became known as *limeys* after the Admiralty issued orders for regular rations of lime juice.)

The first oranges were thought to have been planted near St. Augustine. The warm climate, high rainfall and sandy soil combined to produce ideal growing conditions, and the trees soon spread. Within 200 years new settlers in Florida found thickets of 'wild' citrus and assumed it was a native plant. The first major expansion of the orange industry came in 1870s as farmers realized that Florida-grown fruit might replace the two million or so oranges imported every year from the Mediterranean. After 1900, citrus production moved from small, family-run groves to large-scale commercial production. Today, more than 96% of Florida's orange crop is turned into juice.

Epiphytes

Epiphytes are plants that grow on other plants but do not harm their 'hosts.' They are not parasites – they do not burrow into a tree to suck out nutrients; they simply live on the tree's trunk and branches. (Ecologically, we would call the relationship between a tree and its epiphytes commensal: one party of the arrangement, the epiphyte, benefits – it gains growing space – and the other party, the tree, is unaffected.) How do epiphytes grow if they are not rooted in the host tree or in the ground? Stems and leaves absorb water and nutrients from the air, and eventually, by collecting bits of debris that blow by, each epiphyte develops its own bit of soil, into which it is rooted. Orchids are among the most famous kinds of epiphytes.

One of Florida's most spectacular epiphytes is Spanish moss (*Tillandsia usneoides*; Plate L), which hangs from live oaks and other trees in silvery-gray curtains. The plant is not a true moss but is related to the pineapple; both belong to the plant family Bromeliacae. Native Americans called Spanish moss 'tree hair,' and early colonists fed the plant to their livestock and mixed it with mud to make caulk for their cabins. Later, the moss was used in furniture, and in the 1840s mattress manufacturers in Liverpool, England, were importing American Spanish moss to stuff mattresses. In the 1930s moss gathering was an important industry in Florida. The plant was harvested and sent to commercial moss gins, where it was cleaned, straightened and baled. More than 10,000 tons of Spanish moss, worth $2.5 million, was harvested and ginned in 1939. Synthetic fibers eventually replaced moss as furniture padding, but the plant is still collected and sold for the arts and crafts trade.

Major Habitats and Common Plant Species

People have inhabited Florida for 10,000 years, but their impact on the land has been slight until quite recently. In the last 100 years, the growth of urbanization, agriculture, and the citrus industry has radically and obviously altered the state's landscape. But Florida's vegetation has also been transformed, albeit less obviously, by the lack of fire. Historically, lightning fires were a regular natural phenomenon. Today, roads, agriculture, and urban areas limit the spread of fire, and most areas burn much less frequently than they used to. Without fire, oaks and other hardwoods move in to dominate what was once open pine forest, and shrubs and herbs are overwhelmed by palmetto. The result is a very different-looking landscape from the one discovered by Ponce de Leon in 1513.

While Florida lacks the topographic relief typical of many states, subtle changes in elevation, drainage patterns, and climate create a diverse landscape. The difference between semi-arid scrub and marsh may be only a few meters in elevation. A large number of plant communities have been identified and described for the state, but for convenience and brevity we have limited ourselves to a brief overview of the major upland, freshwater, and coastal ecosystems.

Upland Ecosystems

Prairie habitat

Dry Prairies

Florida's dry prairies are superficially similar to the prairies of the central and western USA in that both are nearly treeless, grass-covered plains; however, the two differ in plant species and several other features. Florida's dry prairies (Habitat Photos 12, 13) are open, flat, grassy expanses, covered by grasses, palmetto and wildflowers. The vegetation is dominated by species such as wiregrass (*Aristida stricta*), broomsedge (*Andropogon virginicus*), arrowfeather (*Aristida purpurascens*), and love grasses (*Eragrostis* spp.), interspersed with clumps of saw palmetto (*Serenoa repens;* Plate E) and scattered patches of low shrubs including fetterbush (*Lyonia lucidia*), staggerbush (*L. fruticosa*) and dwarf blueberry (*Vaccinium myrsinites*). As in other prairies of the USA, large areas of Florida's native dry prairie have been converted into cattle pasture. The largest area of dry prairie in the state occurs north and west of Lake Okeechobee along the Kissimmee River; other prairies on public lands include Paynes Prairie State Preserve and Juniper Prairie Wilderness in the Ocala National Forest.

Pine Flatwoods habitat

Pine Flatwoods

Pine flatwoods (Habitat Photos 18, 19) characteristically occur in low, flat areas, on acidic, sandy soils. Depending on drainage patterns, different types of pines predominate. Longleaf pine (*Pinus palustris*; Plate C) is the dominant tree on well-drained soils, slash pine (*P. elliotti*) on sites of intermediate wetness, and pond pine (*P. serotina*) on poorly drained sites. The pine canopy in flatwoods tends to be open; the pines self-prune their lower branches, leaving a large gap between the canopy and the shrub layer. This openness promotes an extensive low shrub layer of saw palmetto (Plate E), gallberry (*Ilex glabra*), fetterbush, staggerbush, wax myrtle (*Myrica cerifera*), and huckleberry (*Gaylussacia dumosa*).

Flatwoods cover about 50% of Florida's land area and are also common throughout the southeastern coastal plains of Georgia and the Carolinas. The first settlers called these forests 'pine barrens' or 'pine flatwoods,' probably because of their monotonously flat nature. Early writers described the original pine flatwoods as open enough to drive a wagon through, but most of Florida's pine flatwoods have changed markedly in structure and plant composition since Spanish settlement in the 1500s. Historically, spring and summer lightning ignited fires that burned through the underbrush, killing oak and other tree seedlings. The fire-adapted pines, herbs and grasses survived, creating an open, light-filled forest, or 'a savanna with pine trees.'

Today, roads and urban development have created fire barriers and the natural lightning fires, which once maintained the open nature of flatwoods, are now quickly extinguished. Fire control has favored the development of a dense understory, with more shrubs and fewer herbs. More recently, vast areas that were once pine flatwoods have been converted to alternative land uses such as pine plantations, crop land, improved pastures, and urban development. The combined result is that there are probably only a few pine flatwood stands in existence that resemble those of the past. Visitors to Tosohatchee State Reserve near Orlando can see some of Florida's pristine pine flatwoods, in addition to hardwood hammocks and several types of wetlands. Apalachicola and Osceola National Forests also contain good examples of natural flatwoods.

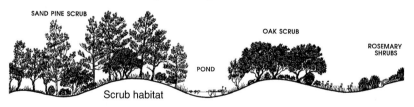

Scrub habitat

Scrub

Early travellers described areas of Florida scrub (Habitat Photo 23) as 'concealed deserts' fit for nothing. This unique plant community has many endemic plants and is maintained by intense, infrequent fires. Sand pines (*Pinus clausa*; Plate E) occupy the canopy layer and the understory vegetation is dominated by evergreen oaks, including the stunted-looking scrub oak (*Quercus myrtifolia*), sand live oak (*Q. geminata*), and Chapman's oak (*Q. chapmanii*). Clumps of saw palmetto (Plate E), rusty lionia (*Lyonia ferruginea*) and Florida rosemary (*Ceratiola ericoides* Plate G) are interspersed with lichen (*Cladonia* spp.) mats and large patches of open, white sand. All the plants are adapted to the hot, dry, nutrient-poor conditions, and fire. The cones of sand pines remain on the trees for years, opening and releasing their seeds only in response to the heat of a fire. Florida rosemary releases a chemical into the ground to stop its own seeds from germinating. The seeds remain in the sand and germinate only after fire kills the mother plant. The advantage to the seeds germinating only after a fire is that competition from other plants is greatly reduced.

Florida's scrub is a remnant of an older and much more extensive ecosystem. Small patches of scrub occur along a series of ancient dunes running north to south through the middle of north and central Florida. The largest block of scrub lies in and around the Ocala National Forest. Good examples of coastal scrub can be seen at Joshua Dickinson State Park and Merritt Island National Wildlife Refuge on the Atlantic coast, and St. Vincent Island on the Gulf coast.

SMALL WOODY SHRUBS   LONGLEAF PINES
High Pine Sandhills habitat

High pine sandhills (Longleaf pine-oak sandhills)

The high-pine ecosystem (Habitat Photo 20) is park-like and characterized by an open overstory of mature longleaf pine (Plate C), with a fairly complete ground cover of grasses, principally wiregrass (*Aristida stricta*), and forbs, interspered with a scattering of deciduous oaks. Turkey oak (*Quercus laevis*) predominates in Florida's high pine regions, which are typically found on upland sandy areas. While tree species diversity in these pine-oak sandhills is low, there are a great variety of herbaceous (non-woody) plants such as wiregrass, piney woods dropseed (*Sporobolus junceus*), bracken fern (*Pteridium aquilinum*), gopher apple (*Licania michauxii*), golden aster (*Pityopsis graminifolia*), sparkleberry (*Vaccinium arboreum*), and pawpaw (*Asimina incárna*).

Fire is a dominant factor in this community, to such an extent that the high pine area has been called 'the forest that fire made.' Many animals of this habitat escape fires by retreating to burrows. Prior to European settlement, the longleaf pine-oak ecosystem once stretched nearly unbroken from southeastern Virginia to east Texas, but little remains today. Cattle grazing, logging, habitat conversion, and fire suppression have combined to change the character of this once vast landscape. Efforts to restore the high pine community have focused on burning during spring and summer, which mimics the historical fire regime associated with lightning fires. Wekiwa Springs State Park and Riverside Island in the Ocala National Forest are good places to see examples of the longleaf pine-oak ecosystem.

LIVE OAK   MAGNOLIA   FALLEN TREE   HICKORY
Temperate Hardwood Hammocks habitat

Temperate hardwood hammocks

In Florida, the word 'hammock' means shady place, and the name is applied to any hardwood-dominated forest. Vines, epiphytes, and Spanish moss are often conspicuous on hammock trees. There are several hammock types, but in general, hammock soil is more fertile than soil under pine flatwoods, and there is a well-developed layer of humus and leaf mould. Hammocks in north Florida (Habitat Photo 21) contain the largest number of species of trees and shrubs per unit area in the continental USA. Panhandle hammocks resemble other lowland hardwood forests of the southeastern USA, but differ in that they contain a high number of locally endemic plants, as well as many species at the southern terminus of their ranges (e.g. beech, *Fagus grandifolia*, and white oak, *Quercus alba*).

In north Florida, hardwood forests in low-lying, damp areas are sometimes dominated by one or two species, such as in the cabbage palm–red bay (*Sabal palmetto–Persea borboinia*) hammock. Where this type is mixed with other species, it often includes sweet gum (*Liquidambar styraciflua*; Plate F), loblolly pine (*Pinus taeda*), live oaks (*Quercus* spp.), holly (*Ilex opaca*; Plate H), and several species of ash (*Fraxinus* spp.) Live oak-cabbage palm hammocks in central Florida often border larger lakes and rivers. A common hammock type in north-central Florida is the magnolia–holly–ironwood–hop hornbeam forest (*Magnolia grandiflora–Ilex opaca–Carpinus caroliniana–Ostrya virginiana*). It is not unusual to find dogwood (*Cornus florida*), pignut hickory (*Carya glabra*), red maple (*Acer rubrum*; Plate D), hackberry (*Celtis laevigata*), and live oaks (*Quercus* spp.) in this diverse association. Hammocks on slightly drier sites are often dominated by large live oaks (*Quercus virginiana*) and hickories (*Carya* spp.), with a mixture of other oaks (*Quercus* spp.) and the occasional pine, cabbage palm (Plate A), or magnolia. Coastal hardwood hammocks occur as narrow bands along parts of the Gulf and Atlantic coasts; these sometimes extend to the edge of coastal marshes. Myakka River State Park, San Felasco Hammock State Preserve, and Highlands Hammock State Park contain excellent examples of Florida's hardwood hammocks.

Tropical hardwood hammocks

As you approach Miami International Airport, the plane circles over the emerald-green sawgrass of the Everglades. Sprinkled throughout this sea of grass are numerous tear-drop-shaped tree islands, rising above the water on rocky lime-stone outcrops. Geologists believe these islands were once ancient coral reefs, which died when the oceans receded, some 120,000 years ago. These rock islands and many of the Florida Keys are covered with tropical hardwood hammocks, a rapidly shrinking ecosystem with a unique flora.

Tropical hardwood hammocks (Habitat Photos 14, 15) are evergreen, broad-leaved forests, filled with tree species usually found in the Bahamas and Greater Antilles. Plant diversity is high, with over 35 species of trees and more than 60 species of shrubs and small trees. Common canopy trees include gumbo limbo (*Bursera simaruba*; Plate B), pigeon plum (*Coccoloba diversifolia*), live oak (*Quercus virginiana*; Plate C), strangler fig (*Ficus aurea*), cabbage palm (*Sabal palmetto*; Plate A), wild tamarin (*Lysiloma latisiliqua*), and mastic (*Mastichodendron foetidissimum*). Understory trees and shrubs include lancewood (*Nectandra coriacea*), inkwood (*Exothea paniculata*), red mulberry (*Morus rubra*), black ironwood (*Krugiodendron ferreum*), West Indies cherry (*Prunus myrtifolia*), crabwood (*Ateramnus lucidus*), and wild coffee (*Psychotria nervosa*). Woody vines, such as the devil's claw (*Pisonia aculeata*), muscadine grape (*Vitus rotundifolia*), Virginia creeper (*Parthenocissus quinquefolia*), and poison ivy (*Toxicodendron radicans*) are common. The tropical temperatures are also favorable for epiphytes – orchids, bromeliads, and ferns are abundant in many tropical hammocks.

The majority of tropical hammocks have been lost to development in south Florida, but relatively large areas of them remain on Key Largo and one of the best examples of tropical hammock is on Lignum Vitae Key, which is located off the lower end of Lower Matecumbe Key.

Freshwater Ecosystems

Freshwater marshes (including the Everglades)

Marshes are characterized by shallow standing water, low emergent vegetation and occasional trees. As many as 15 different types of marshes and wet prairies have been described in Florida, differentiated mainly on the basis of their dominant plants. Sawgrass (*Cladium jamaicensis*; Plate L) dominates the Everglades, whereas other Florida marsh systems are dominated by species such as water lily (*Nymphaea odorata*), cattail (*Typha* spp.), maidencane (*Panicum hemitomon*), pickerelweed (*Pontederia lanceolata*, *P. cordata*; Plate K), arrowhead (*Sagittaria latifolia*), and fire flag (*Thalia geniculata*). The last four species above have flag-shaped leaves, and marshes where these species predominate are called 'flag marshes.'

Which particular set of plant species predominate at a site is determined largely by fluctuating water levels and fire frequency. Because the seeds of most species cannot germinate under water, the kinds of seeds available and the length of the dry season determine which species will gain a foothold. Once established, their subsequent spread is primarily vegetative. The percentage of time a marsh is flooded (*hydroperiod*) also influences plant associations. Water lily, for example, can tolerate long periods (more than 9 months) of flooding, but cattail cannot. Water lilies are not found in marshes where fires occur more than once a decade but sawgrass is. Sawgrass responds particularly fast to fire, growing to a height of as much as 40 cm (16 in) within 2 weeks of being burnt.

Marshes are not uniformly distributed throughout Florida. There are few marshes in the Panhandle and the northern portion of the peninsula because these areas tend to be elevated and well drained. The greatest expanse of marsh is the Everglades in south Florida, but there are also extensive marshes associated with the floodplain habitats of the St. Johns and the Kissimmee rivers.

The smaller marshes and lakes along Florida's central ridge change regularly as drainage patterns change, and a single site may be a lake, a marsh, or dry land all within a relatively short time span. Paynes Prairie near Gainesville is a famous example of this phenomenon. In 1774, when the naturalist William Bartram visited the area, it was a dry savannah. A hundred years later it was a lake, and today it is a marsh.

The author Marjory Stoneman Douglas described the Everglades, Florida's most famous marsh, as a 'river of grass,' and a river it is, albeit a slow one. This vast marsh was originally 100 km (60 miles) wide and covered an area of 10,000 sq km (3860 sq miles), nearly a third of Florida. The Everglades begins as the overflow from Lake Okeechobee and flows slowly to the ocean, down an almost imperceptible slope of 3 cm per km (2 in per mile). It takes almost a year for water from Lake Okeechobee to reach the ocean.

The Everglades have become synonymous with Florida, attracting millions of visitors each year, but drainage, flood control structures, and water management activities have had profound effects on this unique wetland (see p. 49). More than 65% of the original marsh has been drained and 'reclaimed,' and what was once Everglades now contains 40% of Florida's human population and produces half the winter vegetables sold in the USA. The present extent of Everglades marsh habitat is shown in Map 1 (p. 9).

CYPRESS DOME   CYPRESS STRAND

FLATWOODS

Swamp habitat

Swamps

Due to its flat topography and high water tables, Florida is rich in swamps. Swamps are basically forested wetlands, but there the simplicity ends. At least 13 different types of freshwater swamps exist in the state, but it is the blend of temperate and tropical plant species that make Florida's swamps unique among North American wetlands.

Florida's freshwater swamps are usually dominated by cypress trees. Cypress is a deciduous conifer (hence the name 'bald cypress'), which drops its needles in November and regains them again in March. Throughout a cypress swamp you will see hundreds of knobby looking conical stumps protruding above the water around the base of the tree. These cypress 'knees' grow to about a meter (3 ft) in height and allow the tree to absorb oxygen. Strangely, despite the fact that cypress trees spend most of their lives up to their knees in water, cypress seeds cannot germinate in water. Thus, regeneration of cypress trees depends on fluctuating water levels.

Bald cypress (*Taxodium distichum*; Plate B) is usually the dominant tree in river swamps throughout the state, but along rivers and lakes in north Florida it is often found in association with tupelo (*Nyssa aquatica*), Ogeechee lime (*Nyssa ogeche*), red maple (*Acer rubrum*; Plate D), and a variety of other flood-tolerant species. Along linear drainages bald cypress often occur in narrow strips, called strands. Cypress 'domes' are often seen in wet prairies and flatwoods. The trees in the shallower edge of the swamp are shorter than those in the deeper center, giving the stand its dome-like appearance. Pond cypress (*Taxodium ascendens*), black gum (*Nyssa silvatica*) and various bay species (*Persea* spp.) are also found in acidic stillwater swamps. Swamps dominated by bay trees are called bayheads or baygalls; those dominated by one or more shrub species of titi (*Cliftonia monophylla, Cyrilla racemiflora*) are called titi swamps. Cypress trees usually host large numbers of epiphytes; the most common is ball moss (*Tillandsia recurvata*; Plate I), a close relative of Spanish moss. Clumps of ball moss are often sold in souvenir shops as 'air plants.'

Cypress wood is greatly prized for its strength and resistance to rot. Around World War II it was in great demand for bridges, boats, barrels and wood paneling. By 1950 almost every swamp in the state had been logged for its large cypress trees. Conveniently, the trees grow near rivers and lakes and were easily transported to sawmills. You can still see the giant stumps of these ancient cypress trees as you canoe the Ichnetucknee or Oklawaha rivers.

Few stands of virgin cypress remain in Florida. Corkscrew Swamp Sanctuary contains an excellent stand of old-growth bald cypress. The Big Cypress National Preserve is not, despite its name, known for the size of its cypress trees. The preserve is named for the vast area it covers, about one-third of which is dominated by dwarf pond cypress (also called hat-rack cypress).

Lakes

The fact that Florida has a large number of different types of lakes usually comes as a surprise to visitors and residents alike. There are about 7800 lakes in the state, covering roughly 6% of the landscape. However, the vast majority of Florida's lakes are small (only five have surface areas greater than 100 sq km, 40 sq miles), and many are quite shallow, less than 5 m (16.4 ft) deep. Even Lake Okeechobee, the largest lake in the state, has a maximum depth less than 5 m. More than half of all the lakes occur in a 14-county area of central and north Florida; fittingly, they are particularly numerous in Lake County.

Most of Florida's lakes are seepage lakes, with no inflow or outflow. They are fed by rainfall and runoff filtering in from the basins surrounding the lakes. Florida's lakes run the gamut from extremely oligotrophic (poorly nourished), clear, sand-bottomed lakes to hypereutrophic (well-nourished), algae-filled lakes near muck farms and sewage plants.

Exotic water plants introduced to Florida's lakes have caused major changes in many lakes by clogging the waterways and changing chemical conditions in the water. Two of the most problematic species are water hyacinth (*Eichhornia crassipes*) and hydrilla (*Hydrilla verticillata*). In some lakes, biologists have been able to control hydrilla with introduced Asiatic Grass Carp, but efforts to control water hyacinth with herbicides have been relatively unsuccessful.

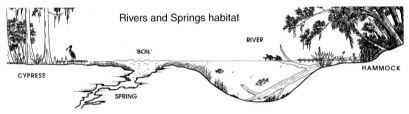

Rivers and Springs habitat

RIVER

'BOIL'

CYPRESS

HAMMOCK

SPRING

Rivers and springs

Before the advent of roads and railways, river travel was the best way to explore interior Florida. Navigable rivers formed the backbone of the state's transportation system and steamboats operated regular routes on the Apalachicola, St. Johns and Oklawaha rivers. Today, river travel, either by canoe, kayak or pontoon boat, is still one of the best ways to see the state's natural areas. Florida's larger rivers are often called 'blackwater' rivers, as decaying leaves and other organic matter turn the water a dark tea-color. The state's outstanding rivers, besides those mentioned above, include the Myakka, Loxahatchee, St. Marys, and Suwannee.

Peninsular Florida is also home to one of the world's largest concentrations of freshwater springs. There are over 300 named springs in the state, most of them located in the north and central regions. Florida's springs are artesian, with water pressure forcing the water back up through vertical holes in the limestone. Some of the holes open into caverns, through which flow underground rivers. The largest springs are known as first-magnitude springs, where flow rates meet or exceed 3 million gallons per hour. Florida has 27 first-magnitude springs, more than a third of the first-magnitude springs in the USA. Homosassa Springs, Ichetucknee Springs, and Silver Springs are some of the best known.

Many of the larger springs are major tourist attractions, used extensively for fishing, snorkeling, tubing, swimming, and cave diving. The crystal clear water bubbling up from the underground limestone remains all year at a constant temperature of about 20 to 23 °C (68 to 73 °F). On a summer day, with air temperatures in the low 30s °C (90+ °F), the water feels deliciously cold, but during winter freezes, the 20 °C (68 °F) water is much warmer than the freezing air temperature. During these cold spells the comparative warmth of the spring water attracts large numbers of manatees.

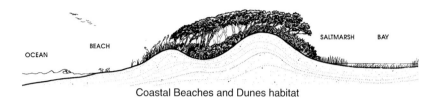

Coastal Beaches and Dunes habitat

Coastal Ecosystems

Beaches, dunes, and salt marshes

Florida has the longest shoreline of any state in the USA except Alaska. Over 1200 km (750 miles) of its coastline consists of sandy beaches, primarily in the form of offshore barrier islands. These long, narrow, shifting spits of sand are home to some of the most beautiful beaches in the USA. Little Talbot Island and Caladesi Island State Park are good examples of barrier island beaches. As you travel about the state you will notice that the texture of beach sand changes quite dramatically from place to place. Beaches on Sanibel Island in southwestern Florida are made up almost entirely of shell fragments, whereas Panhandle beaches are almost pure quartz sand and squeak like snow when you walk on them.

The Atlantic coast is known as a 'high energy' coastline. Strong waves pound the shore year-round, maintaining an open sandy beach backed by a ridge of dunes. The dune vegetation consists of pioneer species, able to establish and maintain themselves in the constantly shifting sands. Typical dune plants are railroad vines (*Ipomoea* spp.), sea oats (*Uniola paniculata*; Plate L), and beach (sand) cordgrass (*Spartina patens, S. bakeri*; Plate N). Behind the dunes the vegetation segues into saw palmetto (Plate E) and dwarf scrubby oaks, coastal hammock forests, or cabbage palm savannah, depending on which part of Florida you are in. Guana River State Park, Cayo Costa State Park, and St. Joseph Peninsula State Park contain outstanding examples of some of Florida's most pristine beaches and dunes.

Other parts of Florida's coastline have more mud than sand. These 'low energy' coastlines have minimal wave action and the water is often shallow for hundreds of meters offshore. Salt marshes thrive in the intertidal zone, with black needlerush (*Juncus roemerianus*) and smooth cordgrass (*Spartina alterniflora*) dominating the vegetation. The highest areas of the marsh are covered with saltgrass (*Distichlis spicata*), glass wort (*Salicornia* spp.) and sea ox-eye daisies (*Borrichia* spp.). Salt marshes can be seen in the Gulf Hammock area on the Gulf coast, and on the Atlantic coast along the Intracoastal waterway near Washington Oaks State Park.

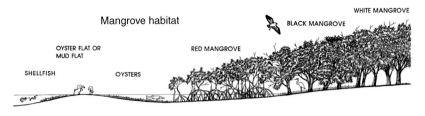

Mangrove habitat

WHITE MANGROVE

BLACK MANGROVE

RED MANGROVE

OYSTER FLAT OR
MUD FLAT

SHELLFISH

OYSTERS

Mangrove

The word *mangrove* comes from a combination of the Spanish word for mangrove tree (mangle) and the English word for a stand of trees (grove). Mangroves are tropical trees that grow in areas exposed to salt water, usually around bays, lagoons, and other protected coastal areas. Florida's mangrove forests are found on both coasts, from Cedar Key in the Gulf around to St. Augustine on the east coast. About 90% of Florida's mangroves are in the four southern counties of Lee, Collier, Monroe, and Dade. Excellent examples of mangrove forests can be seen in Ding Darling National Wildlife Refuge, Collier Seminole State Park, and the Ten Thousand Islands area of southwest Florida. Mangroves flourish where there is little wave action, and in areas that have relatively large tidal ranges. The two most commonly seen species are the red (*Rhizophora mangle*; Plate D) and the black mangrove (*Avicennia germinans*). The red mangrove, with its characteristic prop roots (roots that arise from the trunk and branches and shallowly penetrate the soil below the tree), grows in dense stands and occurs closest to the ocean. The prop roots extend only a few centimeters into the waterlogged soil and allow oxygen to diffuse into the plant. Red mangrove has small yellow waxy flowers and produces seeds that look like miniature cigars. The seeds float and drift with the tide until they lodge somewhere, sometimes great distances from the parent tree. Black mangrove is found farther inland. It lacks prop roots but is surrounded by a carpet of finger-like projections (pneumatophores) that poke up through the soil and promote oxygen exchange. Still farther inland, in the highest part of the intertidal zone, the vegetation segues into white mangrove (*Laguncularia racemosa*), buttonwood trees (*Concocarpus erectus*), sea grape (*Coccoloba uvifera*; Plate E), and saltbush (*Baccharis halimifolia*).

Mangrove forests protect the shoreline and provide valuable habitat for a wide range of animals. They are important nursery areas for fish, shrimp, and lobster; many wading birds nest and roost in mangroves.

Coral reefs

Florida has a variety of reef types along its eastern and southern coastline. Bank reefs formed by ivory tree coral (*Oculina varicosa*) occur offshore at depths of 50 to 100 m (160 to 330 ft) from Jacksonville south to St. Lucie Inlet. Worm reefs, constructed by a tropical marine worm (*Phragmatopma lapidosa*), are found in the intertidal zone from Cape Canaveral to Key Biscayne. The state's most special reefs are the shallow water, tropical reefs of the Florida Keys (also known as the Florida Reef Tract). These are the only living, tropical coral reefs in the continental USA. Reefs in the Keys are similar in species composition and structure to those found in the Caribbean and the Bahamas.

Some 40 species of coral are found in the Florida Keys. Fire corals, named for the burning sensation caused by microscopic stinging organs, are found in a wide range of reef habitats. The octocorals, which include the sea whips, sea plumes, sea fans, and soft corals, are extremely abundant in some reef habitats. These corals share the trait of having eight tentacles on their polyps, hence the name. Stony corals, false corals, and anemones add to the incredible richness of the reef system.

South Florida's coral reefs are known as *fringing reefs*: they grow outward from the coastline and develop mostly in shallow water. The reefs on the seaward side protect those on the inside from wave action of the open ocean, making these portions of the reef the most favorable for coral growth. Reef ecosystems are extraordinarily complex, and support a great variety of algae, invertebrates, plants, and fish (see Chapter 11). John Pennekamp Coral Reef State Park is a good place to see coral reefs.

Chapter 3

PARKS AND RESERVES

- *Introduction*
- *Getting Around*
- *The Great Florida Birding Trail*
- *Fishing*
- *Canoeing*
- *Manatees*
- *Panhandle (PAN)*
- *North Florida (NFL)*
- *Central Florida (CFL)*
- *South Florida (SFL)*
- *Keys and Other Islands (KEY)*

Introduction

The parks, reserves, and wildlife viewing sites described below were selected because they are the ones most often visited by ecotravellers or because they have a lot to offer ecotravellers. The animals profiled in the color plates are keyed to these parks in the following way: the profiles list the geographical regions (Panhandle – PAN, North Florida – NFL, Central Florida – CFL, South Florida – SFL, Keys and Other Islands – KEY) in which each species is likely to be found; and the parks listed below are arranged by the same geographical regions. Park locations and geographical regions are shown in Map 2 (p. 28). Tips on increasing the likelihood of seeing mammals, birds, reptiles or amphibians are given in the introductions to each of those chapters.

Florida has three national parks, three national forests, 29 national wildlife refuges, and 150 state parks. However, good opportunities for wildlife viewing are not confined to parks and reserves. In winter, for instance, you can see manatees around the warm water effluents of the Tampa Electric Company's power plants and thousands of wintering waterfowl on wetlands owned by Florida's water management districts. The information in this chapter will point you to some of these sites and give you a brief idea of the habitats and wildlife you may see.

Without question, the best maps of Florida can be found in the *Florida Atlas and Gazetteer* (1997), published by DeLorme, P.O. Box 298, Freeport, Maine 04032; tel (207) 865–4171; http://www.delorme.com. Each 2.5 cm (1 in) on these maps equals 3.7 km (2.3 miles). Clear symbols show you exactly where you can fish, hike, bike, and launch a canoe. *The Florida Wildlife Viewing Guide*, by S. I. Cerulean and A. J. Morrow, Falcon Publishing, Inc., Helena, Montana, is an extremely useful guide to specific wildlife viewing sites across Florida. As well as outlining the wildlife you are likely to see at each site, this guide lists handicapped access, restaurants, lodging, picnic areas, boat ramps, and other useful information.

National parks usually encompass environmental features of national or international significance. They are dedicated to preserving and protecting outstanding natural areas, while encouraging recreation. The world's first national park, Yellowstone, was established in 1872, and since then some 40 other national parks have been established throughout the USA. Everglades, Biscayne Bay and the Dry Tortugas are Florida's three national parks. All have excellent facilities, including exhibits, trails, resident naturalists, and guided walks. There is a US$10 per car fee to enter Everglades National Park, but there is no entrance fee for Biscayne Bay or the Dry Tortugas.

National forests are managed by the U.S. Forest Service, primarily for timber, but cattle grazing, mining, drilling for oil and hunting, as well as hiking, birding, etc., are also permitted. There is no entrance fee for national forests. The *national wildlife refuge system* dates from 1903, when President Theodore Roosevelt proclaimed Florida's Pelican Island a federal wildlife sanctuary. Today, the U.S. Fish and Wildlife Service administers the operation and management of more than 500 federal refuges, of which there are 29 in Florida. Many of these national wildlife refuges were acquired to provide rest stops for migrating birds, and most are fairly intensively managed. Wetlands are drained and reflooded for migrating birds, corn and other grains are planted to provide food for birds, and some areas are burned to promote new growth. Most national wildlife refuges permit hunting in season. Facilities are usually minimal, and it is a good idea to bring your own drinking water, insect repellent and snacks. There is no entrance fee for most national wildlife refuges.

Florida's 150 *state parks* were established to preserve and protect the state's natural and cultural heritage. Many state parks have campgrounds and a few have rental cabins, but 80% or more of the land area is preserved in its natural condition. State parks are open from 8 a.m. to sunset every day of the year; entrance fees are US$3.25 to $4.00 per carload of people. Walk-ins and bicyclists are $1.00 per person. There may be additional fees for camping, tours and museum entrances. Ask any park ranger where you can pick up a free copy of the *Florida State Park Guide*, or call (805) 488–9872. If you call the telephone number listed next to the park or viewing site below you will usually get a detailed recorded message with directions, facilities and other useful miscellaneous information. The Florida Park Service also has an excellent web site at http://www.dep.state.fl.us/parks/. The site has an interactive map on which you can find descriptions of all Florida state parks and information on accommodations, handicapped access, opening hours and many other details.

Getting Around

By European and other standards, rental cars and gasoline are unbelievably inexpensive in Florida. Almost all visitors to Florida rent a car – apart from a guided tour, there really is no other way to get to out-of-the-way ecotourist sites. Florida also differs from most ecotourism destinations in that it is easy to get information over the telephone even at the last minute. Want to find out the exact directions to a birding site listed in this guide? Buy a US$10.00 telephone card at any gas station or corner grocery store and phone the number listed beside the site before you go. Are the manatees in at Blue Spring? Call. Need to know if the area you want to visit has a reputable canoe outfitter? Call (863) 494–1215 (see below). Want to know which birds are being seen in the Miami area? Call the Tropical Audubon Society Birding hotline recording for area sightings (305) 667–PEEP (7337). Other rare bird alert hotlines include: Statewide (561) 340–0079, Lower Keys (305) 294–3438, Northern Florida (912) 244–9190, and Northwest Florida (850) 934–6974.

The Great Florida Birding Trail

Usually, only local birders know the best birding sites in an area. The Great Florida Birding Trail was designed to give visitors access to those special places that only the locals know. Sponsored by the Florida Fish and Wildlife Conservation Commission, the Florida Park Service, Florida Audubon and the Florida Department of Transportation, the 3200-km (2000-mile) trail ties together well-known birding spots with more obscure, lesser-known sites. Sites along the trail were nominated by local birders, and selected to maximize sightings of the more than 470 bird species that have been seen in the State. The trail has been designed to be birder-friendly for both experts and amateurs. Trail guides tell you which species you can expect to see at each site, and what to expect in terms of logistics – a short walk, a driving loop, or a long hike.

The trail's first part, the East Florida Section, covering about 190 sites along the East Coast and parts of Central Florida, opened in November 2000. Other sections (West Florida, Panhandle Florida, and South Florida) will open in the future at roughly 18-month intervals. The trail consists of a series of driving loops, each one containing 5 to 10 sites that highlight different natural communities and ecosystems. The east Florida section runs from the Georgia line in Nassau County north of Jacksonville, down to St. Lucie County on the Atlantic Coast, with an inland loop through the Lake Wales Ridge area, north to Marion County. Stops along the way are marked with signs featuring a Swallow-tailed Kite.

Birders are encouraged to flex their economic muscles by downloading 'birder calling cards' from The Great Florida Birding Trail web site. Conservation groups suggest that if birders leave calling cards every time they stay in a hotel, eat at a restaurant, or spend money in a store, communities will recognize the proportion of their business that comes from birders. Local communities along the Great Florida Birding Trail are highly supportive of the project because it brings bird-watchers into rural areas that rarely attract tourists. Ultimately, one of the project's main goals is to conserve bird habitat by providing economic incentives for its protection. Commemorative trail maps are available at nature centers, state parks, tourist development councils, or at one of the gateway sites: for the East Florida Section these include Merritt Island National Wildlife Refuge and Fort Clinch State Park. Maps and information can also be downloaded from the Great

Florida Birding Trail Website at http://www.floridabirdingtrail.com, or requested on-line. For more information call 800–922–0664.

Fishing

Florida is a fisherman's paradise. The state has hundreds of freshwater lakes, rivers and canals, and saltwater fishing enthusiasts have access to thousands of kilometers of coastline. Full or half-day fishing charters are available in most coastal towns. If you would like to fish while you are in Florida, you will need a fishing license. A non-resident can buy a 7-day freshwater fishing license for US$16.50 and a 7-day saltwater fishing license for US$15.00. Children under the age of 16 do not need a license. The money from the license fee is used to improve and restore fish habitat, conduct research, enforce the law, and educate the public. To receive an instant license, call 1–888–FISH–FLORIDA (347–4356).

Canoeing

Because Florida is so flat and many of the best- and least-travelled wild places are on or near the water, canoeing is a good way to go. Try it: you will love it. If you choose a weekday and leave early in the morning, you can drift through the 'Real Florida' and get very close to some actual wildlife. Most natural areas in Florida have canoe rental outfitters associated with them, but if you want to be sure, contact the Florida Professional Paddlesports Association at www.paddleflausa.com; PO Box 1764, Arcadia, Fl 34265; tel (863) 494–1215. Tell them where you want to go and they will give you the name of a good canoe rental outfit in that area.

Manatees

Unquestionably, seeing a manatee in the wild is an extraordinary experience. Not surprisingly, many people want to see manatees when they are in Florida. Call the Save the Manatee Club at 1–800–432–5646 for a list of places you can see manatees, or visit their excellent web site at http://www.savethemanatee.org. In winter, especially during cold weather, manatees tend to gather at certain predictable places. A few of these are Blue Spring State Park near Orlando, (904) 775–3663; Crystal River, (352) 563–2088; and the warm-water discharge canal of Tampa Electric Company's generating plant on Tampa Bay, (813) 228–4289. Between December and March, if you visit one of these sites in the morning of the day after a cold front has passed through, you are virtually guaranteed to see manatees. For a wildlife enthusiast it's an exciting experience, and however much you dislike the crowds, remember, just by being part of the crowd you are helping to preserve this extraordinary mammal. Of course, a chance encounter with a manatee is probably one of the most exciting canoeing experiences you will have. Manatees feed on submerged grasses and have even been seen with their heads out of the water, grazing on bank vegetation. They sometimes gather near canoe

Panhandle (PAN)
1. Blackwater River State Forest
2. St. George Island State Park
3. St. Joseph Peninsula State Park
4. St. Marks National Wildlife Refuge
5. Wakulla Springs State Park
6. Florida Caverns State Park

North Florida (NFL)
7. Lower Suwannee National Wildlife Refuge
8. Ichetucknee Springs State Park
9. Little Talbot Island State Park
10. Guana River State Park
11. Ocala National Forest
12. Fort Matanzas National Monument
13. Washington Oaks State Gardens
14. Paynes Prairie State Preserve

Central Florida (CFL)
15. Blue Spring State Park
16. Highlands Hammock State Park
17. Caladesi Island State Park
18. Myakka River State Park
19. Pelican Island National Wildlife Refuge
20. Hillsborough River State Park
21. Lake Kissimmee State Park

22. Canaveral National Seashore
23. Merritt Island National Wildlife Refuge
24. Chassahowitzka National Wildlife Refuge
25. Homosassa Springs State Wildlife Park
26. Crystal River National Wildlife Refuge

South Florida (SFL)
27. 'Ding' Darling National Wildlife Refuge
28. Sanibel-Captiva Conservation Foundation
29. Corkscrew Swamp Sanctuary
30. Collier Seminole State Park
31. Fakahatchee Strand State Preserve
32. Big Cypress National Preserve
33. Jonathan Dickinson State Park
34. Arthur R. Marshall Loxahatchee National Wildlife Refuge
35. Everglades National Park

Keys and Other Islands (KEY)
36. Biscayne National Park
37. John Pennekamp Coral Reef State Park
38. Lignumvitae Key State Botanical Area
39. National Key Deer Refuge
40. Bahia Honda State Park
41. Dry Tortugas National Park

Map 2 Florida, showing locations of parks and reserves, main cities and highways, and the five regions used in the book to describe animal ranges.

and boat launching points. While canoeing, the surprisingly loud, explosive 'POOOF' sound of a manatee exhaling can alert you to their presence.

Panhandle (PAN)

The least populated and most lightly visited portion of Florida, the Panhandle region (Map 2, p. 28) of northwestern Florida, contains some of the state's most beautiful natural areas. The region's rolling, hilly terrain more closely resembles that of areas in Alabama and Georgia than that of peninsular Florida. The highest point (105 m, 345 ft) in Florida is located near the town of Lakewood, which is almost on the Alabama border. Drained by several large rivers, the region has extensive pine and hardwood forests, springs and swamps. Barrier islands, beaches, and tidal marshes fringe most of the Gulf coast. Panhandle beaches are famous for their white 'sugar' sand, composed of quartz washed down from the Appalachian Mountains by ancient rivers. East of the town of Apalachicola, the beaches and barrier islands give way to a vast salt marsh and the coastline is accessible only by boat. Though it takes about five hours to drive from Orlando to Tallahassee, the region's parks and beaches are well worth the trip. The western Panhandle is in the central time zone, so times there are an hour 'earlier' than in the rest of the state.

Blackwater River State Park (Tel: (850) 957–6140)
Northeast of the Panhandle town of Milton, the 74,270-hectare (183,381-acre) Blackwater River State Forest protects a large expanse of longleaf pine habitat, as well as several pitcher plant bogs. The area is also known for its population of Red-cockaded Woodpeckers, an endangered species. A 13-km (8-mile) drive passes through the woodpecker colony, and nest trees are marked with white paint. Birding is best in the spring and summer. The Blackwater River and Juniper Creek are classified as 'Outstanding Florida Waters' and are popular among canoeists. Canoe rental is available.

St. George Island State Park (Tel: (850) 927–2111)
Just offshore from Apalachicola, St. George Island is a long narrow barrier island joined to the mainland by a causeway. The 795-hectare (1962-acre) park is at the eastern end of the island and it has 14 km (9 miles) of undeveloped and unspoiled beaches. This park is mainly for birders, especially just after a winter cold front has passed through. Northern Gannets, wading birds, and sea ducks, including Common Goldeneyes, are often seen from shore in winter. Birders also like the area for wintering waterfowl and St. George is well known as a good place to see songbirds, hawks and falcons during spring and fall migrations. Loggerhead Sea Turtles nest on the beach in summer.

St. Joseph Peninsula State Park (Tel: (850) 227–1327)
A long narrow claw of land, the St. Joseph Peninsula points north towards Callaway and Panama City. The 1020-hectare (2516-acre) park is bounded on three sides by the waters of St. Joseph Bay and the Gulf of Mexico, and consists of white sand beaches and tall, striking dunes with sheltered waters on the bay side. This is an outstanding birding area, noted as one of the best places in the eastern USA for observing hawks during the fall migration. Eagle Harbor is at the narrowest point on the peninsula and an excellent place to observe raptors. The species

most commonly seen are Sharp-shinned Hawks, Broad-winged Hawks and American Kestrels. Eagle Harbor is also good for sea ducks in winter. Shorebirds and wading birds are abundant and birders rank this as the best spot in Florida to see Peregrine Falcons. Monarch butterflies pass through in autumn, on their long migration to Mexico.

St. Marks National Wildlife Refuge (Tel: (850) 925–6121)

About 32 km (20 miles) across, the refuge encompasses some 27,135 hectares (67,000 acres) on Apalachee Bay, about 32 km (20 miles) south of Tallahassee. Over 270 bird species have been recorded in the refuge's salt marshes and tidal flats, hardwood swamps and hammocks. The main purpose of the refuge is to provide habitat for wintering waterfowl. By early December, some 20 species of ducks and two species of geese can usually be seen in the refuge's wetlands. A variety of wading and shorebirds also winter here, and Bald Eagles can be seen nesting in winter. While the winter concentration of waterbirds is St. Marks' main attraction, spring and fall also are good times to see migrants.

The visitor center just past the fee station has some excellent exhibits and a sighting log that will alert you to sighting of any rare birds or other wildlife. You can buy a wildlife drive guide at the visitor center. The Lighthouse Road is the refuge's main artery. About 11 km (7 miles) long, it is the only road in the refuge open for the public to drive on. Many pools along the road offer good places to see wading birds and other waterbirds. Hiking trails and dike roads crisscross the refuge and provide access to the site's more remote regions. Alligators are often seen sunning themselves on the dikes, and refuge biologists estimate there may be 2500 or more of these large reptiles on refuge lands. In October and November a variety of butterflies migrate through the refuge; many of them are attracted to the wildflowers along the dike roads and around the lighthouse. The fall (late October to early November) migration of Monarch butterflies is particularly spectacular as they pause on this last landfall before flying across the Gulf of Mexico.

Wakulla Springs State Park (Tel: (850) 224-5950)

About 16 km (10 miles) south of Tallahassee, the state's capital, Wakulla Springs State Park is a popular weekend destination. The central attraction of this 1160-hectare (2860-acre) park is one of the world's largest and deepest freshwater springs. The spring produces about 1.5 million liters (400,000 gallons) per minute and forms the headwaters of the Wakulla River. The river flows through a good example of old growth cypress swamp. Over the years the spring has been a great source of fossils of Ice Age mammals. The spring is a popular place for swimming and snorkeling; guided boat tours of the river and glass-bottomed boat tours of the spring are available. When the park is not too crowded, the boat tours offer a surprisingly good opportunity to get near to and photograph waterbirds, turtles, and alligators. Sit on the right side of the boat, as this provides the best view of birds and other wildlife along the shore. The park is especially good for parents with children.

Florida Caverns State Park (Tel: (850) 482–9598)

Located 5 km (3 miles) north of the town of Marianna, this park covers 520 hectares (1284 acres) and the caves protect dazzling formations of stalactites, stalagmites, soda straws, columns, and draperies. It is one of the unique natural areas in the state and the park can get quite crowded during the summer season.

North Florida (NFL)

Sparsely populated compared with the central and southern part of the state, North Florida (Map 2, p. 28) contains some unexpected gems for the ecotraveller. The average tourist rarely visits the area's national wildlife refuges and state parks. Timber companies own much of the land along the Gulf coast and the area has few roads and towns. The Gulf coast is a vast region of salt marshes and tidal flats that are difficult to explore and easy to get lost in. North-central Florida is home to the majority of the state's extraordinarily beautiful natural springs, and there are several fairly easy canoe trips down spring runs and rivers that leave you with a real feel for what Florida must have been like 200 years ago. The Atlantic coast is heavily developed, but you can find quiet places in the middle of the beach frenzy. The beach at Washington Oaks State Gardens is almost within shouting distance of the huge crowds of college kids that spend Easter Break at Crescent Beach, yet it is almost deserted. Other Atlantic barrier islands like Little Talbot Island State Park are equally secluded.

Lower Suwannee National Wildlife Refuge (Tel: (352) 493–0238)

This refuge contains 21,160 hectares (52,257 acres) of coastal salt marsh, bottom-land hardwoods and cypress swamp. When combined with the neighboring off-shore Cedar Keys National Wildlife Refuge, the area forms one of the largest undeveloped river delta–estuarine systems in the USA. More than 250 species of birds have been recorded. Bald Eagles, Osprey and Swallow-tailed Kites are regularly seen. There are many miles of walking and biking trails but the main part of the refuge is accessible only by boat. Boat rentals and guided nature tours are available.

Ichetucknee Springs State Park (Tel: (352) 497–2511)

Ichetucknee is an Indian word meaning 'pond of the beaver.' This 890-hectare (2200-acre) park encloses the northern portion of the Ichetucknee River and its associated river swamps and hardwood hammocks. Originating in a series of nine springs, the Ichetucknee River flows southwest for 9.6 km (6 miles) before it joins the Santa Fe River. This exquisite little river has become one of the most popular natural attractions in Florida. During the months of June, July, and August, thousands of people rent inner tubes and float downstream, snorkeling and swimming along the way. No matter how crowded it is, kids love the experience, and even grouchy older ecotravellers have been known to have a good time. During times of peak use, only 750 tubers a day are allowed on the prettier, upper portion of the run, and it is best to arrive early in the morning. Avoid weekends at all costs. Outside the summer busy season this is one of Florida's most beautiful canoe trips. Canoe and tube rentals are available from several local vendors just outside the park.

Little Talbot Island State Park (Tel: (904) 251–2320)

This unspoiled Atlantic barrier island contains over 8 km (5 miles) of wide sandy beaches, dunes, and a maze of salt marshes and tidal creeks. Behind the dunes are ancient live oaks in a splendid coastal hardwood hammock. River Otters, Raccoons, Marsh Rabbits, and a variety of shorebirds inhabit the salt marshes, and fiddler crabs are commonly seen. Loggerhead Sea Turtles nest along the beach in summer. Nearly 200 species of birds have been recorded from the park, including Caspian Terns, Royal Terns, and Common Loons. The observation deck at the south end of the park is a good place to watch for gannets and sea ducks. In summer you can rent canoes and bicycles to explore the island.

Guana River State Park (Tel: (904) 825–5071)

This 970-hectare (2400-acre) park is located on a barrier island 16 km (10 miles) north of St. Augustine. Adjoining the park to the north is the 4860-hectare (12,000-acre) Guana River Wildlife Management Area. Though they are managed by two separate authorities, both reserves are treated as a single conservation area. (However, you should be aware that hunting is permitted on the wildlife management area during hunting season.) Bounded by the Atlantic Ocean and the Intracoastal Waterway, the park contains 16 km (10 miles) of beach and dunes, as well as salt marshes, maritime hardwood hammock, and pond pine flatwoods. The site was occupied by Indians (there are extensive shell middens) and later by the Spanish, British and early American settlers. The dikes and ditches remain, as do the rubble of a mill, houses and a graveyard. More than 226 bird species have been recorded, and on a good day in winter one can often see 60 species. In winter, Guana Lake impoundment is a good place to see migratory ducks, White Pelicans, Osprey and many shorebirds. Three species of sea turtles nest on the beaches. There are few facilities. An outdoor kiosk near the dam has bird lists and a trail guide.

Ocala National Forest (Tel: (352) 669-3152)

Established in 1908, the 153,900-hectare (380,000-acre) Ocala National Forest is the oldest national forest in the eastern USA. However, it can be a disappointing experience for the ecotraveller because of the intense human activity. Logging, tree planting, controlled burns, hunting and off-road vehicles are just some of the activities you may encounter. Despite these distractions, there are at least two worthwhile trips for the ecotraveller in the Ocala National Forest. One is the Juniper Creek canoe run. For a small fee you can rent a canoe at Juniper Springs and paddle down the 11-km (7-mile) (4-hour) canoe trail formed by Juniper Springs and nearby Fern Hammock Springs. The wild and scenic trip passes through some of the finest semi-tropical forest in the continental USA. Avoid the peak summer months because the run becomes overcrowded. For a whole day of canoeing, you can rent a canoe from one of several private outfitters just outside the forest and paddle the 30-km (19-mile) Oklawaha River Run. Alligators and turtles abound. This trip is best made in spring or fall.

Fort Matanzas National Monument (Tel: (904) 471–0116)

This 105-hectare (260-acre) historical site, 22 km (14 miles) south of St. Augustine, has a Spanish fort that was built in 1740 and plenty of wildlife to interest ecotravellers. The National Park Service operates a free ferry to the fort on Rattlesnake Island. On the short trip across the Matanzas River Bottle-nosed Dolphins are frequently sighted. From the boardwalk and nature trail you may see Gopher Tortoises, and during spring and fall many migrating songbirds stop in the hammock vegetation. Gray Kingbirds breed here in spring and summer. Just south of the monument entrance the tidal flats of the inlet attract Brown Pelicans, terns, Black Skimmers and many other sea and shorebirds.

Washington Oaks Gardens State Park (Tel: (386) 446–6780)

A few miles south of Fort Matanzas is the 157-hectare (389-acre) Washington Oaks State Gardens. This small park lies between the Atlantic Ocean and the Intracoastal Waterway. The hammock forest on the Intracoastal Waterway side provides good birding in fall and spring. On the ocean side, opposite the main entrance sign to the Intracoastal side of the park, is a narrow road that leads to a parking lot behind the dunes. This provides access to one of north Florida's most unusual and least crowded public beaches. Unique rock outcrops of coquina – fossilized sea shells bound together by a matrix of dissolved calcium carbonate – protrude from the sand. Tidal pools and unusual rock formations make this beach great fun for older kids (and ecotravellers).

Paynes Prairie Preserve State Park (Tel: (352) 466–3397)

In 1774, the naturalist William Bartram called this area just south of Gainesville, the 'great Alachua Savannah.' Today, the preserve protects 8500 hectares (21,000 acres) of marsh and wet prairie. The area is best known as one of the major wintering grounds for migratory Sandhill Cranes. Between late October and March thousands of Sandhill Cranes gather on the prairie. Early morning and late afternoon are the best times to see and hear the birds calling. On warm days in February and March, dozens of alligators bask on the canal banks along La Chua Trail, which is on the north and east side of the prairie. La Chua Trail is also a good place for birding, especially in the winter, when cranes, eagles, hawks and wading birds are common.

Central Florida (CFL)

Central Florida (Map 2, p. 28), the region that divides temperate and subtropical Florida, extends from coast to coast, and south from Ocala to Lake Okeechobee. The citrus belt begins here, and freezes in this area and southwards are rare occurrences. The subtropical influence is also evident in the increased presence of cabbage palms in wet areas. As well as being home to Orlando and its gigantic complex of theme parks, the central portion of the state is Florida's retirement mecca. The population density increases dramatically and hundreds of golf courses, mobile home communities, retirement communities, shopping malls, churches and funeral homes dot the landscape. Somewhat amazingly, if you know where to look, there are still many wild places left. An hour's drive from Orlando one can be birdwatching on Merritt Island National Wildlife Refuge or canoeing to the Gulf on the Chassahowitzka River. Along the Lake Wales Ridge you can see some of the last remnants of Florida's unique scrub ecosystem.

Blue Spring State Park (Tel: (386) 775–3663)

About 48 km (30 miles) north of Orlando, this 1050-hectare (2600-acre) park is known as an excellent place to see manatees. A handicapped accessible viewing platform offers great views of manatees and fish. When winter cold fronts sweep down from the north, manatees leave the colder 16 °C (60 °F) waters of the St. Johns River and congregate in the warmer 22 °C (72 °F) waters of the spring. On cold days it is not uncommon to see 50 or more manatees floating in the clear waters near the observation platform. However, because there is little food for manatees in the springs, they must leave to feed in the river during the day. If you are visiting the spring on a cold winter morning expressly to see manatees, go early. This park gets extremely crowded on weekends and during the peak summer season.

Highlands Hammock State Park (Tel: (863) 386–6094)

This beautiful 3300-hectare (8140-acre) park, near Sebring, was one of Florida's four original state parks. Opened to the public in 1931, this land's designation as a state park was one of the earliest examples of 'grass-roots' public support for environmental preservation. A great place to see some of Florida's habitats, the park encompasses virgin hardwood forest with 1000-year-old oaks, one of the few surviving virgin cabbage palm hammocks, cypress swamp, pine flatwoods, sand pine scrub and marshes. The park's 177 bird species include the Florida Scrub Jay, Pileated Woodpecker, Red-shouldered Hawk, Wood Stork, and Swallow-tailed Kite. One of the last sightings of the Ivory-billed Woodpecker was made here in 1967. Birding is excellent in the park during fall migration. There are nine trails in the park; all can be walked in 4 to 5 hours (or rent a bicycle and ride). Bring insect repellent in the summer.

Caladesi Island State Park (Tel: (727) 469–5918)

Accessible only by public ferry, this 475-hectare (1170-acre) park consists of six undeveloped Gulf coast barrier islands, with beautiful beaches and great swimming and shelling. Bottlenose Dolphins are often seen offshore and Loggerhead Sea Turtles nest on the beach. This is a great place to follow Raccoon and Gopher Tortoise tracks in the sand; you can often follow what appears to be a Raccoon's entire night's ramblings. The ferry departs hourly. For ferry information call (813) 734–5263.

Myakka River State Park (Tel: (941) 361–6511)

Just south of Sarasota, this 11,700-hectare (28,876-acre) protected area is Florida's largest state park. It is famous for its abundant wildlife and scenic beauty. The park includes one of the best examples of dry prairie habitat in southwest Florida. There are 64 km (40 miles) of hiking trails. More than 19 km (12 miles) of the Myakka River flows through the western portion of the park and its lakes and floodplain marshes are a haven for waterfowl and wading birds. Herons, ibis, egrets, Purple Gallinule, Limpkins and other wading birds abound. Many waterfowl, including widgeon, pintail, and teal winter here. Both Fulvous and Black-bellied Whistling Ducks have been seen in the marshes. More than 250 bird species have been recorded in the park. Canoe rentals are available.

Pelican Island National Wildlife Refuge (Tel: (772) 562-3909)

Tiny Pelican Island (only 1.2 hectares, 3 acres), off the east coast of Florida, holds a unique place in American conservation history. In 1903 President Theodore Roosevelt set aside Pelican Island as a 'preserve and breeding ground for native birds,' and with this designation the area became the first national wildlife refuge in the USA. The refuge is approachable only by boat and encompasses about 2025 hectares (5000 acres) of mangrove islands and waterways. In addition to birds, the area protects a large population of manatees and provides a vital nursery for juvenile sea turtles. There are two bird-nesting seasons, one starting in late November, the other in late March. Winter is the best time to visit. Nesting birds include the Brown Pelican, Common Egret, Snowy Egret, Reddish Egret, Great Blue Heron, Little Blue Heron, Tricolored Heron, Black-crowned Night Heron, White Ibis, Glossy Ibis, Double-crested Cormorant and Anhinga. Wood Storks began to nest here in the 1960s and there are now two Wood Stork rookeries. Unless you have a private boat, the only way to see the rookeries is from a local charter tour boat. Chartered cruises from Sebastian, the closest town, take about one and a half hours.

Hillsborough River State Park (Tel: (813) 987–6771)

Only 19 km (12 miles) north of the city of Tampa, this 1600-hectare (3950-acre) park gets a lot of use. However, several miles of nature trails give visitors the chance to wander through hammocks of live oaks, sabal palms, and hickories bordering the Hillsborough River. The best birding is on the nature trail along the river. You may see River Otters, alligators, and turtles if you canoe the river. Canoe rentals are available.

Lake Kissimmee State Park (Tel: (863) 696–1112)

Twenty-four km (15 miles) east of Lake Wales, the 2040-hectare (5030-acre) Lake Kissimmee State Park contains a rich variety of Florida habitats. The park is surrounded by citrus groves and Lake Rosalie, Tiger Lake and Lake Kissimmee, the state's third largest lake. Habitats in the park include wet prairies, pine flatwoods, hardwood swamp, and oak hammock. The scrubby flatwoods near the gate support many Florida Scrub Jays. The park has 50 species of plants and animals that are either threatened, of special concern, or endangered. The bird list includes more than 200 species, including Bald Eagles, Swallow-tailed Kites, Sandhill Cranes, Burrowing Owls and an occasional Crested Caracara. There are 21 km (13 miles) of hiking trails in the park; an observation tower at the picnic area overlooks Lake Kissimmee. The endangered Whooping Crane is being reintroduced to Florida in the park's prairies. Canoe and boat rentals are available.

Canaveral National Seashore (Tel: (321) 267–1110)

Canaveral is one of 10 National Seashores in the country. Managed by the National Park Service, this site covers 23,300 hectares (57,600 acres) and protects 38 km (24 miles) of beach – the longest stretch of undeveloped beach on Florida's congested Atlantic Coast. Turtle Mound, which is located near the north end of the seashore boundary, is an excellent birding spot for fall migrants. Numerous raptors can be seen from the two platforms, and it is the best land-site in Florida for observing sea birds, especially in late fall on days with strong northeasterly winds. Behind the beaches and dunes lies Mosquito Lagoon, a long tidal estuary fringed by marshes, hardwood hammocks and mangroves. This is one of Florida's great birding hot-spots – over 300 bird species have been identified in the area. Together with neighboring Merritt Island National Wildlife Refuge, the site attracts major concentrations of wintering shorebirds and waterfowl. During spring and fall migrations, the area attracts large numbers of songbirds and hawks. The beach at Canaveral is an important nesting ground for three species of sea turtles. Between 3000 and 4000 Loggerhead Sea Turtles nest here each year, along with 300 or more Green Sea Turtles, and a few Leatherback Sea Turtles. Between May and August park rangers and volunteers patrol the beach each night, looking for new nest sites. They stake out a square of wire mesh screen over each nest to prevent Raccoons from digging up the eggs. Turtle hatchlings can get out through the openings in the mesh. The main entrance is at Apollo Beach, on A1A, 11 km (7 miles) south of New Smyrna Beach. There are a few parking areas and boardwalk access to the beach, but little else in the way of services. The number of people you see declines rapidly with increasing distance from the parking areas. Biting insects (especially on the Mosquito Lagoon side) are numerous in summer. Both Canaveral and Merritt Island are closed during space-shuttle launches.

Merritt Island National Wildlife Refuge (Tel: (321) 861-0667)

Merritt Island National Wildlife Refuge is located on the grounds of the Kennedy Space Center, east of Titusville. The 56,700-hectare (140,000-acre) refuge shares a common boundary with Canaveral National Seashore, and together the two areas rank as one of Florida's major attractions for wildlife enthusiasts. Three hundred and thirty species of birds have been documented in the refuge. Approximately half of the refuge consists of brackish estuaries and marshes; the remainder is coastal dunes, pine flatwoods, and palm and oak hammocks. An estimated 5000 alligators inhabit the refuge, and manatees use the northern Banana River area during spring. A manatee observation deck is located on the northeast side of Haulover Canal. Loggerhead and Green Sea Turtles nest on the beaches in summer. Black Point Wildlife Drive is an excellent 11-km (7-mile) self-guided tour through the marshes. Stop and pick up a brochure at the entrance to the drive. In winter, this is a good place to see waterfowl and wading birds, as well as alligators and occasionally River Otters. There is a visitor information center 6 km (4 miles) east of Titusville. Biting insects are numerous in summer. Both Canaveral and Merritt Island are closed during space-shuttle launches.

Chassahowitzka National Wildlife Refuge (Tel: (352) 563-2088)

Located 6 km (4 miles) south of Homosassa Springs, the 12,560-hectare (31,000-acre) Chassahowitzka National Wildlife Refuge includes the scenic Chassahowitzka River and large areas of coastal marshes, estuaries and hardwood swamps. The refuge is accessible only by boat, but it is relatively simple matter to rent a canoe and paddle down the Chassahowitzka River to the Gulf. The trip is highly recommended. Take lunch and spend the day canoeing the river and some of the side streams. River Otters, alligators, turtles and wading birds are commonly seen. Manatees regularly use the river in winter and often hang out by the canoe launch point. Winter and spring are good times to see some of the 250 bird species recorded in the refuge. Avoid weekends.

Homosassa Springs State Wildlife Park (Tel: (352) 628-5343)

If you want a chance to see some of Florida's native animals and birds close up, this is the place. One of Florida's old tourist attractions has now been turned over to the state and currently serves as a rehabilitation center and refuge for manatees that have been orphaned or injured in the wild. A large underwater observatory centered on a natural spring allows visitors to get a close up look at manatees and many species of fish. Left over from the days when the park was a tourist attraction, there are also several exhibits of captive animals, including Black Bear, Bobcat, River Otter and alligator.

Crystal River National Wildlife Refuge (Tel: (352) 795-7961)

The Crystal River National Wildlife Refuge was established in 1983 to protect the endangered West Indian (Florida) Manatee. Made up of nine islands totaling about 19 hectares (46 acres), the refuge provides critical winter habitat for about 300 manatees. The refuge is accessible only by boat, but many boat rentals, charters and guided tours operate out of the small town of Crystal River, about 10 km (6 miles) north of Homosassa Springs. The best time to see manatees is January to March, especially just after a cold front. Avoid weekends, and observe speed zone and sanctuary restrictions.

South Florida (SFL)

South Florida (Map 2, p. 28) extends from Lake Okeechobee south to the tip of the peninsula. A hundred years ago most of south Florida was wetlands, and the region was sometimes described as 'nine-tenths water, one-tenth swamp.' The topography is flat, and almost all the land in south Florida is less than 8 m (26 ft) above sea level. This is where most of Florida's population lives, but west of Miami the development stops abruptly. Beyond this line is what remains of the upper Everglades. Sawgrass marshes dotted with occasional clumps of palms stretch to the horizon. Driving across the upper Everglades on a highway known as the Alligator Alley (I-75), you pass large yellow signs warning 'Panther Crossing.' More than 30 underpasses were installed on the highway to allow Florida Panthers to cross the roadway. The climate in this region is well and truly tropical; palms, bougainvillea, limes, mangos and other tropical plants appear in city gardens, and tree ferns and epiphytes hang from the trees. Several important natural areas have been preserved: Corkscrew Swamp Sanctuary, the Fakahatchee Strand State Preserve, 'Ding' Darling National Wildlife Refuge, and Jonathan Dickinson State Park to name but a few. After driving through Miami you may doubt that south Florida holds anything of interest for the ecotraveller, but we think you will be surprised.

'Ding' Darling National Wildlife Refuge (Tel: (239) 472–1100)

It is easy to see why Sanibel Island is one of Florida's renowned resort areas. Beautiful beaches, with great shelling, combined with a small town atmosphere makes it one of the most attractive vacation sites in Florida. The tiny island also contains two outstanding wildlife viewing sites, the best known of which is the world famous J. N. 'Ding' Darling National Wildlife Refuge. The refuge occupies over 2025 hectares (5000 acres) of the island and annually attracts hundreds of thousands of visitors from all over the world. A new visitor center with excellent information packets and numerous trails for walking, bicycling or driving make getting around easy. It is difficult not to see birds on the 8-km (5-mile) long Wildlife Drive. Over 50 species of wading and shorebirds frequent the refuge, and Wood Storks, White Ibis, Yellow-crowned Night Herons, and Great and Snowy Egrets are common. At times, as much as a third of the USA population of Roseate Spoonbills can be in the refuge. At low tide – the best time to visit – the mudflats are often covered with shorebirds, including American Oystercatchers and Black-necked Stilts. This is a site you can visit for several days and still see new sights and wildlife. Winter is the best time to visit but be prepared for crowds.

Sanibel-Captiva Conservation Foundation (Tel: (239) 472–2329)

Also on Sanibel Island, this 450-hectare (1100-acre) nature center is less heavily visited than the nearby 'Ding' Darling National Wildlife Refuge. An excellent nature center, it provides information and posts recent wildlife sightings. Seven short trails take you through the area, and a boardwalk lets you get a close look at marsh grass habitat and its birds.

Corkscrew Swamp Sanctuary (Tel: (239) 348–9151)

Owned and managed by the National Audubon Society, this 4455-hectare (11,000-acre) sanctuary is a must-see, with outstanding opportunities for wildlife photography. Corkscrew contains the largest remaining stand of old-growth bald-cypress in the country. Some of the trees are estimated to be over 500 years old.

A 3-km (2-mile) self-guided boardwalk trail gives you a rare glimpse of South Florida before human settlement. From the boardwalk you get great close-up views of tree ferns, orchids and bromeliads. Alligators, lizards, turtles, and River Otters also are commonly spotted. Over 200 bird species have been seen in the sanctuary, including Swallow-tailed Kite, Barred Owl, Limpkin, Anhinga, Green Heron, and American Bittern. It is not unusual to see 40 to 50 species of birds in a day. Corkscrew also has the largest nesting colony of Wood Storks in the USA. The Wood Storks usually begin to nest in December, sometimes within full view of the boardwalk. Most years nesting lasts from February to May. The visitor center has useful free booklets and specific wildlife sightings are posted daily at the trailhead. Most visitors come between Christmas and Easter, but Corkscrew is a good place to visit any time of the year.

Collier Seminole State Park (Tel: (239) 394–3379)

About 27 km (17 miles) southeast of Naples, Collier Seminole State Park is just west of the Fakahatchee Strand Preserve. Nearly two-thirds of this park's 2600 hectares (6423 acres) consists of mangrove forest. But there also are cypress swamps, salt marshes and a tropical hardwood hammock, dominated by trees that are characteristic of coastal forests in the West Indies. Gumbo-limbo, royal palms, buttonwood, strangler fig, bromeliads, and ferns abound. For the adventurous, the 22-km (13.5-mile) Mangrove Wilderness canoe trail is a great way to get a close look at a mangrove swamp. Winter is the best time to visit; in summer the mosquitoes are ferocious. Canoe rentals are available.

Fakahatchee Strand State Preserve (Tel: (239) 695–4593)

About 10 km (6 miles) north of Everglades City, this 26,325-hectare (65,000-acre) preserve is one of the wildest areas left in Florida. The preserve extends from Alligator Alley (as Interstate Highway 75, which cuts east to west across the southern part of the Florida peninsula, is locally known) in the north to Everglades National Park and Ten Thousand Islands in the south. Fakahatchee Strand contains North America's largest stand of native royal palms, and the area is famous for its orchids, rare ferns and bromeliads. This forested wetland was logged for cypress, and today the logging roads, called 'trams,' provide the only way to get around. Most of the trams are overgrown with vegetation but some have been cleared for hiking. The area is one of the strongholds for the endangered Florida Panther. White Ibis, Glossy Ibis, Roseate Spoonbills, herons, egrets, Barred Owls and Red-shouldered Hawks are regularly observed. The 610-m (2000-ft) Big Cypress Bend boardwalk (off U.S. Highway 41) provides access to an old-growth cypress stand. Off Highway 29, a graded gravel road known as Janes Scenic Drive will take you about 18 km (11 miles) into the swamp. Visitor facilities are extremely limited.

Big Cypress National Preserve (Tel: (239) 695–1201)

Named for the size of the area it covers rather than the size of its trees, the Big Cypress Preserve covers 295,250 hectares (729,000 acres) of South Florida. Located between Naples and Miami, next to Everglades National Park, the preserve consists mostly of dwarf pond cypress scattered through vast areas of marsh. The preserve also encompasses cypress domes and strands interspersed with hardwood hammocks. Public access is minimal. The Loop Road south from Monroe Station provides a scenic 42-km (26-mile) drive through the prairies and marshes, but it is a single-lane gravel road. Watch out for potholes. A visitor center is located on U.S. Highway 41 at Oasis.

Jonathan Dickinson State Park (Tel: (772) 546–2771)

Located about 11 km (7 miles) north of Jupiter, this 4660-hectare (11,500-acre) park includes large areas of endangered coastal sand pine scrub, and pine flatwoods. Scrub Jays, Gopher Tortoises, and several lizard species are commonly seen. Cypress and mangrove wetlands flank the Loxahatchee River, which in 1985 was designated a 'National Wild and Scenic River.' Birds here include Osprey, White Ibis, and Anhingas. Canoe rentals are available but avoid weekends and the peak summer season.

Arthur R. Marshall Loxahatchee National Wildlife Refuge (Tel: (561) 734–8303)

The main entrance to Loxahatchee is off U.S. 441, west of Boynton Beach. This 59,700-hectare (147,392-acre) refuge contains the largest remaining tract of northern Everglades habitat. Unlike the more open southern Everglades, this refuge contains thousands of small tree islands formed on floating peat mats. The refuge is downstream from one of Florida's most intensively farmed areas, and agricultural runoff has caused many problems. Despite this, birding is often excellent. Wintering waterfowl, especially Blue-winged Teal, Ring-necked Ducks, Wood Ducks and Fulvous Whistling Ducks concentrate here. You also may see Snail Kites, Black-necked Stilts, Spotted Sandpipers, Anhinga, Limpkins, and ibis. Most of the refuge is underwater or swampy and not accessible by road or foot. Paths are laid out in a grid-like pattern, alternating with canals. Check with the visitor center first for helpful information.

Everglades National Park (Tel: (305) 242–7700)

Everglades National Park is huge. More than 606,688 hectares (1.5 million acres) in area, it is the largest remaining subtropical wilderness in the continental USA. Everglades is also unique, being one of only three sites on Earth to have been declared a UNESCO World Heritage Site, an International Biosphere Reserve, and a Wetland of International Importance. However, unless you know what to expect and where to look, Everglades can be disappointing for the visitor. It is incredibly flat. Looking out across miles and miles of sawgrass is like looking at the ocean or the prairies in the USA's Midwest; after a while you long for a little relief. Below we have listed a few short wildlife viewing trips. For a more complete list of the programs and facilities available at Everglades, write to Everglades National Park, 40001 State Road 9336, Homestead, Florida, or log on to the Park Service's Everglades web site at http://www.nps.gov/ever/home.htm.

The watershed of the Everglades begins in central Florida's Kissimmee basin, and covers most of South Florida. Early settlers viewed the Everglades as a dangerous swamp in need of reclamation. Work on digging drainage canals began in the 1880s and continued until the 1960s. Today 50% of South Florida's former wetlands no longer exist. Over the years, miles of canals and levees have been built and hundreds of gates, spillways and pumping stations now stabilize and control this once-dynamic wetland system. But wading birds and much of the other wildlife of the Everglades depend on annual cycles of drought and flood. The renowned rookeries of herons, egrets and storks have shrunk by 95% since the 1930s. But despite this, the Everglades is still an amazing place to visit. Most tourists go in winter because mosquitoes practically close the place in summer. Even if you are tempted to brave the insects, don't bother. The summer rainy season also means birds and other wildlife are widely dispersed and difficult to see. When you do go, plan ahead. Stop at the visitor center and ask for bird lists, trail guides, and viewing information. There are no provisions or facilities in the park except at Flamingo, at the end of a 60-km (38-mile) road. Take drinking water.

Park headquarters to Flamingo. A 60-km (38-mile) drive with numerous potential stops along the way. Whatever you do, don't be tempted to simply drive to Flamingo and back without getting out of the car; many visitors do just this, then complain that they have not seen anything. Stop at the Royal Palm area; two short trails there, the Gumbo Limbo trail and the Anhinga trail, will take you to Taylor Slough, one of the richest wildlife areas in the park. Most of the birds have become habituated to the presence of humans. Alligators abound, as do turtles, herons, egrets, and Anhingas.

Shark Valley. Ask at the visitor center for directions to the Shark Valley loop trail. Many visitors miss this part of the Everglades but it is well worth a look. Walk or bicycle (rentals available) the 24-km (15-mile) loop road to an observation tower. A two-hour tram ride is also available. There are plenty of alligators along the road and you may see Wood Storks, Purple Gallinules, bitterns, and other wading birds in the marshes.

Ten Thousand Islands. If you are feeling really adventurous, you can make a week-long canoe trip through the Ten Thousand Islands, from Everglades City to Flamingo. Permits are required for the trip and tides can be strong, so only seasoned canoeists should consider making the trip. Request a canoe guide for the Everglades from the National Park Service or check their web site. For shorter trips, you can rent a canoe at Flamingo.

Keys and Other Islands (KEY)

Just south of Miami, the Florida Keys (Map 2, p. 28 and Map 3, p. 41) trail away to the southwest, ending at Key West. The Overseas Highway (a section of U.S. 1) begins at Key Largo and runs for 180 km (114 miles) over 42 bridges and causeways to Key West. The Dry Tortugas, considered a highlight of any birding trip to south Florida, are about 110 km (70 miles) west of Key West. Geologically, the Keys consist of a shallow layer of sand over small patches of ancient coral reef; most of the islands rise only a few meters above the ocean. All fresh water must be piped in or collected from rainfall. The Dry Tortugas National Park relies for fresh water solely on a rain catchment system and a small desalinization plant. Coral reefs extend along the east side of the Keys, from Biscayne National Park through John Pennecamp Coral Reef State Park and out to the Dry Tortugas. Winter is the peak tourist season in the Keys and the parks and reefs are usually very crowded. The area is slightly less crowded in early fall and late spring. Before starting out for Key West, birders should call the Rare Bird Alert hotline for the lower Keys (305) 294–3438.

Biscayne National Park (Tel: (305) 230–7275)
Fourteen km (9 miles) east of Homestead, the 73,500-hectare (181,500-acre) Biscayne National Park contains a small stretch of the mainland, a large area of Biscayne Bay and a number of barrier islands. Ninety-five percent of the park is underwater. In 1992, this section of the coast was ground zero for Hurricane

Parks
Big Cypress National Preserve
Everglades National Park
1. Biscayne National Park
2. John Pennekamp Coral Reef State Park

3. Lignumvitae Key State Botanical Area
4. National Key Deer Refuge
5. Bahia Honda State Park
6. Dry Tortugas National Park

Map 3   The southern tip of Florida, showing locations of the Florida Keys and Everglades National Park.

Andrew; the storm eliminated the park's visitor center (since rebuilt) before moving on to destroy much of the town of Homestead. The park offers an excellent introduction to coral reefs and marine fishes. Most visitors to the park come by private boat, but glass-bottomed boat trips, canoes rentals and scuba and snorkeling trips are available.

John Pennekamp Coral Reef State Park (Tel: (305) 451–1202)

Named for the late John D. Pennekamp, a Miami newspaper editor, this state park is situated on the Atlantic Ocean side of Key Largo. The park extends 5 km (3 miles) into the ocean and is approximately 40 km (25 miles) long. Pennecamp and the adjacent Florida Keys National Marine Sanctuary cover approximately 460 sq km (178 sq miles) of coral reefs, seagrass beds, and mangrove swamps. In this park the wilderness is underwater. Forests of living coral, sponges, shrimp, crabs, turtles, lobsters and nearly 600 species of fish are found here. In places, the coral reef is near the surface, providing excellent opportunities for snorkeling.

However, you should be aware that the reef can be reached only by boat. You cannot see the reef by snorkeling from shore. Most people come to swim, snorkel and fish, but you can also see some interesting birds in winter, including Caspian Terns, Common Terns, Bonaparte's Gulls and Scissor-tailed Flycatchers. Breeding birds include White-crowned Pigeons, Gray Kingbirds, Black-whiskered Vireos, and the Cuban form of the Yellow Warbler. You can pick up a copy of the park's bird list at the excellent visitor center. Pennecamp receives more than a million visitors a year and can get quite crowded. Motor boats, canoes, kayaks, snorkeling and scuba equipment can be rented.

Lignumvitae Key Botanical State Park (Tel: (305) 664–2540)

This 110-hectare (280-acre) pristine site, between Upper and Lower Matecumbe Key, is one of the best remaining examples of a tropical hammock. Because it is accessible only by boat, not many people make the trip. But this is the original Florida, well worth a visit. The island's name comes from a small, gnarled-looking tree, the *Lignum vitae*, which is native to Central America and the Bahamas. The area is a living botanical example of Florida's Caribbean connections; you can see strangler fig, mastic, poisonwood, pigeon plum, mahogany, Jamaican dogwood, gumbo limbo and many other tropical tree and shrub species. The island also supports a population of brightly colored tree snails (*Liguus fasciatus*). Birds include White-crowned Pigeons, Mangrove Cuckoos, Black-whiskered Vireos, gulls, and wading birds. The island is accessible only by boat from Indian Key Fill. The three-hour round-trip boat tour operates Thursday through Monday. Call (305) 664–4815 for information on boat service.

National Key Deer Refuge (Tel: (305) 872–2239)

Located on Big Pine Key, the National Key Deer Refuge was created to protect the miniature White-tailed Deer found only in the Keys. Today, cars are the deer's major 'predator;' some 15% of the population is killed by cars each year. Early morning and evening are the best times to observe these deer, especially along Key Deer Boulevard and on No Name Key. (DO NOT feed the deer; it encourages them to hang around at the side of the road.) Birds often seen in the refuge include the Roseate Spoonbill, Great White Heron, and Mangrove Cuckoo. There is also a local population of very pale-colored Raccoons.

Bahia Honda State Park (Tel: (305) 872–2353)

Nineteen km (12 miles) south of Marathon on U.S. 1, Bahia (pronounced BAY-uh) Honda is Florida's southernmost state park. The name of the park means 'deep bay' and reflects the Spanish influence in this area. The park protects all of Bahia Honda Key, a narrow strip of land bordered by the Gulf of Mexico on one side and the Atlantic Ocean on the other. Bahia Honda has been ranked as one of the best beaches in the USA and most visitors come to swim, fish, and snorkel, attracted to the tropical beach and clear blue-green water. Inland from the beaches is a dense tropical hardwood hammock with gumbo-limbo, silver palm, key thatch palm and yellow satinwood. The Silver Palm Nature Trail gives visitors an opportunity to walk through the otherwise impenetrable vegetation. You may see Smooth-billed Anis, White-crowned Pigeons, Black-whiskered Vireos and Mangrove Cuckoos. Least Terns nest on the beach. Brown Pelicans, Magnificent Frigatebirds, Double-crested Cormorants, and Laughing Gulls can be seen year-round. In winter, White Ibis, Common Terns and Royal Terns are frequently seen. Kayaks, bicycles, and snorkeling equipment can be rented.

Dry Tortugas National Park (Tel: (305) 242–7700)

Most people don't realize that the Keys don't end at Key West. Almost 110 km (70 miles) farther out in the Gulf of Mexico lies a small cluster of islands known as the Dry Tortugas, one of North America's most remote national parks. Because the Tortugas are so far off the beaten path they still offer adventures for the eco-traveller and especially rich rewards for birding enthusiasts. The Tortugas were discovered by Ponce de Leon in 1530; he named them Las Tortugas for the numerous sea turtles he found in the surrounding waters. Later the word 'Dry' was added to the name to warn mariners that there was no fresh water on the islands. The islands are located in the middle of the migratory flyway between North and South America and are known worldwide for their extraordinary bird-life. A spring visit to this remote park is considered the highlight of a birding trip to Florida. Spring and fall migrations can produce many surprises, and the island's bird list (285 species) is full of 'accidental' species from South America or the West Indies, such as Variegated Flycatchers, Thick-billed Vireos, and Loggerhead Kingbirds. Late-winter cold fronts blow flocks of weary warblers, vireos and other songbirds onto the islands. Nesting birds start to arrive in March, and between April and September thousands of Sooty Terns, Brown Noddies, and Roseate Terns nest on Bush Key. Other notable nesting birds include the Magnificent Frigatebird and Masked Booby. In addition to birding opportunities, the park also offers excellent snorkeling and scuba diving sites. Sea turtles, including the Hawksbill, Loggerhead, Green and Atlantic Ridley, are seen in the clear shallow water. Access to the Tortugas is by ferry, chartered boat, or seaplane: (305) 294–2587 or (800) 648–6269. The boat trip takes 3 to 5 hours, seaplane about 45 minutes. There is no lodging available, and visitors must bring camping equipment and all provisions including water.

Chapter 4

ENVIRONMENTAL THREATS AND CONSERVATION PROGRAMS

by Holly Freifeld, Ph.D.

- *Major Environmental Threats*
- *Conservation Programs*
  Return of the Whooping Crane
  The Florida Panther: Teetering on the Brink?
  Bald Eagle Recovery
  Save the Florida Manatee!
  Sea Turtles
  Florida Forever
  Battle For the Everglades
- *Environmental Close-up 1: Alien Nation: Non-native Species in Florida*

Major Environmental Threats

Many residents and visitors see Florida as a paradise. But, like all places that people find particularly attractive, Florida faces challenges in safeguarding and restoring its natural landscapes. Florida's burgeoning human population, over 15 million in 1999 and with nearly 700 new arrivals each day, results in the loss of native habitats and other pressures that compromise the land's ability to support native plants and animals.

Native forest is being removed at a rate of about 81,000 hectares (200,000 acres) each year to make way for the infrastructure to support new Floridians. Forests are being replaced by pine 'plantations' that produce pulp for the paper products industry. The web of roads that fragments what's left of the native ecosystems grows ever more complex – Florida has almost two miles of road per square mile (0.8 km of road per sq km).

Agriculture – citrus, vegetables, and sugar cane – covers about 3 million hectares (7.5 million acres), or 22% of the state. Gigantic water-control projects to support commercial agriculture and control flooding have changed the natural flow of water through Central and South Florida. These changes have caused possibly irreparable damage to the Kissimmee River drainage and Everglades, which formed the largest wetland in North America and was home to literally millions of birds and other animals. The run-off of pesticides and chemical fertilizers from agriculture also has far-reaching, long-term impacts on wildlife. For example, recent research reveals that chemical pollutants in Lake Apopka damage the hormone balance in American Alligators and disrupts their breeding.

Finally, the accelerating human activity in Florida over the past century has resulted in the arrival of hundreds of new plants and animals, and some of these non-native organisms prey on or displace the state's native species. The numbers of endangered and threatened species reflect the impact of human activities on Florida's wildlife. In 1997, the state's Fish and Wildlife Conservation Commission listed 117 animal and 413 plant species as endangered, threatened, or 'of special concern.' Of these, 50 animals and 54 plants are also listed as threatened or endangered by the federal government.

In spite of, or perhaps because of, this apparently dismal situation, Florida has one of the most active conservation communities in the country, comprised of state and federal agencies, private organizations, research scientists, and citizen groups. Following are descriptions of some major conservation projects in the state; these are only a sampling of the many projects and initiatives now dedicated to protecting Florida's native wildlife.

Conservation Programs

Return of the Whooping Crane

According to historical records, Whooping Cranes (Plate 25; p. 125) have never been abundant. At most, 1000 to 2000 of the huge white birds inhabited North America's wet prairies in the 1800s. With hunting, egg collecting, and the conversion of prairies for agriculture, 'Whooper' numbers dwindled to fewer than 20 in the 1930s, and they were listed as endangered in 1967. In addition to protection from hunting and conservation of habitat, establishment of additional populations was deemed critical to the crane's recovery. Today, the total population is just over 400. The main flock of wild Whoopers, 190 birds, nests in the Northwest Territories, Canada, and winters in coastal Texas. Most of the rest live in captivity.

Because of the high quality crane habitat (and healthy populations of Sandhill Cranes) on the Kissimmee Prairie, the U.S. Fish and Wildlife Service chose the area as the site for a Whooping Crane reintroduction project. Fourteen young, captive-bred, Whoopers were released in 1993 to inaugurate a non-migratory Florida population. Since that first release, the Florida Fish and Wildlife Conservation Commission has released and monitored 19 to 48 young cranes each year. The annual releases will continue until the population reaches 125 individuals, including 25 breeding pairs. This will take time. Although more than 180 cranes have been released, some are killed by Bobcats each year. In 2000, Florida's Whooping Crane population stood at 75. The project shows important signs of success, however, including two chicks hatched and reared in the spring of 2000. Although neither survived to fledge, these were the first wild Whooping Cranes hatched in the USA in over a century – a major milestone.

The Florida Panther: Teetering on the Brink?

Fifty to 70 wild panthers in South Florida are all that remains of a population that once inhabited most of the southern USA. Like other large predators in North America, the Florida Panther (Plate 62; p. 209) was seen as a threat to livestock and human safety, and the big cat was hunted out as human settlement expanded in the 1800s and early 1900s. As Florida has lost more and more wild lands to development, the shy, solitary panther has been driven into the last extensive hardwood hammocks and pine forests near the southern tip of the peninsula. Panthers need large territories, and today they must cross highways that traverse their habitat in Big Cypress National Preserve and elsewhere. Collision with cars is today the greatest human-related cause of panther deaths. Other threats include continuing habitat loss, social strife (among panthers forced into increasingly smaller areas of acceptable wild habitat), concentration of toxic heavy metals in their prey, and long-term genetic consequences of inbreeding.

The Florida Panther (actually a subspecies of the Mountain Lion, or Puma, which occupies large sections of western North America and parts of Central and South America) was listed as endangered in 1967, and a recovery plan was issued by the U.S. Fish and Wildlife Service in 1981. Over 50 panthers have been radio-tracked since the 1980s to generate information about their preferred habitats, territory size, principal prey (White-tailed Deer), and other characteristics critical to conservation. Ongoing efforts by federal and state agencies to reverse the panther's decline include protection of more panther habitat (e.g., the Florida Panther National Wildlife Refuge, established in 1989); assessment of large, wild areas in Florida and adjacent states for reintroduction of panthers; release of female Texas Pumas in 1995 to increase genetic diversity in the Florida subspecies; creation of wildlife crossings and underpasses to reduce roadkills; and public awareness programs.

Bald Eagle Recovery

Bald Eagles (Plate 29; p. 119), as well as other birds of prey and some seabirds, suffered major declines in the mid-1900s as a result of eggshell thinning caused by the pesticide DDT in the birds' prey. Since DDT was banned in the USA in 1972, the number of Bald Eagle nests in Florida has grown from 120 to nearly 700. Bald Eagles are still listed as threatened by the state and the federal government, however (see p. 122). In Florida, increasing habitat loss and disturbance are the main obstacles to the bird's complete recovery. Bald Eagles primarily feed on fish, and require access to open water with abundant prey. They typically nest in tall trees with a good view of the surrounding area. Development of lake shores and wetlands for housing and recreation may alter or destroy the habitat and prey base that eagles need, and human disturbance during breeding can cause eagles to abandon their nests.

Bald eagles have been observed nesting near human development in Florida, but whether this behavior is unique to some pairs or eagles are generally adaptable to human disturbance is unknown. Since 1997, The state Wildlife Conservation Commission has conducted a satellite-tracking study to determine the effects of rapid development on the nesting habitat of Florida eagles. Each year, about 20 young eagles are fitted with 5-year satellite transmitters. This study documents where the eagles choose to nest when they mature, and thus aids in impact assessment and establishing guidelines for new housing and other development in eagle habitat. The study also provides valuable information about the movements of young eagles, identifying the high-quality (least-disturbed) habitat in northern Florida that they require for part of the year. More information about this study and maps of the movements of the tracked birds may be found on the Internet at: http://wld.fwc.state.fl.us/eagle/.

Save the Manatee!

Florida is the winter home to the only population of manatees in the USA. West Indian Manatees (Plate 68; p. 212) in Florida (where they are usually referred to as Florida Manatees or, simply, Manatees) are essentially tropical animals, migrating up to 320 km (200 miles) seasonally and relying on warmer inland or South-coastal waters in winter. Because manatees are so mobile, inhabit inland waterways as well as coastal areas, and are difficult to see, estimation of their population in Florida has been difficult. Current estimates put their numbers between 2000 and 3000.

Manatees suffer habitat loss as Florida shorelines are developed and shallow-water seagrass beds disappear, but the primary human-related cause of mortality is collisions with boats. The increase in human population in the state has led to increased motorized boat traffic – and more collisions – in places frequented by manatees, such as the St. Johns River, Indian River, and Tampa Bay. Other causes of mortality include entanglement in fishing gear and crushing and drowning in gates of navigation locks and dams.

The Florida Manatee is protected under the Marine Mammal Protection Act and the US Endangered Species Act. Manatees are also listed as endangered by the Florida Endangered and Threatened Species Act and the Manatee Sanctuary Act. The first comprehensive plan for manatee recovery was completed in 1989 by a coalition of federal and state agencies, conservation organizations, and private industry. Conservation strategies now in practice include a network of manatee sanctuaries, such as at Crystal River National Wildlife Refuge (p. 36) and Blue Spring State Park (p. 33), posting of boat speed regulations and cautionary signs in areas where manatees travel and forage, and public education programs. In 1981, the non-profit Save the Manatee Club was established by former Florida Governor Bob Graham and singer/songwriter Jimmy Buffett to increase public awareness of manatee conservation issues in Florida and support recovery and research projects on manatees worldwide.

In spite of these efforts, however, researchers have found only slight increases in manatee populations in sanctuary areas, and manatee deaths from human-related causes rise every year in Florida. By September of 2000, there was already a record annual high in manatee deaths: 231, of which 70 were caused by boat collisions. Governor Jeb Bush called a 'Manatee Summit' in October 2000, during which all interested parties discussed measures for dealing with the escalating mortality. The Summit participants identified three priorities: more and better enforcement of boat speeds and restrictions, an interagency consensus on habitat requirements and protection, and a significant reduction in new marinas and boat slips. Current information about Florida's manatees can be found at the website of Save the Manatee Club, http://www.savethemanatee.org.

Sea Turtles

Florida is a vital site, nationally, for study and conservation of sea turtles (Plates 8 and 9; p. 82). Six of seven species of sea turtles are listed as threatened or endangered by the USA government, and five of these have been observed in the state's coastal waters. Florida beaches are important nesting habitat for three species: Loggerhead (more than 15,000 nesting females), Green (up to 1000), and Leatherback (only 30 to 60). The Atlantic coast of Florida includes the single most important nesting site for Loggerheads in the western hemisphere. The Archie Carr National Wildlife Refuge, the only sea turtle refuge in the country, protects nesting habitat for one quarter of the loggerhead population.

Humans are responsible for the worldwide declines in sea turtle populations. Adults and eggs are taken for food, and nesting beaches are destroyed by development and disturbed by beach vehicles. Nesting females and hatchlings are disoriented, often fatally, by artificial light from coastal homes and roads. Turtles also drown in fishing nets and other debris, and die of strangulation or malnutrition when they mistake plastic bags and other floating garbage for food items. One major step forward in sea turtle recovery was the development of Turtle Excluder Devices (TEDs), 'escape hatches' for turtles caught in shrimp nets. In 1989, legislation made the installation of TEDs mandatory in all shrimp nets in the USA.

Protection of nesting females, hatchlings, and their habitat is a top priority in federal and state sea turtle programs. Since 1979, more than 1100 km (700 miles) of Florida's beaches have been surveyed annually to monitor nesting activity. These surveys and other studies generate information critical for designating new sites for habitat protection and light-control during the nesting season. The sale of sea turtle license plates in Florida generates increased public awareness and funding for turtle research in the state. Satellite transmitters affixed to turtles in Florida and elsewhere, for example, have revealed their international travels through thousands of miles of ocean. This information has turned turtle conservation into a global issue.

Florida Forever

The State of Florida has one of the most aggressive conservation and recreation land acquisition programs in the USA. In the past 30 years Florida has spent more than $3.7 billion to conserve approximately 1.5 million hectares (3.8 million acres) of land for environmental purposes. During the 1990s alone, the state acquired 400,000 hectares (one million acres) for conservation purposes, including rivers, bays, estuaries, and reefs, as well as inland forests, wetlands, and prairie areas. In 1999 the Florida Legislature passed a new program known as 'Florida Forever.' This bill authorized new funding and the sale of bonds to continue the state's outstanding land acquisition programs. 'Florida Forever' provides $300 million per year for land acquisition and environmental restoration. Fifty percent of this budget is dedicated to acquiring land for conservation and nature-based recreation, another 30% to protecting water resources, and about 10% to augmenting existing state parks, forests, wildlife management areas, greenways, and trails. Some funds can go to assist county-based land conservation programs, as well. Over 20 Florida counties have or are in the process of developing their own land acquisition programs.

Battle for the Everglades

The Everglades has the unique distinction among national parks of also being designated a UNESCO World Heritage Site, an International Biosphere Reserve, and a Wetland of International Significance. The 600,000 hectares (1.5 million acres) of Everglades National Park, however, along with Big Cypress National Preserve and other protected areas, is a fraction of what 200 years ago was an immense subtropical wetland. The annual flood of Lake Okeechobee fed the slow, south-flowing sheet of water that was the Everglades' lifeblood. This flow nourished the 'River of Grass,' the swamp forests, and, ultimately, an extraordinary abundance of wildlife. In the late 1800s, millions of wading birds – egrets, storks, ibises, spoonbills – nested in huge colonies, supported by the rich aquatic ecosystem.

The Everglades were deemed 'valueless' by the state legislature early in Florida's history, and by 1911 a massive drainage program had already begun to 'reclaim' the wetlands. In the 1950s, canals, levees, dikes, floodgates, and pumps began to divert more water to respond to human needs: flood control, agriculture, and development. By the late 1960s, 280,000 hectares (700,000 acres) were drained and converted to sugarcane plantations and other commercial agriculture (the Everglades Agricultural Area or EAA). The flow of water in south Florida is determined now by urban and agricultural demands for water. Much of what isn't diverted to the greater Miami–Ft. Lauderdale area or to the EAA flows in 'flood-control' canals straight into the ocean. Today, less than 30% of the original flow makes its way to the Everglades from Lake Okeechobee.

During the past 50 years, the natural hydrologic cycle of the Everglades has been completely disrupted. The wetlands are starved for water, and much of what is permitted to flow south is polluted with synthetic nutrients and other agricultural run-off. Over half of the original marsh has been drained and channelized, and non-native and nutrient-loving plants are choking out the native vegetation. Ninety percent of the waterbirds are gone.

In response to growing public concern and warnings from scientists that the last remnants of the Everglades are dying, Congress in 1996 authorized the Central and South Florida Project Comprehensive Review Study (the 'Restudy'). This was a feasibility study for a 30- to 40-year plan that proposes to restore the Everglades natural processes through a series of engineering projects that reroute the water flow. While government policy and most scientists advocate the restoration of the Everglades, the plan outlined in the Restudy has come under fire from those who seriously question its ecological benefits. The issue has become a complex and politically charged battle between conservation interests and the multi-million-dollar sugar industry, which receives substantial federal subsidies. In October 2000, the $7.8 billion budget for the restoration plan was passed in the U.S. House of Representatives. Charging that this plan is insufficient, some conservationists advocate buying back the whole EAA instead, and effecting a wholesale restoration of the shallow sawgrass marsh. At the highest market cost, buying back that land would cost some $3.5 billion, roughly half of the budget for the

Everglades restoration plan. Saving the Everglades has become a national issue, and while the plan continues its journey through the USA Congress, all sides are engaged in heated debate on the ground.

Environmental Close-up 1
Alien Nation: Non-native Species in Florida

Holly Freifeld, Ph.D.

Florida harbors a broad diversity of native ecosystems and species, many of which are rare or unique in the USA. Native Florida communities and organisms, however, are embattled by enemies that often are invisible to the untrained eye: non-native, or *introduced*, species. Introduced species are those that have arrived and become established in Florida with the direct or indirect assistance of humans. In the past 200 years, and particularly since Florida's development boom began in the late 19th century, more than 1000 non-natives plants and animals have become established here.

The introduction of these species may be deliberate or accidental. Some insect species have been introduced intentionally to control other alien pests. For example, in the first *biological control* experiment in the USA, three South American insects that specifically attack alligatorweed were introduced to Florida in the 1960s to control this invasive aquatic plant. Accidentally introduced species may be escaped or released cage pets, such as South Florida's parrots (p. 139), or unintentional 'hitch-hikers' that arrive by airplane, truck, or boat; the latter method may have been how the Cactus Moth arrived in the Keys to threaten the endemic prickly pear. Like cage pets, some ornamental plants are escapees. The infamous Brazilian pepper (see below) meandered out of the garden with the help of natural forces, such as birds, mammals, and winds, which dispersed its seeds. High-speed transportation (trucks, airplanes, etc.) exacerbates the problem by increasing the chances that 'hitch-hikers,' such as plant seeds and insects and their eggs, will survive the trip between states and countries. In addition, as the volume of traffic increases with the growing human population, opportunities for humans to inadvertently transport species proliferate as well.

It's difficult to imagine how a few individual eggs, seeds, or birds can explode into an ecological menace, but only time, not a large army, may be necessary for an invader to lay claim to the territory. In one notorious example, five North American Muskrats released in Czechoslovakia in 1905 were sufficient to found a population that spread over most of Europe. Similarly, two releases of 80 European Starlings (p. 177) in New York in the 1890s have resulted in a plague of millions that covers most of North America, and the escape of a handful of Gypsy Moth caterpillars in the 1860s resulted in the defoliation of large areas of New England.

Until only a few decades ago, it was believed that introduced species were largely confined to habitats already disturbed by humans – cities and towns, agricultural lands, harvested timberlands. These areas typically are where introductions of non-native species take place, but some non-natives clearly are able to invade native communities. Three characteristics of Florida make the state especially susceptible to encroachment by alien species. First, Florida's climate is favorable to a far wider range of species than, say, the climate of northern Minnesota, with its months of freezing temperatures, snow, and ice. Second, Florida is virtually an island. Its long peninsula has ocean on all sides and is bounded by colder climate to the north. This island geography results in an isolated flora and fauna that may be more 'naïve' and susceptible to alien trespassers than continental communities. Third, development and other human-caused disturbance has greatly fragmented Florida's natural environment and created more potential areas of introduction and 'incubation' for alien species. Combined with the other two natural conditions, this third characteristic significantly increases the state's vulnerability to invasion by introduced species.

Alien invaders pose a serious threat to native species in several ways.

(1) They may prey upon native species. Non-native mammals, such as Wild Pigs and Red Foxes, prey on native reptiles and their eggs, small mammals, and invertebrates.
(2) Non-natives may interfere with native species; with access to resources they need, such as sunlight, food, and/or breeding sites. Non-native ants, such as the aggressive Fire Ant, infest the entire state, and have in many areas displaced native ants.
(3) Alien invaders may hybridize with close relatives that are natives and cause their extinction by genetic means. The popular and colorful ornamental plant *Lantana camara* interbreeds with the native *Lantana depressa*, which occurs only in Florida. *Lantana camara* thus is hybridizing *Lantana depressa* out of existence. Similarly, domestic ducks (Mallards), which have free-living populations in some areas, have been found to interbreed with the Mottled Duck, which occurs only in Florida and a few other places.
(4) Non-natives may alter whole communities or ecosystems. *Hydrilla*, an escaped ornamental aquarium plant, now chokes over 39,000 hectares (96,000 acres) of Florida's lakes and waterways. This plant forms dense mats near the surface that prevent light from reaching native plants on the bottom, slows water and nutrient circulation, and alters water chemistry.

Many alien animal species, especially in South Florida, are exotic pets that were accidentally or deliberately set free. The year-round warm, humid conditions have proven comfortably similar to the tropical homes of dozens of birds and reptiles, fish, and even monkeys that hail variously from the tropical Americas, Asia, and Africa. Monk Parakeets, Common Mynas, pythons, piranhas, electric eels, and Rhesus Monkeys are just a few of the extraordinary animals that have recently become free-living in Florida.

In general, though, the least-flashy non-natives often are those that cause the greatest ecological damage and are hardest to control. To catch sight of a Wild Pig, for example, is rare, yet perhaps half a million of these large, non-native mammals roam Florida's forests and swamps. Perhaps the most destructive non-native mammal species in the state (or anywhere they are introduced), pigs devour understory plants and tree seedlings and root deep into soils in search of insects, worms, and the eggs of reptiles, including the endangered Gopher Tortoise and sea turtles. These activities, along with the pig's predilection for wallowing in low, wet areas, destroy the natural structure of the vegetation, increase erosion, facilitate dispersal of non-native plants, and create stagnant pools where mosquitoes breed. Wild Pigs are also a reservoir for a host of diseases that can be transmitted to wildlife and domestic livestock, including the pseudorabies virus that can infect the endangered Florida Panther. Pigs are wily animals, and a challenge to control without intensive (and expensive) fencing and hunting programs.

Non-native plants are the most insidious and widespread of invaders – the worst of them completely overrun native ecosystems. In spite of on-going management efforts, millions of acres in Florida presently are dominated by non-native plants. More than 900 alien plant species have become established here in the past two centuries and represent over 25% of the entire flora. People unfamiliar with Florida's natural landscapes may not realize that they're looking at 100% imported vegetation when they see Brazilian pepper (Plate F) choking highway edges and old fields, or Australian *Melaleuca* (Punk; Plate C) forests in the Everglades.

Brazilian pepper forms low, dense stands that cover more than 3500 sq km (1300 sq miles) in Central and South Florida. This shrub excludes virtually all other plants, and both birds and mammals eat and disperse its seeds. Native birds do nest in Brazilian pepper forest; however, the average number of birds nesting in these forests is as low as 25% of the number found in native pine forests. Although most common in places already disturbed or where fire is suppressed, Brazilian pepper has crept in around native mangrove forests in the southwest of Everglades National Park, and may influence the abandonment of colonies of sea- and waterbirds from some mangrove areas.

Melaleuca, also known as the paperbark tree, was introduced to Florida in 1906. The tree grows quickly and soaks up water; it was believed in South Florida that planting it would help dry up the swamps and reduce the risk of malaria. In the 1940s, *Melaleuca* seed was aerially broadcast over the eastern Everglades, ostensibly to aid in draining the wetlands for conversion to agriculture. Today, this tree is one of the state's most troublesome invasive plants, spreading at the rate of 6 hectares (15 acres) per day. It has invaded over a dozen native plant communities, where it shades out other plants and provides virtually no resources or habitat for native animals. Mature *Melaleuca* forests now spread within the Everglades in areas once dominated by native Sawgrass (Plate L), destroying habitat for native species and disrupting the circulation of water through the wetland. More than US$ 2.2 million is spent annually trying to control the tree.

Land managers in Florida agree that dealing with non-native species is a huge challenge that requires extraordinary amounts of time, labor, and capital. They agree, too, that it is a top conservation priority in the state, along with slowing habitat loss. Strategies for the management of any particular invader may involve mechanical removal, application of chemicals, and introduction of biological control species.

Efforts to control *Melaleuca*, Brazilian pepper, Hydrilla, Fire Ants, and some of the other worst invaders are still largely experimental or are aimed at preventing their further spread and protecting the native species they may threaten. Each alien species has a unique life history, and few have been studied sufficiently to determine the best means of control. Some significant successes, however, indicate that the investment of resources and time is worthwhile. For example, the Asian Citrus Blackfly was eradicated by parasitic wasps introduced for that purpose (after chemical treatments failed), and the Giant African Snail was eradicated by hand picking and poisoned bait. Complete eradication of a non-native species usually is possible only if the invasion is caught early, or if the invader requires very specific habitats or other resources. Although eradication may be the goal of alien species management programs, control is often more realistic. The South American water hyacinth (Plate M) is one species that may be impossible to eradicate – it disperses easily, and even a small clump floating downstream can found a new population. Water hyacinth covered about 49,000 hectares (120,000 acres) of Florida's lakes and streams 50 years ago, but covers less than 1600 hectares (4000 acres) today, after several decades of intensive management using mechanical, chemical, and biological controls.

Invasion of natural systems by introduced species is a serious conservation problem worldwide. In the USA, Florida is second only to Hawaii in its abundance of introduced species and the severity of their impacts on native flora and fauna. Long-term protection of Florida's environment from alien species requires research to determine the best control methods, strict guidelines to minimize fragmentation of native habitats, and vigilance to prevent the introduction of more new species.

Chapter 5

HOW TO USE THIS BOOK

- *Some Definitions*
- *Information in the Family Profiles*
- *Information in the Color Plate Sections*

The following chapters will help you to identify many of Florida's most common animal species, and provide information about the animals themselves and the families to which they belong. The information is divided into sections that are intended to make everything as clear as possible – not only for those who are familiar with natural sciences but for the less specialized ecotraveller as well. It may therefore be useful to explain some of the terms we have used, and the sense in which we have used them.

Some Definitions

Natural history, a familiar enough term, we have used to mean general background information on the natural habits of animals, especially their ecology, distribution, classification and behavior.

Ecology is the study of the way living things interact with their physical environment and with each other. These interactions account for almost everything that we find most fascinating about the world's flora and fauna. What an animal eats, how it forages, how and when it breeds, how it survives the rigors of climatic extremes, why it is the shape and size it is, why it has large ears or a long nose or sheds its tail, are all aspects of animal ecology. Of particular interest to an ecologist are the interactions between different species, which can usually be categorized quite distinctly according to how one relates to another. These relationship terms are summarized below.

Competition is an ecological relationship in which neither of the interacting species benefits. Individual animals of two species are in competition when they use the same resource – a certain type of food, nesting holes in trees, etc. – and there is an insufficient supply to meet the demands of both. As a result, each species is less successful than it could be if it did not have to compete with the other.

Predation is an ecological interaction in which one species (the predator) benefits while the other species (the prey) is harmed. If a cat eats a mouse, that is an example of predator eating prey; but predation also includes those interactions where the predator eats only part of the prey and the prey often survives.

Parasitism is another relationship in which one species benefits and the other is harmed. The difference is that in a parasitic relationship the parasite feeds slowly on the *host* species and usually does not kill it. Leeches and ticks are common parasites.

Mutualism is an ecological relationship that benefits both participants. For example, plants and their pollinators engage in mutualistic interactions. Take bees and flowers, for instance: the bee gets food, nectar or pollen, from the plant's blossom, and the plant benefits because the bee transports pollen to another flower and thus enables the plant to reproduce. Central America offers a famous case of mutualism involving several species of acacia plants and the ants that live in them. The ants feed on the nectar the plants produce, and in return they obtain shelter from the acacias and defend the acacias from plant-eating insects. Sometimes the species have interacted so long that they can no longer survive without each other: this is termed *obligate mutualism*. For instance, termites cannot digest wood without the help of protozoans, single-celled animals that live in their guts; at this point in their evolutionary histories, neither the termites nor their internal helpers can live alone.

Commensalism is a relationship in which one species benefits but the other is not affected in any way. Epiphytes (p. 13) such as orchids and bromeliads grow on tree trunks and branches but seem not to harm the trees or help them. A classic example of commensalism is the relationship between remora and shark. The remora is a fish that attaches itself to a shark, by means of a suction cup on its head, in order to catch scraps of food that the shark leaves behind. It is not, as may seem at first glance, a parasite, because it does not harm the shark; nor does it apparently offer any benefit to the shark. Cattle Egrets (p. 112) are commensals: they follow cattle closely, often perching on their back, eating whatever insects and other small animals are flushed out by the cattle moving around their pasture.

Symbiosis, originally from the Greek words for 'living together,' is a term that includes some of these ecological interactions. Usually symbiosis suggests that the two interacting species do not harm each other; therefore mutualism and commensalism can be described as symbiotic relationships.

Information in the Family Profiles

The rest of this book is devoted to the animals themselves: the insects, fish, amphibians, reptiles, birds and mammals of Florida. First we present 'family profiles' that mainly describe the ecology, behavior, and conservation status of Florida's most common and conspicuous animals. Then, in the color plate sections, we present color illustrations of these species, together with brief notes that will allow you to identify animals and the regimes in which they are found.

Classification, Distribution, and Morphology

Each family profile generally opens with information on the family's classification, geographic distribution, and morphology (shape, size and coloring).

Classification (or taxonomy) is important because it helps us to understand how animals are grouped or related. Classification levels are summarized below:

Kingdom Animalia. Aside from plant information, all the species detailed in the book are members of the animal kingdom.

Phylum Chordata, Subphylum Vertebrata. Most of the species in the book are vertebrates, animals with backbones; exceptions are the insects (p. 223) and the corals and other marine invertebrates (p. 226).

Class. The book covers several vertebrate classes, such as Amphibia (amphibians), Reptilia (reptiles), Aves (birds) and Mammalia (mammals), and invertebrate classes, such as Insecta (insects).

Order. Each class is divided into several orders, the animals in each order sharing many characteristics. For example, one of the mammal orders is Carnivora, which includes mammals with teeth specialized for eating meat: dogs, cats, bears, raccoons and weasels are all carnivores.

Family. A family is a sub-division of an order. Each family contains closely related species that are very similar in form, ecology and behavior. The family Canidae, for instance, contains all the dog-like mammals – coyote, wolf, fox, dog. Animal family names end with the suffix *-idae* (*-inae* denotes a subfamily).

Genus. Subdivision of the family. Each genus contains a group of species that are considered to have evolved from a common ancestor. Plural of 'genus' is 'genera.'

Species. The lowest classification level; at this level, different individuals are similar enough to breed with each other and produce living, fertile offspring.

Here, for example, is the classification of the Bobcat (Plate 62).

Kingdom	Animalia, with more than a million species.
Phylum	Chordata, Subphylum Vertebrata, with about 40,000 species.
Class	Mammalia (mammals), with about 4000 species.
Order	Carnivora, with about 246 species; includes bears, weasels, skunks, raccoons, mongooses, wolves, foxes, civets, genets, cats, and hyenas.
Family	Felidae, with 36 species; includes all the cats.
Genus	*Lynx,* with 4 species worldwide; lynxes and bobcats.
Species	*Lynx rufus,* the Bobcat.

Some of the family profiles in the book actually cover animal orders; others describe families or subfamilies.

The distribution of species can vary tremendously. Some species are found only in very limited areas, whereas others range over several continents. Distributions can be described in a number of ways. An animal or group is sometimes said to be *Old World* or *New World* (see Map 4, p. 57); the former refers to parts of the globe known to Europeans before Columbus (Europe, Africa, and Asia) while the latter refers to the Western Hemisphere – North, South and Central America. Florida obviously is in the New World. The terms *tropical* and *temperate* refer to climate regions of the Earth; the boundaries of these zones are determined by lines of latitude. The *tropics*, always warm, are the regions of the world that fall within the belt from 23.5 degrees North latitude (the Tropic of Cancer) to 23.5 degrees South latitude (the Tropic of Capricorn). The world's *temperate zones*, with more

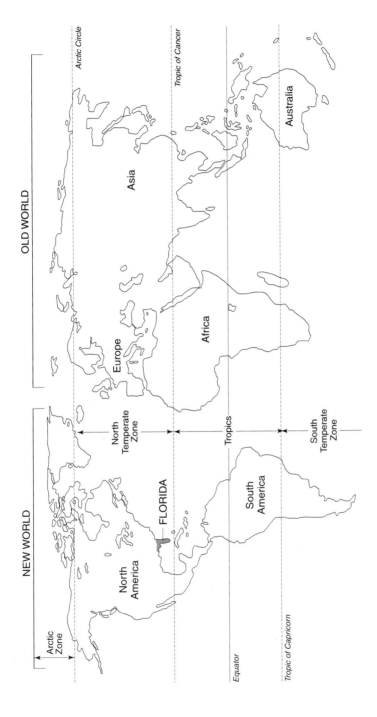

Map 4 Map of the Earth showing the position of Florida; Old World and New World zones; and tropical, temperate, and arctic regions.

seasonal climates, extend from 23.5 degrees North and South latitude to the Arctic and Antarctic Circles, at 66.5 degrees North and South. While Florida is located in the temperate zone, its climate is classified as *subtropical*, a term that refers to a region bordering a tropical zone. Transforming Florida's climate from temperate to subtropical is the maritime influence of the Caribbean Sea and the Gulf of Mexico.

Several terms help to define a species' distribution and describe how it attained its distribution.

Range. The particular geographic area occupied by a species.

Native or *Indigenous*. Occurring naturally in a particular place.

Introduced. An introduced species occurs in an area because, intentionally or not, people have brought it there; it is the opposite of a native species. For instance, more than 30 species of reptiles and amphibians have been introduced to south Florida from the Caribbean and South America. *Melaleuca*, a native Australian plant, was introduced and has spread over much of south Florida.

Endemic. A species, a genus, an entire family, etc., that is found in a particular place and nowhere else.

Cosmopolitan. A species that is widely distributed throughout the world.

Ecology and Behavior

The Ecology and Behavior sections summarize what is known about the basic activities of a group of animals – where and when the animal is usually active, what it eats, and so on.

Activity location – *Terrestrial* animals pursue life and food on the ground. *Arboreal* animals do the same in trees and shrubs. Many of the latter have *prehensile* tails, long and muscular, which they wrap around branches to support themselves as they move about or feed. *Cursorial* refers to animals that are adapted for running along the ground. *Fossorial* animals are proficient diggers and spend their lives underground.

Spatial behavior – *Territories* are areas that animals defend; *home ranges*, which are not necessarily defended, are areas over which an animal lives and searches for food.

Activity time – *Nocturnal* animals are active at night, *diurnal* ones by day, and *crepuscular* ones at dusk and/or dawn.

Food preferences – Most animals eat more than one type of food; a carnivorous mammal will occasionally eat plant material, for instance. But generally, animal species can be assigned to one of the feeding categories below:

> *Herbivores* are predators that prey on plants.
> *Carnivores* are predators that prey on animals.
> *Insectivores* eat insects.
> *Granivores* eat seeds.
> *Frugivores* eat fruit.
> *Nectarivores* eat nectar.
> *Folivores* eat leaves.

Piscivores eat fish.
Omnivores eat a variety of things.

Breeding

These sections present the basics on each group's breeding particulars – type of mating system, special breeding behaviors, duration of egg incubation or *gestation* (pregnancy), as well as information on nests, eggs and young.

Mating systems – A *monogamous* mating system is one in which one male and one female establish a pair bond and contribute fairly evenly to each breeding effort. In *polygamous* systems, individuals of one sex have more than one mate (i.e., they have a harem): in *polygynous* breeding systems, one male mates with several females, and in *polyandrous* systems, one female mates with several males.

Condition of young at birth – *Altricial* young are born in a relatively undeveloped state, usually naked of fur or feathers, eyes closed and unable to feed themselves, walk or run from predators. *Precocial* young are born more developed, with open eyes and soon able to walk and even feed themselves.

Ecological Interactions

These sections present intriguing relationships between species.

Notes

These sections include interesting snippets of information about profiled animals, including folk tales, that do not fit in elsewhere in the account.

Status

In the Status sections we indicate the conservation status of each group: its relative abundance or rarity, whether populations are increasing or declining, and whether any special measures are being implemented. Because this book concentrates on the more common animals in Florida, few of the profiled species are immediately threatened with extinction. However, to distinguish the degree of threat to the different species we have adopted the following terms:

Endangered species are in imminent danger of extinction; they are highly unlikely to survive without the most urgent intervention by conservation specialists. Populations are small and individuals rarely seen.

Threatened species are those whose numbers are declining rapidly, but if conservation measures are enacted in time, and the causes of their decline identified and remedied, they may be prevented from moving to endangered status.

Vulnerable to threat or *Near-threatened* are terms for species that are thought to be susceptible, often because their habitat is itself under threat of destruction.
   Where appropriate, we have also included threat classifications from the Convention on International Trade in Endangered Species (CITES) and the United States Endangered Species Act (USA ESA). CITES is an international agreement to protect the world's threatened species by regulating trade in wild animals and plants among the 130 or so participating countries. The regulated species are listed in separate appendixes according to status. CITES Appendix I lists endangered

species in which all trade is prohibited. Appendix II lists threatened/vulnerable species, those that are not yet endangered but may soon be; and Appendix III lists species that are protected by the laws of individual countries that have signed the CITES agreements.

The USA's ESA works in a similar way, listing endangered and threatened species and, among other provisions, strictly regulating trade in those animals. A major difference is that the ESA also lists species that are endangered or threatened by any action or condition (for example, hunting, habitat loss, small population size), not just international trade.

Information in the Color Plate Sections

Pictures. Among amphibians, reptiles and mammals, the male and female of a species usually look alike, although there are often size differences. For many species of bird, however, the sexes usually differ in color pattern and even anatomical features. If only one individual is pictured you may assume that male and female look pretty much alike. Where there are major differences, however, both male and female are depicted.

Name. The common English name for each profiled species is shown along with the scientific, or Latin, name, and common local names, if any.

ID. This section offers a brief description of each animal, which, along with the pictures, should allow most species to be identified.

The length of a reptile or amphibian is normally the *snout–vent length* (SVL), which is measured from the tip of the snout to the vent, unless we specifically note that the tail is included in the measurement provided. The *vent* is the opening (sexual and waste-voiding) on their belly that lies near where the rear limbs join the body. Therefore, long tails of salamanders and lizards, for instance, are not included in SVLs, nor are the long legs of a frog. The exception is snakes, however: in most cases, the length we give for a snake is its total length.

For mammals, measurements are generally the length of head and body, separate from the length of the tail.

Birds are measured from tip of bill to end of tail. For birds commonly seen flying, such as seabirds and hawks, wingspan measurements (wingtip to wingtip) are often added. We divided passerine birds (the small, perching, birds; p. 103) into *large* (those that are more than 30 cm, or 12 in, long); *mid-sized* (between 15 or 18 cm, 6 or 7 in, and 30 cm, 12 in); *small* (10 to 15 cm, 4 to 6 in); and *very small* (less than 10 cm, 4 in).

Habitat/Region. These sections indicate the regions and habitat types in which each species occurs, with symbols for the types of habitats it prefers and the regions of Florida where each species may be found. We have attempted to show not only the areas where the animal is known to occur but also those in which it probably occurs, based on its known range and the type of habitat it prefers. Habitat symbols are not given for a few species that are found almost entirely in towns and cities.

Explanation of habitat symbols:

= Dry Prairies (p. 14)

= Scrub (p. 15)

= Pine Flatwoods (p. 14)

= High Pine Sandhills (p. 16)

= Temperate Hardwood Hammocks (p. 16)

= Tropical Hardwood Hammocks (p. 17)

= Freshwater. For species typically found in or near lakes, streams, rivers, marshes, swamps.

= Saltwater. For species usually found in or near the ocean or ocean beaches.

REGIONS (see p. 9 and Map 2, p. 28):

PAN Panhandle
NFL North Florida
CFL Central Florida
SFL South Florida
KEY Keys and Other Islands

Example

Plate 62b

Bobcat
Lynx rufus

ID: A tall, long-legged cat, about three times the size of a large domestic cat. The tail is short, pointed ears have a tuft of black hair at the tip. Total length 80 to 110 cm (31.5 to 43 in), including tail (9 to 15 cm; 3.5 to 6 in). Fur is pale brown to olive-brown with scattered black spots. Underparts are white with black spots.

HABITAT: Occurs in a wide variety of habitats, from forested areas to agricultural fields. Also found on tree islands in sawgrass marshes in Everglades and Big Cypress Preserve.

REGION: PAN, NFL, CFL, SFL

Chapter 6

AMPHIBIANS

- *General Characteristics and Natural History*
- *Seeing Amphibians in Florida*
- *Family Profiles*
  1. *Salamanders*
  2. *Toads and Toad-like Frogs*
  3. *Treefrogs*
  4. *True Frogs*
- *Environmental Close-up 2: Frog Population Declines*

General Characteristics and Natural History

The word amphibian is derived from the Greek *amphibios* and means, literally, 'both lives.' The name refers to the fact that the great majority of amphibians undergo *metamorphosis* (or transformation) early in life; they hatch from eggs laid in water to begin life as aquatic larvae, or tadpoles, then change shape, grow legs, and become land dwellers. There are exceptions of course: some amphibians spend their whole lives in water and others are permanent land dwellers; but most lead double lives in keeping with their name.

The first amphibians appeared about 360 million years ago. Early amphibians were the first vertebrates to colonize the land, and the group has retained a close affinity with water. They have thin, glandular skin, which works as an adjunct to the lungs in gas exchange (breathing). Because the skin must be kept wet to function effectively, amphibians are restricted to moist habitats. Amphibians lack claws, and most have four toes on the front feet. The majority of species return to fresh water to lay their eggs, but some deposit their eggs in moist places on land.

Class Amphibia currently contains about 4700 species, but new species are being discovered almost every week, mainly from the New World tropics. Experts believe the species count will soon rise above 5000. The Amphibians are separated into three main groups. The largest group, with about 4100 species, is the *frogs* (order Anura, 'without tails'), followed by the *salamanders* (order Caudata, or 'tailed' amphibians) with 430 species. The third group, the *caecilians* (order Gymnophiona) consists of about 170 species of little known amphibians, many of which look like large earthworms. Caecilians are found exclusively in the tropical regions of Africa, Asia and Central and South America. Florida has no caecilians but the state is home to 32 species of frogs and 26 species of salamanders. Frogs and *toads* are the most numerous of the amphibians, and the most recognizable. Adult frogs and toads are tailless, and most move by jumping or hopping. They have long hind limbs, large eyes, and a smooth or warty skin. The most aquatic ones have webbed feet.

When asked the difference between a frog and a toad, most people would say that frogs are smooth, long-legged creatures that jump and live in water, while toads are dry, warty, stout-bodied animals that hop. Most of the time this would be correct, but there are enough exceptions to confuse the issue, and several families contain both 'frog-like' and 'toad-like' species. Experts suggest the correct solution is to refer to all tailless amphibians as frogs, and to use the word toad in a narrower sense, solely for the members of family Bufonidae. *Bufonid toads* have a pair of *parotid glands* behind their eyes. These bulging glands produce a toxin that protects them from being eaten. The introduced Giant Toad (Plate 1) is the only toad in Florida that is large enough to produce enough toxin to be dangerous to humans and pets.

All adult frogs and toads are carnivores. They sit and wait for insects to come to them; when one moves within range, they lunge forward, using their tongue and jaws to grab the food, then swallow it whole. They will also pursue some prey by hopping along the ground. The aquatic dwelling tadpoles are herbivores and feed mainly on algae, bacteria, and plankton.

Metamorphosis – the transformation of an animal from one stage of its life history to another – is a distinctive characteristic of all amphibians. In frogs and toads, metamorphosis involves a complete reorganization of both external and internal structures. As the frog or toad changes from an aquatic to a terrestrial lifestyle, the mouth, skull, gastrointestinal tract, and reproductive tract metamorphose. The large tail is completely resorbed, the larval teeth are shed and the mouth is enlarged. The tadpoles' long coiled intestine, important for digesting its largely vegetarian diet, becomes greatly shortened, to accommodate its future carnivorous diet. Salamanders also undergo metamorphosis but the changes are less dramatic because larval salamanders look like miniature adults with external gills. Larval salamanders are also carnivorous, so no changes in the gastrointestinal tract are required.

Frogs are found worldwide, in habitats ranging from deserts to mountains and tropical forests. They are found on all continents, except Antarctica, and most islands. Like fish and reptiles, frogs are cold-blooded (*ectothermic*), which means that their body temperature varies with the environmental temperature. Many Florida frogs spend their lives in dry upland habitats and only migrate to wetlands to breed. Frogs can be quite conspicuous especially during the breeding season. Some of them are brightly colored, and in many species, males have loud, distinctive advertisement calls that attract females to their position in a pond. Frogs also have other types of calls: a *rain call*, which is probably territorial; an *alarm call*, which they give when grabbed by a predator; and a *release call*, which is given when a male is accidentally grabbed sexually by another male.

The name salamander comes from the Greek 'fire-lizard;' it was once believed that these lizard-like creatures could walk through fire unscathed. Salamanders likely acquired their legendary reputation because they appeared to crawl through fire; but in reality they had probably crawled out of logs thrown onto the fire.

Salamanders are Florida's least-familiar type of amphibian. They live mainly in temperate areas, although one group, the *lungless salamanders*, is also found in tropical America. Salamanders typically have elongated bodies, long tails and two pairs of legs, although the eel-like *amphiumas* have four tiny non-functional legs and *sirens* have a long eel-like body, external gills and a single prominent pair of legs behind the gills. Some salamanders are completely terrestrial, others are aquatic. Fully-aquatic salamanders such as *hellbenders, mudpuppies,* amphiumas and sirens are found in rivers, lakes, ponds and swamps. Terrestrial species, such as *mole salamanders,* live under rocks and logs and often burrow into the ground, and migrate to ponds for breeding. Other salamanders live along the edges of small streams or on hillsides and never come to water. In common with other amphibians, salamanders have a smooth, moist, non-scaly skin that acts as a respiratory surface. For the skin to function effectively it must remain moist, so most salamanders are restricted to damp or wet habitats.

All salamanders are carnivorous, feeding on insects, mollusks, worms and other invertebrates. Unlike frogs and toads, which have loud calls, salamanders are voiceless. Compared with other amphibians, the salamanders have fairly advanced breeding habits; some have *internal fertilization* (see p. 66), and many species show parental care of their eggs.

Seeing Amphibians in Florida

Florida has the richest concentration of amphibians of any state in the USA. Many species are common and easily seen. Frogs are most easily spotted at night during or just after rain. Though it sounds unlikely, the best frog hunting is done driving slowly along a lightly travelled blacktop road, especially if the road runs near a pond or a swamp. Some nights, after a spring shower, there are so many frogs and toads bouncing in the headlights in front of your car that it is difficult to avoid squashing them. Toads are attracted to insects that come to porch and street lights after dark. Wherever landscapers have installed outdoor lighting to help people find their way between housing complexes, you can usually find one or two toads camped beneath each light.

All Florida frog species have distinctive calls, and most species can be identified by their voices at breeding ponds. You can purchase tapes of frog calls and learn which species are associated with which calls. Standing by a pond in the evening can be a rewarding exercise, as even an amateur can usually distinguish six or seven different frog calls. If you are trying to find a calling frog or toad, move quietly towards the source of the sounds but do not shine your flashlight at it until you are a few feet away. You usually will need to stop moving and switch off the light when the frog stops calling, or it may depart. A frog illuminated by a beam of light usually freezes, allowing itself to be approached quite closely. Playing of a recording of the calling frog will stimulate it to begin calling again.

Salamanders and newts are more difficult to find. They are small and do not vocalize. Even at night, when they are active and hunting, they typically sit with only their head protruding from the vegetation. Salamanders, usually males, will sometimes wander across roads during winter and spring rains. Sirens are often found under floating mats of aquatic plants or caught by fishermen. With a light at night look for salamanders in the shallows of streams and ponds, and under leaf mats. You can sometimes find terrestrial salamanders if you carefully turn over rocks and logs, but be careful to turn things back the way you found them.

A word of caution: amphibians are sensitive creatures with moist, delicate skins. If you pick up amphibians, do so carefully and with clean hands. Insect repellent or other chemicals on your clothes or body are easily and quickly absorbed through their skin and can kill them.

Family Profiles

1. Salamanders

Salamanders superficially resemble lizards but they lack scales and have smooth, glandular skin. These long-bodied, long-tailed amphibians have four, two or no legs, and toes that lack claws. Many have tails that are flattened from side to side for swimming. Found almost exclusively in the Northern Hemisphere, they range in size from the MEXICAN LUNGLESS SALAMANDER, at only 4 cm (1.5 in) long, to the CHINESE GIANT SALAMANDER, at 1.8 m (6 ft). Worldwide there are approximately 450 species of salamanders in 9 families. Florida is particularly rich in salamanders, with 26 species representing 6 families. The largest family of salamanders, the *lungless salamanders* (family Plethodontidae), with 270 species in North, Central and South America, is represented in Florida by 13 diverse but rather nondescript species. Most are long and slender with relatively long tails, four legs, and a groove (the *nasolabial groove*), which extends from the nostril to the upper lip. (The groove is thought to be a sensory receptor for chemicals, helpful in finding food and mates.) As their name suggests, they all lack lungs; they breathe by absorbing oxygen through their skin. The most unusual member of this group is the GEORGIA BLIND SALAMANDER (Plate 6), an eyeless, cave-dwelling species that retains its gills as an adult.

The *sirens* (family Sirenidae) and amphiumas (family Amphiumidae) are sometimes known as the *eel-like salamanders*. Sirens, found only in the southeastern USA and Mexico, are so divergent from other salamander families that they were once placed in their own order. There are only four known species in this family and all of them are found in Florida. Sirens are completely aquatic, but like eels they can travel short distances overland in rainy weather. They have three pairs of external gills and a single pair of small, weak forelimbs behind the gills. Amphiuma are found only in the USA, where they are commonly known as 'Congo eels.' These large aquatic salamanders have long eel-like bodies, gill slits and four tiny, non-functional legs. The exceptionally large adult TWO-TOED AMPHIUMA (Plate 7) can exceed 1 m (3.3 ft) in length.

Mole salamanders (family Ambystomatidae) are so named because they burrow and live underground. They have broad blunt heads, four legs and smooth, boldly marked skin. Three of the four Florida species are quite small – about 7.5 to 10 cm (3 to 4 in) long – but the fourth, the TIGER SALAMANDER (Plate 5), at 15 to 20 cm (6 to 8 in), is the largest terrestrial salamander in the eastern USA. Mole salamanders are found only in North America.

Newts (family Salamandridae) are found in the USA, Europe, Asia and North Africa. Adults are slender with four legs, a long tail, and rough skin. Most adult newts are terrestrial. STRIPED NEWTS (Plate 5) are primarily an upland species but they come to ponds to breed.

Mudpuppies and *waterdogs* (family Proteidae) are a largely North American family, named for the erroneous belief that they can bark like dogs. They are completely aquatic and remain their entire lives in a permanent larval state, with red feathery external gills and four fully developed legs. Only one species (not illustrated) is found in Florida.

Natural History

Ecology and Behavior

Salamanders are an amazingly diverse-looking group of animals with correspondingly varied lifestyles. Terrestrial species like lungless salamanders live under logs, bark, in moss and beneath rocks, and mole salamanders often burrow deep into the soil. Salamanders are always found in moist places and usually hide by day and emerge at night to forage. Most species are cryptic and rarely seen but the DWARF SALAMANDER (Plate 6) and the RUSTY MUD SALAMANDER are sometimes found crossing roads at night during rainy weather. TIGER SALAMANDERS occasionally wander into swimming pools and become trapped. Aquatic forms such as waterdogs, sirens and amphiumas live in streams, swamps, ponds, marshes, drainage canals, and lakes. GREATER SIRENS (Plate 7) and amphiumas are sometimes caught by fishermen.

Both larval and adult salamanders are carnivorous. They feed on small invertebrates such as insects, spiders, slugs, worms, crayfish, aquatic insect larvae, and even small fish. Salamanders in turn are preyed upon by snakes, turtles, birds, and mammals, and many species defend themselves by secreting toxic or sticky substances from skin glands. The SLIMY SALAMANDER (Plate 6) gets its name from the glue-like slime that it secretes from its skin when alarmed.

Breeding

Unlike frogs, salamanders are voiceless; males do not call to advertise territories or attract mates. Instead, males and females probably locate each other by following scent trails. Once the two sexes meet, there is an elaborate courtship ritual of nudging, nose-tapping, bumping and chin-rubs, followed by mating. Males deposit a *spermatophore* (a tiny capsule containing sperm) on the ground, and the female picks it up with her *vent* (the opening on her belly that provides entry and exit for both reproductive and excretory systems). The eggs are thus fertilized within the female's body.

Most salamanders lay their eggs in water but some species deposit their eggs on land. Florida salamanders typically breed in late winter and spring, but two species, MARBLED (Plate 5) and FLATWOODS SALAMANDERS breed in autumn, making small nests and laying their 100 or so eggs in sites that will shortly be flooded by heavy winter rain. Once covered with water, the eggs hatch within two or three days. MOLE SALAMANDERS (Plate 5) migrate to ponds to mate and lay eggs. In many salamander species, the female attends the clutch of eggs through the 30+ day incubation period. Some simply guard the eggs, but others coil themselves around the eggs and keep them moist with their skin secretions. Young typically hatch from the eggs into an aquatic larval stage, but some species go through the larval stage in the egg and the young emerge from the egg looking like miniature adults. A few salamanders, such as the MUDPUPPY, STRIPED NEWT, GEORGIA BLIND SALAMANDER, and Mole Salamander, are *paedomorphic*, meaning they have gills and resemble larvae all their lives, even when sexually mature.

Ecological Interactions

Because amphibians are secretive and difficult to see, their numbers are usually underestimated, and their role in an ecosystem is often undervalued. It is comparatively easy to detect frogs because of their vocalizations, but because salamanders are silent and secretive they usually remain unknown and unnoticed. However, in many parts of the world salamanders and other amphibians are the most abundant land vertebrates. They are major consumers of invertebrates and vital food sources for fish, snakes, birds and mammals. Salamanders and other amphibians can reach astonishingly high densities. In a long-term ecological study in the Hubbard Brook Forest in New Hampshire, the total weight of salamanders alone was calculated to be about twice that of birds at their breeding peak, and about equal to that of small mammals.

Notes

Some salamanders can inject poison into would-be predators. When attacked, the European SHARP-RIBBED NEWT and the SPINY NEWT have the ability to push their sharp, pointed ribs out through poison glands in their skin. The ribs lacerate the skin of the predator, and the poison enters the cuts, causing intense pain.

Status

None of Florida's salamanders are listed as endangered by state or federal authorities, but the ONE-TOED AMPHIUMA, SEAL SALAMANDER, GEORGIA BLIND SALAMANDER, FOUR-TOED SALAMANDER, MANY-LINED SALAMANDER, and STRIPED NEWT are listed as rare by FCREPA (Florida Committee on Rare and Endangered Plants and Animals).

Profiles

Mole Salamander, *Ambystoma talpoideum*, Plate 5a
Tiger Salamander, *Ambystoma tigrinum*, Plate 5b
Marbled Salamander, *Ambystoma opacum*, Plate 5c
Striped Newt, *Notophthalmus perstriatus*, Plate 5d
Peninsula Newt, *Notophthalmus viridescens*, Plate 5e

Three-lined Salamander, *Eurycea longicauda*, Plate 6a
Slimy Salamander, *Plethodon grobmani*, Plate 6b
Southern Dusky Salamander, *Eurycea auriculatus*, Plate 6c
Dwarf Salamander, *Eurycea quadridigitata*, Plate 6d
Georgia Blind Salamander, *Haideotriton wallacei*, Plate 6e
Two-toed Amphiuma, *Amphiuma means*, Plate 7a
Greater Siren, *Siren lacertina*, Plate 7b
Lesser Siren, *Siren intermedia*, Plate 7c
Dwarf Siren, *Pseudobranchus axanthus*, Plate 7d

2. Toads and Toad-like Frogs

Toads (family Bufonidae) are heavy-set amphibians with short back legs and a broad, rounded snout. They have warty, dry-looking skin that allows them to live in relatively dry habitats. Most species also have large prominent toxin-secreting *parotid glands* on the shoulder area of the back, one behind each eye.

Toads live on all continents except Antarctica, and they are also absent from Madagascar and Greenland. They are not native to Australia but have been introduced there. Worldwide there are some 350 *bufonid* toad species, four of which occur in Florida. As a group, toads have the widest range of sizes of any of the frog families, ranging from the immense, dinner-plate-sized GIANT TOAD (at 20 cm, 8 in; Plate 1) to the tiny OAK TOAD (at 3 cm, 1.2 in; Plate 1); both of these species occur in Florida.

Outside the Bufonidae, a few families of frogs also are called toads. They include the *spadefoot toads*, the *clawed* and *Surinam toads* and the *disc-tongued toads*. Of these, only the EASTERN SPADEFOOT (family Pelobatidae; Plate 1) and the EASTERN NARROWMOUTH TOAD (family Microhylidae; Plate 1) are found in Florida.

Natural History
Ecology and Behavior
Adult toads are mainly terrestrial and usually dig burrows or spend the day sheltering in holes made by other animals. Except when breeding, they are found in relatively dry habitats. They do not jump like frogs but move either with short hops, or with a crawling run. As they cannot escape by moving fast, most species discourage predators by secreting toxins from their skin glands – mainly from the parotid glands on the shoulders. The GIANT TOAD can squirt toxic secretions from its parotid glands up to 1 m (3.3 ft) into the eyes or mouth of a would-be predator. Spadefoot toads have evolved to live in semi-arid habitats. They burrow in the soil and remain there for days or weeks. Their digging is aided by the unique spade-like *tubercules* (knob-like projections) on their hind feet – they shuffle their feet, turn their body from side to side, and sink into the ground like a corkscrew. All toads are carnivorous. They feed on small invertebrates such as insects and spiders.

Breeding
Many toad species are *explosive breeders* – on a single night thousands of individuals of both sexes gather at temporary pools to mate and lay eggs. At the water, males call to attract females, often in unison, while females come and go. There are many more males than females at these temporary pools and males will jump on and attempt to mate with just about anything that moves. Other toads are *prolonged breeders*. In these species, breeding activity typically lasts for several months, and they use the same reliable breeding sites year after year. The Florida species have varied advertisement calls; the call of the SOUTHERN TOAD (Plate 1) is a penetrating, rapid trill, while the call of the smaller OAK TOAD is a series of loud peeps. The voice of the introduced GIANT TOAD is a distinctive low-pitched trill that now has become a common night sound in south Florida. During mating and egg-laying, males clasp the female in a grip known as *amplexus*, releasing sperm onto the eggs as they are extruded. The dark-colored eggs are typically laid in long, paired, jellied strings, one from each ovary. The jelly protects the eggs physically, and because it contains toxins, discourages predators. The strings of eggs are often wound around aquatic vegetation or glued to rocks. Even a small toad is capable of laying many thousands of eggs, and a Giant Toad can deposit up to 25,000 eggs. Eggs hatch in a few days, releasing *tadpoles* (larval young), which feed and grow. After a few weeks, the tadpoles metamorphose into toadlets and leave the water.

Notes
Ephemeral ponds that appear suddenly after heavy rains are vital breeding places for the majority of Florida frogs and toads. Because these ponds are temporary

they lack fish, turtles and other predators that prey on frog eggs and tadpoles. Many frogs and toads are so dependent on these ephemeral, fluctuating pools that they do not reproduce successfully in permanent waters.

Status
There are no threatened or endangered toads in Florida.

Profiles
Giant Toad, *Chaunus marinus*, Plate 1a
Oak Toad, *Anaxyrus quercicus*, Plate 1b
Southern Toad, *Anaxyrus terrestris*, Plate 1c
Eastern Spadefoot, *Scaphiopus holbrookii*, Plate 1d
Eastern Narrowmouth Toad, *Gastrophryne carolinensis*, Plate 1e
Greenhouse Frog, *Eleutherodactylus planirostris*, Plate 4a

3. Treefrogs

The *treefrogs* (family Hylidae) are the archetypal tropical frogs, used by artists and illustrators the world over to represent the tropics. Typically, treefrogs are small and narrow-waisted, with flattened bodies, long slender limbs, large heads and huge laterally-placed eyes. They have adhesive discs on their toes that permit them to cling to and climb among leaves and branches. These adhesive toe pads even allow them to cling to glass, and in summer you can often see GREEN and SQUIRREL TREEFROGS (both Plate 2) on the outside of windows, gobbling up insects attracted to the light. There are some 700 species of *hylids* worldwide. Florida's hylid frogs are contained in 5 genera and number 16 species, two of which are introduced. They are generally divided into three groups, the *treefrogs* (9 species), *cricket frogs* (2 species), and *chorus frogs* (5 species). Cricket frogs and chorus frogs are small, 2.5 to 3.9 cm (1 to 1.5 in) long and tend to be terrestrial. The BARKING TREEFROG (Plate 2) is Florida's largest native treefrog at 5.7 cm (2.2 in), but the introduced CUBAN TREEFROG (Plate 2) can attain a length of 12.7 cm (5 in).

Natural History
Ecology and Behavior
As their name suggests, treefrogs are mostly arboreal, spending much of their time climbing among leaves and twigs. A few species, such as the FLORIDA CRICKET FROG (Plate 3), lack large toe pads and have returned to a terrestrial existence. The majority of treefrogs are nocturnal, passing the daylight hours sheltered in tree crevices or on vegetation. They emerge at night to feed on insects. Many treefrogs can change color like a chameleon, and species such as the GREEN TREEFROG and the GRAY TREEFROG are dark olive-brown or charcoal when they are cold or stressed, but become bright green at other times. Male treefrogs typically call while perched on vegetation near water, but BARKING TREEFROGS call while floating in open shallow ponds and SQUIRREL TREEFROGS call from the shoreline.

Breeding
Treefrogs have an extraordinarily wide array of reproductive strategies. Female MARSUPIAL FROGS, a treefrog that occurs in South America, carry their tadpoles in pouches or depressions on their backs, while *leaf frogs*, another type of South/Central American treefrog, attach their eggs to leaves that hang over water.

When the eggs hatch, the young drop into the water to continue their development as tadpoles. In species that typically deposit eggs over streams, the eggs are particularly large so that the tadpoles that hatch out are large and powerful enough to stand up to the water current.

All Florida hylids breed in ponds, streams or marshes. Females deposit 10 to 1500 eggs in small clumps while *amplexed* (mating) with a male, which fertilizes the eggs as they are extruded. The eggs are attached to submerged vegetation or allowed to float free, and hatch into tadpoles within a few days. In Florida, some treefrogs breed in winter, others in spring and summer. Winter cold fronts usually bring rain to north Florida, precipitating winter breeding in the SOUTHERN CHORUS FROG (Plate 3), ORNATE CHORUS FROG (Plate 3), and SPRING PEEPER (Plate 3). These three species can be heard calling between November and March. The BARKING TREEFROG, PINE WOODS TREEFROG (Plate 2), SQUIRREL TREEFROG, and GREEN TREEFROG are spring and summer breeders. They can be heard calling between March and September. LITTLE GRASS FROGS and FLORIDA CRICKET FROGS call practically all year.

Notes

Visitors to Florida often marvel at the sheer volume and variety of sound that thousands of frogs of a dozen different species can produce. And it is not just visitors. Irate residents have been known to contact scientists at the Florida Museum of Natural History and the University of Florida's Department of Wildlife Ecology and Conservation to complain about 'frog noise' and ask if anything can be done. The frog sounds most people hear are made by males – female frogs are largely mute. A calling frog keeps its nostrils and mouth closed and uses the muscles of the body wall to pump air back and forth across the vocal cords, which are located between the vocal sac (the inflatable pouch on its throat) and the lungs. Most frogs call to advertise their presence to females and to repel other males from their territory. As you might guess, frog calls are highly species-specific, and many North American frog species are named for their calls. The PIG FROG (Plate 4) sounds like a grunting pig, the BARKING TREEFROG sounds exactly like a distant pack of hounds, and the BULLFROG (Plate 4) gets its name from its deep-pitched, fog-horn-like call that reminds many people of a bellowing bull.

Status

The PINE BARRENS TREEFROG, which occurs only in three small, separated areas of the eastern USA, is listed as Endangered by FCREPA (Florida Committee on Rare and Endangered Plants and Animals) and listed as a Species of Special Concern by the Florida Fish and Wildlife Conservation Commission.

Profiles

Barking Treefrog, *Hyla gratiosa*, Plate 2a
Squirrel Treefrog, *Hyla squirella*, Plate 2b
Cuban Treefrog, *Osteopilus septentrionalis*, Plate 2c
Green Treefrog, *Hyla cinerea*, Plate 2d
Pine Woods Treefrog, *Hyla femoralis*, Plate 2e
Florida Cricket Frog, *Acris gryllus dorsalis*, Plate 3a
Southern Chorus Frog, *Pseudacris nigrita nigrita*, Plate 3b
Spring Peeper, *Pseudacris crucifer*, Plate 3c
Ornate Chorus Frog, *Pseudacris ornata*, Plate 3d

4. True Frogs

The *true frogs* (family Ranidae) have the widest distribution of any frog family. More than 650 species live in almost all parts of the world except the polar regions, Madagascar, New Zealand, and most of Australia. True frogs, or *ranids*, are what many people regard as typical frogs. They are streamlined and narrow-wasted, with long muscular hind legs and webbed back feet. Their skin is smooth and often green, brown or some combination of both colors. For the most part, ranids are agile jumpers and swimmers, rarely found far from water.

Natural History
Ecology and Behavior

True frogs such as PIG FROGS, BULLFROGS and SOUTHERN LEOPARD FROGS (all Plate 4) live in or on the edges of water, in lakes, ponds, ditches, and other wet habitats. They spend much of their time around the margins of ponds or floating in shallow water. True frogs feed mainly on insects, but also on crayfish, fish and smaller frogs. They in turn are fed on by wading birds, fish, snakes, turtles, and mammals. Because they are eaten by so many other creatures, ranids are very alert to danger. The splashing noise you hear as you walk along a pond or lakeshore is usually made by these frogs leaping into the water.

In Florida, the one exception to the generally aquatic nature of the true frogs is the GOPHER FROG (Plate 4), which resides in the same dry sandhill habitats that support colonies of Gopher Tortoises. Gopher Frogs spend most of their lives in and around Gopher Tortoise burrows. They eat insects, large spiders, other frogs and toads. When alarmed, Gopher Frogs often retreat into the tortoise burrow.

Breeding

Ranids reproduce in a fairly standard amphibian manner. Breeding is usually initiated by rain, and males call from ponds and streams to attract females. Most Florida species breed during the spring but some, like the GOPHER FROG and SOUTHERN LEOPARD FROG, can be heard calling during just about any month of the year except July and August. Gopher Frogs migrate, often long distances, to breed in temporary ponds formed after heavy rain. Males have a distinctive loud snoring call.

During mating, eggs are released by the female into the water and are immediately fertilized by sperm from the *amplexing* (mating) male. The eggs are attached to submerged vegetation, or allowed to float free, and hatch into tadpoles within a few days. BULLFROG eggs often form huge floating rafts of up 20,000 eggs, which hatch into highly conspicuous tadpoles up to 7 cm (3 in) long. The tadpoles of several ranid species overwinter before metamorphosing. BULLFROG and PIG FROG eggs turn into tadpoles in summer and do not become frogs until April of the following year. This may seem like a long time, but Florida Bullfrogs actually develop quite fast compared with their northern relatives. In the northern USA, where waters are cooler and the growing season is shorter, bullfrog tadpoles can take 2 years to become frogs.

Notes

Frogs' legs are prized as an epicurean treat in many cultures, and in other parts of the world they are an important part of subsistence diets. Most species are edible, but it is only the larger ones, such as the American Bullfrogs, that are large enough to make harvesting and preparation economically profitable. In Florida, the PIG

FROG and the BULLFROG have long been considered staples of the frog-leg industry. They are hunted at night from boats using lights and a miniature pitchfork known as a 'frog gig.' (A commercial freshwater fish dealer's license is required to take for sale or to sell frogs.) To satisfy our insatiable demand for frogs' legs, the USA imports more than 562,500 kg (1.25 million lb) of frogs' legs annually, mostly from Bangladesh and Indonesia.

Status

The GOPHER FROG is listed as threatened by FCREPA (Florida Committee on Rare and Endangered Plants and Animals) and is designated a Species of Special Concern by the State of Florida. The FLORIDA BOG FROG, an endemic species of western Florida, is also listed as a Species of Special Concern.

Profiles

Pig Frog, *Lithobates grylio*, Plate 4b
Bullfrog, *Lithobates catesbeiana*, Plate 4c
Gopher Frog, *Lithobates capito*, Plate 4d
Bronze Frog, *Lithobates clamitans*, Plate 4e
Southern Leopard Frog, *Lithobates sphenocephala*, Plate 4f

Environmental Close-up 2
Frog Population Declines

The Problem

For over a decade, scientists have reported that many populations of frogs, toads, and salamanders are declining in numbers. Some populations, and in fact entire species, have disappeared entirely. Several major questions are being asked:

(1) How widespread is the problem?
(2) Are amphibian population declines a special case, happening for reasons unrelated to the general loss of biodiversity?
(3) If there is a generalized worldwide amphibian decline, what are the causes?

The available data indicate a widespread pattern of amphibian declines. There are reports from low elevations and high elevations, from the USA, Central America, the Amazon Basin, the Andes, Europe, and Australia. Habitat loss almost certainly contributes to general declines in population sizes of amphibians, and in this sense, amphibian declines are part of the worldwide loss of biodiversity. But what is going on with amphibians seems to be more extreme than the declines seen in other animals. Why would amphibians be more vulnerable? One reason is that because amphibians have thin, moist skin that they use for breathing, chemical pollutants found in the water, soil, and air are able to enter their bodies easily. Secondly, many amphibians are exposed to double jeopardy: because they live both on land (usually in the adult stage) and in the water (usually the egg and larval stages), they are exposed to environmental contaminants, vagaries of the weather, and other potential factors affecting survivorship in both habitats.

So what could be causing the observed declines of amphibians? One possible cause is environmental pollution, for example *acid rain* – rain that is acidified by various atmospheric pollutants, leading to lake and river water being more acidic.

Acidic water is known to decrease fertilization success because sperm become less active and often disintegrate. The eggs that are fertilized often develop abnormally. Another suggestion is that the increased level of ultraviolet (UV) radiation, due to the thinning of the protective atmospheric ozone layer, might be damaging. Frogs often lay their eggs in shallow water directly exposed to the sun's rays, tadpoles often seek shallow water where the temperatures are warmer, and some juvenile and adult frogs bask for warmth. Studies have shown that increased levels of UV light kill some species of frog eggs and can interact chemically with diseases and acid rain to increase amphibian mortality rates. Another possible cause is global warming. Some species of amphibians may not be able to adapt to the warmer, drier climate the world is currently experiencing. For example, drought during a severe El Niño year in 1986–1987 has been implicated in the declines and disappearances of 40% (20 of 50 species) of the frog species (including the now likely extinct Golden Toad) that lived in the vicinity of Monteverde, Costa Rica. The frogs may have died directly from dessication (drying out), or they may have been so stressed that they became more vulnerable to disease, fungus, or wind-borne environmental contaminants. Another cause of some population declines is a parasitic chytrid fungus that has been identified from Central and South America, the USA, Europe, and Australia. The fungus seems to infest especially the victims' bellies – the area where frogs take up water through the skin. Thus, one speculation is that the frogs may be suffocating and drying out. Another possibility is that the fungus may release toxins that are lethal to the frogs when they are resorbed into the skin. Scientists are wondering where the killer fungus will show up next, and what is stressing amphibians to make them more vulnerable to pathogens such as fungus. They're also wondering if people (including researchers and ecotourists) could inadvertently be spreading the fungus on their shoes and boots. Perhaps non-human animals, such as insects, are spreading the fungus as well.

The Controversy

Not all biologists agree that amphibian declines are a phenomenon over and above the worldwide decline in biodiversity. Scientists who study natural fluctuations in size of animal populations point out that populations of many animals cycle between scarcity and abundance. Many insects are known for their wildly fluctuating population sizes. Population levels of vertebrates also fluctuate with environmental conditions such as food availability and density of prey. For example, voles and lemmings, small rodents of the arctic tundra, are well known for one year being at low population densities (a few per acre or hectare) but several years later, being at very high densities (thousands per acre or hectare). Skeptics point out that, unless those sounding the alarm of amphibian declines can show that the declines are not part of natural cycles, it is too early to panic. They emphasize that the only way to document natural population cycles is to monitor amphibian populations during long-term field studies. Unfortunately, few such studies have been done.

Those scientists who believe that widespread amphibian declines are more than merely natural fluctuations argue that we need to act *now*. Although they agree that we need to initiate long-term studies, they believe we can't wait for the conclusions of such studies 10 or 20 years down the road before we try to reverse the situation. At that point, they argue, it will be too late to do anything but record extinctions.

The Future

The controversy will continue. The important consequence of the debate is that many investigators are working on the problem, considering many different possible causes, from climatic change to a parasitic fungus. A major problem is that even if the scientific consensus right now were that disease, fungi, pollution, climate change, increased level of UV radiation, or some combination, were causing worldwide amphibian declines, the interest and resources are currently lacking to do anything about it on the massive scale required. Because amphibians and reptiles are not uniformly liked and respected, preservation efforts for these animals, except for special cases like sea turtles, will always lag behind conservation efforts made on behalf of birds and mammals. Fortunately, however, because the current conservation emphasis is on preserving entire ecosystems, rather than particular species, amphibians will benefit even if they don't have feathers or fur.

Chapter 7

REPTILES

- *General Characteristics and Natural History*
- *Seeing Reptiles in Florida*
- *Family Profiles*
  1. *Crocodilians*
  2. *Turtles*
  3. *Colubrid Snakes*
  4. *Venomous Snakes – Elapids*
  5. *Venomous Snakes – Viperids*
  6. *Geckos*
  7. *Iguanids – Anoles and Spiny Lizards*
  8. *Skinks and Whiptails*
  9. *Glass Lizards*
- *Environmental Close-up 3: Living with Alligators*

General Characteristics and Natural History

Reptiles have been around since the late Paleozoic Era, some 300 million years ago. The most primitive reptiles currently known to science were small, agile, terrestrial, lizard-like creatures whose fossilized remains were found in giant tree stumps that date from the late Carboniferous Period, some 315 million years ago. Descendents of these early reptiles include 7000+ species that today inhabit most regions of the Earth.

Reptiles have several distinctive characteristics:

(1) Their skin is covered with dry horny scales that reduce water loss from the body surface. Unlike amphibians, which must live in moist places lest they dry out, reptiles can remain on land for extended periods and are able to survive and thrive even in arid areas.

(2) Compared with amphibians, reptiles have larger and more efficient lungs, heart and circulatory system.

(3) Reptile reproduction is not tied to water. Unlike amphibians, which typically

go through an aquatic larval stage, reptiles lay eggs encased in tough leathery shells, or bear their young alive.

(4) Most reptiles deposit their eggs in a burrow or mound and leave them to hatch unattended. The young are not fed or protected, they simply hatch and crawl away. A few species of skinks and snakes remain with the eggs, guarding them until they hatch. Female pythons coil around their eggs, keeping them warm with heat produced by muscle contractions. Crocodilians have the most elaborate parental care of all the reptiles; females guard the nest, assist the young in hatching, and protect hatchlings.

Reptile biologists recognize three major groups of reptiles alive today.

The *Crocodilians* (order Crocodylia) are powerful predators that live along the shores of swamps, rivers and estuaries. Adapted to a semi-aquatic lifestyle, they have short legs, a large body, a long laterally compressed tail and huge head. Their eyes and nostrils are set high on their head and remain above the water while the rest of the animal is submerged. On land, crocodilians can lift their bodies off the ground and walk or run for short distances. They swim with sideways strokes of their muscular tail. There are some 23 crocodilian species distributed throughout the tropical and subtropical regions of the world.

The *Chelonians*, or *turtles* and *tortoises* (order Chelonia), are reptiles with bony shells. The shell consists of two parts, a *carapace* covering the back, and a *plastron* covering the belly. The two parts are connected with boney bridges on each side. Many turtles can pull the head and limbs into the shell when danger threatens, but they don't all retract the head in the same way. One group (pleurodirans) curls the head back into the shell in a sideways maneuver, and these are often called *side-necked turtles*. The other group (cryptodirans) curls the head back into the shell in a vertical or S-shaped maneuver. Turtles' unique body armor is obviously a highly successful design, because chelonians were around before the dinosaurs and have changed comparatively little in their 250-million-year history. Today, some 260 species live throughout the world, on all continents except Antarctica. Most turtles are aquatic; tortoises are turtles that live primarily on land. The *sea turtles* live out their lives in the oceans, females coming ashore only to lay eggs. Different lifestyles have led to different shell designs. The land-based tortoises usually have high domed shells, while aquatic turtles tend to have lower, more streamlined shells. In highly aquatic species like sea turtles and softshell turtles, the bones in the shell have decreased in size, leaving large spaces known as 'fontanelles.' Sea turtles have strong flipper-like front and hind legs.

The third reptile group (order Squamata) contains the roughly 3300 species of *lizards*, and 3500 species of *snakes*.

Lizards are the most successful of the reptiles, and they are the most abundant vertebrate animals in many habitats. Ecologists suspect they owe this ecological success primarily to their efficient predation on insects and other small animals and to their low daily energy requirements. Lizards probably first appeared in the Triassic Period, 245 to 200 million years ago, and the fossil record shows that most of the body plans of today's lizard families were already established nearly 200 million years ago. Lizards survived the massive extinctions that wiped out the dinosaurs 65 million years ago, and today they are found worldwide in deserts, savannahs, and tropical and temperate forests. One species even occurs above the Arctic Circle. Lizards swim, climb, run and glide. Some have specialized toes for climbing smooth surfaces or running on sand, others have become legless and resemble snakes. (One legless group, known as *worm lizards*, has a representative in Florida, the FLORIDA WORM LIZARD, Plate 13; it is small, usually about 25 cm, 10 in, long, and spends most or all of its life underground in dry, sandy soils; it resembles a large earthworm.) Most lizards are small, agile insect predators, but others eat plants, or prey on amphibians, other lizards, mammals, birds, and even fish. Many lizards are active during the day, but geckos, some skinks, and burrowing lizards are nocturnal.

Lizards often defend territories with threat displays, which include color changes, 'push up' displays, tail waving, and extending the throat fan, or *dewlap*. A few, like the largely nocturnal geckos, vocalize to attract mates and defend territories. There are 17 species of native lizards in Florida, but a further 33 species have been introduced to the state at one time or another. Most of the introduced species are restricted to south Florida; some are confined to only a few blocks of a suburban neighborhood.

Snakes are the most recently evolved of the reptiles, having first appeared in the early Cretaceous Period, about 135 million years ago. Though their fossilized remains are rare, it is generally believed they evolved from burrowing lizard-like creatures. About 45 snake species occur in Florida.

Snakes have no legs, no eyelids, and no external eardrums. When most people think of snakes, one of the first words that come to mind is scaly. Unlike fish scales, which are attached to the fish's skin, a snake's scales are part of the skin. Snakes use their scales for protection and locomotion. When moving in a straight line a snake uses its belly scales, moving them forward in a continuous series of waves; the traction of the scales against the surface propels the snake forward.

The most obvious distinguishing feature of snakes is their shape. The long spinal column has 200 to 400 vertebrae (humans have only 32) and many of the internal organs have been reduced in size or offset from one another to fit inside this slender tube shape. Many snakes have only one lung, and females of extremely slender species have only one oviduct.

All snakes are carnivorous and several groups have evolved glands that manufacture poisonous *venom* that can be injected through the teeth. The venom immobilizes and kills the prey, which is then swallowed whole. Other snakes pounce on and wrap themselves around their prey, squeezing it until it suffocates. The majority of snakes are non-venomous, seizing prey with their mouths and relying on their size, strong jaws and curved teeth to subdue it. Snakes generally rely on vision and smell to locate prey, although members of two families have thermal sensor organs on their heads that detect the heat of prey animals.

Snakes are an extremely successful group. The 3500+ snake species outnumber all the other reptile groups combined and are found worldwide except Arctic regions, Antarctica, Iceland, Ireland, New Zealand, and some small oceanic islands. Part of the reason snakes have been so successful is because of their ability to devour prey that is larger than their heads (they have highly modified skulls with mobile jawbones that can separate and move to accommodate large prey as it is swallowed). This unique ability provides snakes with major advantages over other animals. Because they eat large items, snakes can survive long periods without feeding – many snakes are thought to eat only a few times a year. As they need to hunt only infrequently, snakes can spend long periods hidden and secluded, safe from predators. Snakes are prey for hawks and other predatory birds, as well as some mammals. Coral snakes, king snakes and indigo snakes routinely eat other snakes.

Seeing Reptiles in Florida

Florida is a great destination for the ecotourist interested in reptiles. Unlike mammals, which are nocturnal and often difficult to see, alligators, turtles, and lizards are usually active during the day and many of them are quite commonly seen. AMERICAN ALLIGATORS (Plate 8) are abundant in most of Florida's parks, and can be found basking in the sun on canal banks and beside rivers and lakes. You would have to be extremely unlucky to leave Florida without seeing a wild alligator. But remember, alligators can be dangerous. NEVER feed or try to catch one. Not only is it a violation of law, but you may endanger your own or the 'gator's life (alligators classified as nuisance animals are killed and disposed of by licensed trappers). Always keep pets and young children away from the water's edge.

Several lizard species are easy to find and interesting to watch. Geckos are so common in buildings in parts of South Florida that they are called 'house lizards.' These nocturnal lizards are easy to track down by their squeaks and chuckles. By sitting quietly on a park bench during mid-morning or late afternoon you can easily observe anoles and skinks hunting, courting, defending territories and going about their daily lives. Construction rubble, trash piles, and abandoned buildings attract many different reptiles – SOUTHEASTERN FIVE-LINED SKINKS (Plate 15), for example, can often be found under old wooden boards or piles of trash. EASTERN FENCE LIZARDS (Plate 14) are most often seen on logs on the ground or the lower part of standing dead trees.

Turtles and tortoises are more difficult to see. You can often locate GOPHER TORTOISES (Plate 12) by their distinctive burrows. If there are fresh tracks on the large sand apron of the burrow, you can wait and watch from a distance and sooner or later you may see the tortoise emerge to feed. Aquatic freshwater turtles can often be seen basking on the bank of ponds and lakes or on logs. A canoe trip is a good way to see both turtles and alligators. Sea turtles only come ashore at night to lay their eggs in spring and summer. They are most often seen on the southern beaches of the Atlantic coast of Florida and on the beaches of Lee and Collier counties of the Gulf coast. All sea turtles are strictly protected, and nesting beaches are often patrolled by volunteer groups. Unfortunately, you are also likely to see many turtles and tortoises hit on the highway, as they are often killed trying to cross roads. Be careful – people are killed each year in Florida while trying to rescue turtles on roads.

As for snakes, you may be lucky enough to see a BLACK RACER (Plate 16) crossing a dirt road, or notice a ROUGH GREEN SNAKE camouflaged among the leaves and stems of a bush. BANDED WATER SNAKES and FLORIDA GREEN WATER SNAKES (both Plate 17) can sometimes be spotted in the bank vegetation near a canal or lake, or basking on a dock. Watch for water snakes, cottonmouths, and mudsnakes while driving at night, especially along highways with wet roadside ditches.

A small minority of Florida's snakes are venomous, and these should be avoided. Rattlesnakes will coil and rattle if they feel threatened, and the COTTONMOUTH (Plate 19) will coil and open its mouth in a wide, 180-degree gaping yawn. Though not many people will get close enough to see, non-venomous snakes can generally be distinguished by their round pupils. For those concerned about snakebite, statistics are on your side: you have a much better chance of being killed by lightning in Florida than dying of snakebite. Approximately one fatality per year occurs in Florida from snakebite, compared with an average of 10 people per year killed by lightning.

Family Profiles

1. Crocodilians

Crocodilians are the only survivors of the Archosauria, an ancient group that included the dinosaurs. They are the most advanced of living reptiles and many of their features are more similar to mammals or birds than to other reptiles. All modern crocodilians are semi-aquatic and all have a similar body shape. They have a large head, long tubular body and four legs. A long powerful tail accounts for about half the animal's length. Protruding eyes, equipped with movable eyelids, are on top of the head, and valvular nostrils are located on top at the end of the snout. A skin flap protects the ear canal. Some 23 crocodilian species live in tropical and subtropical areas of the world and range in size from Cuvier's Dwarf Caiman, which grows to about 1.5 m (5 ft) long, to the Indo-Pacific Crocodile, which can be up to 7 m (23 ft) long. Three species of crocodilians are found in Florida. The AMERICAN ALLIGATOR (Plate 8) is found in wetlands and water bodies throughout Florida. The AMERICAN CROCODILE (Plate 8) is restricted to a small population in the extreme southern tip of Florida. It is found in coastal swamps and rivers, primarily in mangrove swamps, but occasionally a few miles inland. The COMMON CAIMAN is an introduced species that has become established in a limited area of South Florida. They are thought to have originated from animals imported for the pet trade. The largest known population is on Homestead Air Force Base in Dade County, but individuals have been sighted as far north as Lake Jessup, and as far south as Florida City.

Alligators, crocodiles and caiman are quite difficult to tell apart. In general, the snouts of alligators and caiman tend to be broad and rounded, whereas those of crocodiles are longer and more pointed. The American Crocodile is similar in appearance to the American Alligator but the crocodile is usually grayish brown, rather than black. It has a narrower snout in which the fourth tooth of the upper jaw is visible even when the mouth is closed. In alligators, this tooth is not visible when the mouth is closed. Crocodiles and caimans often bask with their mouths open, a behavior rarely seen in alligators.

Natural History
Ecology and Behavior

Visitors to Florida are always surprised to discover that AMERICAN ALLIGATORS are one of the most commonly seen wildlife species in the state. Alligators can be found in every county in Florida, but they are most common in the major river drainage basins and large lakes in the central and southern portion of the state. Many of them live out their lives in close proximity to people. You can see 2.4 to 3 m (8 to 10 ft) alligators in lakes and ponds on the campus of the University of Florida in Gainesville, in 'barrow pits' along freeways, and even in water hazards on golf courses. Alligators spend much of their time basking along waterways or cruising in the water, with only their eyes and nostrils above the surface. Until you have seen a few, they can be quite difficult to detect in the water, but look for a low 'V'-shaped wake with small bumps (nostrils) at the apex. On land, alligators usually move slowly, but they can put on surprising bursts of speed over short distances.

Alligators and crocodiles are carnivores. Hatchlings and young eat insects, snails, frogs, small fish and invertebrates, but by the time they reach 2 m (6.5 ft) in length they are feeding on fish, turtles, snakes, and waterbirds. In Florida, adult alligators consume so many apple snails that biologists once believed they were the alligator's major food. Current thinking is that alligators eat snails to aid digestion. Alligators are truly opportunistic feeders and will eat almost anything, including aluminum cans, fishing lures, sticks and stones. They have strong jaw muscles for biting and holding prey, but they do not chew – food is swallowed whole.

Breeding
AMERICAN ALLIGATORS reach maturity at about 8 to 13 years old, by which time they are about 2 m (6 or 7 ft) long. Courtship starts in April and mating occurs in early May. During the breeding season males call with loud, throaty roars to attract mates and warn off other males. The sound is intense and can be heard for 150 m (500 ft) or more. Most of this bellowing occurs in the early morning and late afternoon and seems to be contagious; when one animal starts, all the neighbors soon join in. In June and early July females move into marshy areas of lakes and rivers to nest. They construct mounded nests of vegetation, sticks, and mud in which they lay 35 to 50 goose-egg-sized eggs. The mother remains near the nest throughout the 65-day incubation period, protecting the eggs from predators. The temperature inside the nest chamber determines the sex of the young. Low temperatures, below 30 °C (86 °F), result in females, while high temperatures, above 34 °C (93 °F), yield males. Nest temperatures between these two extremes produce young of both sexes.

In mid-August, as the young are about to hatch they start to make high-pitched grunting calls. The female responds to these calls by removing the nesting material covering the young, releasing the 15 to 20 cm (6 to 8 in) long hatchlings from the nest. Young alligators remain in dense vegetation near the nest for several months after hatching, and they often stay in the general vicinity until they are two or three years old. Nevertheless, mortality rates for young alligators are high; in their first two years of life, an estimated 80% are eaten by wading birds, raccoons, otters, fish, and other alligators.

Ecological Interactions
In Florida, female Florida Redbelly Turtles (Plate 11) often lay their eggs in alligator nests. This behavior has several potential advantages for the turtles. Alligator nests provide stable temperature and humidity for both turtle and alligator eggs, and while protecting her own eggs, the female alligator protects the turtle eggs against raccoons and other would-be egg predators. However, laying eggs in an alligator nest is risky – alligators have been seen to attack redbelly turtles. Biologists believe the thick, high-domed shell of this turtle is an adaptation that helps it survive alligator attacks. Close examination of the carapaces of redbelly turtles often show tooth marks and deep gouges, evidence of unsuccessful attacks by alligators.

Notes
Living close to alligators, as many Floridians do, is not without risk, but there are relatively few attacks. Twenty people have been killed by alligators in Florida

since 1948. There are typically four to five attacks per year that result in people needing medical treatment or hospitalization. These attacks are usually by large males, 3 m (10 ft) or larger. The Florida Fish and Wildlife Conservation Commission receives over 10,000 alligator-related complaints per year. Most of these involve what is known as 'nuisance 'gators' – alligators that show up in backyards, swimming pools, golf course water hazards, and drainage ditches. If the alligator in question is deemed to be a genuine nuisance, licensed trappers are brought in to remove it. It is illegal for anyone other than an employee or representative of the Conservation Commission to remove an alligator from the wild.

Florida's 7500 freshwater lakes attract swimmers, water-skiers and fishermen from all over the world. A few simple DOs and DON'Ts make it possible for people and alligators to coexist:

(1) DO use common sense. Swim with a partner. Never swim at night or dusk, when alligators usually feed. Avoid areas with thick vegetation along shorelines.
(2) DON'T swim outside of posted swimming areas or in waters that might contain large alligators.
(3) DON'T feed alligators. It is illegal. When alligators become familiar with handouts, they lose their fear of people and begin to associate people with food.

Status

Most crocodilian species worldwide were severely reduced in numbers during the 20th century. Several were hunted almost to extinction for their skins. Today, only the COMMON CAIMAN is hunted in large numbers, particularly in the Pantanal region of Brazil. All crocodilians are listed by the international CITES agreements, preventing or highly regulating trade in their skins or other parts, and their numbers have been steadily rising during the past 20 years. However, most of the 23 crocodilian species are still threatened or endangered. The AMERICAN CROCODILE is considered threatened by Florida state and is CITES Appendix I and USA ESA listed as threatened. The AMERICAN ALLIGATOR is classified as threatened by both Florida and federal agencies. The COMMON CAIMAN, although not listed as threatened, is protected in Florida because it is similar in appearance to alligators.

Profiles
American Crocodile, *Crocodylus acutus*, Plate 8a
American Alligator, *Alligator mississippiensis*, Plate 8b

2. Turtles

Turtles have been around a long time and they have remained relatively unchanged since the late Triassic Period, some 200 million years ago. By the time of the dinosaurs, turtles already looked very much as they do today. Fossil turtles found in Florida's springs and rivers were twice as large as today's well-known Galapagos Tortoises. The largest known turtle was a fossil sea turtle, *Archelon*, which was about the size of a mid-sized car. It was more than 4 m (13 ft) long and is estimated to have weighed about 2700 kg (5940 lb).

Turtles and tortoises are instantly recognizable because of their shells. The upper shell, the *carapace*, is either covered with plates (*scutes*) or leathery skin. The lower shell is called the *plastron*. Most turtles can draw their heads and legs partly or completely inside their shells for protection. Many turtles spend much of their lives in and around water and most of them lay their eggs on land.

The 260 living turtle species are usually grouped into 12 families. Turtles are found on every continent except Antarctica. Florida is home to 25 species of turtles representing seven families. Two families comprise the *sea turtles*. These specialized turtles spend their entire lives at sea, except for the short time it takes the female to dig a nest hole and lay her eggs. Sea turtles have non-retractile flippers and heads. Their fore and hind limbs are modified as flippers, and they swim with powerful wing-like beats of their fore flippers. They use their hind flippers to steer and stabilize themselves. Five species of sea turtles live in Florida's coastal waters: the LEATHERBACK SEA TURTLE (Plate 8) is the only species in family Dermochelyidae, and the other four species are in family Cheloniidae.

Other turtle families with representatives in Florida include:

(1) *Snapping turtles*, family Chelydridae, which are large aquatic turtles with massive heads, powerful hooked beak-like jaws, and long tails, all traits that make them easy to recognize.

(2) *Basking and box turtles*, family Emydidae, which are small and medium-sized turtles; most of the box turtles are terrestrial and the basking species are primarily aquatic.

(3) *Mud and musk turtles*, family Kinosternidae, which are small, aquatic turtles with high domed shells.

(4) *Softshell turtles*, family Trionychidae, which have very long necks, narrow heads, long, slender, snorkel-like noses, and legs that look like flippers. As might be expected from their name, softshells have soft, flexible shells that feel like leather.

(5) *Terrestrial tortoises*, family Testudinidae, of which the GOPHER TORTOISE (Plate 12) is the only Florida representative.

In some parts of the world people use the word 'turtle' as a generic term for all these shelled reptiles, whereas in Britain and the USA, terrestrial forms are called 'tortoises' and aquatic (freshwater and marine) forms are called 'turtles.' In America, the term 'terrapin' is used for brackish and saltwater basking and box turtles. Additionally, some species of basking turtles are called 'cooters' and 'sliders.'

Natural History
Ecology and Behavior
Sea turtles. LEATHERBACKS are the giants of the turtle family, and the heaviest living reptile. These enormous turtles can grow to be over 1.8 m (6 ft) long, 3.6 m (12 ft) wide across the front flippers, and weigh as much as 600 kg (1320 lb). The track of a Leatherback on the beach often measures more than 2 m (6.5 ft) across. Leatherbacks do not have scutes or plates like most other turtles but are covered with a leathery hide that feels like tough rubber. Leatherbacks are omnivorous but seem to prefer jellyfish. Nesting females have been reported from both coasts of Florida. The GREEN TURTLE (Plate 9) is so called because of the color of its fat. This herbivorous turtle feeds during the day in shallow waters where sea grasses are abundant. The HAWKSBILL (Plate 9) is one of the smaller sea turtles. It is usually found near coral reefs and in shallow coastal waters. It feeds on jellyfish, sponges and mollusks. Only a few nests have been found in Florida, but small (15-cm, 6-in) young are sometimes seen around the coral reefs of the Florida Keys.

The LOGGERHEAD (Plate 8) is probably the best-known turtle in Florida because it nests on beaches during the summer months. Its name comes from its conspicuously large head. The Loggerhead has powerful, crushing jaws, which it uses to catch fish, squid, crabs, sea urchins and sponges. This turtle may be seen anywhere along Florida's coastline. KEMP'S RIDLEY (Plate 9) is one of the world's rarest and most endangered turtles. These small sea turtles do not breed in Florida but young are sometimes seen in the Crystal River and Cedar Key areas.

Snapping turtles. Snapping turtles spend most of their lives underwater, lurking on the bottom of lakes, swamps and slow-moving rivers. Their lifestyle is so sedentary that their shell may acquire a thick growth of algae. Snappers are predators, feeding on fish, insects, carrion and waterfowl. They can be highly aggressive, and large individuals have been known to cause injury to unwary swimmers. When on land they move slowly but they will not hesitate to strike if picked up or disturbed. When molested, snappers can release a strong odor from their musk glands. Rather than basking in the sun like other turtles, snappers prefer to rest in warm shallow water, sometimes buried under a thin layer of mud, with only their eyes and nostrils exposed. The snapping turtles profiled here are the COMMON SNAPPING TURTLE and ALLIGATOR SNAPPING TURTLE (both Plate 10).

Basking and box turtles. Most of the turtles in this family are aquatic, but some, such as the box turtles, spend their lives on land and rarely swim. Box turtles are found mostly in woodlands, pine flatwoods, and fields, whereas the basking turtles (terrapins, cooters and sliders) live in rivers, swamps and lakes, where they can often be seen basking on logs and riverbanks. They eat aquatic vegetation, insects, snails and aquatic invertebrates. The basking and box turtles profiled here are the DIAMONDBACK TERRAPIN (Plate 10), BOX TURTLE (Plate 12), CHICKEN TURTLE (Plate 11), BARBOUR'S MAP TURTLE (Plate 10), FLORIDA COOTER (Plate 11), and FLORIDA REDBELLY TURTLE (Plate 11).

Mud and musk turtles. These turtles live in lakes, rivers and ponds, and are sometimes considered to be pests because they will often take bait off a fishing line. Their diet is largely snails, insects, tadpoles, algae, and cabbage palm seeds. All turtles in this family have musk glands and give off a strong offensive odor when annoyed. Because of this, these turtles are often called 'stinkpots' or 'stinkin-jims.' The mud and musk turtles profiled here are the STRIPED MUD TURTLE and the STINKPOT (both Plate 12).

Softshell turtles. Softshells have strong, knife-like mandibles that are almost as powerful as the jaws of a snapping turtle. Softshells are commonly seen floating on the surface of lakes and ponds. They eat invertebrates and small fish. The softshell profiled here is the FLORIDA SOFTSHELL (Plate 12).

Terrestrial tortoise. Florida's only true tortoise is the GOPHER TORTOISE (Plate 12), a large tortoise with a high, domed, gray or light brown carapace. It is typically found in pine/turkey oak upland areas, sandy scrub habitats, and coastal dunes. This turtle digs burrows, which may be 9 m (30 ft) long and 5 m (16 ft) deep. The sand excavated from the burrow is deposited over a wide apron just outside the burrow entrance. Gopher Tortoises feed on grasses and herbaceous plants.

Breeding
Sea turtles spend their lives at sea but come ashore to lay their eggs. Different species prefer different kinds of beaches; LEATHERBACKS choose long, rock-free

beaches, while HAWKSBILLS prefer sandy coves. Females come ashore at night, and climb the beach to a suitable spot above the high tide line. At this point, they often stop and thrust their nose into the sand while making wide sweeps with their front flippers. If the site is suitable, the female digs a half-meter (1 to 2 ft) deep nest cavity with her rear flippers. She lays 50 to 175 eggs, then fills in the hole, tamping the sand down with her body. LOGGERHEADS press the sand down with their knees, KEMP'S RIDLEYS tamp the sand by rocking their shell vigorously from side to side, making a thumping noise that is audible at some distance. The entire nesting process takes about two hours, and before the female returns to the sea, she disguises the nest site by sweeping sand over the spot with her flippers. Females nest every two or three years, but in breeding years will sometimes lay several clutches. The eggs hatch simultaneously after about two months. The young turtles dig their way up out of the nest, then scuttle down to the ocean. The mortality rate for both eggs and hatchlings is enormous. Just above the high-tide line on many Atlantic coast beaches in south Florida you can see large pieces of wire mesh pegged to the sand. These cover turtle nests, and the mesh has been placed there to stop raccoons, armadillos, dogs and other predators from digging up the eggs. Hatchlings are also vulnerable both on land and in the ocean – only about 2% to 5% survive the first few days of life.

Freshwater turtles and tortoises lay fewer eggs than do marine turtles. BARBOUR'S MAP TURTLE lays a dozen or so eggs twice a year, while the various cooters lay 8 to 24 eggs as many as six times a year. FLORIDA COOTERS construct an unusual 3-hole nest, digging one deep center hole and shallower 'false nest' holes on each side. The female lays most of the eggs in the center hole, putting only one or two eggs in each of the false nests. The false nests are thought to distract predators from the main nest, although in most cases predators appear to find all the eggs.

Ecological Interactions

The GOPHER TORTOISE is not a creature one would intuitively select as pivotal to a community. Slowly stumping through the sandhills of Florida, it lives life at a leisurely pace. Individual tortoises may live to be 60 years old. Females lay about six eggs a year. Each tortoise digs several burrows throughout its home range, and once ensconced, may occupy the same holes for decades. The burrows are virtually the only shelters available in the Florida uplands, and by digging them the tortoise inadvertently provides a home for an array of other creatures. Some species like Gray Fox and Eastern Diamondback Rattlesnakes are regular visitors, but also use other refuges. Others, like the Florida Mouse and Gopher Frog, live almost exclusively in Gopher Tortoise burrows. Since scientists began to use fiber optic probes to look down the 10-m (33 ft) deep holes, they have discovered that tortoise burrows are busy places. Opossums and Eastern Indigo Snakes come and go. Pale wingless crickets with huge antennae scurry along the ceiling, and mice excavate minute side tunnels for their own separate living quarters. On dark damp days, the nocturnal Gopher Frog emerges to sit near the mouth of the burrow.

The Gopher Tortoise is a *keystone species* in Florida's xeric (dry) communities, meaning that its behavior, its presence, affects the survival of many other species. Its burrows not only provide homes for many commensal species, but the digging also returns leached nutrients to the surface. When lightning fires sweep through the sandhills, Gopher Tortoise burrows become a refuge for just about everything small that walks or crawls. More than 300 invertebrate species and 42 vertebrate species use these burrows as a refuge. Gopher Tortoises have been heavily affected by development. Roads have fragmented their living space, and many are killed each year by cars.

Notes

That tortoises and turtles can live to great age and attain great size have always been some of their most fascinating characteristics. In Japan, turtles are regarded as symbols of happiness and good luck because of their longevity. In Chinese and Indian mythology, huge tortoises help hold up the world. Fossil tortoises measuring nearly 3 m (10 ft) long were widely distributed in Asia during the Pleistocene Period, but today's much smaller giant turtles are just over 1 m (3.3 ft) long and confined mainly to remote islands. Giant tortoises roamed Florida up through the end of the Pleistocene. It has been suggested that Paleo-indians may have eaten the local giant tortoises into extinction. Though it is difficult to establish accurate ages for wild turtles, it is known that they typically live longer than other vertebrates. A Radiated Tortoise, said to have been a gift from Captain Cook to the King of Tonga, died in 1966 at the reported age of 189. In another case, five tortoises from the Seychelles were moved to the nearby island of Mauritius in 1776, and became a popular attraction at the Royal artillery barracks. The last survivor died in 1918 when it fell into a pit. It was at least 152 years old and probably nearer to 200 when it died.

The largest freshwater turtle in the USA is the ALLIGATOR SNAPPING TURTLE. Individuals weighing over 90 kg (198 lb) have been found, making this one of the largest freshwater turtles in the world. The largest specimens come from the most northern parts of this species' distribution. One famous snapper that lived in Fulk's Lake in Indiana was described as being 'as big as a dining room table,' with an estimated weight of 227 kg (500 lb).

Size is not always the best indicator of longevity because box turtles, which are small, also appear to have a long natural life span. Because these turtles were often seen and easily caught, it was popular in the past to carve one's initials and a date on their shells, and there have been several apparently valid cases of individuals that were more than 100 years old. One Eastern Box Turtle found in the state of Rhode Island in 1954 bore the initial 'G' and the date 1836, as well as a later date, 1890.

Status

Among the sea turtles, the GREEN, HAWKSBILL, KEMP'S RIDLEY, and LEATHERBACK are classified as endangered (CITES Appendix I and USA ESA listed), and are fully protected under state and federal law. They are threatened by collisions with powerboats, incidental capture and entanglement in fishing nets, and loss of beach nesting habitat. Recent surveys indicate that probably no more than 375 adult female GREEN turtles nest in Florida. Most of these nests are at Melbourne beach, Hutchinson Island and Jupiter Island. Only a few KEMP'S RIDLEY nests have been found in Florida, but juveniles and adults are seen off the east coast. The world population of Kemp's Ridleys has declined dramatically, from an estimated 40,000 females in 1947 to fewer than 600 adult females today. HAWKSBILLS are probably second only to the Kemp's Ridley in terms of endangerment. Their nesting beaches are difficult to protect because nests are widely spaced. The LOGGERHEAD is considered threatened (USA ESA). Many coastal communities have lighting ordinances called 'Lights out for Turtles,' which are designed mainly to encourage hatching Loggerheads to head for the ocean rather than be drawn to an artificial light source. The GOPHER TORTOISE is listed by Florida's Fish and Wildlife Conservation Commission as a Species of Special Concern.

Profiles

Leatherback Sea Turtle, *Dermochelys coriacea*, Plate 8c
Loggerhead Sea Turtle, *Caretta caretta*, Plate 8d
Kemp's Ridley Sea Turtle, *Lepidochelys kempii*, Plate 9a
Green Sea Turtle, *Chelonia mydas*, Plate 9b
Hawksbill Sea Turtle, *Eretmochelys imbricata*, Plate 9c
Common Snapping Turtle, *Chelydra serpentina*, Plate 10a
Alligator Snapping Turtle, *Macroclemmys temminckii*, Plate 10b
Diamondback Terrapin, *Malaclemys terrapin*, Plate 10c
Barbour's Map Turtle, *Graptemys barbouri*, Plate 10d

Florida Redbelly Turtle, *Pseudemys nelsoni*, Plate 11a
Florida Cooter, *Pseudemys peninsularis floridana*, Plate 11b
Chicken Turtle, *Deirochelys reticularia*, Plate 11c
Yellow-bellied Slider, *Trachemys scripta scripta*, Plate 11d
Stinkpot, *Sternotherus odoratus*, Plate 12a
Striped Mud Turtle, *Kinosternon baurii*, Plate 12b
Gopher Tortoise, *Gopherus polyphemus*, Plate 12c
Box Turtle, *Terrapene carolina*, Plate 12d
Florida Softshell, *Apalone ferox*, Plate 12e

3. Colubrid Snakes

Despite the rumors, Florida is not full of deadly, aggressive snakes. Though people often imagine the tropics to be 'dripping' with snakes, in reality, snakes are quite difficult to see even when you go looking for them. Snakes in general are amazingly cryptic; most rely on camouflage and simply lie still until danger has passed. The two exceptions are the rattlesnakes (Plate 19) – which coil and rattle if they feel threatened – and the COTTONMOUTH (Plate 19), which will coil and open its mouth in a wide, gaping threat. Though not many people will get close enough to see, non-venomous snakes can generally be distinguished by their round pupils (the exception in Florida being the highly venomous EASTERN CORAL SNAKE; Plate 19). Those concerned about snakebite can relax; very few visitors to Florida are bitten by venomous snakes and it is doubtful you will see any of them.

The 45 species of snakes in Florida belong to three major families. The largest and most diverse family is Colubridae, which contains more than two-thirds of the world's 3500+ species of snakes. The 39 *colubrid* species in Florida are not venomous, athough there are venomous colubrid species in other parts of the world. All snakes in the other two families, the Elapidae (p. 89) and Viperidae (p. 90), are venomous.

Natural History
Ecology and Behavior

There is enormous diversity in the colubrid snakes. Even among the Florida colubrids, there are water snakes, arboreal insect-eating green snakes, highly specialized crayfish snakes, and death-feigning hognose snakes.

Aquatic colubrids in Florida include the FLORIDA GREEN WATER SNAKE, BANDED WATER SNAKE, MUD SNAKE, BROWN WATER SNAKE, and the STRIPED CRAYFISH SNAKE (all Plate 17). *Water snakes* are common in or near shallow lakes, ponds, marshes, canals and roadside ditches. Brown Water Snakes often bask in the sun, and several can sometimes be seen basking together on a fallen tree or on a branch overhanging the water. Water snakes feed mainly on frogs, fish and tadpoles. If cornered or annoyed, they will strike viciously and can inflict a deep, painful bite. Also found in aquatic habitats, but quite docile by nature, the secretive Striped Crayfish Snake is most often found among the roots of water hyacinth and other aquatic plants in swamps, ponds and slow-moving rivers. It can sometimes be seen crawling on roads in the evening, just at dusk. This snake has a highly specialized diet. It feeds almost entirely on crayfish, which it holds with its coils and swallows tail first. Unlike the other water snakes, Striped Crayfish Snakes are not aggressive and do not bite.

The ROUGH GREEN SNAKE (not illustrated) is very common throughout Florida but extremely difficult to see. This small snake's pale green, slender body is so well camouflaged that even when you are looking directly at it, it is almost impossible to see among the leaves. Green snakes are non-aggressive and rarely bite. When confronted by a predator, they simply move a short distance, then freeze. Rough Green Snakes spend most of their time in shrubs and bushes, hunting for spiders, crickets and moths.

Florida's terrestrial snakes include the handsome BLACK RACER (Plate 16), a shiny black snake with a white chin. It is regularly seen in suburban areas. Black Racers hunt during the daytime and are often seen moving quickly with their head held high above the ground as they search for prey. The INDIGO SNAKE (Plate 16) is perhaps the largest non-venomous snake in North America; individuals up to 2.6 m (8.6 ft) have been recorded. With its glossy blue-black skin and red or white throat, the Indigo is justly considered one of America's most beautiful snakes. Through much of Florida, this day-active snake uses Gopher Tortoise burrows and other holes for shelter. It is sometimes seen hunting on canal and pond banks, looking for small mammals, frogs, and other snakes. The PINE SNAKE (Plate 18) is a burrower, and research in northern Florida shows that it spends a lot of time underground in the tunnels of the Pocket Gopher, a medium-sized burrowing rodent. The Pine Snake gains entrance to these tunnels via the mounds of soil pushed up by the Pocket Gopher as it digs its tunnel. The mounds are displaced soil. The snake first locates the hole (now plugged) through which the Pocket Gopher pushed up the soil from its tunnel. Using its cone-shaped head and thick muscular body, the snake then pushes its way through the plugged hole and into the gopher's tunnel, where it probably preys on young gophers. Pine Snakes also feed on mice, woodrats, rabbits, and ground-nesting birds.

Kingsnakes, such as the EASTERN KINGSNAKE (Plate 18), are well known for their appetite for other snakes and their immunity to the bites of venomous snakes. Kingsnakes are constrictors, and they can kill and eat large poisonous snakes, including Cottonmouths and rattlesnakes. Hognose snakes, such as the EASTERN HOGNOSE SNAKE (Plate 16), are specialized toad-hunters, but they also feed on frogs and lizards. Prey are located by scent in the leaf litter and soil, and rooted out by the snake with its large head and plow-like upturned nose. The Eastern Hognose Snake is also known as the 'puff adder' or 'puffer,' because of its unusual defensive behavior. A frightened hognose will flatten its head and neck and hiss, sometimes striking at the aggressor with its mouth closed. If the antagonist persists, the snake will writhe convulsively, regurgitate, defecate, and turn belly-up with its tongue hanging out of its mouth. If then placed right side up, some hognose snakes will immediately revert to the belly-up position. The color patterns of many individual Eastern Hognose Snakes are similar to those of pygmy rattlesnakes and may be an example of mimicry.

Radio-tracking data for Florida snakes indicate that individual snakes live in a specific space. Male Indigo Snakes and Pine Snakes occupy areas of more than 100 hectares (247 acres); several females live in smaller areas within a male's range. Smaller snakes, such as the RINGNECK SNAKE (not illustrated), use smaller areas of only a hectare (2.5 acres) or less.

Breeding
Relatively little is known about the breeding of most colubrid snakes in the wild. Males travel in search of females, using their olfactory senses to detect the pheromones left by sexually receptive females. Once a female is located, a male may spend several days courting her before mating occurs. Snakes have internal fertilization. Males have a pair of penis-like structures, the *hemipenes*, which lie in the base of the tail. The surface of the hemipenes area is covered with spines and projections, apparently used by the male to find the vent of the female and fix the hemipenes in place in order for copulation to begin. There is no enclosed sperm duct and sperm flows along an external groove in the hemipenes.

Because larger females lay more eggs per clutch, males prefer to mate with larger females. Big female FLORIDA GREEN WATER SNAKES have been known to give birth to up to 128 young at one time. Some colubrids lay eggs, others give birth to live young. *Oviparous* (egg-laying) snakes such as rat snakes and racers lay 4 to 30 elongated white eggs in a damp secluded place – usually in a rotten log or under a rock. Typically the female covers the eggs and departs; there is no parental care. MUD SNAKES are unusual in that they are one of the few colubrid species that remain at the nest and tend the eggs. Mud snakes build underground flask-shaped nests, which have been found to contain 11 to 104 eggs. Though it is not known for sure, herpetologists strongly suspect the large number of eggs in a single nest may be the product of more than one female; in other words, mud snakes may nest communally. Garter snakes, ribbon snakes, water snakes, and the STRIPED CRAYFISH SNAKE give birth to live young (*ovoviviparous* reproduction). Water snakes even have a placenta, which nourishes the young.

Female colubrids do not necessarily breed every year – some breed every 2 years or every 5 years. After mating, a female can store sperm and use it later. In fact, one captive indigo snake had fertile eggs 4 years after the last time she was housed with a male.

Ecological Interactions
The majority of colubrid snakes are long and thin, which is at least partly an adaptation for speedy movement – they escape from predators and capture prey by moving rapidly. A light, slender body-plan also permits many arboreal colubrids to traverse gaps between tree branches. In contrast to the slender colubrids, most of the vipers (p. 90; Plate 19) are heavy-bodied and rely on their bite, rather than speed, for protection and hunting. As *sit-and-wait* predators, vipers tend to move around a lot less than colubrids. Biologists who study snakes know that temperature regulates a snake's life, and is the key to understanding their ecology. Snakes are cold-blooded animals – they inhabit a world in which the outside temperature governs their activity. Unlike birds and mammals, which generate their own body heat,

snakes' body temperatures are determined by how much heat they obtain from their physical environment. They have some control over their body temperature, but it is behavioral rather than physiological. They can move into the sun to elevate body temperature, or retreat to the shade to lower it. But snakes must 'sit out' hours or days in which the air temperature is either too high or too low. This dependence on external temperature affects most aspects of snakes' lives, from date of birth, to food requirements, to the rapidity with which they can strike at prey. For instance, in cold weather snakes are less successful at capturing prey. However, their metabolism slows when they are cold, which means they need less food. At lower temperatures, snakes probably grow more slowly, reproduce less frequently, and live longer.

Notes

All of Florida's water snakes, and especially the BROWN WATER SNAKE and the dark form of the BANDED WATER SNAKE, are often confused with the venomous Cottonmouth, because they live in the same types of habitats. Due to these mistaken identifications, many Banded Water Snakes are killed each year when they emerge to bask on logs or boat docks.

Status

Several colubrid snakes are threatened in Florida, including the ATLANTIC SALT MARSH SNAKE and the eastern subspecies of the INDIGO SNAKE, which are both listed as threatened by federal and state authorities. The BIG PINE KEY RING-NECK SNAKE, SHORT-TAILED SNAKE, the lower Keys population of the FLORIDA BROWN SNAKE, RIMROCK CROWN SNAKE, and the lower Keys population of the FLORIDA RIBBON SNAKE (a subspecies of ribbon snake slightly different from the one in Plate 18) are all listed as threatened by the state of Florida. The Short-tailed Snake is endemic to Florida. This rare species is monotypic (the only species in its genus), and is threatened because its habitat is under intense development pressure for citrus production and housing development. Habitat loss and coastal development threaten the other species.

Profiles

Eastern Hognose Snake, *Heterodon platyrhinos*, Plate 16a
Corn Snake, *Elaphe guttata*, Plate 16b
Yellow Rat Snake, *Elaphe obsoleta*, Plate 16c
Indigo Snake, *Drymarchon couperi*, Plate 16d
Black Racer, *Coluber constrictor*, Plate 16e

Florida Green Water Snake, *Nerodia floridana*, Plate 17a
Striped Crayfish Snake, *Regina alleni*, Plate 17b
Banded Water Snake, *Nerodia fasciata*, Plate 17c
Mud Snake, *Farancia abacura*, Plate 17d
Brown Water Snake, *Nerodia taxispilota*, Plate 17e

Eastern Kingsnake, *Lampropeltis getula*, Plate 18a
Eastern Garter Snake, *Thamnophis sirtalis*, Plate 18b
Eastern Ribbon Snake, *Thamnophis sauritus*, Plate 18c
Pine Snake, *Pituophis melanoleucus*, Plate 18d

4. Venomous Snakes – Elapids

The snakes of family Elapidae are found mainly in Australia, Asia and Africa, and these *elapids* include some of the world's most feared snakes, such as *cobras, mambas, kraits* and *sea snakes*. They have rounded pupils, narrow snouts and straight, hollow, non-retractable fangs located at the front of the upper jaw. Their venom is mainly *neurotoxic* (interferes with nerve function, causing paralysis of the limbs and respiratory failure) and extremely dangerous. In the USA the only representative of this family is the Coral Snake, which is known as the EASTERN CORAL SNAKE (Plate 19) in Florida and the southeastern USA. These small (most are about 76 cm, 2.5 ft, long), slender, pretty snakes are marked with black and red bands separated by yellow rings. The old saying 'Red touches yellow, kill a fellow' can be used to separate this coral snake from its non-venomous colubrid mimics, the Scarlet King Snake and Scarlet Snake. In the latter two species, the bands are similarly colored but red bands touch black bands ('Red touches black, friend of Jack').

Natural History
Ecology and Behavior
Coral snakes are quite common in many habitats. They live in rotting logs and decaying vegetation and are sometimes found around houses by people raking leaves or digging in compost piles. Coral snakes feed on other snakes and lizards, particularly glass lizards. Even when provoked, coral snakes rarely strike like other snakes, and people are rarely bitten by this non-aggressive species. But when it is pinned down, this snake will strike rapidly in a sideways motion. The EASTERN CORAL SNAKE'S neurotoxic venom is more virulent than the venom of any other snake in North America. Coral snakes in Florida are most often seen in March and April and in October and November. If you come across one of these snakes, leave it alone – THESE SNAKES SHOULD NOT BE HANDLED.

Breeding
Coral snakes breed in late spring. During May and June, females lay a single clutch of about 6 sausage-shaped eggs, each about 3.5 cm (1.4 in) long. The eggs hatch in late summer or early fall. Newly hatched coral snakes are about 16.5 to 18.5 cm (6 to 7 in) long.

Ecological Interactions
Despite the coral snake's conspicuous warning coloration, it is preyed upon by king snakes, kestrels and hawks. However, would-be predators sometimes discover that this snake has warning coloration for a reason. K. Brugger of the U.S. Fish and Wildlife Service saw an adult male Red-tailed Hawk land in a meadow with an 80-cm (31-in) coral snake in its talons. As she watched, the bird 'became progressively uncoordinated and unresponsive and finally collapsed.' When Brugger examined the dead hawk she found it had several small fang punctures in its feet and legs.

Status
The EASTERN CORAL SNAKE is common in Florida and not considered threatened.

Profile
Eastern Coral Snake, *Micrurus fulvius*, Plate 19b

5. Venomous Snakes – Viperids

Vipers, family Viperidae, are heavy-bodied, venomous snakes with a sophisticated system of injecting venom. Long, hollow, hinged fangs move forward into a stabbing position when a viper strikes. When the snake closes its mouth the fangs retract and lie flat against the palate. The only vipers that occur in the New World are the *pit-vipers*, so called because of the facial pit found between each eye and nostril. These pits are heat-sensitive organs that can detect differences of less than 0.22 °C (0.4 °F). Because prey animals, especially warm-blooded prey, have body temperatures different from that of the environment, these allow pit vipers to detect potential victims. *Rattlesnakes, copperheads*, and COTTON-MOUTHS (Plate 19) are all pit-vipers. Some 290 species of vipers occur worldwide, from southern Canada to Argentina, and across Africa, Europe, and Asia. There are 17 species of viperids in North America, four of which occur in Florida.

Natural History
Ecology and Behavior
The COTTONMOUTH, or Water Moccasin as it is also sometimes called, gets its name from the whitish color of the inside of its mouth, which is displayed when the snake makes its characteristic open-mouth threat. Cottonmouths are large, heavy-bodied, dark gray-brown snakes, with abruptly tapering tails. These snakes are opportunistic hunters, known to take fish, frogs, birds, small mammals and rabbits. They are sometimes seen in wading bird rookeries, feeding on young birds that have fallen from nests. Cottonmouths swim well and generally live near water. When swimming, this snake inflates its lung, so that much of its body floats. In contrast, the Banded, Brown, and Florida Green Water Snakes (with which the cottonmouth is often confused) swim with only their head and neck above the water's surface. Cottonmouth venom is *hemotoxic*, destroying red blood cells and resulting in considerable tissue damage.

Cottonmouths are known to live at high densities. In the early 20th century, commercial snake hunters claimed to be able to kill 300 in a single night. Recent scientific studies suggest that in some habitats, Cottonmouths reach densities of 700 per hectare (280 per acre).

The EASTERN DIAMONDBACK RATTLESNAKE (Plate 19) is the largest venomous snake in the USA and the most dangerous snake in Florida. Rattlesnakes are named for the distinctive rattle on the tip of their tail. The rattle consists of loosely connected, dry, horny scales that produce a characteristic buzz when the tail tip is rapidly vibrated. Each time the snake sheds its skin a new segment is added to the base of the rattle. The number of rattle seqments does not equal the age of the snake, because rattlesnakes may shed their skin several times per year and segments break off. Diamondbacks have a striking range of 1 m (3 ft) and their bite can deliver a large quantity of hemotoxic venom. Diamondbacks are most often seen in early morning or evening. They hunt by both actively foraging and using sit-and-wait ambush techniques, preying on rabbits, squirrels, gophers, rodents and birds. They often lie in wait for prey beside logs, in dense stands of palmetto, and among the roots of fallen trees. Once bitten, the prey is released and allowed to crawl off and die. The snake then follows the scent trail and swallows the victim, usually head first. In Florida these snakes are active for most of the year, but in cold weather they hibernate in tortoise burrows, hollow logs or stumps, and under leaning trunks of saw palmettos.

The DUSKY PIGMY RATTLESNAKE (Plate 19) is a quick-to-strike, feisty little snake, but despite this, its bite is rarely fatal. Small fangs and small amounts of hemotoxic venom make it less dangerous than its larger relatives, though it can still pose a hazard to children, dogs and cats. Like other pit-vipers, pigmy rattlesnakes are sit-and-wait predators; they sit coiled and immobile, waiting for suitable prey to come within striking distance. Juvenile pygmy rattlesnakes have sulfur-colored tails that they wave to lure frogs and lizards to within striking distance. One study of these snakes found that they sometimes stayed in the same location for two to three weeks. In Florida, pigmy rattlesnakes feed chiefly on anolis lizards, treefrogs and Leopard Frogs. In other areas they rely more heavily on small mammals.

Breeding
COTTONMOUTHS, EASTERN DIAMONDBACK RATTLESNAKES, and DUSKY PIGYMY RATTLESNAKES all bear live young. Cottonmouths typically breed annually, giving birth to 3 to 12 young in August and September. Female Eastern Diamondbacks reproduce every third or fourth year. It is thought that females need more than a year to rebuild their stores of body fat to a level at which they can breed. The same holds true for the pigmy rattlesnake; only about half the adult females in the population give birth in any year. After birth, pigmy rattlesnakes remain clustered together near their mother for several days. Newborn pigmy rattlesnakes are tiny; they weigh 4 to 5 g (0.1 to 0.2 oz), and when coiled are not much larger than a quarter coin.

Notes
Snakes have always fascinated people. Their serpentine movements and ability to 'rejuvenate' themselves by shedding their skins combine to make them intriguing. However, to many people the most fascinating aspect of snakes is their potential to kill animals many times larger than themselves with a pinprick bite.

Venomous snakes are found in three families, Colubridae, Elapidae, and Viperidae, the last family having the most highly developed venom injecting apparatus. Snake venom is produced in glands in the upper jaw and is usually associated with specialized teeth or 'fangs,' which are grooved or hollow and serve to deliver the venom into the body of the prey. Snake venom is a complicated cocktail of substances, but there are four general categories:

(1) Hemotoxins, which cause a breakdown of blood cells and lead to bruising and internal bleeding;
(2) Neurotoxins, which affect the nervous system, attack the brain's respiratory center and result in depressed breathing;
(3) Coagulants, which cause blood to clot; and
(4) Anti-coagulants, which cause profuse bleeding.

Venoms may contain several or all of these components, which may act in concert; but in general, the venom of pit-vipers, such as the three species profiled here, is hemotoxic, whereas the venom of *coral snakes* (p. 90) is neurotoxic.

Statistics compiled by the World Health Organization indicate that some 30,000 people in the world die each year from snakebite. Most live in rural agricultural areas of Southeast Asia, West Africa and tropical America. Approximately 6000 people are bitten by snakes in the USA each year but the majority involve non-venomous species and require no treatment. Approximately a dozen people die of snakebite in North America each year.

Status
None of Florida's pit-vipers are considered threatened.

Profiles

Dusky Pigmy Rattlesnake, *Sistrurus miliarius barbouri*, Plate 19a
Cottonmouth, *Agkistrodon piscivorus*, Plate 19c
Eastern Diamondback Rattlesnake, *Crotalus adamanteus*, Plate 19d

6. Geckos

If you notice small lizards moving around your Florida house, or motel room at night, they are probably *geckos*, most of which are *exotics*, or non-native species. Geckos have managed to fill a vacant niche in Florida. There are no native nocturnal lizards in the state and geckos have successfully taken advantage of this. They have become 'house lizards,' and moved into buildings, where they hunt insects attracted to artificial lights. The more than 900 species of geckos, family Gekkonidae, are spread throughout tropical and subtropical areas of the world.

Geckos have stout, flattened bodies, short legs, and large eyes. All Florida geckos lack a functional eyelid. They lick the eye scale with the tongue to clean away dirt. Flat, adhesive toe pads allow them to climb smooth surfaces and walk across ceilings. On the bottom of the fingers and toe pads, a series of miniscule hair-like structures (*setae*) provide attachment to walls and ceilings by something akin to surface tension – the same property that allows some insects to walk on water.

Seven species of gecko breed in Florida, but only one, the FLORIDA REEF GECKO (not illustrated), is native; the others have been introduced. The MEDITERRANEAN GECKO (Plate 13) has the most widespread distribution of any gecko in Florida. It is almost always found in houses and buildings, rarely on trees or vegetation.

Natural History
Ecology and Behavior

Most lizards are *diurnal* (active during daylight) but geckos are nocturnal. They use their big cat-like eyes to help them to hunt at night, picking off insects near artificial lights. Geckos are sit-and-wait predators; instead of wasting energy actively searching for prey, they sit for long periods, waiting for unsuspecting insects to venture a bit too near, then lunge, grab, and swallow. Geckos rely chiefly on their *cryptic coloration* and their ability to flee rapidly to escape predators. When seized, geckos give threat displays and bite. They also have the ability to shed their tails in an instant (tails later regrow), and this escape mechanism is used so often that it is almost impossible to find a gecko with its original tail.

Unlike most lizards, geckos have well-developed vocal cords and communicate with one another with surprisingly loud chirps, clicks and squeaks. The word 'gecko' approximates the sound of the call from some Asian species.

Breeding

Almost all geckos are egg-layers. Mating occurs after a round of courtship, which involves a male displaying to a female by waving his tail around, followed by some mutual nosing and nibbling. Geckos typically lay one or two shelled eggs, but a female may lay several clutches a year. Florida's native gecko, the FLORIDA REEF GECKO, places her single, sticky, white egg under damp logs, boards or debris, where it incubates for 2 months before hatching. The MEDITERRANEAN GECKO breeds only during warmer months, and females may nest communally in attics and other secluded sites in houses. Females lay 2 eggs, and incubation takes about 48 days. Young geckos break out of the egg by piercing the shell with two sharp pointed egg teeth. There is no parental care; the eggs and the tiny geckos are on their own.

Notes
The world's smallest reptile is the Caribbean Dwarf Gecko. At 4 cm (1.6 in) long, this tiny creature is shorter than its name.

Status
Florida's only native gecko, the FLORIDA REEF GECKO, is not considered threatened.

Profile
Mediterranean Gecko, *Hemidactylus turcicus*, Plate 13d

7. Iguanids – Anoles and Spiny Lizards
The family Iguanidae is a large, diverse assemblage of lizards with a variety of lifestyles. Many in the family are brightly colored and have adornments such as crests, spines or throat fans. Some 628 species in 60 genera are found in the Americas, Madagascar and Fiji. They range in size from tiny *anolis lizards*, or *anoles*, only a few centimeters in total length and a few grams in weight, to GREEN IGUANAS, which may be 2 m (6.5 ft) long. In Florida, the *iguanids* are represented by 16 species of anoles, *basilisks, iguanas, fence swifts, horned lizards*, and *curly-tailed lizards*. Only three of these species are Florida natives, the others being exotics.

Natural History
Ecology and Behavior
Anoles are the most commonly seen lizards in Florida. Many people think they are 'chameleons' because they can quickly change color from bright emerald-green to brown. Anoles are day-active and are often seen basking on trees, shrubs and walls, or displaying to one another. Male anoles have a large throat fan, or *dewlap*, which they display when courting or defending a territory. Anoles feed on insects. Of the eight anole species in Florida, only the GREEN ANOLE (Plate 14) is native.

Spiny lizards are also called swifts, or fence lizards. The EASTERN FENCE LIZARD (Plate 14) is dichromatic – the sexes are colored differently. Adult males have bright blue patches on the throat and lateral margins of the belly, while the belly of the female is buffy white with gray spots. Newly hatched young look like females. Fence lizards are day-active and often seen sunning themselves on trees, fallen logs, and fences. However, their scaly, light gray- to dark-colored backs makes detection difficult on most woody surfaces. Fence lizards feed on insects. The FLORIDA SCRUB LIZARD'S (Plate 14) name describes its preferred habitat, as this species is confined to the remaining patches of Central Florida's sandy scrub. It eats ants, beetles and crickets and is usually seen foraging on the ground.

Breeding
Anoles lay a single egg at 14- to 17-day intervals throughout the warmer months of the year. The egg is laid in a moist place, which sometimes includes the soil around potted household plants. Incubation time depends on temperature and can be anywhere from a month to nearly two months. Fence and scrub lizards may lay several clutches of eggs during the summer months. Fence lizards lay

6 to 10 eggs in rotting wood or at the base of a clump of grass. The eggs hatch in 6 to 8 weeks, and hatchlings begin to appear in June. Reproduction in scrub lizards is a little slower; they lay 2 to 4 eggs, which hatch in 8 to 10 weeks.

Status

None of Florida's iguanid lizards is listed as threatened or endangered by state or federal agencies.

Profiles

Florida Scrub Lizard, *Sceloporus woodi*, Plate 14a
Brown Anole, *Anolis sagrei*, Plate 14b
Eastern Fence Lizard, *Sceloporus undulatus*, Plate 14c
Green Anole, *Anolis carolinensis*, Plate 14d

8. Skinks and Whiptails

The *skinks* (family Scincidae) are a large family containing about 1000 species of small and medium-sized lizards with a worldwide distribution. They occur throughout the warmer parts of the globe. Skinks are easy to recognize. They are slim-bodied with relatively short limbs, and smooth, shiny round scales that combine to produce a satiny look. Many skinks are 5 to 9 cm (2 to 4 in) long, not including the tail, which can easily double an adult's total length. Skinks have tails that break off easily if the tail is held or seized. The tail continues to wriggle while the skink escapes, distracting the predator. There are seven native skinks in Florida, the five illustrated in Plate 15 plus the EASTERN FIVE-LINED SKINK and COAL SKINK. The most commonly seen species is the GROUND SKINK, which is often observed wriggling across lawns or through dead leaves.

Whiptails (family Teiidae) are a New World group of about 200 species, distributed throughout the Americas. Most are tropical. *Teiids* are small to medium-sized, slender lizards, known for their highly alert and active behavior. They have long, slender, whip-like tails, which are often twice the length of their bodies. They range in length from 7 to 12 cm (3 to 5 in). Three species of teiids are established in Florida, but only one, the SIX-LINED RACERUNNER (Plate 13) is native.

Natural History

Ecology and Behavior

Skinks are day-active, largely terrestrial lizards that feed on insects. A few species are arboreal and some are burrowers. Skinks use their limbs to walk, but when the need for speed arises they move by making rapid wriggling movements with their bodies, snake fashion, with little assistance from their legs. Sand skinks and mole skinks have very reduced limbs and are often referred to as 'sand swimmers.' Skinks are secretive and wary. They are sometimes heard making small rustling sounds in the leaves as they dash away. Skinks spend much of their time hidden under rocks, vegetation or leaf litter. The MOLE SKINK is sometimes found in the sandy 'push-ups' of Pocket Gophers or in mounds of burrowing beetles. When threatened, the Mole Skink dives into the sand. The SOUTH-EASTERN FIVE-LINED SKINK is one of Florida's most common lizards. It makes its living on the ground, scratching through dead leaves and plants in search of insects. When alarmed, it vanishes into the dead leaves or sometimes takes to the water. BROADHEADED SKINKS are arboreal and usually found in damp forested habitats, where they feed largely on beetles and beetle larvae. The FLORIDA SAND SKINK has very small, reduced legs, tiny eyes and a translucent lower eyelid. This species spends most of its time underground, where it feeds on termites, ants and insect larvae.

Teiids, or *racerunners*, as they are also known, are active terrestrial hunters. They move rapidly, in short bursts of speed, and are often seen scratching through dead leaves and loose sand in search of insects. Some species also eat plant material. Racerunners are active in the morning and spend a great deal of time basking between bouts of feeding. The SIX-LINED RACERUNNER is very common in dry habitats, especially in sand dune areas at the beach. It is a speedy, active lizard, most often seen moving about during the heat of the day. If you are at the beach or walking along a sandy road and hear an intermittent rustling noise in the dry leaves, it is most likely a Six-lined Racerunner chasing insects.

Breeding
Female MOLE, FIVE-LINED, and BROADHEADED SKINKS create a nesting chamber and guard their eggs after laying them, sometimes coiling around them until they hatch. Incubation may take 55 to 65 days. The GROUND SKINK is the only Florida skink known to lay several clutches. Females lay 2 to 5 eggs at 4-week intervals. The SIX-LINED RACERUNNER lays two clutches of 1 to 6 eggs, which hatch in about 48 days. The young are nearly 7.5 cm (3 in) long at hatching.

Notes
Many lizards, including the skinks, whiptails, and geckos, have what many might regard as a self-defeating predator escape mechanism: they can detach a large portion of their bodies, leaving it behind for the predator to attack and eat while they make their escape. The process is known as *tail autotomy* – 'self removal.' Owing to some special anatomical features of the tail vertebrae, the tail is only tenuously attached to the rest of the body. If the animal is grasped forcefully by its tail, the tail breaks off easily. The tail then wriggles vigorously for a while, diverting the predator's attention for the instant it takes the now-tailless lizard to find shelter. A new tail grows quickly to replace the lost one; however, the replacement tail is never as tapering or the same color as the original tail.

Is tail autotomy successful as a life-saving tactic? Most evolutionary biologists would argue that of course it is, otherwise it could not have evolved to be part of lizard's present-day defensive strategy. Additional support for the value of the tactic is to be found in the stomachs of predators. For instance, some snakes that have been caught and dissected were found to have only skinks in their stomachs – not whole bodies, just tails! Further evidence comes from the findings of field biologists. It is not uncommon in broad-scale surveys involving hundreds of small lizards to find that 50% or more of the animals captured have regenerating tails; this indicates that tail autotomy is a common and successful tactic for staying alive.

Status
The BLUE-TAILED MOLE SKINK (a subspecies of the mole skink shown in Plate 15) and the FLORIDA SAND SKINK are listed as threatened species by both state (Florida Fish and Wildlife Conservation Commission) and federal (US Fish and Wildlife Service) authorities. Both species live in the sand pine scrub habitat of central Florida, which is rapidly being destroyed by development.

Profiles
Six-lined Racerunner, *Aspidoscelis sexlineatus*, Plate 13c
Florida Sand Skink, *Eumeces reynoldsi*, Plate 15a

Broadheaded Skink, *Eumeces laticeps*, Plate 15b
Ground Skink, *Scincella lateralis*, Plate 15c
Southeastern Five-lined Skink, *Eumeces inexpectatus*, Plate 15d
Mole Skink, *Eumeces egregius,* Plate 15e

9. Glass Lizards

The family Anguidae consists of about 90 lizard species, most of which inhabit the northern hemisphere. They are widely distributed in both the New World and Old World. *Anguids* have bony plates (*osteoderms*) beneath the skin scales that make these lizards look and feel hard and rigid. Some anguids have short legs, others are legless. Florida is home to four quite similar-looking legless species known as *glass lizards*, so named for their very long, and fragile tails. Three of four species of glass lizard in Florida have *fracture planes* (weakened areas within or between vertebrae that will cleave easily) in their tail vertebrae, which facilitates a 'break,' or separation, of the tail if grabbed (see p. 96). The tail regenerates in these species.

Because glass lizards are legless, they are often mistaken for snakes. These beautiful, shiny lizards can be distinguished from snakes by their visible ear openings, eyelids, and small scales on the belly. When they move, glass lizards seem stiffer and less flexible than snakes, which is probably due to the osteoderms under the scales. They are the largest of Florida's native lizards, but the most secretive and difficult to see.

Natural History
Ecology and Behavior
EASTERN GLASS LIZARDS (Plate 13) spend most of their lives burrowing through soil and piles of leaves in search of insects. They feed on insects and spiders. These lizards may be found in both moist and dry habitats. Glass lizards sometimes grow to a meter (3.3 ft) or more in length and are stunningly beautiful, impressive-looking reptiles. They can sometimes be seen basking on the edge of paved rural roadways or crossing sandy roads in the late afternoon. Glass lizards will allow themselves to be approached, but if you try to pick one up, it will thrash around wildly, and probably scare you into dropping it.

Breeding
In midsummer, female glass lizards lay 5 to 20 round white eggs in a nest at the base of a grass clump or beneath a log. The female stays with the eggs until they hatch, 50 to 65 days later.

Status
The EASTERN GLASS LIZARD is not considered threatened or endangered, but the MIMIC GLASS LIZARD, which occurs only in the Panhandle and in Nassau County, is a Species of Special Concern in Florida. It is designated as vulnerable, but at present there are not enough data to support listing it as threatened or endangered.

Profile
Eastern Glass Lizard, *Ophisaurus ventralis*, Plate 13a

Environmental Close-up 3:
Living with Alligators

Huge bird-like tracks, each bigger than a human hand, are neatly imprinted in the mud in front of a lakefront home in Orlando. The cause: escaped Ostriches from the local zoo? No, the perpetrators are more reptilian in nature. A sign beside a small pond outside a Sanibel Island hotel tells the story: it reads 'WARNING! DO NOT FEED THE ALLIGATORS.' Similar notices grace a roadside ditch near a shopping center along Interstate Highway 95 and around a small lake in the middle of the University of Florida campus. Indeed, throughout Florida, on golf courses, ponds, lakes and canals, signs warn people to stay away from alligators.

Visitors to Florida are amazed and slightly horrified that these formidable looking reptiles are so omnipresent. Though most Floridians have learned to coexist with alligators, the potential for conflict still exists. A rapidly increasing human population has led to an increase in the number of complaints about alligators in backyards, swimming pools, golf course water hazards, and other places where they are not wanted. The Florida Fish and Wildlife Conservation Commission receives more than 10,000 alligator-related complaints each year. Licensed trappers remove and kill more than 4000 of these 'nuisance' alligators each year.

Most wild alligators are fairly skittish. In areas where boating, fishing and controlled hunting are allowed, they generally hide and watch humans only from a distance. However, despite the fact that Florida law prohibits the feeding of wild alligators, in some places visitors and residents have fed alligators until they have lost their fear of humans. One guidebook even recommends feeding them marshmallows! But don't be fooled. Feeding alligators conditions them to associate humans with food handouts – an immensely undesirable trait. And this is what causes 'nuisance' 'gators.

Humans and alligators have shared the lakes and marshes of Florida for many centuries. Native Americans occasionally hunted alligators for food, but it was not until the Industrial Revolution in Europe that the fashion industry began producing alligator-skin products. Leather made from alligator skin was in great demand for boots, shoes, travel bags, saddlebags, purses, card cases, and belts. Commercial hunting of alligators reached a peak after the American Civil War (1860s), and huge numbers of alligators were killed in a short time. In 1888, in the Cocoa Beach area of Florida, 10 hunters killed 5000 alligators in a single season. At this time it was commonplace for each alligator hunter to kill 200 to 400 animals per year.

By the early 1900s, most alligator skins were being used for boots and shoes, ladies' handbags and belts. Demand for skins increased as supplies dwindled. Florida records show that while 190,000 skins were traded in 1929, the number fell to 120,000 in 1934, and continued to decrease until 1943, when only 6800 skins were traded. A century of unrestricted hunting had depleted the seemingly inexhaustible supply of these prehistoric-looking reptiles. In 1944 Florida introduced legislation protecting alligators during the breeding season and prohibiting the killing of alligators less than 1.2 m (4 ft) in length. But populations continued to decline, and it was not until 1970, when federal laws prohibited the interstate shipment of alligators, that protective measures finally began to take effect.

With protection, alligators began to repopulate areas where they had once been hunted almost to extinction. Numbers rebounded so successfully that state wildlife authorities began an experimental hunting program in 1981, and in 1988, controlled hunting was begun throughout much of Florida.

Today, professional trappers and hunters, and thrill-seeking members of the general public, can apply to harvest a limited number of alligators each year. Applications must be made to the office of the Florida Fish and Wildlife Conservation Commission by June 1 each year. Up to 500 applicants are randomly selected from the several thousand that apply. Usually, each participant is allowed to take five or six alligators that are more than 1.2 m (4 ft) long. If selected, applicants must complete a training and orientation program. Applicants must also purchase an alligator-trapping license, which costs US$250.00 for a resident and $1000 for a non-resident. A three-night hunting trip with a professional guide, lodging, meals, transportation, and with luck, a dead 'gator, costs about $3500 per hunter.

There are about 40 professional alligator hunters in Florida; most of them trap 'nuisance' 'gators for the state. These licensed trappers are self-employed and make a living by selling the skins and meat. The market for skins is highly variable from year to year; they can vary in price from US$20 to $45 per foot (30 cm), but have averaged about $25 per foot over the past 10 years. Alligator meat is sold to restaurants and wholesalers, and brings US$5 to $7 per pound ($11 to $15 per kg).

Alligators are also being farmed and ranched on a large scale in Florida and Louisiana. There are currently more than 350,000 'gators on about 150 farms (captive-bred stock) and ranches (wild-caught stock), and captive breeding produces some 20,000 hatchlings annually – about 10% of total production. Controlled egg collection from the wild provides additional eggs to ranches. Long-term studies of egg harvesting have shown that alligator populations remain stable, even when up to 50% of located nests are collected for ranching.

Alligator management in the USA is now based on a combination of farming, ranching, nuisance alligator control, and direct cropping of wild animals. Under these management programs, alligator populations have remained stable and are even increasing in some areas. Sustainable use of alligators in the USA generates more than US$60 million annually, and provides major incentive to retain alligator habitat and tolerate these potentially dangerous reptiles. Fees from hunts provide funding for alligator management, regulation, enforcement and research.

Chapter 8

BIRDS

by Dennis Paulson

Slater Museum of Natural History, University of Puget Sound

- *Birds: Animals to Watch*
- *General Characteristics and Natural History*
- *Seeing Birds in Florida*
- *Family Profiles*
  1. *Loons and Grebes*
  2. *Pelicans and Their Relatives*
  3. *Long-legged Waders*
  4. *Waterfowl*
  5. *Raptors*
  6. *Chickenlike Birds*
  7. *Cranes, Limpkin, and Rails*
  8. *Shorebirds*
  9. *Gulls, Terns, and Skimmers*
  10. *Pigeons and Doves*
  11. *Parrots*
  12. *Cuckoos*
  13. *Owls*
  14. *Nightjars*
  15. *Hummingbirds*
  16. *Kingfishers*
  17. *Woodpeckers*
  18. *Flycatchers*
  19. *Swallows and Swifts*

20. *Crows and Jays*

21. *Titmice and Nuthatches*

22. *Wrens*

23. *Kinglets and Gnatcatchers*

24. *Thrushes*

25. *Mockingbirds and Thrashers*

26. *Miscellaneous Perching Birds*

27. *Vireos*

28. *Warblers*

29. *Blackbirds and Starlings*

30. *Tanagers and Cardinal Grosbeaks*

31. *Sparrows and Finches*

- *Environmental Close-up 4:* **Why Is Florida So Full of Exotic Birds?**

- *Environmental Close-up 5:* **The Advantages of Colonial Nesting**

Birds: Animals to Watch

Florida is a birdy state; you will see birds everywhere you go, and you will hear them when you don't see them. Even if the day's wildlife viewing includes few mammals or reptiles or amphibians, birds will be seen frequently and often in large numbers. The reason for this pattern is that birds as a group are active during the day and are visually conspicuous. Only the fishes on a tropical coral reef and the herds of large mammals in Africa can give you the same satisfaction in wildlife viewing as you can get from birdwatching. In addition, birds are probably the most vocal of animals, singing or calling throughout the day as they pursue their activities. But why are birds so much more conspicuous than other vertebrates? The reason goes to the essential nature of birds: they fly. The ability to fly is among nature's premier anti-predator escape mechanisms. Animals that can fly well are relatively less prone to predation than those that cannot, and so they can be reasonably certain of daily survival even while being somewhat conspicuous in their behavior. Birds can fly quickly from dangerous situations, taking to the air to escape land-bound predators, for example. Flightless land vertebrates, tied to the ground or the plants that grow in it, are easy prey unless they are quiet, concealed, and careful; very large or fierce; or equipped with special defense mechanisms such as spines, hard shells, or poisons.

A fringe benefit of birds being the most frequently encountered kind of vertebrate is that birds are, to the ecotraveller, entirely innocuous. Typically the worst that can happen from an encounter is a soiled shirt. Contrast that with close encounters with certain insects (any one of Florida's mosquito species), fishes ('Jaws' and his descendants), reptiles (poisonous snakes and large crocodilians come to mind), and mammals (bears or panthers). Better yet, birds do not always depart with all due haste after being spotted, as do most other types of vertebrates. Again, their ability to fly and thus easily evade our grasp permits many birds, when confronted with people, to go about their business (keeping one eye at all times on the intruders), allowing us extensive time to watch them. Not only are birds among the safest animals to observe and the most easily discovered and watched, but they are among the most beautiful. Experiences with Florida's birds will almost certainly provide some of any trip's finest, most memorable moments. A human visitor at a colony of wading birds, for instance, with a half-dozen or more species and many hundreds of individual birds in view, has all senses stimulated to the maximum, far past the familiar and bordering on the overwhelming. That soiled shirt is surely worth it.

General Characteristics and Natural History

Birds are vertebrates that can fly. They began evolving from reptiles during the Jurassic Period of the Mesozoic Era, perhaps 150 million years ago, and saw explosive development of new species occur during the last 50 million years or so. Debate about their exact ancestors (were they in the same group as the *Velociraptor* made famous by the movie *Jurassic Park*?) at this time is intense. As diverse as birds are now, it is thought that there were even more species prior to the Ice Ages. The development of flight is the key factor behind birds' evolution, their historical spread throughout the globe, and their current ecological success and arguable dominant position among the world's land animals. Flight, as mentioned above, is a fantastic predator-evasion technique, but it also permits birds to move over long distances in search of particular foods or habitats, and its development opened up for vertebrate exploration and exploitation an entirely new and vast theater of operations – the open air.

At first glance, birds appear to be highly variable animals, ranging in size and form from 135 kg (300 lb) ostriches to 4 kg (10 lb) eagles to 3 g (a tenth of an ounce) hummingbirds. Some extinct birds were about twice the size of living ostriches! Actually, however, when compared to other types of vertebrates, birds are remarkably standardized physically. The reason is that, whereas mammals or reptiles can be quite diverse in form and still function as mammals or reptiles (think how different in form are lizards, snakes, and turtles), if birds are going to fly, they more or less must look like birds, and have the anatomy and physiology of birds. The most important traits for flying are (1) feathers, which are unique to birds; (2) powerful wings, which are modified forelimbs; (3) hollow bones; (4) warm-bloodedness; and (5) efficient respiratory and circulatory systems. These characteristics combine to produce animals with two overarching traits – high power and low weight, which are the twin dictates that make for successful flying machines. Bats, the only flying mammals, have followed a similar evolutionary pathway.

Currently about 9700 species of birds are recognized. Bird classification is in a state of flux at this time, with several competing systems. Depending on which system is followed, birds are divided into 23 to 30 orders, and 145 to 170 families. For our purposes, we can divide birds into *passerines* and *non-passerines*. Passerine birds (order Passeriformes) are the perching birds, with feet specialized to perch on tree branches. They are mostly the small land birds with which we are most familiar – swallows, robins, wrens, finches, sparrows, etc. – and the group includes more than 50% of all bird species. The remainder of the birds – seabirds and shorebirds, ducks and geese, hawks and owls, kingfishers and woodpeckers, and a host of others – are divided among the other orders. Of the passerines, about three-quarters are *songbirds*, those with a more complex syrinx (the *syrinx* is the sound-producing organ, located where the trachea branches into two bronchi leading to the lungs, that produces the beautiful songs we associate with birds). The other fourth of the passerines consists of the flycatchers and their relatives, which are mostly confined to the New World Tropics and do not produce true songs (although they are quite able to communicate vocally).

Seeing Birds in Florida

Most of Florida's common birds and some of its uncommon ones are illustrated in this book. Large birds (most of them in Florida associated with water) are often out in the open, active at all times of day, and relatively easy to find. Small birds take a little more effort. The best way to spot them is to follow three easy steps:

(1) BRING BINOCULARS on your trip. They need not be an expensive pair, but binoculars are essential for birdwatching, or 'birding,' as its practitioners call it. They also work for viewing butterflies, mammals, reptiles, and any other wildlife that might not be at close range when encountered.

(2) Look for birds at the correct time. They are often most active, and vocalize most frequently, during early morning and late afternoon, and so can be best detected and seen during these times. That is especially true when it is hot at midday, often the case in Florida.

(3) Be quiet as you walk along trails or roads, and stop periodically to look around carefully. Not all birds are noisy, and some, even brightly colored ones, can be quite inconspicuous when they are in dense vegetation. Some species are so well camouflaged that hearing them is almost always the best way to find them. A car serves as an effective moving blind, and driving slowly along country roads is a great way to see birds.

It would be a shame to leave Florida without seeing at least some of its spectacular birds, such as frigatebirds, storks, spoonbills, cranes, oystercatchers, kites, and turkeys. If you have trouble locating such birds, ask people – tour-guides, resort employees, park personnel – about good places to see them. Many people visit Florida in winter to escape cold weather in the north, but also because Florida's heat, humidity, and humming mosquitos are less of a problem then. But for those especially interested in birds, any time of year is a good time to visit. The breeding season is from February to June, and song, courtship behavior, and then young birds can be seen throughout that period; a few species have earlier or later seasons. A very large number of Florida's birds come to the state in winter from farther north, so winter is a great season in which to visit, as you can see both the birds that are resident all year and the host of winter visitors. During spring and fall, there are a large number of species, and sometimes great numbers of individuals, that are present only during these migration seasons. With luck, you may come upon a migratory 'wave,' when large numbers of passerines or shorebirds are present briefly in one spot on their way north or south. During summer, a small but select group of species appears that have wintered in the Caribbean or South America. These birds, including Swallow-tailed Kites and Gray Kingbirds, are some of the specialties that make Florida a birding destination.

Family Profiles

1. Loons and Grebes

Loons and *grebes* are diving birds, not closely related to one another but similarly modified for a life spent foraging for fish underwater. Their similarities include compact bodies, sharply pointed bills, relatively small wings, short (loons) or virtually absent (grebes) tails, short legs, and feet modified for underwater propulsion. Their differences are apparent as soon as one looks at their feet, which in loons have the front three toes connected by webs, as in most swimming birds. Grebe feet, however, are not webbed, but their toes have lobes extending out from them. The result is the same: birds of both groups are amazingly fast swimmers underwater, where they pursue and capture fast-moving fishes. Being such effective divers handicaps them greatly for the terrestrial world, however; because of the structure of their legs and feet, neither of them can move about on land. When a grebe or loon washes up on the beach, the best it can do is propel itself back into the water with a series of grasshopperlike hops and flops.

Worldwide, there are five species of loons, family Gaviidae, and 22 species of grebes, family Podicipedidae. Only the three species profiled here are common and widespread in Florida; in addition, the RED-THROATED LOON and EARED GREBE are regular winter visitors to the northern part of the state. Loons and grebes are *countershaded* – dark above and light below – like many birds that swim underwater. With light coming from above, the back of a countershaded bird (or fish or dolphin) is illuminated, and the underside is shadowed, and this causes them to blend amazingly with the water. All loons and most grebes have bright, contrasty breeding plumages and dull, brown to black non-breeding plumages on their head, neck, and upperparts; the PIED-BILLED GREBE (Plate 20) changes plumage less than the others. The COMMON LOON (Plate 20) and HORNED GREBE (Plate 20) have bright red eyes, visible at close range. Loons are easily distinguished from grebes by their much larger size and relatively shorter necks; they are also much more often seen in flight.

Natural History
Ecology and Behavior
Loons and grebes breed on fresh water but spend much of their year on salt water, where feeding conditions are better and the surface remains unfrozen in winter. They are among the most accomplished diving birds, disappearing below the surface with a thrust of their powerful feet and reappearing many meters away, perhaps with a fish held crosswise in their bill. In Florida, loons are seen in shallow

bays, where they capture bottom fishes such as gobies and flounders. PIED-BILLED GREBES are characteristic of just about all freshwater bodies, while HORNED GREBES are more likely to be seen on the ocean. Grebes have a special adaptation to deal with a fish diet; they swallow their own feathers, which apparently protect their stomach lining from sharp fish bones until the bones are sufficiently digested to pass down the rest of their gut.

Breeding

Both loons and grebes form *monogamous* pairs, the male and female forming a *pair bond* and sharing in all parental care, including nest-building, incubation of the eggs, and brooding and feeding of the young. They typically unite with their mate of the previous year, if both are still alive, when they encounter one another at the breeding lake. If one of the mates doesn't show up, the other has no hesitation in mating with another bird. Both loons and grebes have striking courtship displays, the loons displaying in flight and moving in unison on or under the water, and the grebes standing up breast to breast and shaking their heads simultaneously or taking brief runs across the water's surface; all this activity is accompanied by loud vocalizations. The PIED-BILLED GREBE is the only member of the two groups that breeds in Florida, and its courtship is more sedate than most members of its family.

The nesting habits of both groups are somewhat similar, but the differences tell a nice ecological story. Their nests are big piles of aquatic vegetation at or on the water, as neither kind of bird can move about on land. Loon nests are built right at the shore, where the adults can slide on and off them; grebes, even less agile at maneuvering on a solid substrate, build floating nests. In both cases, vegetation is added to the nest continually, as it decays (and sinks, in the case of grebe nests). Loons typically lay 2 eggs and presumably cannot rear more than 2 young in the large lakes where they breed. Some lakes at which loons nest contain no fish at all, and the adults, which are strong flyers, must travel to nearby, larger lakes to find food. Grebes, weaker flyers, must find productive (high-nutrient, fish-containing) waters on which to nest, and they can thus feed more young, so their clutches range from 4 to 6 eggs. Both sexes incubate the eggs alternately for 23 to 31 days in loons, 20 to 25 days in grebes. Young loons are plain-colored but still stand out in the open waters of large lakes; young grebes have strikingly striped heads, presumably to facilitate the adults' finding them among marsh vegetation. In both families, the adults feed the young until they are able to fly, 7 to 11 weeks after hatching. Because loons migrate during the day, the birds can keep together visually, so the young may remain with their parents in migration. Young and adult grebes part soon after the young can feed themselves.

Lore and Notes

'Crazy as a loon' refers not to the dramatic aerial and aquatic courtship chases of a pair of loons on their breeding grounds but instead to the weird but beautiful calls they give at that time. Loons often call at night, and their loud tremolos coming off a quiet northern lake are enough to produce chill bumps. All loons have memorable voices, although the typical flight call of the RED-THROATED LOON sounds more like the croaking of a giant frog than the musical notes coming from the throats of its near relatives.

Status

The COMMON LOON, although much reduced in numbers as a breeding species in the lower 48 states because of increased human disturbance to its breeding lakes, is still abundant in Canada and Alaska, in areas where wilderness prevails. No North American grebes are at risk, but several South American species are rare and local, and the ATITLAN GREBE of Guatemala has apparently been extirpated from its sole location, Lago Atitlán. Habitat destruction was probably less to blame than the introduction of Largemouth Bass from North America, which decimated the community of small native fishes on which the grebes fed.

Profiles
Pied-billed Grebe, *Podilymbus podiceps*, Plate 20b
Horned Grebe, *Podiceps auritus*, Plate 20c
Common Loon, *Gavia immer*, Plate 20d

2. Pelicans and Their Relatives

The large seabirds treated in this section are members of the order Pelecaniformes: pelicans, of the family Pelecanidae (8 species worldwide on fresh and salt water, 2 common in Florida); cormorants, Phalacrocoracidae (37 species worldwide on fresh and salt water except oceanic islands, 1 common resident and another rare winter visitor in Florida); anhingas, Anhingidae (3 species occupying fresh waters of most of the tropical latitudes, 1 in Florida); boobies, Sulidae (9 species in the oceans worldwide, with 1 rare breeder and 3 non-breeding visitors to Florida); tropicbirds, Phaethontidae (3 marine species, all with tropical marine distributions, 2 species rare visitors to Florida); and frigatebirds, Fregatidae (5 species with tropical marine distributions, 1 in Florida). All members of the order are considered related because they all have *totipalmate* feet, with all four toes connected by webs (reduced in frigatebirds); this makes them excellent swimmers. They all also share the characteristic of much reduced or closed nostrils.

Pelicans are very large birds with compact bodies and short tails but long and fairly broad wings for gliding and soaring. Their huge, long bills and large bill pouches give them a distinctive appearance at rest or in flight and make them known even to people who have never seen one in nature.

Cormorants are fairly heavy-bodied large birds; they rest low in the water when swimming, typically with their bill pointing upward. They are unusual among seabirds in that, after foraging, they leave the water to roost on dry land. Cormorants have long, snaky necks, strongly hooked bills, and large completely webbed feet, all of which are very useful adaptations for fish-catching birds. With their webbed feet acting as swimming paddles, cormorants can easily swim rapidly enough to capture their fishy prey. Cormorants also have relatively long tails, unlike most other diving birds. Their long tail provides them with agility in flight, which allows them to land above the water on rocks, cliff ledges, pilings, and tree branches. In contrast, loons and grebes and diving ducks just splash into the water when they land. Adult cormorants are typically all black or black above and white below, with some variations on these themes. Immatures are usually duller, often brownish. At close range, cormorants are actually quite beautiful, as most of them have bright emerald-green or blue-green eyes and bright colors on their naked facial and throat skin.

Anhingas are closely related to cormorants and are similar to them in many ways. For example, both are blackish with long tails, but Anhinga tails are much longer. Anhingas also have very long, thin necks, and their bills are longer and end with sharp points. Anhingas are also known as *darters*, the name owing to the way the birds swiftly thrust their necks forward to spear fish. Because of their long necks, they are also called *snakebirds*.

Boobies are large seabirds known for their sprawling, densely packed breeding colonies and their spectacular plunges into the ocean from heights to pursue fish. They are unmistakable pointy birds, with long, pointed bills; long, narrow, pointed wings; and long, pointed tails. They are colored in shades of white, black, and brown, often with brightly colored feet. The term *booby* apparently arose because the nesting and roosting birds seemed so bold and fearless toward people, which was considered stupid. Actually, the fact that these birds bred on oceanic islands meant that they had few natural predators, so they had never developed, or had lost, fear responses to large mammals such as people. The three largest species, called *gannets*, breed in temperate waters of the North Atlantic and off South Africa and southern Australia.

Tropicbirds, considered among the most striking and attractive of tropical seabirds, are mid-sized white or white-and-black birds with two very long, thin central tail feathers, called *streamers*, that provide the birds an unmistakable flight silhouette. They have very short legs unsuited for walking on land (and so they spend most of their time in the air or out at sea).

Frigatebirds are large soaring birds, mostly black, with long pointed wings that span up to 2 m (6.5 ft) or more, and a long, forked tail that is usually carried like a closed pair of scissors until it spreads wide when the bird twists and turns in flight. Their feet are very small for their size, and they neither stand on the ground nor swim with them; perching is on branches of trees and shrubs. Males have red throat pouches that they inflate, balloonlike, during courtship displays. Females and immatures have extensive white coloration below.

Natural History
Ecology and Behavior

Pelicans, cormorants, and their relatives feed mainly on fish and have developed a variety of ways to catch them. Pelicans eat fish almost exclusively. Most pelican species feed by swimming on the water and jabbing their huge beaks in the water repeatedly, capturing fish in the expansive pouch and then allowing the water to drain out before they swallow. BROWN PELICANS (Plate 21) are the only pelicans that also plunge from the air, sometimes from considerable altitude, to dive for meals. Their pouch is used similarly to scoop up fish (to 30 cm, 1 ft, long), which are swallowed as quickly as possible so the bird can again take off. Pelicans are ungainly looking but are nonetheless excellent flyers, and they use updrafts to soar high in the air. A flight of pelicans, passing low and slow overhead, in perfect V-formation or in a single line, is a stirring sight. Of special note is that adult pelicans, so far as it is known, are largely silent.

Cormorants are the ultimate fishing machines, and it is a shame that we can't observe them and other diving birds under water very easily (they flee from Scuba divers). Scientists who could watch these birds below the surface without disturbing them would add greatly to our understanding of underwater foraging. Cormorants feed primarily on bottom fishes, but some species feed in groups on surface and midwater schooling fishes such as herrings and anchovies. Cormorants can swallow fishes of greater diameter than their heads, as their throat and neck skin is quite elastic. If you watch a feeding cormorant long enough, you are sure to see it bring up a fish and manipulate it at the surface for a while to assure that it is dead. A live fish going down a bird's gullet might erect spiny fins and get stuck, killing the bird; this has happened often enough that there are numerous notes about it in ornithological journals.

ANHINGAS (Plate 21) use their sharply pointed bills to spear fish (occasionally young turtles, baby crocodiles, and snakes). Cormorants are social birds, foraging, roosting, and nesting in groups, but Anhingas are somewhat territorial, defending resting and feeding areas from other birds. The very long tails of Anhingas are used to give the birds added lift as they migrate by soaring on *thermals* (bubbles of air rising from the heated ground), just as hawks do.

Boobies, which also eat squid, plunge-dive from the air (from heights of up to 15 m, 50 ft, or more) or surface-dive to catch fish underwater. Sometimes they dive quite deeply, and they often take fish unaware from below, as they rise toward the surface. The reduced or closed nostrils in this group keep seawater from rushing into their lungs as they plunge-dive. Tropicbirds are often seen flying alone or in pairs over the ocean or near shore, or inland, circling in valleys and canyons. They eat fish, squid, and crustaceans, which they obtain by flying high over the water, spotting food, hovering a bit, then plunging down into the water to catch the meal. They rarely feed within sight of land, preferring the open ocean. They travel far and wide on oceanic winds, and individuals banded in the Hawaiian region have been spotted at sea 8000 km (5000 miles) away.

Frigatebirds also hunt for their food while on the wing, sometimes soaring effortlessly for hours at a time. Their flight is as graceful as any living bird, and they are so light that their skeleton actually weighs less than their feather coat! They swoop low to catch flying fish that leap from the water (the fish leap when they are pursued by larger, predatory fish or dolphins), and also to pluck squid and jellyfish from the wave tops. They even drink by flying low over the water's surface and sticking their long bill into the water. Although their lives are tied to the sea, frigatebirds cannot swim and rarely, if ever, enter the water voluntarily; with their very long, narrow wings, they have difficulty lifting off from the water. To rest, they land in trees on remote islands.

Breeding

Pelicans and their relatives usually breed in large colonies on small oceanic islands (where there are no mammal predators) or on islands or tree groves in lakes (which predators have difficulty reaching). Some breed on cliff ledges or in rock crevices on the ground (tropicbirds), some in trees or on tops of shrubs (frigatebirds and Anhingas, also some species of pelicans, cormorants, and boobies), and some on the bare ground (most boobies, pelicans, and cormorants). Where people have introduced small mammals such as rats (which feed on seabird eggs and nestlings) to islands, reproductive success is often dramatically reduced, and colonies can be wiped out completely. Most species are monogamous, mated males and females sharing in nest-building, incubation, and feeding young. High year-to-year fidelity to mates, to breeding islands, and to particular nest sites is common.

Pelican and cormorant nests are big, bulky structures of branches and twigs in tree colonies and typically piles of seaweeds in island colonies. Pelicans lay 2 or 3 eggs, which are incubated for 30 to 37 days; usually only one young is raised successfully. Cormorants lay 3 to 5 chalky bluish-white eggs and incubate them for 28 to 34 days. Nestlings are black and featherless at birth and very reptilelike in appearance. They grow relatively slowly, as the clutch is large for a fish-eating bird, and the parents must work hard to feed that many young. The young fledge after about 5 to 8 weeks. Anhingas construct stick and leaf nests in trees or bushes. Three to 5 eggs are incubated for 4 to 5 weeks, and the chicks fledge 5 weeks after hatching. Boobies usually lay 1 or 2 eggs, which are incubated for about 45 days. Usually only a single chick survives to fledging age (one chick often pecks the other to death).

Tropicbirds breed in nests hidden in rock cavities on steep cliffs, and ornithologists have speculated that the WHITE-TAILED TROPICBIRD (Plate 22) may have bred in Fort Jefferson at the Dry Tortugas in Florida. A single egg is incubated by both parents, in shifts of 2 to 5 days. The egg hatches in 40 to 45 days, after which the youngster is fed by the parents for 10 to 14 weeks, until fledging. MAGNIFICENT FRIGATEBIRDS (Plate 20) lay a single egg that is incubated for about 50 days; male and female spell each other during incubation, taking shifts of up to 12 days. Young remain in and around the nest, dependent on the parents, for up to 6 months or more, and are even fed after the birds go to sea; parental care in frigatebirds lasts longest of any birds. In most seabirds, young are fed when they push their bills into their parents' throats, in effect forcing the parent to regurgitate food stored in its *crop* – an enlargement of the lower portion of the esophagus. Seabirds reach sexual maturity slowly (in 2 to 5 years in boobies, 5 years in tropicbirds, 7+ years in frigatebirds) and live long lives (frigatebirds and boobies live 20+ years in the wild).

Ecological Interactions

Many ecological interactions are complex, involving a chain of events in which three or more species interact. The relatively inconsequential interaction of one species with another may represent an excellent opportunity for a third. For example, although cormorants nest in relatively inaccessible places, they are nevertheless subject to nest predation during disturbances. Crows living near a cormorant colony, for instance, know exactly when the approach of Bald Eagles or humans causes the nesting cormorants to take flight, and they arrive promptly to pillage temporarily unprotected eggs.

Frigatebirds are a treat to watch as they glide silently along coastal areas, but they have some highly questionable habits – in fact, patterns of behavior that among humans would be indictable offenses. Frigatebirds practice *kleptoparasitism*: they 'parasitize' other seabirds, such as boobies, gulls, and terns, chasing them in the air until they drop recently caught fish. The frigatebird then steals the fish, catching it in mid-air as it falls. Their piratic behavior has earned them another name, *man-o-war-bird*. Note that both frigate and man-o-war are names for warships. Frigatebirds are also common predators on baby sea turtles, scooping them from beaches as the reptiles make their post-hatching dashes to the ocean. Another form of kleptoparasitism is shown by birds that attend BROWN PELICANS as they feed. The pelican dives, comes up with a pouch full of fish and water, and then one or more Laughing Gulls immediately land next to its bill, even on top of its head, to try to snag a small fish from the pouch as the pelican maneuvers for swallowing.

Lore and Notes

Some species in this group, including the DOUBLE-CRESTED CORMORANT (Plate 21) and ANHINGA, characteristically hold their wings open for several minutes after arriving at their roost, apparently to get rid of excess water that both weighs them down in flight and perhaps makes it more difficult to stay warm. Wing-spreading is known to be for temperature regulation in Anhingas. It is an amusing sight to see a long line of cormorants standing with spread wings, some of them waving their wings back and forth, presumably to dry them that much faster. One gets a very prehistoric, almost reptilian, impression from cormorants, as they wave their snaky heads about. This effect is heightened on their breeding grounds, where they vocalize with grunts and hisses.

Any visitor to the Florida coast will be struck by the tameness of the BROWN PELICANS. People feed them fish at many docks and bridges, and the pelicans have lost their fear of us, perhaps not always the best thing for a wild bird. Fortunately, we have a much more benign attitude toward fish-eating birds today, not treating them as direct competitors to be eliminated as we did decades ago.

Status

The BROWN PELICAN was listed by USA ESA as endangered over parts of its range, but the species is still common in many areas; in fact, it has come back very satisfactorily from a decline apparently caused by eggshell thinning that was a result of ingesting fish that carried DDT in their tissues. The other members of this group that occur in Florida waters are common either in the USA or the nearby Caribbean and are not considered threatened. However, there are threatened or endangered populations of species of pelicans, cormorants, boobies, and frigatebirds elsewhere in the world, including, for example, ABBOTT'S BOOBY, now limited to a single, small breeding population on the Indian Ocean's Christmas Island (CITES Appendix I and USA ESA listed). Only one member of the pelican order has gone extinct, the SPECTACLED CORMORANT of the western Bering Sea; it was a victim of 19th century sailors who found themselves with inadequate rations in that harsh region.

Profiles

Magnificent Frigatebird, *Fregata magnificens*, Plate 20a
American White Pelican, *Pelecanus erythrorhynchos*, Plate 21a
Brown Pelican, *Pelecanus occidentalis*, Plate 21b
Double-crested Cormorant, *Phalacrocorax auritus*, Plate 21c
Anhinga, *Anhinga anhinga*, Plate 21d
Masked Booby, *Sula dactylatra*, Plate 22a
Brown Booby, *Sula leucogaster*, Plate 22b
White-tailed Tropicbird, *Phaethon lepturus*, Plate 22e

3. Long-legged Waders

This section deals with a group of birds that are very prominent in Florida wetlands, the long-legged waders of the order Ciconiiformes. With the exception of the AMERICAN BITTERN, all the common species of this group are profiled here. All members of the group have long bills, long necks, and long legs, but the members of the three families (herons, ibises, and storks) discussed are quite distinct from one another. In most of these water birds, the sexes look alike but adults and immatures are sometimes very differently colored. *Herons* and *egrets*, together with the similar but quite elusive wading birds called *bitterns*, constitute the heron family, Ardeidae, which includes 58 species distributed over most of the world's tropical and temperate regions. This group is a very important one in Florida, with 12 common species that are much in evidence as a visitor travels through the marshy countryside. Herons frequent all sorts of aquatic habitats, including densely vegetated marshes and swamps as well as the shorelines of lakes and bays. The CATTLE EGRET (Plate 23) feeds entirely on land, however. Herons and egrets are, in general, highly successful birds. Typically the white species of the family have been called egrets, although the REDDISH EGRET (Plate 23) comes in two color forms, a white and a dark, as does the GREAT BLUE HERON (Plate 25)! The immature LITTLE BLUE HERON (Plate 23) is also white, further confusing the issue.

Herons and egrets are the tallish birds standing upright and still in shallow water or on the shore, staring intently into the water. They have slender bodies, long necks (which can be folded into a Z shape when perched, giving them a short-necked, hunched appearance), long, pointed bills, and long legs with long toes. Herons have very large, broad wings for their size and fly slowly, with neck curved and mostly resting on the back, again producing the effect of a short-necked bird. Most are either attired in understated shades of gray, brown, blue, or green, or are largely or entirely snow-white. From afar most are not strikingly patterned, but close-up, many are exquisitely marked with small colored patches of facial skin or broad areas of spots or streaks. Their feathers are large and lax and are lifted away from the body by the breeze, and most species develop ornate plumes, lengthy feathers extending from the head, breast, or back, during the breeding season. Most herons are social when nesting and feeding, and their dark or white colors make them conspicuous to others of their species for social interactions. Bitterns, however, are solitary; they are brown and streaked, camouflaged for their lives in dense marshes.

The 33 species of *ibises* and *spoonbills* (family Threskiornithidae) are globally distributed; 2 ibises (plus another rare species) and a single spoonbill are common in Florida. Ibises and spoonbills differ from herons in having much smaller, sleeker feathers, in flying with necks outstretched and with rapid wingbeats, and in having very differently shaped bills and feeding habits. The head is bare of feathers in some members of this family. Ibis bills are long, thin, and curved downward. Spoonbills are easily recognized by their bills, long and expanded at the end like a flattened spoon. The ROSEATE SPOONBILL (Plate 24), large, pink, and spoon-billed, must be one of the easiest birds on earth to identify.

Storks (family Ciconiidae) are wading birds that occur worldwide in tropical and temperate regions; there are 17 species, but only 3 occur in the New World, the WOOD STORK (Plate 25) commonly in Florida. Storks are huge, ungainly looking – and so unmistakable – wading birds. Most species are largely white or black and white, although a few are touched up with pink markings. They have broad wings like herons but fly with faster wingbeats, and they also soar high in the air on thermals like eagles and pelicans. Most storks are very large, and they have long, heavy bills; some species, including our Wood Stork, have largely unfeathered heads and necks. This 'pattern baldness' and the soaring habit may make it a bit easier to believe that their closest relatives are now considered to be the New World vultures (see p. 118).

Natural History
Ecology and Behavior
Herons and egrets stand stock-still or walk about slowly and stealthily in shallow water and sometimes on land, searching for their prey, mostly small vertebrates, including fish, frogs, and the occasional turtle, and small invertebrates such as shrimps and crabs. On land, they take mostly insects, but also other invertebrates and even vertebrates such as small rodents and lizards. Both GREAT BLUE HERONS and GREAT EGRETS (Plate 23), being large, have an especially varied diet. A Great Blue Heron can easily capture a fish 38 cm (15 in) long, big enough

to present quite a challenge in swallowing. CATTLE EGRETS have made a specialty of following grazing cattle and other large mammals, walking along and grabbing insects, lizards, and frogs that are flushed from their hiding places by the moving cattle. A typical pasture scene is a flock of these egrets scattered through a cattle herd, with several of the white birds perched atop the unconcerned bovines. Many herons spend most of their foraging time as *sit-and-wait* predators, standing motionless in or adjacent to the water, waiting in ambush for unsuspecting prey to wander within striking distance. Whether stationary or stalking, they shoot their spearlike bill out with lightning speed, grabbing or stabbing the prey in a flash. Typically, the larger herons are easier to spot because they tend to stay out in the open while foraging and resting; smaller herons, easier prey for predators, tend to stay more hidden in dense vegetation in marshy areas. Most herons are active during the day, but *night-herons* forage at least partly nocturnally. YELLOW-CROWNED NIGHT-HERONS (Plate 24) are especially fond of crabs, and they have a heavy bill to handle these formidable prey items.

Ibises and spoonbills are gregarious birds that feed in marshes and shallow bays, the spoonbills largely restricted to salt water. Ibises insert their long bills into the soft mud bottom and poke about for food – insects, snails, crabs, frogs, tadpoles. They feed by touch, not vision: whatever the bill contacts that feels like food is grabbed and swallowed. Spoonbills also feed by touch, sweeping their flattened bills back and forth through shallow water or nearly liquid mud, quickly grabbing fish or crustaceans that they contact. Storks feed by walking slowly through fields and marshy areas looking for suitable prey, essentially anything that moves: small rodents, young birds, frogs, reptiles, fish, earthworms, mollusks, crustaceans, and insects. WOOD STORKS also feed by touch, moving rapidly through shallow water with slightly open bill tip below the surface. They typically breed during the dry season, when drying-up ponds may be virtually writhing with their favorite foods; thus they can fail to breed during unusually wet or dry years. These birds are excellent flyers, often soaring high overhead for hours during hot afternoons. They are known to fly 80 km (50 miles) or more daily between roosting or nesting sites and feeding areas.

Breeding
Almost all of these wading birds breed in monogamous pairs within breeding colonies of various sizes. Bitterns are solitary nesters. Herons are known for their elaborate courtship displays and ceremonies, which continue through pair formation and nest-building. Generally nests are constructed by the female of a pair out of sticks procured and presented to her by the male. Nests are placed in trees or reed beds. Both sexes incubate the 3 to 7 eggs for 16 to 30 days, and both feed the young for 35 to 50 days before they can leave the nest and feed themselves. The young are *altricial* – born helpless; they are raised on regurgitated food from the parents. Ibises and spoonbills also make stick nests, mixed with green vegetation, in trees or reed beds. Two to 4 eggs are incubated for about 3 weeks, and young fledge 6 to 7 weeks after hatching. Storks first breed when they are 3 to 5 years old. They build platforms of sticks in trees. Sometimes they add new material each year, which results eventually in enormous nests. Their 2 to 4 eggs are incubated for 4 to 5 weeks, and chicks remain in the nest for 50 to 90 days after hatching. Interestingly, the few species of ibises and storks that live in desert areas nest in small colonies on cliff ledges.

Ecological Interactions

Herons and egrets often lay more eggs than the number of chicks they can feed. For instance, many lay three eggs when there is sufficient food around to feed only two chicks. This is contrary to our usual view of nature, which we regard as having adjusted animal behavior through evolution so that behaviors are finely tuned to avoid waste. Here's what biologists suspect goes on: females lay eggs one or two days apart and start incubating before they finish laying all their eggs. The result is that chicks hatch at intervals of one or more days, so the chicks in a single nest are different ages and therefore different sizes. In years of food shortage, the smallest chick dies because it cannot compete for food delivered by the parents against its larger siblings, and also because, it has been discovered, the larger siblings attack it (behavior called *siblicide*). The habit of laying more eggs than can be reared as chicks may be an insurance strategy evolved by the birds to maximize their number of young; in many years, true, they waste the energy they invested to produce third eggs that have little future, but if food is plentiful, all three chicks survive and prosper. Apparently, the chance to produce three surviving offspring is worth the risk of investing in three eggs, even though the future of one is very uncertain.

Lore and Notes

The CATTLE EGRET is a common, successful, medium-sized white heron that, until recently, was confined to the Old World, where it made its living following herds of large mammals. Originating in Africa and southern Asia, its 'hosts' are still elephants and rhinos, among many others. What is so interesting about this species is that, whereas many of the animals that have recently crossed oceans and spread rapidly into new continents have done so as a result of people's intentional or unintentional machinations, these egrets did it themselves. Apparently the first ones to reach the New World were from Africa. Perhaps blown off course by a storm, they first landed in northern South America in about 1877. During the next decades the species spread far and wide, finding abundant food where tropical forests were cleared for cattle grazing. Cattle Egrets have now colonized much of northern South America, Central America, all the major Caribbean islands, and eastern and central North America, as far west as California. The first one seen in Florida was in 1941 or 1942, and nesting was observed in 1953. By 1976, there were thought to be 200,000 birds in the state, and in recent years they have been known to outcompete some of the other small herons for nest space at mixed colonies.

Storks in folklore are generally assigned very positive personality traits. Europe's WHITE STORK, which nests on the roofs of buildings in villages, is highly respected by people and, because of its annual returns, is considered a symbol of continuity and reliability. Some Europeans believe that good luck will befall a family after a stork builds a nest on their house (excluding the possibility of a stopped-up chimney). A common legend, repeated by Aristotle, is that storks have such strong family ties that younger storks will feed older family members during their declining years.

Status

Had this book been written a century earlier, many of Florida's egrets and herons would have been on the list of species of concern. The long, filamentous plumes of egrets, called *aigrettes* in the feather trade, were much sought for ladies' hats. ROSEATE SPOONBILL wings were used in their entirety for pink fans. The birds were shot in great numbers by plume hunters to fill this need, and ultimately the awareness of this slaughter helped bring about the start of the conservation movement on this continent. The killing by plume hunters of Guy Bradley, a National Audubon Society warden hired to protect the birds, surely added to the fuel that fired this movement. Nowadays, all the birds profiled here are common in Florida, although some of them, such as REDDISH EGRETS and Roseate Spoonbills, are quite local as breeding birds, and one of them, the WOOD STORK, is considered endangered (listed as such by USA ESA). Its populations plummeted in southern Florida in the last half of the 20th century, primarily because the great alterations that took place in the natural ebb and flow of fresh water in the area wreaked havoc with their specialized needs for foraging habitat (see above).

Profiles

Cattle Egret, *Bubulcus ibis*, Plate 23a
Snowy Egret, *Egretta thula*, Plate 23b
Great Egret, *Ardea alba*, Plate 23c
Reddish Egret, *Egretta rufescens*, Plate 23d
Tricolored Heron, *Egretta tricolor*, Plate 23e
Little Blue Heron, *Egretta caerulea*, Plate 23f
Green Heron, *Butorides virescens*, Plate 24a
Least Bittern, *Ixobrychus exilis*, Plate 24b
Yellow-crowned Night-Heron, *Nyctanassa violacea*, Plate 24c
Black-crowned Night-Heron, *Nycticorax nycticorax*, Plate 24e
Roseate Spoonbill, *Ajaia ajaja*, Plate 24f
Wood Stork, *Mycteria americana*, Plate 25a
Great Blue Heron, *Ardea herodias*, Plate 25d
Glossy Ibis, *Plegadis falcinellus*, Plate 25e
White Ibis, *Eudocimus albus*, Plate 25f

4. Waterfowl

Members of family Anatidae are universally recognized as *waterfowl*. They are aquatic birds distributed throughout the world in habitats ranging from open seas to high mountain lakes. The family includes 158 species of *ducks*, *geese*, and *swans*, distributed throughout the globe but especially common and diverse in temperate regions. Waterfowl are much less prominent features of the waterbird assemblage in Florida than they are farther north, and the 38 species known from the state are mostly highly migratory birds that breed in northern North America and spend the winter in the southern USA, including Florida. The 15 profiled here also include several tropical resident species that have moved into the state from the south or west, and two other tropical species, the BLACK-BELLIED WHISTLING-DUCK (Plate 26) and MUSCOVY DUCK (Plate 26), that have become naturalized widely in Florida from escaped or released captives.

Waterfowl vary greatly in size and coloring, but all share the same major traits: characteristic duck bills on big heads on rather long necks, pointed wings for strong flight, short tails, and relatively short legs with webbed toes. The group divides neatly into swans and geese on one hand, in which the sexes look alike and plumages tend toward white, gray, or brown, and ducks on the other hand, in most of which males are much brighter than females and are among the gaudiest of our birds. A special feature of many ducks is the *speculum*, a rectangular patch of contrasty, often iridescent, color on the rear edge of the wing near the body; it is prominent in flight and usually partially visible on the resting bird. Male ducks are unusual in bearing a bright, species-specific plumage throughout the winter (normally thought of as the non-breeding season) and holding that plumage through spring, until the females are nesting. The males then molt into a dull plumage in which they look very much like the mostly brown, camouflaged females. This dull non-breeding plumage, which occurs during the summer, is called *eclipse* plumage. Waterfowl are also unusual in having a simultaneous flight-feather molt during the late summer, in which all of the wing feathers are dropped at once, and the birds become flightless. During this time, they usually remain on the water, where they are safe from terrestrial predators. This molting strategy allows them to replace their wing feathers more rapidly than can be done by birds that molt these feathers sequentially over a period of months.

Natural History
Ecology and Behavior
Waterfowl, as their name implies, are birds of wetlands, spending most of their time in or near the water. Geese are the most terrestrial waterfowl, most species spending a large amount of time grazing on terrestrial vegetation such as grasses and sedges. The ducks are divided into *diving ducks* and *dabbling ducks*. Divers, such as scaups and mergansers, plunge underwater for their food; dabblers, such as mallards, wigeons, and teals, take food from the surface of the water or submerge their heads to reach food at shallow depths. When they reach underwater, their rear ends tip up into the air, and a flock of duck behinds all tipped up at once is one of nature's more ludicrous sights. Ducks vary from virtually pure *herbivores* (wigeon spend much time grazing like geese, teal eat seeds of aquatic plants) to pure *carnivores* (mergansers eat fish, goldeneyes eat snails and shrimps, eiders and scoters eat bivalves), but many species eat both plant and animal matter.

In the non-breeding season, almost all waterfowl gather together in flocks, usually of their own species but sometimes mixed. Small ducks fly in clumps, larger ones such as scoters and eiders fly in lines, and geese and swans are well known for their V-formations. Lines and V-formations are thought to allow a modicum of energy saving in these birds because the turbulence produced by the wingtips of the bird in front of them furnishes some lift for the bird behind. This still has not been shown for sure; a good alternative explanation is that the formations allow the birds to organize their flying together with a minimum of accidents!

Breeding
In ducks of the temperate zone, males begin their courtship early in winter, each species with a different courtship behavior that shows off its distinctive color patches. This of course is why their bright breeding plumage is held through the winter, when males and females are together and interacting, and lost in mid-summer, when females have already mated and are on their nests. Males fight among themselves for the privilege of courting an individual female, and unmated females are badly harassed, sometimes by a whole flock of unmated males. Because copulation involves getting on the female's back and often submerging her, females are sometimes killed in these situations. Ducks place their nests on the ground (dabblers, eiders), or on the water's surface (scoters, scaups) in dense vegetation, or in tree holes (WOOD DUCKS, Plate 28, and mergansers). Typically nests are lined with down feathers that the female plucks from her own

belly; in those species that nest in the open, the down is brown and pulled over the whitish eggs to hide them whenever the female leaves the nest to forage. Females of temperate-zone ducks perform all of the breeding duties, including incubation of the 4 to 12 eggs and shepherding and protecting the ducklings. As soon as females are on their nest with a full clutch of eggs, the males desert them and begin their molt into eclipse plumage. In the tropics, ducks are non-migratory, and permanent pair bonds are easier to maintain, so parental care is shared there by many duck species, including the whistling-ducks, in which both sexes incubate. Geese and swans also have lifelong pair bonds, during which male and female share many of the breeding duties; the female incubates the 3 to 7 eggs herself, but the male stays nearby and helps raise the young. In these larger species, the presence of the male is a significant asset in protecting the young, so there has been strong evolutionary pressure for monogamy.

Young waterfowl are *precocial*, able to run, swim, and feed themselves soon after they hatch. They remain with the adult female or pair until full-sized and able to fly well, at one or two months of age in the smaller ducks, ranging up to four months in large swans. Young geese and eiders from several broods are often seen in a *crèche* (a group of young from several families that cluster together), which may be better protected from predators by the presence of additional caregivers. Young geese and swans remain with their parents and migrate south in family groups, in some species the groups staying together through the next spring migration. In ducks, on the other hand, the female deserts the young at about the time they fledge, and they move south separately. Most ducks mature in their first year, but the larger swans may not breed until they are four or more years of age.

Lore and Notes

Ducks, geese, and swans have been objects of people's attention since ancient times, chiefly as a food source. These birds typically have tasty flesh, are fairly large and thus economical to hunt, and are usually easier and less dangerous to catch than many other animals, for example, large mammals. Because they were much used as food, a few species of waterfowl were first domesticated thousands of years ago. The MALLARD is familiar in its many domestic forms, ranging from iridescent black (Cayuga duck) to pure white (Peking duck). The MUSCOVY DUCK, native to Latin America, is another common farmyard inhabitant in many parts of the world, and it is one of only two New World birds that have been domesticated for food (can you think of the other?). Wild ducks also adjust well to the proximity of people, to the point of taking food from them – a practice that surviving artworks show has been occurring for at least 2000 years.

Hunting ducks and geese for sport is also a long-practiced tradition. As a consequence of these long interactions between ducks and people, and the research on these animals stimulated by their use in agriculture and sport, a large amount of scientific information has been collected on the group; many of the ducks and geese are among the most well-known of birds. In fact, many North American duck species have hunters to thank not only for research studies but even for their very existence. The system of national wildlife refuges that superbly protects waterfowl in North America was created primarily to keep duck populations large for hunting, and much of the cost of the refuges is covered by fees paid annually by hunters for federal and state duck stamps (beautiful paintings of waterfowl on stamps that must be attached to hunting licenses).

One of the most used waterfowl 'products' is goose and duck down, the down feathers that waterfowl use to line their nests. Eider down is unexcelled as an insulating material and is much in demand for filling jackets and sleeping bags. In regions where the birds are common, people encourage eiders to nest at high densities by protecting their loose colonies from predators. The down is collected from each nest at the beginning of incubation, and the female replaces it readily; the second batch is taken after the ducklings leave the nest. Interestingly, eiders defecate on their eggs, perhaps to protect them from predators that are very sensitive to smell; the stink of an eider nest can be detected a few meters away. The eider-down industry has presumably developed a way to deodorize the down.

Status

Waterfowl are much affected by human actions, in particular the draining of wetlands. Even in the USA, which has a stated federal policy of 'No net loss of wetlands,' wetlands are continually being destroyed. Although – as any visitor can testify – Florida still has a lot of water, it has suffered more than many other states through alteration of historic wetlands, from channelized rivers in the north to vastly reduced water flow through the Everglades. As one example, channelization of the Kissimmee River resulted in a 90% decrease of waterfowl populations inhabiting that area. The status of the TRUMPETER SWAN (which does not occur in Florida) provides an example of another activity that has affected waterfowl: although much of the breeding range of this species was on inaccessible lakes in southern Alaska and northern British Columbia, it was nevertheless reduced to a tiny remnant of its former numbers by the 1930s, mostly as a result of hunting on its winter range. However, with full protection, it has flourished and continues to increase.

Profiles

Fulvous Whistling-Duck, *Dendrocygna bicolor*, Plate 26a
Black-bellied Whistling-Duck, *Dendrocygna autumnalis*, Plate 26b
Muscovy Duck, *Cairina moschata*, Plate 26c
Mottled Duck, *Anas fulvigula*, Plate 26d
Hooded Merganser, *Lophodytes cucullatus*, Plate 26e
Red-breasted Merganser, *Mergus serrator*, Plate 26f

Northern Pintail, *Anas acuta*, Plate 27a
Northern Shoveler, *Anas clypeata*, Plate 27b
Green-winged Teal, *Anas crecca*, Plate 27c
Blue-winged Teal, *Anas discors*, Plate 27d
American Wigeon, *Anas americana*, Plate 28a
Wood Duck, *Aix sponsa*, Plate 28b
Ring-necked Duck, *Aythya collaris*, Plate 28c
Lesser Scaup, *Aythya affinis*, Plate 28d
Ruddy Duck, *Oxyura jamaicensis*, Plate 28e

5. Raptors

Raptor is another name for *bird of prey*, birds that make their living hunting, killing, and eating other animals, usually other vertebrates. When one hears the term raptor, one usually thinks of soaring hawks that swoop to catch rodents, and of speedy, streamlined falcons that snatch small birds out of the air. Although these are familiar forms of raptors, the families of these birds are large, the members' behavior diverse. The two main raptor families are the Accipitridae, containing the *hawks*, *kites*, and *eagles*, and the Falconidae, including the *falcons* and their tropical relatives. The reasons for classifying the two raptor groups separately have to do with differences in skeletal anatomy and hence, presumed differences in evolutionary history. They differ substantially in nesting behavior as well. Owls (p. 144), which are nocturnal birds of prey, can also be considered raptors. Raptors are common and conspicuous animals in many parts of Florida. Many are birds of open areas, above which they soar during the day, using *thermals*, currents of heated air, that rise from the sun-warmed ground to support and propel them as they search for meals. But raptors are found in all types of habitats, including wetlands and the sea coast as well as forests and woodlands.

The *accipitrid* hawks are a worldwide group of 238 species. Florida is home to 14 regularly occurring species – the OSPREY (Plate 29), 4 kites, 8 hawks, and an eagle – and four rare visitors from the north and west that do not occur annually. Falcons likewise are worldwide in their distribution. There are 63 species, of which three are regular in Florida. Some falcons have very broad distributions, with the PEREGRINE FALCON found almost everywhere. Peregrines may have the most extensive natural distribution of any bird.

Raptors vary considerably in size and in patterns of their generally subdued color schemes, but all are similar in overall form – we know them when we see them. They are fierce-looking birds with strong feet, hooked, sharp claws, or *talons*, and strong, hooked and pointed bills. Females are usually larger than males, in some species noticeably so. Most raptors are variations of gray, brown, black, and white, usually with brown or black spots, streaks, or bars on various parts of their bodies. The plumages of these birds are actually quite beautiful when viewed close-up, which, unfortunately, is difficult to do. Males and females are usually alike in color pattern, the NORTHERN HARRIER (Plate 31) and AMERICAN KESTREL (Plate 32) being conspicuous exceptions. Juvenile raptors often spend several years in *subadult* plumages that differ in pattern from those of adults. In Florida, falcons can be distinguished from hawks by their long, pointed wings, which allow the rapid, acrobatic flight for which these birds are justifiably famous.

The New World *vultures* are another group we include here because of tradition, but in fact, recently established evidence argues conclusively that storks rather than hawks are their closest relatives. Among the similarities between New World vultures and storks is the fact that they are the only birds that defecate on their feet to cool them evaporatively; a group name for the two might be 'foot-poopers.' Birds at the very pinnacle of their profession, eating dead animals, vultures are highly conspicuous and among the most frequently seen birds of rural Florida. That they feast on rotting flesh does not reduce the majesty of these large, soaring birds as they circle for hours high over field and forest. Their family, Cathartidae, has only seven species, all confined to the Americas; several are abundant but one (the CALIFORNIA CONDOR) is close to extinction. They range from southern Canada to Tierra del Fuego, with several of the species sporting wide and overlapping distributions. The two largest members of the family are known as *condors*, the California and ANDEAN CONDORS, and they are among the most spectacular birds anywhere. The BLACK VULTURE (Plate 29), one of the most frequently encountered birds of tropical America, is very common around garbage dumps. It and the TURKEY VULTURE (Plate 29) are the two Florida species.

Vultures are large birds, with wingspans to 1.8 m (6 ft); the huge condors have wingspans of 3 m (10 ft)! Vultures generally are black or brown (but the tropical KING VULTURE is largely white), with hooked bills and curious, unfeathered heads whose bare skin is richly colored in red, yellow, or orange. Turkey Vultures, in fact, are named for their red heads, which remind people of turkey heads. The rather chickenlike feet of vultures, not suited for either carrying or tearing prey, proclaim them quite different from the other raptors. Male and female vultures look alike; males are slightly larger than females.

Natural History
Ecology and Behavior

Raptors are meat-eaters; most hunt and eat live prey. BALD EAGLES (Plate 29) have a reputation as carrion eaters, but they will also take live and healthy prey of many kinds. Raptors usually hunt alone, although, when mated, the mate is often close by. Hawks, eagles, and falcons take mainly vertebrates, including items up to the size of salmon, geese, and young deer. Fish are the sole food of OSPREYS and very important in the diet of Bald Eagles. When a hawk makes a capture, the prey is snatched with the sharply pointed and curved talons and usually killed by the puncturing of internal organs by those same talons. Falcons kill by a swift bite to the base of the skull with their specially toothed and notched bill. In both groups, the very sharp-edged bill is then used to dissect the prey into bite-sized morsels.

Florida's raptors can be divided into groups based on how they pursue and capture prey. *Falcons* are long-winged, high-speed bird chasers, from the duck-eating PEREGRINE FALCON to the sparrow-eating AMERICAN KESTREL. Most people are familiar with stories of Peregrines *stooping* (diving vertically from height to gain speed and force) at speeds of 160 kph (100 mph) or more to grab or knock from the sky an unsuspecting bird. The fish-eating Osprey, in a group of its own, dives to the water surface from flight. *Kites* tend to be relatively delicate raptors, often taking invertebrate prey, although three of the four Florida species take small vertebrates as well. SWALLOW-TAILED KITES (Plate 30) fly through the canopy and pluck baby birds from nests and lizards and katydids from branches. One species, the SNAIL KITE (Plate 30), specializes almost completely on one kind of freshwater snail, which it daintily removes from the shell with its long, pointed bill. *Harriers*, including the NORTHERN HARRIER, look for small birds and mammals while drifting low over the ground, their wings held up in characteristic fashion and – just as in the unrelated owls – their large ears tuned to the sound of potential prey. *Accipiters*, including the COOPER'S HAWK (Plate 31), are forest-based bird chasers with long legs that can reach into dense shrubbery after their prey; the largest species also take small mammals. *Buteos*, including the RED-SHOULDERED HAWK (Plate 32) and RED-TAILED HAWK (Plate 32), hunt from the air, either soaring or hovering, and take primarily rodents and other small mammals. The SHORT-TAILED HAWK (Plate 32), however, is a bird specialist. Bald Eagles pluck fish and water birds from the surface of the water or search the seashore for dead fish and marine mammals.

Many raptors are territorial, a solitary individual or a breeding pair defending an area for feeding and, during the breeding season, for reproduction. Displays that advertise a territory and may be used in courtship consist of spectacular aerial twists, loops, and other acrobatic maneuvers. Although many raptors are common birds, typically they exist at relatively low densities, as is the case for all *top predators* (a predator at the pinnacle of the food chain, preyed upon by no other animal). That is, there usually is enough food to support only one or a pair of a species in a given area. For example, a typical density for a small raptor species, perhaps one that feeds on mice, is one individual per sq km (0.4 sq miles). A large eagle that feeds on rabbits may be spaced so that a usual density is one individual per thousand sq km (386 sq miles).

Most vultures soar during the day in groups, looking for carrion. TURKEY VULTURES can find carcasses in deep forest and beneath objects, strongly implicating smell, as opposed to vision, as the method of discovery. They can move many miles daily in their search for dead animals. BLACK VULTURES, supplementing their taste for carrion, also occasionally kill animals, usually newborn or those otherwise defenseless. Some of the vultures, especially the Black Vulture, also eat fruit. Black Vultures often congregate in large numbers at feeding places, and it is common to find a flock of them at any rural dump. With their superb eyesight, fine-tuned sense of smell, and ability to survey each day great expanses of habitat, vultures are surpassingly good at locating dead animals. No mammal species specializes in carrion to the degree that vultures do, presumably because no mammal could search such large areas each day.

Breeding

Hawk and eagle nests are constructed of sticks that both sexes place in a tree or on a rock ledge (on the ground in harriers). Nests are often lined with freshly collected green leaves, which are thought to produce chemicals that deter nest parasites that could harm the young birds. The female (both sexes in eagles and some kites and sometimes assisted by the male in the OSPREY) incubates the 1 to 6 eggs (only 2 or 3 in the larger species) for 26 to 45 days and gives food to the nestlings. In all raptors, the male hunts for and feeds the female during the egg-laying, incubation, and early nestling periods. Both sexes feed the young when they get a bit older. Youngsters can fly at 4 to 12 weeks of age, depending on species size. After fledging, the young remain with the parents for several more weeks or months until they can hunt on their own. Falcon breeding is similar but differs in a few particulars. Falcons lay their 3 to 6 eggs in a tree or rock cavity or on a ledge but do not construct a nest; in this they are quite different from hawks. Some of them, in fact, lay their eggs in abandoned nests of other birds; for example, MERLINS use crow and magpie nests. Incubation is from 28 to 35 days, performed only by the female. The young fledge after 4 to 7 weeks in the nest.

Vultures are monogamous breeders. Both sexes incubate the 1 to 3 eggs, which are placed on the ground in protected places or on the floor of a cave or tree cavity. Eggs are incubated for 34 to 41 days in the Florida species; both sexes feed the young regurgitated carrion for 2 to 5 months until they can fly. Young vultures at the nest site very rarely become food for other animals, and it has been suggested that the stench of the birds and the site, awash as they are in decaying animal flesh, keeps predators (and everything else) away.

Ecological Interactions

Although the AMERICAN KESTREL is the common resident falcon in Florida, other falcons are common during migration and winter. Bird-eating falcons such as MERLINS and PEREGRINES hit birds in flight with their talons or closed foot, stunning the prey and sometimes killing it outright. Fast as falcons are, an individual prey bird, even one caught unaware in the open, has a fairly good chance of escaping these avian killing machines. Most bird-eating hawks, falcons included, have a success rate of only about 10%. Smaller birds that are chased may not be as fast as falcons, but they can turn on a smaller circle, and often they can continue to evade their pursuer until the falcon gives up or the potential prey finds cover. Birds in groups have two additional defenses. First, each individual in a group benefits because the group, with so many eyes and ears, is more likely to spot a falcon at a distance than is a lone individual, thus providing all in the group opportunities to watch the predator as it approaches and so evade it. This sort of anti-predation advantage may be why many animals stay in groups. Second, some flocks of small birds, such as sandpipers, which usually fly in loose formations, immediately tighten their formation upon detecting a flying falcon. The effect is to decrease the distance between each bird, so much so that a falcon flying into the group at a fast speed and trying to take an individual risks injuring itself – the sandpipers form an almost solid wall of birds. Starling flocks take this one step further and sometimes dive as a group on a hawk, trying to injure or at least intimidate it.

BLACK and TURKEY VULTURES roost communally, the two species often together. A common observation has been that once an individual finds a food source, other vultures arrive very rapidly to share the carcass. Biologists strongly suspect that the group roosting and feeding behaviors of these birds are related, and that the former increases each individual's food-finding efficiency. In other words, a communal roost serves as an *information center* for finding food. Researchers believe that vultures may locate the probable position of the next day's food while soaring high in the late afternoon, before they return to the roost. In the morning, the ones that detected potential carcasses set out from the roost to locate the food, with others, less successful the previous day, following in the general direction. Thus, on different days, the birds take turns as leaders and followers, and all benefit from the communal roosting association.

Lore and Notes

Large, predatory raptors have doubtless always attracted people's attention, respect, and awe. Wherever eagles occur, they are chronicled in the history of civilizations. Early Anglo-Saxons were known to hang an eagle on the gate of any city they conquered. Some North American Indian tribes and also Australian Aboriginal peoples deified large hawks or eagles. Several countries have used likenesses of eagles as nation symbols, among them Turkey, Austria, Germany, Poland, Russia, and Mexico. Eagles are popular symbols on regal coats of arms, and one of their kind, a fish-eater, was chosen as the emblem of the USA. People have had a close relationship with falcons for thousands of years. Falconry, in which captive falcons are trained to hunt and kill game at a person's command, is a very old sport, with evidence of it being practiced in China 4000 years ago and in Iran 3700 years ago. One of the oldest known books on a sport is *The Art of Falconry*, written by the King of Sicily in 1248. Falconry reached its pinnacle during medieval times in Europe, when a nobleman's falcons were apparently considered among his most valued possessions.

Europeans first arriving in the New World thought the region's vultures evil – 'the sloth, the filth, and the voraciousness of these birds, almost exceeds credibility,' wrote one impressionable Englishman in the late 1700s. But the native peoples, especially in hot, humid areas where rotting of corpses occurs quickly, generally thought well of these carrion-eaters. Ancient Mayans called the KING VULTURE 'Oc,' including it frequently in their artworks. Vulture feathers were used in Mayan headdresses. Mayans apparently believed that vultures, when near death, changed into armadillos; the proof being that both were 'bald.'

Status

SNAIL KITES have a broad range from Florida and Cuba to tropical Middle and South America and are fairly common in many tropical areas where there are extensive marshes; however, they are listed as Endangered in the USA. There, also called the Everglades Kite, they occur over only small sections of Florida. During the 1960s, owing to destruction and draining of their marsh habitats, the entire Florida population was believed to number no more than 25 individuals, but they have increased substantially since then, and by the 1990s, there were 700 or more birds in the state. Snail kites are extremely specialized in their feeding; in fact, they are *monophagous* – eating only one thing, freshwater apple snails. This high degree of specialization is one of the kites' biggest problems, because periodic droughts lead to very low food availability and, therefore, to crashes in the kite population.

Another widespread tropical raptor, the CRESTED CARACARA (Plate 32), is represented in Florida by an even smaller population and is listed as Threatened in the state. Caracaras are not imperiled by loss of prey species, as they are very generalized predators. But carrion features strongly in their diet, and that, of course, represents a constant danger, as most of the easily located dead animals in Florida nowadays are road kills. The SHORT-TAILED HAWK is another tropical hawk that reaches its northern limit in Florida, and it may be no more common than the kite or caracara.

The USA's national symbol, the BALD EAGLE, has been closely associated with the rise of environmentalism in North America. In the early part of the 20th century, Alaska fishermen declared war on this fish-eating species; 100,000 eagles were killed. Bald Eagles declined dramatically during the period of DDT use (the middle part of the 20th century), with populations reaching a low of about 400 pairs in the lower 48 states. DDT becomes more concentrated as it passes up the food web (*bioconcentration*), so eagles that ate seabirds that ate fish that ate invertebrates that had DDT in their tissues were greatly at risk. Listed as Endangered in most of the lower 48 states in 1967, the species has recovered very well with the banning of DDT in its range in 1970. It was 'downlisted' to Threatened status in all of the lower 48 states in 1995, and in 1999, a proposal was made to remove it completely from the Endangered Species list. It remains very well protected by the Bald Eagle Protection Act of 1940, which makes it a serious crime to kill or disturb an eagle.

Similarly, the PEREGRINE FALCON was drastically affected by DDT, the effects of which are to cause problems in calcium metabolism such that eggs receive less calcium in their shells; these eggs are thinner than normal and actually crack under the weight of the incubating bird. Populations of the most widespread breeding American subspecies of this falcon were listed as Endangered in the USA in 1970 and Canada in 1978. With DDT no longer used in the USA and Canada, falcon populations began to increase slowly. They were aided by an extensive program of releasing captive-bred young in nest boxes to which some of them would return to breed; several thousand birds were released in this way. This program, called *hacking*, has been used for raptors worldwide with some success. Peregrines were 'downlisted' from Endangered status in 1999.

Profiles

Black Vulture, *Coragyps atratus*, Plate 29a
Turkey Vulture, *Cathartes aura*, Plate 29b
Osprey, *Pandion haliaetus*, Plate 29c
Bald Eagle, *Haliaeetus leucocephalus*, Plate 29d
White-tailed Kite, *Elanus leucurus*, Plate 30a
Mississippi Kite, *Ictinia mississippiensis*, Plate 30b
Swallow-tailed Kite, *Elanoides forficatus*, Plate 30c
Snail Kite, *Rostrhamus sociabilis*, Plate 30d

Cooper's Hawk, *Accipiter cooperii*, Plate 31a
Sharp-shinned Hawk, *Accipiter striatus*, Plate 31b
Broad-winged Hawk, *Buteo platypterus*, Plate 31c
Northern Harrier, *Circus cyaneus*, Plate 31d
Short-tailed Hawk, *Buteo brachyurus*, Plate 32a
American Kestrel, *Falco sparverius*, Plate 32b
Red-tailed Hawk, *Buteo jamaicensis*, Plate 32c
Red-shouldered Hawk, *Buteo lineatus*, Plate 32d
Crested Caracara, *Caracara cheriway*, Plate 32e

6. Chickenlike Birds

The order Galliformes, with 282 species, includes the *gallinaceous birds* of the world. They are usually called 'chickenlike birds' for want of a better inclusive term. Indeed, chickens are domesticated members of the group; the RED JUNGLEFOWL is actually the wild form of the domesticated chicken. Most members of this group live in Eurasia and Africa, but several groups of gallinaceous birds originated in the New World, including the *New World quails*, family Odontophoridae, and *turkeys*, family Meleagrididae.

Chickens and their relatives are stocky, with short, broad, rounded wings, shortish legs with heavy claws adapted for ground scratching, short, thick, chickenlike bills, and short or long tails – with some of the pheasants having tails to 1.5 m (5 ft) long. Some species, particularly among the pheasants, are exquisitely marked with bright colors and intricate patterns. The long tails of male peafowl (actually the uppertail coverts!) are, of course, among nature's most ornate and colorful constructions. Others, however, mostly smaller and so more at risk from predators, are duller and more camouflaged in their typical on-the-ground habitats. The sexes can look alike or different; males of some species are much larger than females.

The 31 species of New World quails are native to North, Central, and South America. Members of this family, including the NORTHERN BOBWHITE (Plate 33), are like small chickens – plump, short-winged, and strong-legged, and preferring to run rather than fly. Many of them have crests or topknots, making them look perky, and their fleet-footedness does nothing to dispel that image. They spend much of their time on the ground, although they roost at night up in shrubs and trees. Most of them have loud, characteristic calls (surely to make up for their skulking habits), and the *bob-white* announcement of the male Northern Bobwhite is a spring sound over most of the eastern USA.

Turkeys are known to everyone, but perhaps not everyone knows the WILD TURKEY (Plate 33) as the ancestor of the bird that preoccupies many Americans on Thanksgiving Day. Turkeys are unmistakable large chicken-relatives with brightly colored naked head and wattles, iridescently barred plumage, and a huge tail fanned during display. Wild Turkeys are native to eastern North America and the highlands of Mexico. The species was domesticated in Mexico many centuries ago, and the subspecies occurring in Mexico has a white tail tip; domestic birds in the USA wandering around at roadsides are easily distinguished from their wild relatives by a white- rather than buff-tipped tail. Many ornithologists and birders are familiar with another species of turkey, the OCELLATED TURKEY of southern Mexican and Guatemalan forest edge, which is even more garishly colored than its northern relative.

Natural History
Ecology and Behavior
Quails and turkeys are terrestrial birds that feed and nest on the ground. Most flights are very brief, but over short distances, such as when making a sudden, quick escape from a potential predator or a hunter, these birds are powerful, swift aviators. With their short, rounded wings, they are not built for sustained flight, and few gallinaceous birds are migratory. Even the grouse of the far northern forests and arctic tundra are resident all year there, among the few birds that are. Gallinaceous birds are mostly vegetarians, eating seeds and other plant matter such as shoots, berries, and roots (grouse eat mostly leaves), as well as some insects and other small invertebrate animals. They scratch the ground with their large feet, clearing away vegetation and soil, looking for buried goodies. Most species are gregarious, and the species profiled here travel in small family or multi-family groups called *coveys* – of up to 30 individuals.

Breeding
Gallinaceous birds are popular among ornithologists who study bird mating systems because so many of the species are *promiscuous*, with no pair bond between males and females. Some of the promiscuous species form *leks*, communal displays that may include several dozen males spread out over a traditional 'dancing ground.' Dominant males keep subordinate ones away from favored parts of the lek, which are usually toward the center of the group (battles among males have led to natural selection for large size, and some male grouse of other species, in other parts of the world, are almost twice the size of females). Females enter the lek from time to time, wandering through the males and raising the display fervor to a frenzy; the females may then wander out the other side of the lek or may approach a particular male and indicate readiness to mate. Mating occurs quickly. Then the female goes away to her own territory and lines a shallow depression on the ground with grasses and other plant material for a nest.

Turkeys follow this promiscuous pattern, males strutting about and displaying to whatever females will pay attention. The females lay their 10 to 15 eggs in a ground nest and incubate them for 25 to 31 days, then shepherd the young around while they feed themselves. The young take several months to become independent. Quails deviate from the galliform norm by forming pair bonds and sharing parental care. Bobwhite females lay 12 to 16 eggs, and both sexes incubate them for 23 to 24 days. The young take 3 to 4 weeks to reach full size and independence. One of the most interesting things about gallinaceous birds is the development of their young, which are amazingly *precocial*, able to run after their parents and begin pecking at small prey just hours after hatching. Precocial young, tiny and conspicuous because of their movements, are greatly at risk from predators. Ducklings at least live in the water, so they are safe from most land-based predators. Baby quail and turkeys, on the other hand, are tasty tidbits for just about any carnivorous bird or mammal, and their way of coping with this is to grow miniature but functional wings very rapidly. They can fly at 6 to 12 days of age, at least giving them an even chance of survival. It's a startling sight to see a brood of diminutive quail burst into the air as they are approached.

Ecological Interactions
Chickens and their relatives have more than one line of defense. They have short, stiff wings and specially adapted flight muscles that allow for amazingly quick takeoffs and rapid acceleration. When approached closely, they take off like a rocket, and this, combined with the loud whirring sound of their wings, produces a *startle effect* that surely must save many from predators. Many a hunter, birder, or woodsperson who has encountered these birds can attest to how well it works.

Lore and Notes
Pheasants and peafowl, with their ornate plumage and long tails, have an associated rich mythology, appearing in ancient Greek, Buddhist, and Hindu legends, among others. The Buddha was sometimes shown riding on a displaying peacock. Early Christians apparently regarded the peacock as a symbol of immortality. Turkeys, on the other hand, have not seemed to garner as much respect. Those we see in the barnyard don't seem especially bright, and calling someone a 'turkey' is a substantial insult in the USA. However, Wild Turkeys are in fact reasonably intelligent birds, one of the most difficult gallinaceous birds for hunters to bag, and worthy in every way of our respect. Benjamin Franklin, who proposed this species as the USA national bird, knew this full well. But the Bald Eagle was the more glamorous of the two, and the nature of that conspicuous predatory bird apparently appealed to the USA's founding fathers better than that of the skulking seed-eater.

Status
Both of the gallinaceous birds native to Florida are doing well, recipients of much attention by state agencies because of their status as game birds. Around 2 million bobwhite are taken by hunters in the USA every year, and their populations continue to flourish. Only loss of habitat threatens either of these species, and, fortunately, the bobwhite at least does well in disturbed habitats. The turkey, on the other hand, needs well-developed forests for roosting and winter cover, and Florida populations are associated with mature pine flatwoods, cypress swamps, and stands of hardwoods along rivers.

Profiles
Northern Bobwhite, *Colinus virginianus*, Plate 33e
Wild Turkey, *Meleagris gallopavo*, Plate 33f

7. Cranes, Limpkin, and Rails

All of the birds of this group are members of the order Gruiformes, which contains a varied group of water and forest birds. There are 15 species of *cranes*, family Gruidae; members of the family occur on all continents but South America. Two species of cranes occur in North America, and both of them in Florida, although the WHOOPING CRANE (Plate 25) is recently introduced into the state. These are large, long-necked and long-legged wading birds that stride across prairies and wetlands. The tallest of them stand as high as a person. Cranes are colored in shades of gray, white, and black, usually quite conspicuous in their open-country habitats. They are sometimes confused with herons, which are also tall wading birds, but the two are very different. Both groups have long, pointed bills, but the crane bill is less compressed than the heron bill, and the nostrils are *perforate* (see-through). Most cranes have a patch of red, naked skin on top of their head, and their very large *tertial* (inner wing) feathers give the appearance of a bustle. Cranes forage by walking steadily, while herons stand very still and watch for the movements of nearby prey. Cranes fly with their neck fully extended, often in flocks, but herons fly singly, with their neck folded back. Cranes are very vocal, with sonorous, rolling gooselike calls, while herons are restricted to guttural croaks. Northern-hemisphere cranes are, in general, highly migratory, moving to distant wintering grounds, but in Florida, the SANDHILL CRANE (Plate 25) has both resident (non-migratory) and migratory populations.

Limpkins, family Aramidae, are smaller relatives of cranes that have much the same shape, with long legs, neck, and bill, but they are colored differently, much better camouflaged for a life among tall marsh vegetation.. The single species, the LIMPKIN (Plate 24), is confined to the New World tropics, extending north into Florida, where it is locally common in freshwater marshes. Its wailing calls are characteristic sounds of Florida swamps and marshes, loud and eerie enough that a close bird vocalizing will make your hairs stand on end.

The *rails*, family Rallidae, are a worldwide group of often secretive small and medium-sized birds of wetlands and forest floors. The chief characteristics permitting this lifestyle usually are long legs and very long toes that distribute the birds' weight, allowing them to walk among marsh plants and across floating vegetation without sinking. The 143 species include *crakes*, *gallinules*, and *coots* as well as rails. Coots and gallinules resemble ducks when swimming, but they do not have ducklike bills, and their feet are not webbed; the toes of coots are lobed, however, to aid them in swimming and diving. Most rails are bedecked with camouflage colors, their browns, russets, and grays blending into the dense vegetation through which they move. A few species, for example the PURPLE GALLINULE (Plate 33), are anything but camouflaged. Rails can pass through amazingly tight spaces because their bodies are very narrow – they are, in fact, thin as a rail.

Natural History
Ecology and Behavior

Cranes are usually seen in pairs or flocks in wet meadows or fields, resting or foraging by striding slowly across their open habitat with a watchful eye for prey. They are omnivores, eating a wide variety of small vertebrates (baby birds in nests are a special delicacy) and large invertebrates, as well as seeds, tubers, grasses, and sedges – just about anything in their environment that they can swallow. In migration, cranes gather in flocks that move slowly northward or southward, reminiscent of geese and swans as they move overhead, calling as they go. Unlike waterfowl, they use the rising air of thermals just as migrating raptors do, circling higher and higher on set wings, then gliding off in the appropriate direction to find another thermal and repeat the maneuver. Their long wings with primary flight feathers separated at the end (into 'fingers') look very much like the wings of eagles. Florida's cranes are sometimes seen high in the air.

Most rails are highly secretive, often heard giving characteristic calls but rarely seen in the dense marshes that are their homes. An exception is the

CLAPPER RAIL (Plate 33), a coastal species that is often seen foraging at the edge of a salt marsh or mangrove swamp, especially near dawn and dusk. PURPLE GALLINULES, although spectacularly conspicuous, can be just as shy as rails, darting into the dense vegetation at the least sign of danger, but the species that swim in open water – COMMON MOORHEN (Plate 33) and AMERICAN COOT (Plate 33) – are much more conspicuous and familiar. Coots, in fact, are among the most common and successful water birds in many parts of the world. Rails tend to be omnivores, eating both plant and animal foods, with the emphasis on animal, including insects, crayfish, frogs, and even snakes. Coots, however, are vegetarians, feeding at the surface and diving for the leaves and stems of aquatic plants.

LIMPKINS are the pickiest members of this group in their diet. Just like the Snail Kite, they prefer apple snails to anything else, although they will take freshwater mussels whenever they can find them. They forage by poking around in shallow water, finding the snails by touch, then cracking open their shells to devour the inhabitants – very different from the finesse of a Snail Kite extracting the snail with its bill. Researchers can easily distinguish snails eaten by kites or Limpkins (see below why researchers might study these two birds).

Breeding

In early spring, SANDHILL CRANES begin their impressive courtship behavior, often referred to as 'dancing,' that includes jumping in the air, giving elaborate bows and wingspreads, and pulling up and tossing of bits of plant material and soil. Cranes are monogamous and mate for life, and pairs defend large territories. The nest is a big pile of vegetation gathered by the adults, often in the middle of an extensive marsh or wet prairie but elevated sufficiently to keep the eggs dry. The 2 eggs laid are incubated by both sexes for 29 to 32 days. The young leave the nest soon after hatching and are fed by the adults at first; gradually they learn how to feed themselves. They first fly at about 9 to 10 weeks of age, then remain with their parents for their first year, accompanying them during migration.

LIMPKINS build nests much like those of cranes, but sometimes well up in trees; the Limpkin is a much more arboreal bird than any crane. Usually 4 to 8 eggs are laid, but the incubation period is poorly known. Much as in cranes, the young leave the nest very soon and follow the adults about. Rails build their nests out of the leaves of aquatic plants such as cattails, usually just above the water surface in dense vegetation. COMMON MOORHENS and AMERICAN COOTS build similar but larger nests, the latter sometimes floating right out in the open. The members of this family lay large clutches, typically of 5 to 10 or more eggs; some coot nests contain many more eggs, probably laid by more than one female. Both sexes incubate the spotted eggs for 17 to 23 days. The young are precocial, able to move about soon after hatching, but the adults feed them for several weeks, then shepherd them about for up to 6 to 8 weeks until they are independent. Young coots and gallinules have brightly colored heads and bills, presumably so the adults can find their young hiding in the vegetation. In both moorhens and PURPLE GALLINULES, young from earlier broods may help feed their siblings from the following brood.

Ecological Interactions

One interaction found in many marshes in the New World tropics is distinctly at odds with theories about competition in nature. Here are two bird species, LIMPKIN and Snail Kite, that specialize on a single prey type, the apple snail. Usually when two species compete for the same resource, one of them is a bit more successful and so the other faces starvation and local extinction. In this case, however, the two specialists seem to specialize in where and how they take their common prey, and this must alleviate the pressures of direct competition. The kites take snails at and near the surface in deep water by flying over the marsh and grabbing with their raptorial feet. The Limpkins take the snails living in shallow water by wading and probing with their long bills. As long as marshes have shallow and deep sections, and as long as snails inhabit both of them, this counterintuitive coexistence will likely persist.

Lore and Notes

Cranes are a symbol of good luck, happiness, and long life in Japan, and they are everywhere in Japanese art and daily life. In part as a consequence of the atomic bombs dropped in Japan during World War II, school children all over the world now make *origami* cranes, cleverly folded pieces of paper, as a demonstration of their desire for world peace. The courtship 'dances' of cranes have also influenced the dances of the Native people of North America, Australia, and Africa, and one wonders how many modern ballet choreographers have been similarly influenced.

Status

SANDHILL CRANES are abundant across most of western North America, although some of the eastern and southern USA populations have diminished greatly with the destruction of wetlands. The Florida resident population may number somewhere around 4000 birds at present; the migratory population annually averages about 35,000 individuals. The federal government and many state governments have programs to maintain this striking species, but even more effort has been put into the recovery of the WHOOPING CRANE, the only other crane to breed in North America. One of America's most spectacular birds, the Whooper was very nearly lost to extinction. It nested widely in northern North America and wintered along the Gulf Coast, but it was subject both to hunting during migration and to disturbance on its nesting grounds; by 1941, it was thought that no more than two dozen of them remained. With complete protection, public education, and a substantial captive-breeding program, numbers gradually increased to the present total of several hundred birds. There is a large captive flock and also a substantial population that nests in Wood Buffalo National Park in Canada and winters on the Texas coast. Beginning in 1993, captive-bred birds were released annually in an attempt to start a second, non-migratory, flock in Florida, but mortality is very high in the released birds (powerline strikes, Bobcat predation), and the success of this endeavor remains to be seen. Not out of danger, the Whooping Crane is at least holding its own at present.

Florida's rails are still common, but many rail species have gone extinct. Members of this group, although seemingly weak flyers, have an amazing ability to reach oceanic islands, where they remain and evolve into *endemic* species, occurring nowhere else in the world. On smaller islands that lack predators, there is a further tendency for the rails to evolve flightlessness, which suits them fine until humans come along and introduce rats, cats, dogs, and other predators that find the flightless rails easy prey. Few of them have survived.

Profiles

Sandhill Crane, *Grus canadensis*, Plate 25b
Whooping Crane, *Grus americana*, Plate 25c

Limpkin, *Aramus guarauna*, Plate 24d
Purple Gallinule, *Porphyrula martinica*, Plate 33a
Clapper Rail, *Rallus longirostris*, Plate 33b
Common Moorhen, *Gallinula chloropus*, Plate 33c
American Coot, *Fulica americana*, Plate 33d

8. Shorebirds

Shorebirds are long-distance migrants. Many of them breed at high latitudes and winter in the tropics, so large numbers of them pass through Florida in migration or spend their winters there. They are among the reasons this state is a compelling destination for the serious birder. Shorebird flocks on beaches and mudflats may contain up to a dozen or more species, ranging greatly in size and coloration. Both their bill shape and their overall coloration are strongly influenced by their non-breeding habitat, whether sand or mud or rock or marsh or open water, so Florida is a good place to become acquainted with shorebirds and their adaptations. Most of the species that winter in or migrate through the state breed on open tundra and forest ponds and marshes across Alaska and Canada. However, some species, for example the KILLDEER (Plate 34), are very wide-ranging and are found throughout the year in the state, while others, such as the BLACK-NECKED STILT (Plate 35), are tropical in origin, breeding in Florida and wintering in South America.

Shorebirds are traditionally placed along with the gulls in the avian order Charadriiformes. They are global in distribution and often occur in large numbers – the primary reason being that the sandy beaches and mudflats on which they forage usually teem with their food. There are several families, four of which require mention. The *sandpipers* (family Scolopacidae) are a worldwide group of 88 species. Twenty-seven of them occur regularly in Florida, and another 9 species are irregular visitors, mostly from western North America or Europe (shorebirds are well-known as long-distance wanderers). The *plovers* (family Charadriidae), with 66 species, likewise have a worldwide distribution but are more common in the tropics. Seven species occur regularly in Florida, and another species is a rare visitor. The *avocets* and *stilts* (family Recurvirostridae) are a worldwide family of 11 species, of which two occur in Florida. Finally, a single species of *oystercatcher* (family Haematopodidae) occurs in the state; this family of 11 species also occurs on all continents.

All shorebirds, regardless of size, are recognizable as shorebirds. They walk or run on sandy beaches, mudflats, or rocks, or wade in shallow fresh or salt water; the waders typically have long, slender legs. The sexes look alike, or nearly so, in most shorebirds (but see under Breeding). They are usually drably colored during the non-breeding season, darker above and lighter below – perfectly camouflaged on the sand, mud, or vegetation on which they forage. Many shorebirds molt into a bright breeding plumage, and this plumage can be seen briefly in spring in Florida, before the birds leave for breeding destinations. Florida sandpipers are generally slender birds with straight or curved bills of various lengths, each adapted to feeding in a specific habitat and even at a specific depth below the surface of the sand or mud. Plovers are small to mid-sized, thick-necked shorebirds with short tails and straight, relatively thick bills. They are mostly shades of gray and brown above and white below, but some have bold color patterns such as a broad white or dark band on the head or chest. A few Florida plovers are boldly marked with large areas of black in the breeding season. Finally, the AMERICAN OYSTERCATCHER (Plate 34) is an unmistakable large black and white shorebird with a bright red, chisel-shaped bill; it feeds on sandy beaches. The AMERICAN AVOCET (Plate 35) and BLACK-NECKED STILT are similarly strikingly colored shorebirds, with long bills, necks, and legs; both wade in shallow water.

Some of the small shorebirds, such as SANDERLINGS (Plate 36), resemble amusing wind-up toys as they spend hours running up and down the beach, chasing, and then being chased by, the outgoing and incoming surf. Shorebirds are often conspicuous and let themselves be watched, as long as the watchers maintain some distance. When in large flying groups, sandpipers such as DUNLINS (Plate 37) and SEMIPALMATED SANDPIPERS (Plate 36) provide some of the most compelling sights in nature, as their flocks rise from sandbar or mudflat to fly low and fast over the surf, wheeling quickly and tightly in the air as if they were a single organism, or as if each individual's nervous system were joined to that of the others.

Natural History
Ecology and Behavior
Shorebirds are typically seen in the open, associated with coastlines and inland wetlands. They are all excellent flyers, but when chased they often seem to prefer running to flying away. Sandpipers characteristically forage by moving slowly and steadily forward, picking their food from the ground or using their bills to probe for it in mud or sand. In the breeding season, most of them eat insects and spiders, but in migration and on their marine and freshwater wintering grounds, they take many kinds of small invertebrates, including worms, snails, and crustaceans. They will also snatch bugs from the air as they walk and from the water's surface as they wade or swim. The larger species, such as godwits and curlews, with longer bills, probe deep in the mud for large worms and small crabs. Plovers forage by alternately running and stopping to pick prey from the surface, and they can easily be distinguished from sandpipers at a great distance by this characteristic behavior. Oystercatchers have a bill surpassingly well adapted for cracking open shells or stabbing partially open oysters so they relax their protective valves. *Phalaropes* are the most unusual shorebirds; although members of the sandpiper group, these tiny shorebirds spend much of their life on the ocean's surface, where they pick planktonic crustaceans from the top few centimeters of the water. They often *spin* (swim in small circles), creating a vortex that draws tiny invertebrates closer to the surface.

Some shorebirds, for example SPOTTED SANDPIPERS (Plate 36) and SANDERLINGS establish winter feeding territories along stretches of beach; they use the area for feeding for a few hours or for the day, defending it aggressively from other members of their species. On the other hand, most sandpipers and plovers are gregarious birds, often seen in large groups, especially when they are travelling. Flocks of thousands of DUNLINS and SEMIPALMATED SANDPIPERS are commonly observed. Several species make long migrations over expanses of open ocean, a good example being the RED KNOT (Plate 37), which flies nonstop over the Atlantic between North American breeding grounds and South American wintering locales.

Breeding
The arctic tundra resounds through the 24-hour daylight of summer with the songs that are given by sandpipers and plovers as they perform their spectacular

display flights. In many species, males defend rather large territories and attract females to them, as is typical of most birds. However, shorebirds breed in a greater variety of ways than other birds. Most species breed in monogamous pairs that defend breeding territories and share in parental care. Others are *polygynous*, the males in species such as RUFFS coming together in communal displays called *leks*. Females are attracted to these groups but mate with only one of the males; certain males mate with more than one female. In this system, males provide no parental care. Other species practice *polyandry*, the least common type of mating system among vertebrate animals, in which some females have more than one mate in a single breeding season. This type of breeding is exemplified by the SPOTTED SANDPIPER. In this species, the normal sex roles of breeding birds are reversed: the female establishes a territory on a lakeshore that she defends against other females. More than one male settles within the territory, either at the same time or sequentially during a breeding season. After mating, the female lays a clutch of eggs for each male. The males incubate their clutches and care for the young. Females may help care for some of the broods of young provided that there are no more unmated males to try to attract to the territory. In phalaropes, also polyandrous, there has been a substantial switch in sex roles; females are distinctly larger and more brightly colored than males (quite unusual in the bird world) and actively court the smaller, duller males. After laying her eggs in a nest constructed by the male, a female contributes no additional parental care.

Most shorebird nests are simply shallow depressions in the ground in which the eggs are placed; some of these *scrapes* are lined with dead leaves or lichens, which apparently are excellent insulating material, holding in the heat generated by the incubating bird's body. Sandpipers, plovers, avocets, and stilts typically lay 4 relatively large eggs, this exact clutch size probably determined by how many eggs can be successfully incubated. Incubation, depending on species, is by the male alone, the female alone, or both parents, for 20 to 28 days. Oystercatchers lay clutches of 3 eggs, which are incubated for 24 to 29 days by both male and female. Like waterfowl and quails, shorebird young are precocial, that is, soon after they hatch they are mobile, able to run from predators, and can feed themselves (but oystercatchers and snipes feed their young). One or both parents usually stay with the young to lead them to feeding areas and guard them until they can fly, 2 to 5 weeks after hatching.

Shorebirds are famous for their *distraction displays*, in which one or both parents flop along the ground as if they have a broken wing or are otherwise incapacitated. A predator that might go for their eggs or young instead follows the apparently guaranteed meal that the adult represents, and is lured away from the young until the adult, having accomplished its goal, flies away.

Ecological Interactions

Shorebirds often gather in very large flocks at what are known as *staging areas*, sites where the birds can find abundant food and put on the fat they need for long-distance migration. In some species, only a few such sites exist on the route between breeding and wintering ground, and the birds put enormous pressure on the invertebrates on which they feed. In fact, shorebirds are the main avian predators on intertidal invertebrates. When researchers construct exclosures on mudflats to keep sandpipers and plovers out of small areas, the invertebrates within those exclosures remain at much greater densities than in the areas where the birds can feed freely.

Lore and Notes

The manner in which flocks of thousands of birds, particularly shorebirds, fly in such closely regimented order, executing abrupt maneuvers with precise coordination, such as when all individuals seem to turn together in a split second in the same direction, has puzzled biologists and engendered some research. What is the stimulus for the flock to turn – is it one individual within the flock, a 'leader,' from which all the others take their 'orders'? Or is it a stimulus from outside the flock that all members respond to in the same way? And how are the turns coordinated? Everything from 'thought transference' to electromagnetic communication among flock members has been advanced as an explanation. After studying films of DUNLINS flying and turning in large flocks, one biologist suggested that the method birds within these flocks use to coordinate their turns is similar to the way people in a chorus line know the precise moment to raise their legs in sequence or how 'the wave' in a sports stadium is coordinated. That is, one bird, perhaps one that has detected some danger, such as a predatory falcon, starts a turn, and the other birds, seeing the start of the flock's turning, can then anticipate when it is their turn to do the same – the result being a dazzlingly quick wave of turning coursing through the flock. To acknowledge where he got it, the researcher called his idea the *chorus-line* hypothesis.

Birds are very hot animals, their body temperatures averaging around 40 °C (104 °F). Because of this, the temperature of the air around them, except in the world's hot deserts, will always be lower than their body temperature. Birds' feathers give them the insulation they need to maintain their high body temperature, but they lose heat from uninsulated parts of their bodies: their eyes, bill, and feet. The response of shorebirds to this heat-loss problem is easy to see. When they are not active, many of them will tuck their bill under their shoulder feathers, pull one leg up within the body feathers, and close their eyes. They are not necessarily sleeping (if you watch them you will see an eye open and close at intervals), but they are conserving heat. They also furnish much amusement to the human onlooker who sees one of them hopping rapidly down the beach on one leg, just to avoid putting that other leg out in the air. When you see a one-legged shorebird; it is very unlikely that it has lost the other leg; we have even seen them attempting to feed while hopping on one leg.

Status

Shorebirds were hunted for the pot at the end of the 19th and beginning of the 20th centuries, and many species had declined to obvious rarity before the Migratory Bird Treaty Act of 1918 was enacted into law. Signed by the United States and Great Britain (for Canada), the act gained real power when it was also signed by Mexico in 1936, thereby protecting all birds of North America. Sadly, it was perhaps too late for the ESKIMO CURLEW, a small curlew that bred on Arctic tundra and wintered on the pampas of southern South America. While the AMERICAN GOLDEN-PLOVER, BUFF-BREASTED SANDPIPER, and other species with similar distribution and migration routes recovered from the market hunting, the curlew did not, and it is either extinct or so rare that years go by with no definite sighting.

The fact that shorebirds are so picky about where they stop in migration makes it obvious that an environmental catastrophe at even one of a species' major stop-over sites would not bode well for that species. In other words, even a very abundant species can be at risk if its populations are highly concentrated at any time of the year.

Profiles

Black-bellied Plover, *Pluvialis squatarola*, Plate 34a
Snowy Plover, *Charadrius alexandrinus*, Plate 34b
Wilson's Plover, *Charadrius wilsonia*, Plate 34c
Semipalmated Plover, *Charadrius semipalmatus*, Plate 34d
Killdeer, *Charadrius vociferus*, Plate 34e
American Oystercatcher, *Haematopus palliatus*, Plate 34f
Marbled Godwit, *Limosa fedoa*, Plate 35a
Black-necked Stilt, *Himantopus mexicanus*, Plate 35b
Greater Yellowlegs, *Tringa melanoleuca*, Plate 35c
Lesser Yellowlegs, *Tringa flavipes*, Plate 35d
American Avocet, *Recurvirostra americana*, Plate 35e
Willet, *Catoptrophorus semipalmatus*, Plate 35f

Spotted Sandpiper, *Actitis macularia*, Plate 36a
Sanderling, *Calidris alba*, Plate 36b
Least Sandpiper, *Calidris minutilla*, Plate 36c
Semipalmated Sandpiper, *Calidris pusilla*, Plate 36d
Western Sandpiper, *Calidris mauri*, Plate 36e
Solitary Sandpiper, *Tringa solitaria*, Plate 36f
Dunlin, *Calidris alpina*, Plate 37a
Short-billed Dowitcher, *Limnodromus griseus*, Plate 37b
Long-billed Dowitcher, *Limnodromus scolopaceus*, Plate 37c
Red Knot, *Calidris canutus*, Plate 37d
Common Snipe, *Gallinago gallinago*, Plate 37e
Ruddy Turnstone, *Arenaria interpres*, Plate 37f

9. Gulls, Terns, and Skimmers

The family Laridae contains 105 species, including eight *jaegers* and *skuas*, 50 *gulls*,
44 *terns*, and three *skimmers*. Florida's waters are inhabited by 4 jaegers and skuas,
16 gulls, 14 terns, and a skimmer, although 13 of these 35 species are very rarely
seen in the state. Terns, on the average, are distributed more in the tropics than
are gulls and jaegers, so they are more prominent in Florida than in other parts
of North America. Members of this family (called *larids* as a group) are long-
winged, long-distance fliers; the ARCTIC TERN has the longest migration route of
any bird. Jaegers and skuas are brown or brown and white. Most adult gulls and
terns are gray and white, with bright colors restricted to their eyerings, bills, and
legs (sometimes very bright). Gulls typically have either an all-white or an all-dark
head in breeding plumage, while many terns have a black cap in that plumage.
Terns (and *noddies*, which are a type of tern) are generally smaller and more
slender-bodied than gulls, with more buoyant flight. Jaegers and skuas, because of
their heavy, hooked bills, brown coloration, and predatory nature, seem allied to
the hawks and eagles, but in fact they are very closely related to the gulls.

Natural History

Ecology and Behavior

The members of this bird family are mostly fish-eaters. Terns dive for their fish.
They fly well above the water surface and watch for prey, often hovering in one
place to get a better view, then plunge their entire body into the water, beak-first,
to capture the fish. Then they take off, get rid of much of their water load with a

vigorous shake, quickly flip the fish around to swallow it headfirst or carry it crosswise in their bill to bring it to hungry young birds. Some terns, while on their freshwater breeding grounds, pick insects from the surface. Skimmers are close relatives of terns, but they have adopted a very different feeding method. They fly slowly along the water's surface with their very long lower mandible slicing through the water. When they contact a fish, the upper mandible closes immediately, the skimmer lifts higher in the air and swallows the fish, then returns its knifelike bill to the surface. A human observer can't help but be amused when the skimmer hits a submerged stick and its head rotates it up into the air; but the skimmer, unfazed, goes right back to feeding. BLACK SKIMMERS (Plate 38) often feed at night, when they have been seen running into a utility wire, doing a complete 360° somersault around the wire, and carrying on! Gulls also dive into the water for fish, but they don't usually go as deep as terns, and they often pick their prey from the surface. Gulls are much more variable in foraging behavior than the rather conservative terns; in addition to fish, they eat dead animals floating on the sea surface or on the beach, hunt for invertebrates by walking around in the intertidal zone (they have longer legs than their relatives), follow plows to pick up unearthed worms and grubs, and use all sorts of other human activities as food sources (see below).

Kleptoparasitic behavior (one animal taking prey from another) is common in gulls and terns. A tern that has been unsuccessful in foraging may harass another tern carrying a fish until it drops it; and gulls perform this sort of behavior all the time, not only on smaller species but on their own. It is easy to observe this wherever gulls are fed by humans, either on purpose or as a consequence of our propensities for producing garbage. Around fish-processing plants, fishing boats, garbage dumps, and even drive-in restaurants, large gulls such as HERRING GULLS (Plate 38) hang around and gather up waste, and they seem to spend as much time chasing one another for tidbits as they do finding their own. In fact, the energy spent by a bunch of gulls chasing one with food in its bill seems far out of proportion to the energy gained by stealing the item – especially when it makes the thief the object of another chase! LAUGHING GULLS (Plate 38) are conspicuous kleptoparasites when Brown Pelicans are feeding (see that species, p. 107). Jaegers and skuas (offshore visitors to Florida) are consummate kleptoparasites, gaining much of their food that way while at sea.

Breeding

All members of the larid family practice *courtship feeding*, in which the male presents a recently caught fish to the female with which he will breed. This ritual not only makes and strengthens the pair bond but also gives the female extra metabolic energy to put into her developing eggs. The eggs growing within the female's body may make her too heavy and slow to be a successful predator, so courtship feeding by the male may sometimes be very important in providing nutrition to breeding females. Courtship behavior in gulls and terns involves much calling. Courtship in terns is especially spectacular. Members of a pair, next to one another, fly higher and higher and then come swooping down in a long, spiral flight with depressed wings, a *pas de deux* with no music other than the sounds of the sea and the birds' own voices. Gull courtship occurs on the ground and involves movements of the head, with bows and head-ups and choking motions; the long, loud calls of courting males ring through the colony at the height of the mating season. Jaeger courtship is rather similar to that of gulls, with fewer vocalizations.

In most members of this group, the nest is an open cup on the ground, usually lined with whatever plant material is available. At lower latitudes, most gulls and terns breed in colonies on islands, where they are safe from ground predators. Arctic-nesting species breed as solitary pairs on the open tundra, where visibility is such that they can see predators approaching from far away and, if necessary, leave their nest in time to avoid the nest being located. BONAPARTE'S GULLS (Plate 38) breed in forested areas at the edge of small lakes. They build somewhat flimsy stick nests in trees, probably because, being white and very conspicuous, they would be subject to intense nest predation if they nested on the ground. Jaegers lay 2 eggs, gulls and terns typically 3, but many tropical-island-breeding species such as SOOTY TERNS (Plate 22) and BROWN NODDIES (Plate 22), both of which breed in large numbers at the Dry Tortugas, lay only one; they have to fly long distances to find food, and it is impossible for them to feed more than one young. Perhaps to get some shade, Brown Noddies build their nest of small sticks up in shrubs; Sooty Terns nest out in the open in the intense tropical sun and must shade their eggs at all times to avoid them being fried. Incubation is for 23 to 28 days in jaegers, 23 to 30 days in gulls, and 20 to 38 days in Florida terns. Larids protect their nests vigorously, diving on approaching predators and hitting them from behind with strong feet. They react the same way to human intruders, and the only ways you can protect yourself are to wear a floppy hat or keep your eyes on the approaching birds; they won't hit you from the front. After one aggressive experience with a large gull, you'll never forget it. Even delicate terns, when they hit you, typically elicit four-letter Anglo-Saxon words such as 'ouch.'

All of these birds have *semiprecocial* young. They are fluffy and alert soon after hatching, but unlike the precocial young of shorebirds and waterfowl, which leave the nest area quickly after hatching, larid young remain at or very near the nest and are fed by the adults for up to two or three months, until they are well able to fly. These birds often breed in large colonies, and the young, especially of terns, often associate in large groups away from the nests. How do adults recognize their own young and vice versa? It is all vocal; an adult coming in with fish begins to call, and its own chicks answer it from the group. They all sound about the same to us, but apparently not to each other. Gulls and especially terns follow their parents around for weeks after they fledge, often able to cajole a feeding out of them, and terns have even been seen feeding young on their wintering grounds, months after leaving the nesting area.

Ecological Interactions
Although jaegers, gulls, and terns are closely related, they don't usually have amicable relationships with one another. Kleptoparasitism has already been discussed, but predation also occurs, by jaegers and gulls on tern chicks and eggs. On the North Atlantic coast of North America, HERRING GULLS nearly wiped out colonies of small terns before gull-control programs reduced gull populations on and around the tern nesting islands. These programs have remained ongoing, to protect both terns and Atlantic Puffins from the double hazards of kleptoparasitism and predation.

Lore and Notes
Gulls are smart birds, no doubt about it; they have to be to compete with crows to take advantage of human largesse. This can best be seen in parking lots of grocery stores and restaurants, where an open dumpster attracts flocks of these birds,

vying for edible bits of garbage. The ensuing squabbles give insights into bird behavior – the advantages of large size, the dominance of adults over immatures, types of aggressive displays, and the different behavior styles of different species. Some people, of course, would rather watch avian interactions in more pleasant surroundings. Both gulls and crows have learned to pick up clams from the shoreline, fly up with them to heights of 10 m (33 ft) or so, then drop them on rocks until they break open. Gulls must be delighted with all the jetties, bridges, roads, and parking lots that we have added to their environments, because they use all of these as clam-smashers. Immature gulls go through a learning period during which they become able to distinguish a hard asphalt road from a soft sandy beach.

Status

Gulls are among the most successful of birds, especially the larger species, as they have learned to coexist with and even take advantage of human populations. The rarest gulls and terns of the world (none of which breed in Florida) have specialized breeding habitats that may be in short supply. Florida's only breeding gull, the LAUGHING GULL, breeds all along the coast and will be successful as long as the state retains nesting islands as sanctuaries. LEAST TERNS (Plate 39) have made up for the loss of some of their nesting beaches by breeding widely around the state on gravel roofs. The Dry Tortugas, home to a number of terns that breed nowhere else in the USA, are well protected, and the species there probably have only two potential problems: oil spills, and climatic changes that might decimate populations of common small prey fishes. The ROSEATE TERN (Plate 39) is the only member of this family that is USA ESA listed in Florida, and it is considered Threatened in the state, with a small nesting population scattered around the Lower Keys, probably Caribbean in origin.

Profiles

Bonaparte's Gull, *Larus philadelphia*, Plate 38a
Laughing Gull, *Larus atricilla*, Plate 38b
Ring-billed Gull, *Larus delawarensis*, Plate 38c
Herring Gull, *Larus argentatus*, Plate 38d
Great Black-backed Gull, *Larus marinus*, Plate 38e
Black Skimmer, *Rynchops niger*, Plate 38f
Roseate Tern, *Sterna dougallii*, Plate 39a
Least Tern, *Sterna antillarum*, Plate 39b
Forster's Tern, *Sterna forsteri*, Plate 39c
Sandwich Tern, *Sterna sandvicensis*, Plate 39d
Caspian Tern, *Sterna caspia*, Plate 39e
Royal Tern, *Sterna maxima*, Plate 39f
Sooty Tern, *Sterna fuscata*, Plate 22c
Brown Noddy, *Anous stolidus*, Plate 22d

10. Pigeons and Doves

The *pigeon* and *dove* family, Columbidae, is a highly successful group, represented, often in large numbers, almost everywhere on dry land, except for Antarctica and some oceanic islands. There are 313 species in this family, and they inhabit almost all kinds of habitats, from semi-deserts to tropical moist forests, to high-elevation mountainsides. Their continued ecological success must be viewed as at least somewhat surprising, because pigeons are largely defenseless creatures and quite edible, regarded as a tasty entree by human and an array of nonhuman predators. Smaller species generally are called doves, larger ones pigeons, but there is a good amount of overlap in name assignments. They are quite diverse in tropical latitudes, but Florida, at the edge of the tropics, has only three native species, the WHITE-CROWNED PIGEON, MOURNING DOVE, and COMMON GROUND-DOVE (all Plate 40). Because pigeons and doves have been introduced widely around the world by people to lands where they are not native, there are two additional species in Florida, the ROCK DOVE (domestic pigeon) from Europe and WHITE-WINGED DOVE (Plate 40) from the American Southwest. Furthermore, the EURASIAN COLLARED-DOVE (Plate 40) is a recent immigrant from the Bahamas, into which it was introduced from Europe. Additionally, five pigeons from the Caribbean and one from western North America are or have been rare visitors to the state.

All pigeons are generally recognized as such by almost everyone, a legacy of people's familiarity with domestic pigeons. Doves and pigeons are plump-looking birds with compact bodies, short legs, short necks, and small heads. Bills are small, straight, and slender. Typically there is a conspicuous patch of naked skin, or *cere*, over the nostrils at the base of the bill. Although many of the Old World pigeons are easily among the most brightly colored of birds (Polynesia's MANY-COLORED FRUIT-DOVE, for instance), the New World varieties generally feature understated grays and browns in their plumage, although a few also have white patches in their wings or bold patterns of black spots. Many have splotches of iridescence, especially on necks and wings. In the majority of species, male and female are generally alike in size and color, although females are often a bit duller than the males.

Natural History
Ecology and Behavior
Most pigeons are at least partly arboreal, as are fruit-doves, but most of the smaller doves are ground-dwellers. Our familiar ROCK DOVE lives in cliffs naturally, so it is not surprising it takes so well to buildings and bridges, nesting on narrow ledges. Pigeons and doves eat primarily seeds and fruit, both ripe and unripe. Those species that forage on the ground move along the leaf-strewn forest floor or open field with the head-bobbing walk characteristic of their kind. Owing to their small, weak bills, they eat only what they can swallow whole; 'chewing' is accomplished in the *gizzard*, a muscular portion of the stomach in which food is mashed against small pebbles that are eaten by pigeons expressly for this purpose. This, and their liking for weed seeds, is why you see so many doves flying up from the roadside. Pigeons are strong, rapid flyers, which, along with their cryptic color patterns, provide their only defenses against predation. Most pigeons are gregarious to some degree, staying in groups during the non-breeding portion of the year; some gather into large flocks. Visitors to Central or South America from North America often are struck by the relative scarcity of sparrows; it is in large part the pigeons of the region that ecologically 'replace' sparrows as predominant seed-eaters.

Breeding
Pigeons are monogamous breeders. Some breed solitarily, others in colonies of various sizes. Nests are shallow, open affairs of woven twigs, plant stems, and roots, placed on the ground, on rock ledges, or in shrubs or trees. Reproductive

duties are shared by male and female. This includes nest-building, incubating the 1 or 2 eggs, and feeding the young, which they do by regurgitating food into the nestlings' mouths. All pigeons, male and female, feed their young *pigeon's milk*, a nutritious fluid produced in the *crop*, an enlargement of the esophagus used for food storage. During the first few days of life, nestlings receive 100% pigeon's milk, but as they grow older, they are fed an increasing proportion of regurgitated solid food. Incubation time ranges from 11 to 28 days, depending on species size. Nestlings spend from 11 to 36 days in the nest. Parent pigeons of some species give *distraction displays* when potential predators approach their eggs or young; they feign injury as they move away from the nest, luring the predator away.

Ecological Interactions

The great success of the pigeon family – a worldwide distribution, robust populations, the widespread range and enormous numbers of ROCK DOVES – is puzzling to ecologists. At first glance, pigeons have little to recommend them as the fierce competitors any hugely successful group needs to be. They have weak bills and therefore are rather defenseless during fights and ineffectual when trying to stave off nest predators. (They do, however, have very loosely attached feathers, and many a predator has caught a dove and come away with nothing more than a mouthful of feathers – pfffft!) They are hunted by people for food. In several parts of the world they compete for seeds and fruit with parrots, birds with formidable bills, yet pigeons thrive in these regions and have spread to many more that are parrotless. To what do pigeons owe their success? First, to reproductive advantage. For birds of their sizes, they have relatively short incubation and nestling periods; consequently, nests are exposed to predators for relatively brief periods and, when nests fail, parents have adequate time to nest again before the season ends. At lower latitudes, many species breed more than once per year, and MOURNING DOVES in Florida may bring off up to five broods a year. Also, the ability of both sexes to produce pigeon's milk (see above) to feed young may be an advantage over having to forage for particular foods for the young. Second, their ability to capitalize on human alterations of the environment points to a high degree of hardiness and adaptability, valuable traits in a world in which people make changes to habitats faster than most organisms can respond with evolutionary changes of their own.

Status

Pigeons and doves in most parts of the world are common, even abundant birds. Some species have even benefited from people's alterations of natural habitats, expanding their ranges, for example, where forests are cleared for agriculture – the MOURNING DOVE is a good example. But a number of New World and Old World pigeons are threatened or endangered, mostly from a combination of habitat loss (generally forest destruction), reduced reproductive success owing to introduced nest predators, and excessive hunting. Many currently threatened birds are restricted to islands, and several pigeons fall into this category; in fact, of the 10 pigeon species known to have become extinct during the past 200 years, 9 were island-bound.

North America's PASSENGER PIGEON, a medium-sized, long-tailed member of the family, suffered dramatic extinction. Because of its habits of roosting, breeding, and migrating in huge flocks, it was easy for people to kill many thousands of them at a time, shipping the bodies to markets and restaurants in large cities through the mid-1800s. It is estimated that when Europeans first settled in the New World, there were more than five billion Passenger Pigeons, a population size perhaps never equaled by any other bird, and that they may have accounted for up to 25% or more of the birds in what is now the USA. It took only a bit more than 100 years to kill them all; the last one died in the Cincinnati Zoo in 1914. In addition to the horrendous toll taken on their populations, their commitment to colonial breeding may have doomed them, as populations fell to such low numbers that birds couldn't form colonies. But it is oversimplification to blame hunting and coloniality entirely for the demise of this splendid bird. One of its most important foods was the beech nut, an abundant food source because beech trees dominated forests all across the northeastern USA. These forests were cut down surprisingly quickly after European settlement, and it is now thought that the loss both of large trees in which to nest and of beech nuts on which to feed also hastened the end of the Passenger Pigeon.

Profiles
White-crowned Pigeon, *Columba leucocephala*, Plate 40a
Eurasian Collared-Dove, *Streptopelia decaocto*, Plate 40b
Mourning Dove, *Zenaida macroura*, Plate 40c
White-winged Dove, *Zenaida asiatica*, Plate 40d
Common Ground-Dove, *Columbina passerina*, Plate 40e

11. Parrots

Everyone knows *parrots* as caged pets, so discovering them for the first time in their natural surroundings is often a strange but somehow familiar experience (like a dog-owner's first sighting of a wild coyote). One has knowledge and expectations of the birds' behavior and antics in captivity, but how do they act in the wild? Along with toucans, parrots are probably the birds most symbolic of the tropics. The 360 parrot species that comprise the family Psittacidae (the 'p' is silent) are globally distributed across the tropics, with some species extending into subtropical and even temperate areas, and with a particularly diverse and abundant presence in the Neotropical and Australian regions. The *psittacids* one sees in Florida represent successful introductions; none of them is a native. Of over 60 species of parrots that have been seen outside of cages in the state, 7 appear to be naturalized at present, but their numbers wax and wane. Florida has a persistent parrot presence, and visitors can expect to see these tropical creatures, especially in the southern part of the state. The 3 species profiled here are among the most likely to be seen. Parrots in the tropics are most numerous in forested lowland areas, but the introduced and naturalized species in Florida are commonly associated with suburban areas with abundant fruit trees. They roost in groups in traditional trees, so the best way to see them is to find out where they roost and be there early morning or late afternoon.

Consistent in form and appearance, all parrots are easily recognized as such. They share a group of traits that set them apart from all other birds. Their typically short neck and compact body yield a form variously described as stocky, chunky, or bulky, although the long-tailed ones look distinctly more elegant. All possess a short, hooked, bill – surprisingly hawklike – with a hinge on the upper mandible that permits great mobility and leverage during feeding. They use this *prehensile maxilla* even for climbing, as you can easily see in the nearest pet store if you have no parrots in your neighborhood. Finally, their legs are short, and their feet, with two toes projecting forward and two back, are adapted for powerful grasping and a high degree of dexterity – more so than any other bird. The basic parrot color scheme is green, but some species, especially among the macaws and lories, depart from basic in spectacular fashion, with gaudy blues, reds, and yellows. Green parrots feeding quietly amid a tree's high foliage can be impossible to see, even for experienced birdwatchers. Male and female parrots usually look alike or nearly so. Ornithologists name parrots by size: *parrotlets* are small birds (as small as 10 cm, or 4 in) with short tails; *parakeets* are also small, with long or short tails; *parrots* are medium-sized, usually with short tails; and *macaws* are large (up to 1 m, or 40 in) and long-tailed. Don't worry if not every species is 'correctly' named.

Natural History
Ecology and Behavior

Parrots are noisy, highly social seed and fruit eaters, flocks of them heading in mornings for feeding areas and back to their night roosts in the evening. A first encounter may be when a raucous, squawking flock takes flight explosively from a forest tree heavily laden with fruit, or, in Florida, from a similar tree in a park or backyard. Parrots are almost always encountered in flocks, even up to dozens of birds. The flocks are made up of many mated pairs, and these pairs are usually quite noticeable as the birds fly from tree to tree. In flight, parrots are easily identified by their family-specific silhouette: thick bodies, big heads, and short, rounded wings distinctly arched downward; tails may be short or long. Parrots generally are not considered strong flyers, but flocks twisting and turning through the trees appear to be moving very rapidly, their shrill calls echoing in the air after they have disappeared. Most do not need to undertake long-distance flights; they are fairly sedentary in their habits, with some regular movements as they follow the seasonal progressions of fruit ripening and flower blossoming.

Parrots use their special locomotory talent to clamber methodically through trees in search of seeds, fruits, and flowers (the lories of the Australian region are nectar-feeders), using their powerful feet to grasp branches and their bills as, essentially, a third foot. Just as caged parrots, they will hang at odd angles and even upside down, the better to reach some delicious morsel. Parrot feet also function as hands, delicately manipulating food and bringing it to the bill. Parrots feed mostly on fruits and nuts, buds of leaves and flowers, and on flower parts and nectar. They are usually considered frugivores, but careful study reveals that when they attack fruit, it is usually to get at the seeds within. The powerful bill slices open fruit and crushes seeds. As one bird book colorfully put it, 'adapted for opening hard nuts, biting chunks out of fruit, and grinding small seeds into meal, the short, thick, hooked parrot bill combines the destructive powers of an ice pick (the sharp-pointed upper mandible), a chisel (the sharp-edged lower mandible), a file (ridged inner surface of the upper mandible), and a vise' (F. Stiles and A. Skutch 1989). Thick, muscular parrot tongues are also specialized for feeding, used to scoop out pulp from fruit and nectar from flowers.

Bear in mind that the usual thought of parrots as tropical forest birds is dispelled on visiting Australia, where the great array of species varies from white to black and all colors of the rainbow in between, and you will see more species in open country than in forests. Our familiar pet-store BUDGERIGAR, one of the species established in Florida, comes from Australia. Budgerigars inhabit the dry center of the continent, where they move about in large flocks hunting grass seeds, more like a finch than a classical parrot.

Breeding

Parrots can teach us a lot. Parrot mating is monogamous, parrot pairing is usually for life, and parrot lives are lengthy! Breeding is very poorly documented for the established species in Florida, but most nesting has been seen in the spring. Parrots typically breed in cavities, most commonly in dead trees but also in holes in earth banks or the ground itself, and some species in termite nests. Very few build exposed nests, but the MONK PARAKEET (Plate 41) builds a huge communal stick nest, each of several pairs having their own 'apartment' in it. A female parrot lays 2 to 8 eggs, which she incubates alone for 17 to 35 days while being periodically fed regurgitated food by her mate. The helpless young of small parrots are nest-bound for 3 to 4 weeks, those of the huge macaws, 3 to 4 months. Both parents feed nestlings and fledglings.

Ecological Interactions

Many fruit-eating birds are fruit seed dispersers, but apparently not so parrots. Their strong bills crush seeds, and the contents are digested. For example, in one study in southern Central America, an ORANGE-CHINNED PARAKEET was examined after it fed all morning at a fig tree. It had in its digestive tract about 3500 fig seeds, almost all of which were broken, cracked, or already partially digested. Therefore, the main ecological interaction between parrots and at least some fruit trees is that of seed predator. Because parrots eat fruit and seeds, they are attracted to farms and orchards and in some areas are considered agricultural pests, with implications for their future populations (see below). Some species, in fact, have had population explosions when introduced into areas with fruit plantations. Macaws and other parrots often congregate at *licks*, exposed riverbank or streamside clay deposits. The clay that is eaten may help detoxify harmful compounds that are consumed in their seed, fruit and leaf diet, or may supply essential minerals that are not provided by a vegetarian diet. Some ecotour destinations are based on lick locations, e.g., in Peru and Bolivia, where visitors reliably find parrots to watch at traditional clay licks.

Lore and Notes

Parrots have been captured for people's pleasure as pets for thousands of years. Greek records exist from 400 BC describing parrot pets. Ancient Romans wrote of training parrots to speak and even of how they acted when drunk! The fascination stems from the birds' bright coloring, their ability to imitate human speech and other sounds, their individualistic personalities (captive parrots definitely like some people and dislike others), and their long life spans (up to 80 years in captivity). Likewise, parrots have been hunted and killed for food and to protect crops for thousands of years. Some Peruvian Inca pottery shows scenes of parrots eating corn and being scared away from crops. Charles Darwin noted that in Uruguay in the early 1800s, thousands of parakeets were killed to prevent crop damage. Macaws, the largest parrots, are thought to have been raised in the past for food in the West Indies; their feathers have been used as ornaments and have had ceremonial functions, and the same is true of lorikeets in New Guinea.

Status

About 90 parrot species are considered vulnerable, threatened, or endangered worldwide. Hunted intensively for the pet trade and for sport, they have been reduced in many tropical countries, and some island species have gone extinct. None of the parrots in Florida is native, but the state once did have a native parrot, the CAROLINA PARAKEET. At one time found all over Florida and much of eastern USA, the bird was gone by 1910, perhaps, like the Passenger Pigeon, a victim of overhunting, habitat destruction, and its own sociality. Parrots are subject to three powerful forces that, in combination, take heavy tolls on their numbers: they are primarily forest birds, and forests are increasingly under attack by farmers and developers; they are considered agricultural pests by farmers and orchardists owing to their seed and fruit eating, and are persecuted for this reason; and they are among the world's most popular cage birds. Without additional protection, more and more of the world's parrots will probably soon be threatened.

Profiles

Monk Parakeet, *Myiopsitta monachus*, Plate 41a
Yellow-chevroned Parakeet, *Brotogeris chiriri*, Plate 41b
White-winged Parakeet, *Brotogeris versicolorus*, Plate 41c

12. Cuckoos

Many of the *cuckoos* and *anis* ('AH-neez') are physically rather plain but behaviorally rather extraordinary: as a group they employ some of the most bizarre breeding practices known among birds. Cuckoos and anis are both included in the cuckoo family, Cuculidae, which, with a total of 143 species, enjoys a worldwide distribution in temperate and tropical areas. Five species occur in Florida – three cuckoos and two anis. Cuckoos are mainly shy, solitary birds of forests, woodlands, and dense thickets. Anis are the opposite: gregarious animals that spend their time in small flocks in savannahs, brushy scrub, and other open areas. Anis are among those birds that make one wonder where they perched before the advent of fences. A notable relative of the cuckoos and anis is a common ground bird of scrub desert areas of Mexico and southwestern USA, the GREATER ROADRUNNER of cartoon fame.

Most cuckoos are medium-sized, slender, long-tailed birds. Males and females mostly look alike, attired in plain browns, reddish browns, and grays, sometimes with streaked or spotted upperparts. Commonly, cuckoos have conspicuous alternating white and black bands on the underside of their tail. Old World cuckoos are more diverse and more colorful than those in the New World, some of them with brightly colored skin around the eyes or large patches of bright rufous; there are even iridescent black and metallic green species. Cuckoos have short legs and bills that curve downwards at the end. Anis are conspicuous medium-sized birds, glossy black all over, with iridescent sheens particularly on the head, neck and breast. Their bills are exceptionally large and keeled above.

Natural History
Ecology and Behavior

Most cuckoos are arboreal, but roadrunners and anis feed on the ground. All members of the family eat insects, apparently having a special fondness for caterpillars. They even safely consume hairy caterpillars, which are avoided by most potential predators because they taste bad or contain sickness-causing noxious compounds. Cuckoos have been observed to snip off one end of the hairy thing, squeeze the body in the bill until the noxious entrails fall out, then swallow the harmless remainder. They may also beat the caterpillar on a limb until its hairs come off. Many of the larger ground-dwelling cuckoos eat vertebrates such as small lizards and snakes as well as insects, and roadrunners even take small birds when they can catch them.

The highly social anis forage in groups. Frequently they feed around cattle, grabbing the insects that are flushed out of hiding places by the grazing mammals. They eat mostly insects, but also a bit of fruit. Anis live in groups of 8 to 25 individuals, each group containing 2 to 8 adults and several juveniles. Each group defends a territory from other groups throughout the year. The flock both feeds and breeds within its territory.

Breeding

Cuckoos are known in most parts of the world for being *brood parasites*, although only about 50 of the species should be so categorized. Brood parasites build no nests of their own, and the females lay their eggs in the nests of other species. These other birds often raise the young cuckoos as their own offspring, usually to the significant detriment of their own, often smaller, young. Many of the parasitic cuckoos lay their eggs in the nests of *host* species that are much smaller than they are. The result is that the host parents often end up bringing food to the nest to feed cuckoo nestlings that are not only much larger than their own offspring (who cannot compete for food against the larger cuckoos and starve), but which may be much larger than the parents themselves – a phenomenon that provides a never-ending stream of striking photographs in biology books.

Most brood-parasitic cuckoos occur in the Old World, and those occurring in Florida do not practice this habit but are instead typically monogamous breeders. The male feeds the female in courtship, especially during her egg-laying period. Both sexes build the plain platform nest that is made of twigs and leaves and placed in a tree or shrub. Both sexes incubate the 2 to 6 eggs for about 10 days (their short incubation period is typical of their brood-parasite relatives, allowing their eggs to hatch first and their young to dominate the nest), and both parents feed the young. In several species, the young hop out of the nest before they have been flight-certified, to spend the several days before they can fly flopping around in the vegetation near the nest, being fed by their parents.

Anis, consistent with their highly social ways, are *communal breeders*. In the most extreme form, all the individuals within the group contribute to a single nest, several females laying eggs in it; up to 29 eggs in one nest have been noted. Many individuals help build the stick nest and feed the young. Although at first glance it would seem as if all benefit by having the group breed together, females contributing eggs to a common nest which all build, defend and tend, actually it is the dominant male and female within each group that gain most. Their eggs go in the nest last, on top of the others that sometimes become buried. Also, some females roll others' eggs out of the nest before they lay their own; thus, it pays to lay last. In some species, several nests are built by pairs within the group's territory. Ani breeding usually occurs during the wet season, when insects are most abundant.

Lore and Notes

YELLOW-BILLED CUCKOOS (Plate 41) are often called 'rain crows,' because their loud calls may herald a coming storm. The *kakakakakaka-kow-kow-kow-kow-kow-kowp-kowp-kowp* ringing through the woods is a characteristic summer sound in Florida. The name *cuckoo* and the sound of the cuckoo clock come from the calls made by a common member of the family, the EUROPEAN CUCKOO.

Status

None of the cuckoos or anis that occur in Florida is currently considered threatened, but the SMOOTH-BILLED ANI (Plate 41) went from a relatively rare bird to a fairly common and widespread resident of southern Florida in historic times, then its fortunes reversed for some reason, and it has become quite uncommon again. Population surges such as this are well known in birds but not always well understood.

Profiles

Yellow-billed Cuckoo, *Coccyzus americanus*, Plate 41d
Mangrove Cuckoo, *Coccyzus minor*, Plate 41e
Smooth-billed Ani, *Crotophaga ani*, Plate 41f

13. Owls

Although some *owls* are common Florida birds, most of them are *nocturnal*, active at night, and so are rarely seen. One species of regular occurrence, the BURROWING OWL (Plate 42), is often seen during the day, and sharp-eyed observers regularly spot roosting BARRED OWLS (Plate 42) along trails through forested areas. Most owls are members of the family Strigidae, a worldwide group of 156 species; the only other owls are 17 species of the barn owl family, Tytonidae. Florida has a moderate number of owls, with six regularly occurring species and three rare visitors. Owls are readily recognized as such because of several distinctive features. All have large heads with forward-facing eyes; small, hooked bills; plumpish-looking bodies because of their large, fluffy feathers; and sharp, hooked claws. Most have short legs and short tails. Owls are clad mostly in mixtures of gray, brown, black, and white, the result being that they are highly camouflaged against a variety of backgrounds. Males and females look alike, although females are a bit larger.

Natural History

Ecology and Behavior

Most owls are forest dwellers, but there are a few species in tundra, grassland, and marshes. They are considered to be the nocturnal equivalents of the day-active birds of prey – the hawks, eagles, and falcons (p. 118). Most owls hunt at night, taking prey such as small mammals, birds (including smaller owls), and reptiles; smaller owls specialize on insects, earthworms, and other small invertebrates. You may see owls during the daytime in Florida, but very few of them will be hunting; even BURROWING OWLS, often spotted at the mouth of their burrow, usually wait until dark to forage. Owls hunt by sight and by sound. Their vision is very good in low light, the amount given off by moonlight, for instance, and their hearing is remarkable. They can hear sounds that are much lower in sound intensity (softer) than can most other birds, and their ears are positioned on their heads asymmetrically, the better for localizing sounds in space. This means that owls in the darkness can hear small rodents moving about on the forest floor, quickly locate the source of the sound, then swoop and grab. Additionally, owing to their soft, loose feathers, the flight of owls is essentially silent, permitting prey little chance of hearing their approach.

Owls kill their prey by biting, much in the fashion of falcons. They swallow small prey whole, then instead of digesting or passing the hard bits, they regurgitate bones, feathers, and fur in compact *owl pellets*. These are often found at the base of trees where owls perch and, when pulled apart, tell the story of an owl's favored cuisine. In winter, some northern owls store prey for later consumption (that is, they *cache* it). For instance, a dead mouse might be placed in a clump of spruce needles, where it quickly freezes. To thaw it later, the owl will tuck the frozen mouse under its belly as if incubating an egg. Owls maintain territories that they defend by their deep hooting and higher-pitched whistled calls (hoots and toots). As might be expected in night birds, vocalizations as much as appearance serve to distinguish species.

Breeding

Owls are monogamous breeders. They do not build nests themselves, but they take over nests abandoned by other birds or nest on broken-off stumps or in cavities such as tree holes; a few small species have taken to nesting boxes. Incubation of the 1 to 10 or more eggs (often 2 to 4) is usually conducted by the female alone for 4 to 5 weeks, but she is fed by her mate. At first, the female broods the young while the male hunts and brings meals, then both feed the young as they grow larger. Because incubation begins soon after the first egg is laid, the eggs hatch in sequence, and a nest may include everything from an unhatched egg up to a two-week old chick. If the parents can bring in enough food, all the young survive, but if food is scarce, the smaller young, which don't beg as energetically as the older ones, don't get fed, and eventually starve to death. Female SNOWY OWLS have been seen feeding one of these freshly dead young to a larger sibling – the economy of nature. Because owl broods are often fairly large, the young in tree-cavity nests may have to leave them before they attain full size. The young climb out and hop onto nearby branches until they settle down on a preferred branch; they are called *branchers* at this point by students of owl biology. The parents continue to feed them until they are 4 to 6 weeks old.

Lore and Notes

Their big heads and forward-directed eyes give owls a peculiarly human look, and this, together with their habit of sitting still when we see them, rather than rushing about like chickadees and warblers, has given them a reputation for wisdom. But they're not especially wise – in most cases when we spot them, they've just been awakened from a sound sleep. The forward-facing eyes of owls are a trait shared with few other animals: humans, most other primates, and, to a degree, cats. Eyes arranged in this way allow for almost complete binocular vision (one eye sees the same thing as the other), a prerequisite for good depth perception, which, in turn, is important for quickly judging distances when catching prey and especially important when you're doing it at night. The very large eyes of owls (those of a GREAT HORNED OWL, Plate 42, being about the size of human eyes) take up so much space that the eyes cannot move much; thus, owls must swivel their heads to look left or right. An owl can turn its head over a very wide angle (more than 180 °), but, contrary to what you may have heard, it can't turn it around completely.

Owls have a reputation for fierce, aggressive defense of their young; many a human who ventured too near an owl nest has been attacked and had damage done. A book by the famous British bird photographer, Eric Hosking, is entitled *An Eye for a Bird*. Most readers don't realize that the title is a direct reference to losing an eye to a TAWNY OWL as Mr. Hosking was photographing a nesting pair.

Status
All Florida owls are secure, as far as we know, but owls *are* harder to keep track of than most birds. SHORT-EARED OWLS have inexplicably declined in parts of their North American range, perhaps because of the disappearance of both marshy wetlands and natural grasslands, their preferred habitats. BURROWING OWLS are probably the species of greatest concern in Florida, as their nesting sites in sandy soil are taken up by one housing development after another. They sometimes benefit by clearing of the land, but the benefit may be transient, ending when the plot of land is developed. Their nesting sites are carefully protected on various golf courses and university campuses, where they often attract some notoriety. The most famous owl from the standpoint of conservation in North America is, of course, the SPOTTED OWL, which usually requires for breeding large sections of undisturbed, old-growth forest and has diminished greatly with the logging of much of that forest in the Pacific Northwest.

Profiles
Barn Owl, *Tyto alba*, Plate 42a
Eastern Screech-Owl, *Megascops asio*, Plate 42b
Barred Owl, *Strix varia*, Plate 42c
Great Horned Owl, *Bubo virginianus*, Plate 42d
Burrowing Owl, *Athene cunicularia*, Plate 42e

14. Nightjars
Members of the family Caprimulgidae are known as *nightjars*, probably because the call of the first-named species, the EUROPEAN NIGHTJAR, is sufficiently loud to jar the silence of the night. In North America these birds have been called *goatsuckers*, although they certainly do not suck the milk of goats, as legend has it. Nightjars are a group of 79 species spread over most of the world's land masses. Their closest relatives are probably the owls, and some recent classification schemes place the two in the same avian order. There are three common nightjars in Florida and two rare ones; the ANTILLEAN NIGHTHAWK (Plate 43) is found only in the Keys, where it breeds sporadically.

Nightjars have a very characteristic appearance. They have relatively long wings, either rounded (most species) or pointed (the *nighthawks*), medium or long tails, and big eyes. Their small, stubby bill gives no hint of the huge mouth that they open in flight to scoop up flying insects. Many species have bristles around their mouth. They all have a comb on their middle toenail, probably to aid in preening, for which their bill is poorly suited. With their short legs and weak feet, they are poor walkers – flying is their usual mode of locomotion. The plumage of these birds is uniformly cryptic: mottled, spotted, and barred mixtures of browns, grays, tans, and black. They often have white patches on their wings or tails that can be seen only in flight.

Natural History
Ecology and Behavior
Most nightjars are night-active birds, with some, such as the nighthawks, becoming active at twilight (*crepuscular* is the term for such a habit). They feed on insects, which they catch on the wing, either with repeated forays from perched locations on the ground or on tree branches, or, as is the case with the COMMON NIGHTHAWK (Plate 43), with continuous, often circling flight.

Nightjars sometimes gather at night near bright lights to feast on the light-drawn insects. Because of their camouflage coloring, they are almost impossible to see when perched, and most of them are not seen during the day unless they are accidentally flushed from their roosting spots, which are either on the ground or on tree branches. They are unique in perching on tree branches with their body oriented parallel to the branch rather than across it.

Breeding

Nightjars breed monogamously. No nest is built. Rather, the female lays her one or two eggs on the ground, perhaps in a small depression in the soil under the branches of a tree, or on a rock or sandbar. Around human developments, COMMON NIGHTHAWKS are known for placing their eggs on bare, gravelly rooftops. In the Florida species, the female alone incubates for 19 to 21 days, and both parents feed insects to the young. Nightjars engage in *broken-wing displays* if their nest is approached by a predator or a person, and this behavior can be very distracting, just as intended. They flop about on the ground, often with one or both wings held out as if injured, making gargling or hissing sounds, all the while moving away from the nest. They also may jump toward the source of disturbance with open mouth and loud hissing – enough to make most people back off!

Lore and Notes

One of the nightjar family, North America's COMMON POORWILL, may be the only bird known actually to hibernate, as some mammals do, during very cold weather. During their dormant state, poorwills save energy by reducing their metabolic rate and their body temperature, the latter by about 22 °C (40 °F). The strange name of CHUCK-WILL'S-WIDOW (Plate 43) refers to the vocalization that this nightjar calls out repeatedly, night after night, during the warm Florida spring.

Status

None of the Florida nightjars are threatened, although the ANTILLEAN NIGHTHAWK has become less common in recent years, perhaps even excluded from some breeding territories by its close relative, the COMMON NIGHTHAWK, which has become more common in the Keys. In the New World, the WHITE-WINGED NIGHTJAR of Brazil and the PUERTO RICAN NIGHTJAR (USA ESA listed) occur in very limited areas and are endangered. The former is known from only a few old specimens and a few modern sightings in Central Brazil. Little is known about the bird, but the area of modern sightings falls within a national park, offering some hope for its survival. The Puerto Rican Nightjar occupies dry forest areas of southwestern Puerto Rico; only about 800 pairs remain.

Profiles

Chuck-will's-widow, *Caprimulgus carolinensis*, Plate 43a
Common Nighthawk, *Chordeiles minor*, Plate 43b
Antillean Nighthawk, *Chordeiles gundlachii*, Plate 43c

15. Hummingbirds

Hummingbirds are birds of extremes. They are among the most easily recognized kinds of birds – the smallest and undoubtedly among the most beautiful, albeit on a diminutive scale. Fittingly, much of their biology is nothing short of amazing. The hummingbirds comprise a large family, Trochilidae, with 322 species.

Hummingbirds are restricted to the New World and primarily to the tropics; although Florida is just about tropical, there are only two regularly occurring and five rare species in the state, and most of the rare species are stragglers from the West during migration. The variety of forms encompassed by the family, not to mention the brilliant iridescence of most of its members, is indicated in the names attached to some of the groups: emeralds, sapphires, sunangels, comets, metaltails, fairies, woodstars, pufflegs, sabrewings, thorntails, and lancebills. Although Florida species are primarily birds of woodland and suburbs, hummingbirds elsewhere occupy a broad array of habitat types, from exposed high mountainsides at 4000 m (13,000 ft) to mid-elevation deserts to sea level tropical forests and mangrove swamps, as long as there are nectar-filled flowers to provide necessary nourishment.

Almost everyone can identify hummingbirds: tiny birds, usually gorgeously clad in iridescent metallic greens, reds, and violets. Their name refers not to their musical activity (most merely say 'chip') but to the sound their wings make as the birds whiz by at high speeds. Most hummers are in the range of only 6 to 13 cm (2.5 to 5 in) long, although South America's GIANT HUMMINGBIRD reaches 20 cm (8 in). The smallest among them resemble nothing so much as large bees. Florida species weigh about 3 g (1/10 oz) – as light as a penny. Bill length and shape varies extensively among species, each bill closely adapted to the precise type of flowers from which a species draws its liquid food. Males are usually more colorful than females, and many of them have *gorgets*, bright, glittering throat patches in red, blue, green, or violet. Hummers have tiny legs and feet and are included with the swifts, another small-footed bunch, in the avian order Apodiformes.

Natural History
Ecology and Behavior

Owing to their many anatomical, behavioral, and ecological specializations, hummingbirds have long attracted the research attention of biologists; the result is that we know quite a bit about them. These highly active birds that are so entertaining to watch are most often studied for one of four aspects of their biology: flying ability, metabolism, feeding ecology, and defense of food resources.

(1) Hummers are capable of very rapid, finely controlled, acrobatic flight, more so than any other kind of bird. Their wings are modified to allow for perfect, stationary *hovering* flight and also for the unique ability to *fly backwards*. The secret to these maneuvers is the hummers' ability to rotate the wing on its own axis and thus get power on both the downstroke and upstroke. Their wings vibrate at a speed beyond our ability to see each stroke – up to 80 times per second. Because people usually see hummers only during the birds' foraging trips, they often appear never to land, remaining airborne as they zip from flower to flower, hovering briefly to probe and feed at each. But they do perch between flights, providing opportunities to get good looks at them.

(2) Hummingbirds have very high metabolisms, a necessary condition for small, warm-blooded animals. To pump enough oxygen and nutrient-delivering blood around their little bodies, their hearts beat up to 10 times faster than human hearts – 600 to 1000 times per minute. To obtain sufficient energy to fuel their high metabolism, hummingbirds must eat many times each day. Quick starvation results from an inability to feed regularly. At night, when they are inactive, they burn much of their available energy reserves, and on

cold nights, if not for special mechanisms, they would surely starve to death. The chief method to avoid energy depletion on cold nights is to enter into a sleep-like state of *torpor*, during which the body's temperature is lowered to just above that of the outside world, from 17 to 28 °C (30 to 50 °F) below their daytime operating temperatures, saving them enormous amounts of energy. In effect, they set the thermostat down and hibernate overnight.

(3) All hummingbirds are *nectarivores* – they get most of their nourishment from consuming nectar from flowers. They have long, thin bills and specialized tongues to suck nectar from long, thin flower tubes, which they do while hovering. Because nectar is mostly a sugar and water solution, hummingbirds need to obtain additional nutrients, such as proteins, from other sources. Toward this end they also eat small insects and spiders, which they catch in the air or pluck off spider webs.

(4) Hummers are typically highly aggressive birds, energetically defending individual flowers or feeding territories from all other hummingbirds, regardless of species. This is always size-mediated – large species are able to dominate small ones.

Predators on hummingbirds include small, agile hawks and also frogs and large insects, such as praying mantises, that ambush the small birds as they feed at flowers. Even large spider webs and sticky plant seeds sometimes catch hummingbirds. Another hazard, not so easy to document, is the long migration some species make between their breeding and wintering habitats. The RUBY-THROATED HUMMINGBIRD (Plate 43) migrates from eastern USA to the Caribbean and Central America and back, even crossing the wide expanse of the Gulf of Mexico.

Breeding
Hummingbirds are promiscuous breeders in which males attempt to mate with as many females as possible and females supply all the parental care. The following refers to the common Florida breeding species, the RUBY-THROATED. A male on his territory advertises for females by performing a wonderful oval display flight. He flies back and forth in an arc like a pendulum, making whirring sounds with his wings. A female enters the territory and, following an intense courtship display in which the male repeatedly buzzes her and may even drive her down to the ground, mates. Afterwards, she leaves the territory to nest on her own. Nests are placed on small horizontal branches of trees, usually within 6 m (20 ft) of the ground. On the outside, nests have a coating of lichens, which is carefully applied by the female and probably provides both camouflage and waterproofing. The female lays 2 eggs, incubates them for 11 to 16 days, and feeds regurgitated nectar and insects to her young for about 21 days, until they fledge.

Ecological Interactions
The relationship between hummingbirds (nectar consumers) and the flowering plants from which they feed (nectar producers) is mutually beneficial. The birds obtain a high-energy food that is easy to locate and always available because various flowering plant species, as well as groups of flowers on the same plant, open and produce nectar at different times. The flowering plants, in turn, use the tiny birds as other plants use bees – as pollinators. The nectar is produced and released into the part of the flower that the hummer feeds from for the sole reason of attracting the birds so that they may accidentally rub up against the parts of the

flower (anthers) that contain pollen grains. These grains are actually reproductive packets that the flower very much 'wants' the bird to pick up on its body and transfer to other plants of the same species during its subsequent foraging, thereby achieving for the flower cross-pollination with another member of its species. Flowers that are specialized for hummingbird pollination place nectar in long, thin tubes that fit the shape of the birds' bills and also protect the nectar from foraging insects. Hummingbird-pollinated plants often have red, pink, or orange flowers, colors that render them easily detectable to the birds but indistinguishable from the background environment to insects, most of which lack red color vision. Furthermore, these flowers are often odorless because birds use color vision and not smell to find them, and this prevents visits from inappropriate pollinating insects that use odor to guide them.

Lore and Notes

Hummingbirds have become more common in many areas, and many of them are extending their geographic ranges, because of hummingbird feeders. For example, numerous hummingbirds native to western North America have been found in Florida in winter, far from their normal breeding or winter range. To attract hummingbirds, boil a mixture of one part sugar to four parts water, fill a hummingbird feeder with the cooled liquid, hang it up somewhere, and the next hummer that flies by will stop without a doubt. Vacationers often take a hummingbird feeder with them to attract these animated little birds to their camp sites.

Status

Florida's hummingbirds are doing fine, prospering in part because so many people put out feeders for them, but many species in tropical countries are rare if not endangered. This is not surprising, considering that many species occur in limited geographic areas and choose forested habitats, where habitat destruction is rampant.

Profiles

Ruby-throated Hummingbird, *Archilochus colubris*, Plate 43d

16. Kingfishers

Kingfishers are bright-colored birds most often encountered along rivers and streams or along the seashore. Classified with the motmots, bee-eaters, and several other colorful tropical bird families in the order Coraciiformes, the 95 kingfisher species of the family Alcedinidae range throughout the tropics, with a few of them pushing deeply northward and southward into temperate areas. Only six kingfisher species reside in the New World, and only one of them makes it to Florida. Kingfishers are all of a similar form: large heads with long, robust, straight bills, short necks, short legs, and, for some, large, bushy crests. The kingfisher color scheme in the New World is also fairly standardized: dark green or blue-gray above, white and/or chestnut-orange below. Old World kingfishers are much more varied in size and shape, and, belying their names, many are terrestrial predators, feeding on insects and lizards in tropical forests and savannahs.

Natural History
Ecology and Behavior

Many kingfishers, as the name suggests, are fish eaters (that is, they are *piscivores*). Usually seen hunting alone near water, they sit quietly, attentively on a low perch

– a tree branch or a telephone wire – while scanning the water below. When they locate suitable prey, they swoop and dive, plunging head-first into the water (to depths of 60 cm, 24 in) to seize it. If successful, they quickly emerge from the water, return to the perch, beat the fish against the perch to stun it, then swallow it whole, head first. Thus, kingfishers are sit-and-wait predators of the waterways. They will also, when they see movement below the water, hover over a particular spot before diving in. BELTED KINGFISHERS (Plate 44) commonly fly out 500 m (a quarter mile) or more from a lake's shore to hover 3 to 10 m (10 to 33 ft) above the water, searching for fish. Kingfishers fly fast and purposefully, usually in straight and level flight, from one perch to another; often they are seen only as flashes of blue darting along waterways. Kingfishers are highly territorial, aggressively defending their territories from other members of their species with noisy, chattering vocalizations, chasing, and fighting.

Breeding

Kingfishers are monogamous breeders that nest in holes. In the BELTED KING-FISHER, both members of the pair defend the territory in which the nest is located, and both take turns digging the 1 to 2 m (3 to 6 ft) long nest burrow into the soft earth of a river or stream bank. In recent times, road excavations near water have become prime habitat for kingfisher nests. Both parents incubate the 6 or 7 eggs for a total of 22 to 24 days. The young are fed increasingly large fish by both parents until they fledge at 27 to 29 days old. Fledglings continue to be fed by the parents for another three weeks. At some point after they are independent, the parents expel the young from the territory. Many juvenile kingfishers apparently die during their first attempts at diving for food. Some have been seen 'practicing' predation by capturing floating leaves and sticks.

Lore and Notes

Kingfishers are the subject of a particularly rich mythology, a sign of the bird's conspicuousness and its association with water throughout history. In some parts of the world, kingfishers are associated with the biblical Great Flood. It is said that survivors of the flood had no fire and so the kingfisher was chosen to steal fire from the gods. The bird was successful, but during the theft, burned its chest, resulting in the chestnut-orange coloring we see today. According to the ancient Greeks, Zeus was jealous of Alcyone's power over the wind and waves and so killed her husband by destroying his ship with thunder and lightning. 'In her grief, Alcyone threw herself into the sea to join her husband, and they both turned immediately into kingfishers. The power that sailors attributed to Alcyone was passed on to the Halcyon Bird, the kingfisher, which was credited with protecting sailors and calming storms' (D. Boag 1982). Halcyon birds were thought to nest 7 days before and 7 days after the winter solstice, and these days of peace and calm were referred to as *halcyon days*.

Status

The BELTED KINGFISHER remains abundant throughout much of North America. None of the New World species is rare, but some kingfisher species on islands in the South Pacific are threatened by destruction of their forest habitats, and a few island populations have already become extinct.

Profiles

Belted Kingfisher, *Ceryle alcyon*, Plate 44a

17. Woodpeckers

We are all familiar with *woodpeckers*, at least in name and in their cartoon incarnations. These are industrious, highly specialized birds of the forest; where there are trees in the world, there are woodpeckers (excepting only Australia and some island groups). The woodpecker family, Picidae, includes 216 species, from the 9 cm (3.5 in) *piculets* to large woodpeckers up to 50 cm (20 in) long. Eight regularly occurring species and one rare species occur in Florida, and they occupy diverse wooded habitats. Woodpeckers have strong, straight, chisel-like bills, very long tongues that are barbed and often sticky-coated, and toes that spread widely, firmly anchoring the birds to tree trunks and branches. They come in various shades of black and white, brown, and olive-green, usually with small but conspicuous head or neck patches of red or yellow, more prominent in males. Some have red or brown crests. A few woodpeckers are quite showy, mostly in striking patterns of red, black, and white, and the RED-HEADED WOODPECKER (Plate 44) exemplifies this showiness. Because of the tapping sounds they produce as they hammer their bills against trees and wooden structures, and owing to their characteristic stance – braced upright on tree trunks – woodpeckers often attract our notice and so are frequently observed forest-dwellers.

Natural History

Ecology and Behavior

Woodpeckers are associated with trees and are adapted to cling to a tree's bark and to move lightly over its surface, searching for insects. They also drill holes in bark and wood into which they insert their long tongues, probing for hidden insects. They usually move up tree trunks in short hops, using their stiff tail as a prop. Woodpeckers find most of their insect prey on the surface or below the bark of twigs, branches, and trunks of many kinds of trees. They also are not above a bit of flycatching, taking insects on the wing, and many tropical species supplement their diets with fruits, nuts, and nectar. The YELLOW-BELLIED SAPSUCKER (Plate 44) uses its bill to drill small holes in trees that fill with sap, which is then eaten. Some woodpeckers, including the NORTHERN FLICKER (Plate 45), also forage on the ground, especially for ants.

Woodpeckers sleep and nest in cavities that they excavate in trees. They hit trees with their bills for three very different reasons: for drilling bark to get at insect food; for excavating holes for roosting and nesting; and for *drumming*, sending signals to other woodpeckers. The characteristic drumming sound, equivalent to the spring song of songbirds, is much more rapid than those steady or irregular taps that indicate feeding or digging a new home. Woodpeckers typically fly with a characteristic up-and-down (*undulating*) flight.

Breeding

Woodpeckers are monogamous, but some species live in family groups of up to a dozen or more birds. In the RED-COCKADED WOODPECKER (Plate 45), one or more males from the previous year's brood may join the pair to help raise their young; by doing this, a young male has a chance of inheriting a territory, perhaps a better life strategy than going out and attempting to find an unoccupied one in a limited habitat. A mated male and female woodpecker carve a nesting hole in a tree and typically line the cavity with wood chips. In Florida woodpeckers, both sexes incubate the 3 to 8 eggs for 12 to 18 days, males typically taking the entire night shift. Young are fed by both parents for 20 to 30 days until they fledge. Juveniles often remain with the parents for several months more, or longer in those species in which groups associate throughout the year.

Ecological Interactions

Woodpeckers are often used as examples of the evolutionary consequences of competitive interactions in nature. One way for ecologically similar species to avoid competition is to specialize on prey of different sizes. Woodpeckers, most of which forage on bark for insects, are very similar ecologically, and different-sized woodpeckers do indeed specialize on different-sized prey, thereby reducing the negative effects of competition. There are small (for instance, DOWNY WOODPECKER, Plate 45), medium-sized (NORTHERN FLICKER), and large (PILEATED WOODPECKER, Plate 45) woodpeckers. When there are two or more woodpecker species of about the same size inhabiting the same place, these potential competitors usually forage in different ways, or for different items – again, eliminating competition that could drive one of the species to extinction in the region in which they overlap. Where only one species is present, and intense competition is relaxed, the two sexes may diverge in bill length to allow them to exploit a greater breadth of resources. This is what has happened with the HISPANIOLAN WOODPECKER of the West Indies.

Woodpeckers use dead trees or dead branches in live trees for most of their foraging and nesting. Dead wood is softer than live, thus easier to chip away, and it is often infested with boring beetles. Woodpeckers are usually considered beneficial by people, because they consume great quantities of insects such as tree borers that can significantly damage forests. On the other hand, the persistent early-morning drumming of a Northern Flicker on the side or roof of a house can drive a home-owner to distraction.

Because other birds use tree holes for roosting and/or nesting, but do not or cannot dig holes themselves, sometimes the carpenter-like woodpeckers end up doing the work for them. Many species, ranging from swallows to small owls and small ducks, occupy deserted woodpecker holes. More problematically, some birds 'parasitize' the woodpecker's work by stealing holes. For instance, European Starlings, although smaller than flickers, have been observed evicting them, as well as other woodpeckers, from their nest holes. RED-BELLIED WOODPECKERS (Plate 44) appear to be better at resisting starlings than are RED-HEADED WOODPECKERS; the former has increased in recent years, while the latter has decreased.

Lore and Notes

Woodpeckers damage trees and buildings and also eat fruit from gardens and orchards (especially cherries, apples, pears, and raspberries) and so in some regions are considered significant pests and treated as such. Sapsuckers drill holes in living trees to eat the sap that flows from them and the insects attracted to fermenting sap, and enough sapsucker holes can lead to diseased and damaged trees. None of these species equaled for newsworthiness the male NORTHERN FLICKER at Cape Canaveral that continually drilled holes in what the bird must have thought was soft wood, but what was actually the hardened foam protective covering of an about-to-be-launched space shuttle's nose cone. The launch was delayed for several days while ornithologists and technicians figured out how to move the troublesome bird from the area.

Status

One Florida woodpecker is at risk and another former resident is, sadly, on the list of extinct species. The large and spectacular IVORY-BILLED WOODPECKER was common in southeastern swamp forests when Europeans began to colonize the continent, but the woodpeckers were tame, very conspicuous, and easily shot. More important, they were probably dependent on the mature trees of old-growth forest for nesting and foraging. The eastern forests were logged surprisingly rapidly as the East was settled, and birds such as the Ivory-bill that needed about 8 sq km (3 sq miles) of undisturbed forest for each pair could not persist. Their numbers had dropped markedly by the end of the 19th century, and only a few birds persisted to nearly the middle of the 20th century. They are gone now, and a similarly precarious population of the species in eastern Cuba has probably met the same fate.

The RED-COCKADED WOODPECKER could well follow its larger cousin, although much effort is being expended to prevent this fate, supported financially because the species is listed as Endangered (USA ESA). The Red-cockaded has disappeared from many of its former haunts, along with the disappearance of the old-growth Longleaf Pine forests it frequents. Both logging and fire suppression (permitting deciduous trees to invade pinelands) have been blamed for the habitat alteration that has affected these birds so strongly. Pairs maintain very large territories of 40 to 60 hectares (100 to 150 acres), so they have great difficulty in finding enough habitat in a mosaic of clear-cut and regrowing pinewoods. The largest population in the USA is now in Florida's Apalachicola National Forest, and that population continues to decline. Not the least of their worries are Southern Flying Squirrels, which act as both competitors for nest sites and predators on their eggs and young.

Profiles

Yellow-bellied Sapsucker, *Sphyrapicus varius*, Plate 44b
Red-headed Woodpecker, *Melanerpes erythrocephalus*, Plate 44c
Red-bellied Woodpecker, *Melanerpes carolinus*, Plate 44d
Red-cockaded Woodpecker, *Picoides borealis*, Plate 45a
Downy Woodpecker, *Picoides pubescens*, Plate 45b
Pileated Woodpecker, *Dryocopus pileatus*, Plate 45c
Northern Flicker, *Colaptes auratus*, Plate 45d

All of the bird groups considered below are *passerine*, or *perching birds*, members of Order Passeriformes (see p. 103).

---

18. Flycatchers

The *flycatchers* comprise a huge group of birds that is restricted to the New World but is broadly distributed over most habitats from Alaska and northern Canada to the southern tip of South America. They are the first *passerine* birds discussed in this book. The flycatcher family, Tyrannidae, is considered among the most diverse of avian groups. With 394 species, flycatchers usually contribute a hefty percentage of the avian biodiversity almost anywhere in the New World. For instance, it has been calculated that flycatchers make up fully one tenth of the land bird species in South America, and perhaps one quarter of Argentinian species. Many species extend into North America, and Florida has 10 regularly occurring species and the surprising number of 16 rare visitors, migrants from all over North America and strays from the nearby Caribbean.

Flycatchers are mostly small birds, at the smallest extreme some of the world's tiniest, at 7 g (1/4 oz). Their bills are usually broad and flat, the better to snatch flying bugs from the air. Tail length is variable, but some species have very long, forked tails, which probably aid the birds in their rapid, acrobatic, insect-catching maneuvers. Most flycatchers are dully turned out in shades of gray, brown, and olive-green, but many tropical species have bright yellow in their plumage, and a few are quite flashily attired in, for example, bright expanses of vermilion. A great many of the smaller, drabber flycatchers, clad in olives and browns, are extremely difficult to tell apart in the field, even for experienced birdwatchers, and some of Florida's species look so similar that even specimens in the hand may be difficult to distinguish; they probably tell each other apart by their voices. Two of the species that visit Florida in winter, the SCISSOR-TAILED FLYCATCHER and VERMILION FLYCATCHER, are among the most gaudy birds of North America. Flycatcher sexes are usually similar in size and coloring.

Natural History
Ecology and Behavior
Flycatchers are common over a large array of different habitat types, from high mountainsides and lowland moist forests to treeless plains and grasslands, marshes, and mangrove swamps; they are especially prevalent in rainforests. In Florida, many species inhabit forests, although the EASTERN KINGBIRD and GRAY KINGBIRD (both Plate 46) are birds of open country. As their name implies, most flycatchers are *insectivores*, obtaining most of their food by employing the classic flycatching technique. They perch motionless on tree or shrub branches or on fences or telephone wires, then dart out in short, swift flights to snatch from the air insects that enter their field of vision; they then return to the same perch to repeat the process. After a period of scanning the sky in vain, they will move to another perch. Many flycatchers also fly up to and snatch insects from foliage, and many tropical species also supplement their diets with fruits. Some of the larger flycatchers will also take small frogs and lizards, and some even consider small fish and tadpoles delicacies to be plucked from shallow edges of lakes and rivers. Almost all of the relatively few flycatchers that have been studied inhabit exclusive territories that mated pairs defend for all or part of the year.

Breeding
Flycatchers are mainly monogamous. Many tropical flycatchers are known for spectacular courtship displays, males showing off to females by engaging in aerial acrobatics, including flips and somersaults. In some monogamous species, males help the females build nests. Some tropical species build roofed nests or globular hanging nests placed in trees or shrubs, others build mud nests that they attach to vertical surfaces such as rock walls, and still others place their nest in holes in trees or rock crevices. Florida flycatchers all build cup nests, except for the GREAT CRESTED FLYCATCHER (Plate 46), which nests in a tree hole and has the unusual habit of inserting a shed snake skin into its nest lining. The skin, which often hangs partway out the entrance hole, may deter some potential nest predators from entering the cavity! Florida flycatchers generally lay 3 to 5 eggs that are incubated by the female for 12 to 18 days; the nestlings fledge when 12 to 18 days old. Flycatchers, as do all passerines, have *altricial* nestlings, born naked, blind, and helpless, that slowly develop the ability to take care of themselves as they grow while in the nest.

Ecological Interactions

Some flycatchers show marked alterations in their lifestyles as seasons, locations, and feeding opportunities change. Such ongoing capacity for versatile behavior in response to changing environments may contribute to the group's great ecological success. An excellent example is the EASTERN KINGBIRD's drastic changes in behavior between summer and winter. Breeding during summer throughout much of North America, these flycatchers are extremely aggressive in defending their territories against other birds and defending their eggs and young against all sorts of predators; they feed exclusively at that time on insects. But a change comes over the birds during the winter, as they idle away the months in South America's Amazon Basin. There, Eastern Kingbirds congregate in large, non-territorial flocks with apparently nomadic existences, and they share fruiting trees with a host of resident tropical fruit-eaters.

Lore and Notes

Of all the groups of birds, it is probably among the flycatchers that the most undiscovered species remain. This distinction is owing to the group's great diversity, its penetration into essentially all terrestrial habitats, and the inconspicuousness of many of its members. In fact, as people reach previously inaccessible locations – hidden valleys, cloud-draped mountain plateaus – in the remotest parts of South America, previously unknown flycatchers are indeed found. New species of flycatchers were described in 1981 from Peru, in 1987 and 1992 from Brazil, and in 1988 from Colombia. The last of Florida's flycatcher species was described in 1895, however.

Status

Florida's flycatchers are faring well, but members of this family elsewhere in the world have suffered from habitat destruction. Several species known only from southeastern Brazil, for example KAEMPFER'S TODY-TYRANT, are considered at great risk, because they have been sighted only a few times in recent years. That part of the world has had the vast majority of its forested habitats cleared for agricultural use, negatively affecting many forest bird populations. Brazil's newly described RESTINGA TYRANNULET is found only along a stretch of beach that is rapidly being developed for recreation.

Profiles

Eastern Wood-Pewee, *Contopus virens*, Plate 46a
Acadian Flycatcher, *Empidonax virescens*, Plate 46b
Eastern Phoebe, *Sayornis phoebe*, Plate 46c
Great Crested Flycatcher, *Myiarchus crinitus*, Plate 46d
Gray Kingbird, *Tyrannus dominicensis*, Plate 46e
Eastern Kingbird, *Tyrannus tyrannus*, Plate 46f

19. Swallows and Swifts

Swallows are easily identified by their habit of catching insects on the wing during long periods of sustained flight. Members of the family Hirundinidae, they are a group of songbirds, 89 species strong, with a worldwide distribution. Seven regularly occurring species and three rarities are found in Florida. Swallows are small, streamlined birds, 11.5 to 21.5 cm (4.5 to 8.5 in) in length, with short necks, bills, and legs. They have long, pointed wings, and most of them have forked tails, adapted for moving rapidly through the air with high maneuverability. Some are colored in shades of blue, green, or violet, but many are gray or brown. The sexes look alike in most species, although male and female PURPLE MARTINS (Plate 47) are quite different.

Swifts, although superficially resembling swallows, are actually only distantly related; they are not even classified with the passerines. The 99 species of swifts (family Apodidae) are, in fact, most closely related to hummingbirds. Only a single species is a common bird in Florida, the CHIMNEY SWIFT (Plate 47), which breeds through much of the state and winters in South America. Three additional species visit the state rarely. Swifts, like swallows, are slender, streamlined birds, with long, pointed wings. They are 9 to 25 cm (3.5 to 10 in) long and have very short legs and very small bills. Their tails can be short or quite long and forked. The long-tailed species are more agile in flight, and the short-tailed ones have their tail feathers stiffened and pointed to support the birds as they cling to vertical surfaces. The sexes look alike: sooty-gray or brown, with white, grayish or reddish rumps or flanks, and some of the darkest species are glossed with iridescence above. Although swifts are common birds in many parts of the world, they are much less well known than are swallows, owing to the fact that their pattern of almost perpetual flight hampers detailed observation.

Natural History
Ecology and Behavior
Among the birds, swallows and the unrelated swifts represent pinnacles of flying prowess and aerial insectivory. It seems as if they fly all day, circling low over water or land or flying in erratic patterns high overhead, all the while snatching insects from the air. The length of a swallow's tail and the depth of its fork are good indicators of where it forages. CLIFF SWALLOWS have a very short, unforked tail, and they forage high in the air, mostly gliding around in circles as they search for insects. TREE SWALLOWS (Plate 47), with tail slightly forked, are more agile flyers, turning more readily to chase elusive prey, but they still fly well above the ground. BARN SWALLOWS (Plate 47), with a very long, deeply forked tail, forage near the ground, where they must be able to turn very suddenly to capture low-flying insects and avoid obstacles.

Perpetual flight was in the past so much the popular impression of swifts that it was actually thought that they never landed – that they remained in flight throughout most of their lives (indeed, it was long ago believed that they lacked feet; the family name, Apodidae, comes from *Apus*, which means 'without feet'). They do land, however, to roost at night and when breeding. When they do, some species use their clawed feet and stiff tail to cling to and brace themselves against vertical structures, much like woodpeckers, although they don't move around like woodpeckers. They normally don't land on the ground and may not be able to take off from horizontal surfaces. A swift spends more time airborne than any other type of bird, regularly flying all night, and even copulating while in the air (a tricky affair, apparently: male and female are partially in free fall during this activity). Swifts are also aptly named, as they are among the fastest flyers.

Some swallows, for example the TREE SWALLOW, are able to winter fairly far north because they can subsist on berries if insects are scarce. Not quite so aerially restricted as swifts, swallows land more often, often resting during the hottest parts of the day. At dawn and dusk, swallows seem always to be airborne, and their calls are sometimes heard from overhead during the night-time.

Breeding

PURPLE MARTINS are the only common breeding swallow in Florida, but BARN, CAVE, and NORTHERN ROUGH-WINGED SWALLOWS (Plate 47) also breed locally. Some species of swallows breed in dense colonies of dozens to a thousand or more nesting pairs. Although swallows are thought of as monogamous like so many other passerines, colonial breeding furnishes abundant opportunities for deviating from this mode. Male BANK SWALLOWS are ready to attempt copulation with any female, and thus when the female of a pair leaves the nest early in the reproductive cycle, her mate will fly right behind her to keep other males away. Many female CLIFF SWALLOWS lay part of their clutch in a nearby nest, if given the opportunity, a literal example of the saying 'don't put all your eggs in one basket' and with the same reasoning. If the swallow's own nest is unsuccessful, that of the neighbor may survive, and the swallow's reproductive efforts are not entirely in vain.

Swallows have adapted amazingly well to human presence, and many species nest on barns, houses, bridges, and other structures. Purple Martins nest colonially in 'martin houses' all over Florida, having largely abandoned tree cavities. In Mexico, Cave Swallows are common inhabitants of Mayan ruins, and those that breed in southern Florida do so under bridges. Northern Rough-winged Swallows nest in burrows in sand banks or in human-furnished structures such as drainpipes! Most Barn Swallows presently nest associated with people but originally they must have attached their mud cup nests to cliffs and cave mouths. Species that build mud nests must find their mud somewhere, so this need determines where they can nest, although in Florida it's usually not too far to the nearest mud puddle. Most swallows line their nests with plant material and then an inner coat of feathers, obviously of value for insulation, and feathers are in great demand among these birds. A single white duck feather in a farmyard might be plucked from the ground by a swallow, which is then chased around and around by others of the same species, the feather dropped and caught in midair repeatedly until one bird finally gets it into its nest. In Florida swallows, either the female alone or both sexes incubate the 3 to 7 eggs for 13 to 18 days. The nestlings fledge after 18 to 36 days, and the parents continue to feed them for several days after that, the young often 'parked' in conspicuous groups on dead tree branches or fence wires.

Swift courtship is impressive and – of course – in flight. Often birds glide in tandem with wings upraised, not dissimilar to the beautiful courtship flights of terns. Swifts are monogamous and most are colonial breeders, but some species nest solitarily. The sexes share breeding chores. Nests consist of plant pieces, twigs, and feathers glued together with the birds' saliva. In the CHIMNEY SWIFT, 4 to 5 eggs are incubated for 19 to 21 days, with young fledging at 28 to 30 days of age. And, as its name implies, this swift and some others associate with human architecture just as readily as do swallows.

Ecological Interactions

Because swallows depend each day on capturing enough insects, their daily habits are largely tied to the prevailing weather. Flying insects fill the air on warm, sunny days but are relatively scarce on cold, wet ones. Therefore, on good days, swallows can catch their fill of bugs in only a few hours of flying, virtually anywhere. But on cool, wet days, they may need to forage all day to find enough food, and they tend to fly low, where under such conditions insects are more available. They are especially attracted to water at that time, perhaps because it is easiest to capture low-flying insects when they are not flying among plants or because aquatic insects continue to emerge from ponds and lakes even during cool weather. Sometimes hard freezes along the USA's North Atlantic coast drive thousands and even millions of TREE SWALLOWS down the Florida Peninsula, where they appear in clouds over the Everglades.

Lore and Notes

The result of the close association between people and swallows is that, going back as far as ancient Rome, swallows have been considered good luck. Superstitions attached to the relationship abound; for example, it is said that the cows of a farmer who destroys a swallow's nest will give bloody milk. Arrival of the first migratory BARN SWALLOWS in Europe is considered a welcoming sign of approaching spring, as is the arrival of CLIFF SWALLOWS at Capistrano, an old Spanish mission in California. The swallows don't actually return to Capistrano on the same day each year, but their arrival dates are close enough to be notable.

Status

Swallows are among the more successful birds of the world, in part because many of them have incorporated the products of our architects and construction workers as nesting sites. Nevertheless, two species of swallows, the RED SEA SWALLOW in the Middle East and the WHITE-EYED RIVER MARTIN in Thailand, are known only from one or a few specimens taken on their wintering grounds; their breeding sites are unknown, and they are obviously very rare if not extinct. Many tropical swifts are so poorly known that we have no idea if their status should be cause for concern.

Profiles

Purple Martin, *Progne subis*, Plate 47a
Chimney Swift, *Chaetura pelagica*, Plate 47b
Tree Swallow, *Tachycineta bicolor*, Plate 47c
Northern Rough-winged Swallow, *Stelgidopteryx serripennis*, Plate 47d
Barn Swallow, *Hirundo rustica*, Plate 47e

20. Crows and Jays

The *crows* and *jays* are members of the Corvidae, a passerine family of 118 species of worldwide distribution. Four species are common residents in Florida, two crows and two jays; all are profiled here. *Corvids* are known for their versatility, adaptability, and undoubted intelligence; jays, in addition, are strikingly handsome. Members of this group are also usually quite noisy, and the *caw* of the AMERICAN CROW (Plate 48) and *jeeah, jeeah* of the BLUE JAY (Plate 48) are among the best-known of bird vocalizations.

Members of the family are large for passerine birds, the COMMON RAVEN being the largest songbird. Corvids have robust, fairly long bills and strong legs and feet; tail length varies from short in *nutcrackers* to very long in *magpies*. Jays hop, but the usual locomotion on the ground of the larger crows and ravens is a jaunty walk that, at higher speeds, could easily be called a drunken swagger. Species on the crow side of the family are all or mostly black, but jays are attired in bright blues, purples, greens, yellows, and white. American jays tend to be blue, and many have conspicuous crests (for example, the BLUE JAY).

Natural History
Ecology and Behavior

Crows and jays eat a large variety of foods and so are considered *omnivores*. They feed on the ground, but also in trees, taking bird eggs and nestlings, carrion, insects, and fruits and nuts. Bright and versatile, they are quick to take advantage of new food sources and to find food in agricultural and other human-altered environments. All use their feet to hold food down while processing it with their bills. Hiding food for later consumption, *caching*, is practiced widely by the group. You can watch a crow or jay that has been fed a peanut, for example, hop over the ground for a while, find an acceptable spot, and push the peanut into the ground by a few blows with its powerful bill. It then stands back, surveys the situation, and then pulls a few leaves and bits of moss over the spot. Sometimes it seems like a major production. Caching is what allows members of this family to be resident at high latitudes and altitudes, because they can use their stored food throughout the winter. GRAY JAYS can cache up to 1000 items in a 17-hour summer day in Alaska, more than one per minute, and their salivary glands produce a sticky saliva that allows them to stash their caches just about anywhere. The memory they have had to evolve to remember where they have hidden so many individual tidbits surely plays a part in the substantial intelligence of this group, which is at the peak of bird braininess.

Corvids are usually quite social, and Florida's species are no exception. AMERICAN CROWS gather in large flocks at winter roosts, and jays often wander through the forest in small groups of relatives, 5 to 10 strong, that forage together within a restricted area, or *home range*. Many jays are raucous and noisy, giving loud calls, some of them harsh and some of them musical, as the foraging flock straggles from tree to tree.

Breeding

Courtship feeding is common in corvids, the male feeding the female before and during incubation, which she performs alone in most species (males are known to help out at times in both BLUE JAYS and FISH CROWS, Plate 48). Bulky, open nests, constructed primarily of twigs, are placed in trees (or on cliff ledges in some ravens). In Florida corvids, 3 to 6 eggs are incubated for 15 to 18 days, and the young are then fed in the nest by both parents for 2 to 3 weeks in jays and 3 to 5 weeks in crows. Quite a few jays of lower latitudes, for example the FLORIDA SCRUB-JAY (Plate 48), breed cooperatively. Generally the oldest pair in the group breeds, and the other members serve only as *helpers*, assisting in nest construction and feeding the young. The helpers are usually offspring from a previous year, and by helping, they hope to inherit the territory and move up to breeding status when the adult of the same sex of the breeding pair dies.

Ecological Interactions

The omnivory of corvids also drives them to be predators on bird nests – generally on species that are smaller than they are, of which there are many. Jays, crows, ravens, and magpies all tear up nests and eat eggs and nestlings. They are considered to be responsible for a significant percentage of the nest predation on many songbird species, particularly those with cup nests.

Owing to their seed-caching behavior, corvids are important to trees as dispersal agents. In eastern North America, for example, the BLUE JAY'S acorn-burying habit must surely result in the maintenance and spread of oak forests, and the CLARK'S NUTCRACKER does the same for certain species of pines in the western mountains. This is because corvids never find all the seeds they've stashed. The best caching corvid from a plant's standpoint is a very active but somewhat forgetful one!

Lore and Notes

Corvid folklore is rife with tales of crows, ravens, and magpies as symbols of ill omen. This undoubtedly traces to the group's frequent all-black plumage and habit of eating carrion, both sinister traits. COMMON RAVENS, in particular, have long been associated in many Northern cultures with evil or death, although these large, powerful birds also figure more benignly in Nordic and Middle Eastern mythology.

Status

The FLORIDA SCRUB-JAY is considered Threatened (USA ESA), as its very specific sand-pine/oak scrub habitat has diminished very greatly in historic times, much of it lost to orange groves. No one can deny the irony of well-meaning environmentalists decrying the loss of scrub-jay habitat as they drink their breakfast orange juice! Otherwise, Florida's corvids remain unthreatened; in fact, the others are all probably increasing in numbers, because the intelligence of the species in this family seems to fit them well for coexisting with humans. FISH CROWS, for instance, have greatly expanded their range in southern Florida in recent years. All of these species raid garbage cans, eat pet food, and scrounge for French fries at Florida's many drive-in restaurants. They are among the short list of species that are often called human *commensals* (commensals are animals that feed in association with other animals; p. 55), and the species on that list should remain on the planet long after many less adaptable species have disappeared.

Profiles

Blue Jay, *Cyanocitta cristata*, Plate 48a
Florida Scrub-Jay, *Aphelocoma coerulescens*, Plate 48b
American Crow, *Corvus brachyrhynchos*, Plate 48c
Fish Crow, *Corvus ossifragus*, Plate 48d

21. Titmice and Nuthatches

There are 53 species of *chickadees* and *titmice*, family Paridae, and 25 species of *nuthatches*, family Sittidae. The members of these families are characteristic forest birds of all north temperate regions, although nuthatches also occur in the lowland tropics in Asia, and titmice occur throughout forested parts of Africa. Florida's woodlands hold a chickadee, a titmouse, and three nuthatches. Chickadees (called 'tits' in the Old World) are small, active, gray or brown or reddish birds with dark caps and throats and contrasty white cheek patches. Their bills are short and pointed, thicker at the base than those of some other insect-eaters. The wings of chickadees are short and their tails long; they are not strong flyers, and all species are resident all year, even at high latitudes. Titmice are similar but lack the fancy head pattern and have a jaunty crest to make up for it. Nuthatches have considerably longer bills and shorter tails than chickadees and are usually blue-gray above and paler below, with dark caps.

Natural History
Ecology and Behavior

Chickadees are very social and move about the countryside in small flocks during the non-breeding season. These *feeding flocks* may be joined by a few nuthatches and other birds and provide characteristic sights and sounds of temperate-zone forests. The birds in these flocks probably stay in touch as they move through the forest by their regular vocalizations (usually some variation of *chick-a-dee dee dee* in the chickadees). The pointed bills of chickadees, small but strong, are used to catch insects and pound open seeds. Chickadees often feed by hanging upside down and sometimes hover beneath a branch to pluck a small insect from it. Owing to these feeding specializations, chickadees can spend the winter at high latitudes. This is because, although their insect food is in dormant stages in winter, the chickadees can extract insect eggs and pupae from beneath leaves and twigs. Nuthatches use their long, slender bills to probe into cracks in tree bark and pry up loose pieces of bark. They also move out onto small branches and probe moss clumps and leaf masses. Like crows and jays, chickadees and nuthatches cache thousands of seeds in the fall and visit their caches throughout the winter, when times are hard. Their memories seem as good as those of their larger relatives.

Breeding

The species in these groups are the smallest hole-nesting birds. We think of wood-peckers as being able to dig nest holes in tree trunks, but it is a bit more surprising to learn that a tiny chickadee or nuthatch can do the same. Both chickadees and nuthatches excavate their own nests in dead trunks or branches or enlarge small natural cavities. WHITE-BREASTED NUTHATCHES may grab an insect and smear it around the edge of the nest hole or may plaster mud around the hole, either activity perhaps to deter predators. Hole-nesting birds tend to lay large clutches of eggs, because their young are relatively well protected from predators, and they can thus stay in their nests for a longer time than the young of cup-nesters. Accordingly, the industrious adults can capture enough prey items to feed a larger number of more slowly growing offspring. Florida's titmice lay 5 to 8 eggs, which are incubated for 11 to 14 days, and the young leave the nest after about 13 to 17 days. Nuthatches lay 5 to 9 eggs, which are incubated for about 12 to 14 days, and the young fledge about 2 to 3 weeks after hatching. In both families, only the female incubates.

Ecological Interactions

Small insectivorous birds such as the ones discussed here eat billions of insects each year. However, they probably have relatively little effect on insect popula-tions, because they are likely to eat the species that are more common and switch to other species when their preferred prey becomes rare. Then the original prey species, relieved of predator pressure, probably increases again. One interesting phenomenon that occurs in foraging animals is the formation of a *search image*. When a particular prey type is common, the animals that feed on it apparently quickly develop a clear picture of that organism in their mind and can pick it out from the background more readily. When the prey decreases, either because of heavy predation pressure or some other reason, the search image can switch to another prey item. This attribute in birds has been thought to have contributed to the almost unbelievable diversity of forms of tropical insects. Presumably many of them evolved bizarre shapes so they were not part of a group of insects for which certain birds had developed a search image.

Lore and Notes

The BROWN-HEADED NUTHATCH (Plate 49) of Florida pinewoods is one of the very few tool-using birds. Some individuals learn to break off small pieces of bark and use them to pry up other such pieces and dislodge insects that would otherwise be inaccessible.

Status

All members of this group are doing reasonably well in Florida – at least there are many of them still present – but the demise of mature pinelands is certainly reducing the numbers of BROWN-HEADED NUTHATCHES, which are as restricted to pines as their much rarer associate, the Red-cockaded Woodpecker (p. 154). Oddly, the WHITE-BREASTED NUTHATCH is less restricted to pines but has decreased even more in Florida.

Profiles

Carolina Chickadee, *Poecile carolinensis*, Plate 49a
Tufted Titmouse, *Baeolophus bicolor*, Plate 49b
Brown-headed Nuthatch, *Sitta pusilla*, Plate 49c

22. Wrens

Wrens are small, brownish passerines with an active manner and characteristically upraised tails. The 75 wren species comprise a group for the most part confined to the Western Hemisphere and much more diverse in the tropics than at high latitudes. Among other traits, wrens are renowned for their singing ability, vocal duets, and nesting behavior. Nests are often placed in crannies and crevices within buildings or other structures. In fact, many wrens nest in naturally occurring cavities, hence the family name, Troglodytidae; *troglodytes* are cave dwellers. Wrens are slender-billed insect-eaters, and some of them, for example the HOUSE WREN (Plate 49), root about near and in human settlements, looking for their prey. Wrens are colored mainly in shades of brown or reddish brown, with white, gray, and black markings. Their wings and tails are usually embellished with finely barred patterns. Some of them are tiny, weighing in at 10 g (1/3 oz). Wrens have rather short, broad wings and because of this are poor flyers – yet some of them make lengthy migrations. The sexes look alike. Their tails may be the group's most distinguishing feature, much of the time being held stiffly erect, at military attention. Tails are waved back and forth during displays, both for courtship and aggression. Holding the tail up is characteristic of small songbirds of many families that inhabit dense thickets, as do many wrens; wrens of open habitats such as deserts and rock cliffs keep their tails down.

Natural History

Ecology and Behavior

Wrens are *cryptically colored* and fairly secretive in their habits. They hop and poke around through forest undergrowth, thickets, grasslands, and marshes, searching for insects. Some are restricted to rocks and canyon sides. They are *insectivorous*, except for a few desert species that frequently eat berries and seeds. Some wrens forage in places foreign to most birds – under logs and into rock crevices and seemingly impenetrable tangles. In fact, it is easier to mistake a wren for a mouse than another bird! Wrens at lower latitudes remain in pairs all year and defend winter territories in which they will nest during the breeding season. Some of the larger tropical wrens spend their days in small family flocks, and, perhaps safer because of larger size and social behavior, are a bit more conspicuous than is typical of wrens. After the breeding season, wrens use their nests as roosting places – or 'dormitories,' as one researcher puts it. The vocalizations of wrens have been studied extensively, and some are at the very pinnacle of bird-song complexity. A pair will call back and forth as they lose sight of each other while foraging in thickets, keeping in contact. In some species, mated pairs sing some of the bird world's most complex duets, male and female rapidly alternating in giving parts of a continuous song, so rapidly and expertly that it sounds as if one individual utters the entire sequence. Such duets probably function as 'keep-out' signals, warning *conspecific* (same species) individuals away from the pair's territory, and in maintaining the pair bond between mated birds. CAROLINA WRENS (Plate 49) have one of the loudest and most characteristic songs of Florida's woodlands.

Breeding

Wrens are mainly monogamous, but some tropical species breed *cooperatively*, with members of the small family group helping out at the single nest of the parents. Many wrens construct their untidy nest in tree cavities; others build elaborate nests in the open, roofed and with inconspicuous side entrances. In some wren species, for example the MARSH WREN that breeds in Florida salt marshes, the male builds many more nests on his territory than his mate (or mates, in *polygynous* species) can use, apparently as a courtship signal. These multiple nests may also confuse predators, which check a few nests, find them empty, and ignore the rest. The 4 to 8 eggs laid by the wrens that occur in Florida are incubated by the female for 12 to 16 days. Nestlings are fed by both parents for about 12 to 19 days, until fledging. Wrens are prodigious breeders, with fairly large clutches and often two broods per year.

Ecological Interactions

Several wren species, including the HOUSE WREN and MARSH WREN, puncture the eggs of birds of other species that nest nearby. Biologists are not sure why they do this, but by doing so they certainly lessen the number of birds with which they must compete for food.

Lore and Notes

There are so many wonderful aspects of nature that books can scarcely contain them. Think, for example, of the geographic distribution of animals and plants. Why are some species widely distributed and others not? The WINTER WREN occurs all around the Northern Hemisphere, including on small islands in the North Atlantic Ocean and Bering Sea. Its distribution is measured in millions of square kilometers. Similarly common in New England, southern Alaska, the Himalayas, and the English countryside, its distribution is especially impressive because it is a tiny bird that spends more of its day creeping about the forest floor or in and out of rock piles than flying over long distances. However, many populations are migratory, and individual wrens must have substantial wing power to be able to fly from Ontario to Georgia or from Finland to Israel. A not-distantly-related species, the COZUMEL WREN, occurs only on tiny Isla Cozumel off the Yucatán Peninsula, its entire range about 350 sq km (135 sq miles). Given the powers of flight of the even smaller Winter Wren, why can't the Cozumel Wren reach the Mexican mainland, about 18 km (11 miles) away?

Status

No wren is known to have gone extinct, but Mexico has two wrens of such restricted distribution that they are certainly vulnerable to extinction because of introduced predators (eating the wrens) and herbivores (eating their habitat) on their home islands. The SOCORRO WREN and CLARION WREN are restricted to the Revillagigedo Archipelago off the west coast of Mexico, where they live on small, offshore islands. These islands are even smaller than Cozumel, mentioned above. A natural catastrophe such as a hurricane could eliminate either species just as readily as changes caused by human activities.

Profiles

Carolina Wren, *Thryothorus ludovicianus*, Plate 49d
House Wren, *Troglodytes aedon*, Plate 49e

23. Kinglets and Gnatcatchers

There are six species of *kinglets*, placed in their own small family, Regulidae, which occurs all across the Northern Hemisphere; the RUBY-CROWNED KINGLET (Plate 50) is common throughout Florida in winter, and another species occurs in small numbers. The BLUE-GRAY GNATCATCHER (Plate 50), a common Florida resident, is in the *Old World warbler* family, Sylviidae, with 383 species. This family includes many of the common small songbirds of Eurasia and Africa. Kinglets and gnatcatchers are the tiniest passerine birds in Florida. Kinglets are active little birds, olive-green above and whitish below, with conspicuous pale wing bars and either stripes or an eyering attracting attention to their head. All species have bright colors on their crown, in the male Ruby-crowned a fiery-red crown patch that is hidden most of the year but can be exposed and erected during singing, courtship, and antagonistic interactions. This patch is a good example of a *coverable badge*, a patch of color that can be hidden or exposed depending on the bird's motivation. Gnatcatchers are similarly active but are blue-gray, without wing bars and with long black and white tails that are expressively waved.

Natural History

Ecology and Behavior

Kinglets are frenetically active as they move through the forest, seemingly never slowing down in their search for insects, hanging and fluttering under branches as much as they are on top of them. Their prey is sufficiently abundant that kinglets are among the most common small birds in forests. Both kinglets and gnatcatchers are sometimes seen together in mixed feeding flocks, when their rather similar styles of foraging can be compared. Although these small birds tend to breed and feed in the forest canopy, during migration and winter they can be seen all the way down to the low shrubbery. They sing thin, wiry songs, although the RUBY-CROWNED KINGLET song starts at a high frequency and then descends to a loud, musical warble, surprisingly forceful for such a tiny bird.

Breeding

Kinglets and gnatcatchers are monogamous, pairs defending territories in the breeding season. Kinglets are northern breeders, but the BLUE-GRAY GNATCATCHER breeds commonly almost throughout Florida. Kinglets build small nests of varied materials, usually including lichens and mosses, that hang between slender branches high in trees and are usually well camouflaged under a canopy of leaves.

Gnatcatchers nest lower but have equally fancy nests, usually on top of a slender branch. Kinglets lay surprisingly large clutches for open-nesting birds, the 7 to 9 (rarely to 12!) eggs incubated by the female for 13 to 15 days. The young fledge in about 14 to 19 days. Gnatcatchers lay 4 to 5 eggs that both parents incubate for 11 to 15 days, and their young fledge in about 10 to 15 days.

Status

Fortunately, small songbirds of wide distribution in the Temperate Zone are usually not at risk of extinction, and thus kinglets should be among the last birds to qualify for endangered-species listing. However, some of the Old World warblers are restricted to specific river valleys, mountain ranges, or tropical islands. The ALDABRA WARBLER, restricted to the island of Aldabra in the Seychelles Islands in the Indian Ocean, is probably extinct, but the SEYCHELLES WARBLER, similarly restricted to the nearby island of Cousin, is stable at a population of several hundred birds, probably as a consequence of the island being taken over as a nature preserve and intensively managed. Even if thriving, populations on small islands are always at risk of being wiped out by a single environmental catastrophe such as a typhoon, a fire, or something as seemingly inconsequential as a lighthouse-keeper's cat.

Profiles

Ruby-crowned Kinglet, *Regulus calendula*, Plate 50a
Blue-gray Gnatcatcher, *Polioptila caerulea*, Plate 50b

24. Thrushes

The 179 species of *thrushes* inhabit most terrestrial regions of the world. Eight species occur regularly in Florida, and another two are rare and irregular visitors. Although many people would recognize a bird as a thrush, the family Turdidae has few defining features that set all its members apart from other groups. One such characteristic, perhaps a bit esoteric, is a *booted tarsus*, which means the horny covering on the lower legs is not divided into scales as in most birds. As could be expected, so large an assemblage of species is sure to include a significant amount of variation in appearance, ecology, and behavior. Thrushes as a group are tremendously successful birds, especially when they have adapted to living near humans and benefiting from our environmental modifications. Some thrushes are among the most common and recognizable park and garden birds, including North America's AMERICAN ROBIN (Plate 50). Thrushes are slender-billed birds, and the North American species range from 15 to 24 cm (6 to 9.5 in) in length. Most thrushes are not brightly colored; instead, they come in drab browns and reddish browns, grays, and black and white. The *bluebirds* are glorious exceptions, with bright blue or blue and orange males and duller blue females, and the EASTERN BLUEBIRD (Plate 50) is surely one of the most striking of Florida's songbirds. Other than in these species, the sexes are similar in appearance. In the nest and for a short while after they leave it, the young of most thrushes are clad in distinctively spotted plumages.

Natural History

Ecology and Behavior

Among the thrushes are species that employ a variety of feeding methods and that take several different food types. Many eat fruits (*frugivorous*), some are primarily *insectivorous*, and most are at least moderately *omnivorous*, taking both plant and animal foods. Although generally arboreal, most thrushes also forage on the ground for insects, other arthropods, and, a particular favorite with AMERICAN ROBINS, delicious earthworms. Ground-foraging thrushes hop and run along the ground, stopping at intervals and cocking their heads to peer downwards. They are not listening for worms, as was popularly believed before researchers showed that the eyes were the only sense organs involved. Bluebirds hunt in open country and are good at hovering over a meadow while looking for insects below.

Thrushes are residents of many kinds of habitats – forest edge, clearings, and other open areas such as shrubby areas and grasslands, gardens, parks, suburban lawns, and even farmlands. Some of them are quite social, spending their time during the non-breeding season in flocks of the same species, feeding and roosting together. Many of Florida's thrushes breed to the north and pass through the state in spring and fall on their way to the tropics or stay through the winter, although the American Robin, EASTERN BLUEBIRD, and WOOD THRUSH (Plate 50) all breed in the state.

Breeding
Thrushes breed monogamously, male and female together defending exclusive territories during the breeding season. Nests, usually built by the female and placed in the branches of trees and shrubs or in crevices, are cup-shaped, made of grass, moss, and similar materials, and lined with mud by some species. Three to 5 eggs are incubated by the female for 12 to 16 days. Young are fed by both parents for 10 to 14 days prior to their fledging and, in some species, for another several weeks after fledging. In the hole-nesting EASTERN BLUEBIRD, the young may not fledge until 18 to 19 days old, as hole nesters typically have more young than open nesters, so each young bird gets fed at a slower rate and grows more slowly.

Ecological Interactions
The AMERICAN ROBIN represents a rather unusual way of life. It does much of its foraging on the ground in the open, yet it needs trees for nesting, so it is distinctly a forest-edge bird. Because of this, it has thrived on a continent in which not only are forests opened up by logging and development of cities and towns, but also trees are planted everywhere on the prairies. Thus much of the lower 48 states and southern Canada has become optimal robin habitat, and the populations of this species have probably increased as much as those of any bird of North America in historic times. That is certainly the case in Florida, where the bird has extended its breeding range greatly.

Lore and Notes
English colonists in the New World gave the AMERICAN ROBIN its name because it resembled England's common ROBIN – both birds are thrushes, and both have reddish breasts. The New World bird, however, is more closely related to Europe's BLACKBIRD, also a common garden bird. Not content with incorrectly labeling birds that were new to them with English names, British settlers around the world, many of them surely homesick, imported birds from the British Isles to their new domains so that familiar birds would surround them. Some of these released birds, such as House Sparrows and European Starlings, have become abundant North American birds.

Status
The BICKNELL'S THRUSH is a rare migrant through Florida on its way between its limited breeding grounds in the mountains of northeast USA and southeast

Canada and its poorly known wintering grounds in the West Indies. With both breeding and wintering range restricted and a forest-based distribution, it is among the Neotropical migrants most at risk, with habitat loss at both ends of its lengthy migration route.

Profiles

Eastern Bluebird, *Sialia sialis*, Plate 50c
Hermit Thrush, *Catharus guttatus*, Plate 50d
Wood Thrush, *Hylocichla mustelina*, Plate 50e
American Robin, *Turdus migratorius*, Plate 50f

25. Mockingbirds and Thrashers

The family Mimidae consists of 34 species of mid-sized, slender-looking (because of their long tails) songbirds; they are known variously as *mockingbirds*, *thrashers*, and *catbirds* and called *mimids* as a group. The group is restricted to the New World, and most species occur in tropical latitudes. Three species are common in Florida, and another three visit the state rarely, two from the West and one from the Bahamas. The northernmost species, in the USA and southern Canada, are migratory. Most are brown or gray with lighter underparts, which are often streaked or spotted; the BROWN THRASHER (Plate 51) is an especially colorful member of the family. Within a species, the sexes generally look alike.

Natural History

Ecology and Behavior

Mimids are mostly birds of the ground, shrubs, and low trees. They forage on the ground in open areas and gardens for insects and other small invertebrate animals, and also take some fruit, especially notable in NORTHERN MOCKINGBIRDS (Plate 51). These birds, as a group, are known for their virtuoso singing performances, their highly intriguing ability to mimic closely the songs of other species, and their aggressive territoriality during breeding seasons. Many a person who wandered innocently across a mockingbird territory during the nesting season has been hit on the head by the swooping birds.

Breeding

Mimids are monogamous. Cup nests are built of sticks and leaves by both sexes or by the female alone. Similarly, either the female (catbirds and mockingbirds) or both sexes (thrashers) incubate the 3 to 4 eggs for about 11 to 14 days. Young are fed in the nest by both sexes for 9 to 13 days until they fledge.

Ecological Interactions

Mockingbirds are among the most fiercely protective of territorial birds. They defend their territories against not only other mockingbirds but often other species as well. When flocks of American Robins descend on southern Florida cities in winter, the resident NORTHERN MOCKINGBIRDS go into a frenzy of robin chasing, always finding still another robin in their favorite fruiting tree after having just chased several away. Some mockers, either smarter or more exhausted than their neighbors, eventually give up the uphill battle.

Lore and Notes

Members of this family are accomplished mimics, as the name of the family implies (named after the mockingbird genus *Mimus*, meaning 'the mimic'). Although thrashers and catbirds both indulge in some mimicry, NORTHERN

MOCKINGBIRDS are especially able mimics of most of the bird species in their area. You might hear one giving almost perfect calls of a Northern Cardinal, Red-bellied Woodpecker, Gray Kingbird, and Tufted Titmouse interspersed among their own characteristic thrice-repeated song phrases. For a long time, ornithologists thought that this mimicry enhanced the mockingbirds' abilities to drive other bird species from their territories, but recent research indicates it's more basic than that. Males that have a greater song repertoire are apparently more attractive to females, and a simple way to increase song repertoire is to learn the vocalizations of other species and add them to the mix.

Status

Florida mimids are common birds, as they all adapt well to human-altered landscapes. Nearby, the Caribbean's BAHAMA MOCKINGBIRD and PEARLY-EYED THRASHER have also adapted well to people, perhaps because they thrive in *second-growth* (forests that have been cut and are re-growing) habitats. Farther east, the WHITE-BREASTED THRASHER of forested habitats on Martinique and St. Lucia is one of the rarest of West Indian birds, endangered on both of its islands.

Profiles

Northern Mockingbird, *Mimus polyglottos*, Plate 51b
Brown Thrasher, *Toxostoma rufum*, Plate 51d
Gray Catbird, *Dumetella carolinensis*, Plate 51e

26. Miscellaneous Perching Birds

The four birds discussed here are all passerines but are not closely related; each represents the only member of its family that occurs commonly in Florida. *Waxwings*, family Bombycillidae, are fairly small, soft-plumaged, silky brown birds with yellow tail tips (red in a Japanese species), jaunty, pointed crests, and wing-feather tips modified to look like little red drops of wax. There are three species of waxwings distributed around the Northern Hemisphere, of which only the CEDAR WAXWING (Plate 51) occurs in Florida.

Shrikes are slightly larger black, gray, and white birds with long tails and heavy, hooked bills. The 30 species of shrikes, family Laniidae, are found widely in the Old World, with Africa the center of diversity of the group. Only two species occur regularly in North America, the LOGGERHEAD SHRIKE (Plate 51) in Florida.

There are 65 species of *pipits* and *wagtails*, family Motacillidae, and they are wider-ranging, with pipits on every continent and wagtails throughout Eurasia and Africa. Pipits are small brown birds with paler underparts and streaked breasts, usually with white outer tail feathers that show in flight; the AMERICAN PIPIT (Plate 51) of Florida, at 15 cm (6 in), is typical of its family. Pipits are supremely adapted for ground living, with long toes and especially long hind claws to furnish additional support as they walk. Most other ground-dwelling passerine birds have curved claws and hop rather than walk; they belong to bird families adapted for tree- and shrub-living but include some members that forage on the ground. Pipits, like their cousins the wagtails, pump their tails up and down as they walk, a good recognition mark (although shared by another common open-country bird in Florida, the Palm Warbler).

Bulbuls of the family Pycnonotidae are native to the Old World – Africa and Asia – but have been introduced elsewhere, as they are much-loved birds for their sprightly demeanor and musical calls. The RED-WHISKERED BULBUL (Plate 60) was long ago accidentally introduced near Miami but has not flourished there and remains very locally distributed. There are 138 species of bulbuls, most of them average-looking, in fact, rather drab, songbirds, but some of them bear striking crests, and others, for example the Red-whiskered, are quite brightly marked. Most species have longish tails and slender bills. Many bulbuls are skulkers in streamside thickets or rainforest understories, but others are much more conspicuous residents of forest edge and semi-open country.

Natural History
Ecology and Behavior

The four birds profiled here are very different from one another. CEDAR WAXWINGS are primarily fruit-eaters, forming nomadic flocks during winter and roaming the countryside looking for trees and shrubs that have held their berries through the fall. They also eat fruit in summer on the breeding grounds but switch their diet to take more insects then, even catching some of them in the air, from a perch like a flycatcher or from the air like a swallow. Their bill is flattened somewhat like the bill of a flycatcher, and their wings are pointed somewhat like those of swallows, so they are well adapted to capture insects. Just about any shape bill is adequate for eating soft fruits.

Bulbuls are also fruit-eaters, so they are somewhat similar ecologically to waxwings (and in fact many are conspicuously crested), but they are not closely related. Bulbuls often flock, but the flocks are more sedentary and don't gather in tight groups flying over the countryside as waxwings do. They also glean insects from leaves and twigs as well as flycatching aerially. The RED-WHISKERED BULBUL, like many in its family, feeds on a great variety of fruits, including at least several dozen exotic species in southern Florida. It has become an agricultural pest in some areas but has not reached sufficient numbers to do so in its limited Florida range.

Shrikes are predatory songbirds that hunt small vertebrates and large invertebrates from a perch in the open, alert to all signs of movement around them. In completely open country, they can hover over a spot and dive down on a prey animal just about as effectively as a hawk. They kill with a quick bite through the spinal cord with their heavy, notched bill. Shrikes have an interesting way of *caching* prey that probably stemmed from the inability of the shrike's passerine feet, not at all like those of a hawk or owl, to hold prey firmly while tearing off bite-sized pieces. Thus the shrike had to wedge or snag its prey somehow to hold it in place – on a large thorn, for instance. A mouse or sparrow or grasshopper so secured was then available for the shrike to return to later to finish its meal. Shrikes have been known to return to such a cache – mummified but perhaps still edible – months after it was made. Sharp-eyed observers from time to time see one of these shrike caches on a stiff branch or thorn, or on a barbwire fence where this sign of civilization is prevalent. LOGGERHEAD SHRIKES eat primarily large insects but are quite willing to chase down and catch a lizard or small bird that makes itself available.

The AMERICAN PIPIT is an open-country bird that breeds on arctic and alpine tundra and winters mostly along coastlines and in grasslands. It may be seen in flocks in winter in open areas, for example beaches, tide flats, and agricultural lands, anywhere in Florida. Pipits walk or run through open areas, where the vegetation is usually quite short, and pluck their insect prey from the ground. The fine bill indicates a confirmed insectivore. Pipits are often invisible until flushed, when they ascend, circle, and either fly away or drop back to the ground. They come down in jerks, as if descending an invisible stairway, and their loud, two-noted calls sound enough like 'pi-pit' to be memorable.

Breeding
These birds are all typical passerines, with monogamous mating and cup nests built in trees and shrubs (on the ground in the pipit, often sheltered by over-hanging rock or grass). Waxwings have no song as such, but courtship feeding is charming to watch in the CEDAR WAXWING, with the male 'capturing' berries and feeding them to the female. Pipits sing from the air, and the male AMERICAN PIPIT has a lengthy song flight, ascending up to 30 m (100 ft) or more in the air and then gliding back down, singing all the way. Flight songs make it possible for open-country birds to advertise their territories and attract mates much more effectively than if the birds were confined to the ground. Both sexes construct the nest in waxwings and shrikes, but only the female performs that task in pipits and bulbuls. The female (both parents in the RED-WHISKERED BULBUL) incubates the 4 to 6 eggs in all four species. Incubation lasts about 2 weeks, and the young fledge in another 2 weeks after hatching (slightly longer in the shrike), with both sexes providing their food.

Ecological Interactions
Shrikes are noteworthy for the very large size of their territories. As they eat many small vertebrates, they are eating higher up on the food chain than most passerines; therefore, they need much more space to find an adequate number of small birds, rodents, and lizards than would be needed by an insect-eater such as the pipit, or fruit-eaters such as the waxwing and bulbul.

Lore and Notes
'Waxwing' refers to the waxlike modified feather tips of all species in the family. 'Shrike' comes from the same source as 'shriek,' originally a bird with a shrill cry. Shrikes are also called 'butcher birds' because of their habits of hanging their prey on thorns and branches. 'Bulbul' is a Persian word, perhaps referring the calls of a common species in that part of the world.

Status
Waxwings must surely be more common and widespread than they were originally on this continent, because very large numbers of them seem dependent on planted fruit trees. Such trees are common, for instance, all across the Great Plains, where no trees, much less fruiting trees, grew a few centuries ago. Shrikes, on the other hand, are much less common, perhaps because of a decline in their prey populations. Populations of LOGGERHEAD SHRIKES have declined to nearly zero in the northeastern USA, while those in the South and West remain healthy. This decline was first thought to indicate some significant environmental problem, but researchers more recently have come to the conclusion that many open areas (optimal shrike habitat) in the Northeast have grown up into closed woodland (poor shrike habitat) since the early farming days.

Much of the world is open space, and it would seem surprising that birds of open country, including pipits, would be vulnerable to habitat destruction. But in fact, natural grasslands (*steppes*) are among the most threatened environments. Because our temperate-zone grain crops (wheat, corn, rye, sorghum) are grasses, areas of grassland are the natural places to plant them, and in North America in particular, scarcely any of the original grassland remains. Many grassland species, for example the SPRAGUE'S PIPIT and Greater Prairie-Chicken of the American Great Plains, have become scarce in most parts of their ranges.

Profiles

Loggerhead Shrike, *Lanius ludovicianus*, Plate 51a
Cedar Waxwing, *Bombycilla cedrorum*, Plate 51c
American Pipit, *Anthus rubescens*, Plate 51f
Red-whiskered Bulbul, *Pycnonotus jocosus*, Plate 60c

27. Vireos

Vireos are small birds of the family Vireonidae, with 52 species widely distributed in North and South America. Shrikes are perhaps their nearest relatives, and on closer look, one can see that the bill of vireos is hooked somewhat like that of a shrike, perhaps because vireos tend to eat larger prey than other insect-eating birds of about their size. Most species are olive-green to gray-brown, often with some yellow below, their only conspicuous markings stripes or eyerings on their head; some species have white or red eyes. A few tropical species (the *peppershrikes* and *shrike-vireos*) are larger and much more brightly colored, conspicuously marked with chestnut or even entirely bright green. Five common and five rare species of vireos have been recorded in Florida, and all the common species are profiled here. The WHITE-EYED VIREO (Plate 52) is resident in the state, and the BLUE-HEADED VIREO (Plate 52) spends the winter; the other species are summer visitors.

Natural History
Ecology and Behavior

Vireos are quintessential *gleaning* birds; they move slowly along branches and twigs, checking the surface of twigs and leaves thoroughly and looking for relatively large insects. They are much less 'flitty' than similar-sized warblers and small flycatchers and can be identified in the field just by their behavior. Because they are slow-moving, they are less likely to join mixed feeding flocks than are other small birds, such as chickadees, gnatcatchers, kinglets, and warblers.

Breeding

Vireos breed in monogamous pairs that share parental care about equally. Males of some species sometimes sing from the nest while incubating, seemingly a counterproductive behavior in a world of predators with good ears! The cup nests of vireos are almost always built in the fork of two divergent twigs well out on a tree or shrub branch. They are constructed of a great variety of materials, including grass stems, leaves, lichens, mosses, twigs, rootlets, and pieces of bark. The 3 to 5 eggs are incubated by both parents (by only the female in RED-EYED and BLACK-WHISKERED VIREOS, both Plate 52) for 12 to 15 days, and the young fledge after 9 to 15 days. Vireos are among the most frequent hosts to the nestlings of parasitic cowbirds (p. 178), and in some species these parasites cause the loss of all vireo nestlings in well over half the nests.

Lore and Notes

Vireos are among the most persistent singers, perhaps compensating for their generally drab appearance. At midday in a north Florida swamp, the only song you hear may be the persistent and monotonous warbled phrases of a RED-EYED VIREO. Similarly, that sharp *chick-bew, deedle-deedle-do-wee, chick* issuing again and again from a dense tangle in the Florida Keys is sure to be a WHITE-EYED VIREO. Like many birds of dense vegetation, vireos are also surpassingly curious, and by making a *psshhh-psshhh-psshhh* noise repeatedly, you can attract them to the edge of their thicket or woodland home for a close view.

Status

Florida's vireos in general are flourishing, and the BLACK-WHISKERED VIREO has pushed its way northward along both Florida coasts since its colonization from the Caribbean in the 19th century. Two North American vireos, the BLACK-CAPPED VIREO and BELL'S VIREO, are in jeopardy. The Black-capped is Endangered (USA ESA), its populations greatly reduced in historic times and extirpated from large parts of its originally limited range in the oak-juniper forests of Oklahoma and Texas. Habitat destruction, mostly for development, is responsible for the great decrease, but brood parasitism from Brown-headed Cowbirds is also a serious problem. Cowbirds have been trapped in great numbers near vireo breeding sites, with some positive results, but developments continue to threaten habitats, as relatively few birds are protected on reserves. The story is the same for California populations of Bell's Vireos, which have declined by over 90% in historic times. It also is a habitat specialist, breeding in narrow strips of *riparian* (waterside) vegetation in the central and southern parts of the state. Flood-control projects, invasion of exotic species, development, and – of course – cowbird parasitism have all contributed to its decline. More recently, the Black-whiskered Vireo has attracted attention in Florida. A coastal species, its numbers have been adversely affected by recent die-offs of large areas of mangroves from freezes and hurricanes, and it may be increasingly adversely affected by the colonization of Florida by both Brown-headed and Shiny cowbirds.

Profiles

White-eyed Vireo, *Vireo griseus*, Plate 52a
Red-eyed Vireo, *Vireo olivaceus*, Plate 52b
Black-whiskered Vireo, *Vireo altiloquus*, Plate 52c
Yellow-throated Vireo, *Vireo flavifrons*, Plate 52d
Blue-headed Vireo, *Vireo solitarius*, Plate 52e

28. Warblers

Warblers are small, active birds that occur in all wooded habitats, as well as brushy second-growth and even marshes. American warblers (family Parulidae), also known as *wood warblers*, are a group of 115 species with wide distribution over the New World. Members of this family are brightly colored, predominantly yellow or greenish, often mixed with varying amounts of gray, black and white; a few have even more color, with patches of red and orange. A few are brown like thrushes or wrens, to match the forest floor where they live. They are beautiful little birds and among the favorites of all birders, because of their quick movements and great diversity, and this same diversity makes them important birds in the *boreal forests* (northern forests) of North America, making up more of the birdlife in many such forests than all other birds combined. Many warblers migrate long distances to tropical wintering grounds, where they are especially evident in areas of disturbed woodland, where resident tropical species are less common. Florida, on a major migration pathway between breeding and wintering grounds, is home to 35 regularly occurring species and another 6 species that visit only rarely; one former visitor is presumed extinct. Because it extends almost into the tropics, Florida is home to more species of warblers in winter than any other state of the USA; a dozen species can be found easily at Christmas-time on the southern mainland.

Natural History

Ecology and Behavior

Warblers are commonly found in forested and shrubby habitats; in migration and winter many of them move into parks and gardens. They forage in lively fashion, mainly for insects and spiders; in the winter, some of them pierce berries to drink juice and partake of nectar from flowers. Most of them capture their prey by *gleaning*, a very common behavior in insectivorous birds in which the bird moves slowly along branches or hops from branch to branch, looking for insects on twigs and leaves. Some species specialize in creeping along larger branches and tree trunks to do this, even *probing* like a nuthatch or creeper; the BLACK-AND-WHITE WARBLER (Plate 54) is a good example of this foraging type. Some species also forage by *hover-gleaning*, in which they hover briefly next to or beneath a leaf and pluck an insect or spider from it. Others capture flying insects by *sallying* into the air after them, as true flycatchers do. This can be seen commonly in Florida wherever flocks of YELLOW-RUMPED WARBLERS (Plate 53) gather, and it is especially spectacular in the AMERICAN REDSTART (Plate 54), when you see a brilliant black and orange male flutter through the air in pursuit of a tiny moth. Still other warblers forage on the ground, good Florida examples being the PALM WARBLER (Plate 53) and OVENBIRD (Plate 55).

Breeding

In the breeding season, warblers are territorial birds, a male and a female defending a piece of real estate from other members of their species. Many warblers have two different types of songs, one to advertise their territory ownership and repel other males of their species, and another to attract females. Warblers are monogamous, but partners do not necessarily make equal contributions to breeding efforts. They build open cup or roofed nests in trees or shrubs or on the ground. Surprisingly, even some treetop foragers build ground nests, which may be safer from predators just because they are not so obvious when nestled into the ground. Usually the female alone builds the nest and incubates the 4 to 6 eggs for 11 to 13 days; the male may feed his incubating mate. Young fledge after 8 to 13 days in the nest.

Ecological Interactions

For many years, North American scientists interested in warblers and other migratory songbirds concentrated their research on the birds' ecology and behavior during breeding, essentially ignoring the fact that the birds spent half of each year wintering in the tropics, many of them in Mexico and Central America. Now, with the realization that the birds' biology during the non-breeding season is also important for understanding their lives, their ecology and behavior during the winter have become areas of intense interest. Researchers are now addressing a diverse set of questions. Are species that are territorial during breeding also territorial on their wintering grounds, and if so, in what way? Why do some birds remain territorial and solitary, but others move about in flocks, either with their own species or in multispecies mixed flocks? Do individual birds return to the same spot in the tropics each year in winter as they do for nesting during the

North American summer? Do species have similar diets on breeding and wintering grounds, or do some of them change drastically? Do migratory birds compete for food on their wintering grounds with those species that remain all year in the tropics? Why do some species retain their bright, species-specific breeding plumage in their winter habitat, whereas others molt into an entirely dull plumage?

Lore and Notes

Warblers are among the favorites of North American birders because they are brightly colored, active, very diverse, and highly migratory. 'Warbler waves' in the eastern states may involve migratory movements of a dozen or more species, and with the right conditions in spring and fall, trees can be full of these beautiful little birds. The BLACKPOLL WARBLER breeds all across the boreal forests of Canada and Alaska and winters primarily in South America; thus it has one of the longest migration routes of any small bird of the Americas. These birds leave Alaska in fall and fly all the way to the Atlantic coast, feeding voraciously in the Canadian Maritimes or New England. They then set out on a 3800 km (2400 mile) flight over the Atlantic Ocean to northern South America, where most of them arrive safely but much lighter, having burned up the extensive stores of fat they deposited under their skin during their pre-migratory feeding frenzy. Each fall, natural selection takes its toll on those birds not effective enough as foragers to put on the weight needed for the flight. Some of these birds are fortunate and land in Bermuda, but even then they may be out of luck, because on those small oceanic islands they may not find enough food to meet their needs for a further flight. Blackpolls are uncommon in fall in Florida, appearing mostly when easterly winds deposit some of the oceanic migrants onshore. On the return flight in spring, Blackpolls move through the islands of the Caribbean and are then much more common in the state, but still largely confined to the Keys and the peninsula.

Status

No warbler is threatened in Florida, but the BACHMAN'S WARBLER of southeastern swamps is recently extinct, perhaps lost because of the destruction of thickets of giant canes, the tall grasses in which they nested. Habitat destruction on their wintering grounds in Cuba might have also played a part in their demise. KIRTLAND'S WARBLER of jack-pine forests near the Great Lakes and the GOLDEN-CHEEKED WARBLER of juniper woodlands in Texas are just holding their own, threatened as much as anything by intense pressure from Brown-headed Cowbirds. Cowbirds are *brood parasites*, laying their eggs in the nests of other birds. The young cowbirds are usually larger and grow faster than their nest mates, and thus are able to obtain more food from their 'parents,' causing the parents' real young to starve. It is thought that aggressive programs to control cowbird populations have greatly reduced that particular threat to these two warblers. However, *natural succession* (the continued growth and change in species composition of shrubs and trees) constantly changes the landscape and, in the preferred habitats of these warblers, is producing habitats that are less favorable for them. In addition to cowbird trapping, controlled burning is now being used to set back succession and keep habitats in their optimal states for these two rare species.

Migrant birds, including many warblers, are also vulnerable to habitat destruction in their winter range. So much tropical lowland and mid-elevation forest has been destroyed that this loss surely has had an effect on populations of wintering birds (so-called *Neotropical migrants*) there, as well as the resident tropical species. Fortunately, at least some of the migrants do well in disturbed habitats. A recent controversy involves growing conditions for coffee, plantations of which have replaced natural forest in many areas. Where the upper story of shade trees is left intact (above low-growing coffee plants), or fast-growing leguminous trees are planted, this 'shade coffee' supports substantial populations of birds (enough so that these wintering grounds could rightly be called 'coffee grounds'). Where the shade trees are removed ('sun coffee'), very few birds persist. Imagine the environmental effect if all coffee drinkers insisted on shade coffee!

Profiles

Yellow-rumped Warbler, *Dendroica coronata*, Plate 53a
Northern Parula, *Parula americana*, Plate 53b
Prairie Warbler, *Dendroica discolor*, Plate 53c
Pine Warbler, *Dendroica pinus*, Plate 53d
Palm Warbler, *Dendroica palmarum*, Plate 53e
Black-and-white Warbler, *Mniotilta varia*, Plate 54a
Yellow-throated Warbler, *Dendroica dominica*, Plate 54b

Orange-crowned Warbler, *Vermivora celata*, Plate 54c
American Redstart, *Setophaga ruticilla*, Plate 54d
Prothonotary Warbler, *Protonotaria citrea*, Plate 54e
Yellow-breasted Chat, *Icteria virens*, Plate 55a
Common Yellowthroat, *Geothlypis trichas*, Plate 55b
Hooded Warbler, *Wilsonia citrina*, Plate 55c
Kentucky Warbler, *Oporornis formosus*, Plate 55d
Ovenbird, *Seiurus aurocapillus*, Plate 55e

29. Blackbirds and Starlings

The family Icteridae includes 97 species, arrayed in a variety of types called *blackbirds, cowbirds, grackles, meadowlarks, orioles, caciques (kah-SEE-kays)*, and *oropendolas*; they vary extensively in size, coloring, ecology, and behavior. These *icterids*, or *New World blackbirds*, are highly successful and conspicuous birds throughout their range, which encompasses all of North, Central, and South America. Most icterids are tropical in distribution, and about 14 regularly-occurring and 3 rare species occur in Florida; an additional species, the SPOT-BREASTED ORIOLE, was introduced and is now established in the Miami area. The wide ranges of sizes, shapes, colors, mating systems, and breeding behaviors of these birds attract frequent interest from avian researchers, and diversity is the key to comprehending the members of this family.

Icterids are medium to quite large passerines; the largest in Florida is the male BOAT-TAILED GRACKLE (Plate 58). Bills are usually sharply pointed and conical. Black is the predominant plumage color in the group, but many combine it with bright reds, yellows, or oranges. In some species, the sexes are alike (particularly in the tropical species), but in others, females look very different from males, often more cryptically outfitted in browns, grays, or streaked plumage. Pronounced size differences between the sexes, females being smaller, are common; male oropendolas, for instance, may weigh twice as much as females. Bills and eyes are sometimes brightly colored.

Grackles, common in city areas, are iridescent black birds with slender bills and long tails. The name 'blackbird' is applied to a variety of species, many of them marsh dwellers; the name stems from confusion among early colonists in North America, who confused common icterids such as the RED-WINGED BLACKBIRD and COMMON GRACKLE (both Plate 58) with the European Black-bird, a thrush related to the American Robin. Orioles are small, bright, often exquisitely marked birds in yellow or orange mixed with black and white, whose preferred habitat is forest and woodland. Meadowlarks are grassland birds, streaky brown above and yellow or red below. Oropendolas are spectacular, larger birds of tropical forests that breed in colonies. Caciques, which also usually breed in colonies, are smaller, sleeker black birds, frequently with red or yellow rumps and yellow bills. Cowbirds are black and brown like other blackbirds but have short, sparrowlike bills.

There are 114 species of starlings, family Sturnidae, occurring widely in the Old World but especially diverse in Africa and tropical Asia. One species, the EUROPEAN STARLING (Plate 60), was long ago introduced into the USA and has spread throughout much of temperate North America, including Florida, where it is now common. Two tropical species, the COMMON MYNA (Plate 60) and HILL MYNA, were introduced into southern Florida, and at least the former seems to be well established with growing populations. Starlings are the Old World equivalent of blackbirds, occurring in all habitats but typically represented by birds that are all or mostly black and tend to be gregarious in nature. Just as in blackbirds, there are many exceptions to this generality, as some starlings are plain brown and others are brilliantly colored. In fact, starlings are among the most iridescent of birds, and the glossy starlings and their relatives of open savannah country in Africa are especially spectacular.

Natural History
Ecology and Behavior

Icterids occur in all sorts of habitat types – woodlands, thickets, grassland, marshes, forest edges, and the higher levels of closed forests – but they are especially prevalent in more open areas. Their regular occupation of marshes has always been viewed as interesting, as they are not obviously adapted for living in aquatic environments – they do not have webbed feet, for example, nor are they able to float or dive. They eat a wide variety of foods including insects and other small animals, fruit, and seeds. Fruit-eaters are predominant among those species, for example oropendolas, that live in tropical forest canopies. Some are fairly omnivorous, as befitting birds that frequently become scavengers in urban and suburban settings. A common feature of the group is that seed-eaters (*granivores*) during the non-breeding periods become insect-eaters during breeding, and feed insects to their young. Icterids use a particular feeding method not widely used by other birds, known as *gaping* – a bird places its closed bill into crevices or under leaves, rocks or other objects, then forces the bill open, exposing the previously hidden space to its prying eyes and hunger. Outside of the breeding season, icterids, particularly the blackbirds and grackles, typically gather in large, sometimes enormous, flocks that can cause damage to roosting areas and agricultural crops. Blackbirds are regularly 'controlled' in areas in the USA where they inflict crop damage.

Starlings have many habits similar to those of blackbirds, including their basic one of feeding by gaping, for which their long, flattened, pointed bills are similarly modified. Like the icterids, there are fruit-eating starlings of tropical forests and seed-eating species of open country. One major difference is that there are many marsh-breeding icterids (South America is a wet continent) but none among the starlings (Africa is a dry continent). Again like blackbirds, some starlings travel in large flocks during the non-breeding season, foraging in a characteristic way: the flock moves forward by the rearmost birds flying over and landing at the advancing edge – a characteristic rolling motion.

Breeding

Icterid species pursue a variety of breeding strategies. Some, such as the orioles, breed in classically monogamous pairs, male and female defending a large territory in which the hanging pouch nest is situated. But others, including many caciques and the oropendolas, nest in colonies, where males display continuously and attempt to attract several females each. Our familiar RED-WINGED BLACK-BIRD is similarly polygynous, males defending territories and attracting as many females as they can – the average is three or four, the record 17! BOAT-TAILED GRACKLES are also highly polygynous, but COMMON GRACKLES and the other breeding icterids in Florida are usually monogamous. Perhaps most intriguing to scientists who study mating systems is that some very closely related icterid species have very different mating systems and breeding behaviors.

Icterid nests range from hanging pouches woven from grasses and other plant materials to open cups lined with mud to roofed nests built on the ground, hidden in meadow grass. Nests are almost always built by females. The female also incubates the 2 to 6 eggs, for 10 to 15 days, while the male guards the nest. Nestlings are fed for 11 to 20 days either by both parents (monogamous species) or primarily by the female (polygynous species). Cowbirds are brood parasites, building no nests themselves. Rather, females, after mating with one or more males, lay their eggs in the nests of other species – other icterids as well as other birds – and let host species raise their young (see below). By doing this, female BROWN-HEADED COWBIRDS (Plate 60) can lay as many as 40 eggs per season, greatly increasing their reproductive potential.

Starlings are not as varied as blackbirds in their mating systems; most are monogamous, and the much-maligned EUROPEAN STARLING is a model of bi-parental care, the sexes sharing in constructing the nest, incubating the 4 to 6 eggs for about 12 days, then feeding the young for about 3 weeks until they leave the nest. COMMON MYNAS, of tropical origin, have smaller clutches (typically 3 or 4 eggs) and may feed their young at a slower rate, as their fledgling period is of the order of a month. Most starlings are hole nesters, bringing large quantities of twigs, leaves, grass, and human artifacts into woodpecker holes, natural cavities, or human-provided cavities as varied as openings in streetlights and lamp poles or blocked drainpipes. Starlings are successful competitors against most other hole nesters, including the woodpeckers that make the holes that are such valued resources to other species.

Ecological Interactions

Cowbirds are *brood parasites* – including Florida's BROWN-HEADED COWBIRD. The parasitic cowbird lays eggs in the nests of other species, the *hosts*, and her young are raised by the foster parents. Some of the cowbirds specialize on other icterids as hosts – for example, the GIANT COWBIRD (of Central and South America) parasitizes only caciques and oropendolas and the SCREAMING COWBIRD (of South America) parasites only a single icterid, the BAYWING. Some host species have evolved the abilities to recognize cowbird eggs and eject them from their nests, but others have not. The cowbirds benefit from the interaction by being freed from defending a nesting territory and from nest-building and tending chores – what must amount to significant savings of energy and also decreased exposure to predators. The host species suffer reproductive harm because a female cowbird often ejects a host egg when she lays her own (when the nest is left unguarded). Also, more often than not, the cowbird's young are larger than the host's own, and are thus able to outcompete them for food brought to the nest by the adult birds. The host's own young often starve or are significantly weakened. Because of these harmful effects, the very successful cowbirds are believed to be responsible for severe population declines in North America of several species of small passerine birds. Because one population in these interactions benefits and one is harmed, the relationships between cowbirds and their hosts is *parasitic* – social parasitism in this case. How can brood parasitic behavior arise? Evolutionary biologists posit that one way would be if, long ago, some female cowbirds that built nests had their nests destroyed midway through their laying period. With an egg to lay but no nest in which to place it, females in this situation may have deposited the eggs in the nests of other species, which subsequently raised the cowbird young.

Status

The icterid group includes some of the most abundant birds of the Western Hemisphere, such as RED-WINGED BLACKBIRDS, COMMON GRACKLES, and BROWN-HEADED COWBIRDS. However, several tropical icterids are endangered: Puerto Rico's YELLOW-SHOULDERED BLACKBIRD (USA ESA listed), Brazil's FORBES' BLACKBIRD, and the MARTINIQUE ORIOLE and MONTSERRAT ORIOLE of the Lesser Antilles. A few others in South America are in serious trouble from combinations of habitat destruction, brood parasitism, and the pet trade.

Profiles

Eastern Meadowlark, *Sturnella magna*, Plate 58a
Red-winged Blackbird, *Agelaius phoeniceus*, Plate 58b
Boat-tailed Grackle, *Quiscalus major*, Plate 58c
Common Grackle, *Quiscalus quiscula*, Plate 58d
Orchard Oriole, *Icterus spurius*, Plate 59c
Baltimore Oriole, *Icterus galbula*, Plate 59d
European Starling, *Sturnus vulgaris*, Plate 60a
Common Myna, *Acridotheres tristis*, Plate 60d
Brown-headed Cowbird, *Molothrus ater*, Plate 60e

30. Tanagers and Cardinal Grosbeaks

Tanagers comprise a large New World group of beautifully colored, small passerine birds, most of which are limited to tropical areas. They are among the tropics' most common and visible birds, primarily owing to their habit of associating in flocks of several species that gather in the open, often near human habitation, to feed in fruit trees, and they are a treat to watch. All told, there are 252 species of tanagers (family Thraupidae), the group including the *typical tanagers*, the *honeycreepers*, and the *euphonias*. There are two regularly occurring and two rarely occurring species of this family in Florida. North American tanagers are all migratory, wintering somewhere in the tropics. Tanagers inhabit all forested and shrubby areas of the American tropics, over a wide range of elevations, and are particularly numerous in wet forests and forest edge areas. Not devotees of the dark forest interior, they prefer the lighter, upper levels of the forest canopy and more open areas; some prefer low, brushy habitat.

Tanagers are compact birds with fairly short, thick bills and short to medium-long tails. Their outstanding physical attribute is their bright coloring – they are strikingly marked with patches of color that traverse the entire spectrum, rendering the group among the most fabulously attired of birds. It has been said of the typical tanagers (genus *Tangara*) that they must 'exhaust the color patterns possible on sparrow-sized birds.' Yellows, reds, blues and greens predominate, although a relatively few species buck the trend and appear in plain blacks, browns, or grays. The species present even in a single flock on the slopes of the Andes may show all the colors of the rainbow, and a single individual of some species, for example the PARADISE TANAGER (black, blue, green, yellow, and red), can dazzle with its color pattern. The sexes look alike in the majority of species, but some are strongly dimorphic. Euphonias are small, stout tanagers, many of them glossy blue-black above, with yellow foreheads, breasts, and bellies. Honeycreepers are also usually brilliantly colored, with bright blues and greens emphasized. Some have brilliant yellow or red feet.

There are 42 species of *cardinal grosbeaks* of the family Cardinalidae, a primarily Neotropical group with representatives extending well up into North America, primarily in summer. Members of the group are called *cardinals*, *grosbeaks* (these two groups large species with large bills) and *buntings* (small species with small bills). There are six regularly occurring and two rare species in Florida. Most of these birds are very colorful, with blues, yellow, and reds predominating, although some species (and the females of many of them) are drab brownish or greenish. The PAINTED BUNTING (Plate 56) rivals any tropical bird in coloration, not surprising because – after all – it is a tropical bird, spending over half its life on its tropical wintering grounds. Fortunately for Floridians, the southern part of the state is included in that range, so bird enthusiasts regularly get to see these breathtakingly beautiful little birds at their bird feeders. Members of this family are mostly smallish birds, similar to tanagers in size, but unlike the tanagers, they are seed-eaters, with deep, conical bills that provide them the mechanical advantage necessary to crack seeds. The largest-billed species, as you might expect, eat the largest seeds. All the Florida species are migratory, with the exception of the NORTHERN CARDINAL (Plate 56), which is one of the least migratory of all birds. In that species, even the northernmost populations are resident, providing a flash of tropical color at a snow-covered bird feeder.

Natural History
Ecology and Behavior
In tropical areas, many tanager species associate in mixed-species tanager flocks, sometimes together with other types of birds. Finding five or more tanager species in a single group is common in the tropics, but in Florida the two regularly occurring species, the breeding SUMMER TANAGER (Plate 55) and the migratory SCARLET TANAGER, will not be found in flocks. A tanager flock, or single tanagers, will settle in a tree full of ripe fruit such as berries and enjoy a meal. These flocks move through forests or more open areas, searching for fruit-laden trees. Although tanagers mostly eat fruit, some also take insects from foliage or even out of the air. And although most species are arboreal, a few are specialized ground

foragers, taking seeds and insects. Tanagers usually go after small fruits that can be swallowed whole, such as berries, plucking the fruit while perched. After plucking it, a tanager rotates the fruit a bit in its bill, then mashes it and swallows. Ecologists divide frugivorous birds into *mashers*, such as tanagers, and *gulpers*, such as trogons and toucans, which swallow fruit whole and intact. One explanation is that mashing permits the bird to enjoy the sweet juice prior to swallowing the rest of the fruit. This fits with the idea that mashers select fruit based partially on taste, whereas gulpers, which swallow intact fruit, do not.

Cardinals, grosbeaks, and buntings feed on seeds according to the size of both the bird and the bill. The larger ones eat a variety of seeds, from large to small, while the smaller ones are restricted to small seeds. For example, the very small INDIGO BUNTINGS (Plate 56) and PAINTED BUNTINGS feed on weed seeds in open areas and at forest edges. Some of the tropical grosbeaks also eat quite a bit of fruit.

Breeding

Most tanagers appear to breed monogamously. Breeding in the tropics is usually concentrated during the transition from dry to wet season, when fruit and insects are most plentiful, but in Florida, the SUMMER TANAGER breeds in the season its name indicates. Summer is distinctly the favorable season for bird breeding in Florida, as it corresponds to both the warm season and the rainy season. In many tropical tanager species, male and female stay paired throughout the year, but the sexes go their own way in the non-breeding season in the North American migratory species. Males of many species give food to females in *courtship feeding*, and during courtship displays make sure that potential mates see their brightly colored patches. Either the female alone or the pair builds a cup nest in a tree or shrub. In the North American migratory tanagers, the 3 to 5 eggs are incubated by the female only for 11 to 14 days, and young are fed by both parents for about two weeks prior to their fledging and for another one to two weeks after fledging.

The cardinal grosbeak group are monogamous breeders with open cup nests, typically built by females low in trees and shrubs. They lay 3 to 5 eggs, which the female (both parents in the ROSE-BREASTED GROSBEAK) incubates for 11 to 14 days. The young fledge after a further 9 to 14 days, and in the species that often have two broods per season, the male will take over their feeding while the female begins to lay another clutch of eggs.

Ecological Interactions

Tanagers, as mashing frugivores, sometimes drop the largest seeds from the fruits they consume before swallowing but, nonetheless, many seeds are ingested; consequently, these birds are active seed dispersers. Some ecologists believe tanagers to be among the most common dispersers of tropical trees and shrubs, that is, they are responsible for dropping the seeds that grow into the trees and shrubs that populate the areas they inhabit. Euphonias, for example, are crucial for the mistletoe life cycle because, after eating the berries, they deposit their seed-bearing droppings on tree branches, where the seeds germinate, the mistletoe plants starting out there as epiphytes.

The INDIGO BUNTING is another good example of a species that changes its habits from breeding to wintering grounds. In summer, Indigo Buntings are familiar as bright blue birds that sing loudly and cheerily from dead branches and telephone wires throughout the day. If another male bunting appears, there is an immediate territorial chase. On the wintering grounds, for example the Yucatán

Peninsula of Mexico, where they are especially common, Indigo Buntings occur in flocks of silent little brown birds (they change their plumage twice a year) that fly up from the edges of corn fields.

Lore and Notes

Tanagers illustrate two interesting points about migration and bird plumages. The tropical species tend to be *monomorphic*, males and females looking the same. This is because, being resident, they defend all-year territories, and both sexes are brightly colored to facilitate quick and easy recognition by others of their own species in a territorial interaction. Temperate-breeding tanagers, on the other hand, are all *dimorphic*, the males bright and the females dull. They migrate into their breeding grounds, and the male needs to be bright to be quickly recognizable when he begins to sing and defend a territory. A receptive female arrives at the territory, the pair mates, and the female quickly lays eggs and begins to incubate them. Being bright would actually be a disadvantage for a bird sitting on an open-cup nest, so females are drab and quite different-looking from their fancy mates. The second point is that these migratory birds move into the territories of resident tanager species during the winter, and it might be advantageous then to be dull and inconspicuous, and indeed male SCARLET TANAGERS, brilliant red with black wings and tail, molt into greenish birds in the non-breeding season, looking much like their mates. SUMMER TANAGERS, which do not migrate as far and don't spend the winter in the range of as many tropical species, do not change plumage at that time, the males remaining red. We often find two closely related species with very different appearance because of differences in their lifestyles.

Status

A number of tropical tanagers, especially in Colombia and Brazil, but even as far north as southern Mexico, are considered threatened or endangered, primarily owing to habitat loss. The North American species range from mature forest to second growth and are secure as long as good-sized patches of woodland remain in both breeding and wintering areas. The same is true for the cardinal grosbeaks.

Profiles

Summer Tanager, *Piranga rubra*, Plate 55f
Indigo Bunting, *Passerina cyanea*, Plate 56a
Painted Bunting, *Passerina ciris*, Plate 56b
Blue Grosbeak, *Guiraca caerulea*, Plate 56c
Northern Cardinal, *Cardinalis cardinalis*, Plate 56d

31. Sparrows and Finches

The names *sparrow*, *bunting*, *finch*, and *grosbeak* have been long applied to small birds with conical bills adapted for cracking seeds, and these birds are not all closely related. The largest group of birds that have received these names belongs to the family Emberizidae – the *New World sparrows* and *Old World buntings*. This is a large, diverse, almost worldwide group of 157 species that includes some of Florida's most common and visible passerine birds. Members of this family occur just about everywhere in the New World, in all kinds of habitats and climates, from Alaska and northern Canada south to Tierra del Fuego. Florida is home to 20 species of the sparrow/bunting family, with another 11 as rare visitors. Many of the species of regular occurrence leave Florida during the summer, breeding in the northern part of the continent, but some of them, for example the EASTERN TOWHEE (Plate 56) and BACHMAN'S SPARROW (Plate 57), remain throughout that season.

For our purposes here, we will speak of all birds in this group as sparrows. Sparrows are generally small birds, with relatively short, thick, conical bills, that are specialized to crush and open seeds. In some species, the upper and lower halves of the bill can be moved from side to side, the better to manipulate small seeds. Sparrows have relatively large feet that they use in scratching the ground to find seeds; they scratch by pushing backwards with both feet at once, and towhees make enough noise doing so that you might think there was a good-sized mammal in the bushes. Coloring varies greatly within the group, but the plumage of most is the epitome of camouflage for a ground bird, various shades of brown and gray, with streaked backs; towhees are the biggest, brightest sparrows. Distinctions among the species are typically seen in their head and breast patterns; the sexes generally look alike.

The HOUSE SPARROW (Plate 60), one of the globe's most widespread and well-known birds, is a member of family Passeridae, the *Old World sparrows*, a group of 36 species of small open-country birds. Many of them, including House Sparrows, are drably costumed in brownish streaked plumages; male and female sometimes look alike, although they are quite distinct in the single species profiled here. Although not closely related, members of both this and the previous family are called sparrows; note that they evolved independently the same conical bill adapted for eating seeds that caused them to receive the same name.

There are 140 *finches* in the Fringillidae, a family found on all the forested continents but Australia. The greatest diversity of species is in the North Temperate zone, and most of the tropical species occur on higher mountains, although a few of them have become specialized for desert life. Finches occur in all temperate forest types, but no species occurs in tropical rain forest, probably because most tropical forest trees have seeds too large even for the larger-billed finch species to crack open. Finches are seed-eating birds with conical bills, the high base of the bill furnishing mechanical advantage for cracking seeds. Larger finches eat larger seeds and have considerably stronger bills, and the smallest finches – *redpolls* and *siskins* – have more slender bills adapted for opening tiny seeds; most species fit in between these extremes. Many finches are colorful, with reds and yellows predominating in otherwise brown-streaked plumages. Males are brighter than females in most species. Close to the tropics and with no mountains to speak of, Florida has relatively few finches, and the only really common and widespread one is the AMERICAN GOLDFINCH (Plate 59).

Natural History
Ecology and Behavior

Sparrows are mostly seed-eaters, although they feed insects to their young, as do most passerine birds. They are birds of thickets, forest edge, and open country, foraging mostly on the ground or at low levels in shrubs or trees. Because many species spend large amounts of time in thickets and brushy areas, they can be quite inconspicuous. Their songs vary from buzzy and insectlike (species of open grassland) to loud and musical (especially species of dense thickets). The sweet, whistled song of the WHITE-THROATED SPARROW (Plate 57) can sometimes be heard in spring before the birds migrate back to their Canadian breeding grounds, and the resident BACHMAN'S SPARROW also has a very pleasing song; for the other extreme, check out the resident population of the GRASSHOPPER SPARROW. Some sparrows show local *song dialects*, with all the birds in one region singing more or less similarly and birds in another region sounding quite different.

Most species are strongly territorial, a mated pair aggressively excluding other members of the species from sharply defined areas. These territorial proclivities usually disappear in winter, although SONG SPARROWS (Plate 57), among a few other species, maintain winter territories as well. Some species within the group travel in small flocks during the winter; the DARK-EYED JUNCO, an uncommon visitor to Florida, is a good example of this behavior.

Old World sparrows are more social than the American sparrows, often nesting in loose colonies and always going around in flocks after breeding. HOUSE SPARROWS may form into flocks of hundreds, sometimes thousands of birds, at which time they can become significant agricultural pests on cereals and grains. That species, having been introduced from its native Eurasia to most other parts of the world, now flourishes over vast stretches of the Earth, essentially wherever there are people, excepting rainforests, deserts, and arctic tundra areas. House Sparrows live in and near cities and towns at elevations from sea level to 4500 m (14,700 ft); they have been seen feeding on upper floor ledges of New York City's Empire State Building. Members of the Old World sparrow family eat mostly seeds but will eat or attempt to eat a great variety of things, including insects and plant buds and leaves. House Sparrows are fond of food that has been discarded by people (French fries being a perennial favorite).

Finches are the most confirmed seed-eaters among the birds. One of the more recently evolved families, their evolutionary radiation probably occurred during the similar radiation of the flowering plants, especially woody plants of the North Temperate zone. Many finches are specialists, eating seeds of a particular size range in their environment and thus often specializing on particular trees. For example, redpolls are especially fond of birch seeds and siskins fond of alder seeds, so flocks of these tiny seed-eaters can often be found in the non-breeding season by checking groves of their favorite trees. They are not specialists to the point of starving to death without their preferred seeds, however, and most species of the family come readily to bird feeders stocked with mixed bird seeds. Many birds of other families are also seed-eaters, but those birds feed insects to their young, the insects a good source of the protein that the young need for growth. True finches, on the other hand, can raise their young on a seed diet.

Breeding

Most sparrows are monogamous breeders. The female of the pair usually builds a cup-shaped nest out of grasses and fine rootlets. Nests are concealed on the ground or low in a shrub or tree. Females of the Floridian species in this family incubate 3 to 5 eggs for 10 to 14 days. Both males and females feed nestlings, which leave the nest after 7 to 12 days, in some cases before they can fly, but are fed for another 2 to 3 weeks. Most sparrows, especially those that breed southerly, have two broods per season.

HOUSE SPARROWS are also monogamous, nesting in trees or in cavities in buildings, and both parents constructing messy-looking, ball-shaped nests of straw, grass, and pieces of trash. Two to 4 eggs are incubated by the female for 10 to 13 days; young are fed by both parents and fledge after 14 to 17 days in the nest. Several broods are raised each year, and breeding has been observed in all months at lower latitudes.

Finches breed in monogamous pairs like most other passerines. Courtship feeding is common in this family, the males offering tidbits to their mates at regular intervals. This may serve both to strengthen the pair bond and to add to the female's energy resources while eggs are developing in her body. Nests, of twigs and a variety of finer plant material are constructed by the female, in shrubs and trees in most species. Finches lay clutches of 3 to 6 eggs, and the female incubates them for about 2 weeks. The young remain in the nest for 2 to 3 weeks and are fed by both parents.

Ecological Interactions

Members of the American sparrow family are the most common seed-eating birds in North America. Many of them form flocks in the non-breeding season, and the flocking behavior of several species has been studied from the standpoint of predation. It appears clear that foraging in flocks confers some real advantages. Birds in larger flocks spend more time eating and less time looking around than birds in smaller flocks or single birds, presumably because the more birds there are, the less likely a predator will be able to surprise them. Of course, foraging in a flock isn't all to the good; birds in this situation are pushed into direct competition for resources with their flock mates. To alleviate the problem of constant bickering, birds develop *dominance hierarchies* (first called 'peck order' in chickens). Subordinate birds give way before dominant ones when they encounter a choice food morsel at the same time. This is most easily studied at artificial feeding stations, where birds are forced into competition, but the situation may be a bit more relaxed in nature, where birds are usually spread out more when searching for seeds.

Lore and Notes

In addition to their reputation for ecological success, the New World sparrows are known especially as a group that is the subject of frequent scientific research, and therefore as one that has contributed substantially to many areas of our knowledge about birds. For instance, studies of the North American SONG SPARROW and Neotropical RUFOUS-COLLARED SPARROW provided the basis for much of the information we have about avian territoriality and many other kinds of behavior. Also, the WHITE-CROWNED SPARROW has been the species of choice for many researchers for investigations of bird physiology and the relationships between ecology and physiology, especially with regard to the timing of breeding and migration. Song dialects also have been thoroughly studied in this species.

Because almost everyone is familiar with HOUSE SPARROWS (whether they know it or not) and because they're one of the world's commonest birds, it might seem a waste here to devote to them illustration space and a paragraph or two. But if you think about it, the lowly House Sparrow is actually nothing short of amazing. It's a 30-g (1-oz) dynamo of vigorous, competitive energy. These sparrows have probably been in a close commensal relationship with people since the development of agriculture in the Middle East, 10,000+ years ago, feeding on cereal and grain crops and on seeds left in fields. Ornithological historians suspect that these small brown birds would then have prospered and multiplied during the age of non-mechanized cities, when beasts of burden and transport such as horses perpetually filled streets with their seed-rich droppings. Europeans brought House Sparrows with them when they colonized great sections of the planet during the 17th through 19th centuries. They brought many more of their native bird species also, but relatively few made 'successful' colonizations (meaning, the first few individuals released into new lands survived, thrived, reproduced, and initiated self-perpetuating, range-expanding populations), and fewer still colonized with the swiftness and eventual pervasiveness of the House Sparrow. Its first successful North American introduction evidently occurred during the mid-1850s in New York. It took only 50 years for the birds to reach the Pacific Ocean, essentially colonizing and occupying all suitable habitat on the entire USA mainland. They now also occur over much of sub-arctic Canada, Mexico, and Central and South America, and they are still spreading.

HOUSE FINCHES (Plate 59), as their name implies, also do well around people, and they have also spread from an introduction, in this case from the opposite direction. A common bird of the high plateaus of Mexico and throughout the southwestern USA, this species multiplied as forests were turned into farmland and cities, eventually spreading northward into the Pacific Northwest. Birds from the West that were illegally held captive were released by pet store owners in New York City (there must be something about New York) in the mid-20th century, and in the ensuing 50 years they have increased and spread south and west, meeting and blending with their original populations! They have moved into northern Florida and will probably make it down the peninsula one of these days.

Status

Most of the American sparrows are abundant, but a few have fared poorly, and Florida has been the focus of these problems. The SEASIDE SPARROW is widespread along the Atlantic and Gulf coasts of the USA, but a subspecies restricted to Cape Canaveral, Florida, called the DUSKY SEASIDE SPARROW, became extinct only recently, as its limited habitat was drained, flooded, burned, developed, and poisoned. If those actions weren't enough, some of the changes made in the ecosystem allowed nest predators such as grackles to flourish. In 1967, there were well over 1000 birds; in 1987, the last male died in captivity, after efforts were made to mate it with females of other subspecies. Later studies of DNA showed that even that effort was misguided, as the subspecies chosen for its similar-looking females was in fact distant genetically from the Dusky. Now there is another problem subspecies, the FLORIDA GRASSHOPPER SPARROW, which has been listed as Endangered (USA ESA). With a very limited distribution northwest of Lake Okeechobee, this subspecies needs open prairies, so both grazing and fires in moderation appear to favor it; nevertheless, it is now absent from some areas where it formerly bred.

Profiles

Eastern Towhee, *Pipilo erythrophthalmus*, Plate 56e
Bachman's Sparrow, *Aimophila aestivalis*, Plate 57a
Chipping Sparrow, *Spizella passerina*, Plate 57b
Savannah Sparrow, *Passerculus sandwichensis*, Plate 57c
Swamp Sparrow, *Melospiza georgiana*, Plate 57d
White-throated Sparrow, *Zonotrichia albicollis*, Plate 57e
Song Sparrow, *Melospiza melodia*, Plate 57f
American Goldfinch, *Carduelis tristis*, Plate 59a
House Finch, *Carpodacus mexicanus*, Plate 59b
House Sparrow, *Passer domesticus*, Plate 60b

Environmental Close-up 4:
Why Is Florida So Full of Exotic Birds?

Florida is full of parrots – yes, parrots! No fewer than 64 species of exotic parrots have been seen free-flying in the state, most in the Miami area, and, of these, perhaps as many as 14 species are now established breeders, with populations of some of them growing steadily. Total numbers of hundreds or even thousands of birds have been estimated for Budgerigars, Monk Parakeets, White-winged Parakeets, and Yellow-chevroned Parakeets. Black-hooded, Blue-crowned, Red-masked, Mitred, and Dusky-headed Parakeets, and Red-crowned and Orange-winged Parrots have been estimated in the mere dozens. Interestingly, all of these species come from Central and South America, except for the 'budgie,' from Australia. Perhaps this is merely because so much of the parrot trade, both legal and illegal, comes from the New World Tropics. Sadly, the one parrot that did occur naturally in Florida, the Carolina Parakeet, is long extinct. That species was adapted for life in a temperate climate, so it would not have suffered much competition from the hordes of its tropical relatives, had it survived.

And parrots are not the only non-native birds that have become established in the state. In addition to the widespread Rock Dove (domestic pigeon), European Starling, House Finch, and House Sparrow, the list includes Black-bellied Whistling-Duck (New World Tropics), Muscovy Duck (New World Tropics), Ringed Teal (South America), Purple Swamphen (Old World Tropics), Eurasian Collared-Dove (Europe), White-winged Dove (Southwest USA and south into Tropics), Red-whiskered Bulbul (Southeast Asia), Common Myna (Southeast Asia), Hill Myna (Southeast Asia), and Spot-breasted Oriole (Central America). This assemblage of avian aliens gives a distinctly exotic flavor to birdwatching in southern Florida. In fact, southern Florida has a higher proportion of introduced birds than anywhere else in North America and perhaps anywhere else in the world, with the exception of Hawaii, where the situation is even more extreme.

Why are these birds so successful in southern Florida? After all, captive birds escape or are released in other areas and don't make a go of it. The answer lies in latitude. If you spend time in southern Florida, you will be struck by the tropical ambience. Key West, after all, is only 65 km (40 miles) from the Tropic of Cancer, so southern Florida is almost tropical in the true sense. But it is close enough to the tropics to be warm all year, to have typical tropical rainy and dry seasons, and to be suitable for plants and animals from just about anywhere in the world's tropical zone. So among the native flora are epiphytic orchids and bromeliads and mangroves, all with their origins in the tropics. In addition, almost anywhere you look in the cities, you can find bananas and mangos and guavas, jacarandas and poincianas and bougainvilleas, plants imported from all around the equatorial belt. With a virtually tropical climate and a virtually tropical collection of plants, it's not surprising that many of the animals are tropical, too. Think of crocodiles, manatees, Greenhouse Frogs, and coral snakes among the native fauna, and geckos, Giant Toads, Peacock Bass, and walking catfish among the introduced fauna. Many of the native birds of Florida are tropical – Roseate Spoonbill, Limpkin, Snail Kite, White-crowned Pigeon, Gray Kingbird, and numerous others – so it's not surprising that tropical birds of all kinds flourish here, no matter where in the world they should be.

These exotic species flourish in part because they have relatively few competitors, a result of being at the end of a peninsula, where the diversity of native species is relatively low. This is known as the *peninsula effect*, whereby species diversity decreases as one progresses out a long peninsula. The reasons for this are not very well known, but in this particular case, it is clear that the tip of the Florida peninsula does not represent optimal habitat for many of the birds (and other organisms) that live there. It is just too different in too many ways – climate, soil, and plant communities among them. Going down the Florida peninsula is very much an experience of moving from the temperate zone to the tropics. Even related species respond differently to this change. For example, Carolina Chickadees and Tufted Titmice are common birds over much of south-eastern USA. The titmouse extends down the Florida peninsula into the Big Cypress Swamp, but the chickadee occurs no farther south than the Tampa Bay area. These two birds live in the same habitats in most parts of their range, so ecologists would love to know why the chickadee can't make the grade in the southern Florida habitats in which the titmouse thrives.

One other factor, cultural rather than ecological, is responsible for the abundance of exotics of all kinds in southern Florida. The Miami airport is often the first stop for animals taken from the tropics to be sold in the pet trade (both legally and illegally), and some of these unfortunate animals escape or are released from captivity in transit.

Environmental Close-up 5:
The Advantages of Colonial Nesting

Many of Florida's birds nest in colonies, either on islands (pelicans, frigatebirds, gulls, terns, skimmers) or in trees standing in water (cormorants, herons, ibises, storks). These assemblages of breeding birds are often called 'rookeries' (from the colonial nesting groups of ROOKS, members of the crow family that are common in Eurasia). Many kinds of birds nest in colonies (about 12% of all bird species), so there must be some special advantage in doing so. In fact, there are probably several reasons for colonial nesting in birds.

One important reason is for *safety*. Birds that nest on the ground, as so many marine birds do, are subject to predation by snakes at low latitudes and mammals at all latitudes. One way to *avoid predation* is by nesting on islands or in trees over water, places where snakes and mammals are scarce or have difficulty reaching. But such ideal locations may be in short supply, so many birds may be packed into a relatively small space. This in itself causes breeding densities of some species to be high. But the birds realize real advantages from nesting in groups. Some predators are of a size that an individual bird or pair could not protect their eggs and young from them, but numerous individuals of the nesting species can sometimes gang up on such predators and *prevent predation*. When predators approach colonies of nesting gulls and terns, they are dive-bombed unmercifully and, even if not hit, are so distracted that they may turn around before they reach the first nest. Individual predators do learn to ignore the commotion, however, and some predators are even attracted to the noise and activity of a nesting colony. Both Great Horned Owls and Black-crowned Night-Herons have been known to visit colonies of terns every night and make off with both adult and young birds, the day-active terns having no defense against a nocturnal predator that can reach their offshore sanctuary from a nearby mainland.

Another factor provided by the high density of birds in colonies is *safety in numbers*. Predators enter colonies from their edges, and the peripherally nesting birds are most at risk; central birds may not be threatened at all. Thus, not only does colonial nesting protect against predation, but larger colonies seem less at risk, and this makes colonies of thousands of birds more understandable. Furthermore, another safety factor provided by very large colonies is *predator saturation* (there are too many prey animals for predators to have much effect on their population). Most predators are territorial, and if the colony was in the territory of only one or a pair of predators, the birds could finish their breeding before that pair of predators could take many of their eggs or young. Of course, the overall success of the colony is not applicable to the relatively few birds unfortunate enough to be eaten or to have their nests destroyed.

Besides predation, nesting in colonies also confers *benefits for feeding*. Seabirds such as gulls and terns are by definition marine animals, and nest sites should be situated as near as possible to rich oceanic feeding areas. But if prey species are patchily distributed, and especially if they move about, as fish schools do in the ocean, the best way birds could exploit their prey would be to breed in one spot in the midst of the area in which the prey might be encountered. An island represents a focal point where breeding can be accomplished, and yet the birds can still fly out in all directions to forage for fish and other marine life for themselves and their young. This is very different from the territoriality of terrestrial and freshwater birds, which defend a relatively restricted area in which they can find all or most of their food.

There is also the thought that breeding colonies may serve as *information centers* for birds to learn about good foraging areas. Imagine if you were a heron on a nest in a mangrove swamp, and your neighbors returning from the West all had beaks full of fish, whereas those coming from the East were empty-beaked. In which direction would you fly when it was your turn to go out and bring back a meal for your chicks? The idea of information centers is intuitively pleasing, and there is some evidence that birds do use each other as indicators or guides.

Another very good reason for nesting in colonies is the opportunity a large group provides for *mate-finding*. Most seabirds move over long distances and are spread out all over the ocean, while wading birds are scattered over swamps and marshes and mudflats. By gathering at one place at the right time, they are just about assured of a mate. For the most part, if both members of a pair return to the nesting area, they come together again; this is considered monogamy, even though they go their own ways in the non-breeding season.

Chapter 9

MAMMALS

- *Introduction*
- *General Characteristics of Mammals*
- *Classification of Mammals*
- *Seeing Mammals in Florida*
- *Family Profiles*
    1. *Opossum*
    2. *Armadillo*
    3. *Bats*
       Carnivores
    4. *Raccoon*
    5. *Coyote and Foxes*
    6. *Bear*
    7. *Skunks and Otters*
    8. *Cats*
    9. *Marine Mammals*
    10. *Pigs and Deer*
    11. *Rodents – Mice, Rats, and Pocket Gopher*
    12. *Rodents – Squirrels*
    13. *Rabbits and Hares*
- *Environmental Close-up 6: Reducing Roadkill*

Introduction

Leafing through this book, the reader will have noticed the profiles of many more birds than mammals. Why not include more mammals? There are several reasons for this discrepancy – good biological reasons. One is that, even though the tropics generally have more species of mammals than temperate or arctic regions, the total number of mammal species worldwide, and the number in any region, is less than the number of birds. In fact, there are in total only about 4500 mammal species, compared to 9700 species of birds, and the relative difference is reflected in Florida's fauna. But the more compelling reason not to include more mammals in a book on commonly sighted wildlife is that, even in regions with a high degree of mammalian diversity, mammals are rarely seen. Most mammals are nocturnal. They are also shy, secretive, and usually live in dense cover. We have profiled the more conspicuous ones. We also included several mammals, such as the FLORIDA PANTHER (Plate 62), GOLDEN MOUSE (Plate 65), and LEAST SHREW (Plate 65), which are not easy to see but that are ecologically interesting; and, in the case of the panther, even if few people see them, it is still exciting to know that they are out there.

General Characteristics of Mammals

If birds are feathered vertebrates, mammals are hairy ones. The first group of mammals arose, so fossils tell us, about 245 million years ago, splitting off from the primitive reptiles during the late Triassic Period of the Mesozoic Era. Four main traits distinguish mammals and confer upon them great advantages over other types of mammals. These traits include:

(1) hair on their bodies, which insulates them from cold and protects them;
(2) suckling their young with milk, enabling females to convert just about any type of food into nourishment for offspring;
(3) the bearing of live young instead of eggs, which allows breeding females to be mobile and hence, safer than if they had to sit on eggs for several weeks; and
(4) advanced brains, with the obvious benefits that go along with increased brainpower.

Classification of Mammals

Mammals are quite variable in size and form, many being highly adapted – changed through evolution – to specialized habits and lifestyles. Bats have wings and are the only mammals capable of flight, manatees are somewhat fish-like in form and are specialized for an aquatic lifestyle, and bobcats are finely built for stalking and capturing rabbits. Some, such as *moles* (see, for example, EASTERN MOLE, Plate 66), live out most of their lives underground. The smallest mammals are the *shrews*, tiny insect-eaters that weigh as little as 2.5 g (1/10 oz). Shrews are voracious little predators, usually solitary, that are active on the ground mostly at night (and so are not often seen, but dogs sometimes find them); their high metabolic rates mean that they need to seek food for many hours each day. There are about 30 shrew species in North America, three of which occur in Florida; two, the LEAST SHREW and SHORT-TAILED SHREW, are shown in Plate 65. The largest mammals are the *whales*, weighing in at up to 160,000 kg (350,000 lb, half the weight of a loaded Boeing 747) – as far as anyone knows, the largest animals ever.

Mammals are divided into three major groups, primarily according to reproductive methods. The *monotremes* are an ancient group that lays eggs and still retains some other reptile-like characteristics. Only three species of monotremes survive, the Duck-billed Platypus and two species of spiny anteaters, in Australia and New Guinea. The *marsupials* give birth to live young that are relatively undeveloped. At birth the young climb unassisted across their mother's abdomen into her pouch, where they attach to a nipple and continue their development. Though the name of the group is derived from the Latin *marsupium*, meaning 'pouch,' not all marsupials have pouches. For instance, many of the smaller species of opossums do not have pouches. There are about 240 species of marsupials, including kangaroos, koalas, wombats, and opossums. Marsupials are found mainly in Australia, New Guinea, and South and Central America, but one species, the VIRGINIA OPOSSUM (Plate 61), is found across much of the USA and into southern Canada.

The majority of mammals are *eutherians*, or *true mammals*. These animals are distinguished by having an advanced placenta, which connects the mother to her developing babies, allowing for a long internal development (and so are often called *placental* mammals). This trait, which allows embryos to develop to a fairly mature form in safety, and for the female to be mobile until birth, has allowed the true mammals to become the dominant land vertebrates. The true mammals include those which most people are familiar: rodents, rabbits, cats, dogs, bats, primates, elephants, horses, whales – everything from house mice to ecotravellers.

The 4500+ species of living mammals are divided into about 20 orders and 115 families. Approximately 96 species occur in Florida, of which 63 are terrestrial or fly; the remainder are marine species.

Seeing Mammals in Florida

Mammals are difficult to see. One can go for weeks and see very few of them. A great deal of luck is involved. Fortunately, Florida has a few mammals that are comparatively easy to see. RIVER OTTERS (Plate 61) are often encountered in Florida's rivers and springs. We have watched a River Otter fishing in front of a crowd of 25 or more people at Manatee Springs, and seen a family of five otters playing and racing up and down the bank along the Chassahowitzka River. WEST INDIAN MANATEES (Plate 68) are likewise fairly easy to see, especially when winter cold fronts drive them into springs and the warm water effluents of powerplants. EASTERN FOX SQUIRRELS (Plate 64) are fairly common during the daytime in the high pine sandhills and on golf courses. EASTERN GRAY SQUIRRELS (Plate 64) are a regular feature in most state parks.

Nocturnal animals are more difficult. Bats are easily spotted in the early evening, especially as they flit around ponds and lakes in pursuit of insects. NORTHERN RACCOONS (Plate 61) are common in state parks, and they have learned to beg for food from visitors (don't encourage them!). If you are driving at night, it is common to see opossums and armadillos crossing or foraging beside the road, and WHITE-TAILED DEER (Plate 63) often graze on roadside verges, frighteningly close to traffic.

Although many mammals are difficult to see, you are likely to spot at least traces of them – the tracks they leave in mud and sand. Following an animal's tracks often provides insights into its behavior. *Scats*, or fecal droppings, also indicate a mammal has been present, and the contents of scats are clues to what the animal has been eating. If one waits quietly beside a pond or stream, the chances of seeing critters, as they approach to drink, are greatly improved.

In general, early mornings and late afternoons are good times to look for mammals. Alternatively, take a nighttime stroll with a flashlight. Shine the light up into the trees as well as on the ground and look for bright, shiny eyes reflecting back at you. You may see flying squirrels, opossums, raccoons, and, perhaps, if you are in the right place at the right time, a GOLDEN MOUSE.

Family Profiles

1. Opossum

If you ask someone to name a mammal with a pouch, the odds are that they will say 'kangaroo.' But *marsupials* – named for the marsupium, or pouch, in which they carry their young – come in a wide variety of shapes and sizes. Most of the world's more than 240 marsupial species live in Australia and New Guinea, where they have become the ecological equivalents of carnivores, ungulates, moles, rabbits, rats and more. Of the eight living families of marsupials, three occur in the New World, and only one species, the VIRGINIA OPOSSUM (Plate 61), is found north of Mexico.

The Virginia Opossum has expanded its range significantly during the last century. Before European settlement of North America, the northern limits of its range were Kentucky, Indiana and Ohio, but the species is now found as far north as the Great Lakes and Canada. It is not found in the arid western parts of the USA; and populations in Baja California, British Columbia, Idaho and western Colorado are the results of introductions. In Florida, the Virginia Opossum is abundant and frequently seen, especially as roadkills.

'An opossum hath a head like a Swine, & a taile like a Rat, and is of the Bignes of a Cat. Under her belly shee hath a bagge, wherein shee lodgeth, carrieth, and suckleth her young.' So wrote the English explorer John Smith in 1612, describing a Virginia Opossum. Smith's description needs only little elaboration. Virginia Opossums grow throughout life, resulting in considerable size and weight differences; they range from about 1 kg (2.2 lb) to 6 kg (13 lb), and males are larger and heavier than females. About the size of a domestic cat, they have a pointed nose with long, highly sensitive whiskers, thin, leaf-like ears and a nearly naked prehensile tail that is black at the base and pinkish for the remainder. Virginia Opossums often wrap their tails around branches when they climb to help them balance and hold on, but contrary to popular belief, they rarely hang by the tail. The feet are adapted for climbing, and all the toes, except the opposable thumb on the hind foot, are clawed. Females have a fur-lined pouch on the abdomen. Fur color is highly variable, which results primarily from differences in the color of the *guard hairs* (coarse, rigid, long, pigmented outer hairs). In northern USA and Canada, Virginia Opossums are usually gray, but black opossums are occasionally seen in Florida.

Natural History

Ecology and Behavior

Resting during the day in tree cavities, hollow logs, or underground burrows, VIRGINIA OPOSSUMS typically emerge after sunset in their quest for food. They are omnivorous. Most of their time is spent foraging on the ground, searching for insects, worms, mollusks, small vertebrates and fruits. They also climb well and are sometimes seen feeding on wild cherry, persimmons, or grapes. They will eat just about anything, including carrion, garbage, or pet food. Opossums are found in a variety of forested habitats, including deciduous woodlands, swamps, pine flatwoods, and are more abundant in habitats with or adjoining permanent water. They also survive well in suburban areas and are often considered pests because of their habit of raiding garbage cans.

Breeding

In Florida, VIRGINIA OPOSSUM breeding activity typically begins in January/ February. Young are born in an embryonic state after a 13-day gestation period. The bee-sized babies emerge from the birth canal and make their own way into the mother's pouch, where they attach with their mouth to a nipple. Micro-barbs on the babies' lips and tongue fit into small grooves on the nipples, essentially sealing each young to a teat. Some 20 or more young are born but females have 13 nipples, so only the embryos that succeed in attaching to a nipple survive. The usual litter size is 7. The young grow fast; by 65 days their eyes are open, they are well furred, and can crawl about on their mother as she rests. The young are now the size of large mice and the pouch becomes crowded, making it difficult for the female to walk. At this stage the young begin to ride on the mother's back, grasping wedges of her fur with their mouths and feet. This is a hazardous time of their lives – babies regularly fall off and get left behind. Wildlife rescue services get many phone calls from distressed homeowners who find squawking baby opossums in the backyard after the family dog has chased the mother. When young are about 80 days old, the litter becomes too cumbersome for the mother to carry, and she leaves the kids in a burrow or some other secure den while she forages. By 100 days of age the young are weaned and on their own, and the female has a new litter of young in the pouch. The youngsters begin to forage around the den area, gradually expanding their range, but they are extremely vulnerable at this age: Great Horned Owls, foxes, snakes and other predators kill 90% of newly independent young. Females usually give birth to two litters per year; in exceptional cases they may have three.

Ecological Interactions

Keeping young in a pouch has always been considered more primitive than, and even ecologically inferior to, growing them in a womb. But reproductive biologists have found that the total amount of energy invested in a litter by a female is similar in marsupial and placental mammals; the main difference is that marsupials invest more in lactation, whereas placental mammals invest in gestation. Having young ride around in a pouch does have some advantages over a traditional den. The pouch is a movable nest that allows a female to forage while still keeping her young protected and fed. She can also exploit new sources of food when and where they occur without having to worry about long commutes to the den to nurse her young.

Though they can live to be three or, rarely, four years old in captivity, the majority of wild VIRGINIA OPOSSUMS live less than 2 years. Despite their short lifespan and 'primitive' system of reproduction, Virginia Opossums are some of the most successful animals in North America. They are numerically abundant, they have greatly expanded their geographical distribution, and they do well in human-altered environments. They are survivors.

Notes
VIRGINIA OPOSSUMS are famous for 'playing possum' when they find themselves in danger. During this death-feigning behavior, the opossum lies on its side, mouth agape, with its tongue hanging out. Limp and dead-looking, it may defecate and emit a foul-smelling greenish liquid from its anal glands. While looking at an opossum playing dead, it is difficult to imagine what kind of survival benefits such behavior would have. However, animal behaviorists theorize that by playing dead, the opossum switches off all the potential signals that would stimulate the predator to continue an attack.

Opossums are thought to be immune to the venom of pit-vipers (p. 91); given that snakes are a regular part of the opossum diet, this immunity would seem to be quite beneficial. They also appear to be highly resistant to rabies.

Status
VIRGINIA OPOSSUMS are widespread and successful. While they are short-lived and suffer high mortality, they have the ability to reproduce quickly and prolifically, and they are clearly not threatened or endangered.

Profile
Virginia Opossum, *Didelphis virginiana*, Plate 61a

2. Armadillo

When the Spanish encountered shelled mammals in the New World they gave them the name *armadillo*, meaning 'little armored one.' The NINE-BANDED ARMADILLO (Plate 61) is small, but heavy-bodied, and weighs 4 to 8 kg (8.8 to 17.6 lb). It is nearly hairless and covered with armor-like plates on the head, back, shoulder, rump, and tail, making it difficult to mistake for any other Florida animal. The large plates on the shoulder and pelvic regions are inflexible, whereas those along the back are arranged in eight or nine separate but movable side-to-side bands (hence the name). The leather-like skin beneath the bands provides flexibility and allows the animal to curl its body, but this species cannot form a tight ball, as popularly alleged. The scales on the tail completely encircle it and, like the bands on the back, are somewhat flexible. There is no armor on the soft underparts. Armadillos have short legs with powerful digging claws, a narrow, wedge-shaped head, and a variable number of small, peg-like teeth. The dark ears are large relative to the size of its head. Armadillos belong to family Dasypodidae, a group of 8 genera and 20 species found primarily in the tropical regions of South and Central America. The Nine-banded is the only armadillo whose range extends into the southern USA, where it is found in an area from Texas to Florida, and as far north as Kansas, Missouri, and Tennessee.

Natural History
Ecology and Behavior
The NINE-BANDED ARMADILLO is an opportunistic species that thrives in citrus groves, cattle pastures, fields, gardens, logged forest, pine flatwoods and scrub habitat. It is usually most abundant in moist habitats, near water, and wherever

deep sandy soils provide easy digging.

Armadillos have extremely poor eyesight but keen senses of hearing and smell, which they use to search for food. They shuffle along, nose to the ground, stopping to root with their nose and dig small holes with their forefeet. They are active primarily at night and can often be heard grunting as they root about in the leaf litter, or poke their long noses into holes and crevices in search of arthropods. More than 90% of their food consists of insects and other invertebrates, and they occasionally take reptiles and amphibians, bird eggs, berries and fungi. They are great diggers and each animal excavates a series of underground dens throughout its home range. The burrows, which range from 1 to 5 m (3 to 16 ft) in length, are usually located at the base of stumps, trees, or under brushpiles. When pursued, an armadillo can dig incredibly fast and is capable of disappearing underground in a few seconds. Armadillos often irritate landowners by digging up lawns, golf courses, vegetable gardens, and flowerbeds; such damage often triggers nuisance calls to animal control authorities. Armadillos also cause damage by burrowing under foundations and driveways.

Breeding

NINE-BANDED ARMADILLOS first breed when they are about a year old. They mate in July or August but the fertilized egg does not implant in the female's uterus until late November or December (called *delayed implantation*). The single fertilized egg divides into four cells that separate and develop into four identical embryos. After a gestation period of about 120 days the female produces identical quadruplets in March or April. The young open their eyes within a few hours of birth and they can walk on the first day. They nurse for about two months but begin to accompany their mother on foraging expeditions when they are only a few weeks old. Young remain with their mother for several months.

Ecological Interactions

Armadillos and cars don't get along well. Everyone who travels Florida's highways notices that armadillos seem to make up a disproportionate number of roadkills. This holds true across the southern USA, especially in Texas, where armadillos are known as 'Texas speed bumps'. The problem lies with armadillo behavior. When an armadillo is startled by a predator it may jump three or four feet into the air – straight up. This reaction is usually enough to escape a fox or a Bobcat, but when the predator is a car the results are not so favorable. The jump sends it crashing into the underside of the vehicle. If you want to avoid an armadillo on the road, drive around it. If you try to miss it by straddling it with your wheels, it will jump.

Notes

Armadillos have become key to a global effort to eradicate leprosy. Though the leprosy bacillus was discovered in 1872, scientists were unable to grow it in the laboratory until a century later, when it was discovered that armadillos could carry the disease. Their relatively cool body temperature (32 to 35 °C, 90 to 95 °F) makes them an ideal host for the bacillus and they are now being used in the development of new drugs for treatment of the disease. Armadillos in Texas and Louisiana have tested positive for leprosy and have transmitted it to people. Armadillos in Florida do not seem to carry the disease; tests of 3000 animals showed no evidence of leprosy. However, it is probably a good idea not to handle them.

Status

NINE-BANDED ARMADILLOS were first observed in the USA in 1849, when they were limited to the Rio Grande Valley in Texas. Aided by humans and their own capabilities, these armadillos have undergone an explosive range expansion during the last 150 years, and the species is now found throughout the southern USA. Deliberately introduced to Florida in the 1920s, they then spread quickly throughout the state, and later these Florida armadillos merged with populations that had expanded eastward from Texas. Drought and extended periods of freezing temperatures are thought to be the factors that will limit the northern movement of armadillos.

Profile

Nine-banded Armadillo, *Dasypus novemcinctus*, Plate 61b

3. Bats

Bats are the only true flying mammals. They range in size from Thailand's incredibly small, 2-g (1/10 oz) KITTI'S HOG-NOSED BAT to the SAMOAN FLYING-FOX, which has a wingspan of nearly 2 m (6.5 ft) and weighs up to 1.2 kg (2.6 lb). Most bats feed on insects but different species specialize on a variety of different foods, including nectar, fruit, frogs, fish, and even blood. Bats live throughout the world's tropical and temperate regions and on all but the most isolated islands. The world's 925 or so species of bats make up nearly a quarter of all mammal species – second in number only to the rodents. Because of their nocturnal habits, most bats are difficult to see, and even harder to identify, but they play an extremely important role in their ecosystems.

The living bats are arranged in two major groups. The Megachiroptera consists of a single family and includes the Old World *fruit bats* and *flying foxes*. The Microchiroptera consists of 16 families, which navigate and hunt using echolocation. The 16 bat species found in Florida are all Microchiropteran insect-eaters. Four of the more commonly seen species are profiled in this section.

Bats all share the same basic body plan. Chiroptera, the scientific name for bats (and the name of their order) comes from the Greek 'chiro,' meaning hand, and 'ptera,' meaning wing, and it is the 'hand-wings' of bats that makes them easy to recognize. The wings are made of skin stretched between elongated finger bones and attached to the sides of the body and legs. All bats have clawed thumbs, used mainly for moving around in the roost, and toes with sharp, curved claws that allow them to hang upside down. Many bats also use their claws to catch prey. As mammals, bats have hair, and mammary glands that secrete milk to suckle their young. They are also warm-blooded but can survive periods of time when their body temperature drops to near freezing. A bat with lowered body temperature is said to be in a state of *torpor*.

Natural History

Ecology and Behavior

Unlike the gliding flight of mammals such as flying squirrels or Australian sugar gliders, bat flight involves wings that flap, and, like bird wings, bat wings vary considerably in size and shape. Species like the BRAZILIAN FREE-TAILED BAT (Plate 67) have long narrow wings, which allow them to fly economically and at high speeds. Bats with broad wings fly more slowly but are more maneuverable.

Florida's bats are all insect-eaters. They hunt on the wing, and navigate and locate their prey with 'sonar,' or echolocation. An echolocating bat produces a high frequency, discrete pulse of sound and then receives and interprets the returning echo before producing the next pulse. Microchiropteran bats use vocalizations as their pulsed sound; some species emit the sound through their open mouths, others through their nostrils. Remarkably, both nose- and mouth-emitters can chew and vocalize at the same time. Bats that emit sound pulses through their nostrils are easy to recognize because they often have elaborate leaf-like facial structures known as 'nose leaves').

Locating and tracking insects involves great precision, and bats need to be able to distinguish between a flying moth and a wind-blown leaf. Bats that prey on insects in open areas face a relatively straightforward problem. Species that hunt insects on leaves have a more complex task, and they use different echolocation call types.

As a bat closes in on its prey, it increases the rate at which it produces sound pulses. Bat biologists using bat-detecting equipment to eavesdrop on the echolocation sounds of bats call these rapid pulses a 'feeding buzz.' But like motorists with radar detectors, some insects have evolved the ability to recognize an approaching bat's sonar pulses. Several species of moths, mantids, crickets, katydids and lacewings are able to 'hear' the bat approaching and begin evasive actions. Some insects fold their wings and dive for the ground, others start a series of wild looping aerial maneuvers to evade the bat. Moths that can hear the approach of a bat and respond appropriately stand a 40% lower chance of being eaten. In the ever-escalating arms race, some tropical bats send their pulsed signals at wavelengths that cannot be detected by moths.

Food. For their size, bats have huge appetites. BIG BROWN BATS (Plate 67) weigh 14 to 25 g (0.5 to 0.9 oz) and consume 50% to 100% of their body weight in insects each night. A baby BRAZILIAN FREE-TAILED BAT typically consumes its own weight in milk every day. To produce this much milk, its mother must eat 1.2 times her own body weight in insects. Males and non-nursing female bats generally eat more than 50% of their body weight in insects each day. It is one thing to eat your own body weight in food in 24 hours if you are a lion, and can lie around for 18 hours after the meal, but, if you must eat and fly, large quantities of food can present problems. Bats have a number of adaptations that allow them to eat a lot and still remain light enough to fly. Bats that feed on insects usually remove and reject the less nutritious wings and legs of their prey before starting to feed. They chew very quickly, and their gut is specialized for rapid chemical breakdown of food. A bat can catch a moth, digest the body and pass the indigestible remains as feces in only 20 minutes.

Roosting. Bats avoid predators and temperature extremes by spending the daylight hours in a secure roost site. Roost sites are usually tree cavities, caves and rock crevices, but many bats will also use human-crafted structures, roosting under bridges and culverts, in attics, and under the eaves of buildings. Some tropical bats have highly specialized roosting habits. Southeast Asian *bamboo bats*, for example, roost in bamboo stems, entering the stems through holes bored by beetles. In South America, *sucker-footed bats* have adhesive discs on their wrists that enable them to roost inside unfurling leaves. Other bats fold leaves into 'tents' and roost inside; they bite the veins of leaves so they fold over.

Activity patterns. Most bats leave their roosts around dusk, then fly to foraging sites, which vary by season. Nighttime activity patterns also vary, perhaps serving to reduce competition among species. Some tend to fly and forage intensively in the early evening, become less active in the middle of the night, then resume intensive foraging near dawn; others are relatively inactive early in the evening but more active later on.

The four species profiled below are Florida's most commonly seen bats.

BIG BROWN BAT (Plate 67). This medium-sized bat has long, glossy, chestnut-brown fur and broad, blackish wings. It roosts in attics, hollow trees, outbuildings, culverts and under bridges. When roosting in caves this bat often chooses a spot near the entrance, sometimes in partial daylight. Compared with other bats, the Big Brown Bat is a well-studied species, and much is known of its habits. Banding studies have shown that most of these bats live their lives within 16 km (10 miles) of their birthplace. They typically begin hunting about 20 minutes after sunset, and spend about 90 minutes per night foraging. They feed mainly on beetles, but also eat caddisflies, moths and mayflies. Relatively slow, straight flyers, these bats can be seen hunting over lakes, city parks, and along the edges between forest and fields.

BRAZILIAN FREE-TAILED BAT (Plate 67). A small, conspicuous bat with narrow black wings and a short tail membrane. One of the most gregarious bats in Florida, this species is common in cities and suburbs and roosts in attics, caves, culverts and palm trees. In some parts of the western USA, some free-tailed bat colonies consist of millions of individuals, but in Florida colonies usually contain a few hundred to a thousand bats. Free-tailed bats emerge from their roost shortly after sunset. On cold nights they may forage for a few hours then return to the roost; on warm nights they often fly until 4.00 a.m. They feed on small moths, beetles, winged ants and mosquitos, and are considered to be of great economic importance because they are major insect predators. Brazilian Free-tailed Bats are rapid flyers, with a hard-to-follow erratic flight pattern.

EASTERN YELLOW BAT (Plate 67). One of the largest and most visible bats in Florida, yellow bats start flying well before dark. As long as there are flying insects, these bats are active year-round. They fly slowly, and seem to hunt systematically, hawking back and forth over the same piece of ground. They can be seen over open areas such as lake edges, fields, golf courses, and beaches. They are also common in suburban residential areas. Yellow bats rarely roost in human-crafted structures, preferring clumps of Spanish moss or dead palm fronds as daytime hiding places. Yellow bats take a variety of insects including dragonflies, moths, and beetles.

EVENING BAT (Plate 67). Evening Bats have short, black, narrow wings and blunt, rounded ears. They often roost in colonies in houses and other buildings and because of this are sometimes considered a nuisance. Females typically form maternity colonies of 30 to several hundred individuals. Evening Bats leave their roost shortly after sunset and feed over fields, ponds, and along watercourses. They eat beetles, moths, leafhoppers and caddisflies.

Breeding

Chauve-souris, the French word for bat, means 'bald mouse,' while the German *Fledermaus* translates as 'fluttering mouse.' In names and descriptions bats are often likened to mice and rodents, but when it comes to reproduction they are the very opposite. While a female mouse can have as many five or six litters a year, each with four or five young, most bats produce only a single offspring per year. The BRAZILIAN FREE-TAILED BAT has one young each year, but BIG BROWN BATS, EASTERN YELLOW BATS and EVENING BATS typically have two young each year, usually in May or June. Most young bats can fly when they are 3 weeks old.

Ecological Interactions

Most bats play extremely important roles in their ecosystems. Tropical bats are pollinators and seed dispersers for many food plants, including bananas, breadfruit, mangoes, and dates. Worldwide, insect-eating bats are natural predators of insect pests that cost farmers and foresters billions of dollars. Because they often eat their own weight in insects each night, even a small colony of bats can have a significant impact on the local insect population. A colony of 150 BIG BROWN BATS can eat enough Cucumber Beetles to protect local farmers from tens of millions of the beetle's rootworm larvae each summer. The 20 million BRAZILIAN FREE-TAILED BATS from Bracken Cave in Texas eat approximately 200 tons of insects a night!

In a unique demonstration of the ecological value of insect-eating bats, biologist Greg Richards calculated that the 2 million bats roosting in the National Museum of Cambodia in Phnom Penh annually consumed about 600 metric tons of insects, gleaned from surrounding vegetable farms and rice paddies. To help authorities, who were considering removing the flying mammals, visualize the positive impact of the bats, Richards calculated that each year the bat colony was eating the equivalent in weight of insects of about 4000 family cars. Richards then asked the authorities to visualize the thousands of gallons of insecticide that would have to be purchased, trucked in, and sprayed to control the huge number of insects if the bats were removed. Additionally, the bats were converting the insects to *guano* (bat droppings, a preferred fertilizer) for free – and the guano was bought by the surrounding farmers.

Notes

Bats have frightened people for a long time. There is a huge body of folklore that portrays bats as evil, associated with witches, black magic and death. Undeniably, it was bats' alien lives – their activity in the darkness, flying ability, and strange form – and people's ignorance of bats that were the sources of these superstitions. One of the most common themes in bat folklore is that they become entangled in human hair. Almost everyone knows someone who swears they have had a bat try to get into their hair. In French folklore, the bat is trying to steal hair from people to put on its wings. In other countries a bat in your hair has consequences that range from petty to lethal. Your hair may turn gray, you may become bald, insane, have lifelong headaches, or even be eternally damned. As with most folklore, the idea of bats trying to get into people's hair is probably based on a variation of the truth. Bats often fly low over people walking in the evening, but they are in search of insects, not hair. People and lights tend to attract insects, and insects attract bats.

Status

More than 50% of American bat species are in severe decline or already endangered. The greatest cause of their decline is human persecution and fear. In Florida, bat numbers have declined drastically in recent years. In fact, a 1982 survey of more than 100 Florida pest control companies showed that requests to remove 'nuisance' bats had dwindled to almost nothing.

Two species of bat found in Florida, the INDIANA BAT and GRAY BAT, are listed as endangered by federal (U.S. Fish and Wildlife Service) and state (Florida Fish and Wildlife Conservation Commission) authorities. Both species are extraordinarily vulnerable to natural or human-caused catastrophes because the entire populations concentrate in only a few caves during hibernation. Loss of suitable caves for roosting is thought to be the greatest threat to their survival. The FLORIDA MASTIFF BAT is listed as threatened by FCREPA (Florida Committee on Rare and Endangered Plants and Animals); its decline is thought to have been caused by heavy pesticide spraying for mosquitos. The BIG BROWN BAT, EASTERN YELLOW BAT, and BRAZILIAN FREE-TAILED BAT are all listed by FCREPA as 'status undetermined.' This designation means the species may be endangered, threatened or rare, but there is insufficient information to assign them to a specific category.

Profiles

Big Brown Bat, *Eptesicus fuscus*, Plate 67a
Brazilian Free-tailed Bat, *Tadarida brasiliensis*, Plate 67b
Eastern Yellow Bat, *Lasiurus intermedius*, Plate 67c
Evening Bat, *Nycticeius humeralis*, Plate 67d

Carnivores

The *carnivores* comprise a group of meat-eating mammals that are highly specialized for hunting and killing other animals and feeding on their flesh. The order Carnivora is native to all continents except Australia and Antarctica and includes 12 families and 271 species. Most carnivores, like cats and bears, are terrestrial, but some, like otters, live in fresh water, and others such as seals live in the ocean. The 14 species of carnivores found in Florida include members of seven families: raccoons (Procyonidae), dogs (Canidae), bears (Ursidae), weasels (Mustelidae), cats (Felidae), skunks (Mephitidae), and true seals (Phocidae).

Carnivores have large, conical, *canine teeth* at the front corners of the mouth, used for gripping and holding prey or delivering a killing bite. At the back of the jaw, blade-like *carnassial teeth* function much like scissors, slicing flesh from a carcass. Carnivores have highly developed brains, excellent vision and a keen sense of smell. Their habits and feeding strategies are diverse. Cats are stalk-and-ambush hunters and subsist entirely on meat. Otters and seals hunt in water and feed on fish. Foxes and Coyotes are also meat-eaters, but supplement their diets with insects, fruit, and plants.

Historically, carnivores, particularly larger ones, were considered threats to humans and were hunted and trapped as nuisance animals. The Red Wolf, for example, was once widely distributed in the southeastern USA, but human persecution and habitat change were largely responsible for its extirpation by the late 1800s. Today, carnivores face different pressures. Large carnivores such as bears and Puma are 'landscape animals,' requiring large tracts of interconnected habitats to survive. In Florida's rapidly developing landscape, habitat loss is a major concern and connections between tracts of forested land are being whittled away by roads and urban development. Highway mortality is now the major cause of death for Puma and Black Bears in Florida. However, some of the smaller carnivores, such as raccoons, Coyotes and foxes, are thriving in these altered landscapes. Coyotes and Red Foxes have expanded their ranges into Florida and elsewhere in the USA. Indeed, there are estimated to be 15 to 20 times as many raccoons in North America today as there were in 1930.

4. Raccoon

There are 18 species in the *raccoon* family (Procyonidae), and they are found only in the Americas. They are mostly confined to Central and South America, but the distribution of one species, the NORTHERN RACCOON (Plate 61), stretches northwards to southern Canada. Members of the family, which include such euphoniously named creatures as KINKAJOU, COATI, CACOMISTLE, and OLINGO, typically live in forests and are adept climbers. They are small to medium-sized (1 to 14 kg; 2 to 30 lb) animals, and most members of the family have conspicuous facial markings and long tails marked with alternating light and dark rings. One species, the Kinkajou, has a prehensile tail, which is not banded. *Procyonids* are omnivores; they move with a shuffling, bear-like gait, and forage both on the forest floor and in the trees. Three species occur in North America but only the Northern Raccoon is found in Florida. (The other two are the Coati, which occurs in Texas, New Mexico, Arizona, and south into Mexico and Central America; and the RINGTAIL, which occurs in southwestern USA, Baja California, and Mexico.) Florida's Northern Raccoons are smaller than Northern Raccoons in the northern USA. Adults weigh only 3 to 9 kg (6.6 to 20 lb) and are about the size of a large, stout, domestic cat. They have a bushy tail marked with 4 to 7 alternating brown and black rings, and a black facial mask edged with white above and below.

Natural History
Ecology and Behavior
NORTHERN RACCOONS are usually most abundant near water, especially in swamps, forests near streams, marshes and mangroves. They are omnivorous and opportunistic, and will eat just about anything that they can find. In Florida they feed on crayfish, snails, clams, beetles, frogs, eggs, grubs, fruit, acorns, and corn, as well as garbage and carrion. They often forage near campgrounds and become quite adept at begging for handouts.

Raccoons generally spend the day asleep in a den, which can be a hollow tree, an underground burrow, or an old squirrel nest high in the branches of a tree. They usually begin foraging after dark, but are occasionally seen moving about in the late afternoon. The activity patterns of raccoons living in salt marshes and tidal areas are linked closely to the tides; they become active at low tide and inactive at high tide, sometimes without regard for day or night.

Bobcats, foxes, owls, alligators, and domestic dogs may occasionally kill raccoons, and, in parts of South Florida where large prey are scarce, raccoons make up almost 20% of the Puma's diet. Most rabies outbreaks in Florida are associated with raccoons. Each year raccoons account for 65% of cases of animal rabies in the state.

Breeding
NORTHERN RACCOONS produce one litter per year. In Florida, mating usually begins in December but some young are born in most months of the year. Females usually give birth in a tree den after a gestation period of about 2 months. Females raise the young without assistance from the male. The 3 or 4 young are born fully furred, but with their eyes closed. They open their eyes when they are 2 to 3 weeks old, and begin to move with their mother at about 2 months of age. At this stage of their lives the family is very close-knit, and young raccoons follow their mother and each other very closely. During a 6-year population study

of raccoons in North Florida, we trapped, marked and released hundreds of wild raccoons. In spring, when the young first began to move with their mother, we occasionally captured two or three small raccoons in a single trap. Once there were four tiny raccoons in the same trap. For all to get into the trap before the first one stepped on the plate and triggered the door to close they must have been walking literally nose to tail. On a couple of occasions a female was alone in the trap, but her young were in a nearby tree, watching the trap and calling, presumably for their mother.

Young raccoons are not completely weaned until they are 12 to 16 weeks old and typically remain with their mother through the first winter. Females can breed before they are a year old but most do not breed until their second year.

Ecological Interactions
NORTHERN RACCOONS are among Florida's most common urban animals, frequently seen around parks, campsites, and homes. Under most circumstances they are fun to watch and harmless when left alone. Problems arise because people find it difficult not to feed them. Raccoons are highly intelligent animals that will eat practically anything, and it takes only a few handouts from well-meaning people to teach them that humans are a source of food. When raccoons become conditioned to seeing humans as a source of food, they can become a problem. They raid garbage cans, find their way into garages and sheds, and generally make a nuisance of themselves. Because they can carry distemper and rabies, any physical contact with raccoons is potentially dangerous.

Notes
The word 'raccoon' is thought to be derived from an American Indian word meaning 'one who scratches with his hands.' Because NORTHERN RACCOONS use their hands to search for food, both on land and in water, there is a commonly held belief that raccoons always wash their food before eating it. Even the raccoon's Latin name, 'lotor,' means 'the washer.' However, the belief is not true. The most likely explanation for the 'washing' behavior is that raccoons are not washing the food but feeling for prey like frogs and crayfish beneath the surface. Studies have shown that the dabbling (we interpret it as washing) is a stereotyped behavior pattern used for searching for aquatic food in the wild. Captive raccoons probably 'wash' food as a substitute for their normal feeding behavior.

Status
Most other procyonid species are restricted to the tropics, but NORTHERN RACCOONS have expanded deeply into temperate areas, becoming highly successful. Their diverse diet, prolific reproduction, and capacity to tolerate heat and cold have made them a most effective colonizing species. They began to increase in numbers and expand their range northwards in the late 1940s, extending their range into regions where indigenous people had never seen them before. Indeed, native Indians in Canada have no name for raccoons. It is estimated that there are 15–20 times as many raccoons in North America today as there were in the 1930s.

Profile
Northern Raccoon, *Procyon lotor*, Plate 61e

5. Coyote and Foxes

The world's dogs and dog-like animals comprise the family Canidae. *Canids* are runners. From the widespread, powerful GRAY WOLF to Africa's diminutive FENNEC FOX, and even to 'Rover,' the family dog, the majority of the world's canids are adapted for the pursuit of prey in open areas. Moving lightly on their toes, they can trot for hours in search of a rabbit or put on a burst of speed to catch a deer. Adaptations for this *cursorial* way of life make canids easy to recognize. They typically have large, pointed ears, an elongated, pointed nose, powerful jaws and large canine teeth. The tail is bushy and the long, lightly built legs end in four toes tipped with blunt claws.

Nine of the world's 34 canid species are found in North America, and three of these occur in Florida. The GRAY FOX (Plate 62) is one of Florida's most commonly seen carnivores. Though most are wary, some individuals become quite tame. They are frequently seen at night on unpaved roads, and individuals often allow themselves to be followed for a short distance. The Gray Fox has a wide red-orange strip along both flanks and on the sides of the neck, a black-tipped tail, and it is sometimes confused with the less commonly seen RED FOX, which is a mahogany red and has a white-tipped tail. The foxes are similar in size and weigh 3 to 5 kg (6.6 to 11 lb). A COYOTE (Plate 62) weighs about three times as much as a fox and look like a smaller, bushy-tailed version of the German Shepherd dog. Tracks of dogs and Coyotes are similar in size, but Coyote tracks are longer and narrower. Both the Red Fox and the Coyote were introduced by hunters to Florida, but they may also have arrived in the state via natural range expansions from the north and west.

Natural History
Ecology and Behavior

COYOTES and RED and GRAY FOXES are adaptable and opportunistic carnivores, flexible in their feeding habits and quite tolerant of people. They feed on small animals, fruit, and insects, but they will also eat out of garbage cans, and scavenge road-killed animals. Gray Foxes prey heavily on rabbits, but they also eat rodents, birds, insects, acorns and fruit. Coyotes have a similarly catholic diet but also take domestic livestock, and they are known to be serious predators of sheep and newborn calves. Coyotes also damage watermelon crops by biting chunks out of ripening melons.

All three species are usually active at night, and most often hunt alone. They move at a rapid trot, eyes, ears and nose alert for signs of prey. Red Foxes catch rodents with a characteristic floating 'mouse leap.' In this precision display of aerial acrobatics, the fox first pinpoints the position of the prey using its ears, then springs high into the air and lands with its front paws together on the unsuspecting rodent. A fox can kill a mouse with one of these leaps from almost 5 m (16 ft) away.

The versatile Coyote is found in all habitat types. Gray Foxes are most abundant in hardwood forests, pine-oak woodlands, and brushy fields. They are the only member of the canid family that regularly climbs trees, and have been seen in trees at heights up to 18 m (60 ft). During one study in North Florida, radio-collared Gray Foxes were regularly found resting on the horizontal branches of large live oak trees. Red Foxes avoid the more heavily wooded areas occupied by Gray Fox, preferring the edges of forest, meadows, agricultural fields, and open brush and pastures.

Breeding

RED and GRAY FOXES usually form pair bonds that last year-round. COYOTES have a variable mating system: they may pair for life or for a single season. All three species are typical canids in that both parents guard and feed the pups. Pairs mate during the winter and produce a litter in March or April after a gestation period of about 53 days (63 days for Coyotes). The 4 to 6 pups are born blind and helpless, in an excavated den. Interestingly, Coyotes respond to increasing human persecution by increasing their litter size, thus compensating for population losses. Foxes den in hollow logs and enlarge the burrows of armadillos and gopher tortoises; Coyote dens are much larger, often a dug-out area under a bank or fallen tree. When they are 8 to 12 weeks old, pups abandon the birth den and begin to forage with their parents. Family groups stay together until late summer or early fall, after which the young disperse to find their own home ranges.

Ecological Interactions

COYOTES have a variable and flexible social system. Though the basic social unit is a mated pair and their offspring, Coyotes are also known to live as solitary nomads, in temporary aggregations, and in packs of as many as eight. A variety of factors, including food distribution and availability and level of human persecution, are probably important determinants of the coyote's social system. In Wyoming, researchers found that Coyotes formed packs where carrion was abundant and defendable. Where carrion was scarce and dispersed, Coyotes lived in pairs or as loners.

Status

Traditionally associated with the American West, the COYOTE has now become established throughout the eastern USA. The removal of wolves and Pumas and the conversion of forest to more open habitats have apparently promoted this expansion. Recent observations of Coyotes in New York's Central Park are a testament to their adaptability. Coyotes first appeared in the Florida Panhandle in the 1970s and are now well established throughout the state.

In the 1600s, the southern limit of the RED FOX in eastern North America was probably Quebec, but the species has since greatly expanded its range and is now found as far south as central Florida. (Red Foxes, which may be native to North America, were also brought by people from Europe, where they are also native, and released along the USA's east coast; so the Red Fox in Florida today may have both North American and European recent ancestry.) This range expansion coincided with the clearing of forest for agriculture and the extirpation of wolves in the southern USA.

All three of Florida's canids can coexist with humans, and are able to live in agricultural fields and urban areas. The loss of forest cover and the increasing habitat fragmentation that is accompanying Florida's rapid growth appears to have been especially beneficial to the Coyote and Red Fox.

Profiles

Gray Fox, *Urocyon cinereoargenteus*, Plate 62a
Coyote, *Canis latrans*, Plate 62c

6. Bear

Bears are found worldwide from the Arctic to the tropics, and on all continents except Antarctica, Africa and Australia. They are large, heavily built mammals, with a short tail, powerful limbs, a broad head, and short, rounded ears. Their broad, flat feet have five toes and long non-retractable claws. Bears are the largest of the terrestrial carnivores – male Grizzly and Polar bears may weigh 800 kg (1760 lb). With the exception of the carnivorous Polar Bear, most bears are herbivores, although they will eat fish, scavenge carrion and garbage, and occasionally kill young or disabled ungulates. There are 9 species of bears in the world and 3 of these species, the Polar Bear, Grizzly Bear, and BLACK BEAR (Plate 63) occur in North America. Only the Black Bear occurs in Florida.

The Black Bear is the largest terrestrial mammal in Florida. Females average 82 kg (180 lb) and males 113 kg (250 lb). However, males can grow to be considerably larger – in 1990, a 285-kg (627-lb) male was killed by a car in South Florida. Florida bears are usually completely black, with a brown muzzle and sometimes a light colored chest patch. In South Florida, black-colored bears sometimes lose the black guard hairs (coarse, rigid, long, pigmented outer hairs) and become a woolly brown. Black Bear footprints are as large or larger than the print made by the heel of a human hand pressed into the dirt, and the long, non-retractable claws are usually obvious in the print.

Natural History
Ecology and Behavior

BLACK BEARS use a wide range of forested habitats, from pine flatwoods, hardwood hammocks and sand pine scrub to cypress swamps, mangroves and forested wetlands. Bears often feed in different habitats at different seasons, as foods become available. In early spring they feed on emerging green vegetation. During summer they concentrate on fruits of the saw palmetto, swamp tupelo, cabbage palm, blueberry and gallberry. Hard mast (nuts and acorns) becomes important during fall, and insects, honey, small animals, and carrion supplement their diet year-round.

Except for females and their cubs, bears are solitary animals. Adults often have overlapping home ranges, but they rarely travel or feed together except in the mating season. Studies of radio-collared bears in Florida's Osceola and Ocala National Forests have shown that home ranges are large – female ranges average 28 sq km (11 sq miles) and male ranges average 170 sq km (66 sq miles).

In the northern USA and Canada, both male and female bears hibernate for several months and females give birth during hibernation. In Florida, males, non-pregnant females with large cubs, and subadults sometimes remain active throughout the year or den only for a short time. Pregnant females are the exception. They always hibernate, even in areas where winter temperatures remain warm and food is plentiful. Scientists believe that for bears there must be a deep evolutionary link between the reproductive process and hibernation.

Breeding

Compared with other mammals, bears give birth to extremely small young; cubs weigh only 200 to 450 g (7 to 16 oz), which is approximately 1/250 of the mother's weight (for comparison, human babies weigh approximately 1/20 of the mother's weight). In Florida, female BLACK BEARS are capable of breeding when they are 3 years old, but most are 4 years or older when they produce their first litter. Birth dens are in remote areas, in very dense cover, often a tangle of vines or a thicket of bushes and shrubs. Females give birth in January or February to a litter of 2 or 3 cubs.

The small hairless cubs grow slowly. At 40 days of age they weigh about 1 kg

(2.2 lb) and are fully furred. When they are about 2 months old they leave the den and begin to travel with their mother; however, they continue to nurse until fall and the family does not split up until the cubs are about 16 months old. This long period of maternal investment means that females breed only every other year. Reproduction is closely linked to the availability of food, and in years with little or no fruits and nuts, many females will not have young.

Ecological Interactions

Bears love honey. Florida is the nation's third most important honey-producing state. Each year commercial beekeepers place more than 230,000 hives out in Florida's swamps, woods and citrus groves, and the bees obligingly produce 22.5 million pounds of tupelo, sassafras and orange blossom honey. BLACK BEARS are serious predators on beehives and can cause great economic damage to commercial honey operations. The problem is particularly severe in North Florida between April and June, when the peak of honey production coincides with a natural period of food shortage for the bears. Bears are sometimes shot or poisoned in retaliation when they destroy hives. The Florida Fish and Wildlife Conservation Commission has a bear management program that helps beekeepers with problem bears. They have found that placing hives on high platforms, or surrounding hives with electric fencing, although requiring con-siderable extra work on the part of beekeepers, resolves the majority of bear problems.

Status

The BLACK BEAR is widespread in Florida but its distribution is fragmented and greatly reduced from what it was 100 years ago. The largest remaining bear pop-ulations in the state are found in five public areas: Ocala National Forest, Osceola National Forest/Pinhook/Okefenokee Swamp, Apalachicola National Forest, Big Cypress National Preserve, and Eglin Air Force Base. Accelerating loss of habitat, illegal hunting, and roadkills continue to cause bear numbers to decline – recent estimates put state-wide numbers at 1000 to 2000 individuals. Authorities are attempting to reduce the number of bears killed by cars by putting up bear cross-ing signs at sites where bears frequently cross roads, and including wildlife under-passes in new highway construction projects.

Profile

Black Bear, *Ursus americanus*, Plate 63a

7. Skunks and Otters

Skunks and *otters* are members of family Mustelidae, which contains the 67 species of weasel-like carnivores. Excluding Australia and Antarctica, *mustelids* are found on all continents. They are absent from most oceanic islands, including the West Indies, Madagascar, Sulawesi, New Guinea, and the Philippines. Mustelids are the most diverse family of all the carnivores. They range in size from the 30 to 70 g (1 to 2.5 oz) LEAST WEASEL to the 45 kg (100 lb) SEA OTTER. They are terrestrial (*weasels*), aquatic and semi-aquatic (*otters* and *mink*), or semi-arboreal (*martens*); some are accomplished diggers (*badgers*). Small to medium in size, with long, slen-der bodies and short legs, many mustelids play an important ecological role as major predators of rodents. Others, like otters, are specialized for capturing and feeding on fish, while the long claws of *skunks* are well suited for digging up insects. While skunks have long been considered to be members of the mustelid family, recent molecular studies indicate they are sufficiently distinct to be in their own family (Mephitidae).

Most mustelids have a characteristic and often powerful odor. Their anal glands produce an oily, fetid-smelling fluid known as *musk*, which is stored in sacs near the rectum. The sacs are under voluntary muscle control and can be discharged at will. Most mustelids use this odiferous fluid to scent-mark objects, but skunks have taken things a step further than most, and are known for their ability to spray anal gland fluid on would-be predators.

Five species of mustelids occur in Florida, and of these the MINK and LONG-TAILED WEASEL appear to be rare. EASTERN SPOTTED and STRIPED SKUNKS (both Plate 61) are rarely seen but occasionally appear as roadkills; you can smell the distinctive odor as you drive by. RIVER OTTERS (Plate 61) are the most commonly encountered of Florida's mustelids; it is not unusual to see an otter swimming in one of central Florida's many springs or rivers.

Natural History
Ecology and Behavior

Most mustelids are highly carnivorous, powerful predators capable of killing prey as large as themselves. However, the EASTERN SPOTTED and STRIPED SKUNKS and RIVER OTTER are exceptions to this general pattern. Skunks are recorded from just about every terrestrial habitat type in Florida, but they prefer overgrown fields and farming areas with forest-edge plant communities. As these habitats have disappeared, so have the skunks. Much to the dismay of homeowners, skunks occasionally show up in suburban residential areas. Skunks usually dig their own dens but may use the burrows of foxes, Armadillos or Gopher Tortoises. They spend the day asleep in a den and emerge at dusk to forage, rooting through leaf litter and soil, looking for eggs, insects, snails and small vertebrates such as lizards and perhaps snakes. Occasionally they take fruit and vegetation. Skunks have poor vision, but a keen sense of hearing and smell. Eastern Spotted Skunks are agile climbers, and can scuttle up and down trees like squirrels.

River Otters forage alone or in pairs. They are active during the day and at night, hunting in streams, rivers and ponds for fish, crayfish and other crustaceans. Although otters always remain in or near the water, they spend their inactive time in burrows dug into river banks or other rest sites on land. River Otters are playful, social animals that delight in manipulating shells, sticks and other small objects. Young otters often engage in exuberant play, running in and out of the water, or sliding down the bank.

Breeding

In Florida, EASTERN SPOTTED SKUNKS breed in late winter. Following a 2-week period of delayed implantation (see below), there is a 50- to 65-day gestation period, after which 2 to 9 kits are born. STRIPED SKUNKS breed in February and March, and litters of 1 to10 young are born after a 59- to 77-day gestation period. Young Striped Skunks can 'spray' when they are only eight days old, but cannot aim the spray until their eyes open at about 24 days. RIVER OTTERS breed once a year, and in Florida mating occurs in fall and winter. Though the embryos actually develop for about 8 weeks, gestation can last for 11 to 12 months because of the extended period of delayed implantation. Litters usually consist of 2 to 3 young, which are born fully furred. The young open their eyes after a month and are weaned at about 3 months.

Notes

At least 16 species of mustelids go through an unusual reproductive phenomenon known as *delayed implantation*. In most mammals, the ball of cells known as a *blastocyst* (a very early stage of the developing embryo) implants in the wall of the uterus within a few days of conception. In mammals with delayed implantation, however, the blastocyst floats free in the uterus in a stage of arrested development for periods varying from a few weeks to 10 months. The delay is maintained by low levels of the hormone progesterone, and implantation in some species is thought to be triggered by increasing day length. The mystery is, why do some species, like the WESTERN SPOTTED SKUNK, have a long (200-day) period of delayed implantation, while the closely related EASTERN SPOTTED SKUNK does not? Likewise, RIVER OTTERS in the northern USA undergo an extended period of delayed implantation, but the closely related EURASIAN RIVER OTTER does not. Both species of skunks and otters live at similar latitudes and it is a biological puzzle as to why delayed implantation should benefit the Western Spotted Skunk and the North American River Otter and not the Eastern Spotted Skunk and the Eurasian River Otter.

Status

EASTERN SPOTTED and STRIPED SKUNKS and RIVER OTTERS are not considered threatened or endangered in Florida. However, the Everglades population of the MINK is listed as threatened by state authorities.

Profiles

Eastern Spotted Skunk, *Spilogale putorius*, Plate 61c
Striped Skunk, *Mephitis mephitis*, Plate 61d
River Otter, *Lontra canadensis*, Plate 61f

8. Cats

The 36 species of cats (family Felidae) are found throughout the world, and all of them are easily recognized as cats. They are lithe, muscular predators, with large eyes, sharp, stabbing canine teeth, and retractile claws. The majority of *felids* are spotted or striped. They range in size from about 1 kg (2 lb) – the Asian RUSTY-SPOTTED CAT, South American KODKOD, and South African BLACK-FOOTED CAT are pretty much tied for smallest – to the SIBERIAN TIGER, at more than 300 kg (660 lb). Most cats are solitary and very difficult to see, but sometimes it is enough to know that they are out there, hunting in the same woods and fields that you are walking and driving through. Two species of cats stalk the wilds of Florida: the short-tailed, spotted, 7- to 15-kg (15- to 33-lb) BOBCAT (Plate 62) and the larger, 30- to 60-kg (66- to 132-lb) unspotted PUMA (also known as the Florida Panther; Plate 62). Driving at night in South Florida, you might be lucky enough to see a Puma cross the road or a Bobcat hunting in the fields at twilight.

Natural History

Ecology and Behavior

Cats are stalk-and-ambush hunters, built for a slow, stealthy stalk, and a quick burst of speed. Cats usually hunt from cover, stalking as close as possible, then rushing in for the kill. Large cats use their muscular front legs to hold and grapple, then dispatch the animal with a bite from long, dagger-like canine teeth. Smaller cats use the same stalk-and-ambush tactics but the hunt usually ends with a pounce, and prey is dispatched with a swift bite to the back of the neck. BOBCATS are primarily rabbit-hunters, but they also take just about anything they can catch, including squirrels, opossums, rats, mice, birds and lizards. In the Everglades and Big Cypress National Preserve, Bobcats are a significant predator of White-tailed Deer fawns. Throughout most of North America, deer are the mainstay of the PUMA'S diet. In South Florida, where the remaining Florida Puma live, deer and pigs also feature prominently in the cat's diet. However, where deer are scarce, Puma prey extensively on raccoons, armadillos, rabbits, and small alligators. Both cats can climb well and will take to the trees if pursued by dogs. Scientists use this behavior to capture both Bobcats and Puma for study. The cats are chased with hunting dogs until the cat 'trees;' the cats are then anesthesized using a dart gun. Studies of radio-collared Bobcat and Puma have shown that they range over very large areas. Home range size averaged 519 sq km (200 sq miles) for resident male Puma and 194 sq km (75 sq miles) for resident females. Each male Puma's home range overlapped the smaller ranges of several females. Similarly, the home ranges of each resident male Bobcat overlapped the smaller ranges of one or two females, but home range sizes of Bobcats are much smaller, varying from about 14 sq km (5 sq miles) for females to 37 sq km (14 sq miles) for males.

Breeding

Though they undoubtedly encounter each other when hunting and come to know one another by scent, male and female cats rarely spend any time together except while mating. Females raise their young alone, without any direct help from the male. Female PUMA are usually two and a half or three years old before they have their first litter. The 2 or 3 young are born after a gestation period of 90 days, and weigh about 0.5 kg (1 lb) each. Though adults are uniformly tawny colored, newborn kittens have black spots and black rings on their tails. Kittens first begin to accompany their mother when they are 3 or 4 months old, and are dependent on her for almost 2 years. Thus, females breed only once every 2 years. BOBCATS are more prolific. They are able to breed when they are a year old, and give birth to 2 or 3 kittens after a 62-day gestation period. Young Bobcats stay with their mother until spring of the year following their birth, and females may give birth every year.

Notes

A surprising number of people in Florida claim to have seen all-black Florida PUMA. Literally hundreds of 'sightings' of black Puma occur in Florida every year but none have ever been authenticated. Despite this, reports of black Puma continue to crop up year after year in newspaper reports. While there are black JAGUARS, black LEOPARDS, and even black BOBCATS, there are no skins or specimens of black Pumas. Biologists insist that there are no black Pumas in Florida, and maintain that they should know, because most of Florida's 50 or so Pumas have been radiocollared, photographed and followed since birth. Wildlife authorities ascribe the sightings to large housecats, dogs, excited observers, and/or poor lighting conditions; however, others continue to believe in the beast, arguing that so many people cannot be wrong.

In 1982, the Florida Panther was made the state mammal of Florida.

Status

BOBCATS are common in many parts of the USA and in Florida; they are not considered threatened or endangered. They are classified as a game animal and may be hunted and trapped during the appropriate season. The PUMA has the greatest geographic distribution of all New World felids. Its range extends from northern Canada to the southern tip of South America. In the USA the Puma is common in most western states and it once was found throughout the eastern states. The Florida subspecies was believed to be extinct until a Puma was 'treed' by a hunter at Fish-eating Creek in 1973. Today a small remnant population of 50 to 70 cats survives only in South Florida. The population is fully protected and listed as endangered by the U.S. Fish and Wildlife Service and by state authorities (Florida Fish and Wildlife Conservation Commission).

The 1973 discovery of Puma in southwestern Florida sparked new interest in the cat, and that set in motion a series of efforts by state and federal agencies to 'recover' the population. The goal of the recovery plan is to 'establish three, viable, self-sustaining populations within the historic range of the subspecies.' The recovery effort focused on three major areas.

Reducing the number of road-killed Puma. Despite the vast acreage of the Big Cypress National Preserve and the adjoining Everglades National Park, many Puma are killed while attempting to cross the state's busy highways. Between December 1979 and May 1991, 32 Puma deaths were documented; collisions with vehicles caused 15 (47%) of these deaths. When Alligator Alley, the major east-west highway across South Florida, was upgraded to a four-lane interstate highway (I-75), a 64-km (40-mile) section of the road was fenced and equipped with 36 wildlife underpasses. Animals attempting to cross the road are funneled into the underpasses by 3-m (10-ft) high chain link fence. The effort appears to have been successful. Automatic cameras have photographed Puma and other wildlife using the underpasses and no Puma have been killed on Alligator Alley since the underpasses were built.

Small population. Small populations are vulnerable to catastrophic natural events and the harmful effects of breeding with close relatives. Hoping to address these issues, authorities experimented with the reintroduction of captive-born and wild-caught Puma as a way to either reestablish the cat in vacant areas or to augment the existing population. In 1989 and 1993–94, a total of 26 Puma (some captive-born in Florida, but mainly wild Puma from Texas) were released into remote forested areas in North Florida to test the feasibility of reestablishing the cat in its historic range. Mortality was high. Several cats were killed by cars and hunters, and others had to be removed from the wild because they began to kill domestic livestock. It became clear from these studies that captive-bred cats did not make good candidates for reintroduction. A third experiment was initiated in 1995. Eight wild-caught Texas female Puma were released in south Florida. At least seven of the females bred successfully with Florida puma males, and produced litters.

Habitat Acquisition. Roughly half of the Puma in South Florida live on private land. The Florida Fish and Wildlife Conservation Commission is working with private landowners to preserve key habitat corridors and essential pieces of habitat. In 1989, the Florida Panther National Wildlife Refuge was established, and the U.S. Fish and Wildlife Service has begun the process of acquiring additional habitat.

Profiles

Bobcat, *Lynx rufus*, Plate 62b
Puma (Florida Panther), *Puma concolor*, Plate 62d

9. Marine Mammals

Two types of marine mammals occur in Florida waters and both are seen fairly frequently. *Manatees* are massive (500 to 1650 kg; 1100 to 3600 lb), slow-moving, aquatic mammals found in tropical and subtropical coastal waters. They vaguely resemble a walrus without tusks but are more closely related to elephants and hyraxes than to other marine mammals. The WEST INDIAN MANATEE (Plate 68) is one of four species in the order Sirenia, which also includes the WEST AFRICAN and AMAZONIAN MANATEES, and the DUGONG of India, East Africa and Australia. The West Indian Manatee is a long, plump, cigar-shaped creature with a small blunt head and no visible neck. Manatees have wrinkled, brownish gray skin, often covered on the back with algae and barnacles. The head is blunt, with a broad square snout, and the upper lip is cleft and covered with bristles. The upper right and left lips are flexible and are used to maneuver food into the mouth. The short broad forelimbs have nails, and the tail is broad and paddle-shaped. Females are larger than males.

Dolphins are smaller members of the order Cetacea, which also includes *whales* and *porpoises*. Some 78 species of *cetaceans* occur throughout the world's oceans, coastal waters and larger rivers. Dolphins are the fastest and most agile of the cetaceans. They have elongated, spindle-shaped bodies tapered at both ends, a beak-like nose and mouth, sharp, pointed teeth, and a backwards curving dorsal fin. They are extremely intelligent and have highly developed social systems; most species live in groups.

At least 9 species of dolphins are found in Florida waters; the two most often seen are the COMMON DOLPHIN and the ATLANTIC BOTTLE-NOSED DOLPHIN (both Plate 68). Common Dolphins, also known as Saddle-backed Dolphins, are 1.8 to 2.6 m (6 to 8.5 ft) long, black on the back and upperparts and white below. Bottle-nosed Dolphins are 2.4 to 3.6 m (8 to 12 ft) long, purplish gray to light gray on the back and sides, and white underneath. They have distinctively rounded foreheads.

Natural History
Ecology and Behavior

WEST INDIAN MANATEES rarely venture into deep water, preferring to stay in shallow coastal coves and bays and large, slow-moving rivers. Manatees are very intolerant of cold, and when ocean temperatures drop below 20 °C (68 °F), they seek out warm-water refuges such as natural springs and places where power plants discharge warm water effluent. During Florida's periodic winter freezes, aggregations of 60 to 100 manatees are sometimes seen in the warm waters of Blue Spring near Orlando, and as many as 300 have been counted around power plants near Crystal River and Tampa Bay.

Manatees are herbivores. They eat a variety of aquatic plants including water hyacinth, hydrilla, and sea grass, and may even graze on bank vegetation where it overhangs the water. Manatees must consume about 8% of their body weight each day – for larger individuals this can mean eating 23 to 41 kg (50 to 90 lb) of vegetation a day. When they are not eating, manatees often rest just below the surface, raising their snout every few minutes to breathe. This behavior puts them in great danger from speeding motorboats. The number of boat encounters is so great that almost all manatees have scars on their backs or split tails. In fact, biologists studying manatees use the scars as a way of identifying individuals.

Manatees communicate with one another with a variety of squeaks, chirps, grunts and groans, most of which are audible to humans. These vocalizations seem to be especially important for maintaining contact between mother and calf. In one instance, a mother and calf separated by a floodgate called back and forth for three hours before they were reunited.

COMMON DOLPHINS generally spend their time well offshore, in groups of 10 to several thousand. They are fast swimmers, and feed almost exclusively on fish and squid living near the surface. These dolphins are bow-wave riders and often seem to approach a boat from quite some distance just to ride the bow wave. BOTTLE-NOSED DOLPHINS are the most familiar and best known of all the cetaceans. This is the species that portrays 'Flipper' of TV and movie fame, and the species usually trained to perform for the public in aquariums and theme parks. Bottle-nosed Dolphins are also the species most commonly seen in Florida, as they prefer shallow coastal and estuarine waters. They are frequently seen just beyond the surf line, but rarely in deeper waters. Their diet consists of fish, crabs, shrimp and squid. Bottle-nosed Dolphins are extremely gregarious, and are sometimes seen in groups of up to several hundred.

Breeding
WEST INDIAN MANATEES are capable of breeding when they are 4 or 5 years old. Large numbers of males gather around estrous females, jostling for position and the chance to mate. After a 12- to 14-month gestation period, females usually give birth to a single calf, but twins have been recorded. Newborn manatees weigh 27 to 32 kg (60 to 70 lb) and are about 1.2 m (4 ft) long. They nurse underwater from a nipple located just behind the mother's forelimb. Young manatees are born with teeth and begin eating vegetation when they are only a few weeks old. Calves continue to nurse for 1 to 2 years and remain with their mothers for about 2 years.

BOTTLE-NOSED DOLPHINS breed in March and April and females give birth to a single calf after a 12-month gestation period. The newborn weighs about 14 kg (30 lb) and is about 1.1 m (3.5 ft) long. Young dolphins continue to nurse until they are about a year and a half old.

Status
In winter, Florida harbors the entire USA population of WEST INDIAN MANATEES and annual counts reveal a population of about 2600 individuals. The West Indian Manatee is considered an endangered species (CITES Appendix I and USA ESA listed). They are also protected under the USA's Marine Mammal Protection Act. In an effort to protect manatees, the State of Florida has established manatee sanctuaries and designated speed zones for boats in areas where manatees congregate. BOTTLE-NOSED and COMMON DOLPHINS are CITES Appendix II listed.

Profiles
West Indian Manatee, *Trichechus manatus*, Plate 68a
Common Dolphin, *Delphinus delphis*, Plate 68b
Atlantic Bottle-nosed Dolphin, *Tursiops truncatus*, Plate 68c
Short-finned Pilot Whale, *Globicephala macrorhynchus*, Plate 68d

10. Pigs and Deer

Pigs and *deer* are representatives of order Artiodactyla, the globally distributed hoofed mammals with even numbers of toes on each foot. Other *artiodactyls* include hippos, giraffes, antelope, bison, cattle, gazelles, goats and sheep. Pigs, also called hogs and boars, are largely omnivorous, with low crowned cheek teeth and tusk-like canines. Deer are *ruminants* with high-crowned, ridged teeth. Ruminants are specialized herbivores that have a multi-chambered stomach. They *chew the cud*, or regurgitate and rechew their food, to help digest fibrous vegetation. The pigs, family Suidae, are an exclusively Old World group containing nine species. *Peccaries*, which are pig-like and occur in South, Central, and southern North America, are the New World pig counterparts; three species of peccaries make up the family Tayassuidae. The members of the pig and peccary families share a number of features. They have short legs, short necks, large heads and an oval, disc-like snout. They are unique among the Artiodactyls in their high rate of reproduction. The EUROPEAN WILD BOAR is the most widely distributed of the *suids* in the world, thanks in part to introductions by colonial traders and immigrants. Spanish settlers first brought pigs to Florida in 1539, making Florida one of the earliest states and quite possibly the first state in the continental USA to have a *feral* (domesticated but escaped and living in a wild state) pig population. The widespread practice of allowing domestic pigs to range freely to feed on acorns, nuts and other foods inevitably led to the establishment of feral populations, and the descendants of these Spanish pigs are now found throughout Florida and neighboring southeastern states. These WILD PIGS (Plate 63), also known as Wild Hog or Wild Boar, are highly regarded for their meat and are widely hunted.

The deer family, Cervidae, has 43 species worldwide; one species, the WHITE-TAILED DEER (Plate 63), occurs in Florida. Deer are large mammals with long, thin legs, short tails and big ears. Males have *antlers* that are shed each year and regrown. The White-tailed Deer has a remarkably broad distribution, extending from southern Canada to Bolivia, and varies considerably in size throughout this range. Adult males in northern populations typically weigh 100 to 150 kg (220 to 330 lb), while deer in Florida and the southern USA are about half the size of those in the north. The endangered KEY DEER (Plate 63) in the Lower Florida Keys is the smallest subspecies of White-tailed Deer, adults weighing only 25 to 36 kg (55 to 79 lb).

Natural History
Ecology and Behavior
WILD PIGS are omnivores: they feed on mast (nuts and acorns), mushrooms, fruit, berries, and grass. They will also eat just about any type of animal life, including snakes, frogs, salamanders, ground-nesting birds, insects and carrion. Pigs spend a lot of time rooting in the ground with their broad noses, looking for bulbs, tubers, and anything else edible. An area recently rooted by pigs looks as if it has just been plowed. Pigs forage mainly at night, but where they are not hunted they may be active during the day. They typically travel in small herds composed of several females and their offspring. Adult males are solitary except at breeding time. Home range size varies between 200 to 300 hectares (500 to 750 acres), depending on habitat quality. Puma and dogs are their major predators, but piglets may also be taken by alligators, Bobcats and Coyotes.

Deer are browsers, feeding on twigs, leaves and other herbaceous vegetation. They also graze on grasses, herbs and agricultural crops and eat acorns and other mast, as well as mushrooms and lichens. WHITE-TAILED DEER live in almost every habitat type in Florida, but tend to be most abundant in deciduous forest and forest edge habitats. They forage mainly at night, but in undisturbed areas they can also be seen feeding during the daytime, especially on cloudy days. White-tails form several kinds of social groups, the most common of which is *matrilineal*, which includes a doe, her female offspring of previous years, and their fawns. Adult and subadult males also form groups, and males form *bachelor groups* in winter after they have shed their antlers. Though White-tailed Deer are not territorial, they occupy fairly specific home ranges, which may vary in size from 60 to 500 hectares (150 to 1235 acres). Predators of White-tailed Deer include Puma and dogs. Bobcats and Coyotes are significant predators of fawns.

Breeding
WILD PIGS breed throughout the year. Gestation is about 112 days and litter size varies from 1 to 12. Piglets are able to walk and follow their mother within a few hours of birth. They grow rapidly and are weaned within a few weeks, but continue to travel with their mother for several months. The rutting season for WHITE-TAILED DEER typically begins in fall and lasts for several months. In South Florida, the rut begins in August and fawns are born in February, before the rains begin. Males spar with one another for about a month, then begin to court and mate females. Gestation lasts about 200 days. Females usually give birth to a single fawn the first time they breed, but if food is plentiful they will give birth to twins in following years. Fawns are spotted and weigh about 3 to 4 kg (6.6 to 8.8 lb) at birth. They are able to stand and nurse almost immediately. The mother leaves them hidden in the vegetation for the first 3 or 4 weeks of their lives but returns to nurse them several times a day. Young deer are weaned in 8 to 10 weeks and are fully functional ruminants by the time they are 2 months old.

Notes
Wild Pigs cause serious damage to native fauna and flora. Orchids, lilies, and bog and swamp plants are particularly vulnerable to their rooting behavior. Salamanders and other native amphibians and reptiles are also extremely vulnerable, as many of these species live in moist soil, and under logs and stones – exactly the places where pigs forage. In 1966 the US Forest Service declared that all feral pigs or free-ranging domestic swine in Florida were privately-owned livestock that did not belong on national forest land. Since the 1980s, when the population was estimated to exceed 500,000, the Forest Service has been working to eliminate all feral pigs on national forest land in Florida. Despite these efforts, the feral pig population in Florida is currently stable or expanding.

Status
The diminutive KEY DEER, a subspecies of WHITE-TAILED DEER, is considered endangered by federal (U.S. Fish and Wildlife Service) and state (Florida Fish and Wildlife Conservation Commission) authorities. Currently some 250 to 300 of these tiny deer remain in the lower Keys; the majority live within the boundaries of the National Key Deer Refuge.

Profiles
Wild Pig, *Sus scrofa*, Plate 63b
White-tailed Deer, *Odocoileus virginianus*, Plate 63c

11. Rodents – Mice, Rats, and Pocket Gopher

Rodents are by far the most diverse and successful group of mammals, but they are inconspicuous and difficult to see. The number of rodent species in the world approaches 2000, fully 44% of the approximately 4500 known mammalian species. Probably in every region of the world save Antarctica (which, along with some Arctic islands, are the only places rodents do not occur), rodents are the most abundant land mammals. More individual rodents are estimated to be alive at any one time than individuals of all other types of mammals combined. But despite their abundance, rodents are rarely seen, most likely because they are small, secretive and usually nocturnal. The ecological success of rodents is likely related to their rapid reproduction, efficient specialized teeth and associated jaw muscles, and broad diets. Rodents are characterized by having four large *incisor teeth*, one pair front and center in the upper jaw, one pair in the lower jaw (*cheek teeth*, separated from the incisors, are located farther back in the mouth). The word rodent comes from the Latin *rodere*, to gnaw, and most rodents live up to their name, making their living with their strong, sharp, chisel-like front teeth. These teeth are worn down as they are used, but they keep growing; in some species the incisors grow as rapidly as 2.5 cm (1 in) per month.

Most of the world's rodents are small mouse-like or rat-like mammals that weigh less than 1 kg (2.2 lb); they range, however, from tiny *pygmy mice* that weigh only a few grams to South America's pig-sized CAPYBARA, which can weigh as much as 50 kg (110 lb). Except for the AMERICAN BEAVER, which occurs only in the northern part of the state, most of Florida's 22 species of rodents weigh less than 500 g (1.1 lb).

Natural History
Ecology and Behavior

Florida is home to a variety of mice and rats. The NORWAY RAT and BLACK RAT (both Plate 66) are introduced species, common in urban areas, garbage dumps and shipping wharves. The smaller, slimmer and longer-tailed Black Rat is an agile climber that forages and nests in rafters, attics and in the tree canopy. It will eat virtually anything consumable but prefers vegetable matter. It builds loose, spherical nests of shredded vegetation, cloth, or other suitable material. In Florida, the Black Rat is also called 'the orange grove rat' because it feeds on ripe and fallen fruit in citrus groves. The larger Norway Rat is more terrestrial in its habits. These omnivorous rodents dig long branching tunnels in the ground or beneath logs and garbage piles. The tunnels have rooms for nests and food storage. Seeds, grains, nuts, vegetables and fruits are preferred food items. They often live in colonies of 10 to 20 individuals.

The BEACH MOUSE (Plate 65) prefers sparsely vegetated sandy beaches and weedy old fields. It builds a small tunnel, 0.5 to 1 m (2 to 3 ft) deep, with a nest chamber at the end. An escape tunnel leads from the nest chamber to within a few cm (about an inch) of the surface. These mice feed on grass seeds, herbs and occasionally arthropods. They are primarily nocturnal but are sometimes seen during the day. The FLORIDA MOUSE (Plate 65) is an endemic species and only occurs in longleaf pine and turkey oak sandhills and sand pine scrub forest. They live almost exclusively in Gopher Tortoise burrows, where they dig small side tunnels into the wall of the tortoise burrow. They emerge at night to feed on insects, seeds and other plant material. Acorns of several oak species are particularly important. The strikingly beautiful GOLDEN MOUSE (Plate 65) is especially common in dense woodlands and habitats with thick undergrowth. It is quite arboreal, often nesting and foraging above the ground. Nests are sometimes built in clumps of Spanish moss. Golden mice build feeding platforms above the ground. Their diet consists of seeds, nuts, and berries. In Florida, SOUTHEASTERN POCKET GOPHERS (Plate 66) are sometimes called 'salamanders.' The name is a version of their common name, 'sandy mounder,' which comes from their habit of pushing up mounds of sand as they construct their tunnels. Pocket gophers are muscular, rat-sized animals with long cylindrical bodies and huge buck teeth. They use the massive claws on their front feet to dig tunnels through the earth. They feed on a variety of roots, tubers, and bulbs, and use their cheek pouches (pockets) to carry food. Pocket gophers are rarely seen on the surface; however, the sandy 'push ups' they make as they tunnel are common features in open fields and pine oak woodlands.

Breeding

BLACK and NORWAY RATS are prolific breeders and reproduce year-round. Litter size averages 6 to 9 and they can produce 6 to 8 litters per year. BEACH MICE and GOLDEN MICE also breed throughout the year. Litter size is 2 or 3 for the Golden Mouse and 3 or 4 for the Beach Mouse. The young are weaned by the time they are three or four weeks of age. The FLORIDA MOUSE has small litters, with larger young that develop more slowly. SOUTHEASTERN POCKET GOPHERS can breed during any month of the year. The female gives birth to 1 to 3 young that develop slowly – their eyes do not open until they are 5 weeks old.

Status

BEACH MICE populations have been decimated by beach-front activities and development; consequently, four races, or subspecies, of Beach Mice are listed as Endangered by the Florida Fish and Wildlife Conservation Commission and the U.S. Fish and Wildlife Service. One race is listed as Threatened. The FLORIDA MOUSE is listed as a Species of Special Concern by the Florida Fish and Wildlife Conservation Commission.

Profiles

Beach Mouse, *Peromyscus polionotus*, Plate 65a
Golden Mouse, *Ochrotomys nuttalli*, Plate 65b
Florida Mouse, *Podomys floridanus*, Plate 65c
Black Rat, *Rattus rattus*, Plate 66a
Norway Rat, *Rattus norvegicus*, Plate 66b
Southeastern Pocket Gopher, *Geomys pinetis*, Plate 66d

12. Rodents – Squirrels

When you think of a *squirrel*, the first thing that comes to mind is the familiar perky, little, tree-climbing creature with a long, plume-like tail, found in parks and gardens all over North America and Europe. Though this is a fairly accurate image for most of the squirrels in Florida, not all members of the squirrel family live in trees. The squirrel family, Sciuridae, is classified under the umbrella of the huge group of mammals known as Rodents. The 273 species in the squirrel family are found worldwide and include *prairie dogs, marmots, chipmunks, ground squirrels, tree squirrels* and *flying squirrels*.

Squirrels have a long cylindrical body, short front legs, much longer hind legs, and a long – or sometimes short – bushy tail. The front feet have four toes, each with a sharp, arched claw, and the thumb is reduced, used mainly for holding food. Except for flying squirrels, members of this family tend to be diurnal, and are some of the most visible members of the rodent group. There are four species of *sciurids* in Florida: the EASTERN CHIPMUNK, the ubiquitous EASTERN GRAY SQUIRREL (Plate 64), the handsome and colorful 'giant' EASTERN FOX SQUIRREL (Plate 64), and the tiny SOUTHERN FLYING SQUIRREL (Plate 64). The Eastern Chipmunk (not illustrated) in Florida is restricted to a small area in the far western portion of the Panhandle. It is a small (total length 21 to 28 cm, 8 to 11 in, of which the tail is 8 to 11.5 cm, 3 to 4.5 in) brown, reddish brown, or orangish squirrel with dark and light stripes down its back.

Natural History
Ecology and Behavior
Most squirrels are seed-eaters and many species spend their lives in the trees. The EASTERN FOX SQUIRREL, EASTERN GRAY SQUIRREL, and SOUTHERN FLYING SQUIRREL are arboreal, but all three species also forage on the ground. Gray Squirrels feed mainly on acorns and seeds but they will also eat fungi, berries, fruit and bird eggs. They are often seen burying acorns and nuts. Fox squirrels – so-called because of their striking fox-like tails – have similar habits but spend more time on the ground than the other species. Fox squirrels prefer open park-like habitats with scattered mature pine trees and an open understory. They often run across the ground as they move from tree to tree. In some parts of southwest Florida fox squirrels are quite abundant on golf courses that have retained patches of open pine-oak forest. Both species are strictly diurnal, but fox squirrels do not usually begin foraging until mid-morning. Tree cavities are used as sleeping quarters and birth dens but in some areas large leaf nests are also constructed.

The Southern Flying Squirrel is the only nocturnal member of the squirrel family in North America. It lives primarily in hardwood forests, where it is dependent on tree cavities for den sites. Flying squirrels can sometimes be seen on bright moonlit nights as they glide from tree to tree, and they often reveal their presence by distinctive high-pitched squeaks. These tiny squirrels forage mainly in the trees, feeding on nuts, berries, fruits and insects. During cold weather they roost communally; two dozen or more will sometimes curl up together in a large tree cavity.

Chipmunks are inhabitants of deciduous forests, forest edges, and wooded ravines. They live in underground burrows. Chipmunks are diurnal and forage primarily on the ground but will occasionally climb trees. Their diet consists of seeds and nuts but large numbers of insects are also eaten. Chipmunks have cheek pouches located inside the mouth. While foraging, Chipmunks stuff their cheek pouches with food, to be carried back to the burrow.

Breeding
In Florida, EASTERN GRAY SQUIRRELS usually have two litters per year, one between January and March, the second during June/July. Two to six young are born after a 45-day gestation period. The young are born pink and hairless, with eyes and ears closed. Their eyes remain closed for a comparatively long time, finally opening when they are 4 weeks old. The young are weaned and independent at 8 or 9 weeks old. EASTERN FOX SQUIRREL reproduction is similar to the Eastern Gray Squirrel. SOUTHERN FLYING SQUIRRELS breed in spring and fall, producing 2 or 3 young in each litter, after a 40-day gestation period. The young are independent at 6 weeks of age. Chipmunks breed in early spring and again in summer if conditions are favorable. Two to seven young are born after a 31-day gestation. Young remain in underground nest chambers until they are about 5 to 6 weeks old and are weaned by 2 months of age.

Status

SHERMAN'S FOX SQUIRREL and the BIG CYPRESS FOX SQUIRREL, subspecies, or races, of the EASTERN FOX SQUIRREL, are listed as threatened by Florida state authorities. Because of their extremely limited distribution in the Panhandle, the EASTERN CHIPMUNK is listed as a Species of Special Concern by the Florida Fish and Wildlife Conservation Commission.

Profiles

Southern Flying Squirrel, *Glaucomys volans*, Plate 64a
Eastern Gray Squirrel, *Sciurus carolinensis*, Plate 64b
Eastern Fox Squirrel, *Sciurus niger*, Plate 64c

13. Rabbits and Hares

Rabbits and *hares* were once thought to be rodents, due partly to their chisel-like incisor teeth. However, they are not rodents and are classified in order Lagomorpha, which contains two families, the Leporidae (rabbits and hares) and the Ochotonidae (*pikas*). The 54 species of rabbits and hares are native to most regions of North and South America, Europe, Asia, and Africa, and people have introduced them to many other areas where they were absent, the most notable being Australia. Fifteen species of *leporids* are found in North America, but only three occur in Florida. They are the EASTERN COTTONTAIL and MARSH RABBIT (both Plate 64), which are native to the state, and the introduced BLACK-TAILED JACKRABBIT.

Rabbits and hares are adapted for foraging in open habitats. Large, elongated ears, and an excellent sense of hearing help them detect danger, and their elongated hind feet and powerful hindquarters help them move with a speedy zigzag dash when escaping from predators. When feeding or moving slowly they move with a hopping, or saltatorial, type of gait.

Natural History

Ecology and Behavior

The EASTERN COTTONTAIL is highly adaptable and thrives in practically all Florida habitats except dense forests and swampy areas. Its name is derived from the tail hair that forms a cotton tuft. Cottontails are active mainly at night, but can often be seen feeding at dusk and dawn, and sometimes during the day when the weather is cloudy. They eat grasses, herbs and leaves.

As its name suggests, the MARSH RABBIT is found only in marshy habitats, where water is plentiful. The Marsh Rabbit is slightly smaller and darker than the Eastern Cottontail and its tail hair forms a brown tuft. In South Florida it is found in sawgrass marshes, sugar-cane fields, mangrove swamps, and on canal banks. Marsh Rabbits take to the water readily and swim well – often for considerable distances. They are most active at night and eat a wide variety of wetland plants including water hyacinth, grasses, cattail, rushes, and herbs.

The BLACK-TAILED JACKRABBIT, a native of the western USA, was introduced to the Miami area in the 1930s and 1940s and can now frequently be seen in the open grassy areas at Miami International Airport. They were originally brought in to train racing greyhounds and many escaped into the surrounding countryside.

Breeding

Rabbits are famous for their high reproductive output and the phrase 'breeds like a rabbit' is well founded. A short gestation period, large litters, rapidly developing young and several litters per year combine to make them among the most fecund of mammals. In central and southern Florida, EASTERN COTTONTAILS and MARSH RABBITS breed year round, but in North Florida, few young are born between November and February. Unlike European rabbits, which dig extensive warrens complete with maternity chambers, North American species do not burrow. Females choose a well-camouflaged spot to make a cup-shaped depression in the ground and line the nest with grass and soft breast fur. The nest is covered with grass when the female is away foraging.

Eastern Cottontails give birth to 3 to 6 naked, helpless young after a gestation period of 28 days (a main difference between hares and rabbits is that hares give birth to *precocial* young – born in a fairly developed state, eyes open, fully furred, and nearly ready to move; but rabbit young are *altricial* – born naked, eyes closed, fairly helpless). The female mates again immediately after giving birth, and is often pregnant while she nurses the litter. Young cottontails grow extremely fast. Their eyes open and they are fully furred in a week, and by the end of a month they are weaned and ready to leave the nest. When they leave, the mother is often ready to deliver another litter. Females can breed when they are about 6 months old, and may have 7 to 12 litters per year. Marsh Rabbits are only slightly less prolific. Females give birth to about 3 young after a 37-day gestation period. The young leave the nest when they are about 2 weeks old, but continue to nurse until they become independent, at about 1 month of age. Females in south Florida average 7 litters per year.

Ecological Interactions
By most mammalian standards, the parenting system of rabbits and hares is highly unusual. Males take no part in raising the young and females are absentee mothers. Female rabbits and hares leave their young alone in the nest and return only once every 24 hours to nurse them. Nursing visits are amazingly brief – about 3 minutes in most cases; then, after a brief lick, the mother departs. Female rats, which give birth to similarly undeveloped young, spend 90% of their day cuddled up with their offspring, nursing and grooming them. By contrast, rabbit mothers spend 0.1% of their day with their young. The rabbit's absentee parenting is thought to have evolved as an anti-predator strategy. Rabbits are not very fierce, and faced with a predator, they run rather than fight. By hiding their young and visiting them as infrequently as possible, they reduce the chance of the babies being found by a fox or Bobcat.

Notes
In Europe in the 1400s, the rabbit was a symbol of lust, depicted in paintings and murals as an associate of Venus, the goddess of love. Hares, on the other hand, were said to bring bad luck. Very much like domestic cats, hares were believed to be the familiars of witches, and they were sometimes thought to be witches in disguise. It was considered unlucky even to see a hare. However, the foot of the unlucky hare was a potent charm; kept in your pocket, it was believed to ward off bad luck and ill health. In time, this 'charm' was generalized to a rabbit's foot.

Status
Both the EASTERN COTTONTAIL and MARSH RABBIT are common throughout much of Florida. However, owing to habitat loss and encroaching development, the lower Keys subspecies of the Marsh Rabbit is considered endangered by the U.S. Fish and Wildlife Service and the Florida Fish and Wildlife Conservation Commission.

Profiles
Eastern Cottontail, *Sylvilagus floridanus*, Plate 64d
Marsh Rabbit, *Silvilagus palustris*, Plate 64e

Environmental Close-up 6:
Reducing Roadkill

On Interstate Highway 75 (I-75) between Fort Lauderdale and Naples, motorists speed past large yellow signs emblazoned with the words 'Panther Crossing.' Looking out of the window, there seems to be nothing but featureless swamp for as far as the eye can see, but below the road a wide grassy culvert funnels alligators, deer, bears, bobcats, and sometimes even panthers under the busy highway.

Florida has become a world leader in the rather unusual science of designing and building animal road crossings. The state now has panther crossings in the Everglades, bear crossings near Orlando and even a special snake and amphibian crossing in North Florida. Highway planners and biologists originally came up with the idea of wildlife crossings as a way to reduce the number of endangered Florida Panthers being killed by cars. The idea is catching on and several states and many different countries now have special wildlife crossings for everything from toads to elk.

Driving around Florida, it is difficult not to notice the crushed carcasses of tortoises, opossums, raccoons and armadillos lying beside the highway. Indeed, road-killed wildlife is so common that one enterprising author even produced a book entitled 'Field Guide to Flattened Fauna.' The slim, entertainingly written volume allows motorists to identify the different sized 'splats' on the road as they drive by.

Roads and wildlife just don't mix very well. On a typical four-lane highway that carries 20,000 vehicles per day, one car or truck goes by roughly every four seconds. This creates an almost impenetrable barrier for wildlife. Millions of birds, reptiles, mammals and amphibians are killed each year by vehicles travelling on America's roads. Slow-moving animals like tortoises, turtles, frogs and salamanders are at great risk when they cross roads to reach mating or nesting sites. Wide-ranging animals like bears and Florida Panthers are also vulnerable, simply because they routinely must cross roads.

When Florida Department of Transportation (FDOT) engineers needed to widen I-75 in South Florida, the new, improved highway threatened to isolate some of the few remaining Florida Panthers in the Big Cypress Preserve and contribute to the rising body-count of panthers hit and killed by vehicles. After talking to biologists and studying badger tunnels that people had built in Holland and toad culverts in England, FDOT engineers came up with the design for the Panther Crossings. Constructed at sites where panthers are most likely to cross, each underpass is 30 m (100 ft) across and 2.4 m (8 ft) high. Three-meter (10-ft) high chain link fences along the roadside funnel animals into the crossing points. The project was not cheap. The 36 crossings constructed along a 65-km (40-mile) stretch of I-75 cost US$ 13 million. But the crossings work. Remote cameras have confirmed that panthers, bobcats, deer, raccoons, alligators, wading birds, dogs and even some humans use them. And no panthers have been killed on I-75 since the crossings were built.

Florida Black Bears have been on the state's list of threatened species since 1974. Scientists estimate that some 1000 to 2000 bears currently remain in Florida, but the number of bears killed on the state's highways has increased every year since counts began in 1976. Sixty bears were killed on Florida's highways in 1996, 74 in 1997, and 88 in 1998. More than 40% of all Florida's bear road mortalities occur in and around the Ocala National Forest. The Florida Fish and Wildlife Conservation Commission and the Florida Department of Transportation have identified several areas, including State Road 46, just north of Orlando, as especially deadly highways for bears (watch for bear crossing signs if you are driving this road). Bears are often hit on this road as they try to cross from Wekiwa Springs State Park into the Ocala National Forest. At least 11 bears were killed on a single, 1.6-km (1-mile) stretch of SR 46, so in 1994 the FDOT installed a specially designed experimental 'bear' underpass. Bears now use the crossing regularly, and none have been killed on this stretch of road since the crossing was installed.

Another innovative wildlife crossing can be found on US Highway 441 in north Florida. One short segment of this road has more documented road-kills than any other road in Florida. Thousands of animals from more than 80 species are killed every year on the 3.2-km (2-mile) section of road that passes through Paynes Prairie State Preserve, just south of Gainesville. Most of the casualties are snakes, frogs and turtles. For this problem, a multi-disciplinary task force came up with an innovative solution. A 1.1-m (3.5-ft) high wall with a special lip at the top diverts animals into eight culverts that run beneath the road. The task force got the idea for the design from the walls in zoo serpentariums. The wildlife wall was completed in 2000 at a cost of US$ 2.6 million, and the FDOT and the designers are hoping that the project will become a model for the state and the nation.

Florida also has the USA's first wildlife bridge, an overpass that crosses Interstate 75 in Central Florida, 16 km (10 miles) south of Ocala. Drivers on the Interstate can recognize the wildlife overpass by its landscaping – it is the only bridge over the Interstate with pines and oaks growing on it. The bridge joins two halves of the Florida Greenway and reconnects the woodlands on either side of the highway. (The Marjorie Harris Carr Cross Florida Greenway is a state recreation and conservation area in north-central Florida, a 175-km (110-mile) corridor that traverses a wide variety of natural habitats such as rivers, floodplains, wetlands, and uplands.) Landscape planners hope that the bridge, the bear and panther crossings, and other greenway trails will re-connect Florida's fragmented landscapes, and help reduce the horrible carnage on the state's highways.

Chapter 10

INSECTS AND OTHER ARTHROPODS

by Dennis Paulson

Slater Museum of Natural History, University of Puget Sound

- *General Characteristics and Natural History*
- *Seeing Insects in Florida*

General Characteristics and Natural History

Insects are the most diverse living organisms, with over a million described species and perhaps tens of millions of undescribed ones. No one has estimated the number of species of insects in Florida, but it is surely an impressive number. Like amphibians and reptiles, the body temperature of insects is that of the surrounding air or water (they are all *ectotherms*, ecto = outside, therm = heat), so they flourish in the warm environments of low latitudes. Not only are there many species in the state, but there are a whole lot of individuals! Florida is often called a 'buggy' state, but it surely has fewer mosquitos than Alaska, fewer tarantulas than Texas (in fact, none), and perhaps fewer cockroaches than New York City.

Insects are classified in the phylum Arthropoda and class Insecta. Insects are the only group of arthropods with exactly six legs. Almost all insects are terrestrial, like spiders but unlike the mostly marine crustaceans. Insects have three body parts, a *head*, *thorax*, and *abdomen*. The antennae, eyes, and mouthparts are on the head, the three pairs of legs and usually two pairs of wings are on the thorax, and the reproductive structures are on the abdomen. *Spiders* (Plate 77), *scorpions* (Plate 77), *ticks* (Plate 76), and *mites* (including chiggers; Plate 76) are in the same phylum but class Arachnida. *Arachnids* have eight legs and only two body parts, the *cephalothorax* (combined head and thorax) and abdomen.

Insects vary among themselves tremendously: in where they live, what they eat and how they eat it, how they escape their predators, how they reproduce, and how their immature stages develop. They also vary greatly in how they affect humans, from the predatory wasps that eat caterpillars that are our crop pests, through the beautiful butterflies that please our aesthetic senses, to the fleas and flies, which sometimes carry human diseases. Spiders are much more uniform; all of them are predators that sink their *chelicerae* ('fangs') into their prey and suck out their body juices. They do vary in how they capture their prey, from hunters that lie in wait for insects or chase them down (even underwater!), to the many kinds of web-builders that trap their prey in strong sticky strands (which they spin with remarkable organs called *spinnerets* at their abdomen tip). Scorpions are also predators that dispatch their prey with potent venom injected by the stinger on the tip of their segmented 'tail.' Ticks and mites suck blood from larger animals; they are considered *ectoparasites*.

Because of their great diversity, it is not surprising that insects eat just about everything. What is especially interesting is that they do it in so many ways. Insect groups vary in their basic feeding anatomy, or mouthpart structure. Many insects, for example, dragonflies (Plate 73), beetles (Plate 74), and grasshoppers (Plate 72), have biting mouthparts, consisting of a pair of strong mandibles with which they chew up plant or animal prey. Dragonflies are predators, grasshoppers are herbivores (plant-eaters), and there are so many beetles that among them they eat just about everything (for example, whole families of beetles specialize in carrion-eating). Others, such as butterflies and moths (Plates 69 to 72), have sucking mouthparts, the same structures modified into a long, coiled tube through which they suck nectar produced by flowers. Still others, including bugs (Plate 75) and many types of flies (Plate 76e), have piercing mouthparts, which they insert into plant or animal tissues to deliver venom and suck blood and tissues. Some flies have lapping mouthparts, with which they imbibe exposed liquids; our familiar house fly is among this group.

The reproductive biology of insects varies especially in how they develop to adulthood. Primitive insects such as silverfish exhibit *direct metamorphosis*, the immature going through a series of *molts*, shedding its outer covering each time and growing while it is soft. These immature stages change gradually into the reproductively mature adult. More advanced insects such as grasshoppers, cockroaches, and bugs have an immature stage called a *nymph*, which becomes increasingly adultlike as it goes through a series of molts. The final molt turns the still immature-looking nymph into a mature adult, with reproductive organs, usually with wings, and often looking rather different from the nymph. Dragonflies and mayflies show a variation on this theme, with a nymphlike aquatic larva that changes gradually as it grows, then a dramatic metamorphosis into a flying adult. The most extreme change is undergone by advanced insects such as beetles, butterflies, flies, and wasps, in which there is a *larval*, a *pupal*, and an *adult stage*, all very different from one another. The pupal stage allows the larva to change into the adult, usually adapted for a very different lifestyle from that of its larva. Almost all insects lay eggs, but some aphids and others give birth to live young. Most aphid births are *parthenogenetic*, females giving birth to other females without the benefit of fertilization.

Seeing Insects in Florida

You needn't worry about looking for insects in Florida – they'll come to you. But the ones that come to you may not be the ones you were seeking! Most likely they will be mosquitos, no-see-ums, and deer flies (Plate 76) that visit you for the microscopic amount of blood you can donate to their well-being. If their bites didn't hurt or produce allergic reactions, we often wouldn't notice them; more seriously, a very few of them transmit human diseases (very unlikely in Florida). However, with a modicum of protection, you can get along just fine in the midst of these pesky flies while spending your time looking for the showier creatures that make Florida seem so exotic: the glamorous butterflies and dragonflies, big colorful lubber grasshoppers (Plate 72), and huge orb-weaving spiders.

Many insects, for example butterflies and dragonflies, are sun-lovers, so don't look for them during bad weather. But weather in Florida is mostly good, and in the southern part of the state many insects can be seen right through the winter, when their relatives up North are hidden away in some snug, overwintering shelter. Dragonflies can be found wherever there are lakes, ponds, marshes, and streams. Butterflies are attracted to plants, some for their nectar and others for their leaves, which furnish food for their larvae. Walking Sticks (Plate 72) and lubber grasshoppers, impressive enough by themselves, are often seen as mating pairs. Just as is the case in birds and mammals, different habitats support different species of insects, so look in all sorts of places to see the greatest variety.

Insects are small animals, and one way you can add to your enjoyment of them is to make them larger. You can do this by looking at them through a 10× hand lens, available in nature stores and many book stores. Ten times magnification is much better than the 3× to 5× magnifiers sold 'to reveal the secrets of nature.' Some naturalists carry their lens on a string around their neck, for immediate use, but a pocket will suffice. If you're a birder, already carrying binoculars, you will find that reversing them provides an excellent pair of magnifying glasses. When that next mosquito lands on your arm, don't swat it – study it!

Chapter 11

CORAL REEF WILDLIFE

by Richard Francis

Department of Ichthyology, California Academy of Sciences

Florida contains some remarkably diverse underwater habitats, including crystalline freshwater springs, the shallow-water environments of the Everglades, where huge fish known as gar stack themselves like cordwood during the dry season, as well as a variety of marine environments. Marine environments include the Gulf coast and the Keys, on which I will focus here. Florida's Keys extend almost 300 km (185 miles) from the southern tip of the mainland toward the tropical waters of the Caribbean. For underwater enthusiasts, the Keys are most celebrated for their coral reefs, the only ones to be found in the continental USA. Many American divers first experience coral reef environments on Florida's Keys.

Coral reefs are the marine equivalents of tropical rainforests. As in rainforests, the diversity of life on a coral reef is truly mind-boggling and life's abundance, palpable. In contrast to rainforests, however, where most of the action is beyond view and can be only vaguely appreciated, most of the life on a reef can be experienced directly. Equipped only with mask, snorkel and fins, you can explore environments so different from those in which we spend most of our lives that, by comparison, the Gobi desert, Antarctica, the Congo and New York City are just variations on a single theme.

The Florida Keys represent the northern limit of Atlantic coral reefs. Farther north, the water is not sufficiently warm for sufficiently long. Warm water is essential for reef development, the water must also be shallow and clear enough to allow light to penetrate significantly below the surface. Florida's reefs are confined to the gently sloping continental shelf that extends southward from the mainland, away from the turbidity generated by river runoff. One of the primary threats to these reefs is the increased turbidity that has accompanied the explosive growth of the human population in South Florida.

Because the Keys are at the limit of coral growth, there are fewer species of both invertebrates and vertebrates than in the Caribbean. There are, however, a number of species that flourish on these reefs that are either rare or absent in the Caribbean, such as the beautiful Blue Angelfish (Plate 78). In addition, found here are numerous *subtropical species* (species that occur in regions that border a tropical zone), for which the Keys represent the southernmost extension of their geographic distribution. So the Keys, like the Galápagos Islands in the Pacific, afford an opportunity to explore a zone of contact between tropical and subtropical species.

The coral reef system of the Keys consists of numerous *reef patches* of varying sizes, separated by areas of rubble and sand. The sandy stretches host a suite of animal inhabitants quite distinct from those you will find on the reefs themselves. The *coral rubble*, which often forms a transition habitat between the living reef and the sandy areas, also has a host of creatures unique to it. Another distinct community develops on the *grassbeds* which develop in the more protected, shallow, sandy areas. These grassbeds are important nurseries for many reef fishes, including *snappers, parrotfishes* and some *wrasses*. The most important marine nurseries, however, are provided by the mosquito-infested mangroves (p. 22), which are also home to some of the favorite sportfish, such as Tarpon (Plate 82) and Bonefish (Plate 81). All of these habitats are worth exploring.

It is the coral reefs themselves, however, that are the main attraction for underwater explorers, so I will focus primarily on them. Aside from the *hard corals*, which form the foundation of these reefs, you will notice a tremendous variety of *gorgonians* (Plate 101), including *sea fans* (Plate 101), *sea whips, sea rods* (Plate 101) and *sea plumes*. *Sponges* (Plate 105), including large tube and barrel forms, are another extremely important part of the reef community. The sponges, soft corals and hard corals provide the physical texture of the reef and the background colors, but it is the moving things that usually attract a snorkeler's attention first, and primary among these are the fish. Their variety and number are dazzling. Loose schools of *surgeonfishes* (Plate 79), sometimes a mixture of several species, and *damselfishes* (Plate 85) of various sorts, will attract your attention. As you explore further, you will encounter the large Blue Angelfishes (Plate 78), usually in pairs. These fish pair for life, and exhibit a degree of fidelity that parsons would envy. They are quite curious, and if you avoid rapid movements they will approach and inspect you from a distance, sometimes turning on their sides to get a better perspective. You will have to look more closely to find the much shyer Queen Angelfish (Plate 78), which never stray far from their nooks in the coral. These creatures are well worth the effort, as they are among the most magnificently beautiful fish you will find anywhere in the world.

Butterflyfishes (Plate 78) are closely related to angelfishes. These are among the most spectacular reef inhabitants. There are not nearly as many species of butterflyfishes in Florida and the Caribbean region as in the tropical Pacific, but they are still a prominent component of the reef community. Like the angelfishes, some types of butterflyfishes mate for life. Remarkably, they seem to pair up before they reach sexual maturity, a form of extended courtship. There is evidence that when they initially pair up, their sexes are not yet determined; only after pairing does one member of the pair 'decide' to become a male, and the other a female. Some butterflyfishes are among the few reef fishes to eat live coral.

Although juvenile butterflyfishes look like miniature versions of the adults, the same cannot be said of the angelfishes. Juvenile Blue Angelfishes, for instance, are much more strikingly colored than adults; their jet black body is decorated with circular white lines of increasing diameter, somewhat like a bull's-eye. Such age-related color changes are common among reef fishes. Aside from the angelfishes, such color changes are especially common among damselfishes (Plates 85, 86), wrasses (Plates 90, 91) and parrotfishes (Plate 89). So dramatic are the color differences between young and adult in some of these groups, that they were often classified as different species when first described scientifically. Among many wrasses and parrotfishes the differences in color between juvenile and adult are further complicated by the dramatic sex differences in adult coloration. Again, males and females can look so different that, in some cases, they were once classified as different species. The females are typically fairly drab compared with the males, and hence harder to distinguish. Only experienced divers can discriminate between females of the various parrotfishes; the males, however, are quite easy to identify.

To further complicate matters, some individuals don't appear to be either male or female, but rather like something intermediate between the two. And in fact they are. It turns out that many types of wrasses and parrotfishes are *sex changers*. The Yellowhead Wrasse (Plate 91) is typical. In this species, all individuals mature first as females. Only when they are much older and achieve a certain (relative) size, do some individuals undergo sex change and become males. Sex-changing species are often highly social and the sex change process is regulated by social interactions within the group. In general, only the most dominant individuals become males and enjoy the reproductive privileges that come from being one male among many females. Alas, in some species it gets even more complicated. The Bluehead Wrasse (Plate 91), for example, exhibits two distinct types of male. One type of male, referred to as 'terminal phase,' becomes male only after a sex change, as in the Yellowhead Wrasse. The second male type, or 'initial phase,' matures as a male without undergoing sex change. The initial phase males look just like females, which relates to their reproductive strategy. Whereas the large and colorful terminal-phase males defend a territory and court females, the initial-phase males like to sneak into the vicinity of the courting couple and spew their sperm all over them; they then hastily exit the area before the terminal-phase male can switch from a sexual to an aggressive, fighting mode. Not a terribly efficient way to fertilize eggs, but it works well enough.

The Stoplight Parrotfish (Plate 90) exhibits yet another developmental wrinkle to further complicate sexual matters. Whereas in the Bluehead Wrasse initial phase males stay that way for life, initial-phase Stoplight Parrotfish males can themselves become terminal-phase males after they reach a certain size. So in this species there are two distinct routes to becoming a terminal-phase male; either you mature as a female and later change sex, or you mature as an initial phase male and then become a terminal-phase male. In either case there are not only dramatic color changes associated with these sexual changes, but internal changes – which include changes in the brain – as well. No wonder these fishes gave headaches to early scientists who tried to classify them!

Aside from their complicated sex lives, parrotfishes are notable for their unique feeding habits. The front teeth on each jaw are fused into a beak-like structure from whence they derive their name. With this extremely strong beak they can grind up the cement-like hard corals in order to extract the soft polyps and algae inside. The sounds they make in the process are quite audible underwater. After a hearty meal, parrotfish rid themselves of the non-nutritive coral matrix they have ingested along with the algae by excreting wispy clouds of fine sand, which you will occasionally encounter, suspended in the water. Parrotfish convert incredible amounts of coral into this white sand; and this parrotfish excrement is a significant contributor to those beautiful white sand beaches that attract so many to the tropics and subtropics.

Hamlets (Plate 87) are small members of the seabass family which also exhibit noteworthy sex lives. They are true *hermaphrodites*, possessing both ovaries and testes. Mating, as you might expect, is somewhat unconventional, involving the alternate release of eggs and sperm by each member of a pair, during a process known as *egg trading*. The seabass family also includes the *groupers* (Plates 87, 88), which are some of the most important predatory reef fishes.

Damselfishes exhibit some of the most interesting behavior among the reef inhabitants, particularly during the breeding season. In most coral reef fishes, the eggs, once fertilized, drift in the *plankton* (the oceans' tiny floating organisms) for varying periods before settling out on a suitable reef patch. Parental contribution to their lives ends with fertilization. Damselfishes, however, lay eggs on the bottom in nests carefully prepared by the male. The male then protects the eggs from predators, especially from marauding wrasses and other damselfishes, until they hatch. During this period the males attack anything and everything that comes near, including divers. What they lack in size they more than make up for in pugnacity, and if you come near a nest, they will come at you with a comically menacing demeanor. If you point your finger in their direction, they will try to nip it. It is also interesting to watch the males interact with each other during their constant border wars. Many damselfishes, including Sergeant Majors (Plate 86), maintain territories in clusters, and because this means they have common borders, they are constantly stimulating each other to attack. At territorial boundaries you can observe a characteristic to and fro between males, in which one advances, and then retreats as it drifts into the neighbor's territory, at which point it instantly loses its confidence and the roles are reversed. The back and forth can go on for minutes, usually ending in a stalemate at the boundary, the two combatants just staring at each other across the divide; until that is, an invasion is detected from a different direction. Male damselfishes use up tremendous energy in this way, and by the end of the breeding season they are understandably exhausted. The females take no part in protecting the territory or the eggs.

Though they comprise the largest family of vertebrate animals, *gobies* are often overlooked because of their small size and sedentary habits. Look for them in the rubble, cracks in coral heads, under coral heads, and inside the barrel sponges. Some species are quite beautiful, and several of the most attractive gobies act as *cleaners*, much like some Pacific wrasses. The Neon Goby (Plate 92) is one of the more notable cleaners. It sets up stations at which much larger fish, including *groupers* (Plates 87, 88), *snappers* (Plate 84) and *grunts* (Plate 83) congregate, waiting patiently in line for the cleaners' attentions. This is not at all a frivolous matter; the cleaners remove external parasites and dead scales as they course over the body surfaces of their clients, as well as inside the mouths. To a first-time observer this looks like the fish equivalent of suicide, but after a while the cleaner will emerge from one of the gills, safe and sated. It has been shown that when cleaner fish are removed from a reef patch, the health of the large fish suffers significantly.

To fully appreciate the diversity of life on the reef, you will need to explore it at night as well as by day. When the sun goes down, a completely different cast of characters emerges, much as occurs on land. But the 'shift changes' on land are much more gradual compared with similar transitions on the reef, where in as little as 15 minutes, the daytime contingent disappears and the creatures of the night emerge. As the *anemones* (Plate 106) retract, the *basket stars* (Plate 104) unfurl; as the groupers and snappers retreat to their caves, the *moray eels* (Plate 97) and *octopi* begin to prowl. Some wrasses bury themselves in the sand, while some parrotfishes construct a giant mucous cocoon within which to sleep. Crevices that harbor *squirrelfishes* (Plate 91) and *soldierfishes* (Plate 91) by day are taken over by surgeonfishes and butterflyfishes as the light wanes. The myriad damselfishes are seemingly absorbed by the coral.

No matter how many times you have dived or snorkeled these reefs, you can expect to see something new each time you enter the water. Start with the most obvious – the sponges, sea fans and angelfishes; then, as you become more experienced, begin looking for the little, less obvious creatures, such as the *tunicates* (Plate 105), *brittle stars* (Plate 104), *shrimps* (Plate 102) and gobies. You will be amply rewarded.

REFERENCES AND ADDITIONAL READING

Alderton D. (1988) *Turtles and Tortoises of the World.* Blandford Press, London, UK.

Ashton R. E. and P. Ashton. (1981) *Handbook of Reptiles and Amphibians of Florida, Part One: The Snakes.* Windward Publishing, Miami, FL.

Ashton R.E. and P. Ashton. (1985) *Handbook of Reptiles and Amphibians of Florida, Part Two: Lizards, Turtles and Crocodilians.* Windward Publishing, Miami, FL.

Ashton R.E. and P. Ashton. (1988) *Handbook of Reptiles and Amphibians of Florida, Part Three: The Amphibians.* Windward Publishing, Miami, FL.

Bartlett R.D. and P.P. Bartlett. (1999) *A Field Guide to Florida Reptiles and Amphibians.* Gulf Publishing Field Guide Series, Houston, TX.

Boag D. (1982) *The Kingfisher.* Blandford Press, Poole, UK.

Brown L.N. (1997) *A Guide to the Mammals of the Southeastern United States.* University of Tennessee Press, Knoxville, TN.

Brown R.C. (1998) *Florida's Fossils. Guide to Location, Identification and Enjoyment.* Pineapple Press, Sarasota, FL.

Cerulean S. and A. Morrow. (1998) *Florida Wildlife Viewing Guide.* Falcon Publishing, Helena, MT.

Carr A. (1994) *A Naturalist in Florida: A Celebration of Eden.* Yale University Press, New Haven, CT.

Cogger H.G. and R.G. Zweifel (editors) (1992) *Reptiles and Amphibians.* Smithmark Publishers, New York, NY.

Ernst C.H. (1992) *Venomous Reptiles of North America.* Smithsonian Institution Press, Washington, DC.

Gannon M. (1993) *Florida: A Short History.* University Press of Florida, Gainesville, FL.

Grow G. (1997) *Florida Parks. A Guide to Camping and Nature,* 6th ed. Longleaf Publications, Tallahassee, FL.

Halliday T.R. and K. Adler (editors) (1994) *The Encyclopaedia of Reptiles and Amphibians.* Facts On File, New York, NY.

Humphrey S.R. (1992) *Rare and Endangered Biota of Florida, Vol. I. Mammals.* University Press of Florida, Gainesville, FL.

Jewell S.D. (1995) *Exploring Wild Central Florida: A Guide to Finding the Natural Areas and Wildlife of the Central Peninsula.* Pineapple Press, Sarasota, FL.

Jewell S.D. (1997) *Exploring Wild South Florida: A Guide to Finding the Natural Areas and Wildlife of the Southern Peninsula and the Florida Keys,* 2nd ed. Pineapple Press, Sarasota, FL.

Kale H.W. and D.S. Maehr. (1990) *Florida's Birds. A Handbook and Reference.* Pineapple Press, Sarasota, FL.

Kaufman K. (1996) *Lives of North American Birds.* Houghton Mifflin Co., Boston, USA.

Kurten B. (1996) *Before the Indians*. Columbia University Press, New York, NY.

Mattison C. (1986) *Snakes of the World*. Blandford Press, London, UK.

Mattison C. (1992) *Frogs and Toads of the World*. Blandford Press, London, UK.

Meylan A., B. Schroeder, and A. Mesier. (1995) *Sea turtle nesting activity in the state of Florida 1979–1992*. Florida Marine Research Publication No. 52: 1–51.

Milne L. and M. Milne. (1980) *National Audubon Society Field Guide to North American Insects and Spiders*. Alfred A. Knopf, New York, NY.

Minno M.C. and M. Minno. (1999) *Florida Butterfly Gardening: A Complete Guide to Attracting, Identifying, and Enjoying Butterflies of the Lower South*. University Press of Florida, Gainesville, FL.

Moler P.E. (1992) *Rare and Endangered Biota of Florida, Vol. III. Amphibians and Reptiles*. University Press of Florida, Gainesville, FL.

Myers R.L. and J.J. Ewel (editors) (1990) *Ecosystems of Florida*. University of Central Florida Press, Orlando, FL.

National Geographic Society. (1999) *Field Guide to the Birds of North America*. National Geographic Society, Washington, USA.

Nelson G. (1995) *Exploring Wild Northwest Florida: A Guide to Finding the Natural Areas and Wildlife of the Panhandle*. Pineapple Press, Sarasota, FL.

Nelson G. (1996) *The Trees of Florida: A Reference and Field Guide*. Pineapple Press, Sarasota, FL.

Pranty B. (1996) *A Birder's Guide to Florida*. American Bird Banding Association, Inc., Colorado Springs, CO.

Reynolds J.E. and D.K. Odell. (1991) *Manatees and Dugongs*. Facts On File, New York, NY.

Robertson W.B., Jr., and G.E. Woolfenden. 1992. *Florida bird species: an annotated list*. Florida Ornithological Society, Gainesville.

Rodgers J.A., Jr., H.W. Kale, II, and H.T. Smith. (1996) *Rare and Endangered Biota of Florida, Vol. V. Birds*. University Press of Florida, Gainesville, FL.

Ross C.A. and S. Garnett (editors) (1989) *Crocodiles and Alligators*. Golden Press Pty Ltd, Australia.

Simberloff D., D.C. Schmitz, and T.C. Brown (editors) (1997) *Strangers in Paradise. Impact and Management of Nonindigenous Species in Florida*. Island Press, Covelo, CA.

Stamm D. (1994) *The Springs of Florida*. Pineapple Press, Sarasota, FL.

Stebbins R.C. and N.W. Cohen. (1995) *A Natural History of Amphibians*. Princeton University Press, Princeton, NJ.

Stevenson H.M. and B.H. Anderson. (1994). *The Birdlife of Florida*. University Press of Florida, Gainesville.

Stiles F.G. and A.F. Skutch. (1989). *A Field Guide to the Birds of Costa Rica*. Cornell University Press, Ithaca, NY.

Wilson D.E. and S. Ruff (editors) (1999) *The Smithsonian Book of North American Mammals*. Smithsonian Institution Press, Washington, D.C.

HABITAT PHOTOS

I Freshwater swamps like this one are commonly seen along the Tamiami Trail (US 41). Cypress and other trees like pond apple (*Annona glabra*) are covered with epiphytes, such as wild pine bromeliads (*Tillandsia utriculata*) and the occasional orchid. ©Kerry Dressler

2 The Fakahatchee Strand State Preserve along US 41 has a boardwalk at Big Cypress Bend where visitors can get a unique inside look into a freshwater cypress swamp. Bring insect repellent and wear long sleeves. ©Walter Judd

3 Roadside ditches (or borrow pits) beside highways are good places to look for alligators, wading birds and flowering water plants. ©Kerry Dressler

4 The insectivorous pitcher plant (*Sarracenia flava*) is sometimes seen in wet areas of the Apalachicola National Forest in the Panhandle. ©Kerry Dressler

5 Most of the Chassahowitzka River and National Wildlife Refuge near Homosassa is accessible only by boat. Manatees, alligators, otters and more than 250 species of birds lure ecotourists and professional photographers. ©Kerry Dressler

6 The River Styx in North Florida. Small islands of bald cypress (*Taxodium distichum*) allow other aquatic plants to take root around their buttresses. ©Kerry Dressler

7 Hundreds of Manatees swim into the warmer waters of Florida's springs to seek refuge from the winter cold. Here a park ranger counts Manatees swimming in Blue Spring State Park near Orange City. ©Kerry Dressler

8 Manatees and tourists can mingle in some parts of Crystal River. However, the Park Service has set up Manatee-Protected Areas, enclosed by ropes, into which the Manatees can retreat when tourists become too enthusiastic. ©Kerry Dressler

9 The Anastasia State Recreational Area on Florida's northeast coast is less than 3 km (2 miles) from historic downtown St. Augustine. Camping, fishing, sailboard and kayak rentals, and miles of white sandy beach make this one of North Florida's best-kept secrets.
©Kerry Dressler

10 Florida's wide, white sand beaches draw visitors from around the world. Some, like this beach on Cayo Costa Island, just north of Sanibel, are accessible only by private boat or ferry.
©Kerry Dressler

11 The deep roots of these sea oats (*Uniola paniculata*) stabilize the sand dunes in coastal areas, protecting soil and property from storm damage.
©Kerry Dressler

12 After a particularly wet spring, thousands of American lotuses (*Nelumbo lutea*) bloom on Payne's Prairie, south of Gainesville. The showy 13 to 15 cm (5 to 6 in) flowers bloom for more than a month. ©Kerry Dressler

13 This prairie near Avon Park shows a few of the seasonal flowering plants that visitors can enjoy even at highway speeds in their travels through Florida. ©Brad Stith

14 The Everglades palm (*Acoelorrhaphe wrightii*), mahogany, and other tropical trees mark the edge of Mahogany Hammock in the Everglades National Park. The grass in the foreground is actually growing in water and the hammock is reached by a boardwalk. ©Walter Judd

15 Matheson Tropical Hammock is located just north of Fairchild Tropical Gardens in Coral Gables, south of Miami. Tropical hardwoods, bromeliads and palms are only minutes away from the night life of South Beach. ©Kerry Dressler

16 Small coastal towns, such as Cedar Key in Levy County, draw visitors with their wonderful seafood restaurants, fishing and relaxed lifestyle. ©Kerry Dressler

17 Hundreds of miles of mangroves protect Florida's coastline from storms and provide breeding and nursery areas for fish and other aquatic animals. The small upright roots on the left are Black Mangrove (*Avicennia germinans*), which grows intermingled with the stilt-like Red Mangrove (*Rhizophora mangle*; on the right). ©Kerry Dressler

18 Flatwoods dominated by slash pine (*Pinus elliotii*) or longleaf pine (*Pinus palustris*) and saw palmetto (*Serenoa repens*) are the most common plant community in Florida.
©Walter Judd

19 Juvenile longleaf pines (*Pinus palustris*) appear as vertical bristly poles among taller trees and yellow wildflowers in the upland flatwoods habitat of Putnam County.
©Kerry Dressler

20 Mature longleaf pines (*Pinus palustris*) dwarf a visitor among the campgrounds in the Ocala National Forest in Central Florida.
©Walter Judd

21 This hardwood hammock in North Florida contains huge old southern magnolias (*Magnolia grandiflora*), spreading live oaks (*Quercus virginiana*), and smaller trees like the Devil's Walking Stick (*Aralia spinosa*), named for its spiny trunk, in the foreground. ©Kerry Dressler

22 On Big Pine Key, slash pine (*Pinus elliotii*) and silver palms (*Cocothrinax argentata*) form a unique habitat on outcroppings of ancient limestone. ©Brad Stith

23 On the Lake Wales ridge, evergreen oaks, Florida rosemary (*Ceratiola ericoides*) and open patches of sand typify Florida scrub habitat. Gopher Tortoises (foreground), Florida Scrub-Jays, Scrub Lizards and Sand Skinks inhabit this dry shrub community. ©Brad Stith

24 A sea of grass dotted with tree islands is a common sight to travellers crossing South Florida on Alligator Alley (I-75) and the Tamiami Trail (US 41). The upright fertile fronds of the Giant Leather Fern (*Acrostichum danadifolium*) are visible in the right foreground. ©Kerry Dressler

25 Panther crossing signs can be found on several highways, such as the Tamiami Trail (US 41) and Alligator Alley (I-75), and in Everglades National Park in South Florida. Cars travelling at high speeds are serious threats to the endangered Florida Panthers, which must wander over large areas to find prey and mates. ©Kerry Dressler

Habitat Symbols

= Dry Prairies (p. 14)

= Scrub (p. 15)

= Pine Flatwoods (p. 14)

= High Pine Sandhills (p. 16)

= Temperate Hardwood Hammocks (p. 16)

= Tropical Hardwood Hammocks (p. 17)

= Freshwater. For species typically found in or near lakes, streams, rivers, marshes, swamps.

= Saltwater. For species usually found in or near the ocean or ocean beaches.

REGIONS (see p. 9 and Map 2, p. 28):

PAN   Panhandle
NFL   North Florida
CFL   Central Florida
SFL   South Florida
KEY   Keys and Other Islands

PANHANDLE

NORTH FLORIDA

CENTRAL FLORIDA

N

160 km
100 miles

SOUTH FLORIDA

KEYS and OTHER ISLANDS

IDENTIFICATION PLATES

Plates A–N, 1–106

Abbreviations on the Identification Plates are as follows:

M; male
F; female
IM; immature
B; breeding
NB; nonbreeding

The species pictured on any one plate are not necessarily to scale.

Plant photos by Kerry Dressler
Plant text by Kerry and Robert Dressler

Plate A1
Australian Pine
Casurina equisetifolia (Non-native Invader)
Australian pine family
ID: This invasive tree (to 46 m, 150 ft) from Australia was introduced in the late 1800s as a windbreak and shade tree. It grows rapidly, produces dense shade, and has displaced large areas of native vegetation. Australian pine can tolerate salt and thus is able to grown on beaches, where it has replaced native deep-rooted vegetation that once kept erosion under control. The bark is reddish brown to gray, rough and peeling. The leaves are reduced to tiny scales around the joints of the pine-needle-like branchlets.

HABITAT: Beaches, sandy slopes, and pinelands.

REGION: NFL, CFL, SFL, KEY

Plate A2
Cabbage Palm
(also called Swamp Cabbage)
Sabal palmetto (Native)
Palm family
ID: The cabbage palm is very common throughout Florida. Its trunk is relatively stout and appears latticed with old leaf bases. Leaves are somewhat fan-shaped. 'Hearts of Palm,' cut from the terminal bud of this and other species of palms, can be found on restaurant menus or bought in jars in grocery stores worldwide.

HABITAT: Pinelands, hammocks, swamps, wet forests, and seasonally wet prairies.

REGION: PAN, NFL, CFL, SFL, KEY

Plate A3
Chinaberry
Melia azederach (Non-Native Invader)
Mahogany family
ID: This Asian deciduous tree was introduced as an ornamental around 1830 in South Carolina and Georgia. Since then it has spread south through 23 counties of Florida. The inflorescences (structures made up of several flowers) are showy, made up of small fragrant flowers with 5 lilac petals around a dark purple united stamen. It flowers in March and April. The yellow or yellowish-green fruits are poisonous to humans and some other mammals.

HABITAT: Disturbed areas, fencerows, along highways; also floodplain hammocks, marshes and upland woods.

REGION: PAN, NFL, CFL, SFL

Plate A4
Coconut Palm
Cocos nucifera (Non-Native)
Palm family
ID: This tall (to 24 m, 80 ft) palm is easy to recognize when it is in fruit. The large green coconut fruits can be seen at the base of the palm fronds year-round. The trunk appears swollen at the base and often curved or leaning, with conspicuous rings and vertical cracks. The leaves are feather-like, to 7 m (23 ft) long.

HABITAT: Beaches and towns.

REGION: SFL, KEY

2 Cabbage Palm (*Sabal palmetto*)

1 Australian Pine (*Casuarina equisetifolia*)

3 Chinaberry (*Melia azederach*)

4 Coconut Palm (*Cocos nucifera*)

Plate B1
Bald Cypress
Taxodium distichum (Native)
Cypress family

ID: The trunk of the cypress is enlarged at the base and forms buttresses. Often you will find conical cypress knees (see photo) coming up from the ground around the base. The furrowed bark varies from light brown to dark reddish brown. There are still a number of cypress 'domes' that can be seen from the highway, which look like hills on the flat landscape; these 'domes' are formed by the various sizes of cypress trees.

HABITAT: Ponds, wet depressions, swamps, floodplains, pond and lake margins.

REGION: PAN, NFL, CFL, SFL, KEY

Plate B2
Everglades Palm
(also called Parautis Palm, Saw Cabbage)
Acoelorrhaphe wrightii (Native)
Palm family

ID: This palm can be seen in dense stands bordering the hammocks and tree islands in the Everglades. It can be identified by its growth habit of multiple slender trunks up to 12 m (40 ft) high, which are covered with reddish matted fibers and ends of old leaf bases. Orange fruits that are black when mature are clustered on long inflorescences (structures made up of several flowers).

HABITAT: Wet areas, hammocks and tree islands in Everglades, and towns.

REGION: SFL, KEY

Plate B3
Flowering Dogwood
Cornus florida (Native)
Dogwood family

ID: A small deciduous tree, the dogwood is very striking when it blooms in April and May. The greenish-white flower clusters usually open before the leaves emerge. Later in the year, bright red berries appear. Dogwood is often used by landscapers in towns – especially in Tallahassee and Gainesville – but is also a common tree along highways and roads in North and Central Florida.

HABITAT: Woods and towns.

REGION: PAN, NFL, CFL

Plate B4
Gumbo Limbo
Bursera simaruba (Native)
Torchwood family

ID: Gumbo limbo, with large, crooked branches, an open crown and a stout trunk, can grow to a height of 24 m (80 ft). The distinctive bark is reddish brown to green, and peels away in papery sheets. The tree has a turpentine odor. The flowers, tiny, creamy to greenish white, appear in clusters that bloom from February to April.

HABITAT: Hammocks, shell mounds; mainly coastal.

REGION: CFL, SFL, KEY

1 Bald Cypress (*Taxodium distichum*)

4 Gumbo Limbo (*Bursera simaruba*)

2 Everglades Palm (*Acoelorrhaphe wrightii*)

3 Flowering Dogwood (*Cornus florida*)

Plate C1
Live Oak
Quercus virginiana (Native)
Beech family

ID: The live oak is frequently seen with its broad spreading branches in open fields, where cattle and horses appreciate its shade. The leaves are 13 cm (5 in) long, elliptical to oblong, shiny above and hairy below. The bark is dark brown, ridged and furrowed. The acorns, at 2.5 cm (1 in) long, seem small for so large a tree.

HABITAT: Moist woods, roadsides, and towns.

REGION: PAN, NFL, CFL, SFL

Plate C2
Longleaf Pine
Pinus palustris (Native)
Pine family

ID: This pine can reach 46 m (150 ft) tall, with a rounded crown and spreading branches that curve up at their tips. The needles are 30 cm (12 in) long and usually occur in bundles of 3. The cones reach 25 cm (10 in) long and are egg-shaped to cylindrical.

HABITAT: Sandy uplands, sandhills, and flatwoods.

REGION: PAN, NFL, CFL

Plate C3
Orange
Citrus sinensis (Non-Native)
Citrus family

ID: Florida is synonymous with oranges, which actually were introduced from Southeast Asia. The trees' white flowers are so fragrant they can be smelled inside a car travelling along one of the Interstate highways at 110 kph (70 mph). Millions of acres are harvested commercially in Florida every year, but many more are planted around homes for Floridians to enjoy. Young trunks and branches have very sharp spines, but the trunks become smooth with age. Commercial groves have been restricted by past freezes to Central and South Florida.

HABITAT: Hammocks, shell mounds, and disturbed areas.

REGION: NFL, CFL, SFL, KEY

Plate C4
Punk
(also called Paper-bark, White Bottlebrush)
Melaleuca quinquenerva (Non-Native Invader)
Myrtle family

ID: Melaleuca has formed huge stands of trees in natural areas of Florida. This native Australian tree was first introduced as a landscaping ornamental in 1906. In the 1930s, seeds were scattered by plane in the Everglades to encourage its growth into forests. Now we recognize that these extremely fast-growing trees threaten the Everglades, have displaced native trees, and do not provide the habitat and food that native wildlife need. They can grow 1 to 2 m (3 to 6 ft) per year and are capable of flowering within 2 years from seed. The tree releases a volatile oil into the air, especially when in bloom, that is an allergen. The blooms smell like boiling potatoes.

HABITAT: Disturbed and natural habitats, wet pine flatwoods, and cypress swamps.

REGION: CFL, SFL

Plate C **253**

1 Live Oak, (*Quercus virginiana*)

2 Longleaf Pine (*Pinus palustris*)

3 Orange (*Citrus sinensis*)

4 Punk (*Melaleuca quinquenerva*)

Plate D1

Red Mangrove
Rhizophora mangle (Native)
Red mangrove family

ID: This mangrove is easy to identify by its stilt roots, which are evident at low tide, and its 2.5-cm (1-in) reddish-brown fruit; the fruit germinates while still attached to the tree and forms a long green torpedo-shaped root that descends from the brown fruit. It is a shrub or small tree with star-shaped white or cream flowers.

HABITAT: Tidal swamps.

REGION: PAN, NFL, CFL, SFL, KEY

Plate D2

Red Maple
Acer rubrum (Native)
Maple family

ID: Maples in Florida bloom in December and January. Their flowers are tiny, red and in bunches. The winged fruit is also red and this is what gives the Red Maple its distinctive red appearance at a distance before the leaves develop. In some areas the leaves turn red in the fall before falling from the tree. The bark is dark gray and furrowed.

HABITAT: Wet woods and swamps.

REGION: PAN, NFL, CFL, SFL

Plate D3

Redbud
Cercis canadensis (Native)
Pea family

ID: These trees are easy to spot from January to March because their masses of pink to reddish, pea-shaped flowers bloom before the leaves emerge. Then rounded, heart-shaped, green leaves help them to fade into the upland forests and woods where they occur. Many are planted around homes and along roads for their spring show.

HABITAT: Upland hardwood forests, bluffs, and secondary woods.

REGION: PAN, NFL, CFL

Plate D4

Royal Palm
Roystonea elata (Native)
Palm family

ID: This tall (to 46 m, 130 ft), regal looking palm has a light gray, smooth trunk that may appear swollen at the bottom. The flowers are white to yellow and the fruit, purple. It is used in landscaping in many south Florida cities but can be seen in its natural habitat in Everglades National Park.

HABITAT: Marshes and towns.

REGION: SFL

I Red Mangrove (*Rhizophora mangle*)

2 Red Maple (*Acer rubrum*)

3 Redbud (*Cercis canadensis*)

4 Royal Palm (*Roystonea elata*)

Plate E1
Sand Pine
Pinus clausa (Native)
Pine family
ID: The sand pine normally is about 20 m (65 ft) tall. The trunk has many branches and the 10-cm (4-in) long, yellowish to dark green needles occur in bundles of 2. The cones are 7.5 cm (3 in) long, egg-shaped, and much more compact than in the longleaf pine (Plate C2).

HABITAT: Dunes, sandhills, and sand scrub.

REGION: PAN, NFL, CFL, SFL

Plate E2
Saw Palmetto
(also called Scrub Palmetto)
Serenoa repens (Native)
Palm family
ID: Look beneath pine trees anywhere in Florida and you are likely to see the saw palmetto. It forms clumps of 1-m (3-ft) long, fan-shaped leaves that have very prickly edges. Beneath the foliage the trunks sprawl along the ground, making it almost impossible to walk through. Saw Palmetto is now a popular herbal remedy for kidney ailments, and honey made from its flowers is highly prized.

HABITAT: Pinelands, hammocks, coastal dunes, and sandhills.

REGION: PAN, NFL, CFL, SFL, KEY

Plate E3
Sea Grape
Coccoloba uvifera (Native)
Buckwheat (Knotweed) family
ID: The sea grape grows as a shrub or compact tree with a short gnarled trunk. Its common name comes from the grape-like cluster of green to purplish fruit that ripens from August to September. Leaves are large, roundish, and leathery green. The fruit can be eaten raw or used for jam and jellies. Teas made from the roots, bark and leaves are used as medicinals.

HABITAT: Mainly coastal beaches, hammocks, scrub, dunes, towns.

REGION: NFL, CFL, SFL, KEY

Plate E4
Southern Magnolia
Magnolia grandiflora (Native)
Magnolia family
ID: Magnolias are a symbol of the American South. In April, large flowers can easily be seen high up in these trees, set off by dark green, shiny, leathery, leaves in April. The flowers develop into beautiful, pinkish colored cone fruits that open when ripe to reveal bright red, shiny seeds.

HABITAT: Bluffs, floodplains, dunes, hammocks, and secondary woods.

REGION: PAN, NFL, CFL

1 Sand pine (*Pinus clausa*)

2 Saw Palmetto (*Serenoa repens*)

3 Sea Grape (*Coccoloba uvifera*)

4 Southern Magnolia (*Magnolia grandiflora*)

Plate F1
Sweetgum
Liquidambar styraciflua (Native)
Witch hazel family
ID: The sweet gum is a tall tree (to 37 m, 120 ft) with grayish-brown bark, and twigs that are often winged or ridged. The leaves are deciduous, 5-lobed, and appear star-like. The flowers form dense, green, spherical heads, but the fruits are the most unusual, as they form a dense cluster in a spiny ball.

HABITAT: Moist forests often in wet or swampy areas.

REGION: PAN, NFL, CFL, SFL

Plate F2
Brazilian Pepper
(also called Florida Holly, Christmas Berry)
Schinus terebinthifolius (Non-Native Invader)
Cashew family
ID: Imported as an ornamental in the 1840s from Brazil, this evergreen shrub to tree (to 13 m, 43 ft) has a multi-stemmed trunk and branches that form tangled masses. The leaves are 2.5 to 5 cm (1 to 2 in) long, elliptic and dark green; they give off an aromatic peppery odor when crushed. The large clusters of dark red berries can easily be seen along the edge of Interstates 75 and 95 in Central and South Florida. Wildlife eat the fruit and spread the seeds. The tree has spread and displaced some rare, threatened species of Florida native plants. Chemicals in the leaves, flowers and fruits can irritate human skin and respiratory passages.

HABITAT: Disturbed areas, mangrove swamps, pinelands, hammocks, and along the coasts.

REGION: NFL, CFL, SFL, KEY

Plate F3
Buttonbush
Cephalanthus occidentalis (Native)
Madder family
ID: A shrub to small tree, this plant is easily identified by its white, pin-cushion-like balls of tiny white flowers that bloom in winter through to the summer. The fruits are tiny and seed-like on the rough, brown, woody balls.

HABITAT: Swamps, sloughs, stream banks, depressions, marshes, and edges of ponds and lakes.

REGION: PAN, NFL, CFL, SFL, KEY

Plate F4
Coontie
(also called Florida Arrowroot, Indian Breadroot)
Zamia pumila (Native)
Sago-Palm family
ID: This plant has a short, thick, woody trunk and 7.5-cm (3-in) long leaves that are feather-like and compound, giving the plant a fern-like or palm-like appearance. It produces 20-cm (8-in) long reddish to purplish, velvety cones. Early Native Americans and colonial settlers used to grind and process the trunk as a starch source.

HABITAT: Hammocks, pine-oak woods, scrub, shell mounds, and towns.

REGION: NFL, CFL, SFL

1 Sweetgum (*Liquidambar styraciflua*)

2 Brazilian Pepper (*Schinus terebinthifolius*)

3 Buttonbush (*Cephalanthus occidentalis*)

4 Coontie (*Zamia pumila*)

Plate G1
Elderberry
Sambucus canadensis (Native)
Honeysuckle family
ID: A shrub or small tree, often seen growing along roadsides and on disturbed ground. The branches are upright and leaves are 15 cm (6 in) long, opposite, with 5 to 11 toothed, oval shaped leaflets. The bark is grayish brown and furrowed. Large (40-cm, 16-in, wide) clusters of small white flowers appear in spring and summer. Purplish-black berry-like fruit appears in late summer. The fruit is used to make wine and jellies, and is an important food source for birds and mammals.

HABITAT: Wet open woods, thickets, roadsides, fencerows, and pond margins.

REGION: PAN, NFL, CFL, SFL, KEY

Plate G2
Florida Rosemary
Ceratiola ericoides (Native)
Crowberry family
ID: These rounded shrubs can be seen dotting the landscape in sandy areas of the state. Their leaves are needle-like and dark green on the erect branches. The rusty brown flowers are very small, as is the fruit, which is greenish yellow and berry-like.

HABITAT: Sandhills, scrub, mature coastal dunes, and old inland dunes.

REGION: PAN, NFL, CFL

Plate G3
Oleander
Nerium oleander (Non-Native)
Dogbane family
ID: This introduced, evergreen shrub is included because it is frequently seen as an ornamental along roadsides and in gardens. It is HIGHLY TOXIC, with poisonous sap. The leaves are narrow, elliptic to lance-shaped and dark green, from 5 to 15 cm (2 to 6 in) long. The fragrant showy white to dark pink flowers average 2.5 cm (1 in) across.

HABITAT: Roadside plantings, around homes, landscaping.

REGION: PAN, NFL, CFL, SFL, KEY

Plate G4
Pond Apple
(also called Custard Apple)
Annona glabra (Native)
Annona family
ID: Pond apple is a small tree (to 12 m, 40 ft) with large, leathery leaves and a buttressed base. The large flowers have 3 fleshy green petals and 6 white petals. Blooms hang singly from branches and twigs, and open only at night. This plant's common name comes from the large, fleshy, apple-shaped fruit, which may be up to 13 cm (5 in) long.

HABITAT: Swamps and ponds.

REGION: CFL, SFL

1 Elderberry (*Sambucus canadensis*)

2 Florida Rosemary (*Ceratiola ericoides*)

3 Oleander (*Nerium oleander*)

4 Pond Apple (*Annona glabra*)

Plate H1
Red Buckeye
Aesculus pavia (Native)
Horse-chestnut family
ID: Shrub or small tree (to 3 m, 10 ft) with dark gray to brown smooth bark. Forms dark red 2.5-cm (1-in) long tubular flowers in long clusters in April and May. The fruit, about 5 cm (2 in) long, pear-shaped and brown, contains one to three nut-like seeds.

HABITAT: Moist woods, hammocks, edges of swamps and streams.

REGION: PAN, NFL, CFL

Plate H2
Walter's Viburnum
(also called Small Leaf Viburnum)
Viburnum obovatum (Native)
Honeysuckle family
ID: Shrub to small tree (to 9 m, 30 ft), evergreen, with 5-cm (2-in) opposite leaves. The bark is dark brown to black, furrowed, and may appear to be in plates on older trunks. Flowers bloom in flat white clusters from April to May, followed by red berries.

HABITAT: Moist woods, thickets, stream and river banks, swamps and swamp borders.

REGION: PAN, NFL, CFL, SFL

Plate H3
Yaupon Holly
Ilex vomitoria (Native)
Holly family
ID: A large evergreen shrub that often forms thickets. The stiff, leathery leaves are oval, 2.5 cm (1 in) long, and toothed. The fruit is a bright red, shiny, and berry-like. The plant is frequently used in landscaping and hedges.

HABITAT: Hardwood forests, dunes, coastal maritime forests, near coastal wetlands, wet pine flatwoods, and wet hammocks.

REGION: PAN, NFL, CFL

Plate H4
Cross Vine
(also called Trumpet Flower)
Bignonia capreolata (Native)
Bignonia family
ID: The vine produces masses of red trumpet-shaped flowers in the spring, which can be seen on top of small trees, trailing up trunks of larger trees, or flowing off fence lines. If you cut a stem you will see the 'cross' of its common name.

HABITAT: Upland woodlands, floodplain and lowland woodlands, edges of evergreen shrub-tree bogs and bays, thickets, and fencerows.

REGION: PAN, NFL, CFL

1 Red Buckeye (*Aesculus pavia*)

2 Walter's Viburnum (*Viburnum obovatum*)

3 Yaupon Holly (*Ilex vomitoria*)

4 Cross Vine (*Bignonia capreolata*)

Plate I1
Trumpet Vine
(also called Trumpet Creeper)
Campsis radicans (Native)
Bignonia family

ID: This woody climbing vine has clusters of 7.5-cm (3-in) long, dull, orange-red, trumpet-shaped flowers from April through September. The insides of the flowers are streaked with yellow to red.

HABITAT: Thickets and moist woods.

REGION: PAN, NFL, CFL

Plate I2
Yellow Jessamine
(also called Carolina Jasmine)
Gelsemium sempervirens (Native)
Logania family

ID: An evergreen, perennial, climbing vine with reddish-brown stems and tubular, yellow flowers. This woody blooms December to April and can completely cover a tree or a trellis with thousands of lightly scented, yellow flowers. However, it is extremely poisonous – even its nectar is toxic!

HABITAT: Upland mixed forests, pine flatwoods, bluffs, floodplains, and garden landscaping.

REGION: PAN, NFL, CFL

Plate I3
American Lotus
(also called Lotus-Lily, Water Chinquapin)
Nelumbo lutea (Native)
Lotus family

ID: The lotus has large round bluish-green leaves with a large (25 cm, 10 in) yellow flower on an erect stem. The plants can form huge colonies that cover open wet areas. The fruit is brown and cone-shaped, and holds many nutlet-like seeds.

HABITAT: Streams, ponds, and estuaries.

REGION: PAN, NFL, CFL, SFL

Plate I4
Ball Moss
Tillandsia recurvata (Native)
Pineapple family

ID: Ball moss forms small (25 cm, 10 in) clusters of tangled ball-like masses of greenish to silvery colored wire-like leaves that are found on tree trunks and branches. They bloom from April to October with small flowers in 2.5-cm (1-in) purple spikes.

HABITAT: Scrub, hammocks, and pinelands.

REGION: PAN, NFL, CFL, SFL

Plate I **265**

1 Trumpet Vine (*Campsis radicans*)

2 Yellow Jessamine (*Gelsemium sempervirens*)

4 Ball Moss (*Tillandsia recurvata*)

3 American Lotus (*Nelumbo lutea*)

Plate J1
Florida Sunflower
Helianthus floridanus (Native)
Aster family

ID: There are about 18 species of sunflowers in Florida. The Florida sunflower is one of the six that occur in wetlands. The stems can grow to 1.8 m (6 ft) tall with flowers 5 cm (2 in) across. They have 10 to 12 yellow petals around a dark brownish-purple center. They flower from June through November and are often found in large numbers along roadsides in north-central Florida.

HABITAT: Roadsides, ditches, fields, wet flatwoods, wet prairies, edges of bay or swamp thickets.

REGION: NFL, CFL

Plate J2
Fringed Orchid
Platanthera ciliaris (Native)
Orchid family

ID: A terrestrial orchid that flowers between July and August and can grow as tall as 1 m (3.3 ft). The flower spike is a cluster of bright yellow or deep orange flowers that have a deeply fringed lip; hence the name. The fringed orchid is a protected flower and may not be collected.

HABITAT: Wet pine flatwoods, marshes, wet roadside ditches, and bluffs.

REGION: PAN, NFL, CFL

Plate J3
Golden Canna
Canna flaccida (Native)
Canna family

ID: The golden canna grows to 1.2 m (4 ft) tall and produces large (15 cm, 6 in), beautiful, yellow to golden colored flowers. These striking plants can be seen in bloom from January through September.

HABITAT: Swamps, pond and lake margins, ditches, savannahs, and wet pine flatwoods.

REGION: PAN, NFL, CFL, SFL, KEY

Plate J4
Greenfly Orchid
Epidendrum conopseum (Native)
Orchid family

ID: A small epiphytic orchid that grows on tree branches. It flowers from June through September, producing fragrant blooms that are green with purple markings. The flowers seem to hover above the plant on slender stalks, which perhaps gives the plant its name. This plant is protected in Florida and may not be collected.

HABITAT: Moist upland mixed forests, swamps, and sinkholes.

REGION: PAN, NFL, CFL

1 Florida Sunflower (*Helianthus floridanus*)

2 Fringed Orchid (*Platanthera ciliaris*)

3 Golden Canna (*Canna flaccida*)

4 Greenfly Orchid (*Epidendrum conopseum*)

Plate K1
Milkwort
(also called Wild Bachelor's Button)
Polygala nana (Native)
Milkwort family
ID: This plant forms a clump about 15 cm (6 in) tall with several greenish-yellow clover-like or thimble-like flowers, each on its own stem. The green leaves form a rosette at the base of the plant. It flowers from March through October.

HABITAT: Moist pine flatwoods and coastal swales.

REGION: PAN, NFL, CFL, SFL

Plate K2
Pickerel Weed
Pontederia cordata (Non-Native Invader)
Pickerelweed family
ID: A tall herb with erect, heart- or lance-shaped leaves. The flowers are lavender to blue-purple (occasionally white) on showy spikes. The uppermost petal has a yellow and white splotch. Flowers year round.

HABITAT: Marshes, streams, ditches, and shallow water of lakes and ponds.

REGION: PAN, NFL, CFL, SFL, KEY

Plate K3
Poison Ivy
Toxicodendron radicans (Native)
Cashew (Sumac) family
ID: Poison Ivy can be a low-growing herb or climbing woody vine. Watch for leaves that occur in threes, usually toothed along their edges and widest near the base. In fall they turn from green to orangish red before dropping. The sap can cause a severe allergic reaction in people.

HABITAT: Pine flatwoods, upland hardwoods, upland mixed forests, coastal and tropical hammocks.

REGION: PAN, NFL, CFL, SFL, KEY

Plate K4
Sandspur
Cenchrus incertus (Native)
Grass family
ID: Visitors to Florida do not need to look for this plant, it finds them! This grass grows as high as 50 cm (20 in), but is also found sprawling on the sand where its small, roundish, EXTREMELY sharp burs can go right through an unwary visitor's sneakers or even leather shoes. The burs will adhere to almost anything. This plant blooms year-round.

HABITAT: Beaches, pinelands, sandhills, fields, and disturbed areas.

REGION: PAN, NFL, CFL, SFL, KEY

1 Milkwort (*Polygala nana*)

2 Pickerel Weed (*Pontederia cordata*)

3 Poison Ivy (*Toxicodendron radicans*)

4 Sandspur (*Cenchrus incertus*)

Plate L1
Sawgrass
Cladium jamaicensis (Native)
Sedge family

ID: This sedge grows to 3 m (10 ft) tall and forms huge colonies. Flowers occur in spikelets and the fruits are tiny (0.2 cm, 1/16 in) rounded-ovoid nutlets. The leaves are coarse, gray-green, and sawtoothed on both edges and along the mid-rib. The leaves can catch unwary travellers, leaving long shallow cuts on unprotected arms and legs.

HABITAT: Swamps, brackish marshes, shores, especially in coastal marshes.

REGION: PAN, NFL, CFL, SFL, KEY

Plate L2
Sea Oats
Uniola paniculata (Native)
Grass family

ID: This grass can be seen growing in clumps along the dunes of many Florida beaches. It is a protected plant because of its decreasing populations and its importance in maintaining healthy dunes. It may not be collected. It forms an extensive root system that builds dunes and helps prevent erosion. The seedheads are flat, straw-colored to purplish, and about 2.5 cm (1 in) long.

HABITAT: Coastal grasslands, beach dunes, and coastal strands.

REGION: PAN, NFL, CFL, SFL, KEY

Plate L3
Spanish Moss
Tillandsia usneoides (Native)
Pineapple family

ID: This hanging moss flows from trees in wiry, curly, silvery-scaled stems. It is especially obvious on oak trees. In the past it was collected and dried for use in mattresses and as a packing material. It blooms from April through June but the flowers are almost invisible to the naked eye.

HABITAT: Hammocks, pinelands, and scrub.

REGION: PAN, NFL, CFL, SFL, KEY

Plate L **271**

I Sawgrass (*Cladium jamaicensis*)

2 Sea Oats (*Uniola paniculata*)

3 Spanish Moss (*Tillandsia usneoides*)

Plate M1
Taro
(also called Wild Taro, Dasheen)
Colocasia esculenta (Non-Native Invader)
Arum family

ID: Taro has large, deep green, 'elephant ear' or arrowhead-shaped leaves. It is often seen along the edges of streams and marshes. The inflorescence (structure made up of several flowers) is a fleshy stalk that is enfolded by a green-yellow bract. The flowers are small and densely crowded on a finger-like cluster. Native to India and Southeast Asia.

HABITAT: Along streams, marshes, marshy shores, drainage canals and marshy clearings.

REGION: PAN, NFL, CFL, SFL, KEY

Plate M2
Water Hyacinth
(also called Water-orchid)
Eichornia crassipes (Non-Native Invader)
Pickerelweed family

ID: This Amazonian Basin plant invaded Florida in 1890. It grows aggressively and can double its population in as little as 6 to 18 days, spreading by way of runners to completely clog waterways. Though attractive, it degrades water quality and has altered native plant and animal communities. The flowers, which occur in dense spikes, are lavender with a yellow spot on the uppermost petal.

HABITAT: Lakes, rivers, streams, ditches, and marshes.

REGION: PAN, NFL, CFL, SFL, KEY

Plate M3
Water Lettuce
(also called Water Bonnets)
Pistia stratiotes (Non-Native Invader)
Arum family

ID: This plant is native to Africa and South America, but was seen in Florida as early as 1774. It forms vast floating mats in lakes and rivers that can disrupt navigation and affect natural animal and plant communities. It looks like a lettuce with rosettes of pleated gray-green leaves. The flowers and fruit are very small and not readily noticed.

HABITAT: Ponds, streams, rivers, and canals.

REGION: PAN, NFL, CFL, SFL

Plate M4
Yucca
(also called Spanish Bayonet, Spanish Dagger)
Yucca aloifolia (Non-Native)
Agave family

ID: The leaves of this plant are as sharp as a dagger and dangerous. It is often used in hedges to discourage trespassers. It can grow 2.1 m (7 ft) tall, with a rosette of sword-like leaves climbing its woody trunk. The flowers form a tall showy spray from the top of the plant from April to July. Native to the West Indies and Mexico – where the flowers are used in cooking.

HABITAT: Beaches, coastal grasslands, maritime hammocks, sandhills, disturbed sites, and landscaping.

REGION: NFL, CFL, SFL, KEY

1 Taro (*Colocasia esculenta*)

3 Water Lettuce (*Pistia stratiotes*)

2 Water Hyacinth (*Eichornia crassipes*)

4 Yucca (*Yucca aloifolia*)

Plate N1
Deer Moss
Cladina evansii (Native)
Lichen family

ID: Deer moss appears as small (7.5 to 15 cm, 3 to 6 in), light green to grayish, wiry piles or humps on the ground in scrubby areas. It is actually a lichen – a fungus living symbiotically with algae (in this case, a blue-green alga). The fungus absorbs water and minerals from the environment and the algae provides the photosynthesis to produce carbohydrates. Lichens are slow-growing organisms without roots and are sensitive to pollution. Deer moss, despite the name, is eaten by animals other than deer, such as small rodents (deer eat it, too).

HABITAT: Scrub habitats and sandy areas.

REGION: PAN, NFL, CFL, SFL

Plate N2
Meadow Beauty
Rhexia virginica (Native)
Meadow beauty family

ID: There are many lovely flowers in the Meadow Beauty family in Florida. This pink-flowered herb grows to 1 m (3.3 ft) tall and has hairy, four-sided stems. The young leaves can be used in a salad and the roots have a nutty taste. It flowers between July and October.

HABITAT: Wet pine flatwoods, cypress pond margins, riverbanks, and wet roadsides.

REGION: PAN, NFL, CFL, SFL

Plate N3
Sand Cord Grass
Spartina bakeri (Native)
Grass family

ID: A common sight near the coast, this erect grass forms distinct, tufted hummocks up to 1.8 m (6 ft) tall. The clumps are very obvious and this is the easiest way to identify them. The leaves appear rolled to somewhat flattened and feel sandpapery on the upper surface.

HABITAT: Margins and shallow areas in fresh and salt water; marshes, ditches, dunes, prairies, and shores.

REGION: PAN, NFL, CFL, SFL, KEY

Plate N4
Marsh Fern
(also called Shield Fern)
Thelypteris kunthii
Aspidia family

ID: There are a great variety of ferns in Florida, including 18 varieties of shield ferns. This fern has lance-shaped fronds that taper at the tips. It propagates from a creeping rhizome and grows 30 to 60 cm (12 to 24 in) high. It has stiff hairs along the mid-rib and veins on the fronds.

HABITAT: Along streams, moist or wet forests, cypress swamps, roadside ditches.

REGION: PAN, NFL, CFL, SFL, KEY

1 Deer Moss (*Cladina evansii*)

2 Meadow Beauty (*Rhexia virginica*)

3 Sand Cord Grass (*Spartina bakeri*)

4 Marsh Fern (*Thelypteris kunthii*)

Plate 1a

Giant Toad
Chavnus marinus

ID: A huge grayish-brown toad with a creamy yellow belly. Adults range in size from 15 to 23 cm (6 to 9 in). When threatened it secretes a milky substance from the large glands on the back of its head. A potent chemical (bufotoxin) in this substance is a skin irritant to humans and highly toxic to dogs and cats. Call, heard in spring and summer, sounds like a distant idling tractor.

HABITAT: Urban areas, near canals and ponds. Often seen under street and yard lights, and feeding from dog or cat food bowls. Breeds in shallow pools. An introduced species from Central America, originally released in sugar-cane fields of South Florida to control mice and rats.

REGION: SFL, KEY

Plate 1b

Oak Toad
Anaxyrus quercicus

ID: The smallest toad in the USA; maximum length 3.8 cm (1.5 in). Gray to almost black with a yellowish stripe down the center of the back. There are three to four pairs of light-edged dark spots on the back. Call sounds like a baby chick, a continuous 'cheep-cheep-cheep.'

HABITAT: Found in longleaf pine-turkey oak forest, sand pine scrub and dry hammocks. Breeds in roadside ditches and temporary ponds.

REGION: PAN, NFL, CFL, SFL, KEY

Plate 1c

Southern Toad
Anaxyrus terrestris

ID: A medium-sized toad, to 9.2 cm (3.6 in). Color variable, back can be red, brown, gray or dark charcoal. Distinguished by two large ridges between the eyes that end as knobs just behind the eyes. Large glands behind eyes are kidney-shaped. The belly is light colored, often flecked with black. Males have a dark throat. The call is a long, high-pitched trill.

HABITAT: This toad is a habitat generalist, common in yards and gardens, near porches and street lights. Also in marshes, swamps, wooded hammocks, pine-oak forest and sandy scrub. Breeds in shallow water of ponds and lakes.

REGION: PAN, NFL, CFL, SFL, KEY

Plate 1d

Eastern Spadefoot
Scaphiopus holbrookii

ID: A medium-sized toad, to 7 cm (2.8 in), back brown to olive-brown with yellowish or pale green stripes. The underside is creamy yellow to gray. Large eyes have vertical pupils. Each hind foot has a hard, dark, crescent-shaped 'spade' on the heel. Voice is a loud moaning grunt, sounds like 'quonk' repeated every 10 seconds. Many people are allergic to the substance secreted by the skin glands of this toad.

HABITAT: Rarely seen because of their burrowing habits. Found in pinelands, hammocks, woodland edges and urban areas. Occasionally seen in large numbers on highways after rain. Breeds in shallow pools.

REGION: PAN, NFL, CFL, SFL, KEY

Plate 1e

Eastern Narrowmouth Toad
Gastrophryne carolinensis

ID: Small, plump frog with a pointed head and a fold of skin in back of head. Body black to dark gray with a bluish cast, and irregular patterns on the sides. Maximum length 3.6 cm (1.4 in). Call is a loud sheep-like bleat.

HABITAT: In woodlands, ponds, swamps and marshes, but also in urban and suburban areas, where they are often found in lawns.

REGION: PAN, NFL, CFL, SFL, KEY

Plate I **277**

a Giant Toad

b Oak Toad

c Southern Toad

d Eastern Spadefoot

e Eastern Narrowmouth Toad

Plate 2a
Barking Treefrog
Hyla gratiosa

ID: Florida's largest native treefrog, to 6.8 cm (2.7 in). Coloration varies (and individuals can change) from bright green, greenish brown, to brown, and individuals can be unspotted or marked with round dark spots. The toes end in large adhesive toe pads. Along sides of the body and under front legs is a light stripe bordered by a purplish brown stripe. This frog is named for its call, which sounds like distant dogs barking.

HABITAT: Found in open mixed woodlands, pinelands, and farmland. Breeds in swamps and shallow ponds.

REGION: PAN, NFL, CFL, SFL

Plate 2b
Squirrel Treefrog
Hyla squirella

ID: A small treefrog, maximum length 4.5 cm (1.7 in). Highly variable in color and pattern, and can change color rapidly. Often greenish brown with or without faint blotches on its back and legs. There is usually a light line on the upper lip, and sometimes a dark spot or bar between the eyes. The toe pads are well developed. Named for its rain call, which sounds like a squirrel chattering. Breeding call sounds like a duck – 'quank-quank.'

HABITAT: One of the state's most common frogs. In all habitats, from woodlands to hammocks, swamps, pastures and gardens. Breeds in shallow pools and ditches.

REGION: PAN, NFL, CFL, SFL, KEY

Plate 2c
Cuban Treefrog
Osteopilus septentrionalis

ID: A gray-green mottled treefrog; largest treefrog in the United States. Maximum length 14 cm (5.5 in). Toe pads are very large and obvious.

HABITAT: Pine lands and tropical hammocks, as well as in gardens, around houses and near ornamental fish ponds. Breeds in shallow pools. Introduced from the Caribbean.

REGION: SFL, KEY

Plate 2d
Green Treefrog
Hyla cinerea

ID: Usually a beautiful bright green but may be dull green or gray when hidden or sleeping. A creamy white stripe extends down either side of the body. Maximum length 5.7 cm (2.2 in). Call is a scratchy 'quonk-quonk-quong' often heard during rainstorms.

HABITAT: Found in places with abundant vegetation; breeds in ponds and lakes with cattails, swamps and canals. Often found around buildings, where they feed on insects attracted to the light.

REGION: PAN, NFL, CFL, SFL, KEY

Plate 2e
Pine Woods Treefrog
Hyla femoralis

ID: Highly variable in color and difficult to identify unless in hand. May be brown, gray or light green with dark blotches on the back. Maximum length 4.4 cm (1.7 in). Distinguishing characteristic is a patch of white, yellow, or orange spots on the inner thigh.

HABITAT: Found in pine flatwoods and around lights near houses. Breeds in marshes, ditches, and ponds. Highly arboreal; in trees as high as 9 m (30 ft).

REGION: PAN, NFL, CFL, SFL

Plate 2 **279**

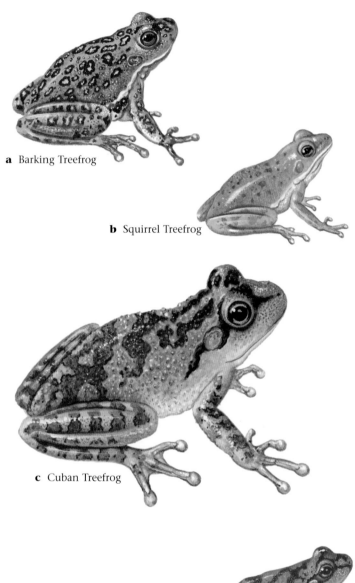

a Barking Treefrog

b Squirrel Treefrog

c Cuban Treefrog

d Green Treefrog

e Pine Woods Treefrog

Plate 3a
Florida Cricket Frog
Acris gryllus dorsalis
ID: A small frog (2.5 cm; 1 in) with rough or warty skin. Highly variable in background color and dorsal pattern, but most are brown, or gray to greenish. Dark diagonal bars often mark the flanks, and stripe of contrasting color along mid-back is usually present. Toward the head end, the stripe splits and outlines a triangular or V-shaped mark just behind the head and between the eyes. Call is a rapid, repeated series of metallic-sounding clicks.

HABITAT: Freshwater habitats, from temporary potholes to ponds, lakes, marshes, and along swamp edges.

REGION: PAN, NFL, CFL, SFL

Plate 3b
Southern Chorus Frog
Pseudacris nigrita nigrita
ID: A small gray frog with rows of dark blotches on the back and legs, which may merge to form stripes. The upper lip is solid white. Maximum length 3.2 cm (1.3 in). Rarely seen but its 'comb clicking' call is often heard. Call sounds like fingernail being pulled over the teeth of a small comb.

HABITAT: Found in pinelands. Breeds in flooded fields and ditches. Often calls from the base of grass clumps at the edge of the water.

REGION: PAN, NFL, CFL, SFL

Plate 3c
Spring Peeper
Pseudacris crucifer
ID: A small frog, maximum length 3.2 cm (1.5 in). Back is smooth, gray-brown to russet red, marked with dark 'X.' There is often a dark strip down each side of the body. The toes end in large toe pads. The call is a series of whistled peeps, often heard on rainy winter nights.

HABITAT: In hammocks near water; breeds in swamps, ponds, and roadside ditches.

REGION: PAN, NFL, CFL

Plate 3d
Ornate Chorus Frog
Pseudacris ornata
ID: A rounded nose and plump body distinguish this species from other chorus frogs. There are three distinct color forms, reddish brown, gray and pale green. All have large dark brown spots or stripes on the sides and sometimes on the back and legs. Males have a dark throat. Maximum length 3.6 cm (1.4 in).

HABITAT: Found in pine and oak uplands. Breeds in ponds, flooded meadows and ditches.

REGION: PAN, NFL

Plate 3 **281**

a Florida Cricket Frog

b Southern Chorus Frog

c Spring Peeper

d Ornate Chorus Frog

Plate 4a
Greenhouse Frog
Euyas planirostris

ID: A small frog, highly variable in color. Back is usually bronze with two clear brown stripes, or may be spotted. Top of head from eyes to snout is pinkish. Underside pale gray. Maximum length 3.8 cm (1.5 in).

HABITAT: Found in gardens, nurseries, woodlands, scrub, beneath fallen leaves, and crevices. Terrestrial breeder, in moist leaves, soil, and under wood. Introduced; has spread throughout Florida and in many places it is the most commonly found frog.

REGION: PAN, NFL, CFL, SFL, KEY

Plate 4b
Pig Frog
Lithobates grylio

ID: This large frog is brownish gray to olive-brown or bright green as an adult, or bronze with dark spots as a juvenile. The snout is pointed. Webbing on the hind foot extends to the tip of longest toe. Maximum length 15 cm (6 in). The call sounds like a pig grunting.

HABITAT: Found in most waterways, including ponds, lakes, rivers, swamps and marshes.

REGION: PAN, NFL, CFL, SFL

Plate 4c
Bullfrog
Lithobates catesbeiana

ID: The largest native frog in North America; reaches a maximum length of 20 cm (8 in). Body is dark olive-green, sides of the face and the lips are brighter green. Hindlegs may be banded with darker stripes. On each side of the back there is a prominent ridge that extends from the rear of the eye, over the top of the tympanum (eardrum), and ends above the front leg. Webbing on hind foot does not extend to tip of longest toe, as it does on Pig Frog. Call is very deep, two or three syllable, 'jug-o-rum.'

HABITAT: Found in ponds and ditches.

REGION: PAN, NFL, CFL, SFL

Plate 4d
Gopher Frog
Lithobates capito

ID: A large, plump, dusky gray frog with scattered black spots. The spots are sometimes outlined with a lighter color. Bronze ridges on either side of the back. Underside is cream colored. Maximum length 11 cm (4.3 in). Distinctive call, sounds like someone snoring.

HABITAT: Found in dry sandy habitats. This frog frequents Gopher Tortoise burrows.

REGION: PAN, NFL, CFL, SFL

Plate 4e
Bronze Frog
Lithobates clamitans

ID: A medium-sized frog; maximum length 10 cm (4 in). Head and back are rich bronze, snout and upper lip may be light brown to bright green. The underside is cream color, sometimes patterned with faint black blotches. Also known as the Banjo Frog, this frog's call is a 'blonk-blonk,' like someone plucking the strings of a banjo.

HABITAT: Found in streams, cypress swamps, ponds and lake edges.

REGION: PAN, NFL, CFL

Plate 4f
Southern Leopard Frog
Lithobates sphenocephala

ID: A medium-sized frog, light brown to dark green with several rows of distinct brown spots. The head is long and pointed, the iris of the eye is gold, and there is a distinct light spot in the center of the tympanum (eardrum). The throat and belly are white. Maximum length 8 cm (3 in). The call has been likened to the sound made when 'slowly rubbing a finger over the surface of a wet balloon.'

HABITAT: Found in most water bodies, including shallow marshes, swamps, and in wet grassy areas.

REGION: PAN, NFL, CFL, SFL, KEY

Plate 4 **283**

a Greenhouse Frog

b Pig Frog

c Bullfrog

d Gopher Frog

e Bronze Frog

f Southern Leopard Frog

Plate 5a
Mole Salamander
Ambystoma talpoideum
ID: A short-bodied, short-tailed salamander with a broad head. Maximum length 12 cm (4.7 in). Back is gray to bluish gray, with darker blotches or blue mottling.

HABITAT: Spends most of its life underground, or under logs, in wet hammocks or pine flat woods.

REGION: PAN, NFL

Plate 5b
Tiger Salamander
Ambystoma tigrinum
ID: This is the largest terrestrial salamander in Florida, reaching 25 cm (10 in) in length. Body color is highly variable, from brown to blackish, marked with irregular, light colored spots. Head is broad, larger than the neck, and the tail is as long or longer than the body.

HABITAT: In moist woodlands, vegetated ponds. Adults are rarely seen, because they spend most of their life underground. Occasionally found trapped in swimming pools.

REGION: PAN, NFL

Plate 5c
Marbled Salamander
Ambystoma opacum
ID: Short and stocky with a broad head. Average length 11 cm (4.3 in). The tail is round, and shorter than the body. The body is black; males are marked with white blotches, females with gray or silver.

HABITAT: Found under damp logs and leaves, and debris in moist and wet hammocks.

REGION: PAN

Plate 5d
Striped Newt
Notophthalmus perstriatus
ID: A small, slender newt, brownish to tan on the back and yellowish on the undersides. Length 8 to 10.5 cm (3 to 4 in). Red stripes run the length of the body and about half way down the tail, where they break up into a series of dashes.

HABITAT: In cypress ponds and temporary ponds in pine sandhills and scrub.

REGION: PAN, NFL, CFL

Plate 5e
Peninsula Newt
Notophthalmus viridescens
ID: A medium-sized, rough-skinned newt, 6 to 8 cm (2.4 to 3 in) in length. The back is dark olive-brown to blackish with very few red spots; the belly is yellowish, peppered with small black spots.

HABITAT: Common in lakes, ponds, ditches, and slow-moving water with abundant aquatic vegetation.

REGION: PAN, NFL, CFL, SFL

Plate 5 **285**

a Mole Salamander

b Tiger Salamander

c Marbled Salamander

d Striped Newt

e Peninsula Newt

Plate 6a
Three-lined Salamander
Eurycea longicauda

ID: A long, slim-bodied salamander, tail as long or longer than the body; length 10 to 13.5 cm (4 to 5.3 in). Body is light brown, with a prominent black stripe down the center of the back, and a black stripe on each side of the body. There are five toes on each foot.

HABITAT: Under rocks, along streams, near seepages, and in caves.

REGION: PAN

Plate 6b
Slimy Salamander
Plethodon grobmani

ID: A slender, black salamander with silvery white flecks on the back and sides. Total length 12 to 17 cm (4.7 to 6.7 in). When alarmed this salamander secretes a glue-like slime from its skin.

HABITAT: In rotting logs, beneath rocks, and under leaves. One of the most commonly seen salamanders in north Florida.

REGION: PAN, NFL, CFL

Plate 6c
Southern Dusky Salamander
Eurycea auriculatus

ID: A large, stout-tailed salamander with a dusky brown body. Lower sides and tail are marked with white or cream spots. Length 8 to 13 cm (3 to 5 in).

HABITAT: Found under rocks, logs, fallen leaves, and in muck along streams and rivers.

REGION: PAN, NFL, CFL

Plate 6d
Dwarf Salamander
Eurycea quadridigitata

ID: A small, slender salamander with a very long tail. Total length 3 to 9 cm (1.3 to 3.5 in). The back is brownish, sometimes patterned with a series of thin V-shaped markings running down the center. A thin dark stripe runs down each side. There are four toes on each hind foot.

HABITAT: Common in wet hammocks, ponds and streams, particularly in mats of sphagnum moss and among the roots of dense aquatic vegetation.

REGION: PAN, NFL, CFL, SFL

Plate 6e
Georgia Blind Salamander
(also called Cave Salamander)
Haideotriton wallacei

ID: A thin, translucent, white or pinkish salamander, 5 to 8 cm (2 to 3 in) in length. The functionless eye is reduced to a small black spot. Delicate feathery external gills are reddish.

HABITAT: In clear cave pools and underground streams. Only in the Marianna area, Jackson County, Florida.

REGION: PAN

Plate 6 **287**

a Three-lined Salamander

b Slimy Salamander

c Southern Dusky Salamander

d Dwarf Salamander

e Georgia Blind Salamander (Cave Salamander)

Plate 7a
Two-toed Amphiuma
(also called Congo Eel)
Amphiuma means
ID: Large, to 1 m (3.3 ft) long, eel-like salamander with four tiny legs, each with two toes. No external gills, but there is a gill slit on either side of the head. Body is dark gray above, lighter on the belly. Will bite hard if handled carelessly.

HABITAT: In muddy or silted water where there is plenty of aquatic vegetation. In the mud of cypress heads, ponds, streams, ditches, and canals. Burrows into the mud when water levels are low.

REGION: PAN, NFL, CFL, SFL

Plate 7b
Greater Siren
Siren lacertina
ID: A stout, heavy bodied, eel-like salamander; adults may be almost 1 m (3.3 ft) in length. Back is greenish brown, sides may be speckled with yellow. Prominent external gills are reddish brown. Fore limbs are well developed with four toes on each foot. There are no hind limbs. Often caught by fisherman using worms as bait.

HABITAT: Found in slow-moving rivers, canals and ditches. Juveniles are often found in mats of floating vegetation. When the water dries up, sirens bury themselves deeply in the mud and become dormant.

REGION: PAN, NFL, CFL, SFL

Plate 7c
Lesser Siren
Siren intermedia
ID: Eel-like, usually gray or blackish with dark spots. Maximum length 66 cm (26 in). Prominent external gills are reddish brown. Fore limbs are well developed with 4 toes on each foot. There are no hind limbs. Adults are very difficult to distinguish from Greater Sirens.

HABITAT: In slow rivers, ponds, ditches, and canals; especially in vegetation choked waterways and *hydrilla* mats.

REGION: PAN, NFL, CFL, SFL

Plate 7d
Dwarf Siren
Pseudobranchus axanthus
ID: A small, slender, eel-like siren with delicate feathery external gills behind the head. The dark back contains three poorly-defined buff stripes and each side is marked with several yellowish stripes. The well-developed front legs have three toes on each foot. There are no hind limbs. Maximum length about 15 cm (6 in).

HABITAT: Found in ponds and swamps; more often in muck and detritus of pond bottoms than in floating vegetation.

REGION: NFL

Plate 7 **289**

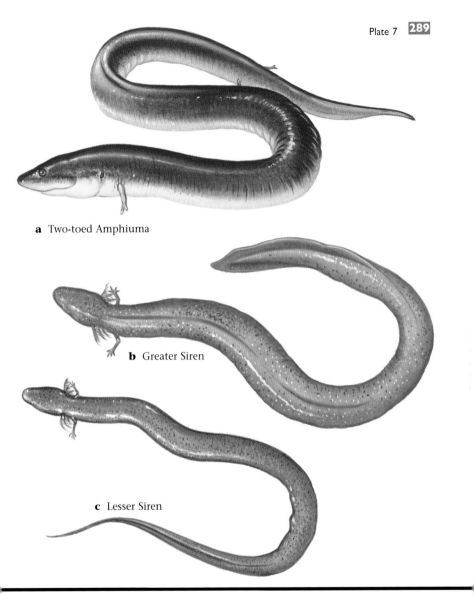

a Two-toed Amphiuma

b Greater Siren

c Lesser Siren

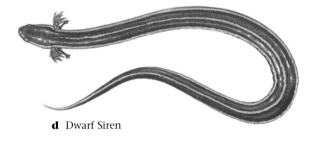

d Dwarf Siren

Plate 8a
American Crocodile
Crocodylus acutus
ID: A large grayish brown or olive crocodile covered with rows of large keeled scales. The snout is long and narrow and, unlike alligators, the fourth tooth of the lower jaw projects outside the upper jaw when closed. Crocodiles often bask with their mouths open, a behavior rarely seen in alligators. Maximum length 4.6 m (15 ft).

HABITAT: Found in coastal mangroves and brackish creeks. Fewer than 2000 individuals in Florida.

REGION: SFL, KEY

Note: This species listed as endangered, CITES Appendix I and USA ESA.

Plate 8b (and book cover)
American Alligator
Alligator mississippiensis
ID: The body and head are black, throat is white to creamy yellow. Snout is broad and rounded. Six raised ridges on back merge into two on the tail. Males occasionally reach 3 m (10 ft), females smaller. Hatchlings are black with yellow crossbands.

HABITAT: Aquatic habitats – lakes, ponds, rivers, canals, swamps, marshes, and mangroves. Abundant in some areas.

REGION: PAN, NFL, CFL, SFL, KEY

Note: This species listed as threatened, CITES Appendix II and USA ESA.

Plate 8c
Leatherback Sea Turtle
(also called Leatherback)
Dermochelys coriacea
ID: Largest of the world's sea turtles, to lengths of 1.7 m (5.5 ft) or more and weights of 550+ kg (1200+ lb). Back is black or brown, smooth, covered with a continuous layer of black, often white-spattered, leathery skin (instead of the hardened plates of other sea turtles); seven ridges along back running front to rear; no claws on limbs; no scales on skin except in youngsters; front limbs up to 1 m (3.3 ft) long.

HABITAT: A turtle of the open ocean, but occasionally found in shallow waters of bays and estuaries. Nests regularly on both coasts of Florida, but in greater numbers on the east coast from Cape Canaveral south to West Palm Beach. Females come ashore at night to lay eggs, preferring beaches with coarse sand. Most nesting recorded between April and August.

REGION: PAN, NFL, CFL, SFL

Note: This species listed as endangered, CITES Appendix I and USA ESA.

Plate 8d
Loggerhead Sea Turtle
(also called Loggerhead)
Caretta caretta
ID: A mid-sized or largish sea turtle with an elongated reddish-brown shell. The head is large, with powerful jaws. The underside of the shell is yellowish and the flippers are reddish brown. Adults weigh 70 to 180 kg (150 to 400 lb) and are 70 to 125 cm (2.3 to 4 ft) long. Hatchlings are brown above, light brown below.

HABITAT: Found in shallow coastal waters, bays, and estuaries. From April to August females come ashore at high tide to lay eggs. The major nesting beaches are between Cape Canaveral and Palm Beach, with almost 40% of all Florida nests near Cape Canaveral. More than 90% of all Loggerhead nesting activity in the world occurs on Florida beaches.

REGION: PAN, NFL, CFL, SFL, KEY

Note: This species listed as endangered, CITES Appendix I, and as threatened, USA ESA.

Plate 8 **291**

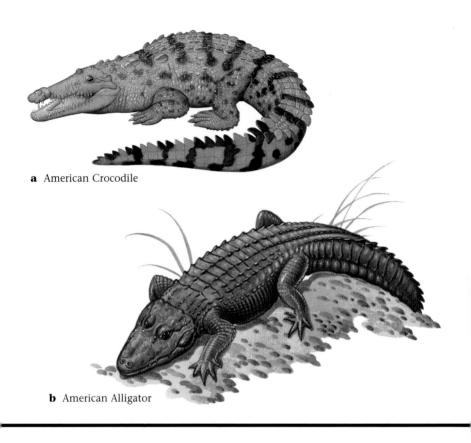

a American Crocodile

b American Alligator

c Leatherback Sea Turtle

d Loggerhead Sea Turtle

Plate 9a

Kemp's Ridley Sea Turtle
(also called Kemp's Ridley, Atlantic Ridley)
Lepidochelys kempii
ID: Relatively small greenish, gray, or yellowish sea turtle with heart-shaped or roundish top shell; central ridge runs along back; bottom shell white or yellowish; grayish or cream-colored head and legs, often with darker markings; to about 70 cm (2.3 ft).

HABITAT: Prefers shallow coast waters. In the Florida Keys it is found in close proximity to red mangrove forest. The only major nesting area in the world for this turtle is off the southern coast of Tamaulipas, Mexico. Nests infrequently in Florida; only seven nesting records from 1989 to 1999, almost all of which were along southwest coast.

REGION: NFL, CFL, SFL, KEY

Note: This species is critically endangered, CITES Appendix I and USA ESA listed.

Plate 9b

Green Sea Turtle
(also called Green Turtle)
Chelonia mydas
ID: A medium-sized sea turtle with black, gray, greenish, or brown heart-shaped back, often with bold spots or streaks; yellowish white underneath; males' front legs each have one large, curved claw; males with longer, thicker tails than females; name refers to greenish body fat; to 1.2 m (4 ft).

HABITAT: Migrates across oceans but feeds in shallow water with abundant submerged vegetation. Nests from June to late September along both coasts of Florida, but in large numbers on the east coast from Cape Canaveral south to West Palm Beach.

REGION: PAN, NFL, CFL, SFL

Note: This species is endangered over parts of its range, CITES Appendix I and USA ESA listed.

Plate 9c

Hawksbill Sea Turtle
(also called Hawksbill, Atlantic Hawksbill)
Eretmochelys imbricata
ID: A small to mid-sized sea turtle; shield-shaped back mainly dark greenish brown; yellow underneath; head scales brown or black; jaws yellowish with dark markings; chin and throat yellow; two claws on each front leg; narrow head and tapering hooked 'beak' give the species its name; to 90 cm (3 ft).

HABITAT: Sometimes found in deep ocean waters but more characteristically associated with rocky places and coral reefs. Occasionally found in shallow coastal waters, including bays, lagoons, and estuaries fringed with mangrove forest. Nests infrequently in Florida; the few nesting occurrences are all from extreme southern portion of the state.

REGION: SFL

Note: This species is endangered, CITES Appendix I and USA ESA listed.

Plate 9   **293**

a Kemp's Ridley Sea Turtle

b Green Sea Turtle

c Hawksbill Sea Turtle

Plate 10a
Common Snapping Turtle
Chelydra serpentina
ID: A uniformly gray-brown turtle with a long tail. The neck is long and the head is large. Shell may be bumpy or smooth but often covered with algae. When alarmed, this turtle releases a strong smelling musk. Maximum length 47 cm (18.5 in); weight 34 kg (75 lb) or more.

HABITAT: Found in marshes, ponds, lakes, and rivers. Basks by floating on the surface of the water, rarely on land. Most active at night. Nests in uplands.

REGION: PAN, NFL, CFL, SFL

Plate 10b
Alligator Snapping Turtle
Macroclemys temminckii
ID: A large turtle, shell dark brown above with three rows of knobby plates. The rear of the top shell is jagged. The head is very large, with a hawk-like bill, and the neck is short. Maximum length 71 cm (28 in); maximum weight 91 kg (200 lb). Avoid handling; can inflict serious bite.

HABITAT: Found in slow-moving waters of large rivers, creeks, lakes and reservoirs. Rarely ventures onto land.

REGION: PAN, NFL

Plate 10c
Diamondback Terrapin
Malaclemys terrapin
ID: The gray to blackish oval top shell has a central keel, and the centers of the plates are orange. The skin on the head and feet is smoky gray speckled with black. The underside is creamy yellow. Maximum length 23 cm (9 in).

HABITAT: All around Florida's coast, in saltwater marshes, estuaries, and lagoons.

REGION: PAN, NFL, CFL, SFL, KEY

Plate 10d
Barbour's Map Turtle
Graptemys barbouri
ID: The olive-gray to dark brown top shell has dull yellow 'U' shaped marks on each plate. The top shell has a prominent keel with black-tipped knobs. There is a large greenish-yellow patch behind each eye and one on the snout. Females are often twice as large as males. Maximum length: males 13 cm (5 in), females 30 cm (12 in).

HABITAT: Large river drainages.

REGION: PAN

Plate 10 **295**

a Common Snapping Turtle

b Alligator Snapping Turtle

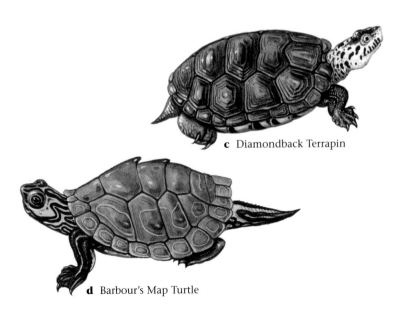

c Diamondback Terrapin

d Barbour's Map Turtle

Plate 11a
Florida Redbelly Turtle
(also called Florida Red-bellied Cooter)
Pseudemys nelsoni
ID: A large turtle with an olive-brown to blackish top shell, patterned with wide faded reddish markings. The underside of the top shell is red or orange. The head, feet and tail are black with bright yellow stripes. The bottom shell is orange or rusty red. Maximum length 34 cm (13.4 in).

HABITAT: Found in fresh to brackish water. Prefers places with abundant vegetation and little water flow, including ponds, lakes, ditches, and canals. Often nests in alligator nests.

REGION: PAN, NFL, CFL, SFL

Plate 11b
Florida Cooter
Pseudemys peninsularis floridana
ID: This common turtle has a dark olive-brown top shell with faint to bright yellowish markings on each plate. The head and feet are dark brown marked with bright yellow stripes. The bottom shell is yellow and unmarked. Maximum length 38 cm (15 in).

HABITAT: In lakes, streams, springs, slow-moving rivers, and well-vegetated waterways.

REGION: PAN, NFL, CFL, SFL

Plate 11c
Chicken Turtle
Deirochelys reticularia
ID: A brownish-green, oblong-shaped turtle, marked with a net-like pattern of yellow. The top shell is edged in yellow, and there is a broad yellow stripe on each front leg. The skin on either side of the tail has bright yellow vertical stripes, and the long neck has yellow stripes. Maximum length 25 cm (10 in).

HABITAT: In weedy ponds, ditches, and canals. Frequently seen basking on aquatic vegetation. Often seen crossing highways, especially in spring.

REGION: PAN, NFL, CFL, SFL

Plate 11d
Yellow-bellied Slider
Trachemys scripta scripta
ID: Medium-sized turtle, maximum length 29 cm (11 in). Dark top shell marked with broad yellowish vertical bars on plates. Belly is yellow with brown blotches. Dark head marked with distinctive broad yellow blotch behind each eye.

HABITAT: Commonly found in ponds, lakes, and streams that have a lot of aquatic vegetation. Frequently basks on logs or mats of floating vegetation.

REGION: PAN, NFL

Plate 11 **297**

a Florida Redbelly Turtle

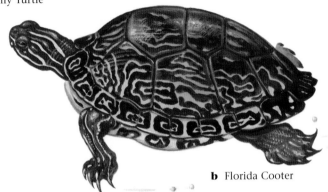

b Florida Cooter

c Chicken Turtle

d Yellow-bellied Slider

Plate 12a
Stinkpot
(also called Common Musk Turtle)
Sternotherus odoratus

ID: A small gray-black turtle with a smooth, high domed top shell. The skin of the head and legs is dark, and the large head has two prominent yellow lines on either side. The bottom shell is small, with ample flesh exposed between the scales. Emits strong musk odor from glands when alarmed.

HABITAT: Common in almost any still-water habitat, including ponds, lakes, and canals. Often seen on land, and they sometimes manage to climb into low trees and shrubs over water to bask.

REGION: PAN, NFL, CFL, SFL

Plate 12b
Striped Mud Turtle
Kinosternon baurii

ID: A small turtle with a smooth domed top shell. The brownish to black top shell has three yellowish or light colored longitudinal lines. The head is small and dark with two stripes on either side of the face. Maximum length 12 cm (5 in).

HABITAT: In shallow water habitats, including swamps, marshes, ponds, and ditches. May be found on land under leaves or logs.

REGION: PAN, NFL, CFL, SFL, KEY

Plate 12c
Gopher Tortoise
Gopherus polyphemus

ID: A large tortoise with a high, domed, oblong top shell, gray or dark brown with prominent growth rings. Front feet are broad and spade-like with heavy claws for digging. Hind feet are round and elephant-like. The neck is short and the head is large and rounded. Maximum length 30 cm (12 in).

HABITAT: Digs burrows, 9 m (30 ft) or more in length, in longleaf pine-turkey oak, oak hammocks, coastal dunes, and open scrub.

REGION: PAN, NFL, CFL, SFL

Plate 12d
Box Turtle
Terrapene carolina

ID: A small terrestrial turtle with a high domed top shell that is brownish black and patterned with radiating yellow stripes. There are two yellow stripes on the side of the face. The underside of the shell is hinged. Most Florida Box Turtles have only three long-clawed toes on each hind foot. Maximum length 16.5 cm (6.5 in).

HABITAT: In open woodlands, pine flatwoods, and fields. Often seen crossing highways.

REGION: PAN, NFL, CFL, SFL, KEY

Plate 12e
Florida Softshell
Apalone ferox

ID: This large turtle can reach a maximum length of 50 cm (20 in). The brown leathery top shell has many small knobs along the front edge behind the head. The head is dark and there is often a yellowish stripe behind each eye. Females are much larger than males. Avoid handling; has an extremely long neck and a nasty bite.

HABITAT: Common in almost any still-water habitat, including ponds, lakes, canals, and swamps. Often seen floating on the surface of the water. Basks on logs and mats of floating vegetation.

REGION: PAN, NFL, CFL, SFL, KEY

Plate 12 **299**

a Stinkpot

b Striped Mud Turtle

c Gopher Tortoise

d Box Turtle

e Florida Softshell

Plate 13a
Eastern Glass Lizard
Ophisaurus ventralis

ID: A large, smooth, legless lizard. Maximum length 1.1 m (3.5 ft). Often mistaken for a snake, but appears less flexible and much less sinuous in its movement. Unlike snakes, glass lizards have eyelids, external ear openings, and lack enlarged belly scales. Young are sandy brown with dark stripes down the sides. Adults are blackish with green spots covering the entire body. Tail breaks off easily and may grow back a different color.

HABITAT: Found in open grassy areas near canals, or in pine-oak woodlands. Often seen crossing sand roads.

REGION: PAN, NFL, CFL, SFL

Plate 13b
Florida Worm Lizard
Rhineura floridana

ID: A large, pink, eyeless, earthworm-like lizard. Maximum length 28 cm (11 in). Body appears segmented because scales are arranged in rings. Head and tail are blunt.

HABITAT: In dry upland habitats with sandy soil, sand pine forest, longleaf pine-turkey oak forests and upland hammocks. Rarely seen because it burrows like an earthworm.

REGION: PAN, NFL, CFL

Plate 13c
Six-lined Racerunner
Cnemidophorus sexlineatus

ID: A large, brown lizard with six yellowish stripes down the back. Maximum length 24 cm (9.5 in). Males have a blue belly and throat. Hind legs are long with a very long fourth toe.

HABITAT: Common in dry, sandy, open habitats such as fields, scrub areas, and dunes along beaches. Active during the heat of the day, it moves fast. Often seen rummaging around in fallen leaves, as it looks for insects.

REGION: PAN, NFL, CFL, SFL, KEY

Plate 13d
Mediterranean Gecko
Hemidactylus turcicus

ID: A small, rough-scaled gecko with large eyes and long tail. Maximum length 12 cm (4.7 in). Grayish with light pink and dark brown spots. There are raised white spots on the back and sides. This gecko changes color – at night becoming light gray to whitish. Voice is a weak squeaking noise, like a mouse.

HABITAT: Found predominantly around human habitation. Introduced.

REGION: PAN, NFL, CFL, SFL, KEY

Plate 13 **301**

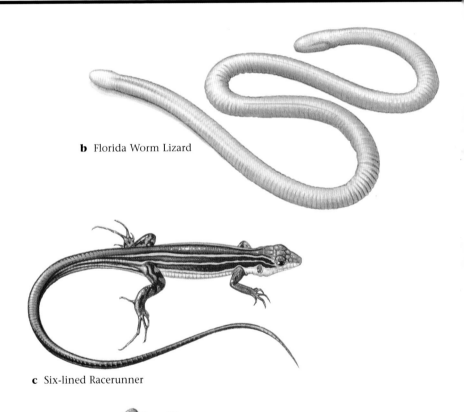

a Eastern Glass Lizard

b Florida Worm Lizard

c Six-lined Racerunner

d Mediterranean Gecko

Plate 14a
Florida Scrub Lizard
Sceloporus woodi
ID: A small, spiny-scaled, gray or gray-brown lizard with a dark brown stripe along each side of the body. Females have zigzag bars across the back. Adult males have a light blue patch on either side of the belly and on throat. Maximum length 13 cm (5 in).

HABITAT: Found in scrub habitats. Often seen foraging on the ground. When alarmed it will run along the ground rather than climb.

REGION: CFL, SFL

Plate 14b
Brown Anole
Anolis sagrei
ID: A long, slender, brown lizard. Males reach 20 cm (8 in) in length, females are smaller. Males have yellowish spots on the back, a ridge down the center of the back, and an orange to pale-yellow, white-edged dewlap (throat sac).

HABITAT: Thrives in disturbed habitats and among ornamental plants. Often seen on the ground or low in trees and shrubs. Common around buildings. An introduced species, becoming more common every year.

REGION: PAN, NFL, CFL, SFL, KEY

Plate 14c
Eastern Fence Lizard
Sceloporus undulatus
ID: A medium-sized, rough-scaled lizard. Maximum length 18 cm (7 in). Females are gray-brown with dark zigzag transverse bars across the back and tail. Males are gray to almost black with 'terra-cotta' markings and dark, shiny blue patches on throat and sides of belly.

HABITAT: Common in sandy pine/turkey oak forest, pine flatwoods, and oak hammocks. Often seen basking on logs, posts or tree trunks.

REGION: PAN, NFL, CFL

Plate 14d
Green Anole
Anolis carolinensis
ID: A medium-sized lizard with a long tail. Usually bright emerald-green, but can change color to brown or gray. Males have a pink or red extendable dewlap (throat sac) and a small ridge down the center of the back. The toes have adhesive pads on the undersides. Maximum length 20 cm (8 in).

HABITAT: In almost every habitat type, including gardens and buildings. Arboreal; often seen head down on tree trunks, fence posts, and bushes.

REGION: PAN, NFL, CFL, SFL, KEY

Plate 14 **303**

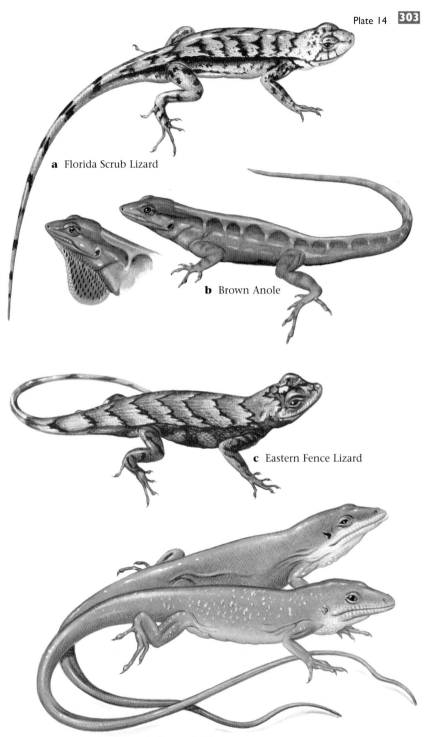

a Florida Scrub Lizard

b Brown Anole

c Eastern Fence Lizard

d Green Anole

Plate 15 (*See also*: Skinks, p. 95)

Plate 15a
Florida Sand Skink
Eumeces reynoldsi

ID: A small, shiny, snake-like lizard with greatly reduced legs. Front legs are tiny and have only one toe; the hind legs are slightly larger with two toes. Body is silvery gray or light brown. Maximum length about 13 cm (5 in), about half of which is tail.

HABITAT: In sparsely vegetated rosemary and sand pine scrub, oak scrub, and patches of loose sand. Because it moves by 'swimming' through loose sand this skink cannot live in areas with many plant roots.

REGION: CFL, SFL

Note: This species is threatened, USA ESA listed.

Plate 15b
Broadheaded Skink
Eumeces laticeps

ID: A very large, shiny lizard that can be identified by size alone. Maximum length 32 cm (13 in). Males are uniform brown, with orange heads during the spring breeding season. Females are grayish brown. Younger females may have pale yellow lines on the sides of the body and a faint line down the center of the back. Juveniles are black with five or seven yellowish stripes and a bright blue tail.

HABITAT: Found in parks, gardens, woodlands, and wet hammocks. In urban parks, some individuals can become quite tame. Arboreal.

REGION: PAN, NFL, CFL

Plate 15c
Ground Skink
Scincella lateralis

ID: A small lizard with a long, round body and tiny legs. Maximum length 13 cm (5 in). Back and sides are light coppery brown with a dark stripe running along the upper portion of both sides.

HABITAT: Found in almost all habitats with ground cover, including woodlands, and near streams and ponds; often seen on lawns. Moves in a snake-like manner. One of Florida's most common lizards.

REGION: PAN, NFL, CFL, SFL, KEY

Plate 15d
Southeastern Five-lined Skink
Eumeces inexpectatus

ID: A large, shiny skink, up to 21 cm (8 in) long. Females are dark chocolate-brown with five yellowish-white stripes down the back. Males may be lighter brown with lighter stripes. Tail brown to bluish. In spring, breeding males have orange heads and cheeks.

HABITAT: Occurs in many types of habitats. Often seen basking on fallen trees, walls, or in piles of trash.

REGION: PAN, NFL, CFL, SFL, KEY

Plate 15e
Mole Skink
Eumeces egregius

ID: A slender lizard with smooth, shiny scales. Maximum length 15 cm (6 in). Small legs, five toes on each foot. Light brown with light stripes extending from nose onto sides. Tail can be pink, red, violet, or blue.

HABITAT: This skink is a 'sand swimmer,' found in dry sandhill and scrub habitats. Frequently seen in the sandy mounds pushed up by pocket gophers, or in the loose sand in the apron of Gopher Tortoise burrows.

REGION: PAN, NFL, CFL, SFL, KEY

Plate 15 **305**

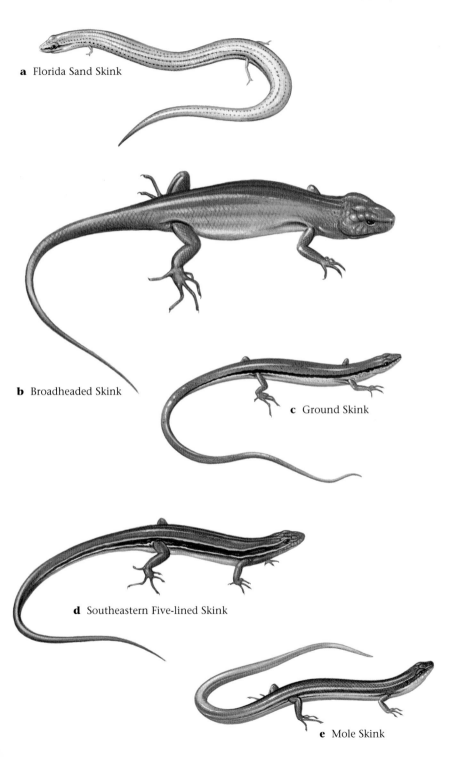

a Florida Sand Skink

b Broadheaded Skink

c Ground Skink

d Southeastern Five-lined Skink

e Mole Skink

Plate 16a
Eastern Hognose Snake
Heterodon platirhinos
ID: A thick-bodied, medium-sized snake; maximum length 1.2 m (3.8 ft). Color highly variable, from uniform black or gray to yellowish with dark blotches. This snake is best distinguished by its pointed upturned snout and wide neck. If disturbed, it will raise its head, flatten its body and neck, hiss, and strike, like a pit-viper. If that fails to deter a predator, it rolls over and feigns death.

HABITAT: Found in dry sandy areas including upland longleaf pine-turkey oak forests, mixed hardwood forests, and brushy fields.

REGION: PAN, NFL, CFL, SFL

Plate 16b
Corn Snake
Elaphe guttata
ID: A slender, beautifully marked snake; varies in background color from gray to yellowish or reddish brown. Along the back is a row of large reddish blotches outlined with black; smaller blotches occur along the sides. The belly is distinctly patterned with black and white squares. Maximum length 1.8 m (6 ft).

HABITAT: Lives in almost any terrestrial habitat, including pine-turkey oak forests, hardwood hammocks, brushy fields, barns and outbuildings. Common.

REGION: PAN, NFL, CFL, SFL, KEY

Plate 16c
Yellow Rat Snake
Elaphe obsoleta
ID: A long snake; adults bright yellow to olive-green with four dark stripes, one along each side and two down back. Head yellow-brown to tan. Some adults with faint to dark blotches on back and sides. Belly is white, light yellow, orange or gray, often with faint blotches or checks. Maximum length 2.1 m (7 ft).

HABITAT: Common along edges of woodland habitats, but also found in farmland, abandoned fields, and old buildings. Highly arboreal.

REGION: PAN, NFL, CFL, SFL, KEY

Plate 16d
Indigo Snake
Drymarchon couperi
ID: The largest snake in Florida; maximum length 2.6 m (8.5 ft). Heavy-bodied, smooth-scaled, and glossy blue-black. Chin and throat are usually cream, orange or reddish.

HABITAT: It is found in dry sandy habitats, including pine flatwoods, oak hammocks, and sandhills where it shelters in Gopher Tortoise burrows. In south Florida it is found in tropical hammocks. Uncommon.

REGION: PAN, NFL, CFL, SFL, KEY

Plate 16e
Black Racer
Coluber constrictor
ID: A shiny black or dark gray snake with large smooth scales. The throat is usually white and the underside paler gray. The large eye has a reddish-brown iris. Maximum length 1.8 cm (5.8 ft).

HABITAT: Occurs in many habitat types; most common in brushy areas near water. Active during the day. This is the most frequently seen snake in suburban areas.

REGION: PAN, NFL, CFL, SFL, KEY

Plate 16 **307**

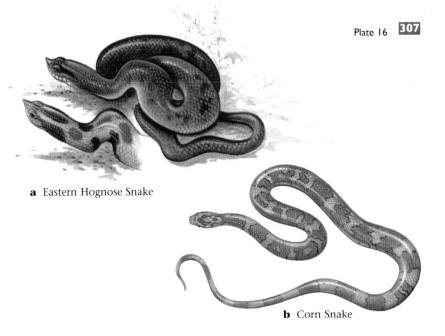

a Eastern Hognose Snake

b Corn Snake

c Yellow Rat Snake

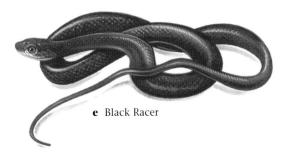

d Indigo Snake

e Black Racer

Plate 17a
Florida Green Water Snake
Nerodia floridana
ID: A heavy-bodied snake, maximum length 1.4 m (4.6 ft). Fairly uniform olive-green to green-brown, but in South Florida some individuals may be reddish. Belly is unmarked, cream-colored.

HABITAT: Found in wetlands with abundant aquatic vegetation – in marshes, ponds, ditches, wet prairies, and coastal wetlands. The most abundant aquatic snake in Florida.

REGION: PAN, NFL, CFL, SFL

Plate 17b
Striped Crayfish Snake
Regina alleni
ID: A small, moderately thick, glossy water snake; maximum length 65 cm (26 in). The back is shiny brown with three very faint, darker, longitudinal stripes. The yellowish belly is usually unmarked.

HABITAT: Found in ponds, lakes, swamps, and canals, especially in places with abundant floating vegetation.

REGION: PAN, NFL, CFL, SFL

Plate 17c
Banded Water Snake
Nerodia fasciata
ID: A medium-sized snake with an oval head and snout and gradually tapering tail. A dark stripe runs from the eye to the corner of the jaw. Background color is reddish to yellowish gray marked with broad dark bands. Belly is pale yellow with squarish spots. Some individuals may be solid dark brown, with almost imperceptible bands. Maximum length 1.6 m (5.2 ft). Often confused with the Cottonmouth.

HABITAT: Wet prairies, coastal wetlands, and near ponds and lakes.

REGION: PAN, NFL, CFL, SFL

Plate 17d
Mud Snake
Farancia abacura
ID: A large, shiny snake, jet-black on the back. Red or pinkish bars on the belly sometimes extend onto the sides. The top of the head is black, chin yellowish. The tip of the tail has an enlarged, sharply pointed scale. Maximum length 2.1 m (6.9 ft).

HABITAT: Found around most shallow freshwater habitats. They prefer areas with dense aquatic vegetation, including marshes, swamps, irrigation canals, and cypress stands.

REGION: PAN, NFL, CFL, SFL

Plate 17e
Brown Water Snake
Nerodia taxispilota
ID: A large, heavy-bodied snake; maximum length 1.7 m (5.6 ft). Body is dull brown, with a row of large square-shaped darker brown blotches along back, and a row of alternating dark blotches on each side. Belly creamy yellow with dark spots. Head is brown with few or no markings, oval in shape and wider than the neck.

HABITAT: Found in rivers, lakes, ponds, ditches, and cypress swamps, especially where there are fallen trees for basking.

REGION: PAN, NFL, CFL, SFL

Plate 17 **309**

a Florida Green Water Snake

b Striped Crayfish Snake

c Banded Water Snake

d Mud Snake

e Brown Water Snake

Plate 18a
Eastern Kingsnake
Lampropeltis getula
ID: A large, smooth, glossy snake; maximum length 2.1 m (6.8 ft). Head and neck are similar in diameter. Color and patterning highly variable. Most often shiny black or brown, marked with many yellowish or white crossbands. Belly is creamy yellow.

HABITAT: Usually near water, including vegetation-filled ponds, canals, wet prairies and marshes; also on tidal flats and in estuaries.

REGION: PAN, NFL, CFL, SFL

Plate 18b
Eastern Garter Snake
Thamnophis sirtalis
ID: Highly variable in color. Body and head dark brown to olive. Three wide, pale-yellow to yellow-brown stripes run down the back, one runs along the middle of the back, and one runs along each side of the body. Maximum length 1.2 m (4 ft).

HABITAT: Found in forests, fields, cypress stands, usually near water in heavily vegetated areas; also in gardens, parks, vacant lots. Common.

REGION: PAN, NFL, CFL, SFL

Plate 18c
Eastern Ribbon Snake
Thamnophis sauritus
ID: A slender, long-tailed snake that resembles the Eastern Garter Snake. Maximum length 1 m (3.3 ft). Background color is olive-green or dull brown. Usually has three bright stripes running longitudinally down back and sides. The head is narrow and pointed. Individuals from Panhandle have vertical white spot in front of the eye.

HABITAT: Usually near water, including marshes, wet prairies, and canal banks. Common.

REGION: PAN, NFL, CFL, SFL, KEY

Plate 18d
Pine Snake
Pituophis melanoleucus
ID: A large, heavy-bodied snake, highly variable in color. Head small; snout pointed, with enlarged rostral scale. Maximum length 2.3 m (7.5 ft). Back is light brown to gray with darker reddish-brown blotches. The blotches become bands near the tail.

HABITAT: Most often found in sandy areas where pocket gophers occur, including longleaf pine-turkey oak and abandoned fields, but also in scrub. Burrows into tunnels of pocket gophers. Uncommon.

REGION: PAN, NFL, CFL, SFL

Plate 18 **311**

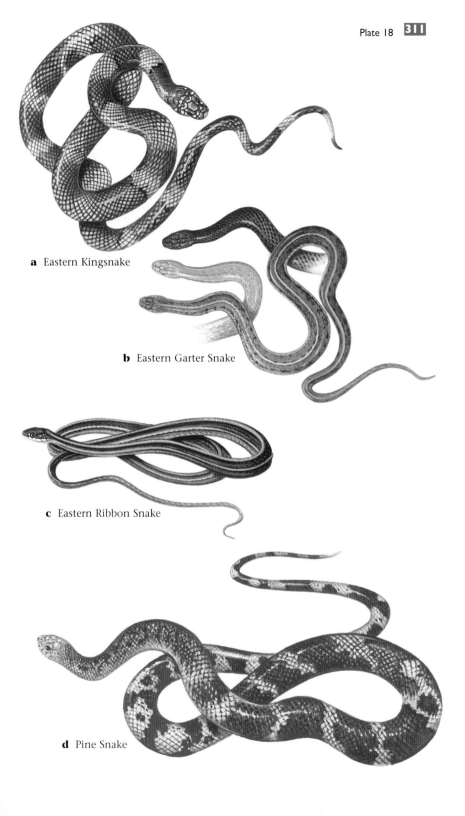

a Eastern Kingsnake

b Eastern Garter Snake

c Eastern Ribbon Snake

d Pine Snake

Plate 19a
Dusky Pigmy Rattlesnake
Sistrurus miliarius barbouri

ID: A small, stout-bodied snake; maximum length 79 cm (31 in), but more commonly about 50 cm (20 in). The rough-scaled back is gray, heavily marked with large dark circular spots. From the base of the head, large reddish-orange spots alternate with the dark spots along the midline of the back. Pupils are vertical. The tiny rattle produces a sound like a buzzing insect, and is difficult to detect more than a few feet away.

HABITAT: Found in both wet and dry areas, in pine flatwoods, palmetto, scrub, grasslands, sawgrass prairies, and hardwood hammocks.

REGION: PAN, NFL, CFL, SFL

Plate 19b
Eastern Coral Snake
Micrurus fulvius

ID: This small, smooth, brightly colored snake has a slender body, small, blunt head and round pupils. Maximum length is 1.2 m (3.9 ft), but more commonly about 76 cm (30 in). Narrow yellow bands separate wider bands of black and red. Diagnostic feature is black snout and broad yellow band across the back of the head and neck.

HABITAT: Found along edges of wooded areas, in longleaf pine-turkey oak forest, particularly where there is a thick layer of leaf litter or plenty of ground cover; also in compost heaps and woodpiles. Common but secretive.

REGION: PAN, NFL, CFL, SFL, KEY

Plate 19c
Cottonmouth
Agkistrodon piscivorus

ID: A large, heavy-bodied snake with a thick head that is much larger than the neck. Tail tapers abruptly. Maximum length 1.9 m (6.2 ft), but more commonly about 91 cm (36 in). Color varies from olive-brown to black, with or without dark crossbands. A dark band extends from behind the eye to the jaw hinge, and the edges of the mouth are light brown or whitish. The pupils are elliptical.

HABITAT: A water snake, found in swamps, along lake margins, and tree bordered marshes; also in salt marshes and on barrier islands.

REGION: PAN, NFL, CFL, SFL, KEY

Plate 19d
Eastern Diamondback Rattlesnake
Crotalus adamanteus

ID: A large, heavy-bodied snake with a broad triangular head that is much larger than the neck. Segmented rattle at the end of the tail. Maximum length 2.4 m (8 ft), but now seldom see one more than 1.5 m (5 ft) long. The rough-scaled back is gray to dark brown, patterned with pale-bordered diamond-shaped dark markings. The head is striped with black and white on the sides.

HABITAT: Lives in almost every type of habitat; most commonly found in palmetto, pine flatwoods, sandhills, abandoned fields, and brushy areas.

REGION: PAN, NFL, CFL, SFL, KEY

Plate 19   313

a Dusky Pigmy Rattlesnake
(VENOMOUS)

b Eastern Coral Snake (VENOMOUS)

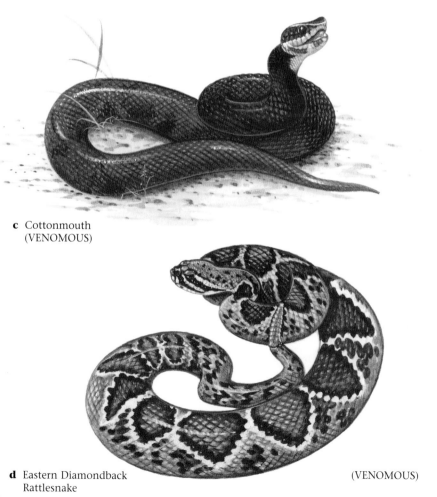

c Cottonmouth
(VENOMOUS)

d Eastern Diamondback
Rattlesnake

(VENOMOUS)

Plate 20a

Magnificent Frigatebird
Fregata magnificens

ID: A large, lightly built, black bird with long, narrow, angled wings. Very distinctive silhouette. Tail is deeply forked. The bill is long and bluish gray, with a down-curved tip. Males have a bright red throat pouch, which is inflated during courtship. Females have a white breast patch. Immature birds have white heads and underparts. Length 1 m (3.3 ft); wingspan 2.3 m (7.5 ft).

HABITAT: Often seen soaring high above coastal areas and mangroves.

REGION: CFL, SFL, KEY

Plate 20b

Pied-billed Grebe
Podilymbus podiceps

ID: A small, stocky, diving bird with a short stout bill. Most commonly seen in winter, when it is brown-gray overall, with a white throat and plain yellow bill. During the breeding season (March to December) bill is white with a vertical black band. Chin and throat are black. These grebes become much more numerous in winter, when northern migrants join the resident population. Length 34 cm (13.5 in).

HABITAT: Lakes, ponds, and brackish water.

REGION: PAN, NFL, CFL, SFL

Plate 20c

Horned Grebe
Podiceps auritus

ID: In winter, white cheeks and throat contrast with drab gray-brown back, crown and nape. White cheek patch extends behind the head. There is a pale spot in front of the eye. Migrant, seen October through April. Length 34 cm (13.5 in).

HABITAT: In protected bays and inlets along the Gulf Coast. Occasionally on large inland lakes.

REGION: PAN, NFL, CFL, SFL

Plate 20d

Common Loon
Gavia immer

ID: A large diving bird. Heavy, sharply pointed bill is gray in color. Plumage white below, gray-brown above. Crown and nape are darker than back. Winter resident, November to April. Length 81 cm (32 in).

HABITAT: Open saltwater and fresh water in large lakes, bays and lagoons.

REGION: PAN, NFL, CFL, SFL

Plate 20 315

a Magnificent Frigatebird

M

F

IM

B

NB

b Pied-billed Grebe

c Horned Grebe

d Common Loon

Plate 21a
American White Pelican
Pelecanus erythrorhynchos
ID: A large white seabird with a long, massive yellow bill and distinctive black wingtips visible in flight. This winter resident is seen in Florida from December to March. Usually found in flocks. Length 1.6 m (5.2 ft); wingspan 2.7 m (8.8 ft).

HABITAT: Occasionally in lakes and coastal areas of North Florida, more common in Central and South Florida, and Florida Bay. In spring and fall large migrating flocks are often seen along the Gulf coast.

REGION: PAN, NFL, CFL, SFL

Plate 21b
Brown Pelican
Pelecanus occidentalis
ID: Large brownish seabird with white or brown neck and yellowish crown. Wings long and broad with light lining. Long, hooked bill has a prominent throat pouch. Immatures uniformly brown-tan with white belly. Males slightly larger than females. Length 1.2 m (3.9 ft); wingspan 2.1 m (6.9 ft).

HABITAT: Coastal areas and lakes.

REGION: PAN, NFL, CFL, SFL, KEY

Plate 21c
Double-crested Cormorant
Phalacrocorax auritus
ID: A large, heavy-bodied, black seabird with an orange throat patch and a heavy, hooked bill. Black webbed feet. Often seen swimming with just its head above water or perched in upright posture on rocks, piers, and docks, drying its outstretched wings. Length 81 cm (32 in); wingspan 1.3 m (4.3 ft).

HABITAT: Lakes, rivers, ponds and coastal waters.

REGION: PAN, NFL, CFL, SFL, KEY

Plate 21d
Anhinga
Anhinga anhinga
ID: A large dark bird with a long, slender, S-shaped neck. Males are greenish iridescent black except for silvery white shoulders and upper wings; females similar except neck and breast are light brown. Often swims with only head and neck above water. Commonly seen perched, drying its outstretched wings. Distinguished from cormorant by sharp spear-like bill and longer tail. Length 89 cm (35 in); wingspan 1.1 m (3.6 ft).

HABITAT: Freshwater ponds, lakes, rivers and swamps.

REGION: NFL, CFL, SFL, KEY

Plate 21 317

IM

IM

a American White Pelican

b Brown Pelican

IM

c Double-crested Cormorant

M

F

d Anhinga

Plate 22 (*See also*: Pelican Relatives, p. 106; Terns, p. 133)

Plate 22a

Masked Booby
Sula dactylatra

ID: A stocky, white seabird. Tail and trailing edges of the wings are black. Bill and feet yellow. In the breeding season, adults have a patch of bare blue skin at the base of the bill. Feeds by plunging straight down into the ocean. Length 81 cm (32 in); wingspan 1.6 m (5.2 ft).

HABITAT: Offshore. Also on sandbars and buoys in the Dry Tortugas.

REGION: PAN, NFL, CFL, SFL, KEY

Plate 22b

Brown Booby
Sula leucogaster

ID: A dark brown seabird with sharply contrasting white underbelly and large white patches underneath wings. Immature birds have light brown underparts. Bill and feet are yellow. Feeds by plunging straight down into the ocean, but also skims the surface for flying fish. Length 76 cm (30 in); wingspan 1.4 m (4.6 ft)

HABITAT: Offshore. Sometimes seen perching on buoys and channel markers.

REGION: PAN, NFL, CFL, SFL, KEY

Plate 22c

Sooty Tern
Sterna fuscata

ID: A medium-sized slender tern, black above, white below with a white patch on the forehead. Tail deeply forked. Bill thin and black. These terns do not dive. They feed by plucking small fish from the water surface. Length 41 cm (16 in); wingspan 81 cm (32 in).

HABITAT: Offshore. Nests in colonies in the Dry Tortugas.

REGION: NFL, CFL, SFL, KEY

Plate 22d

Brown Noddy
Anous stolidus

ID: A medium-sized, dark brown tern with a light gray cap and black bill. Tail is long and wedge-shaped. Does not dive but feeds over the open ocean, plucking small fish from the surface. Length 39 cm (15.5 in); wingspan 81 cm (32 in).

HABITAT: Offshore. Nests colonially in the Dry Tortugas.

REGION: PAN, NFL, CFL, SFL, KEY

Plate 22e

White-tailed Tropicbird
Phaethon lepturus

ID: A spectacular white seabird with black streaks on the back, a black eye stripe, and a yellow bill. White tail has two very long central feathers. Flies with rapid wingbeats and feeds by diving. Length 76 cm (30 in); wingspan 94 cm (37 in).

HABITAT: Offshore. Dry Tortugas and occasionally off South Florida after tropical storms.

REGION: NFL, CFL, SFL, KEY

Plate 22 **319**

a Masked Booby

IM

b Brown Booby

IM

IM

c Sooty Tern

e White-tailed Tropicbird

d Brown Noddy

Plate 23a
Cattle Egret
Bubulcus ibis
ID: Small, chunky heron, all white with yellow bill and uniformly colored legs. During breeding, crest, breast, and back are buff, bill and legs dark red. Distinguished from Snowy Egret and immature Little Blue Heron by smaller size, shorter, thicker bill and neck, overall stockier appearance. An Old World species, dispersed to Florida in 1950s. Often seen in large flocks. Length 51 cm (20 in); wingspan 91 cm (36 in).

HABITAT: Cattle pastures and farms, roadside ditches, other disturbed habitats.

REGION: PAN, NFL, CFL, SFL, KEY

Plate 23b
Snowy Egret
Egretta thula
ID: A smallish, slender, white heron with longish, black bill, black legs, and yellow feet. Like other herons, has long crest, breast, and wing plumes during breeding; feet then turn bright red or orange. Forages actively with rapid movements. Length 61 cm (20 in); wingspan 1 m (3.3 ft).

HABITAT: Wetlands, mangrove swamps, mud flats, and margins of lakes and ponds.

REGION: PAN, NFL, CFL, SFL, KEY

Plate 23c
Great Egret
Ardea alba
ID: Largest all-white heron in Florida; roughly twice the size of Snowy Egret. Smaller than Great Blue Heron. Yellow bill, black legs. During breeding, long breast and wing plumes. Stalks prey with slow stealth. Common. Length 99 cm (39 in); wingspan 1.3 m (4.3 ft).

HABITAT: Wetlands, mangrove swamps, mudflats, and margins of lakes and ponds.

REGION: PAN, NFL, CFL, SFL, KEY

Plate 23d
Reddish Egret
Egretta rufescens
ID: Adult is dark gray with dull reddish-brown head and neck, bluish legs; there is also a white form adult. Breeding plumage is brighter with long plumes typical of most herons; bill is bright pink with black tip. Uncommon, usually solitary. Forages with distinctively rapid, erratic sprints and lunges, frequently with wings half-spread. Length 76 cm (30 in); wingspan 1.2 m (3.9 ft).

HABITAT: Atlantic and Gulf coasts, estuaries, mangrove swamps, and mudflats.

REGION: PAN, NFL, CFL, SFL, KEY

Plate 23e
Tricolored Heron
Egretta tricolor
ID: White underparts contrasting with dark head, back, and wings distinguish this species from Little Blue and other similar-sized herons. Bill long and yellow with black tip, head and back of neck blue, base of neck and wings purplish, back feathers buff-colored during breeding. Length 66 cm (26 in); wingspan 91 cm (36 in).

HABITAT: Salt marshes, estuaries, mangrove swamps.

REGION: PAN, NFL, CFL, SFL, KEY

Plate 23f
Little Blue Heron
Egretta caerulea
ID: Smallish heron, slaty blue with darker purple neck and head, blue-green legs and feet. Bill dark gray with black tip. Breeding colors brighter, plumes long. Immatures are white and may be confused with small egrets. Note yellow and black bill, yellow legs, and slaty wingtips. Length 61 cm (24 in); wingspan 1 m (3.3 ft).

HABITAT: Freshwater ponds and marshes, coastal wetlands.

REGION: PAN, NFL, CFL, SFL, KEY

Plate 23 **321**

IM

a Cattle Egret

b Snowy Egret

c Great Egret

white form

d Reddish Egret

IM

e Tricolored Heron

f Little Blue Heron

Plate 24a
Green Heron
Butorides virescens
ID: Small, stocky, brightly marked heron. Adult has dark green back, blackish cap; neck is white beneath with bright chestnut sides; bill and legs yellowish. Solitary and often cryptic; bursts from cover when alarmed with a loud 'kiyow.' Length 46 cm (18 in); wingspan 66 cm (26 in).

HABITAT: Streams, ponds, swamps, and marshes with woody cover.

REGION: PAN, NFL, CFL, SFL, KEY

Plate 24b
Least Bittern
Ixobrychus exilis
ID: Smallest Florida heron, solitary and secretive. Adult male brown above with black crown, back, tail, and wingtips; throat streaked brown. Female similar but lighter, browner upperparts. Bill and legs yellowish. Bright buff wing patches distinctive in flight. Length 33 cm (13 in); wingspan 43 cm (17 in).

HABITAT: Predominantly freshwater marshes with dense cover of grasses, reeds, or cattails.

REGION: PAN, NFL, CFL, SFL, KEY

Plate 24c
Yellow-crowned Night-Heron
Nyctanassa violacea
ID: Medium-sized, mostly gray heron with pale yellow crown, black face with distinctive white cheek patch, short, thick black bill, and yellow legs. Wings have faint white scalloping. Breeding birds have long white plumes at back of head. Typically cryptic; an ambush hunter. Length 61 cm (24 in); wingspan 1.1 m (3.6 ft).

HABITAT: Interior hardwood swamps, mangrove and other coastal wetlands with brushy cover. Roosts in wetland and swamp trees.

REGION: PAN, NFL, CFL, SFL, KEY

Plate 24d
Limpkin
Aramus guarauna
ID: Medium-large, rail-like bird, dark brown overall with dense white streaking on upperparts that diminishes toward tail. Long neck similar to a heron's; bill long, pinkish, slightly down-curved. Legs and large feet dull gray. Distinctive, wailing cry given at night. Length 66 cm (26 in).

HABITAT: Freshwater streams, lake margins, and swamps. Range in USA almost completely restricted to Florida.

REGION: PAN, NFL, CFL, SFL, KEY

Plate 24e
Black-crowned Night-Heron
Nycticorax nycticorax
ID: Medium-sized, very stocky heron, pale gray with black cap and back. Whitish face and underparts. Breeding birds have long, white plumes at back of neck. Legs yellow. Cryptic, nocturnal. Length 64 cm (25 in); wingspan 1.1 m (3.6 ft).

HABITAT: Lakes, streams, and marshes with dense cover.

REGION: PAN, NFL, CFL, SFL, KEY

Plate 24f
Roseate Spoonbill
Ajaia ajaja
ID: Unmistakable large, rose-pink wading bird with spoon-shaped bill. Head is naked and greenish. Breeding birds have brighter pink wings with magenta or red shoulder areas, rump patch, and breast patch; orange tail; pink legs; black patch on back of head. Side-to-side sweeping of head during feeding is characteristic. Length 81 cm (32 in); wingspan 1.3 m (4.3 ft).

HABITAT: Shallow water in estuaries, coastal wetlands, and mangrove swamps.

REGION: PAN, NFL, CFL, SFL, KEY

Plate 24 **323**

a Green Heron

b Least Bittern

c Yellow-crowned Night-Heron

IM

d Limpkin

e Black-crowned Night-Heron

IM

IM

f Roseate Spoonbill

Plate 25a
Wood Stork
Mycteria americana
ID: Large, heavy-bodied white wading bird with contrasting black flight feathers and tail. Adult has naked, dark gray head. Bill is heavy, dark, slightly down-curved. Legs dark, feet yellow. Flaps slowly and soars on thermals. Unlike herons, flies with neck extended. Length 1 m (3.3 ft); wingspan 1.6 m (5.2 ft).

HABITAT: Swamps, ponds, coastal wetlands.

REGION: PAN, NFL, CFL, SFL, KEY

Plate 25b
Sandhill Crane
Grus canadensis
ID: A large, all-gray bird with long dark legs, fluffy, drooping tail feathers and naked, red crown. Bill is dark and sharply pointed, heron-like. Florida has both resident and migrant populations. Like stork, flies with neck extended. Length 1 m (3.3 ft); wingspan 1.8 m (5.9 ft).

HABITAT: Marshes, wet prairies, grasslands, farm fields, cattle pastures.

REGION: PAN, NFL, CFL, SFL

Plate 25c
Whooping Crane
Grus americana
ID: All white, larger than Sandhill Crane, with red crown and face, black mask. Bill yellowish. Black underwings seen only in flight. Distinguished in flight from Wood Stork by white tail and wing pattern, longer neck, smaller, paler head. Length 1.3 m (4.3 ft); wingspan 2.2 m (7.2 ft).

HABITAT: Marshes, wet prairies, grasslands, and farm fields. Endangered; introduced to Florida.

REGION: CFL

Plate 25d
Great Blue Heron
Ardea herodias
ID: Largest heron. Body blue-gray overall, throat streaked black and white, thighs reddish brown. Head has black stripe above eye. Bill yellow. Like other herons, breeding adult has long plumes on head, back, and breast. All-white south Florida form distinguished from Great Egret by yellowish legs. Length 1.2 m (3.9 ft); wingspan 1.8 m (5.9 ft).

HABITAT: Wide-ranging in coastal and freshwater wetlands, ponds, and lake margins, in wet fields and along roads.

REGION: PAN, NFL, CFL,SFL, KEY

Plate 25e
Glossy Ibis
Plegadis falcinellus
ID: Medium-sized, active, all-dark wading bird with long, decurved bill. In good light, breeding adult is iridescent brownish green or purple with muddy-green bill, grayish legs with dark-red joints. Length 58 cm (23 in); wingspan 91 cm (36 in).

HABITAT: Freshwater and saltwater marshes.

REGION: PAN, NFL, CFL, SFL, KEY

Plate 25f
White Ibis
Eudocimus albus
ID: All white with black wingtips visible in flight. Pinkish face, long, down-curved bill; legs deepen to bright pink or red in breeding season. Gregarious and active. Length 64 cm (25 in); wingspan 97 cm (38 in).

HABITAT: Freshwater and saltwater marshes, lake and stream margins, and mangrove swamps.

REGION: PAN, NFL, CFL, SFL, KEY

Plate 25 **325**

a Wood Stork

b Sandhill Crane

c Whooping Crane

white form

d Great Blue Heron

e Glossy Ibis

IM

f White Ibis

Plate 26a
Fulvous Whistling-Duck
Dendrocygna bicolor
ID: A large, long-necked duck, deep golden overall with a darker stripe down back of neck (broken in male), dark wings, white streaking on flanks, pale rump band visible in flight, black bill and legs. Legs visible extending beyond tail in flight. Most active at night. Loud, two-note whistle is characteristic. Length 51 cm (20 in).

HABITAT: Marshes and farm fields.

REGION: PAN, NFL, CFL, SFL

Plate 26b
Black-bellied Whistling-Duck
Dendrocygna autumnalis
ID: Similar size and shape to Fulvous Whistling Duck, but with distinctive red bill, gray face, white eye-ring and wing patch, all-black rump and tail, and pink or red legs. Lower belly is black, and in flight wings show striking, broad white stripe. Juvenile dull, lacks red bill. Arboreal nester. Whistling call is four notes. Length 53 cm (21 in).

HABITAT: Woodland ponds, streams, and marshes.

REGION: NFL, CFL, SFL

Plate 26c
Muscovy Duck
Cairina moschata
ID: Large, terrestrial duck with irregular patches of rough flesh around eyes and base of bill. Highly variable plumage ranges from all dark, iridescent green-black to all white. Non-native species, native to Central/South America. Length 71 cm (28 in).

HABITAT: Typically abundant in urban and suburban parks and ponds.

REGION: PAN, NFL, CFL, SFL, KEY

Plate 26d
Mottled Duck
Anas fulvigula
ID: All-brown plumage with lighter face, yellow bill, and orange legs in both sexes is similar to female Mallard and Black Duck, but metallic-colored patch (speculum) on Mottled's wing is blue or turquoise and has no white edging. Plumage is darker than Mallard, lighter than Black Duck, and lacks white on tail. Length 56 cm (22 in).

HABITAT: Freshwater or brackish marshes.

REGION: PAN, NFL, CFL, SFL

Plate 26e
Hooded Merganser
Lophodytes cucullatus
ID: Small diving duck with narrow, finely serrated bill. Male has black head and throat with large white patch in crest (most conspicuous when crest is raised), white breast with black band, dark back and wings with lighter stripe. Female is overall brownish with dark back and dull reddish-brown crest. Nests in cavities. Length 46 cm (18 in).

HABITAT: Ponds and lakes, hardwood swamps, and coastal saltwater creeks.

REGION: PAN, NFL, CFL, SFL, KEY

Plate 26f
Red-breasted Merganser
Mergus serrator
ID: Wintering migrant. Male has metallic green head with long, shaggy, double crest, narrow, serrated, orange bill, wide white collar, tawny breast. Back is black, wings with broad white stripe. Female has dull reddish head and crest. Female overall light gray-brown with contrasting white and black patch (speculum) on wing. Length 58 cm (23 in).

HABITAT: Typically coastal, also found on inland lakes and reservoirs.

REGION: PAN, NFL, CFL, SFL, KEY

Plate 26 **327**

a Fulvous Whistling-Duck

b Black-bellied Whistling Duck

c Muscovy Duck

d Mottled Duck

e Hooded Merganser

M

F

f Red-breasted Merganser

M

F

Plate 27a
Northern Pintail
Anas acuta
ID: Large dabbling duck with longish neck. Male has striking white breast with narrow white streak extending up back on neck into chocolate-brown head. Back and flanks gray. Long, sharp central tail feathers extend well beyond wings. Female brown overall with scaly chest and back and blue-gray bill. Wintering migrant. Length: male, 66 cm (26 in); female 51 cm (20 in).

HABITAT: Ponds, freshwater marshes, and grain fields.

REGION: PAN, NFL, CFL, SFL, KEY

Plate 27b
Northern Shoveler
Anas clypeata
ID: Very large, spoon-shaped bill is diagnostic in both sexes. Male has deep green head, white breast, reddish-brown flanks, black primary feathers, some white in black tail. Female mottled brown overall, with orange-edged bill. Wings of both sexes are blue on shoulder. Length 48 cm (19 in).

HABITAT: Freshwater lakes and ponds.

REGION: PAN, NFL, CFL, SFL, KEY

Plate 27c
Green-winged Teal
Anas crecca
ID: Florida's smallest dabbling duck. Male has rich red-brown head with iridescent green ear patch extending to neck, speckled breast, mostly brown-gray body. Female predominantly mottled brown with dark eyeline and white patch under tail. Wintering migrant. Length 37 cm (14.5 in).

HABITAT: Wet prairie, fields, shallow fresh water, and mudflats.

REGION: PAN, NFL, CFL, SFL, KEY

Plate 27d
Blue-winged Teal
Anas discors
ID: Male's blue-gray head with bright white crescent between bill and eye is diagnostic. Male's body is speckled overall; wing has blue patch on leading edge. Female distinguished from Green-winged Teal by slightly larger bill and yellow legs. Length 39 cm (15.5 in).

HABITAT: Shallow ponds, lakes, and freshwater marshes.

REGION: PAN, NFL, CFL, SFL, KEY

Plate 27 329

a Northern Pintail

F

M

b Northern Shoveler

F

M

c Green-winged Teal

F

M

M

d Blue-winged Teal

M

F

M

Plate 28a
American Wigeon
Anas americana
ID: Male has pale crown, bright green eyestripe in finely speckled face, light blue bill with black tip. Chestnut breast contrasts with white belly and black patch under tail. Metallic-colored patch on wing is green with black borders. White wing patches diagnostic in flight. Female lacks head and facial markings, has browner back and dark bill. Migrant dabbler. Length 48 cm (19 in).

HABITAT: Lakes, ponds, estuaries, and coastal wetlands.

REGION: PAN, NFL, CFL, SFL, KEY

Plate 28b
Wood Duck
Aix sponsa
ID: A medium-sized, cavity-nesting duck. Male is brilliantly and ornately patterned with green head and long crest, red eye and base of bill, white cheek patch and throat, russet chest speckled with white. Flanks beige, wings iridescent blue and purple, tail black. Female drab with white eyering and eyeline, finely streaked breast and white belly. Length 47 cm (18.5 in).

HABITAT: Woodland ponds, streams, and wetlands.

REGION: PAN, NFL, CFL, SFL, KEY

Plate 28c
Ring-necked Duck
Aythya collaris
ID: A medium-sized diving duck. Male has dark purple head and neck, black breast, back, and tail, light gray sides with white wedge extending in front of wing toward base of neck. Female brown overall with narrow eyering and eyeline extending back to ear. Both sexes have peaked heads and bills with white ring separating black tip from gray base. Primarily a wintering migrant. Length 43 cm (17 in).

HABITAT: Freshwater lakes, estuaries, and coastal waters.

REGION: PAN, NFL, CFL, SFL, KEY

Plate 28d
Lesser Scaup
Aythya affinis
ID: Very similar to Ring-necked Duck, but bill is paler and uniformly colored. Male has light gray back; white flanks lack wedge in front of wing. Female is dark brown with white patch on face surrounding bill. Primarily a wintering migrant; diver. Length 42 cm (16.5 in).

HABITAT: Deep lakes, estuaries, and bays, sometimes in developed areas.

REGION: PAN, NFL, CFL, SFL, KEY

Plate 28e
Ruddy Duck
Oxyura jamaicensis
ID: Small, chunky, diving duck. Male easily identified by stiff, black tail held erect. Breeding male has bright blue bill, white cheek patch and overall red body; white cheek retained in generally brown winter plumage. Female has dark brown head with prominent white stripe beneath eye, dark brown back with lighter, finely barred breast and sides. Often seen in large groups. Length 38 cm (15 in).

HABITAT: Estuaries and bays, inland lakes and impoundments; typically in deep water.

REGION: PAN, NFL, CFL, SFL, KEY

Plate 28 **331**

a American Wigeon

F

M

b Wood Duck

M

F

c Ring-necked Duck

F

M

d Lesser Scaup

F

M

e Ruddy Duck

F

M

Plate 29a

Black Vulture
Coragyps atratus

ID: Smaller of the two Florida vultures, with bare, dark-gray head and pale bill. Underside of wing in flight shows a whitish area near wingtip. Flaps rapidly and soars with wings held flat. Feet may show beyond short tail. Aggressive and gregarious; often seen in flocks. Length 64 cm (25 in); wingspan 1.4 m (4.6 ft).

HABITAT: Ubiquitous; most common in open country, prairies, agricultural lands, and along roadsides where carrion is abundant.

REGION: PAN, NFL, CFL, SFL, KEY

Plate 29b

Turkey Vulture
Cathartes aura

ID: Most abundant and widespread vulture. Head of adult is bare with red skin extending past nostrils; underside of wing in flight is black in front, grayish behind. Tail longer than Black Vulture. Characteristic shallow 'V' profile in flight, with tipping or rocking motion. Seldom flaps. Often seen in groups, sometimes mixed with Black Vultures, soaring on thermal updrafts. Length 69 cm (27 in); wingspan 1.7 m (5.6 ft).

HABITAT: Ubiquitous; most common in open country, prairies, agricultural lands, and along roadsides where carrion is abundant.

REGION: PAN, NFL, CFL, SFL, KEY

Plate 29c

Osprey
Pandion haliaetus

ID: Arguably Florida's most abundant bird of prey. White head with broad dark eyestripe. Back and wings dark brown above, heavily barred below with dark wingtips and patches at wrists. Throat and belly white. Female has dark streaking across breast. Holds wings slightly angled when soaring. Length 56 to 64 cm (22 to 25 in); wingspan 1.5 to 1.8 m (4.9 to 5.9 ft).

HABITAT: Fishes in open water with wooded margins; lakes, estuaries, bays, and coastal saltwater creeks.

REGION: PAN, NFL, CFL, SFL, KEY

Plate 29d

Bald Eagle
Haliaeetus leucocephalus

ID: Adult is unmistakable: very large with all-white head, neck, breast, and tail, large yellow bill and feet. Upperparts and belly dark brown. Holds wings flat while soaring. Usually seen near or over water; nests high in pines. Length 79 to 94 cm (31 to 37 in); wingspan 1.8 to 2.3 m (5.9 to 7.5 ft).

HABITAT: Lakes, estuaries, bays, and wetlands.

REGION: PAN, NFL, CFL, SFL, KEY

Plate 29 **333**

a Black Vulture

b Turkey Vulture

IM

d Bald Eagle

c Osprey

Plate 30a
White-tailed Kite
Elanus leucurus
ID: A small, uncommon kite with long, pointed wings, most often seen in South Florida. Prominent black shoulder on otherwise gray wing is diagnostic. Wings white and gray beneath, with small black wrist patch. Belly and tail white. Tail is square, fanned when bird hovers. Length 41 cm (16 in); wingspan 1.1 m (3.6 ft).

HABITAT: Wet prairies and marshes.

REGION: PAN, NFL, CFL, SFL

Plate 30b
Mississippi Kite
Ictinia mississippiensis
ID: Florida's smallest kite. Blue-gray overall with lighter head and darker wingtips and tail. Wings each have a light gray and a rusty brown patch. Distinguished from White-tailed Kite by gray underparts and dark tail. Frequently soars over urban areas. Length 37 cm (14.5 in); wingspan 89 cm (35 in).

HABITAT: North Florida hardwood forests, hammocks, and swamps.

REGION: PAN, NFL, CFL, SFL, KEY

Plate 30c
Swallow-tailed Kite
Elanoides forficatus
ID: Large, flashy kite. Long, black, deeply-forked tail and sharply contrasting black and white plumage are distinctive. Head is white, back and wings black; belly white; underside of wings in flight white in front, black behind. Flight is buoyant and agile on long, narrow, angled wings. Often takes and eats prey on the wing. Length 58 cm (23 in); wingspan 1.2 m (4 ft).

HABITAT: Forests and bottomlands with tall pines or cypress.

REGION: PAN, NFL, CFL, SFL, KEY

Plate 30d
Snail Kite
Rostrhamus sociabilis
ID: Stocky, all-dark kite with white patch at base of tail, gray band at end of dark, square tail. Bill is thinner than other kites and more sharply hooked. Male is blackish with red or orange face and feet; female dark brown with white eyebrow and facial patches, orange feet. Specialist feeder on apple snails. Length 43 cm (17 in); wingspan 1.2 m (3.9 ft).

HABITAT: Predominantly in freshwater marshes in South Florida.

REGION: CFL, SFL

Plate 30 **335**

a White-tailed Kite

c Swallow-tailed Kite

b Mississippi Kite

d Snail Kite

Plate 31a
Cooper's Hawk
Accipiter cooperii
ID: Medium-sized forest hawk with broad, relatively short wings and long, rounded tail. Charcoal-gray upperparts contrast strongly with black cap. Breast and legs finely barred with rusty red; in flight, tail white with narrow dark bands. Female larger than male. Length 36 to 51 cm (14 to 20 in); wingspan 74 to 94 cm (29 to 37 in).

HABITAT: Woodlands.

REGION: PAN, NFL, CFL, SFL, KEY

Plate 31b
Sharp-shinned Hawk
Accipiter striatus
ID: Small forest hawk with proportions and markings similar to Cooper's Hawk, but with shorter and distinctly square tail, less contrast between dark cap and back. Size is an unreliable character; female 'Sharpie' may be similar in size to male Cooper's. Wintering migrant; follows passerine prey south. Length 25 to 36 cm (10 to 14 in); wingspan 51 to 71 cm (20 to 28 in).

HABITAT: Woodlands.

REGION: PAN, NFL, CFL, SFL, KEY

Plate 31c
Broad-winged Hawk
Buteo platypterus
ID: Small soaring hawk with light underwings edged with black. Wingtips distinctly pointed. Tail banded black and white. Length 41 cm (16 in); wingspan 86 cm (34 in).

HABITAT: Hardwood and other forests, predominantly in Panhandle and North Florida.

REGION: PAN, NFL, CFL, SFL, KEY

Plate 31d
Northern Harrier
Circus cyaneus
ID: Largish hawk with round head with owl-like facial disks. Wings and tail are long; white rump patch is distinctive. Male is gray above with black wingtips and lighter beneath. Larger female is brown above, light below and heavily streaked, with banded tail. Wintering migrant. Typically forages by flying low over open areas with low or scrubby vegetation. Flight is often 'tippy,' somewhat like Turkey Vulture's. Length 43 to 58 cm (17 to 23 in); wingspan 1 to 1.2 m (3.3 to 3.9 ft).

HABITAT: Open country: fields, wet prairies, marshes, coastal wetlands.

REGION: PAN, NFL, CFL, SFL, KEY

Plate 31 **337**

a Cooper's Hawk

IM

IM

b Sharp-shinned Hawk →

← **c** Broad-winged Hawk

a Cooper's Hawk

M

d Northern Harrier

F

Plate 32a
Short-tailed Hawk
Buteo brachyurus
ID: A mid-sized hawk with two color forms: one with dark brown underparts spotted with white, one with dark helmet and white underparts. All birds have dark face and wingtips, barred flight feathers, and dark band on tail. Range in USA restricted to peninsular Florida. Length 39 cm (15.5 in); wingspan 89 cm (35 in).

HABITAT: Woodlands with nearby prairie or wetland.

REGION: CFL, SFL, KEY

Plate 32b
American Kestrel
Falco sparverius
ID: The smallest and most brightly colored North American falcon, often seen perched on telephone wires. All birds have two black, vertical bars on face, reddish-brown back, and broad, black band at tail end. Male has red crown on blue head, and blue-gray wings; female has reddish-brown wings, barred tail. Length 27 cm (10.5 in); wingspan 58 cm (23 in).

HABITAT: Farm fields, pastures, prairies; nests in tree cavities.

REGION: PAN, NFL, CFL, SFL, KEY

Plate 32c
Red-tailed Hawk
Buteo jamaicensis
ID: Most common large soaring hawk. Stocky with rounded wings. Upperparts dark brown overall with variable white mottling in shoulder feathers. Red tail and dark belly band are distinctive, as are dark wingtips and leading edge in flight. Length 56 cm (22 in); wingspan 1.3 m (4.3 ft).

HABITAT: Widespread across habitat types; most frequent over fields, pastures, prairies, and wetlands.

REGION: PAN, NFL, CFL, SFL, KEY

Plate 32d
Red-shouldered Hawk
Buteo lineatus
ID: Largish hawk with rusty barred underparts, reddish-brown shoulder patch, longish legs and tail. Distinguished from Broad-winged Hawk in flight by rusty patches under wings, white patches behind dark wingtips, and more rounded wings. The loud, measured 'keh-keh-keh' call is a characteristic sound of Florida woodlands. Length 48 cm (19 in); wingspan 1 m (3.3 ft).

HABITAT: Moist woodlands, mixed hardwood, and pine forests.

REGION: PAN, NFL, CFL, SFL, KEY

Plate 32e
Crested Caracara
Caracara cheriway
ID: Striking, long-legged, large-headed bird with black crown and crest, red-orange facial skin. White throat and neck grade into black belly. Wings and back black with white 'windows' near wingtips. Tail barred with dark band at end. May be seen in company with vultures. Length 58 cm (23 in); wingspan 1.3 m (4.3 ft).

HABITAT: Open country, especially palmetto savanna, grasslands, and pastures.

REGION: CFL, SFL

Plate 32   **339**

dark form

light form

b American Kestrel

F

M

a Short-tailed Hawk

c Red-tailed Hawk

d Red-shouldered Hawk

e Crested Caracara

Plate 33a
Purple Gallinule
Porphyrula martinica
ID: A large, dark rail with iridescent green back, rich purple head, neck, and underparts. Forehead shield light blue. Short, thick bill is red with orange-yellow tip. Legs and large, unwebbed feet are yellow. Somewhat cryptic, but more easily seen than many other rails. Length 33 cm (13 in).

HABITAT: Freshwater marshes, swamps; edges of ponds, lakes, canals, and impoundments.

REGION: PAN, NFL, CFL, SFL, KEY

Plate 33b
Clapper Rail
Rallus longirostris
ID: A large, long-billed rail with dark gray face and white throat. Brown wing and back feathers edged with gray. Brownish-gray neck grades into gray- and white-barred sides. Secretive, forages within or at edge of wetland vegetation; seldom flies. Length 37 cm (14.5 in).

HABITAT: All coasts; salt marshes, and mangrove swamps.

REGION: PAN, NFL, CFL, SFL, KEY

Plate 33c
Common Moorhen
Gallinula chloropus
ID: Common freshwater rail. Somewhat similar to Purple Galinule, but slightly larger and stockier, black overall with deep green-brown back and white streaking on flanks. Red forehead shield and yellow-tipped bill. Often forages in small groups, in open water near vegetated edges. Length 36 cm (14 in).

HABITAT: Freshwater marshes, ponds, lakes, canals, and impoundments; less common in salt marshes.

REGION: PAN, NFL, CFL, SFL, KEY

Plate 33d
American Coot
Fulica americana
ID: Most abundant, gregarious, and conspicuous rail. Body is similar to Moorhen in shape but slightly larger, and coots swim like ducks (with which they commonly forage). White bill and shield are characteristic; forehead shield is sometimes dark red. Plumage is black with gray breast and white rump. Large, greenish feet are lobed, making this bird a strong swimmer. Length 39 cm (15.5 in).

HABITAT: Freshwater marshes, ponds, lakes, canals and impoundments; estuaries, bays, and salt marshes.

REGION: PAN, NFL, CFL, SFL, KEY

Plate 33e
Northern Bobwhite
Colinus virginianus
ID: Small, round game bird, more often heard than seen. Call is a loud, ascending, two-note whistle, 'bob-WHITE.' Plumage red-brown, scaled and spotted with white. Male has rusty crest, white throat, and broad, white line through eye. Female has tawny throat and eyeline. Groups typically forage under dense cover. Length 25 cm (10 in).

HABITAT: Pine forests, fields, and pastures.

REGION: PAN, NFL, CFL, SFL

Plate 33f
Wild Turkey
Meleagris gallopavo
ID: Male is dark, iridescent brown-green with dark breast tuft and white barring on wings. Rump and tail feathers have red-brown edges. Head is naked with blue and red skin and red wattle. Female smaller and more drab overall with gray skin on head. Largest chicken-like bird in Florida. Length 94 to 117 cm (37 to 46 in).

HABITAT: Widespread in least-disturbed forests.

REGION: PAN, NFL, CFL, SFL

Plate 33 **341**

a Purple Gallinule

IM

b Clapper Rail

c Common Moorhen

IM

e Northern Bobwhite

F

M

IM

d American Coot

f Wild Turkey

M

F

Plate 34a

Black-bellied Plover
Pluvialis squatarola

ID: Large plover with short, black bill and large eye. Overall pale gray with white feather edges, underparts white with gray streaking. Dark legs. Black patch under wing and white rump in flight are diagnostic. Mostly a winter resident. Length 29 cm (11 in).

HABITAT: Beaches, mud flats; less often seen along inland lakeshores.

REGION: PAN, NFL, CFL, SFL, KEY

Plate 34b

Snowy Plover
Charadrius alexandrinus

ID: Florida's smallest plover, pale with black marks on fore-crown, cheek, and shoulder during breeding. Upperparts uniform gray, underparts white, legs black. Bill slender. Length 16 cm (6.3 in).

HABITAT: Gulf coast beaches and sand flats only, primarily in Panhandle.

REGION: PAN, NFL, CFL, SFL

Plate 34c

Wilson's Plover
Charadrius wilsonia

ID: Small, dark plover with long, heavy bill and pink legs. Upperparts brownish gray, white beneath with single wide neck-ring, black in breeding males. Length 20 cm (8 in).

HABITAT: Beaches, barrier islands, and sand flats.

REGION: PAN, NFL, CFL, SFL, KEY

Plate 34d

Semipalmated Plover
Charadrius semipalmatus

ID: Darkest small plover. Upperparts brown, single neck-ring and fore-crown black in breeding males. Distinguished from Wilson's Plover by smaller size, darker color, tiny orange and black bill, yellow-orange legs, partially webbed feet. Often forages in large groups with other small shorebirds.

HABITAT: Beaches and mudflats.

REGION: PAN, NFL, CFL, SFL, KEY

Plate 34e

Killdeer
Charadrius vociferus

ID: Common inland plover. Dark above, white below with distinctive double neck-rings and orange rump. Legs pale. Loud call, 'kill-dee' or 'dee-dee-dee,' especially when flushed. Erratic flight with deep wingbeats. Length 27 cm (10.5 in).

HABITAT: Fields, pastures, city parks, lake and pond shores.

REGION: PAN, NFL, CFL, SFL, KEY

Plate 34f

American Oystercatcher
Haematopus palliatus

ID: Largest and most striking shorebird, with black head and neck, red eyering, long, heavy, scarlet bill. Upperparts dark brown, wings and rump with white patches that show as a 'V' in flight. Underparts white, legs pink. Loud, rapid, piping whistle when flushed. Length 47 cm (18.5 in).

HABITAT: Beaches, barrier islands, oyster bars, sand and mudflats on both coasts.

REGION: PAN, NFL, CFL, SFL, KEY

Plate 34 **343**

a Black-bellied Plover

NB

B

b Snowy Plover

c Wilson's Plover

d Semipalmated Plover

e Killdeer

f American Oystercatcher

Plate 35a
Marbled Godwit
Limosa fedoa
ID: Large, brownish shorebird. Very long bill is pinkish at base, black and slightly up-curved at tip. Upperparts mottled black and brown, underparts tawny, more barred in breeding plumage. Legs gray. Length 46 cm (18 in).

HABITAT: Beaches and mudflats.

REGION: PAN, NFL, CFL, SFL

Plate 35b
Black-necked Stilt
Himantopus mexicanus
ID: Delicate wader with very long, red or pink legs, long, thin, black bill, contrasting plumage. Upperparts black with white patch over eye, underparts white. Highly vocal, call a loud 'kip-kip-kip.' Length 36 cm (14 in).

HABITAT: Shallow water, freshwater and saltwater wetlands.

REGION: PAN, NFL, CFL, SFL, KEY

Plate 35c
Greater Yellowlegs
Tringa melanoleuca
ID: Medium-sized gray shorebird with long, yellow to orange legs. Head, neck, and flanks gray and slightly streaked, back and wings darker and speckled with white. Underparts white. Bill thinner than Willet's, lighter at base, slightly up-turned. Call is three or more 'tew' notes. Length 36 cm (14 in).

HABITAT: Shallow marshes and lakes, flooded fields, lakes, and mudflats.

REGION: PAN, NFL, CFL, SFL, KEY

Plate 35d
Lesser Yellowlegs
Tringa flavipes
ID: Separated from very similar Greater Yellowlegs by smaller size, all-black, thinner, and very straight bill, higher-pitched and shorter call. Legs never orange. Often forages with Greater Yellowlegs, legs frequently submerged. Length 27 cm (10.5 in).

HABITAT: Shallow marshes and lakes, flooded fields, lakes, and mudflats.

REGION: PAN, NFL, CFL, SFL, KEY

Plate 35e
American Avocet
Recurvirostra americana
ID: Very long-legged wader with long, thin, up-curved bill. Male's bill less curved. Head and neck pale gray, but rusty orange in breeding plumage. Upperparts black with long white wedges in wings. Underparts white. Feeds by sweeping bill from side to side while walking through shallow water. Length 46 cm (18 in).

HABITAT: Primarily coastal wetlands; also flooded fields and ponds.

REGION: PAN, NFL, CFL, SFL, KEY

Plate 35f
Willet
Catoptrophorus semipalmatus
ID: Medium-sized, chunky, gray shorebird with straight black bill. Legs pale blue-gray. Distinctive black-and-white underwing pattern in flight. Winter birds unmarked gray above, lighter underneath. Breeding birds have mottled brown back and wings. Length 38 cm (15 in).

HABITAT: Beaches, mudflats, salt marshes; less common inland in flooded fields and phosphate mine pits.

REGION: PAN, NFL, CFL, SFL, KEY

Plate 35 **345**

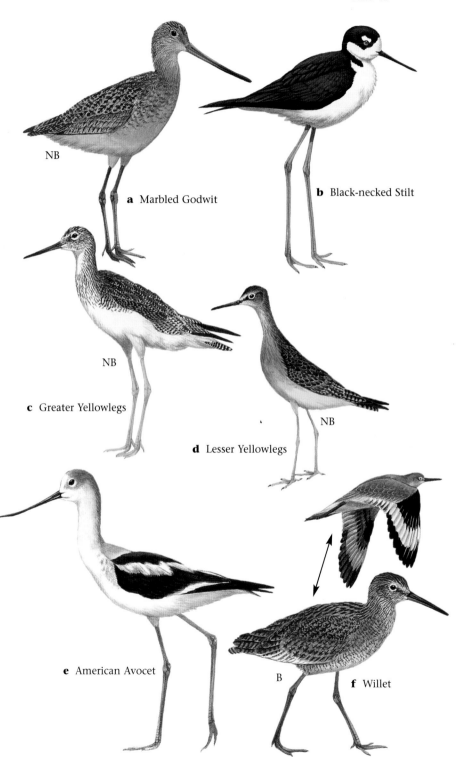

NB
a Marbled Godwit

b Black-necked Stilt

NB
c Greater Yellowlegs

NB
d Lesser Yellowlegs

e American Avocet

B
f Willet

Plate 36a

Spotted Sandpiper
Acititis macularia

ID: Small, inland sandpiper. Gray upperparts, faint barring or scalloping in shoulder area. Gray wash on neck; underparts otherwise white. Bill straight, shorter than Solitary Sandpiper's. Flies with stiff, rapid wingbeats. Typically seen alone or in pairs, standing on rocks, sand bars, muddy shores, bobbing its tail. Length 19 cm (7.5 in).

HABITAT: Streams, ponds, swamps, and marshes.

REGION: PAN, NFL, CFL, SFL, KEY

Plate 36b

Sanderling
Calidris alba

ID: Arguably the most common small sandpiper on beaches; smaller than Red Knot or Dunlin. Pale gray above with black at the wrist. Clear white underparts. Straight black bill is longer than Snowy Plover's. Legs black. Length 20 cm (8 in).

HABITAT: Beaches on both coasts.

REGION: PAN, NFL, CFL, SFL, KEY

Plate 36c

Least Sandpiper
Calidris minutilla

ID: Smallest shorebird. Bill short, thin, and slightly down-curved, legs yellowish (but often obscured by mud). Darker above than Semipalmated or Western Sandpiper, and with brown band across breast. Length 15 cm (6 in).

HABITAT: Beaches, mudflats, marsh and pond edges.

REGION: PAN, NFL, CFL, SFL, KEY

Plate 36d

Semipalmated Sandpiper
Calidris pusilla

ID: Gray upperparts, white underparts, short, thick bill, black legs. Distinguished from Least Sandpiper by lighter plumage, black legs, thicker, straighter bill. Distinguished from Western Sandpiper by stouter appearance, different bill shape, clear white breast. Length 16 cm (6.3 in).

HABITAT: Beaches, mudflats, marsh and pond edges.

REGION: PAN, NFL, CFL, SFL, KEY

Plate 36e

Western Sandpiper
Calidris mauri

ID: Gray above and white below with black legs like Semipalmated Sandpiper, but with longer, thinner, tapered bill, and sometimes with faint streaking in center of breast. Length 17 cm (6.5 in).

HABITAT: Beaches and mudflats.

REGION: PAN, NFL, CFL, SFL, KEY

Plate 36f

Solitary Sandpiper
Tringa solitaria

ID: Gray above; lightly streaked head contrasts with darker, white-speckled back and wings. Like Spotted Sandpiper (also gray above, light below), usually solitary, teeters and bobs; distinguished by slightly larger size and longer bill, darker and more speckled wings. Darker legs than Greater and Lesser Yellowlegs. Length 22 cm (8.5 in).

HABITAT: Streams, ponds, swamps, marshes.

REGION: PAN, NFL, CFL, SFL, KEY

Plate 36 **347**

a Spotted Sandpiper

NB

b Sanderling

NB

c Least Sandpiper

NB

f Solitary Sandpiper

NB

d Semipalmated Sandpiper

NB

e Western Sandpiper

NB

Plate 37a

Dunlin
Calidris alpina

ID: Smallish shorebird, upperparts gray-brown, breast washed with gray. Toward spring may show black belly patch and reddish-brown back feathers. Longish bill is gently down-curved. Legs black. Large flocks. Length 22 cm (8.5 cm).

HABITAT: Primarily coastal: beaches, mudflats, and lagoons; less common inland.

REGION: PAN, NFL, CFL, SFL, KEY

Plate 37b

Short-billed Dowitcher
Limnodromus griseus

ID: Medium-sized, dark shorebird with long, straight bill. Brownish-gray scalloped or mottled upperparts, gray breast. Close view may reveal fine, dark speckles on breast. Call is a soft 'pew-pew-pew.' Typically forages in mud or shallow water; bill moves with 'sewing-machine' motion. Tail appears paler than Long-billed Dowitcher in flight. Length 28 cm (11 in).

HABITAT: Mudflats and shallow water on coasts and on marshes and lakeshores inland.

REGION: PAN, NFL, CFL, SFL, KEY

Plate 37c

Long-billed Dowitcher
Limnodromus scolopaceus

ID: Very similar to Short-billed Dowitcher in appearance and habits. Best separated by voice; Long-billed's call is a single squeaky 'keek.' Also note slightly darker tail in flight, and darker, less spotted breast. Length 29 cm (11.5 in).

HABITAT: Mudflats and shallow water on coasts and on marshes and lakeshores inland.

REGION: PAN, NFL, CFL, SFL

Plate 37d

Red Knot
Calidris canutus

ID: Mid-sized shorebird, pale gray above and white below, with speckled breast and flanks. Bill relatively shorter and thicker than Dunlin's. Legs short and greenish. Early fall birds may show remains of reddish-brown belly and back. Length 27 cm (10.5 in).

HABITAT: Beaches on both coasts.

REGION: PAN, NFL, CFL, SFL, KEY

Plate 37e

Common Snipe
Gallinago gallinago

ID: Short-legged and stocky with very long bill, pronounced dark stripes on head and through eye. Upperparts dark with longitudinal light lines on back; flanks heavily barred, belly white. Cryptic in marsh vegetation; flight is erratic and darting when flushed. Length 27 cm (10.5 in).

HABITAT: Wet prairies, marshes, and lake edges.

REGION: PAN, NFL, CFL, SFL, KEY

Plate 37f

Ruddy Turnstone
Arenaria interpres

ID: Medium-sized and chunky shorebird with short, narrow bill. Head, back, and wings are dark, scaly brownish; underparts white with black bib. Legs orange. Distinctive, high-contrast pattern on back and wings in flight. Typically forages in small groups on beaches; flips debris with bill. Length 24 cm (9.5 in).

HABITAT: Beaches, mudflats, and coastal wetlands; less common inland.

REGION: PAN, NFL, CFL, SFL, KEY

Plate 37 **349**

NB **a** Dunlin

B

b Short-billed Dowitcher

NB

NB

c Long-billed Dowitcher

NB

d Red Knot

B

e Common Snipe

B

f Ruddy Turnstone

NB

Plate 38a
Bonaparte's Gull
Larus philadelphia

ID: Very small, pale gull with dark patch behind eye and black bill. Legs pink or orange. Light gray back and wings, and white wedge on leading edge of wing in flight. Flight is buoyant, tern-like. Wintering migrant. Length 34 cm (13.5 in); wingspan 84 cm (33 in).

HABITAT: Primarily coastal, rarely inland.

REGION: PAN, NFL, CFL, SFL, KEY

Plate 38b
Laughing Gull
Larus atricilla

ID: Florida's only breeding gull. Medium-sized. Breeding birds have black head and red bill. Back and wings dark gray, with black wingtips. Legs red-black. Winter adults have light head washed with gray, darker bill. Length 42 cm (16.5 in); wingspan 1 m (3.3 ft).

HABITAT: Primarily coastal beaches, less common over lakes inland. Nests on barrier islands.

REGION: PAN, NFL, CFL, SFL, KEY

Plate 38c
Ring-billed Gull
Larus delawarensis

ID: Slightly larger and stockier than Laughing Gull. White head mottled with brown, back and wings light gray, wingtip black with white 'windows' near very tip. Bill yellow with black ring near tip, legs yellow. Wintering migrant. Most common gull in Florida, especially inland. Length 45 cm (17.5 in); wingspan 1.2 cm (4 ft).

HABITAT: Coasts and inland lakes and impoundments.

REGION: PAN, NFL, CFL, SFL, KEY

Plate 38d
Herring Gull
Larus argentatus

ID: Large, light-colored gull with brown streaked head, pale gray back and wings, black wingtips with white 'windows.' Heavy, yellow bill has red spot on lower mandible. Legs pink. Wintering migrant. Length 64 cm (25 in); wingspan 1.5 m (4.8 ft).

HABITAT: Beaches on both coasts, and garbage dumps.

REGION: PAN, NFL, CFL, SFL, KEY

Plate 38e
Great Black-backed Gull
Larus marinus

ID: Largest gull; size and black back and wings distinctive. White wingtips. Bill pale to bright yellow; adult with red spot on lower mandible, younger birds with black bill tip. Legs pink. Wintering migrant. Length 76 cm (30 in); wingspan 1.6 m (5.2 ft).

HABITAT: Uncommon, more frequent on Atlantic than Gulf coast.

REGION: PAN, NFL, CFL, SFL, KEY

Plate 38f
Black Skimmer
Rynchops niger

ID: Unmistakable, large tern with heavy, red and black bill. Lower mandible longer than upper is diagnostic. Black cap, back and wings, black stripe in center of shallow-forked tail. Short, red legs. Often flies low, dragging lower mandible through water. Often in large flocks, with other terns. Length 46 cm (18 in); wingspan 1.1 m (3.6 ft).

HABITAT: Both coasts throughout state, inland lakes and flooded fields in Peninsula.

REGION: PAN, NFL, CFL, SFL, KEY

Plate 38 **351**

a Bonaparte's Gull

NB

NB

b Laughing Gull

B

NB

c Ring-billed Gull

NB

Herring Gull

NB

IM

f Black Skimmer

NB

e Great Black-backed Gull

Plate 39a
Roseate Tern
Sterna dougallii
ID: Medium-sized with almost white back and wings, black cap and nape. White underparts have a pink sheen in good light. Black bill is red at base, red-orange feet. Flies with rapid wingbeats. Length 39 cm (15.5 in); wingspan 74 cm (29 in).

HABITAT: Coastal, mainly Dry Tortugas and Keys; casual to rare along Gulf coast, rare elsewhere in state.

REGION: PAN, NFL, CFL, SFL, KEY

Plate 39b
Least Tern
Sterna antillarum
ID: Smallest tern. Black crown and nape. Black through eye creates white window on forehead. Back and wings light gray with darker wingtips. White tail is broad and deeply forked. Longish bill yellow, feet yellow. Often nests on graveled rooftops and other human-made structures. Length 23 in (9 in); wingspan 51 cm (20 in).

HABITAT: Beaches and islands; less common inland.

REGION: PAN, NFL, CFL, SFL, KEY

Plate 39c
Forster's Tern
Sterna forsteri
ID: Small, common tern. Pale gray back and wings, long, deeply forked tail, white underparts. Winter birds have black patch through and behind eye and black bill. Feet red. Distinguished from Roseate Tern by slower, deeper wingbeats, slightly smaller size. Migrant. Length 37 cm (14.5 in); wingspan 79 cm (31 in).

HABITAT: Coastal beaches and salt marshes; inland over lakes and wetlands.

REGION: PAN, NFL, CFL, SFL, KEY

Plate 39d
Sandwich Tern
Sterna sandvicensis
ID: Medium-sized tern with larger head, longer neck and bill than others of similar size. Bill is slender and black with yellow tip. Back and wings pale with darker wedge at wingtip. Tail white and forked. Breeding birds have black cap and nape with short, fluffy crest; winter birds have mottled black cap and crest. Length 38 cm (15 in); wingspan 86 cm (34 in).

HABITAT: Beaches along both coasts, primarily in Peninsular Florida.

REGION: CFL, SFL, KEY

Plate 39e
Caspian Tern
Sterna caspia
ID: Florida's largest tern, with heavy, crimson bill, black wingtips, and broad, shallowly forked tail. Back and wings gray. Breeding birds have black cap, winter birds mottled gray cap. Call is deep and harsh. Length 53 cm (21 in); wingspan 1.3 m (4.3 ft).

HABITAT: Beaches along both coasts, less frequent inland.

REGION: PAN, NFL, CFL, SFL, KEY

Plate 39f
Royal Tern
Sterna maxima
ID: Large tern, similar in appearance to Caspian Tern. Distinguished by more slender, yellow-orange bill, lighter underwings, and slight crest. Winter birds have light, mottled black cap. Voice higher-pitched than Caspian's. Often encountered in large flocks. Length 51 cm (20 in); wingspan 1 m (3.3 ft).

HABITAT: Beaches along both coasts.

REGION: PAN, NFL, CFL, SFL, KEY

Plate 39 **353**

a Roseate Tern

b Least Tern

NB

B

c Forster's Tern

NB

d Sandwich Tern

NB

e Caspian Tern

B

f Royal Tern

B

NB

Plate 40a
White-crowned Pigeon
Columba leucocephala
ID: Large, dark pigeon with rounded wings and square tail. Light cap is pure white in males, gray-white in females. Nests in mangroves, moves inland to feed. Length 34 cm (13.5 in).

HABITAT: South Florida coastal areas and Keys only.

REGION: SFL, KEY

Plate 40b
Eurasian Collared-Dove
Streptopelia decaocto
ID: Overall pale beige dove with browner back and shoulders; black at ends of wings; black band on nape. Breast lighter, tail broader and paler than Mourning Dove's. Non-native species, dispersed to Florida from introduced population in Bahamas. Length 32 cm (12.5 in).

HABITAT: Throughout state but typically restricted to developed areas.

REGION: PAN, NFL, CFL, SFL, KEY

Plate 40c
Mourning Dove
Zenaida macroura
ID: Abundant dove with long, sharply pointed tail. Brownish upperparts with black spots on wings. Underparts lighter with rosy wash in good light. Sad call, 'woo-OO, woo-woo-woo' is a common sound in residential areas. Length 31 cm (12 in).

HABITAT: Throughout state in urban and rural as well as native habitats.

REGION: PAN, NFL, CFL, SFL, KEY

Plate 40d
White-winged Dove
Zenaida asiatica
ID: Stockier than Mourning Dove, with more rounded tail. End of wings black with white crescent at wrist, which shows as a narrow line on perched bird. Red eye surrounded by blue skin. Breeding population introduced; naturally a migrant in South Florida. Length 29 cm (11.5 in).

HABITAT: Primarily in human-modified landscapes.

REGION: PAN, NFL, CFL, SFL, KEY

Plate 40e
Common Ground-Dove
Columbina passerina
ID: Tiny, plump dove. Sleek, brownish back contrasts with scaly plumage on head and breast. Wings with black spots, bright ruddy wingtips best seen in flight. Short tail. Male has slaty blue crown and nape and pink breast and belly; female more drab. Foraging birds frequently bob their heads. Length 17 cm (6.5 in).

HABITAT: Open woodlands, pastures, and fields.

REGION: PAN, NFL, CFL, SFL, KEY

Plate 40   **355**

a White-crowned Pigeon

b Eurasian Collared-Dove

c Mourning Dove

d White-winged Dove

e Common Ground-Dove

M

F

Plate 41a

Monk Parakeet
Myiopsitta monachus
ID: Small green parrot with pale gray forehead, cheek, and breast. Blue on wings seen mostly in flight. Gregarious and noisy. Most common parrot in South Florida, smaller populations throughout state. Introduced species, native to South America. Length 29 cm (11.5 in).

HABITAT: Urban, suburban, and agricultural habitats.

REGION: NFL, CFL, SFL, KEY

Plate 41b

Yellow-chevroned Parakeet
Brotogeris chiriri
ID: Green (a bit lighter than White-winged Parakeet) with darker wingtips and bright yellow wing patches. Smaller than Monk Parakeet, range more restricted. Forages and roosts in small groups. Introduced species, native to South America. Length 22 cm (8.75 in).

HABITAT: Most common in suburban and residential areas in South, less common in Central Florida.

REGION: CFL, SFL

Plate 41c

White-winged Parakeet
Brotogeris versicolorus
ID: Green (a bit darker than Yellow-chevroned Parakeet) with darker wingtips and white and bright yellow wing patches. Smaller than Monk Parakeet, range more restricted. Forages and roosts in small groups. Introduced species, native to South America. Length 22 cm (8.75 in).

HABITAT: Most common in suburban and residential areas in South, less common in Central Florida.

REGION: CFL, SFL

Plate 41d

Yellow-billed Cuckoo
Coccyzus americanus
ID: Upperparts dark brown with reddish-brown primary feathers. Underparts white. Long tail has white feather tips, and shows as strong black and white barring underneath. Narrow yellow eyering. Sharp, down-curved bill has yellow lower mandible. Heard more than seen, call consists of hollow 'tok' and 'ka-klop' notes. Most common and widespread Florida cuckoo. Length 31 cm (12 in).

HABITAT: Woodlands, riparian forests, and orchards.

REGION: PAN, NFL, CFL, SFL, KEY

Plate 41e

Mangrove Cuckoo
Coccyzus minor
ID: Very similar in appearance to Yellow-billed Cuckoo; distinguished by black patch behind eye, tawny underparts, and limited distribution. Voice more gutteral and monotonous. Length 31 cm (12 in).

HABITAT: Coastal mangrove forests from Keys up Gulf Coast to Tampa Bay.

REGION: CFL, SFL, KEY

Plate 41f

Smooth-billed Ani
Crotophaga ani
ID: Large, black cuckoo with iridescent brown wash. Tail is long and broad, frequently wagged when bird is perched. Distinguished from large grackles by deep, heavy bill with flattened shield extending up forehead. Gregarious; often forages in disturbed, scrubby vegetation; often associated with cattle. Length 37 cm (14.5 in).

HABITAT: Scrub, fields, and pastures in subtropical Florida.

REGION: CFL, SFL

Plate 41 **357**

a Monk Parakeet

b Yellow-chevroned Parakeet

c White-winged Parakeet

d Yellow-billed Cuckoo

e Mangrove Cuckoo

f Smooth-billed Ani

Plate 42a
Barn Owl
Tyto alba
ID: Distinctive white, heart-shaped face with dark eyes. Upperparts tawny brown or lighter with pale speckling; underparts range from white to brown. Nests and roosts in cavities in trees, attics, barns, and other seldom-used buildings. Hissing or thin screeching call. Common, nocturnal. Length 41 cm (16 in).

HABITAT: Woodlands, residential and urban areas.

REGION: PAN, NFL, CFL, SFL, KEY

Plate 42b
Eastern Screech-Owl
Megascops asio
ID: Florida's smallest owl, with prominent ear tufts, yellow eyes, and light underparts vertically barred and streaked with brown and black. Upperparts brown in most birds; red and gray forms also present. Call is a quavering, descending trill or a monotone whir.

HABITAT: Widely distributed in native forests and human-modified environments.

REGION: PAN, NFL, CFL, SFL, KEY

Plate 42c
Barred Owl
Strix varia
ID: Medium-large owl with smooth, round head, distinctly marked facial disks, and dark eyes. Brown overall, mottled with white on upperparts and vertically streaked on breast and belly. Characteristic call, 'who-cooks-for-YOU?' often heard during daylight. Nests in tree cavities. Length 53 cm (21 in).

HABITAT: Forests and woodlands throughout state, especially hardwood forests.

REGION: PAN, NFL, CFL, SFL

Plate 42d
Great Horned Owl
Bubo virginianus
ID: Large, stocky owl with fluffy ear tufts; round, cinnamon facial disks, yellow eyes, and white throat. Upperparts mottled brown and tawny. Characteristic call a series of three or more deep, loud hoots, first long note often followed by two short, rapid notes. Crepuscular to nocturnal. Length 56 cm (22 in).

HABITAT: Widespread; often in rural or residential areas.

REGION: PAN, NFL, CFL, SFL

Plate 42e
Burrowing Owl
Athene cunicularia
ID: Small owl with long legs, prominent white facial markings. Brown overall, strongly spotted and barred with white. Flies low, sometimes hovers over prey like a kestrel. Nocturnal. Nests in burrows and forages in open country. Length 24 cm (9.5 in).

HABITAT: Dry prairies, pastures, fields, and golf courses.

REGION: PAN, NFL, CFL, SFL, KEY

Plate 42 **359**

a Barn Owl

red form

b Eastern Screech-Owl

c Barred Owl

d Great Horned Owl

IM

IM

e Burrowing Owl

Plate 43a
Chuck-will's-widow
Caprimulgus carolinensis
ID: Largest nightjar; nocturnal and secretive. Tawny brown and mottled overall with pale band on throat. Rounded wings and long, rounded tail. Far more often heard than seen. Distinctive call is 'chuck-WILL'S-WIDow;' first syllable may or may not be audible. Sometimes observed sitting on road, eyes reflect reddish color in car headlights. Length 31 cm (12 in).

HABITAT: Woodlands and rural areas.

REGION: PAN, NFL, CFL, SFL, KEY

Plate 43b
Common Nighthawk
Chordeiles minor
ID: Common, agile nightjar, like oversized swift; often seen foraging in groups at sunset. In flight, white bars across wings are distinctive. Wings long and pointed, tail long, forked. Mottled black and brown overall with barred underparts. Male has white throat and tail band, female has buffy throat. Characteristic, nasal call, 'peent.' Length 24 cm (9.5 in).

HABITAT: Cosmopolitan in urban and rural areas as well as native habitats.

REGION: PAN, NFL, CFL, SFL, KEY

Plate 43c
Antillean Nighthawk
Chordeiles gundlachii
ID: Almost identical to Common Nighthawk; may appear buffier underneath in good light. Best separated by its call, a three-syllable 'pit-pit-pit.'

HABITAT: South Florida and Keys only.

REGION: SFL, KEY

Plate 43d
Ruby-throated Hummingbird
Archilochus colubris
ID: Florida's smallest bird and, excepting vagrants, its only 'hummer.' Dark metallic green above. Male has shining magenta throat, dark sides and belly. Female has pale underparts with some buff on flanks and speckling on throat. Length 10 cm (3.75 in).

HABITAT: Widespread in wooded, rural, and residential areas.

REGION: PAN, NFL, CFL, SFL, KEY

Plate 43 **361**

a Chuck-will's-widow

b Common Nighthawk

c Antillean Nighthawk

d Ruby-throated Hummingbird

Plate 44a
Belted Kingfisher
Ceryle alcyon
ID: Slate-blue with large, crested head, large bill. White ring around throat and white belly; female has cinnamon sides and band across belly. Harsh, chattering call carries long distances. Ubiquitous but solitary and territorial. Nests in burrows in sandy banks. The only kingfisher in most of the USA. Length 33 cm (13 in).

HABITAT: Along rivers, streams, lake shores, wetlands, estuaries, and salt marshes.

REGION: PAN, NFL, CFL, SFL, KEY

Plate 44b
Yellow-bellied Sapsucker
Sphyrapicus varius
ID: Both sexes have red forehead, black and white facial pattern, black and white wings, black bib, and underparts washed with pale yellow. Male has red throat, female's is white. Wintering migrant. Length 22 cm (8.5 in).

HABITAT: Wooded habitats throughout.

REGION: PAN, NFL, CFL, SFL, KEY

Plate 44c
Red-headed Woodpecker
Melanerpes erythrocephalus
ID: Flashy woodpecker with crimson head and throat, black and white upperparts and white underparts. Bright white wing patches and rump flash conspicuously in flight. Typical call a sudden, loud, and harsh 'quirr.' Often seen on wooden telephone and power poles. Length 24 cm (9.25 in).

HABITAT: Patchily distributed in open forests, woodlands, and residential areas.

REGION: PAN, NFL, CFL, SFL, KEY

Plate 44d
Red-bellied Woodpecker
Melanerpes carolinus
ID: Stocky, bold woodpecker. Back and wings barred black and white, rump white. Face and underparts grayish with reddish patch on belly. Male has bright red hood, female has red nape. Common feeder bird. Length 24 cm (9.25 in).

HABITAT: Most common in open or disturbed woodlands, suburban and residential areas.

REGION: PAN, NFL, CFL, SFL, KEY

Plate 44   **363**

a Belted Kingfisher

F

M

F

M

b Yellow-bellied
Sapsucker

c Red-headed
Woodpecker

d Red-bellied
Woodpecker

F

M

Plate 45a
Red-cockaded Woodpecker
Picoides borealis
ID: Small woodpecker with black and white barred back, black cap, and white cheek. Male's red head tufts rarely visible except on juveniles. Underparts white, with black streaks on flank. Call a single harsh 'sreep' or 'tsik;' voice deeper and more raspy than Downy Woodpecker. Excavates cavities only in live pine trees. Length 22 cm (8.5 in).

HABITAT: Restricted to mature pine forests, and pine-oak woodlands.

REGION: PAN, NFL, CFL, SFL

Note: This species is endangered, USA ESA listed.

Plate 45b
Downy Woodpecker
Picoides pubescens
ID: Smallest Florida woodpecker, with tiny bill. Black and white barred wings, black cheek patch in white face, black crown. Underparts clear white. Back of male's head is red. Distinguished from Red-cockaded Woodpecker by smaller size, solid white back, and voice. Call is a high, squeaky 'peek' or loud, 'bouncing-ball' trill. Length 17 cm (6.75 in).

HABITAT: Fairly ubiquitous in woodlands, suburban and rural areas.

REGION: PAN, NFL, CFL, SFL

Plate 45c
Pileated Woodpecker
Dryocopus pileatus
ID: Largest woodpecker in USA. Almost completely black with bright red crown and crest, white chin, white stripe through cheek and down neck; white under wings flashes in flight. Male has red stripe on throat just below the mandible, white patch visible on closed wing, and red cap extends to base of bill. Red plumage on female restricted to small portion of crest. Length 42 cm (16.5 in).

HABITAT: Widespread in forests and wooded suburbs and rural areas.

REGION: PAN, NFL, CFL, SFL, KEY

Plate 45d
Northern Flicker
Colaptes auratus
ID: Large, stocky, colorful woodpecker. Brown and black barred upperparts, white rump, black bib, tawny breast with large black spots. Yellow underwing visible in flight. Face is beige with gray crown and red stripe on nape. Male has black moustache stripe. Length 32 cm (12.5 in).

HABITAT: Widespread in forests, wooded suburbs, and rural areas; less common in South Florida.

REGION: PAN, NFL, CFL, SFL, KEY

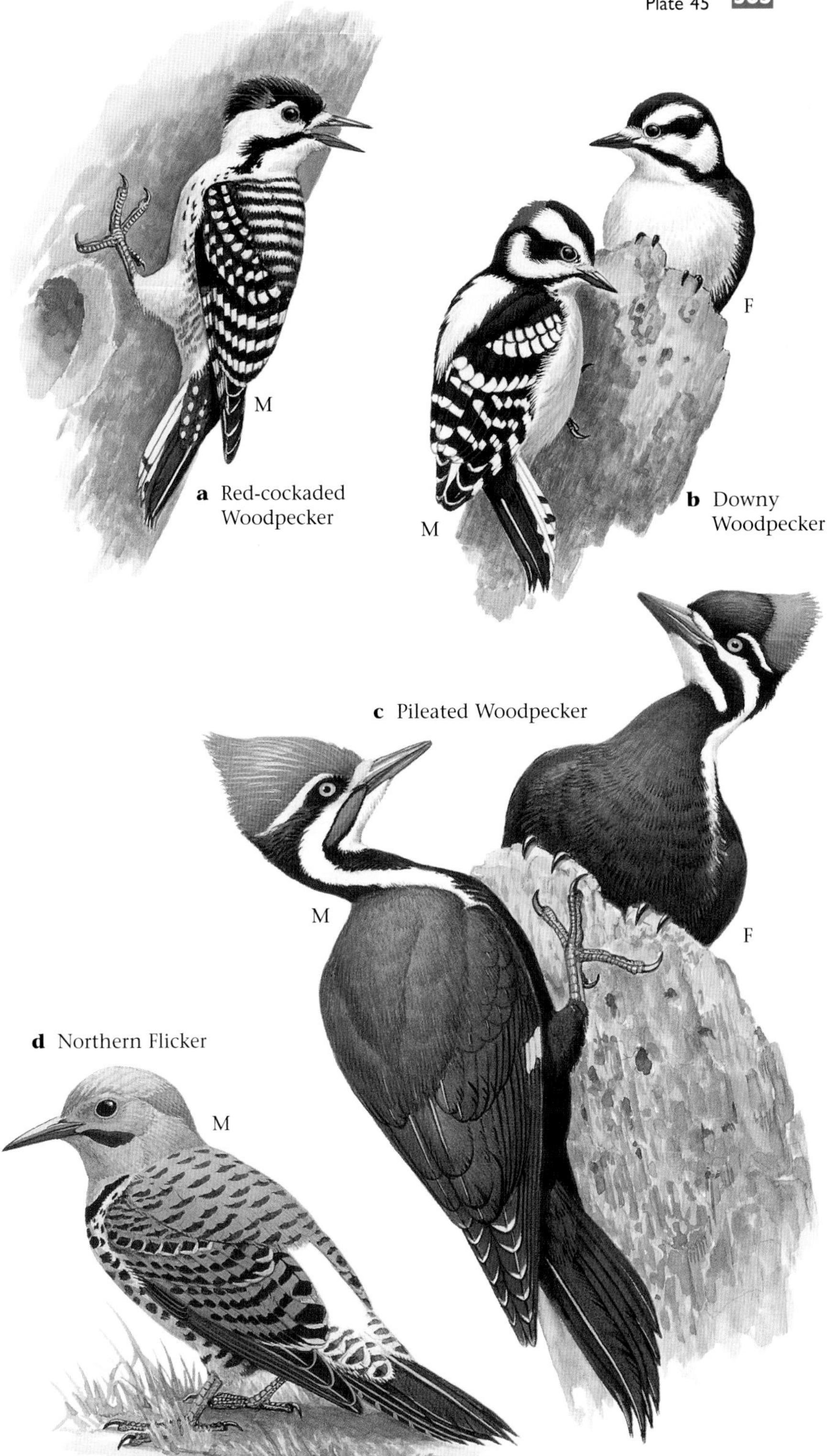

Plate 45　**365**

a Red-cockaded
Woodpecker

M

b Downy
Woodpecker

M

F

c Pileated Woodpecker

M

F

d Northern Flicker

M

Plate 46a
Eastern Wood-Pewee
Contopus virens
ID: Small, dark, and shy flycatcher. Upperparts dark olive-gray above, tail and wings darker. Throat and belly dim white, darker band across breast. Upper mandible of bill black, lower, dull yellow. Says its name, 'pee-a-wee.' Length 16 cm (6.25 in).

HABITAT: Pine forests and pine-oak woodlands, especially in Panhandle and northern half of Peninsula.

REGION: PAN, NFL, CFL, SFL, KEY

Plate 46b
Acadian Flycatcher
Empidonax virescens
ID: Smallest breeding flycatcher in Florida. Drab green above with two bars (pale buff or white) in darker wings. Gray throat, greenish breast band, yellow wash on abdomen. Yellow eyering, lower mandible of broad bill orange-yellow. Length 15 cm (5.75 in).

HABITAT: Lowland forests, hardwood hammocks and swamps.

REGION: PAN, NFL, CFL, SFL, KEY

Plate 46c
Eastern Phoebe
Sayornis phoebe
ID: Medium-sized, drab flycatcher. Dull brown above with darker head, wings, and tail. Underparts white with pale gray or olive wash on sides and breast; fall birds have yellowish belly. Typically sits on exposed perches, pumping its tail; sallies after flying insects. Length 18 cm (7 in).

HABITAT: Woodlands, residential and rural areas, and roadsides throughout state. Only known to breed in western Panhandle.

REGION: PAN, NFL, CFL, SFL, KEY

Plate 46d
Great Crested Flycatcher
Myiarchus crinitus
ID: Large, relatively colorful flycatcher. Olive-brown, crested head and back contrast with gray face and throat, lemon-yellow belly and under tail. Wings darker with chestnut patch, chestnut tail. Length 20 cm (8 in).

HABITAT: Mixed woodlands, residential and rural areas.

REGION: PAN, NFL, CFL, SFL, KEY

Plate 46e
Gray Kingbird
Tyrannus dominicensis
ID: Largest flycatcher in Florida. Gray upperparts with black mask. Thick, black bill. Underparts white, tail slightly forked. Coastal bird, may be seen on power and telephone wires in beach towns. Length 23 cm (9 in).

HABITAT: Beaches, islands on both coasts, and mangrove forests.

REGION: PAN, NFL, CFL, SFL, KEY

Plate 46f
Eastern Kingbird
Tyrannus tyrannus
ID: Large, stocky flycatcher with short bill and striking black and white plumage. Upperparts dark gray with black head, wings, and tail with white band at end. Underparts white. Often perches on exposed branches, utility lines, fences. Sallies after flying insects. Length 22 cm (8.5 in).

HABITAT: Common in rural, agricultural, and disturbed woodland and scrub environments.

REGION: PAN, NFL, CFL, SFL, KEY

Plate 46 **367**

a Eastern Wood-Pewee

b Acadian Flycatcher

d Great Crested Flycatcher

c Eastern Phoebe

f Eastern Kingbird

e Gray Kingbird

Plate 47a
Purple Martin
Progne subis
ID: Largest, darkest swallow. Male appears black, is glossy purplish blue in good light; female duller and gray beneath. Both sexes have forked tail. Like other swallows, flies with rapid wingbeats and short glides. Readily nests in artificial boxes. Length 20 cm (8 in).

HABITAT: Natural and residential open areas, often near water.

REGION: PAN, NFL, CFL, SFL, KEY.

Plate 47b
Chimney Swift
Chaetura pelagica
ID: Fast flier with cigar-shaped body and long, narrow wings. Very short tail. Dusky gray overall with slightly paler throat. Virtually always in flocks and always on the wing. Roost and nest colonially in natural and artificial hollows. Chattering call. Length 13 cm (5.25 in).

HABITAT: Ubiquitous, especially common over urban and rural environments.

REGION: PAN, NFL, CFL, SFL, KEY

Plate 47c
Tree Swallow
Tachycineta bicolor
ID: Dark upperparts with glossy blue or green cast on head, back and shoulders. White cheek patch ends below eye. Wings broad at base, wedge-shaped. Underparts white, tail dark, forked. Huge flocks roost in freshwater marshes. Common to abundant. Length 15 cm (5.75 in).

HABITAT: Open areas near water, often over marshes, lakes, ponds, fields, and prairies.

REGION: PAN, NFL, CFL, SFL, KEY

Plate 47d
Northern Rough-winged Swallow
Stelgidopteryx serripennis
ID: Brown and white swallow. Upperparts dark brown, sometimes with reddish wash; throat and breast faintly streaked. Tail forked. More drab and less gregarious than Tree Swallow. Forages in small flocks, individual pairs nest in holes in sandy banks, culverts, and beneath bridges. Length 13 cm (5 in).

HABITAT: Open areas near water, often over marshes, lakes, ponds, fields, and prairies.

REGION: PAN, NFL, CFL, SFL, KEY

Plate 47e
Barn Swallow
Hirundo rustica
ID: Colorful swallow with long, deeply forked tail, reddish-brown throat, buff or orange-brown underparts. Upperparts deep, metallic blue with reddish-brown patch above bill. Wings sharply pointed. Widespread, but often associated with rural and agricultural areas, marshes.

HABITAT: Widespread in residential and rural areas, in fields, prairies, and open woodlands.

REGION: PAN, NFL, CFL, SFL, KEY

Plate 47 **369**

M

b Chimney Swift

a Purple Martin

F

c Tree Swallow

d Northern Rough-winged Swallow

e Barn Swallow ⟶

Plate 48 (*See also*: Crows and Jays, p. 159)

Plate 48a
Blue Jay
Cyanocitta cristata
ID: Large, attractive, very active songbird. Crest, nape, back, and shoulders purple-blue, wings blue with white bars, tail blue with black bars and white tips on outer feathers. Face gray with black through eye. Underparts gray with black breast band. Diverse raucous and whistled vocalizations; mimics Red-shouldered Hawk calls. Length 28 cm (11 in).

HABITAT: Ubiquitous; common feeder bird.

REGION: PAN, NFL, CFL, SFL, KEY

Plate 48c
American Crow
Corvus brachyrhynchos
ID: Largest passerine bird in Florida. All black with heavy bill. Call is unmistakable 'caw,' deeper than Fish Crow's. Gregarious; opportunistic feeder. Often seen in fields and pastures and on roadside carrion. Length 45 cm (17.5 in).

HABITAT: Ubiquitous; less common in heavily urbanized areas.

REGION: PAN, NFL, CFL, SFL, KEY

Plate 48b
Florida Scrub-Jay
Aphelocoma coerulescens
ID: Large, rounded head, long tail. Light blue head has whitish forehead, gray back contrasts with bright blue wings, rump, and tail. Throat streaked whitish, underparts streaked gray. Florida endemic. Length 28 cm (11 in).

HABITAT: Restricted to scrub habitats in North and Central Florida.

REGION: NFL, CFL

Note: This species is threatened, USA ESA listed.

Plate 48d
Fish Crow
Corvus ossifragus
ID: All black, smaller than American Crow, with relatively longer tail and smaller head and bill. Best distinguished by higher-pitched, less raspy voice. Calls include a high 'caah' and a lower 'uh-uh.' Frequents docks, wharves, and beaches. Length 39 cm (15.5 in).

HABITAT: Coastal: salt marshes, tidal creeks, estuaries; less common inland.

REGION: PAN, NFL, CFL, SFL, KEY

Plate 48 **371**

a Blue Jay

b Florida Scrub-Jay

c American Crow

d Fish Crow

Plate 49a
Carolina Chickadee
Poecile carolinensis
ID: Tiny, active, common songbird. Compact 'no-neck' body with small bill and narrow tail. Cap and throat black, cheek white. Upperparts gray, underparts white with pale buffy abdomen. Gregarious and noisy; often in mixed flocks with titmice, nuthatches, and kinglets. Length 12 cm (4.75 in).

HABITAT: Woodlands, and wooded residential areas. Common feeder bird.

REGION: PAN, NFL, CFL

Plate 49b
Tufted Titmouse
Baeolophus bicolor
ID: Stocky, vocal. Crest and upperparts gray, black forehead. Underparts white with reddish or rusty flanks. Voice highly variable, distinctive song, 'peter, peter, peter.' Length 17 cm (6.5 in).

HABITAT: Woodlands, and wooded residential areas. Common feeder bird.

REGION: PAN, NFL, CFL, SFL

Plate 49c
Brown-headed Nuthatch
Sitta pusilla
ID: Brown cap with gray patch on nape, back, wings, and short dark gray tail. Cheek and throat white, underparts buffy. Bill slender and sharply pointed. Typically forages along tree trunks and branches; acrobatic. Nests in cavities. Length 11 cm (4.5 in).

HABITAT: Open, mature pine forests.

REGION: PAN, NFL, CFL, SFL

Plate 49d
Carolina Wren
Thryothorus ludovicianus
ID: Energetic and highly vocal; sings year-round. Rich brown above with broad white eyeline, white bars on black-barred wings, longish, black-barred tail. Throat white, underparts buffy. Bill thin, slightly down-curved. Typically in underbrush. Length 14 cm (5.5 in).

HABITAT: Brushy woodlands, residential and rural areas; common backyard bird.

REGION: PAN, NFL, CFL, SFL, KEY

Plate 49e
House Wren
Troglodytes aedon
ID: Smaller, more drab and secretive than Carolina Wren, with shorter bill and tail. Upperparts brown with fine black barring, underparts gray with barring on abdomen and undertail coverts. Chattering alarm call. Length 12 cm (4.75 in).

HABITAT: Woodlands and parks, hedgerows, and brush piles.

REGION: PAN, NFL, CFL, SFL, KEY

Plate 49 **373**

a Carolina Chickadee

b Tufted Titmouse

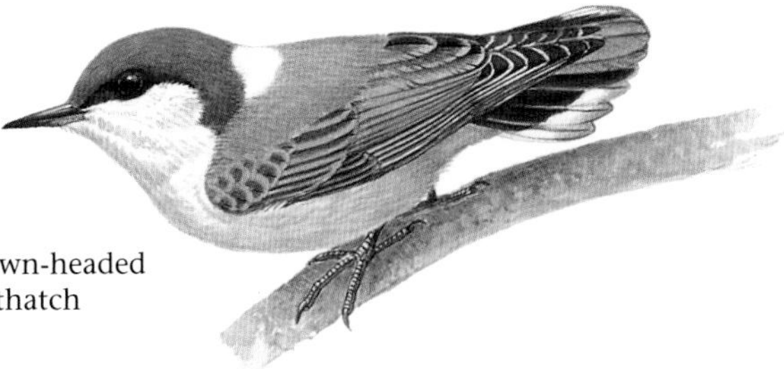

c Brown-headed Nuthatch

d Carolina Wren

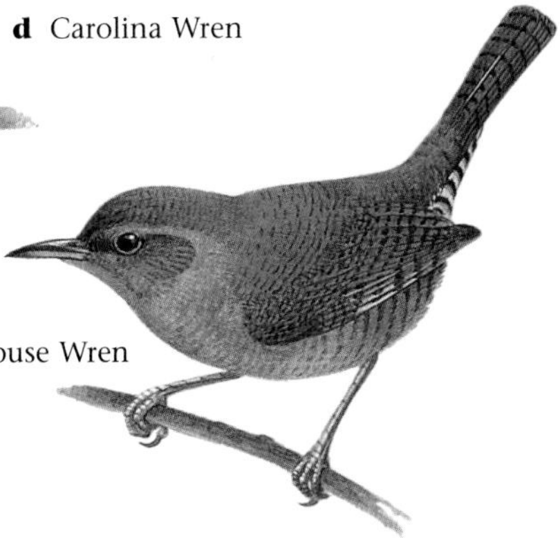

e House Wren

Plate 50a
Ruby-crowned Kinglet
Regulus calendula

ID: Tiny, plump 'no-neck' forest bird with broken white eyering. Upperparts olive-green, wings darker with two white or buffy bars. Tail slightly forked. Red crown rarely visible. Underparts grayish. Habitually flicks wings. Length 11 cm (4.25 in).

HABITAT: Forests and woodlands, and wooded residential areas. Less common in South Florida.

REGION: PAN, NFL, CFL, SFL, KEY

Plate 50b
Blue-gray Gnatcatcher
Polioptila caerulea

ID: Small and slender with white eyering and long tail. Male's upperparts blue-gray, female more gray. Mostly black tail has white outer feathers. Underparts white. Very active, frequently cocks and fans tail. Voice is thin, insect-like. Length 11 cm (4.25 in).

HABITAT: Forests, woodlands, and wooded swamps.

REGION: PAN, NFL, CFL, SFL, KEY

Plate 50c
Eastern Bluebird
Sialia sialis

ID: Male has brilliant blue upperparts, contrasts with cinnamon or red throat, sides of neck and breast; belly white. Female more drab above. Nests in natural and artificial cavities. Often seen in groups on high, exposed perches such as utility wires. Length 18 cm (7 in).

HABITAT: Dry pine forests, and rural areas.

REGION: PAN, NFL, CFL, SFL

Plate 50d
Hermit Thrush
Catharus guttatus

ID: Small brown thrush with whitish eyering and contrasting chestnut or rusty tail. Small, thin bill. Throat and breast buffy with brown spots. Belly white and flanks grayish. Secretive, usually seen on the ground in brushy areas. Length 17 cm (6.75 in).

HABITAT: Moist, open woodlands, hardwood hammocks, and thickets.

REGION: PAN, NFL, CFL, SFL, KEY

Plate 50e
Wood Thrush
Hylocichla mustelina

ID: Large thrush with cinnamon crown, back, and wings, browner rump and tail. Streaked face, prominent white eyering. Underparts pale with large, distinct spots extending to abdomen. Smaller and less conspicuous than Brown Thrasher, and with shorter bill and tail. Length 20 cm (7.75 in).

HABITAT: Deciduous forests, primarily North Florida.

REGION: PAN, NFL, CFL, SFL, KEY

Plate 50f
American Robin
Turdus migratorius

ID: Largest, most common thrush in USA. Male has gray-brown upperparts with darker head and tail, broken white eyering and streaky white throat. Breast and belly deep, rusty red, abdomen white. Bill yellow. Female similar but more drab overall. Length 25 cm (10 in).

HABITAT: Ubiquitous; large winter flocks often seen in residential areas.

REGION: PAN, NFL, CFL, SFL, KEY

Plate 50 **375**

a Ruby-crowned Kinglet

F

M

b Blue-gray Gnatcatcher

F

M

c Eastern Bluebird

F

M

d Hermit Thrush

e Wood Thrush

f American Robin

Plate 51a
Loggerhead Shrike
Lanius ludovicianus
ID: Small, chunky predator with a short, slightly hooked bill. Gray crown, back, and rump, broad black mask, black wings and tail. Wings have white patch at base of primaries, tail edged with white. Distinguished from Northern Mockingbird by black mask, darker wings and tail, smaller white patch in wing. Often seen on utility lines and fences. Length 23 cm (9 in).

HABITAT: Open pine forests, scrubby and disturbed habitats.

REGION: PAN, NFL, CFL, SFL

Plate 51b
Northern Mockingbird
Mimus polyglottos
ID: Gray upperparts, darker wings have white bars and white patch, darker tail has white outer feathers. Throat and underparts gray. Plumage less contrasty overall and more white in wing than Loggerhead Shrike. Well-known singer; often (not always) imitates other birds. Frequently sings at night. Florida's state bird. Length 25 cm (10 in).

HABITAT: Edge habitats, urban, residential, and disturbed areas.

REGION: PAN, NFL, CFL, SFL, KEY

Plate 51c
Cedar Waxwing
Bombycilla cedrorum
ID: Stocky, flocking bird with long crest, black mask, and bright yellow band at end of tail. Head, breast, and back brown, wings and rump gray. Red spots on wings. Belly yellowish, undertail white. Flocks often feed on berries. Constant, high-pitched, buzzing trill is distinctive. Length 18 cm (7.25 in).

HABITAT: Woodlands and swamps, rural and residential areas, less common in South Florida. Common backyard bird.

REGION: PAN, NFL, CFL, SFL, KEY

Plate 51d
Brown Thrasher
Toxostoma rufum
ID: Large, brown songbird, typically forages on the ground. Upperparts red-brown, underparts pale to buff, heavily streaked. Distinguished from Wood Thrush by long, down-curved bill, longer tail, streaked rather than spotted underparts. Conspicuous, active. Length 29 cm (11.5 in).

HABITAT: Woodland edges, brush, residential areas.

REGION: PAN, NFL, CFL, SFL, KEY

Plate 51e
Gray Catbird
Dumetella carolinensis
ID: A shy, dark, relative of the Mockingbird. Charcoal-gray overall with black cap and tail. Tail frequently cocked, revealing reddish-brown undertail coverts. Often heard; typical call a high-pitched, nasal 'myew'. Length 22 cm (8.5 in).

HABITAT: Dense brush and thickets in woodlands and swamps.

REGION: PAN, NFL, CFL, SFL, KEY

Plate 51f
American Pipit
Anthus rubescens
ID: Easily mistaken for a sparrow, but has a thinner bill, longer tail with white outer feathers. Upperparts brown, underparts buffy with dark streaking on breast. Forages on ground, typically walking rather than hopping. Length 17 cm (6.5 in).

HABITAT: Open country: fields, prairies, golf courses, moist ground near lake and marsh edges.

REGION: PAN, NFL, CFL, SFL, KEY

Plate 51 **377**

a Loggerhead Shrike

c Cedar Waxwing

b Northern Mockingbird

d Brown Thrasher

e Gray Catbird

f American Pipit

Plate 52a
White-eyed Vireo
Vireo griseus
ID: Small vireo with distinctive, warbling song beginning and ending with a 'chick.' Gray-green above with darker wings and tail, two pale wing bars. Yellow 'spectacles' around eyes and over base of bill. Eyes pale, bill short. Underparts whitish with yellow wash on flanks. Shy. Length 13 cm (5 in).

HABITAT: Woodlands, swamps, and riparian forests.

REGION: PAN, NFL, CFL, SFL, KEY

Plate 52b
Red-eyed Vireo
Vireo olivaceus
ID: Common vireo with greenish back and darker, browner wings and tail. Gray cap, white eyeline bordered with black. Underparts pale, may grade to yellowish under tail. Red eye visible in good light. Constant singer; typical songs sounds like 'how-are-you? I'm fine.' Length 15 cm (6 in).

HABITAT: Hardwood forests, wooded parks and residential areas. Less common in South Florida.

REGION: PAN, NFL, CFL, SFL, KEY

Plate 52c
Black-whiskered Vireo
Vireo altiloquus
ID: Similar to Red-eyed Vireo, but lacks black above white eyestripe, has black stripe on neck just below mandible, and has longer and heavier bill. Habitat restricted. Length 16 cm (6.25 in).

HABITAT: Hardwood forests and mangrove swamps in Keys and on both coasts; rare in North Florida and Panhandle.

REGION: NFL, CFL, SFL, KEY

Plate 52d
Yellow-throated Vireo
Vireo flavifrons
ID: Yellow-green head and back, wings and tail darker, gray rump. Yellow 'spectacles,' throat and breast, and white belly. Similar Pine Warbler has yellow rump, streaky flanks. Length 14 cm (5.5 in).

HABITAT: Hardwood and mixed hardwood-pine forests, primarily in northern half of state.

REGION: PAN, NFL, CFL, SFL, KEY

Plate 52e
Blue-headed Vireo
Vireo solitarius
ID: Gray-blue head contrasts with olive back, wings, and tail. Wing feathers have yellowish edges. Outer tail feathers white. Prominent white 'spectacles.' Underparts white with streaked, yellow sides. Length 13 cm (5 in).

HABITAT: Widespread in pine forests, hardwood hammocks, and wooded residential areas.

REGION: PAN, NFL, CFL, SFL, KEY

Plate 52 **379**

a White-eyed Vireo

b Red-eyed Vireo

c Black-whiskered Vireo

d Yellow-throated Vireo

e Blue-headed Vireo

Plate 53a

Yellow-rumped Warbler
Dendroica coronata

ID: Very common warbler with streaky, dark upperparts, white wingbars, and bright yellow rump patch. Narrow white eyeline and broken eyering. Male is gray-black with black cheek, white throat and belly, black breast with yellow near wing, and black streaking on flank. Female's pattern similar but browner overall. Often feeds on wax myrtle fruits. Length 14 cm (5.5 in).

HABITAT: Widespread; forms large flocks in cold weather.

REGION: PAN, NFL, CFL, SFL, KEY

Plate 53b

Northern Parula
Parula americana

ID: Blue-gray above with greenish wash on back. Wings and tail darker gray; wings have two bright white bars. Broken white eyering. Throat and breast yellow, belly white. Male has dark and rustyred bands on breast. Often nests in hanging Spanish moss. Length 11 cm (4.5 in).

HABITAT: Hardwood forests and swamps, and well-wooded suburbs.

REGION: PAN, NFL, CFL, SFL, KEY.

Plate 53c

Prairie Warbler
Dendroica discolor

ID: Bright, stocky warbler. Crown and back ochre, wings and tail darker. Faint yellow wingbars. Bright yellow underparts with black-streaked sides. Male has black eyeline and crescent through cheek in yellow face; female's face ochre with yellow area around eye. Length 12 cm (4.75 in).

HABITAT: Coastal mangrove swamps and forests; inland in dense shrubs and pine stands.

REGION: PAN, NFL, CFL, SFL, KEY

Plate 53d

Pine Warbler
Dendroica pinus

ID: Olive upperparts with darker wings and tail, white wingbars; yellow breast, white belly. Male distinguished from Yellow-throated Vireo by olive-green rump, streaking on sides, and absence of 'spectacles.' Female more drab with fainter streaking. Length 14 cm (5.5 in).

HABITAT: Most common in pine forests.

REGION: PAN, NFL, CFL, SFL

Plate 53e

Palm Warbler
Dendroica palmarum

ID: Upperparts olive with faint streaks, reddish-brown cap in breeding, yellow eyebrow. Male has yellow underparts and reddish streaking on flanks in breeding. Female browner with yellow throat and otherwise white underparts. Length 14 cm (5.5 in).

HABITAT: Widespread in edge, open, and disturbed areas, including farmlands and marshes.

REGION: PAN, NFL, CFL, SFL, KEY

Plate 53 **381**

a Yellow-rumped Warbler

F

M

b Northern Parula

F

M

c Prairie Warbler

d Pine Warbler

F

M

NB

e Palm Warbler

Plate 54a

Black-and-white Warbler
Mniotilta varia

ID: Black and white striped head, dark upperparts with white stripes, underparts white with black streaking on sides and under tail. Breeding male has black throat and cheek patch. Behaves like a nuthatch, foraging along tree trunks and limbs. Length 13 cm (5.25 in).

HABITAT: Woodlands, especially hardwoods.

REGION: PAN, NFL, CFL, SFL, KEY

Plate 54b

Yellow-throated Warbler
Dendroica dominica

ID: Upperparts sleek charcoal-gray with two white wingbars. Face is black with white ear patch and long eyebrow. Females have less extensive black on face. Throat and upper breast chrome yellow, underparts otherwise white. Black streaking on flanks. Forages along branches and trunks. Length 14 cm (5.5 in).

HABITAT: Pine forests, mixed hardwoods, and swamps.

REGION: PAN, NFL, CFL, SFL, KEY

Plate 54c

Orange-crowned Warbler
Vermivora celata

ID: Fairly drab warbler, greenish-gray overall with faint streaking on sides of breast. Orange crown patch difficult to see. Best field mark is yellowish patch under tail. Length 13 cm (5 in).

HABITAT: Mixed hardwoods, especially live oaks, shrubby areas.

REGION: PAN, NFL, CFL, SFL, KEY

Plate 54d

American Redstart
Setophaga ruticilla

ID: Distinctive colors and patterns: male black with bright orange patches on flanks, base of flight feathers, and tail. White abdomen and under tail. Female gray and olive above, white beneath, with yellow instead of orange patches. Typically fans tail and flicks wings while perched. Length 13 cm (5.25 in).

HABITAT: Mixed hardwoods throughout state; less common in South Florida.

REGION: PAN, NFL, CFL, SFL, KEY

Plate 54e

Prothonotary Warbler
Protonotaria citrea

ID: Bright, stocky warbler. Male has brilliant yellow head and underparts, paler toward abdomen, white undertail coverts. Back olive, wings and tail gray, no wingbars; white spots in tail. Female's yellow parts darker around head and duller on underparts. Nests in crevices, cavities near water. Length 14 cm (5.5 in).

HABITAT: Hardwood and cypress swamps, and riparian forests.

REGION: PAN, NFL, CFL, SFL, KEY

Plate 54 **383**

a Black-and-white Warbler

F

M

b Yellow-throated Warbler

c Orange-crowned Warbler

d American Redstart

M

F

e Prothonotary Warbler

Plate 55a

Yellow-breasted Chat
Icteria virens

ID: Largest warbler in USA. Unmarked, olive-brown upperparts with long tail. Underparts bright yellow with whitish abdomen and undertail. White 'spectacles.' Black area between eye and bill is bordered in white. Bill short and heavy. Secretive but vocal. Length 19 cm (7.5 in).

HABITAT: Dense brush and thickets.

REGION: PAN, NFL, CFL, SFL, KEY

Plate 55b

Common Yellowthroat
Geothlypis trichas

ID: Male's wide black mask, bordered above with white, is distinctive. Upperparts dark olive, underparts deep yellow. Female's face grayish with faint eyering, underparts duller. Typically nests in dense grasses near ground; usually encountered near water. Length 13 cm (5 in).

HABITAT: Thick vegetation at lake and pond shores, streams, and marshes; also in woodlands.

REGION: PAN, NFL, CFL, SFL, KEY

Plate 55c

Hooded Warbler
Wilsonia citrina

ID: Olive back, wings, and tail. Outer tail feathers white. Face and underparts yellow, area between eye and bill is dark. Male has complete black hood, extending from crown around neck to throat. Female has dark crown only and faint black necklace. Length 13 cm (5.25 in).

HABITAT: Moist forests and woodlands.

REGION: PAN, NFL, CFL, SFL, KEY

Plate 55d

Kentucky Warbler
Oporornis formosus

ID: Similar to Hooded Warbler, distinguished by yellow 'spectacle' in dark face, clear yellow throat, shorter tail. Dark parts more drab on female. Nests and forages close to the ground in dense shrubs. Length 13 cm (5.25 in).

HABITAT: Moist forests, woodlands, and wooded swamps.

REGION: PAN, NFL, CFL, SFL, KEY

Plate 55e

Ovenbird
Seiurus aurocapillus

ID: Upperparts olive, cinnamon cap bordered with black stripes, white eyering. Underparts white with black streaks in lines on breast, paler toward flanks. Legs reddish. Appearance and behavior like a small thrush. Typically forages on the ground in moist woodlands. Length 15 cm (6 in).

HABITAT: Mixed hardwood forests, often near small ponds and streams.

REGION: PAN, NFL, CFL, SFL, KEY

Plate 55f

Summer Tanager
Piranga rubra

ID: Male solid red with slightly darker wings, slightly forked tail. Bill heavy and pale. Female is ochre above with yellow underparts. Typically hidden in foliage high in trees. Length 20 cm (7.75 in).

HABITAT: Open pine and oak woodlands.

REGION: PAN, NFL, CFL, SFL, KEY

Plate 55 **385**

a Yellow-breasted Chat

F

M

b Common Yellowthroat

F

M

c Hooded Warbler

M

F

d Kentucky Warbler

e Ovenbird

f Summer Tanager

M

F

Plate 56a

Indigo Bunting
Passerina cyanea

ID: Male's overall iridescent blue plumage is unmistakable. Female is brown overall with white throat and streaked breast and flanks. Bill small and black, tail slightly forked. No wingbars. Length 14 cm (5.5 in).

HABITAT: Open forests, woodland edges and clearings.

REGION: PAN, NFL, CFL, SFL, KEY

Plate 56b

Painted Bunting
Passerina ciris

ID: Male is among Florida's most colorful songbirds, with purple head, green back, and scarlet rump and underparts; dark wings and tail; red eyering. Female rich green above, yellower beneath. Can be a feeder bird in some areas. Length 14 cm (5.5 in).

HABITAT: Dense undergrowth and thickets.

REGION: PAN, NFL, CFL, SFL, KEY

Plate 56c

Blue Grosbeak
Guiraca caerulea

ID: Superficially similar to Indigo Bunting, but distinguished by larger size, larger, thicker bill, and red-brown wingbars. Male has black surrounding base of bill and blue is deeper, more purplish. Female has clear tan breast, streaked back and rump. Length 17 cm (6.75 in).

HABITAT: Brushy stream banks, marshes, and woodlands.

REGION: PAN, NFL, CFL, SFL, KEY

Plate 56d

Northern Cardinal
Cardinalis cardinalis

ID: Conspicuous, active, finch-like bird with heavy reddish bill and prominent crest. Male is crimson overall with black mask and throat. Female is light brown with lighter underparts and gray mask, reddish in crest, wings, and tail. Length 22 cm (8.75 in).

HABITAT: Woodland edges, riparian corridors, residential and other disturbed areas. Common feeder bird.

REGION: PAN, NFL, CFL, SFL, KEY

Plate 56e

Eastern Towhee
Pipilo erythrophthalmus

ID: Large, long-tailed sparrow. Male has black upperparts, head, and upper breast, with white patch at base of primaries. Flanks rusty red, belly white, undertail buffy. Female has similar pattern but black plumage is brown and wing patch is buffy. Nests and forages on or near the ground. Length 19 cm (7.5 in).

HABITAT: Brushy woodlands, residential and rural areas.

REGION: PAN, NFL, CFL, SFL, KEY

Plate 56 **387**

F **a** Indigo Bunting

M

M

F

b Painted Bunting

M

F

c Blue Grosbeak

M

F

d Northern Cardinal

F

M

e Eastern Towhee

Plate 57a
Bachman's Sparrow
Aimophila aestivalis

ID: Large, chunky sparrow with long, dark, rounded tail. Upperparts gray with brown streaking, brown and gray stripes on crown, buffy-gray face with thin brown line extending back from eye. Unstreaked throat and breast light gray, belly white. Length 15 cm (6 in).

HABITAT: Dry pine forests and scrub palmetto.

REGION: PAN, NFL, CFL, SFL

Plate 57b
Chipping Sparrow
Spizella passerina

ID: Adult has bright reddish-brown crown, white eyebrow, and black eyeline. Gray cheeks, nape, and rump contrast with streaky brown wings and dark, notched tail. Two white wingbars. Breast gray, unstreaked. Bill small, sharply pointed. Length 14 cm (5.5 in).

HABITAT: Widespread in woodland edges, fields, lawns, and gardens. Feeder bird in some areas.

REGION: PAN, NFL, CFL, SFL, KEY

Plate 57c
Savannah Sparrow
Passerculus sandwichensis

ID: Variable. Overall streaked appearance, with upperparts brown to dark brown; underparts lighter, lower belly clear white. Light eyebrow and area between eye and bill may be yellow. Notched tail. Length 14 cm (5.5 in).

HABITAT: Open habitats: prairies, marshes, dunes, and pastures.

REGION: PAN, NFL, CFL, SFL, KEY

Plate 57d
Swamp Sparrow
Melospiza georgiana

ID: Upperparts brown with black streaking and reddish-brown wing patches. Brown stripes on sides of head above dark gray face and white throat. Breast and flanks brown, streaked; belly whitish. Length 15 cm (5.75 in).

HABITAT: Brushy areas near water, edges of streams, lakes, and swamps.

REGION: PAN, NFL, CFL, SFL, KEY

Plate 57e
White-throated Sparrow
Zonotrichia albicollis

ID: Sharply outlined white throat against clear, gray breast is distinctive. Head striped black and either white or buff. Broad eyebrow stripe is yellow in front of eye. Belly white. Upperparts brown with faint wingbars, and unstreaked rump. Length 17 cm (6.75 in).

HABITAT: Widespread in undergrowth in edge habitats, fields, suburban lawns and gardens, and disturbed areas.

REGION: PAN, NFL, CFL, SFL

Plate 57f
Song Sparrow
Melospiza melodia

ID: Heavy, dark sparrow with long, rounded tail. Dark brown upperparts with striped head and gray eyebrow; light breast is heavily streaked brown, with characteristic central spot. Length variable, about 15 cm (6 in).

HABITAT: Woodland edges, brushy fields, suburban gardens, and disturbed areas.

REGION: PAN, NFL, CFL, SFL

Plate 57 **389**

a Bachman's Sparrow

b Chipping Sparrow

c Savannah Sparrow

d Swamp Sparrow

e White-throated Sparrow

f Song Sparrow

Plate 58a
Eastern Meadowlark
Sturnella magna
ID: Black 'V'-shaped bib on yellow underparts is distinctive. Upperparts light, scaly brown; head striped black and white or buff with pale cheek. Flanks streaked with yellow or white. Long, sharp bill, and short tail. Length 24 cm (9.5 in).

HABITAT: Open fields, meadows, and prairies.

REGION: PAN, NFL, CFL, SFL, KEY

Plate 58b
Red-winged Blackbird
Agelaius phoeniceus
ID: Male shiny black overall with crimson shoulder patch edged with yellow. Red patch may not be visible on perched birds. Female brownish above, heavily streaked below. Tail shorter, bill more conical than Common Grackle. Can aggregate in huge flocks. Abundant; common throughout North America. Length 22 cm (8.75 in).

HABITAT: Wet prairies, fields, marshes and meadows.

REGION: PAN, NFL, CFL, SFL, KEY

Plate 58c
Boat-tailed Grackle
Quiscalus major
ID: Long, broad, wedge-shaped tail and male's iridescent blue-black plumage is distinctive. Smaller female is golden-brown and unstreaked, with darker mask, wings, and tail. Brown eye. Small flocks; not as gregarious as Red-Winged Blackbirds. Length 37 to 42 cm (14.5 to 16.5 in).

HABITAT: Salt and freshwater marshes, ponds, lake and stream edges.

REGION: PAN, NFL, CFL, SFL, KEY

Plate 58d
Common Grackle
Quiscalus quiscula
ID: Similar to Boat-tailed Grackle, but smaller, male with purple and bronze iridescence, yellow eye; not as restricted to habitats near water. Female slightly smaller than males and dull; darker than female Boat-tailed. May flock with other blackbirds in winter. Length 32 cm (12.5 in).

HABITAT: Prairies, marshes, citrus groves, urban and suburban parks and residential areas.

REGION: PAN, NFL, CFL, SFL, KEY

Plate 58 **391**

a Eastern
Meadowlark

b Red-winged
Blackbird

M

F

c Boat-tailed
Grackle

M

F

d Common
Grackle

M

F

Plate 59a

American Goldfinch
Carduelis tristis

ID: Small finch with black, white-barred wings and notched, black and white tail. Winter male has brown head and back, sometimes black above bill. Face and throat yellowish, breast buff, flanks brown, belly white. Female more drab, darker brown. Length 13 cm (5 in).

HABITAT: Brushy woodlands and old fields; common feeder bird in some areas.

REGION: PAN, NFL, CFL, SFL, KEY

Plate 59b

House Finch
Carpodacus mexicanus

ID: Dark brown, streaky back, darker wings and tail. Male has brown cap, cheek, and ear patch, red forecrown, throat, and bib. Light belly and flanks have dark streaks. Female streaked brown overall with lighter underparts than back. Introduced species; native to western USA. Length 15 cm (6 in).

HABITAT: Wooded or shrubby urban, suburban, and rural areas; common to abundant feeder bird.

REGION: PAN, NFL, CFL, SFL

Plate 59c

Orchard Oriole
Icterus spurius

ID: Small oriole. Male is chestnut/brick red with black back, tail, head, breast; white wingbar. Female is lemon yellow overall with greenish back, darker wings. Sharply pointed, slightly down-curved bill. Length 18 cm (7.25 in).

HABITAT: Open woodlands and wooded suburbs.

REGION: PAN, NFL, CFL, SFL, KEY

Plate 59d

Baltimore Oriole
Icterus galbula

ID: Larger, stockier, and darker than Orchard Oriole, with straighter, slightly heavier bill. Male is golden orange with black hood and back; black wings with white bar; and black and orange tail. Female dull olive-brown above with darker wings, orange underparts, and variable amounts of black on head. Length 22 cm (8.25 in).

HABITAT: Woodlands and suburbs.

REGION: PAN, NFL, CFL, SFL, KEY

Plate 59 **393**

a American Goldfinch

b House Finch

c Orchard Oriole

d Baltimore Oriole

Plate 60a
European Starling
Sturnus vulgaris
ID: Iridescent black with purple, green, and bronze highlights. Winter birds appear speckled with white or buff. Tail short and square, wings wedge-shaped with broad base in flight. Bill yellow or gray, sharply pointed. May flock with blackbirds. Introduced species, native to temperate Eurasia. Length 22 cm (8.5 in).

HABITAT: Fields and pastures, orchards, urban and suburban environments.

REGION: PAN, NFL, CFL, SFL, KEY

Plate 60b
House Sparrow
Passer domesticus
ID: Breeding male has chestnut nape, gray crown, black throat and bill. Back streaked chestnut and black. Underparts clear gray. Winter males lack black and chestnut marks, bill is pinkish. Females gray-brown overall with streaked back, clear breast, and buff eyestripe. Introduced species, native to Eurasia. Length 16 cm (6.25 in).

HABITAT: Human settlements.

REGION: PAN, NFL, CFL, SFL, KEY

Plate 60c
Red-whiskered Bulbul
Pycnonotus jocosus
ID: Introduced species, native to Old World tropics. Dark brown above with white band at tail end, white underparts. Male has black, erect crest, red ear patch, and red patch under tail. Female lacks red patch on face and has pinkish undertail coverts. Length 18 cm (7 in).

HABITAT: Miami parks and suburbs.

REGION: SFL

Plate 60d
Common Myna
Acridotheres tristis
ID: Dark brown with black head, breast, and white-tipped tail. White wing patch and white patch under tail flash in flight. Bill and legs yellow; teardrop-shaped patch of bare skin behind eye. Gregarious. Introduced species, native to Southeast Asia. Length 25 cm (10 in).

HABITAT: Human-altered landscapes in South Florida.

REGION: SFL

Plate 60e
Brown-headed Cowbird
Molothrus ater
ID: Smaller than other blackbirds or Starling, with shorter, more conical bill. Male is metallic green with dull brown head. Female is grayish brown above, lighter and streaked below. Feeds with tail cocked. Parasitic; lays eggs in the nests of other birds. Length 19 cm (7.5 in).

HABITAT: Open country: woodland and forest edges, urban and suburban areas.

REGION: PAN, NFL, CFL, SFL, KEY

Plate 60 **395**

a European Starling

b House Sparrow

F

M

c Red-whiskered Bulbul

d Common Myna

e Brown-headed Cowbird

M

F

Plate 61a

Virginia Opossum
Didelphis virginiana

ID: About the size of a house cat, with long gray or blackish-gray fur, thin, hairless ears and a long naked tail. Weight 1 to 4 kg (2 to 9 lb). The feet have a thumb-like toe. Females have a fur-lined pouch on the abdomen. Males are larger than females and have no pouch.

HABITAT: Common throughout the state and in virtually all habitats with trees; most abundant in wooded areas adjoining wetlands. Opossums are excellent climbers, often found in backyards and suburban areas. They are one of Florida's most frequently seen road-killed animals.

REGION: PAN, NFL, CFL, SFL, KEY

Plate 61b

Nine-banded Armadillo
Dasypus novemcinctus

ID: Cat-sized, with a rounded back, a sharp nose, and medium length tail. Nine bands of ossified (bony) skin wrap around the middle and there are bony plates on the shoulders and rump. Weight 3.6 to 7.7 kg (8 to 17 lb). Armadillos move with a highly characteristic tiptoe trot – like a clockwork toy.

HABITAT: More common in sandy areas, where soil is easy to dig. Prefer moist sites with thick leaf litter and abundant invertebrates. In extremely dry areas they concentrate around streams and water sources. Tracks are birdlike, showing long middle toes and a line where tail drags. They are frequently killed by cars and their squashed remains are often seen at roadside.

REGION: PAN, NFL, CFL, SFL

Plate 61c

Eastern Spotted Skunk
Spilogale putorius

ID: The smallest of the skunks, about the size of a squirrel. Total length 42 to 52 cm (16.5 to 20.5 in), including tail (16 to 21 cm; 6.3 to 8.3 in). Fur is long and black, marked with white spots and stripes. There is a small white spot in the middle of the forehead and a spot in front of each ear. The tail is long and bushy with a small tuft of white hairs on the tip.

HABITAT: Localized, in open forested areas and habitats with dense ground cover, such as weedy fallow fields, vegetation along fences, brushy areas, saw palmetto and coastal scrub.

REGION: PAN, NFL, CFL, SFL

Plate 61d

Striped Skunk
Mephitis mephitis

ID: About the size of a house cat. Total length 59 to 71 cm (23 to 28 in), including tail (21 to 35 cm; 8.3 to 13.8 in). Fur is long and black with distinctive white stripe on the nose and two white stripes down the length of the back, but stripe length and width is highly variable. The plume-like tail may be tipped with white.

HABITAT: In every terrestrial habitat type, but not abundant. Most often found in forest edges, brushy fields, and sometimes in suburban areas.

REGION: PAN, NFL, CFL, SFL

Plate 61e

Northern Raccoon
(also called Common Raccoon)
Procyon lotor

ID: The size of a large house cat, with a black mask across the eyes and a long bushy tail marked with black rings. Color variable, from pale yellowish to almost completely black. Upperparts are usually grayish brown, underparts pale brown and yellowish. Weight 3 to 6 kg (6 to 13 lb).

HABITAT: Found in every habitat type, strongly associated with water. Common in floodplain hardwood forests with hollow trees and salt marshes. Can be abundant in suburban areas.

REGION: PAN, NFL, CFL, SFL, KEY

Plate 61f

River Otter
(also called Northern River Otter)
Lontra canadensis

ID: A long-bodied, tube-shaped animal with short legs, a small flattened head and a muscular tapering tail. Total length 90 to 110 cm (35 to 43 in), including tail (30 to 40 cm; 12 to 16 in). Legs are short and feet have webbed toes. Fur is a rich brown, paler on the underparts.

HABITAT: In almost every aquatic habitat in the state. Rarely found far from water, but sometimes seen crossing highways when moving between water bodies.

REGION: PAN, NFL, CFL, SFL

Plate 61 **397**

b Nine-banded Armadillo

a Virginia Opossum

c Eastern Spotted Skunk

d Striped Skunk

e Northern Raccoon

f River Otter

Plate 62 (*See also*: Coyote and Foxes, p. 204; Cats, p. 209)

Plate 62a

Gray Fox
Urocyon cinereoargenteus

ID: Small, dog-like animal with a long bushy tail. Total length 80 to 112 cm (31.5 to 44 in), including tail (27 to 40 cm; 11 to 16 in). Fur is gray on the upperparts, white on the belly, orange-red along the legs, sides, neck and ears (the reddish marking often causes it to be mis-identified as a Red Fox, which is orangish above and has black lower legs).

HABITAT: Hardwood forests, pine-oak woodlands, and oak hammocks. Also found in suburban areas.

REGION: PAN, NFL, CFL, SFL

Plate 62b

Bobcat
Lynx rufus

ID: A tall, long-legged cat, about three times the size of a large domestic cat. The tail is short, pointed ears have a tuft of black hair at the tip. Total length 80 to 110 cm (31.5 to 43 in), including tail (9 to 15 cm; 3.5 to 6 in). Fur is pale brown to olive-brown with scattered black spots. Underparts are white with black spots.

HABITAT: Occurs in a wide variety of habitats, from forested areas to agricultural fields. Also found on tree islands in sawgrass marshes in Everglades and Big Cypress Preserve.

REGION: PAN, NFL, CFL, SFL

Plate 62c

Coyote
Canis latrans

ID: Large, dog-like animal resembling a small German Shepherd. Total length 1 to 1.4 m (3.3 to 4.6 ft), including tail (30 to 39 cm; 12 to 15 in). Fur is light gray to yellowish buff on the back. Underparts are white or cream. Tail is bushy with a black tip. Some individuals are almost all black or all white. Coyotes can sometimes be heard howling at night during mating season – late winter and early spring.

HABITAT: Open fields, brushy pastures, woodlands. Expanded its range into state, aided by introductions; currently well established through most of the state.

REGION: PAN, NFL, CFL, SFL

Plate 62d

Puma
(also called Florida Panther, Mountain Lion, Cougar)
Puma concolor

ID: A large, lithe cat with a long tail. Total length 1.5 to 2.5 cm (4.9 to 8.2 ft), including tail (50 to 79 cm; 20 to 31 in). Upperparts are uniformly tawny or grizzled dark brown, underparts are white or buff. Head appears small for a big cat; ears are small and rounded, black on the back. Weight about 36 to 55 kg (80 to 120 lb).

HABITAT: Pine flatwoods, hardwood hammocks, cabbage palm woodlands, and cypress swamps.

REGION: SFL

Note: The Florida population of this species is endangered; USA ESA listed.

Plate 62 **399**

a Gray Fox

b Bobcat

c Coyote

d Puma (Florida Panther)

Plate 63a

Black Bear
Ursus americanus

ID: The largest carnivore in Florida. Heavily built with long black hair. The muzzle is yellowish brown and there may be white markings on the throat and chest. The tail is very short and inconspicuous. Total length 1.3 to 2 m (4.3 to 6.6 ft), including tail (10 to 28 cm; 4 to 11 in). On average, females weigh about 80 kg (175 lb), males about 115 kg (250 lb).

HABITAT: Prefer heavily wooded habitat including swamp forest and undisturbed upland forest. Restricted to five large tracts of public land scattered about state (p. 207).

REGION: PAN, NFL, CFL, SFL

Note: This species is threatened in some USA states; USA ESA listed.

Plate 63b

Wild Pig
(also called Feral Pig, Wild Hog, Wild Boar)
Sus scrofa

ID: Looks like a domestic pig, except thinner and more rangy in appearance. Total length 1.3 to 2 m (4.3 to 6.6 ft), including tail (24 to 33 cm; 9 to 13 in). Hair is coarse and sparse, all black or spotted orange, white, or red. Both sexes have tusks in upper and lower jaws; male tusks are enlarged and obvious, female tusks are inconspicuous.

HABITAT: Swamps, moist hardwood forests, and pine flatwoods.

REGION: PAN, NFL, CFL, SFL

Plate 63c

White-tailed Deer
Odocoileus virginianus

ID: A large animal with long, slender legs. Total length 1.4 to 2 m (4.6 to 6.6 ft), including tail (20 to 35 cm; 8 to 14 in). Coat is grayish brown to reddish brown, underparts are white. Males grow and shed antlers each year. A small-size (22.5 kg, 50 lb, or less) White-tailed Deer race, or subspecies, called the Key Deer, exists in the lower Keys.

HABITAT: In almost all terrestrial habitats. Most common in forest-edge habitats.

REGION: PAN, NFL, CFL, SFL, KEY

Note: The Key Deer, a subspecies of White-tailed Deer (p. 215) is endangered; USA ESA listed.

Plate 63 **401**

a Black Bear

b Wild Pig   IM

c White-tailed Deer

M

"Key Deer"

F

Plate 64a
Southern Flying Squirrel
Glaucomys volans

ID: Less than half the size of a gray squirrel. Total length 21 to 25 cm (8 to 10 in), including flattened tail (9 to 12 cm; 3.5 to 5 in). Active at night. The fine, dense and silky fur is brown, grayish brown or tawny on the upperparts, creamy white on the underparts. The eyes are large and glow red in the light of a flashlight. Glides between trees aided by a *patagium*, a flap of skin along the sides of the body that is attached to front and hind legs. When the legs are extended, the flap of skin stretches into a wing-like surface. At night, their presence is often detected by bird-like chirps and twitters.

HABITAT: In all forested habitats, but they reach highest densities in oak hammocks and mature pine oak woodlands. They depend on hollow trees, dead snags, and cavities for daytime rest-sites and nests.

REGION: PAN, NFL, CFL, SFL

Plate 64b
Eastern Gray Squirrel
Sciurus carolinensis

ID: The most common native mammal east of the Mississippi River. Fur gray above and on the flanks, white on the underparts. Tail is long, bushy, and flattened. Ears are small, rounded, often with a white patch on the back. Total length 40 to 50 cm (16 to 20 in), including tail (19 to 22 cm; 8 to 9 in). Albinos are fairly common, as are 'blondes,' which have pale fur with a gray stripe down the middle of the back.

HABITAT: Hardwood forest, or mixed hardwood and pine forest. Common in urban parks and suburban areas, especially where there are large trees.

REGION: PAN, NFL, CFL, SFL, KEY

Plate 64c
Eastern Fox Squirrel
Sciurus niger

ID: Twice the size of a gray squirrel. Total length 60 to 100 cm (24 to 39 in), including tail (29 to 34 cm; 11 to 13 in). Muzzle and forehead are white. Fur color is variable, ranging from gray, yellowish tan, and reddish brown to completely black. Underparts are usually paler, from white and cream to rusty orange. The striking tail is long and bushy.

HABITAT: Mature open pine flatwoods and high pine forests. Fox squirrels prefer open park-like habitats where trees are scattered and the understory is open. Common on golf courses that have retained large pine and oak trees.

REGION: PAN, NFL, CFL, SFL

Plate 64d
Eastern Cottontail
Sylvilagus floridanus

ID: A large rabbit (800 to 1500 g; 1.8 to 3.3 lb). Upperparts grayish to reddish brown sprinkled with black. The underparts are white except for a brown throat patch. The tail is a white cotton-like tuft and there is a light cream colored ring around each eye. There may be a distinct white spot on the forehead.

HABITAT: Found in most upland habitats except dense forest. Most abundant in brushy fields, forest edges, and grassy openings. Usually absent from wetter habitats, which are occupied by the Marsh Rabbit.

REGION: PAN, NFL, CFL, SFL

Plate 64e
Marsh Rabbit
Sylvilagus palustris

ID: Slightly smaller and darker colored than an Eastern Cottontail, with chestnut-brown to rusty red fur. The tail is small and dark and does not look like the cottontail's white powderpuff. Dark and short ears.

HABITAT: Confined to freshwater and saltwater marshy habitats with pooled water. Particularly common in sawgrass marshes, cypress swamp, canal banks, mangrove swamps, and sugar-cane fields.

REGION: PAN, NFL, CFL, SFL, KEY

Plate 64 **403**

a Southern Flying Squirrel

b Eastern Gray Squirrel

c Eastern Fox Squirrel

d Eastern Cottontail

e Marsh Rabbit

Plate 65a
Beach Mouse
(also called Old Field Mouse)
Peromyscus polionotus
ID: Fur color is extremely variable, ranging from white with a narrow buff-colored stripe down the back (some beach forms) to cinnamon or buff gray. Mice living in areas with light-colored soils are usually pale. The underparts are white and the tail is short. Total length 12 to 13.5 cm (4.5 to 5.5 in), including tail (4 to 5 cm; 1.5 to 2 in)

HABITAT: In early successional stages of abandoned or disturbed fields and other open sandy habitats, such as grass-covered beach dunes, scrub areas behind the dunes, and on barrier islands.

REGION: PAN, NFL, CFL

Note: Some Florida populations of this species are endangered; USA ESA listed.

Plate 65b
Golden Mouse
Ochrotomys nuttalli
ID: This mouse is semi-arboreal with a prehensile tail. It builds arboreal feeding platforms in vines and among Spanish moss. Old bird nests are sometimes used as well. The strikingly beautiful fur is golden or orangish cinnamon on the upperparts. Underparts and feet are white, often tinged with gold. Total length 14 to 18.5 cm (5.5 to 7 in), including tail (6 to 9 cm; 2.5 to 3.5 in).

HABITAT: Dense woodlands with vines and heavy brush or palmettos, especially near water.

REGION: PAN, NFL, CFL

Plate 65c
Florida Mouse
Podomys floridanus
ID: Upperparts are tan or buffy brown mixed with dark hairs. Cheeks, shoulders and lower sides are orangish. Feet are white and the ears are large and rounded. Total length 18.5 to 21 cm (7 to 8 in), including tail (8 to 9.5 cm; 3 to 4 in). Most Florida Mice live in close association with Gopher Tortoise burrows, creating small side tunnels off the main burrow.

HABITAT: In Gopher Tortoise burrows in high, well-drained sandy soils with pine-turkey oak or sand pine scrub vegetation.

REGION: NFL

Plate 65d
Short-tailed Shrew
Blarina carolinensis
ID: Smaller than a mouse, with a cone-shaped head and long pointed nose. Total length 7.8 to 12 cm (3 to 5 in), including short tail (1.3 to 3 cm; 0.5 to 1.2 in). Fur is slate-gray and velvety, slightly darker on the back. Spends much of its time foraging underground or burrowing through deep ground litter.

HABITAT: Most abundant in moist habitats with well-drained soils, especially hardwood forests. Sometimes found in open weedy fields and brushy areas.

REGION: PAN, NFL, CFL, SFL

Plate 65e
Least Shrew
Cryptotis parva
ID: Smaller than the Short-tailed Shrew, with cone-shaped head and long pointed nose. Total length 7 to 9 cm (2.8 to 3.6 in), including tail (1.2 to 2.4 cm; 0.4 to 0.9 in). Fur is grayish brown on the upperparts, distinctly paler on the underside. Forages during the day and at night.

HABITAT: Marshy areas among cabbage palms, dry grassy fields, pine woods, and brushy weedy sites.

REGION: PAN, NFL, CFL, SFL

Plate 65 **405**

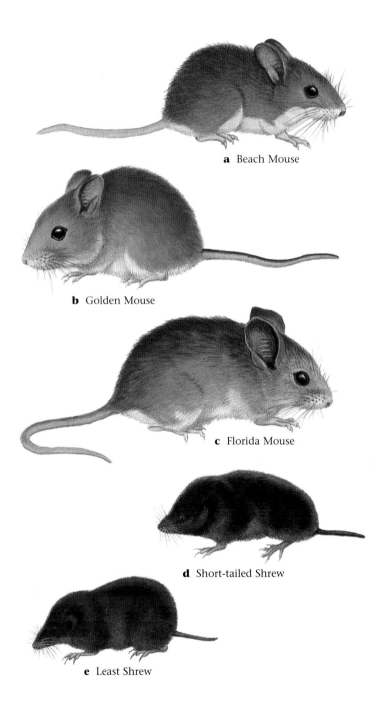

a Beach Mouse

b Golden Mouse

c Florida Mouse

d Short-tailed Shrew

e Least Shrew

Plate 66a

Black Rat
(also called Roof Rat, House Rat)
Rattus rattus

ID: Fur is grayish brown (rarely black) on the upperparts, slate-gray or creamy white on the underparts. The bare tail is longer than combined head and body, and the ears are large and rounded. Total length 32 to 43 cm (12.5 to 17 in), including tail (16 to 26 cm; 6 to 10 in). Smaller than the Norway Rat but has a proportionately longer tail.

HABITAT: Cosmopolitan, in garbage dumps, buildings, warehouses and in all types of forests. These agile rats are excellent climbers, often found in roofs and rafters of buildings, and in the canopy of trees.

REGION: PAN, NFL, CFL, SFL, KEY

Plate 66b

Norway Rat
(also called Brown Rat, Lab Rat)
Rattus norvegicus

ID: Fur is grayish brown on the upperparts, pale gray to grayish brown on the underparts. The bare tail is slightly shorter than the combined head and body length and the ears are large and rounded. Total length 32 to 48 cm (12.6 to 18.9 in), including tail (15 to 22 cm; 6 to 9 in). Has a larger, more robust body than the Black Rat and a shorter tail.

HABITAT: Not as widespread or abundant as the Black Rat. Found mainly in inner cities, shipping wharves, and grain elevators.

REGION: PAN, NFL, CFL, SFL, KEY

Plate 66c

Eastern Mole
Scalopus aquaticus

ID: Fur is thick and velvety, uniformly gray-brown. Tiny eyes are completely covered with skin and the forepaws are broad with partially webbed fingers and toes and large digging claws. The short tail is almost hairless and the snout is long and flexible. Total length 1.2 to 1.4 cm (4.5 to 5.3 in), including tail (1.4 to 2.5 cm; 0.6 to 1.0 in).

HABITAT: In almost all terrestrial habitats, from forests to grassland, but not in waterlogged muck soils.

REGION: PAN, NFL, CFL, SFL

Plate 66d

Southeastern Pocket Gopher
Geomys pinetis

ID: Rat-sized, with huge buck teeth, muscular front legs, massive claws on the front feet, and a short, naked tail. Fur is soft and short, cinnamon to dark brown on the upperparts, buff or tan on the underparts. Total length 23 to 31 cm (9 to 12 in), including tail (7 to 9 cm; 2.7 to 3.5 in). The pocket gopher is named for its distinctive, fur-lined external cheek pouches or 'pockets.'

HABITAT: Most abundant in deep sandy soils. Found in pine-oak forests, open, scrubby flatwoods and open fields. Not found in waterlogged muck soils.

REGION: PAN, NFL, CFL

Plate 66   **407**

two-tone form

black form

brown form

a Black Rat

b Norway Rat

c Eastern Mole

d Southeastern Pocket Gopher

Plate 67a
Big Brown Bat
Eptesicus fuscus

ID: Fairly large bat. Overall brown color except for broad, blackish wings. Underparts are cinnamon and the tail membrane is devoid of hair. Total length 8.7 to 13.8 cm (3 to 5.5 in). Weight 11 to 23 g (0.4 to 0.8 oz). Females slightly larger than males. Flight slow and relatively straight.

HABITAT: Forages near lakes, city parks, and the edges of forests and fields. Roosts in attics, hollow trees, caves, and under bridges.

REGION: PAN, NFL, CFL, SFL

Plate 67b
Brazilian Free-tailed Bat
Tadarida brasiliensis

ID: Small, with nearly uniform brown fur. Wings narrow and black. Tail projects conspicuously beyond tail membrane. Total length 9.5 cm (3.7 in). Weight 10 to 15 g (0.3 to 0.5 oz). Flight rapid and erratic.

HABITAT: Common in cities and suburbs. Often seen feeding at high altitudes. Roosts in colonies in attics, caves, culverts and palm trees.

REGION: PAN, NFL, CFL, SFL

Plate 67c
Eastern Yellow Bat
(also called Northern Yellow Bat)
Lasiurus intermedius

ID: Large, with yellowish-gray to yellowish-brown fur. Wings dark brown. Total length 1.2 to 1.3 cm (3 to 3.5 in). Weight 14 to 20 g (0.5 to 0.7 oz). Females larger than males. Starts flying well before dark.

HABITAT: Forages over lakes, fields, golf courses and beaches. Common in suburban areas. Roosts in clumps of Spanish moss, hollow trees, attics, caves, or dead palm leaves.

REGION: PAN, NFL, CFL, SFL

Plate 67d
Evening Bat
Nycticeius humeralis

ID: Small, fur dark brown above, tawny below. Wings short and narrow. Ears blunt and rounded. Total length 8 to 10 cm (3 to 4 in). Weight 9 to 14 g (0.3 to 0.5 oz).

HABITAT: Forages over fields, clearings, ponds, and along watercourses. Roosts in colonies in houses and abandoned buildings, also in hollow trees and palm fronds.

REGION: PAN, NFL, CFL, SFL

Plate 67 **409**

a Big Brown Bat

b Brazilian Free-tailed Bat

c Eastern Yellow Bat

d Evening Bat

Plate 68a

West Indian Manatee
(also called Florida Manatee, Caribbean Manatee, Sea Cow)
Trichechus manatus

ID: A massive, blimp-like gray aquatic mammal. The thick skin is often covered with barnacles and algae. The snout is broad and square and the large, prehensile lips are studded with whiskers. Forelimbs are dextrous and paddle-like, with nails. Tail is horizontally flattened into one broad flipper. Total length seldom exceeds 3.5 m (11.5 ft). Weight 270 to 1140 kg (600 to 2500 lb).

HABITAT: Shallow bays and estuaries during the warmer months. In winter they move inland to freshwater springs, where they congregate in large numbers.

REGION: PAN, NFL, CFL, SFL

Note: This species listed as endangered, CITES Appendix I and USA ESA.

Plate 68b

Common Dolphin
(also called Saddle-backed Dolphin)
Delphinus delphis

ID: Back is very dark gray to black, sides are marked with saddle-shaped patterns of yellow or tan. Dorsal fin and flippers of many adults are marked with pale gray to white patches. Total length 1.8 to 2.6 m (6 to 8.5 ft).

HABITAT: During the summer, groups of 10 to 100 are often seen 110 km (70 miles) or more off the Florida coast; though they are an offshore species, schools sometimes come closer to shore at the mouths of large rivers.

REGION: PAN, NFL, CFL, SFL, KEY

Plate 68c

Atlantic Bottle-nosed Dolphin
Tursiops truncatus

ID: A light gray to purplish-gray dolphin, with a pronounced beak. Flippers are dark gray, underparts light. Total length 2.4 to 3.7 m (8 to 12 ft). Dorsal fin about 25 cm (10 in) high.

HABITAT: Shallow coastal waters and estuaries. Commonly seen in inshore waters, and just beyond the surf line in open ocean.

REGION: PAN, NFL, CFL, SFL, KEY

Plate 68d

Short-finned Pilot Whale
Globicephala macrorhynchus

ID: A medium-sized whale, total length 4 to 7 m (13 to 23 ft). Completely black above and below, with a bulbous, globe-like head. Gregarious, often seen in groups of 20 to 100 or more. Group strandings occasionally occur on Florida beaches.

HABITAT: Usually found in deeper water, but sometimes forages close to the shoreline.

REGION: PAN, NFL, CFL, SFL, KEY

Plate 68 **411**

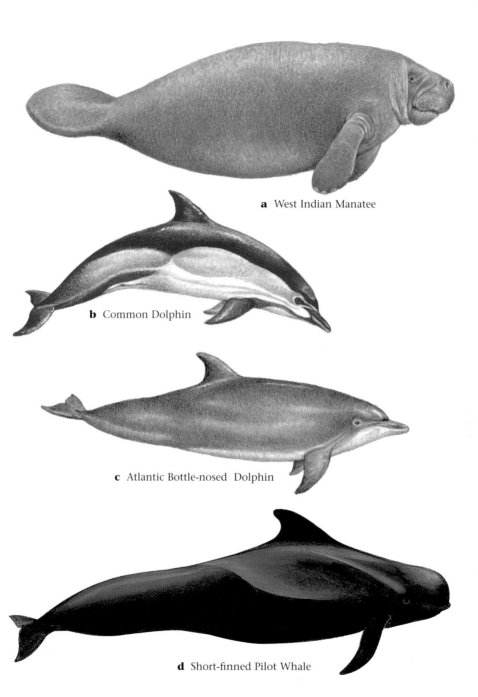

a West Indian Manatee

b Common Dolphin

c Atlantic Bottle-nosed Dolphin

d Short-finned Pilot Whale

Plate 69a

Great Southern White
Ascia monuste

ID: A white butterfly with black or dark brown markings on the outer edges of the forewings. Females have a small dark spot near the center of the forewing. Wingspans range from 4.5 to 6.0 cm (1.8 to 2.4 in). The tips of the antennae are bright blue. Adults can be seen year-round in South Florida. Found in coastal areas and gardens. Southern whites go through periodic outbreaks and in some years thousands can be seen flying along the Florida coast.

Plate 69b

Pipevine Swallowtail
Battus philenor

ID: A large, mostly black butterfly with creamy spots in iridescent blue along the wing borders. Undersides of hind wings have a row of orange spots in metallic blue. Wingspan 6.0 to 9.0 cm (2.4 to 3.5 in). Females are slightly larger than males. Found February to November in sandhills, scrubby flatwoods, and fields. These butterflies are distasteful to predators. They are protected by toxic chemicals found in the caterpillar's host plant, 'snakeroot' (*Aristolochia*).

Plate 69c

Giant Swallowtail
Heraclides cresphontes

ID: One of Florida's largest butterflies. Wings are dark brown or black with broad yellow diagonal bands of yellow spots. The undersides of the wings are mostly yellow with black markings. The hindwings have red eyespots and yellow tails. Wingspan ranges from 8.5 to 11.3 cm (3.3 to 4.4 in). Adults are found February through November in woodlands and citrus groves, throughout the year in South Florida.

Plate 69d

Zebra Swallowtail
Eurytides marcellus

ID: The only black and pale green to white striped butterfly in Florida. The hindwings have a red spot near the very long tail. Wingspans range from 5.5 to 7.9 cm (2.2 to 3.1 in). Sexes are similar. Found from March to December in deciduous woodlands along streams and rivers. Caterpillars are bright green with sky blue, yellow, and black transverse stripes.

Plate 69e

Eastern Tiger Swallowtail
Pterourus glaucus

ID: Florida's largest butterfly. Wingspan ranges from 9.6 to 11.8 cm (3.8 to 4.6 in). This species is easily recognized by four black tiger stripes on the upperpart of the forewings. The innermost stripe on each wing connects with the only black band on the hindwing. Adults are seen February through November in swamps, fields, hammocks and gardens. Adults feed on nectar of many flowers and also visit mud and carrion.

Plate 69f

Black Swallowtail
(also called American Swallowtail)
Papilio polyxenes

ID: A medium-large black butterfly. Upper sides of wings are edged with yellow spots. There are two rows of orange spots on the underside of the hindwings. Wingspan 6.9 to 8.4 cm (2.7 to 3.3 in). Found February through November near wet prairies, roadside ditches, open fields and gardens. Young caterpillars look like bird droppings.

Plate 69 **413**

a Great Southern White

b Pipevine Swallowtail

c Giant Swallowtail

d Zebra Swallowtail

e Eastern Tiger Swallowtail

f Black Swallowtail

Plate 70a

Atala

Eumaeus atala

ID: Males are black and metallic green, females black and blue. Undersides of wings are black with blue spots. The abdomen is bright red. Wingspan about 4.5 cm (1.8 in). The Atala was thought to be extinct in South Florida until 1979, when a small population was discovered on Key Biscayne. The species declined because its host plant, the coontie, was overharvested. With cultivation of the coontie and rearing of Atala larvae, the species has made an amazing comeback.

Plate 70b

Cloudless Sulphur

Phoebis sennae

ID: A large lemon-yellow butterfly. Undersides of the wings marked with small reddish-brown spots. Wingspan ranges from 4.8 to 6.5 cm (1.9 to 2.6 in). Adults are seen in open or brushy fields, gardens, roadsides and beaches. From mid-August until November, thousands of these butterflies can be seen migrating south into Florida.

Plate 70c

Gulf Fritillary

Agraulis vanillae

ID: Mainly orange with black markings. There are three white spots outlined in black on the upper surface of the forewing. The undersurface of the wing is orange with many silver-white spots. Wingspan ranges from 4.9 to 7.4 cm (1.9 to 2.9 in). Found in open fields and gardens. Adults are seen year-round in South Florida. In fall thousands of these butterflies migrate south into Florida from the eastern USA.

Plate 70d

Zebra Longwing

Heliconius charitonius

ID: The Zebra Longwing is Florida's official state butterfly. Its long, narrow, black wings are marked with yellow stripes; wingspan ranges from 4.9 to 8.8 cm (1.9 to 3.5 in). Adults occur in all months of the year in South and Central Florida and move into North Florida by summer. Zebra Longwings are found in hardwood hammocks, fields and gardens. Adults are unusual in that they often sleep in clusters on the same branch. These roosting aggregations sometimes last for weeks.

Plate 70e

Common Buckeye

Junonia coenia

ID: A small to medium-sized butterfly, chiefly brown with orange markings. Forewing has one large eye-spot with a blue pupil, hind wing has one large and one smaller eye-spot. Wingspan ranges from 3.3 to 5.1 cm (1.3 to 2.0 in). Adults are seen in all months of the year but are most abundant from August to October. Found in open weedy fields, pine woods, sandhills, beaches, and gardens.

Plate 70f

Orange Longwing

(also called Orange Julia)

Dryas iulia

ID: A bright orange butterfly with long narrow wings. Upperparts of the wing have narrow brown borders. Females are duller orange. The undersides of the wings are light brown with a white streak at the base of the hindwing. Wingspan ranges from 7.1 to 8.1 cm (2.8 to 3.2 in). Found year-round in hammocks, open fields and gardens.

Plate 70 **415**

a Atala

b Cloudless Sulphur

c Gulf Fritillary

d Zebra Longwing

e Common Buckeye

f Orange Longwing

Plate 71a
Long-Tailed Skipper
Urbanus proteus
ID: A brown butterfly with semi-transparent spots on the forewings. The hindwings have long tails. Wingspan ranges from 3.9 to 4.8 cm (1.5 to 1.9 in). Adults seen throughout the year in South Florida, most common August to October in North Florida. Found in open areas and disturbed sites.

Plate 71b
Monarch
Danaus plexippus
ID: This well-known butterfly is orange with black wing borders and veins. The undersides are similar but paler. Wingspan ranges from 8.1 to 10 cm (3.2 to 3.9 in). Adults and caterpillars are distasteful to predators. Monarchs can be seen in open habitats and disturbed sites. Every year these butterflies migrate north from wintering sites in Mexico. They breed along the way and several generations later they reach southern Canada. In fall they begin the return journey to Mexico.

Plate 71c
Io moth
Automeris io
ID: A large moth, wingspan 5.5 to 7.9 cm (2.2 to 3.1 in). Forewings are yellowish orange or buff-brown. Hind wings have a large prominent eye-spot, with black 'eyebrow' lines below. Caterpillars are vivid emerald-green with two stripes along the side of the body. The top stripe is red, the lower one is white. Their backs are covered with branching, stinging spines. Found in open woodlands; adults are seen flying around lights at night.

Plate 71d
Luna Moth
Actias luna
ID: The pale yellow-green Luna Moth has a long curved tail on its hind wings and a wingspan of 7.5 to 10.5 cm (2.9 to 4.1 in). There is a small eye-spot on each wing. Common but rarely seen, these moths are attracted to lights, and they are sometimes found on window screens or around outdoor lights. The adult moths do not feed and live for only about a week.

Plate 71e
Imperial Moth
Eacles imperialis
ID: A very large moth; wingspan ranges from 8.8 to 10.1 cm (3.5 to 4.0 in). Wings are orangish or yellow with dark flecks and purple-brown patches. Caterpillar bright green, orange or brown (depending on stage), with sparse white hairs. Found in mixed oak-pine woodlands. Adults are seen at lights.

Plate 71f
Polyphemus Moth
Antheraea polyphemus
ID: This huge moth has a wingspan of 10 to 15 cm (3.9 to 5.9 in), and is one of the largest species found in Florida. It has reddish to yellowish-brown wings, each with a distinct oval eye-spot ringed with yellow, blue, and black. Found in forests, orchards, and wetlands; it is also commonly seen flying around lights in urban areas. Adults emerge from their cocoons in the late afternoon and mate the same day. Females lay eggs that evening. Adults survive for only a few days.

Plate 71 **417**

a Long-tailed
Skipper

b Monarch

c Io Moth

d Luna Moth

e Imperial
Moth

f Polyphemus Moth

Plate 72a
Giant Leopard Moth
Ecpantheria scribonia
ID: A large, fairly unmistakable, black and white moth. Body white with black spots, forewings white marked with black open circles. Wingspan about 8.9 cm (3.5 in). Antennae black, legs banded black and white. Found in gardens on orange and banana trees.

Plate 72b
Walking Stick
Anisomorpha buprestoides
ID: Slow-moving, elongated, stick-like insects up to 7.6 cm (3 in) long. Black or dark brown with paler markings. Females are much larger than males. Neither sex has wings. Often found on oak trees as they feed on oak leaves. They can emit a foul-smelling substance from glands on their back.

Plate 72c
Rattlebox Moth
Utetheisa bella
ID: Forewings are red, orange, or yellowish orange, marked with rows of white-ringed black spots. Wingspan about 4.1 cm (1.6 in). Antennae black. Feeds on rattlebox and sweet clover. Found in open areas and edge habitats.

Plate 72d
Southeastern Lubber Grasshopper
Romalea microptera
ID: This large flightless grasshopper is slow and clumsy, and can jump only short distances. Adults are 6.0 to 8.0 cm (2.4 to 3.1 in) long. Body is dull yellow with black markings, wings are short and stubby, hindwings reddish with a black border. Their bright color is a warning coloration; the species contains toxic substances dangerous to birds and mammals. Most commonly seen during July and August, in open woods, fields and along roadsides.

Plate 72e
Oleander Moth
Syntomeida epilais
ID: A startling-looking blue-black moth that mimics a wasp. Also known as the Polka Dot Moth because of the white spots on its body and wings. Wingspan ranges from 4.7 to 4.9 cm (1.8 to 1.9 in). The tip of the abdomen is brilliant scarlet. Caterpillar is orange with tufts of long black hair. Feeds on oleander plants, which are poisonous to mammals. Often seen in gardens of tourist attractions where oleanders are planted.

Plate 72f
Praying Mantis
Stagmomantis carolina
ID: A large insect; adults are over 5 cm (2+ in) in length. May be brown or green in color. The front legs are modified for grasping prey, and the flexible neck can turn in all directions. Flies well for short distances. In brushy fields and gardens.

Plate 72g
Broad-winged Katydid
Microcentrum rhombifolium
ID: A large, bright green, almost perfectly camouflaged insect. Body about 5.7 cm (2.2 in) long. Wings are veined and resemble leaves. Antennae are longer than the body. Can be located by its call – a loud KATY-DID-KATY-DIDN'T. Found in woods, fields, and gardens.

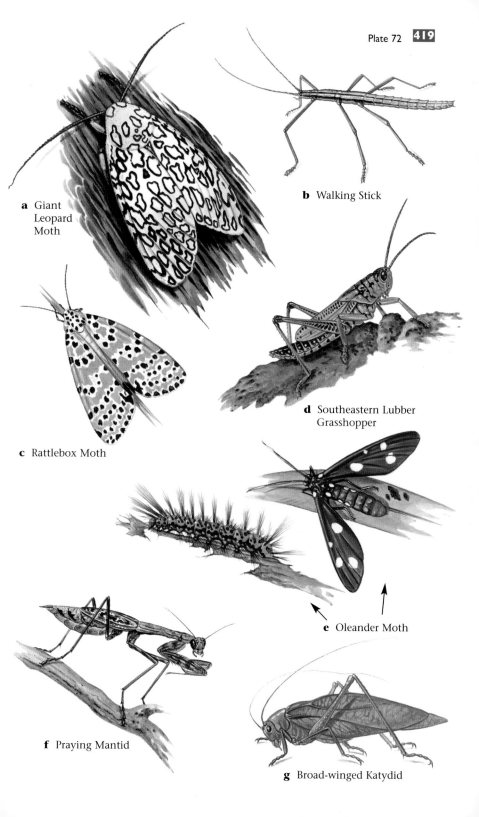

Plate 72 **419**

a Giant Leopard Moth

b Walking Stick

c Rattlebox Moth

d Southeastern Lubber Grasshopper

e Oleander Moth

f Praying Mantid

g Broad-winged Katydid

Plate 73a
Mole Cricket
Gryllotalpa hexadactyla
Body stout, elongated (3.1 cm; 1.2 in), with shield-like covering on body (thorax). Uniformly tan or brown. Enlarged front feet with strong, flat claws for burrowing through soil. Wings narrow. Feeds on roots of grass and other plants; major pest of lawns and golf courses. Found in pastures, moist woods, gardens, and lawns.

Plate 73b
Ebony Jewelwing
Calopteryx maculata
ID: A spectacular black and green damselfly, with broad wings rounded at the tips. Males have metallic green bodies and all-black wings. Females have dull-green bodies and black wings with white spot on tips. Both sexes have long, thin, black legs. Flight pattern is distinctive, with hesitation in wingbeat. Often seen perching on vegetation along streams and rivers. Length 4.5 to 5.5 cm (1.8 to 2.2 in).

Plate 73c
Rambur's Forktail
Ischnura ramburii
ID: Mature male has black back and green sides and a striking blue final segment of the abdomen. Females occur in three color forms: olive, orange-red, and black-green. Wings are transparent, with dark spot at tips. Perches and flies along edges of ponds and marshes. Length 2.6 to 3.5 cm (1.0 to 1.4 in).

Plate 73d
Blue Dasher
Pachydiplax longipennis
ID: Mature male has whitish face, metallic green eyes, and black and yellow striped body. Pale blue abdomen tapers to black tip. Female duller with short blunt abdomen. In juveniles, the abdomen is black and marked above with two interrupted yellow lines. Wings mostly clear. Typically perches on tips of twigs and stems; found near any still water, including ponds, swamps and marshes. Length 2.6 to 4.4 cm (1.0 to 1.7 in).

Plate 73e
Common Green Darner
Anax junius
ID: A large (7.6 cm; 3 in) dragonfly. Distinctive 'bull's-eye' spot on forehead, green body, and bright blue (male) or reddish-brown (female) abdomen. Wings clear. Perches low in vegetation. Often hunts near the ground, flies with hind wings held flat. Also seen near lakes and ponds. Sometimes referred to as 'mosquito hawk.'

Plate 73f
Halloween Pennant
Celithemis eponina
ID: A colorful, medium-sized (3.0 to 4.2 cm; 1.2 to 1.7 in) dragonfly. Dark abdomen with orange-yellow stripe on top. Yellow-orange wings are large and distinctively marked with dark brown bands and spots. Often seen perching on tips of tall vegetation in fields or near ponds and marshes.

Plate 73 **421**

a Mole Cricket

b Ebony Jewelwing

c Rambur's Forktail

d Blue Dasher

e Common Green Darner

f Halloween Pennant

Plate 74a
Cicada
Tibicen sp.
ID: Cicadas are largish (3.8 cm, 1.5 in), usually dark with greenish markings and long, clear membranous wings. Body compact, with large head and bulging eyes. Most growth occurs underground, some species taking 13 years to develop into adults; cicadas emerge and shed larval skins. Song of male cicada is a rapid, buzzing or clicking call. Each species produces a distinctive song. Calls often heard on hot, sultry summer afternoons.

Plate 74b
American Cockroach
Periplaneta americana
ID: A reddish-brown roach, about 3.8 cm (1.5 in) long, with a yellow margin on the rear edge of the head. Antennae are longer than the body. When disturbed, runs rapidly and adults may fly. Immature cockroaches are wingless. Common in moist areas such as basements, sewers, and inside buildings.

Plate 74c
Firefly
Photinus pyralis
ID: Fireflies are not flies but beetles, which produce light signals from their abdomens at night. Beetle about 1.9 cm (0.75 in) long; long wings are blackish or brown, edged with yellow or orange. Fireflies flash to find mates. The male flies over a likely area and flashes, the female responds. Different species can be recognized by the duration and frequency of their flashes. Found in meadows, woodland edges, and close to streams. This firefly is harvested commercially by the biochemical industry.

Plate 74d
Tiger Beetle
Cicindela scutellaris
ID: Elongated body, about 1.6 cm (0.6 in) long. Head, thorax and wings are shiny metallic green; abdomen is dark. They are fast runners, with long legs and long antennae. Voracious predators of small insects. Inhabit open sandy areas.

Plate 74e
Wood Roach
(also called Palmetto Bug)
Eurycotis floridanus
ID: A large (3.0 to 3.8 cm, 1.2 to 1.5 in), clumsy, flightless roach. Black or dark reddish brown. It is also called Stinking Roach, because it exudes a very pungent smell when disturbed or threatened. Occasionally found in leaf bases of cabbage palmetto, but more likely to be in stacks of planks, empty flower pots, under rotting logs or near compost piles. Does not survive well indoors.

Plate 74f
Rhinoceros Beetle
(also called Ox Beetle)
Strategus sp.
ID: Adults are large, over 2.5 cm (1 in) in length, and handsome, but clumsy. Dark brown to shiny black. Male has three horns on thorax; females are smaller and without horns. Adults found in open woods and brushy fields; feed on leaves and fruit. The larvae, or 'white grubs,' live in the soil and eat roots of plants.

Plate 74g
Click Beetle
Orthostethus infuscatus
ID: Named for the audible sound produced by the snapping of a small, fingerlike projection on the underside of the thorax into a groove. If the beetle is placed on its back, this clicking action can flip it into the air, and often results in an upright landing. Beetles have elongate and flattened bodies and a hardened pair of wing shields that fit together tightly. Adults live in decayed wood, under bark, or in the ground. Wireworms are the immature larval stages of click beetles. Larvae are slender, hard-bodied and shiny; most are brown or yellowish.

Plate 74h
Cuban Green Coachroach
Panchlora nivea
ID: An outdoor, tropical roach, not usually found north of Florida. Adults are pale green, about 1.9 cm (0.75 in) long; nymphs (an immature stage) are dark brown. Adults live on plant leaves, but are attracted to lights and are adept flyers.

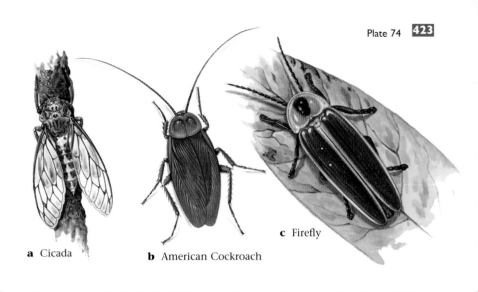

a Cicada **b** American Cockroach **c** Firefly

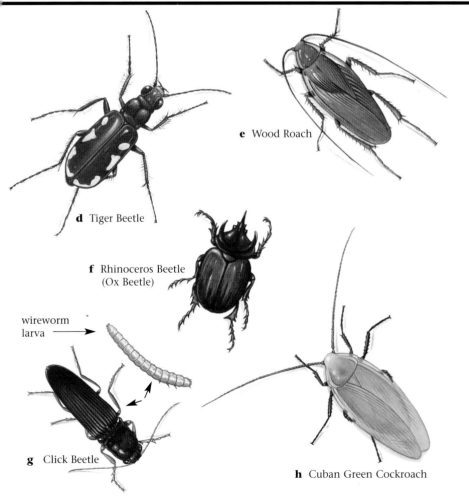

d Tiger Beetle

e Wood Roach

f Rhinoceros Beetle (Ox Beetle)

wireworm larva

g Click Beetle

h Cuban Green Cockroach

Plate 74 **423**

Plate 75a
Mud Dauber
Sceliphron caementarium
ID: A slender black-and-yellow wasp, about 2.5 to 3.0 cm (1.0 to 1.3 in) long, with an obvious waist between thorax and abdomen. Legs are mostly yellow and wings are dark. Female uses mouth to collect moist mud and shape it into balls to form a long tubular cell; each nest comprised of several parallel joined cells. Each cell is filled with paralyzed spiders and female lays single egg on spiders and seals the chamber. Nests are stuck on walls of buildings, under rocks, overhanging cliffs, or other sheltered sites. Harmless insect unless grabbed by hand.

Plate 75b
Eastern Yellow Jacket
Vespula maculifrons
ID: Yellow jackets are black and yellow wasps with a stout body and a definite waist. Their bodies are 1.4 to 2.5 cm (0.6 to 1.0 in) long. Yellow jackets nest under logs, and in crevices. These wasps feed on a wide variety of insects but also forage for sweets around garbage cans and picnic tables. For most people a yellow jacket sting is just a temporary pain, but 0.5 to 1.0 % of the human population is highly allergic to yellow jacket venom.

Plate 75c
Milkweed Bug
Lygaeus kalmii
ID: A brightly colored seed-eating bug, about 1.2 cm (0.5 in) long. Black with red spot on head and red band on thorax. Distinctive X-shaped mark on forewings. Feeds on milkweed seeds, which contain toxic chemicals, and stores chemicals in body as protection against insect predators.

Plate 75d
Fiery Searcher
(also called Caterpillar Hunter)
Calosoma sp.
ID: A large, beautiful beetle, about 2.5 cm (1 in) long. Wing covers are an iridescent, bluish green; head and thorax are black. The legs are blue. As its name implies, this beetle feeds mainly on caterpillars. Hunts at night and hides under bark and in leaf litter during the day.

Plate 75e
Lovebug
Plecia nearctica
ID: This insect's habit of congregating in clouds along roadsides make it an easily recognizable species. About 1 cm (0.4 in) long, Lovebugs have a black head and wings, and orange-red thorax. Common throughout Florida in fall and spring, males and females are often seen joined together, mating. Lovebugs are attracted to car exhaust fumes and can be a serious nuisance to motorists because their squashed bodies clog windshields and radiators.

Plate 75f
Giant Waterbug
Lethocerus griseus
ID: A large (5 cm; 2 in), dark brown bug. Excellent swimmer, pursues and captures prey in the water. Insects, minnows or tadpoles are seized by clamp-like front legs, and strong beak then used to inject powerful venom into victims. May deliver painful bite if handled. Be alert for these bugs in hotel swimming pools.

Plate 75g
Paper Wasp
Polistes sp.
ID: A reddish wasp with a long spindle-shaped abdomen. About 2.5 cm (1 in) long. Reddish-brown wings. Nests are honeycombed and paperlike, made from masticated pulp of fibers scraped from weeds or wood and mixed with secretion from wasp's mouth. The nests are often located under eaves of houses, stadium bleachers, or undersides of large leaves. Sting of wasp is painful and dangerous for people who are allergic to venom.

Plate 75h
Florida Leaf-footed Bug
Acanthocephala femorata
ID: The largest plant-feeding bug in Florida, more than 2.5 cm (1 in) long. Massively built. Produces audible buzz when flying. Dark brown; hind legs are flattened and expanded into a leaf-like shape. Have stink glands on their sides for defense.

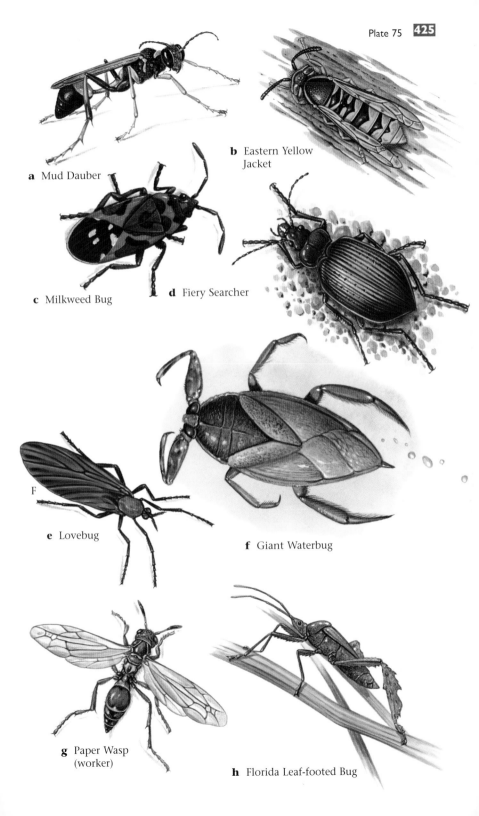

Plate 75 **425**

a Mud Dauber

b Eastern Yellow Jacket

c Milkweed Bug

d Fiery Searcher

e Lovebug

f Giant Waterbug

g Paper Wasp (worker)

h Florida Leaf-footed Bug

Plate 76a
Chigger
Trombicula sp.
ID: Minute blood-sucking mite, barely visible to the naked eye. Reddish-orange color. Also called redbugs, jiggers, and harvest mites or lice. In leaf litter or clinging to grass stems and foliage, they attach to any animal that brushes against them. Do not burrow into skin but pierce it and inject an anti-coagulant. Common points of feeding include feet, legs, around waistline, under belts and elastic bands of underwear. Feeding causes intense itching, but is usually not dangerous.

Plate 76b
Wood Tick
(also called Dog Tick)
Dermacentor sp.
ID: A tiny (0.3 to 0.4 cm; 0.1 to 0.16 in), flattened, pale gray (male) to reddish-brown (female) tick with a hard plate on top of the body. Small dorsal plate of female is silvery. Sometimes called 'seed ticks.' Cling to grass in meadows and on shrubs along forest trails and pathways, waiting to latch onto passing mammal host. Penetrates skin with barbed mouthparts and feeds on blood. Drops off after obtaining blood meal. Tick may be vector of several diseases. Prompt and careful removal of tick head important to reduce chance of infection.

Plate 76c
Deer Tick
Ixodes scapularis
ID: A tiny (0.2 to 0.4 cm; 0.08 to 0.16 in), flattened, reddish-brown tick with a hard plate on top of the body. Sometimes called 'seed ticks.' Sit on vegetation in fields, pastures, and woods, waiting to latch onto passing host. Penetrate skin with barbed mouthparts and feed on blood of mammals. Ticks may be carrying bacteria that cause Lyme Disease. Prompt and careful removal of tick head important to reduce chance of infection.

Plate 76d
Fire Ant
Solenopsis invicta
ID: The 0.5 to 0.9 cm (0.2 to 0.4 in) long Fire Ant is thought to have been inadvertently introduced to the USA from Brazil by a cargo ship dumping ballast. Fire Ants live in underground colonies usually with a single queen. Excavated soil is piled in a mound above. They feed on foliage, insects, and dead animals. These ants are aggressive, 'boiling' out of the ground to attack anything that disturbs the mound. The bite is painful. Leave them alone!

Plate 76e
Deerfly
Chrysops sp.
ID: About 0.7 to 1.0 cm (0.3 to 0.5 in) long, with dark eyes marked with fluorescent green lines. Also referred to as the dreaded 'yellow fly.' Females are blood suckers, and strong flyers, able to keep up with people trying to run away. Males feed mainly on pollen and nectar. Body is yellowish brown with dark bands or spots; clear wings. Active during daylight hours in shady areas.

Plate 76f
Velvet Ant
(also called Cow Killer)
Dasymutilla occidentalis
ID: Though it looks like a large ant, this 2.5 cm (1.0 in) red and black fuzzy-looking insect is really a wasp. Velvet Ants are solitary and often seen moving quickly about on the ground. Males have small wings, females are wingless. They are found in sandy areas, in fields and on the edges of woodlands. Velvet Ants get the name 'cow killer' from their painful sting; the pain is so severe people claim it could kill a cow.

Plate 76g
Carpenter Bee
Xylocopa sp.
ID: About 1.9 to 2.5 cm (0.75 to 1 in) long. Closely resemble Bumblebees except abdomen is shiny metallic greenish black, while abdomen of Bumblebee is hairy. Build nests in solid wood tunnels 7.6 to 10.2 cm (3 to 4 in) deep; entrance hole about 1.3 cm (0.5 in) wide, looks as if it has been made with a drill. Pollinate flowers of passion fruit.

Plate 76 **427**

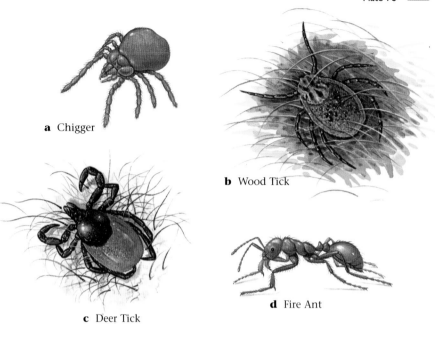

a Chigger

b Wood Tick

c Deer Tick

d Fire Ant

e Deerfly

f Velvet Ant

g Carpenter Bee

Plate 77a
Black Widow Spider
Latrodectus mactans
ID: The female's glossy jet-black body is about 1.3 cm (0.5 in) long, marked with a characteristic red hourglass on the underside of the abdomen. Females are poisonous, but the smaller males are not a threat. Females hang belly up and rarely leave the web. These spiders commonly build their webs near woodpiles, outdoor toilets, and under porches and buildings. The bite feels like a pinprick, and the venom causes muscle spasms and breathing difficulties in humans.

Plate 77b
Silver Argiope
Argiope argentata
ID: Female 1.2 to 1.6 cm (0.5 to 0.6 in); male 0.4 to 0.5 cm (0.1 to 0.2 in). Head/thorax covered with short silver hair; abdomen black to brownish yellow with silver spots. Legs dark and hairy with pale brown and yellow banding. Spins a translucent web, with dense, white, zigzag cross threads that form an X-shaped mark in center. Spider varies zigzag pattern to keep bees from learning to avoid web. Found in fields and gardens.

Plate 77c
Golden Silk Spider
Nephila clavipes
ID: Female is large (2.2 to 2.5 cm; 0.8 to 1.0 in). Head and thorax (cephalothorax) are pale gray, marked with dark spots on each side; abdomen is yellow, orange, or green and marked with white spots. Orange and black bands on legs, with tufts of black hair on first and last pairs of legs. Male is small (0.4 cm; 0.16 in) with drab coloring. Web is large (60 to 90 cm; 2 to 3 ft) and woven with different types of thread and notch-like support lines. Spider adds yellow pigments to its silk to attract small bees. Found in woods, swamps, and shrubs.

Plate 77d
Black and Yellow Garden Spider
Argiope aurantia
ID: Body 2.7 to 4.4 cm (1.1 to 1.7 in) long. Yellow and black patterned abdomen; head/thorax with short silvery hair. Long, hairy legs, marked with reddish-yellow and black bands. Builds large web with thick zigzag pattern radiating from center. Web placed in sunny, sheltered sites in meadows, bushes, and gardens.

Plate 77e
Carolina Wolf Spider
Lycosa carolinensis
ID: Largest wolf spider in North America. Females 2.2 to 3.5 cm (0.9 to 1.4 in); males 1.8 to 2.0 cm (0.7 to 0.8 in). Looks like a gray-brown tarantula, but less hairy. Dark eyes. Dark lateral stripe on abdomen. Hairy legs. Nocturnal, terrestrial hunter, in open fields. Female deposits egg sacs in deep burrow and guards the entrance.

Plate 77f
Scorpion
Centruroides gracilis
ID: Large, brown to tan scorpion, up to 15 cm (6 in) long, but most 5 to 7 cm (2 to 2.75 in). Head/thorax often striped with yellow; abdomen slender and tipped with stinger. Prey seized with pair of large head appendages (pedipalps) that have pincer-like tips; prey stung to death. Nocturnal hunter, often found under bark, stones, in wood piles, and sometimes in old buildings. Painful sting but not dangerous.

Plate 77 **429**

a Black
Widow Spider

b Silver Argiope

c Golden
Silk Spider

e Carolina
Wolf Spider

d Black and Yellow Garden Spider

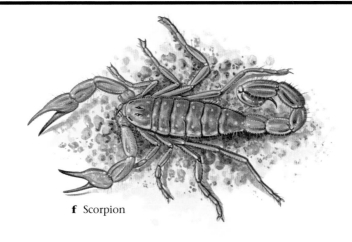

f Scorpion

Lengths given for fish are 'standard lengths,' the distance from the front of the mouth to the point where the tail appears to join the body; that is, tails are not included in the measurement.

Text by Richard Francis

Plate 78a
Queen Angelfish
Holacanthus ciliaris

One of the most spectacular fishes in the Florida/Caribbean area. This rather shy angelfish must be approached slowly. It is fairly common in the protected reefs preferred by snorkelers, where it can be seen poking around coral heads looking for various invertebrates to eat. These fish are highly territorial and usually occur in pairs. (to 45 cm, 18 in)

Plate 78b
Longsnout Butterflyfish
Chaetodon aculeatus

This is a rather shy fish, and unlike most butterflyfishes, tends to be solitary. This fish prefers somewhat deeper water than snorkelers typically explore, and is best observed on SCUBA. As its common name indicates, this species has an elongated snout, which facilitates deep coral probing. The color of this species typically ranges from olive to dusky. (to 10 cm, 4 in)

Plate 78c
Reef Butterflyfish
Chaetodon sedentarius

Closely related to the angelfishes, butterflyfishes are also generally monogamous. This species is fairly common and prefers the tops of coral reefs where it can be easily observed, usually in pairs. Very attractive, but not flashy by butterflyfish standards; look for the vertical black bar through the eye. Like many members of its family, the reef butterflyfish eats live coral. (to 16 cm, 6 in)

Plate 78d
Banded Butterflyfish
Chaetodon striatus

This butterflyfish has prominent vertical black bands on white background; the front-most black band runs through the eye. Usually seen in pairs foraging on reef tops. (to 15 cm, 6 in)

Plate 78e
Spotfin Butterflyfish
Chaetodon ocellatus

This beauty is named for the small black spot on the trailing edge of its dorsal fin. Its snow-white body is fringed by bright yellow dorsal and anal fins. The vertical black stripe that runs through the eye probably serves to deceive predators as to which end is the head. Usually found in pairs cruising over the top of the reef. The best way to get close is to place yourself in their line of travel. They will move away when approached. (to 20 cm, 8 in)

Plate 78f
Blue Angelfish
Holacanthus bermudensis

This beauty is common in Florida and the Bahamas (but is absent in the rest of the Caribbean). Its body color is a grayish blue to grayish purple. Its fins are tinged with yellow. Shy, but curious, look for them on reef tops. (to 36 cm, 14 in)

Plate 78 **431**

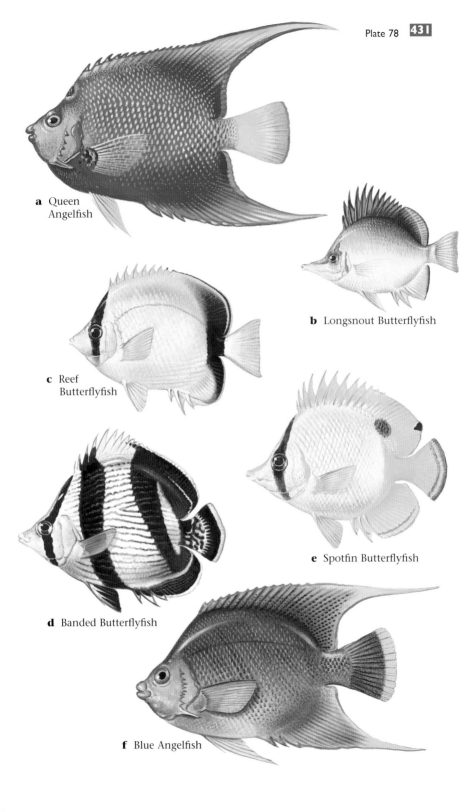

a Queen Angelfish

b Longsnout Butterflyfish

c Reef Butterflyfish

d Banded Butterflyfish

e Spotfin Butterflyfish

f Blue Angelfish

Plate 79a
Ocean Surgeonfish
Acanthurus bahianus
This species is also a color-changer (from dark brown to bluish gray). Fairly common and generally found in loose aggregations, along with Blue Tangs and Doctorfish. Grazers, they are approachable but tend to keep a minimum distance from divers. (to 35 cm, 14 in)

Plate 79b
Blue Tang
Acanthurus coeruleus
This is one of the surgeonfishes, as indicated by the scalpel-like protrusion near the base of the tail, which is deployed in aggressive encounters. Individuals can rapidly change color from a deep purple to powder-blue. Abundant and usually in fairly large groups that move restlessly along reef tops grazing on algae. (to 23 cm, 9 in)

Plate 79c
French Angelfish
Pomacanthus paru
Another large angelfish that can be distinguished from the gray angel by the yellow highlights on its scales. It resembles the Gray Angelfish in both habits and temperament. If you are above them, they will turn toward the horizontal to better keep an eye on you. (to 35 cm, 14 in)

Plate 79d
Rock Beauty
Holacanthus tricolor
This is a common but fairly shy species. They patrol well-defined territories on the reef. The quiet snorkeler will be rewarded by the sight of this striking fish. Yellow areas in the front and tail sections are separated by a large area of black. Also notice the blue highlights around the eye. Juveniles are bright yellow with a blue-ringed black bull's-eye on the body toward the tail. (to 20 cm, 8 in)

Plate 79e
Doctorfish
Acanthurus chirurgus
Very similar in appearance and habits to the Ocean Surgeonfish. They can be distinguished by their vertical body bars, which, however, can be quite faint. This is one of the most abundant shallow water species. (to 25 cm, 10 in)

Plate 79f
Gray Angelfish
Pomacanthus arcuatus
These large angelfish are quite curious and may approach if you remain still. They mate for life and, once formed, a pair is rarely separated by more than a few meters. They consume a variety of invertebrates and are quite active during the day. Much less shy than Queen Angelfish. (to 50 cm, 20 in)

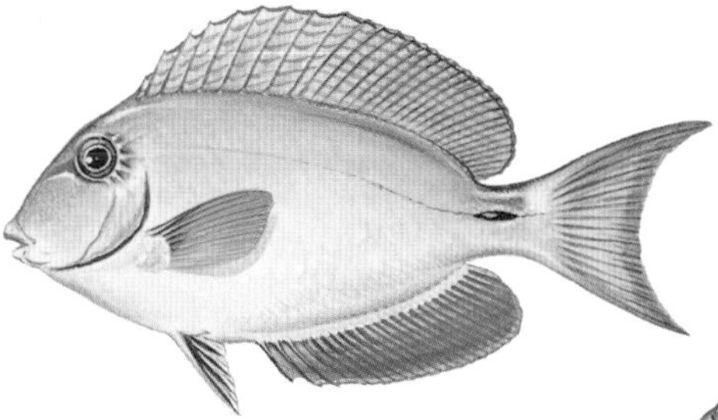

Plate 79   **433**

a Ocean Surgeonfish

b Blue Tang

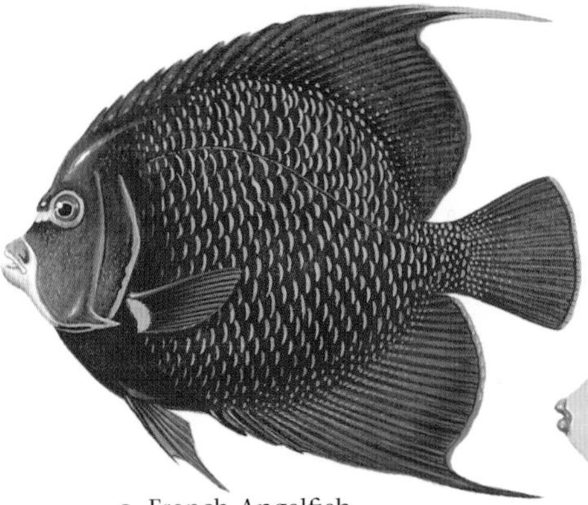

c French Angelfish

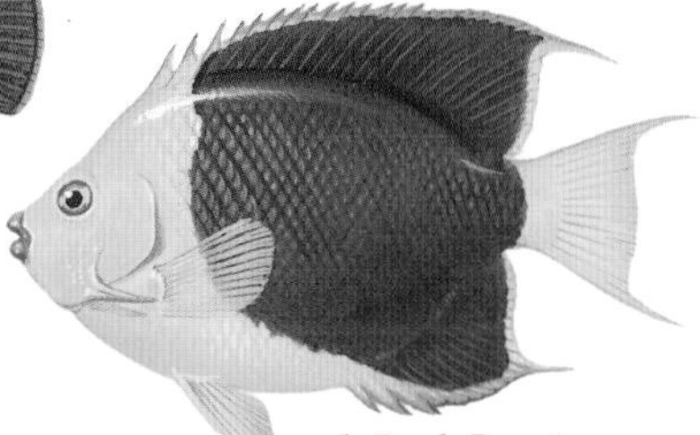

d Rock Beauty

e Doctorfish

f Gray Angelfish

Plate 80a
Houndfish
Tylosurus crocodilus
This species belongs to the needlefish family, of which it is the largest. They are typically found in shallow water over turtle grass beds or small patch reefs, where they tend to drift just below the surface. A favorite food item for Brown Pelicans in the Florida area. They are fairly shy and not easy to see from below. (to 1.5 m, 5 ft)

Plate 80b
Great Barracuda
Sphyraena barracuda
This consummate predator has an impressive array of teeth which it displays while slowly opening and closing its mouth (to assist respiration). Not dangerous, but they can be disconcertingly curious. They may even follow you around the reef. Barracudas exhibit an economy of movement, generally drifting, but capable of rapid bursts should prey approach. (to 2 m, 6.5 ft)

Plate 80c
Horse-eye Jack
(also called Bigeye Jack, Horse-eye Trevally)
Caranx latus
Another common jack found in open water over reefs, usually in small schools. More skittish than Bar Jacks, these fast-moving fish will usually give the snorkeler only a brief glimpse of them. Distinguished by their yellow tails and large eyes. (to 75 cm, 29 in)

Plate 80d
Cero
Scomberomorus regalis
This mackerel has the body shape of a barracuda. It is silvery, with a darker back. Ceros prefer open water but can be seen near drop-offs. (to 1.2 m, 4 ft)

Plate 80e
Lookdown
Selene vomer
This species is much more common in Florida than in the Caribbean. They prefer calm, shallow water, often quite turbid. One of the laterally compressed jacks, its body is silver. (to 30 cm, 12 in)

Plate 80f
Bar Jack
(also called Skipjack)
Caranx ruber
A fast-moving predator that courses over the reefs in groups of variable size. Bar jacks can make surprisingly close passes and you may be lucky enough to find yourself in the middle of a swirling school. This species can be distinguished from other jacks by its black stripe, bordered by bright blue, running from its dorsal fin through the bottom half of the tail. (to 60 cm, 24 in)

Plate 80 **435**

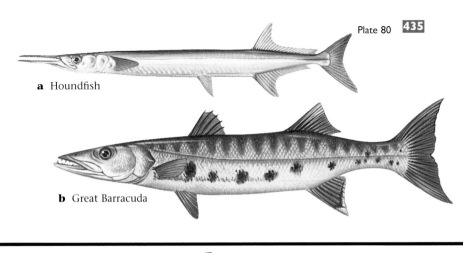

a Houndfish

b Great Barracuda

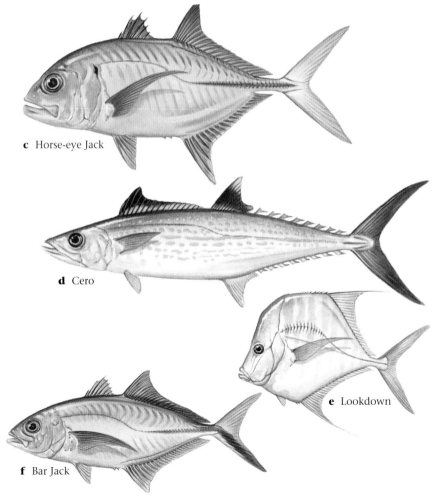

c Horse-eye Jack

d Cero

e Lookdown

f Bar Jack

Plate 81a
Bonefish
Albula vulpes
One of the species most prized by sports-fisherpersons. When feeding, usually found in shallow flats on a rising tide, in the vicinity of mangroves. Tend to prefer the coral rubble when they are not feeding. Bonefish are common but very shy; they must be approached slowly. Not colorful, they are silvery with no characteristic markings. Forked tails and an underslung jaw, somewhat like freshwater suckers. (to 1 m, 3.3 ft)

Plate 81b
Common Snook
Centropomus undecimalis
Another prized sportfish, look for them near mangroves along the mainland coastline. Wary, but not as shy as Bonefish; they can be approached. Snook have a characteristic black line running through the middle of their bodies. The shape of their head is rather unique, like a shallow slide. (to 1.4 m, 4.5 ft)

Plate 81c
White Mullet
Mugil curema
These common fish are found in shallow, open water over sand or other soft bottom habitats. They feed on tiny animals found on bottom detritus or sea grasses. This species has a characteristic black spot at the base of the pectoral fin and very large scales. (to 38 cm, 15 in)

Plate 81d
Striped Mullet
Mugil cephalus
This elongate species has a silvery body, with darker tints. It occurs in large schools in fairly shallow water. (to 91 cm, 3 ft)

Plate 81e
Spottail Pinfish
Diplodus holbrooki
A subtropical species that does not occur in the Caribbean; it can be found primarily where there are grassbeds. Its laterally compressed body is silvery with a black area at the base of the tail. (to 46 cm, 1.5 ft)

Plate 81f
Pinfish
Lagodon rhomboides
This species has a fairly elongate body for a porgy. It is basically subtropical, common in Florida but absent from the Caribbean. Its color is variable, but generally silvery with bluish to greenish tones. (to 35 cm, 14 in)

Plate 81 **437**

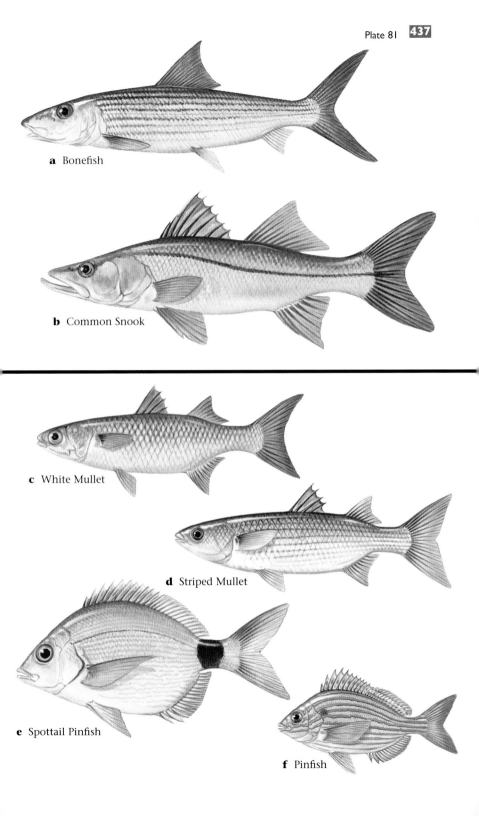

a Bonefish

b Common Snook

c White Mullet

d Striped Mullet

e Spottail Pinfish

f Pinfish

Plate 82a
Tarpon
Megalops atlanticus
This renowned sportfish is quite easy to approach underwater. They tend to form resting schools during the day, often in very specific places. They set out to feed, alone, at night. (to 2.4 m, 8 ft)

Plate 82b
Cobia
Rachycentron canadium
These large grayish fish have slightly protruding lower jaws. They like to hover below cover such as ships and buoys, where they can be readily approached, as they seem completely unafraid. (to 1.8 m, 6 ft)

Plate 82c
Red Porgy
Pagrus pagrus
Another subtropical species; it is silvery with reddish tones and red tail margins. The adults are usually found in deeper water than the juveniles, which tend to hover above reefs. Fairly bold and curious, they may approach if you remain still. (to 91 cm, 3 ft)

Plate 82d
Bermuda Chub
Kyphosus sectatrix
This common species swims in loose schools over reefs, sometimes quite near the surface. Chubs have a characteristic oval shape, silvery body, and dusky-colored fins. (to 76 cm, 30 in)

Plate 82e
Jolthead Porgy
Calamus bajonado
This species has the classic porgy shape, but with a more prominent head. You can find joltheads over patchy reef and sand areas. (to 61 cm, 2 ft)

Plate 82f
Sheepshead
Archosargus probatocephalus
This species is common in Florida, where it can be found near rocky outcrops with adjacent sandy areas. It can be readily distinguished by its oblique black bands (5 or 6) on a silvery background. Sheepshead are fairly curious, and will sometimes come over to observe you, if you appear to be ignoring them. (to 91 cm, 3 ft)

Plate 82 **439**

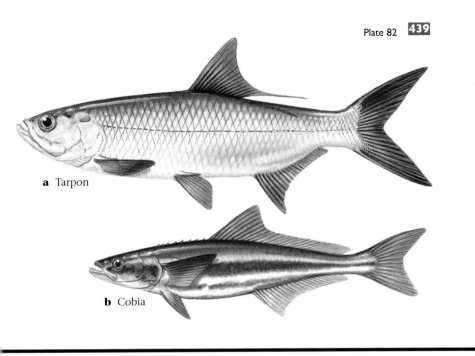

a Tarpon

b Cobia

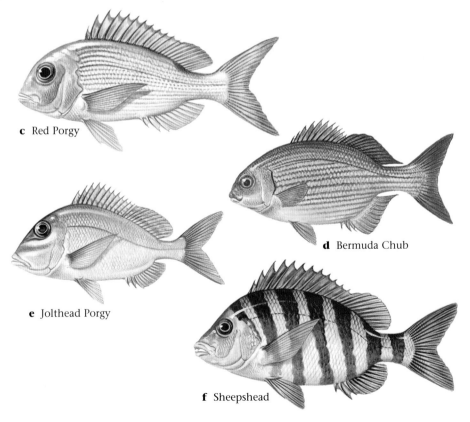

c Red Porgy

d Bermuda Chub

e Jolthead Porgy

f Sheepshead

Plate 83a

French Grunt

Haemulon flavolineatum

Grunts are named for the characteristic sound they make by grinding teeth-like structures in their throats. They are an important group of predators throughout the Florida area and the Caribbean, and are closely related to snappers. Grunts are found on reefs, sandy areas and seagrass beds. The French Grunt is one of the common species in this region. Wavy blue horizontal lines on a yellow body are characteristic. Look for them under ledges. (to 30 cm, 12 in)

Plate 83b

White Grunt

Haemulon plumieri

This grunt species is distinguished by the checkered pattern of blue and yellow on its body, as well as the parallel blue and yellow lines on its long head. Like many grunt species, white grunts seem to drift in groups of variable size; they retreat to cover when approached. (to 45 cm, 18 in)

Plate 83c

Blue-striped Grunt

Haemulon sciurus

This striking fish has bright blue stripes on a golden-yellow body. Also note the dark dorsal fin and tail. This is one of the most wary of the grunt species; patience and slow movements are required in order to approach. (to 45 cm, 18 in)

Plate 83d

Spanish Grunt

Haemulon macrostomum

This species is not as common as other grunts in the Florida reefs. A prominent black stripe runs through the eye to the base of the tail. The body is generally silvery and the fins have yellow borders. (to 43 cm, 17 in)

Plate 83e

Sailor's Choice

Haemulon parra

This handsome grunt has a silvery body with dark highlights. Its fins are quite dusky. They drift in small schools over and between reefs. (to 40 cm, 16 in)

Plate 83f

Margate

Haemulon album

This gray grunt prefers the sand flats between reef patches. Behaviorally a typical grunt; fairly wary but sometimes curious, it tends to drift passively, either alone or in small groups. (to 60 cm, 24 in)

Plate 83 **441**

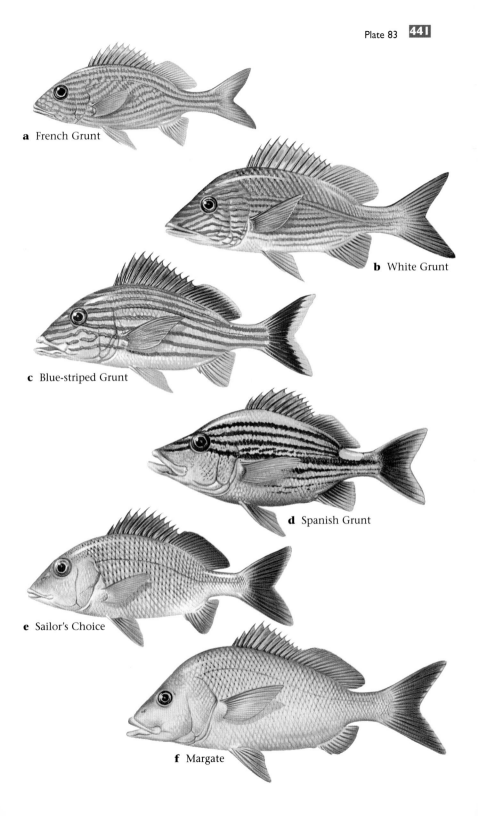

a French Grunt

b White Grunt

c Blue-striped Grunt

d Spanish Grunt

e Sailor's Choice

f Margate

Plate 84a
Porkfish
Anisotremus virginicus
This is one of the more abundant species in the Caribbean, and a favorite for snorkelers. Bright yellow lateral stripes behind two striking vertical black bands distinguish this beautiful grunt. As an added bonus, it is quite easy to approach. (to 40 cm, 16 in)

Plate 84b
Atlantic Spadefish
Chaetodipterus faber
You will not confuse this fish with any other. Laterally compressed like a pompano and shaped like an angelfish (but without the continuous fins), this species gets its name from its supposed resemblance to a suit of playing cards. The body is silver with dark vertical bars which may, however, rapidly fade. They occur in slow-moving schools, sometimes quite large ones, and are fairly approachable. (to 91 cm, 36 in)

Plate 84c
Lane Snapper
Lutjanus synagris
This species is much more common in Florida waters than the Caribbean. It is best distinguished by the black spot below the end of the dorsal fin. (to 38 cm, 15 in)

Plate 84d
Schoolmaster
Lutjanus apodus
This snapper usually occurs in loose schools drifting above the reef. It is quite common but not easy to approach. The body is generally silver and the fins are yellow. (to 60 cm, 24 in)

Plate 84e
Mutton Snapper
Lutjanus analis
Most snappers are favorite food fishes, which tends to make them wary. In protected areas though, they can be approached. Look for them in caves and deep crevices. This species has quite variable coloration, from silver to reddish-brown, but almost always with a black spot near midbody. (to 75 cm, 30 in)

Plate 84f
Red Snapper
Lutjanus campechanus
A subtropical species, closely related to the Caribbean Red Snapper, and a favorite food fish. The red coloration becomes increasingly pronounced toward the dorsal fin and top of the head. Usually in deeper waters, seen only with SCUBA equipment or on your dinner plate. (to 91 cm, 3 ft)

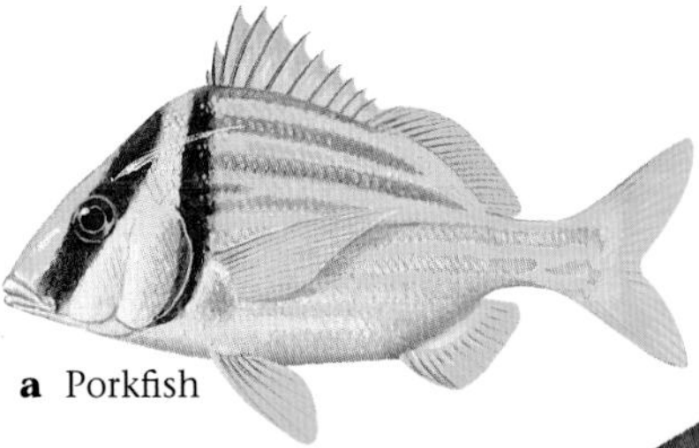

Plate 84 **443**

a Porkfish

b Atlantic Spadefish

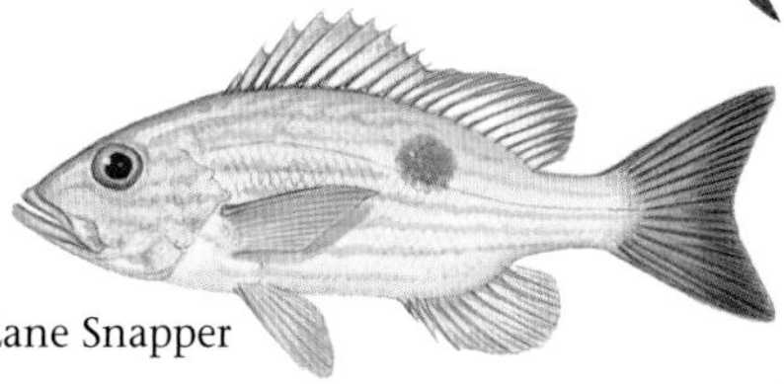

c Lane Snapper

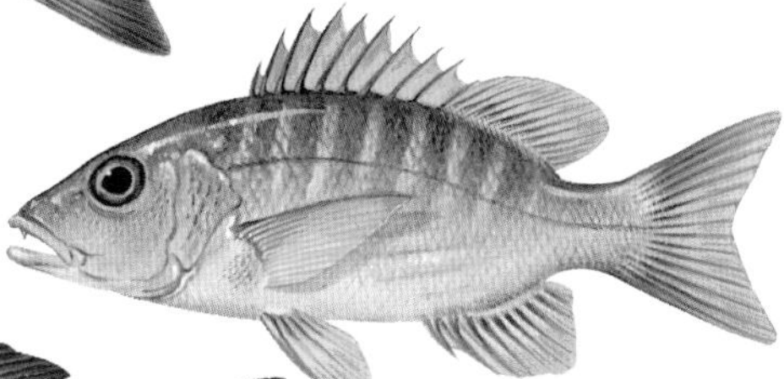

d Schoolmaster

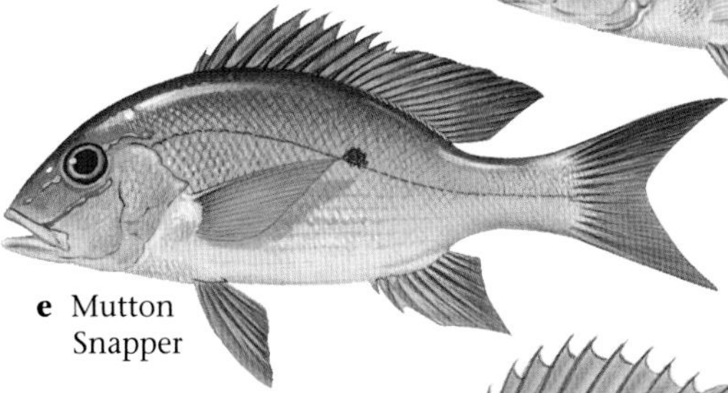

e Mutton Snapper

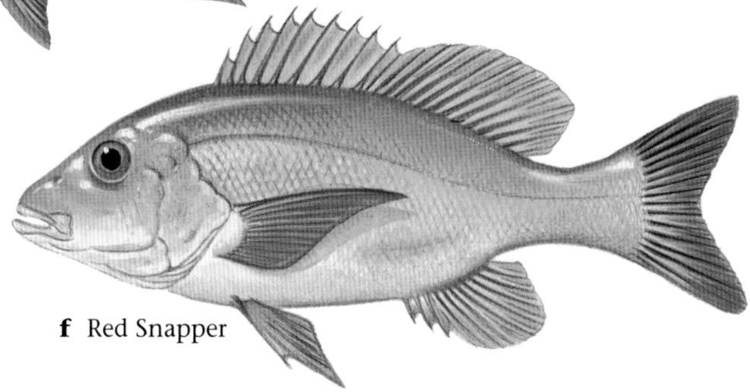

f Red Snapper

Plate 85a
Longfin Damselfish
Stegastes diencaeus
The damselfishes are among the most
entertaining coral reef inhabitants. Highly
territorial and aggressive, especially during the
breeding season when the males are tending the
eggs. Though diminutive, they will even attack
divers, which can be quite comical. This species
is dusky brown throughout and is distinguished by
its relatively long dorsal and anal fins. The
juveniles of this, and most other damselfishes,
differ markedly from adults in coloration. In this
species the juveniles are yellow with distinctive
blue stripes dorsally and a prominent blue-ringed
black spot near the base of the dorsal fin. (to
13 cm, 5 in)

Plate 85b
Cocoa Damselfish
Stegastes variabilis
The adults of this species can be hard to
distinguish from other damsels, but look for a dark
spot at the base of the tail. Juveniles (shown) are
blue above the eye and yellow below. Not as
aggressive as most damsels. (to 13 cm, 5 in)

Plate 85c
Dusky Damselfish
Stegastes fuscus
Very similar to the Longfin Damsel but with
shorter and more rounded fins. Juveniles are
bluish with a bright orange swath running from
the snout to the middle of the dorsal fin. (to 15 cm,
6 in)

Plate 85d
Beaugregory
Stegastes leucostictus
This damsel prefers coral rubble and sandy areas,
and like Cocoa damsels, is relatively
unaggressive. It is not shy, however. Adults are
distinguished from other damsels, such as Longfin
and Dusky, by their yellowish-tinged fins.
Juveniles (shown) closely resemble Cocoa
damsels. (to 10 cm, 4 in)

Plate 85e
Threespot Damselfish
Stegastes planifrons
The adults are a fairly bland dusky color but with
a small yellow crescent above the eye. Juveniles
(shown) are bright yellow with a black spot near
the base of the dorsal fin. Another pugnacious
species that is extremely active and bold. (to
13 cm, 5 in)

Plate 85f
Bicolor Damselfish
Stegastes partitus
This species defends smaller territories than most
damsels. They are aggressive but channel it
toward fishes of about the same size. This species
is easy to identify, with its body divided between a
black fore-region and a white rear. Juveniles have
a lesser black area and a bright yellow triangular
swath originating beneath the chin. (to 10 cm, 4 in)

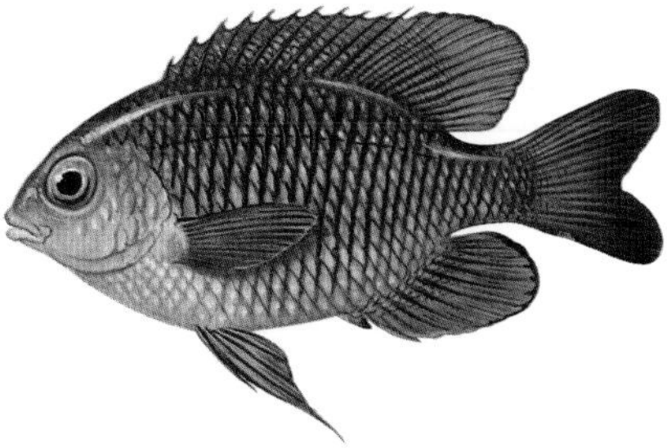

Plate 85 **445**

a Longfin Damselfish

b Cocoa Damselfish

c Dusky Damselfish

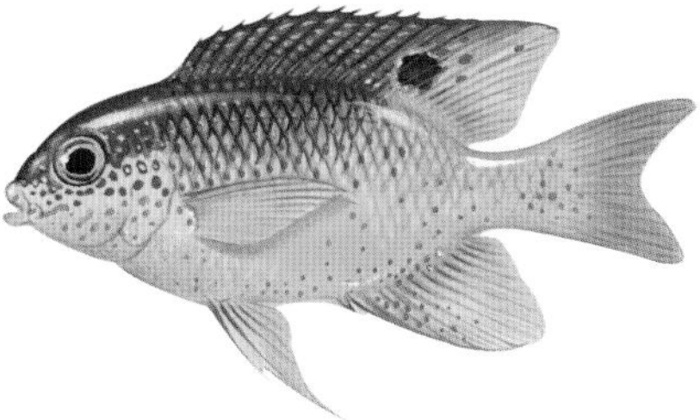

d Beaugregory

e Threespot Damselfish

f Bicolor Damselfish

Plate 86a
Yellowtail Snapper
Ocyurus chrysurus
This abundant species is much more streamlined than most snappers. A distinctive yellow line runs from behind the eye to the base of the tail, which is also yellow. It swims above the reefs in loose schools, and is much less wary than most snappers. (to 75 cm, 30 in)

Plate 86b
Yellowtail Damselfish
Microspathodon chrysurus
Large by damselfish standards, this species has a distinctive yellow tail. The juveniles are spectacular in bright light; their dark blue bodies are covered with electric blue dots. Be aware that the juveniles prefer to hang around skin-irritating fire coral. (to 21 cm, 8 in)

Plate 86c
Blue Chromis
Chromis cyanea
This brilliant blue damsel with a black nape is extremely abundant in midwater, often in very large groups. The tail is very deeply forked. It is most common slightly below typical snorkeling depths, but look for it over drop-offs. (to 13 cm, 5 in)

Plate 86d
Brown Chromis
(also called Yellow-edge Chromis)
Chromis multilineata
Generally tan or brownish-gray with a characteristic black spot at the base of the pectoral fin. The deeply forked tail often has black borders. Similar in habits to the Blue Chromis, with which it often schools. (to 16 cm, 6 in)

Plate 86e
Purple Reeffish
(also called Purple Chromis)
Chromis scotti
Not so much purple as varying shades of blue. The juveniles (shown) are a very deep and bright blue. This is a deeper water species that is best observed on SCUBA. It occurs in small groups near the bottom of deep reefs. (to 10 cm, 4 in)

Plate 86f
Sergeant Major
Abudefduf saxatilis
Probably the most common damselfish, it can be easily distinguished by its five vertical black bars on a silvery gray body. Juveniles have more yellow tones, and the adult males turn dark purplish blue when guarding eggs. They prefer to remain higher above the reefs than most damsels and usually occur in loose aggregations. (to 15 cm, 6 in)

Plate 86 **447**

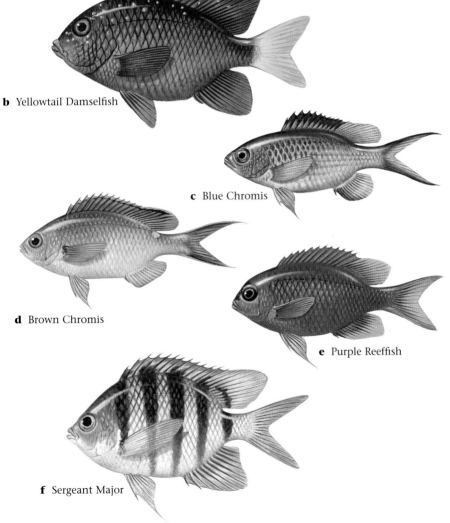

a Yellowtail Snapper

b Yellowtail Damselfish

c Blue Chromis

d Brown Chromis

e Purple Reeffish

f Sergeant Major

Plate 87

Plate 87a
Blue Hamlet
Hypoplectrus gemma
Iridescent blue body often with darker eye. This beautiful species stays close to the bottom and will remain motionless for long periods while being observed. (to 13 cm, 5 in)

Plate 87b
Butter Hamlet
Hypoplectrus unicolor
Common in the Keys, much less so throughout the Caribbean; this hamlet can be distinguished from other species by the black spot at the base of the tail. (to 13 cm, 5 in)

Plate 87c
Tan Hamlet
Hypoplectrus sp.
Not so common as the Butter Hamlet, this is one of the plainest of the hamlets, with its generally uniform brownish coloration. Like all hamlets, it is shy but curious. (to 13 cm, 5 in)

Plate 87d
Jewfish
Epinephelus itajara
The largest grouper in the Caribbean, this species is severely threatened by overfishing, particularly spearfishing. Its appearance is variable but always splotched or mottled. Shy in unprotected areas, but much less so where protected. They spend much of the day inside caves or other protected areas. Groupers, as well as the hamlets, are seabasses of the family Serranidae. Many are suspected to be serial hermaphrodites that are female while young and small, then turn to male when larger. In some of the largest groupers the reverse transition is thought to occur. (to 2.4 m, 7.8 ft)

Plate 87e
Yellowfin Grouper
Mycteroperca venenosa
Many groupers exhibit different color phases. This one varies from black to bright red and white. The only constants are the yellow edges on the pectoral fins and the black fringe at the end of the tail. This is a mid-size grouper, often found resting on sand. It prefers reef-tops near drop-offs. (to 90 cm, 35 in)

Plate 87f
Nassau Grouper
Epinephelus striatus
Another grouper threatened by overfishing. This species has five distinctive brown stripes on its body, but it can change color from a very pale hue to virtually black. A somewhat steeper forehead than most groupers. You can often find them resting on the bottom. (to 1.2 m, 4 ft)

Plate 87 **449**

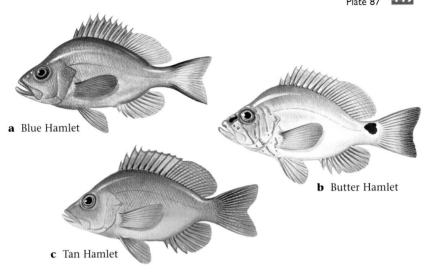

a Blue Hamlet

b Butter Hamlet

c Tan Hamlet

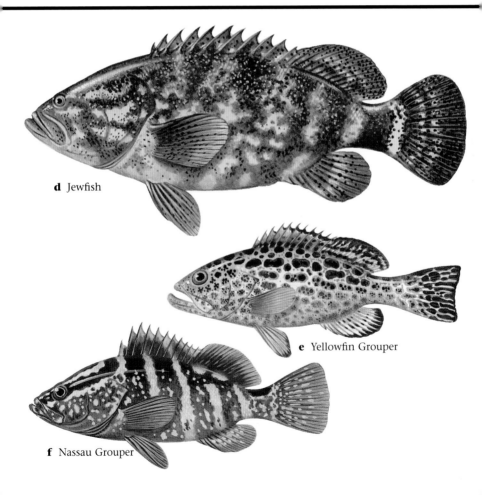

d Jewfish

e Yellowfin Grouper

f Nassau Grouper

Plate 88

Plate 88a

Red Grouper
Epinephelus morio

This mid-sized grouper can be found resting on the bottom by day. Like most groupers, this species has variable coloration; it is most easily confused with the Nassau grouper, which, however, has a distinct black spot at the base of the tail. (to 91 cm, 3 ft)

Plate 88b

Black Grouper
Mycteroperca bonaci

This grouper can be distinguished from others by the black band at the end of the tail, and the thin yellow margins on the pectoral fins. It is generally quite shy. (to 1.2 m, 4 ft)

Plate 88c

Coney
Epinephelus fulvus

This common small grouper exhibits a wide range of color patterns. All individuals have at least a few small spots. They can be quite curious and are more social than most groupers. (to 41 cm, 16 in)

Plate 88d

Graysby
Epinephelus cruentatus

This small grouper is one of the most common in the Florida area. It can quickly change color. Look for the three distinctive black spots at the base of the dorsal fin. (to 35 cm, 14 in)

Plate 88e

Scamp
Mycteroperca phenax

This grouper generally has dark blotches over a lighter background. It can, however, rapidly change the background hue from very pale to very dark. This grouper is not at all shy. (to 61 cm, 2 ft)

Plate 88f

Black Sea Bass
Centropristis striata

This is a subtropical fish, and is more common north of the Keys. It likes shallow water over a hard substrate. The first few dorsal spines are white-tipped in males. (to 61 cm, 2 ft)

Plate 88 451

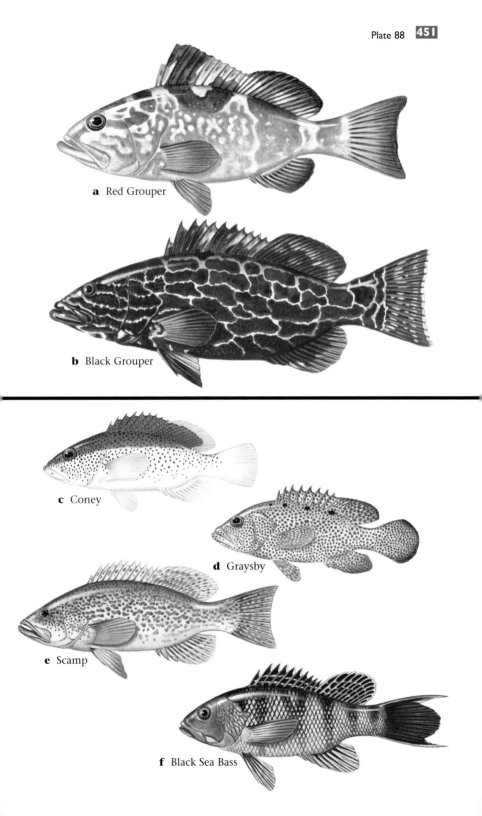

a Red Grouper

b Black Grouper

c Coney

d Graysby

e Scamp

f Black Sea Bass

Plate 89a
Blue Parrotfish
Scarus coeruleus
Parrotfishes are unique grazers. They feed primarily on algae from rocks and coral, and can munch the hard corals with their powerful beak-like mouth. Watch for the wispy white clouds of coral dust that they occasionally void. Parrotfishes are female-to-male sex changers (p. 228) but with a twist. Some males (initial phase males) are born that way, and have a completely different reproductive strategy from the large (terminal phase) males. The latter are solitary and territorial, while the initial phase males tend to congregate with females. Identifying parrotfishes is tricky because of the different color phases associated with their development. Terminal phase males are easiest to identify and it is from their coloration that the common names usually derive. In this species, however, all phases come in beautiful shades of blue, from light to quite dark. Terminal phase males have a squared-off head. This is one of the largest parrotfish species. (to 90 cm, 35 in)

Plate 89b
Queen Parrotfish
Scarus vetula
A medium-sized parrotfish, similar in habits to the Midnight Parrotfish. Terminal phase males have blue-green bodies with striking blue and green markings around the mouth. (to 61 cm, 24 in)

Plate 89c
Midnight Parrotfish
Scarus coelestinus
All phases of this species are midnight blue, with brighter blue splashes around the head. Not wary, but will not allow close approach. Parrotfishes tend to be quite active and stop only to scrape algae off coral. This is one of the larger parrotfish species. (to 76 cm, 30 in)

Plate 89d
Tobaccofish
Serranus tabacarius
This small seabass can be found in very shallow water and is not at all shy. Common in the Florida region where it prefers areas of coral rubble. Tends to hover near the bottom. The common name derives from the horizontal midbody band, which someone, who must have been smoking something else, thought was the shade of tobacco. (to 18 cm, 7 in)

Plate 89e
Redband Parrotfish
Sparisoma aurofrenatum
This species can be observed actively swimming on top of the reef. The terminal phase males are generally green with a reddish anal fin. Also look for the small yellow area on the body toward the head. Females and initial phase males are highly variable in color and can change color as well. (to 28 cm, 11 in)

Plate 89f
Sand Perch
Diplectrum formosum
Another species that is more common in Florida than the Caribbean, it can be found in a variety of habitats. It digs a burrow into which it retreats when it feels threatened. Look for the bluish longitudinal body stripes. (to 31 cm, 12 in)

Plate 89 **453**

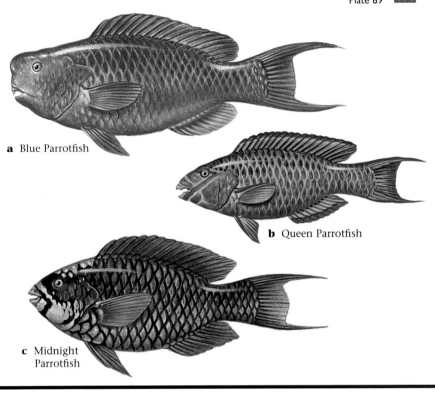

a Blue Parrotfish

b Queen Parrotfish

c Midnight Parrotfish

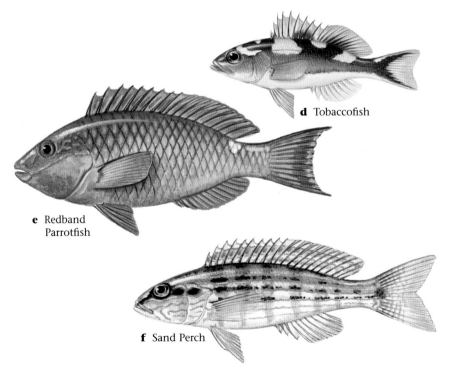

d Tobaccofish

e Redband Parrotfish

f Sand Perch

Plate 90a
Hogfish
Lachnolaimus maximus
This species belongs to the wrasse family, close
relatives of parrotfishes. A favorite food fish
wherever it occurs, it is wary wherever
spearfishing is allowed, but can become quite
tame where protected. Most wrasses exhibit the
complicated reproductive strategy typical of
parrotfishes, as well as various developmental
color phases. This species has only one male
type, which has an off-white, grayish, or reddish-
brown body, with a black swath over the head.
When erected, the dorsal fin has a dramatic
appearance, with several long spines in front. (to
91 cm, 36 in)

Plate 90b
Creole Wrasse
Clepticus parrae
This wrasse is one of the most abundant fishes in
the Caribbean. It prefers the open water over the
top of deep reefs where it occurs in large groups,
often in the afternoon forming long stream-like
schools over the drop-offs. Another wrasse
without distinct color phases, the snout area is
usually dark purple and the front half of the body
dark blue to slate. Older individuals show more
yellow and red in the tail region. (to 30 cm, 12 in)

Plate 90c
Spotfin Hogfish
Bodianus pulchellus
This species is common in Florida but rare in the
Caribbean. Adults are strikingly colored, with a
bright yellow tail region, and bright red throughout
the rest of the body. Juveniles are all yellow. Both
have a black area on the front of the dorsal fin.
Hogfish are in constant motion, and too
concerned with finding food to worry much about
divers. (to 23 cm, 9 in)

Plate 90d
Clown Wrasse
Halichoeres maculipinna
Look for the three vertical red lines on the head in
this variably colored species. Terminal phase fish
have a dark blotch on the side of the body. (to
16 cm, 6.5 in)

Plate 90e
Spanish Hogfish
Bodianus rufus
One of the few wrasse species without distinct
color phases, this common species is constantly
on the move and quite easy to approach. A large
purple area on the upper half of the body behind
the head is characteristic. (to 40 cm, 16 in)

Plate 90f
Stoplight Parrotfish
Scarus viride
One of the more common parrotfishes in the
Florida area. This mid-sized species is
distinguished by a characteristic yellow spot on
the upper part of the gill-cover. Also look for the
crescent-shaped tail. (to 50 cm, 20 in)

Plate 90 **455**

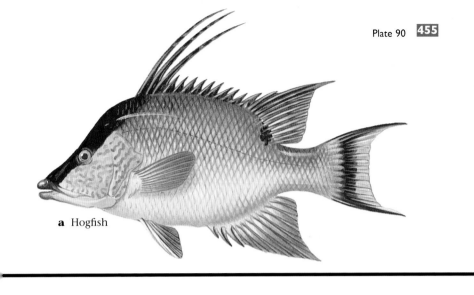

a Hogfish

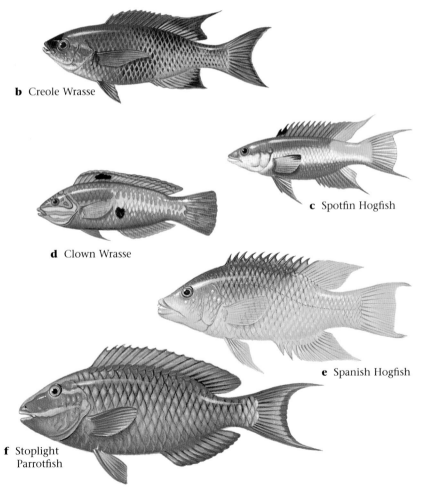

b Creole Wrasse

c Spotfin Hogfish

d Clown Wrasse

e Spanish Hogfish

f Stoplight Parrotfish

Plate 91a
Blackbar Soldierfish
Myripristis jacobis
This member of the squirrelfish family can often be found in caves or other dark recesses swimming upside down. It can be quite curious and approachable. The body is bright red, with a black stripe behind the gill-cover. (to 20 cm, 8 in)

Plate 91b
Squirrelfish
Holocentrus ascensionis
Members of the squirrelfish family are most active at night. By day, you can observe them in protected areas such as rock crevices and inside large barrel sponges preferably in shallow patch reefs. They are not shy and allow close observation. This species is red with white patches and, like all members of the family, has very large eyes. (to 30 cm, 12 in)

Plate 91c
Bluehead Wrasse
Thalassoma bifasciatum
This common wrasse is easy to observe on shallow reefs. Terminal phase males have the bright blue head for which the species is named. Initial phase males and females have a dusky blue color with irregular white stripes. Juveniles have variable color patterns and may act as cleaners (p. 229). (to 18 cm, 7 in)

Plate 91d
Yellowhead Wrasse
Halichoeres garnoti
This species exhibits several distinct developmental color phases. Terminal phase males have the yellow head and forebody for which the species is named, and a dark vertical bar at midbody. Initial phase males and females have a dusky back and yellow mid-region. Juveniles are bright yellow with bright blue horizontal stripe. (to 18 cm, 7 in)

Plate 91e
Slippery Dick
Halichoeres bivittatus
This very common species can be found on reefs as well as adjacent sandy areas and turtle grass patches. Terminal phase males are various shades of green with a darker horizontal stripe at midbody. As to the meaning of the common name, don't ask. (to 20 cm, 8 in)

Plate 91f
Barred Cardinalfish
Apogon binotatus
This species is very common in the Keys, much less so throughout the Caribbean. It can be distinguished by the black bar near the tail. By day it rests in the reef's recesses. (to 11 cm, 4.5 in)

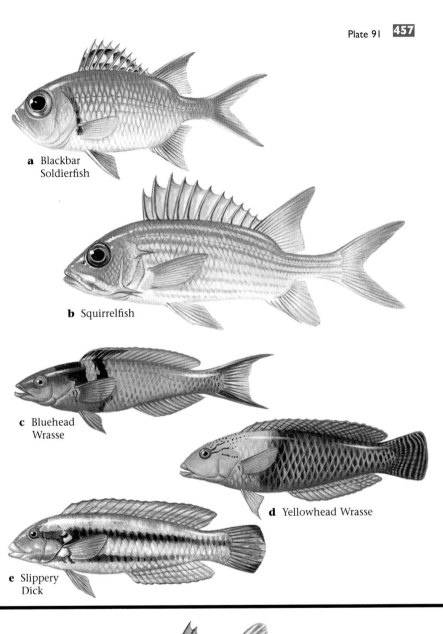

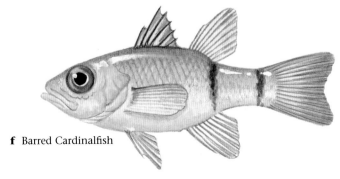

Plate 91 **457**

a Blackbar
Soldierfish

b Squirrelfish

c Bluehead
Wrasse

d Yellowhead Wrasse

e Slippery
Dick

f Barred Cardinalfish

Plate 92a
Glasseye Snapper
Priacanthus cruentatus
Another nocturnal species that can be observed by day in its hideouts. The coloration is variable but it usually has silver bars on the back. Unlike other 'bigeyes' in the area, it prefers shallow reefs. (to 33 cm, 13 in)

Plate 92b
Bigeye
Priacanthus arenatus
This species is best observed on SCUBA because it prefers deep reefs where it drifts in small groups. The body is a uniform but variable shade of red. (to 30 cm, 12 in)

Plate 92c
Flamefish
Apogon maculatus
One of the cardinalfishes, this species is active at night. By day it can be found in various dark places in a variety of habitats, including reefs and docks. One of the species most often seen on night dives. Body color is salmon to bright red; distinctive features are small white lines above and below eye and a black spot behind eye. (to 11 cm, 4 in)

Plate 92d
Neon Goby
Gobiosoma oceanops
Gobies constitute the largest family of fishes, indeed, the largest vertebrate family, yet only the careful observer will be able to enjoy these diminutive fishes. This common goby often acts as a cleaner (p. 229). It often establishes cleaning stations at which several congregate waiting for clients. This is a very attractive fish with its black body bisected by an electric-blue horizontal stripe. (to 5 cm, 2 in)

Plate 92e
Yellowline Goby
Gobiosoma horsti
This species is much shyer than the Neon Goby. Usually found near sponges on reefs of medium depth. It has a black body and a yellow horizontal stripe running from head to tail, including the top of the eye. (to 4 cm, 1.5 in)

Plate 92f
Yellowprow Goby
Gobiosoma xanthoprora
Look for the bright yellow body stripe, and yellow blotch on the snout of this otherwise dark fish. This very shy fish can only be observed if you approach carefully. It tends to retreat into sponges. (to 4 cm, 1.5 in)

Plate 92 **459**

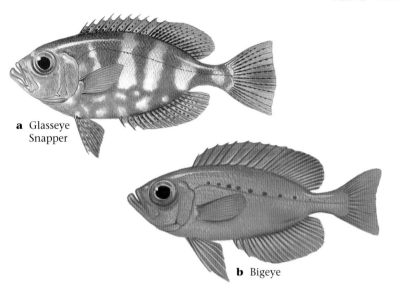

a Glasseye Snapper

b Bigeye

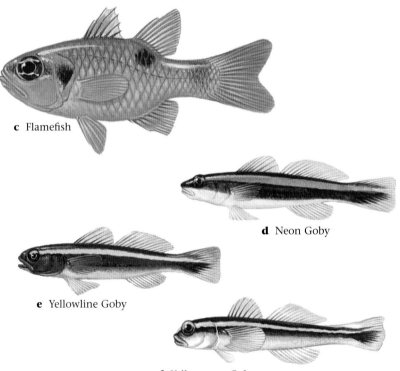

c Flamefish

d Neon Goby

e Yellowline Goby

f Yellowprow Goby

Plate 93a
Wrasse Blenny
Hemiemblemaria simulus
This species closely resembles the yellow initial phase of Bluehead Wrasses (Plate 91), and it is thought to mimic their cleaning behavior in order to get close to unwary fish from which it bites off small pieces of flesh. The body is bright yellow. (to 10 cm, 4 in)

Plate 93b
Redlip Blenny
Ophioblennius atlanticus
Large, by blenny standards, members of this species are also full of personality. They typically sit on an exposed perch, ever watchful for territorial intrusions. Their prominent eyes, which move independently of one another, allow them to monitor events in all compass directions. Their coloration varies from gray to reddish brown; the head is usually darker and redder than the rest of the body. The head looks almost flat in profile. (to 12 cm, 5 in)

Plate 93c
Rusty Goby
(also called Sharknose Goby)
Priolepis hipoliti
The unusual feature of this goby is that it can often be found perched upside down on the roofs of small clefts in reefs or under boulders. This goby is fairly approachable. It has bright orange spots on the dorsal, tail, and anal fins, as well as several dusky body bars. (to 4 cm, 1.5 in)

Plate 93d
Tiger Goby
Gobiosoma macrodon
This goby can be identified by the series of black vertical stripes over a translucent body. It tends to perch on coral and sponges. (to 4 cm, 1.5 in)

Plate 93e
Spotted Goby
Coryphopterus punctipectophorus
This goby has a very pale body with, characteristically, three orange lines extending from the eye tailward above the pectoral fin. It prefers sandy areas between reef patches. (to 5 cm, 2 in)

Plate 93f
Yellowhead Jawfish
Opisthognathus aurifrons
These inhabitants of the sand and coral rubble are fun to watch. They typically excavate burrows in the sand and line the entrance with small bits of coral, which tend to migrate from one burrow to another, as they are perpetually stealing their neighbors' goods. They look like small eels, especially when only the upper half of the body is extended above the surface. The body is pale and the head a very pale yellow. (to 10 cm, 4 in)

Plate 93 **461**

a Wrasse Blenny

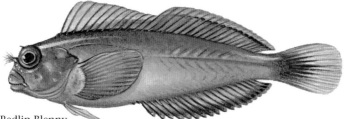

b Redlip Blenny

c Rusty Goby

d Tiger Goby

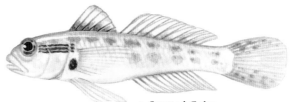

e Spotted Goby

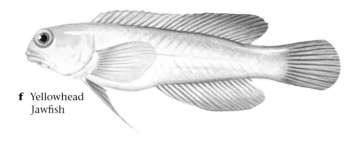

f Yellowhead
Jawfish

Plate 94a

Trumpetfish
Aulostomus maculatus

One of the more distinctively shaped reef creatures, this elongate fish actually looks more like a soprano saxophone than a trumpet. They are usually seen drifting with their head down, which may serve as a sort of camouflage, especially in grass beds or among some gorgonians. They will not tolerate a direct approach but these curious creatures may approach you if you don't flail around too much. (to 1 m, 3.3 ft)

Plate 94b

Gulf Toadfish
Opsanus beta

Like all toadfish, this species is a master of camouflage. It generally waits very still until prey approaches closely enough to gulp. It prefers calm water with seagrass beds and rubble. (to 31 cm, 12 in)

Plate 94c

Peacock Flounder
Bothus lunatus

This flatfish is most active at night. By day you will see them only if you happen to swim close enough to cause them to swim away; otherwise their camouflage is quite effective. This species also prefers sandy areas or coral rubble. The species is named for the striking blue spots on the body and fins. (to 39 cm, 15 in)

Plate 94d

Red-spotted Hawkfish
Amblycirrhitus pinos

The only hawkfish in the Atlantic, this species has brownish-red bars over a whitish-pink background. Look for the red spots on the head and back, including on the dorsal fin. Hawkfish rest on the bottom, using their pectoral fins for support; they move in short bursts. (to 10 cm, 4 in)

Plate 94e

Longlure Frogfish
Antennarius multiocellatus

Though common, this fish is seldom seen, due to its incredible camouflage and reluctance to move. It can change color and shade to match its background. Individuals tend to stay in one spot, so the best way to spot them is to go to a specific place where one is known to reside, otherwise you will have to wait until they move, and they won't move unless inadvertently touched. (to 20 cm, 8 in)

Plate 94f

Barbfish
Scorpaena brasiliensis

Closely related to the Gulf Toadfish, the Barbfish typically has a dark spot above the pectoral fin and two dark bars on the tail. It occurs in a variety of habitats, and it always blends in. (to 36 cm, 14 in)

Plate 94 **463**

a Trumpetfish

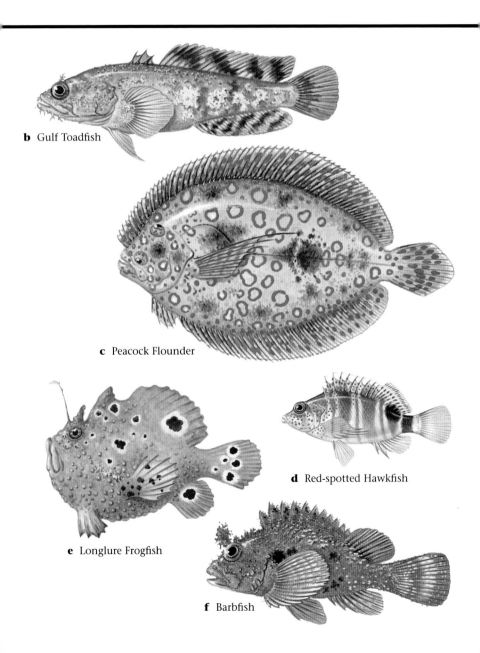

b Gulf Toadfish

c Peacock Flounder

d Red-spotted Hawkfish

e Longlure Frogfish

f Barbfish

Plate 95a
Sand Tilefish
Malacanthus plumieri
Look for these fish in sandy areas, where their large, inverted, conical burrow entrances are easy to spot. They are fairly shy and will retreat to the burrow when approached too closely. But if you are patient, they will eventually emerge and hover over the burrow by undulating their long dorsal and anal fins. (to 60 cm, 24 in)

Plate 95b
Porcupinefish
Diodon hystrix
This member of the puffer family will inflate its body dramatically when threatened, its sharp spines becoming erect during the process. This obviously makes these fish less easy to swallow for any would-be predator. It does not facilitate movement, however, and they can look quite comical when attempting to swim away in this state, furiously beating their pectoral fins. During the day they occupy various recesses. But you can often spot their head peering outward, and they can then be approached quite closely. (to 90 cm, 35 in)

Plate 95c
Queen Triggerfish
Balistes vetula
This is one of the most strikingly beautiful species on the reef. Background body coloration is various shades of purple, blue, turquoise and green, and the head is usually lighter, tending toward yellow; but these fish can rapidly darken or lighten. Irregular black lines radiate from the eye and two striking blue lines run above the mouth. Triggerfish move about primarily by means of the coordinated action of their dorsal and anal fins. Queen Triggers prefer reef tops and coral rubble. This species is fairly shy but your patience will be rewarded. (to 60 cm, 24 in)

Plate 95d
Scrawled Cowfish
Lactophrys quadricornis
Though its color is variable and changeable, individuals generally have bluish markings covering the body. The spine over each eye is characteristic of cowfish, and is the feature for which they were named. They are not easy to spot, and once detected they retreat into crevices. Cowfish can be found in a variety of habitats. (to 46 cm, 18 in)

Plate 95e
Smooth Trunkfish
Lactophrys triqueter
Like puffers, trunkfish manage to negotiate the reefs using their pectoral fins almost exclusively. This species is not wary and allows the diver fairly close inspection. Aside from its peculiar shape and small mouth with those seemingly kissable lips, notice the bulbous eyes, which seem to rotate in various directions like radar dishes. The smooth trunkfish has a dark body with numerous white spots throughout. These spots thin somewhat behind the pectoral fin in older fish and honeycomb markings appear. (to 30 cm, 12 in)

Plate 95f
Striped Burrfish
Chilomycterus schoepfi
This is one of the spiny puffers, or porcupinefishes. It is more common in the Gulf regions of Florida than in the south. Burrfish tend to change habitats with the seasons, preferring grass beds in calm lagoons during the summer, and reefs during the winter. They will inflate only if you really bother them; do not succumb to the temptation. (to 25 cm, 10 in)

Plate 95   **465**

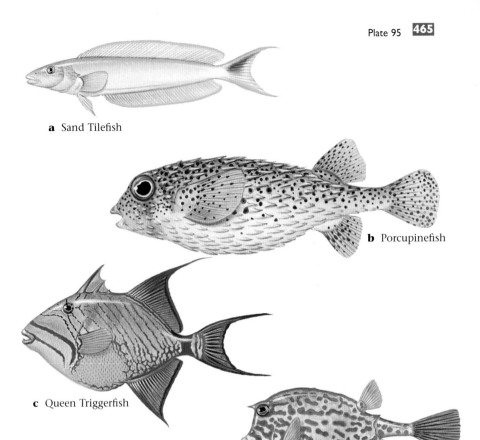

a Sand Tilefish

b Porcupinefish

c Queen Triggerfish

d Scrawled Cowfish

e Smooth Trunkfish

f Striped Burrfish

Plate 96a

Scrawled Filefish
Aluterus scriptus

This very odd-looking fish always seems to have a disheveled appearance because its tail is usually limp. The body coloration is usually a shade of yellow-green, and covered with blue and black spots. Fairly common, filefish drift over the reefs, seemingly without aid of their fins, until they are approached; they then retreat but again without much exertion. These fish are loners. (to 1.1 m, 3.6 ft)

Plate 96b

Black Durgeon
Melichthys niger

One of the more social members of the triggerfish family, this species occurs in groups of variable size, sometimes quite large. Quite common and easy to observe at a distance, it usually does not permit close inspection. The body is black and fins blacker, but with prominent pale blue lines beneath dorsal and anal fins. (to 50 cm, 20 in)

Plate 96c

Spotted Goatfish
Pseudopeneus maculatus

Another variably and changeably colored species, but with three characteristic dark blotches along the midbody. Like all goatfish, this is a bottom feeder; you can generally spot them as they energetically move through sandy areas probing with their barbels for food. (to 28 cm, 11 in)

Plate 96d

Yellow Goatfish
Mulloidichthys martinicus

Goatfish look very much like freshwater catfish, primarily because of the barbels under the lower jaw. Goatfish prefer sandy areas where they can be found, usually in small groups, busily probing the bottom for food. This species has a silvery white body with a yellow midbody stripe. The tail is also yellow. This is one of the more approachable species and it can be found in quite shallow water. (to 40 cm, 16 in)

Plate 96e

Spotted Drum
Equetus punctatus

This handsome fish can be found in protected areas of the reef, under ledges or in various nooks and crannies, where they rest by day. Drums are most active at night. The Spotted Drum and the similar Jackknife Fish have an unusual dorsal fin that is extremely long and directed upward with a slight curve. Striking black and white stripes on the body, and black back and tail with white spots. Quite unafraid, they will allow close inspection if you approach slowly. (to 25 cm, 10 in)

Plate 96f

Ocean Triggerfish
Canthidermis sufflamen

This is more of an open water species, most frequently observed near drop-offs. However, during the nesting season, they can be found in sandy areas between reef patches. Males create large depressions into which the female lays her eggs, which the male then guards until hatching. This species is almost entirely gray but with a prominent black spot at the base of the pectoral fin. (to 65 cm, 26 in)

Plate 96 **467**

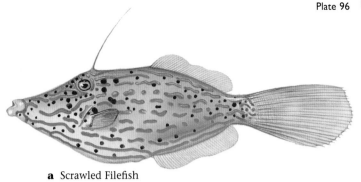

a Scrawled Filefish

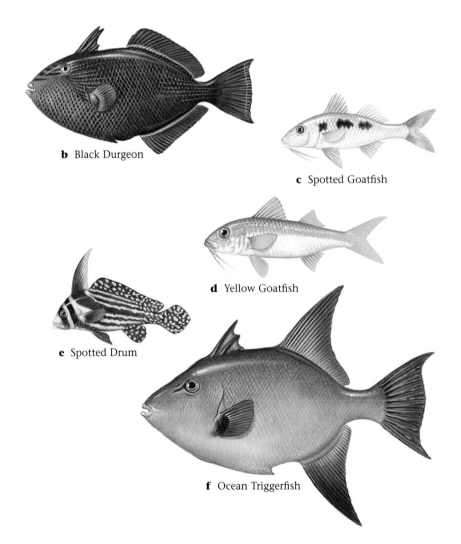

b Black Durgeon

c Spotted Goatfish

d Yellow Goatfish

e Spotted Drum

f Ocean Triggerfish

Plate 97a
Highhat
Equetus acuminatus
More common, and found in more shallow water
than the Jackknife Fish, this drum also prefers
secluded parts of the reef, where it rests by day. It
is fairly unafraid, and can be approached closely.
The dorsal fin is not nearly as long as that of the
Jackknife Fish; its coloration consists of black
horizontal stripes over a grayish background. (to
23 cm, 9 in)

Plate 97b
Jackknife Fish
Equetus lanceolatus
Look for these nocturnal fish in protected and
secluded parts of the reefs, especially near
outcrops and caves. They generally occur
beneath snorkeling depths. They will tolerate a
close approach. The long dorsal fin projects
toward back. A black bar outlined in white runs
through the dorsal fin and along the entire back.
Two additional bars run vertically on the head, the
front one going through the eye. (to 23 cm, 9 in)

Plate 97c
Cubbyu
Equetus umbrosus
This drum is shaped like the Highhat, but lacks the
stripes; also, its dorsal fin is shorter. It, too, rests
in secluded areas of the reef, but is not at all wary
of divers. (to 25 cm, 10 in)

Plate 97d
Sharptail Eel
Myrichthys breviceps
Snake eels are often mistaken for sea snakes by
those who don't realize that there are no sea
snakes in the Atlantic. You can find this species in
a variety of habitats, generally slithering along the
bottom. It is most active at night. (to 1.1 m, 3.5 ft)

Plate 97e
Spotted Moray
Gymnothorax moringa
This species is much smaller than the Green
Moray. They prefer shallow reefs with abundant
rubble, where they can be observed resting by
day, head protruding from their refuge. This
species is more speckled than spotted, seemingly
splattered by black paint. (to 1.2 m, 4 ft)

Plate 97f
Green Moray
Gymnothorax funebris
Largest of the morays, this species occurs in
diverse habitats and is fairly common, even in
shallow water. Morays rest by day in crevices
with only their head protruding. They open and
close their jaws in order to breathe, exposing
their teeth. Though they look menacing, they are
actually quite docile and retreat deeper into the
reef when approached. They quickly become
tame, however, and can be observed quite closely
in some protected areas. All morays are active at
night. (to 2.4 m, 8 ft)

Plate 97 **469**

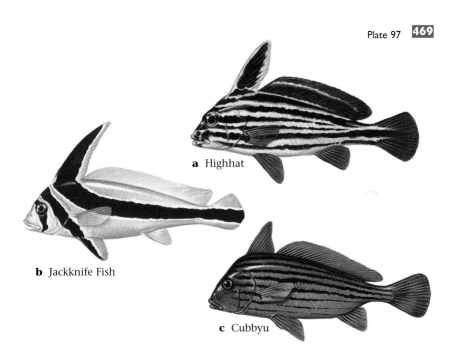

a Highhat

b Jackknife Fish

c Cubbyu

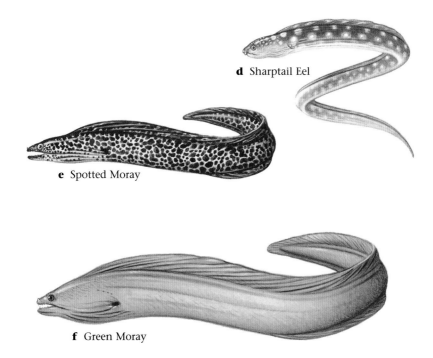

d Sharptail Eel

e Spotted Moray

f Green Moray

Plate 98a

Lemon Shark
Negaprion brevirostris
This species somewhat resembles the bull shark but is much more slender. It frequents inshore waters, where it sometimes rests on the bottom. The second dorsal fin on this shark, which is almost as large as the first, is the easiest way to distinguish this species. Lemon Sharks are potentially dangerous, but should not cause problems if treated with respect. (to 3.3 m, 11 ft)

Plate 98b

Nurse Shark
Ginglymostoma cirratum
This is the shark species you are most likely to observe. Nurse sharks are quite sluggish by shark standards, spending much of their time resting on the bottom. But they do reach impressive sizes and if one happens to swim by, your heart rate will increase. Nurse sharks seem to be missing the bottom half of the tail. Their heads are also larger than those of most sharks. (to 4.2 m, 14 ft)

Plate 98c

Bonnethead
Shyrna tiburo
A small species of the hammerhead family, Bonnetheads can be found in calm, shallow, inshore waters, such as bays, lagoons and estuaries. Its head is shaped like a spade. (to 1.5 m, 5 ft)

Plate 98d

Bull Shark
Carcharhinus leucas
This is the most heavy-bodied of the requiem sharks. Bulls prefer inshore waters and some even migrate hundreds of miles up rivers into freshwater lakes, most notably in Nicaragua. Though fairly common, they are rarely seen. I once watched from shore while a large bull shark approached to within 3 m (10 ft) of a group of snorkelers who, nonetheless, remained unaware of its presence. This species should be treated with utmost respect. (to 3.5 m, 11.5 ft)

Plate 98 **471**

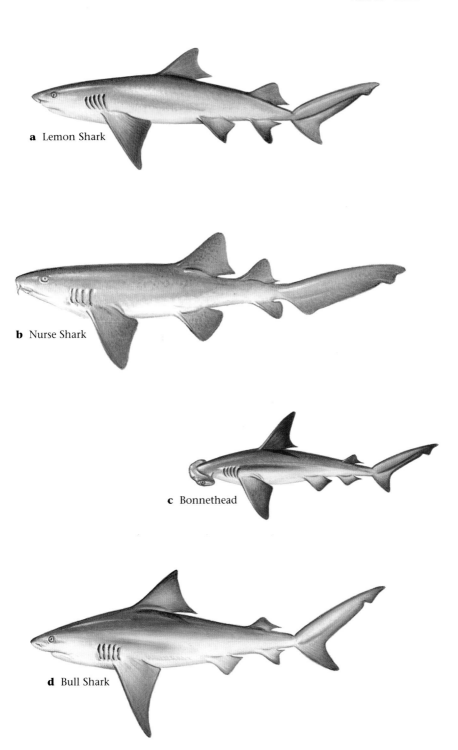

a Lemon Shark

b Nurse Shark

c Bonnethead

d Bull Shark

Plate 99a
Spotted Eagle Ray
Aetobatus narinari
This common and quite handsome species prefers to stay well up in the water column, where it seems to fly through the water with its considerable wing-like fins. They have venomous spines but do not pose any threat to divers. They are quite wary, in fact, and best observed by staying motionless. They often leap out of the water for unknown reasons, and the sound they make upon re-entry is an impressive clap. (to 2.3 m, 7.5 ft)

Plate 99b
Southern Stingray
Dasyatis americana
This common species prefers sandy areas where it lies buried to varying degrees. The name derives from the venomous spine near the base of the tail, contact with which can be exquisitely painful. Because they prefer shallow water, they are a factor to consider while wading in sandy areas. They are quite unafraid and will not move unless you are almost on top of them. (to 1.5 m, 5 ft)

Plate 99c
Hammerhead Shark
(also called Smooth Hammerhead)
Sphyrna zygaena
This species spends most of its time in open water, but they do cruise the reefs on occasion, especially at night. The bizarre head with eyes stuck at each end ensures that this shark will not be confused with any other. They reach impressive sizes and, though quite wary, should be treated with care. (to 3.5 m, 11.5 ft)

Plate 99d
Yellow Stingray
Urolophus jamaicensis
This common ray likes sandy areas between reef patches. It often lies motionless on the bottom, covered with sand, unless molested. Like all stingrays, it has a venomous spine near the tip of the tail. (to 38 cm, 15 in, excluding tail).

Plate 99 **473**

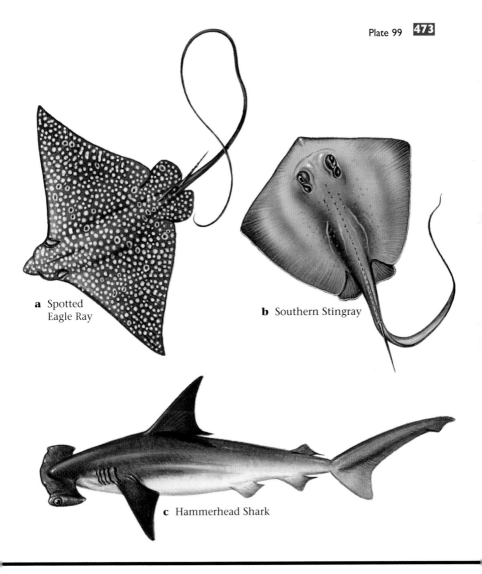

a Spotted
Eagle Ray

b Southern Stingray

c Hammerhead Shark

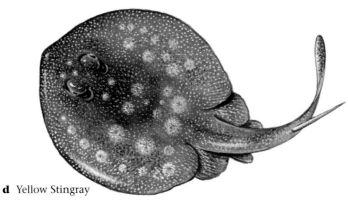

d Yellow Stingray

Plate 100a
Staghorn Coral
Acropora cervicornis
One of the fastest growing coral species, it prefers shallow, calm water. Forms dense tangles of branches in which only the outer tips are alive. Staghorn coral is fragile and subject to storm damage, but it recovers more quickly than most corals due to rapid growth rate.

Plate 100b
Elkhorn Coral
Acropora palmata
Another fast-growing species, it prefers shallow areas with good water movement and wave action. This coral can cover vast areas of shallow bottom, and it is one of the characteristic species living on the shallow fringing reefs off Florida's Keys. The branches are flattened like moosehorns.

Plate 100c
Lettuce Coral
Agaricia agaricites
This common coral often forms plate-like colonies resembling lettuce leaves. It can be found in a variety of environments, including reef walls and mangroves. It can adopt one of several forms, the most common of which is the one that resembles lettuce. (colony size to 1 m, 3.3 ft)

Plate 100d
Fire Coral
Millepora alcicornis
Fire corals are named for their skin-irritating capacity. They can cause welts and swelling in sensitive people, although the effect is usually of short duration. Pictured here is the branching species of fire coral but they can become encrusting on certain substrates. They tend to be brownish-orange but the color is variable. This species prefers deeper, calmer water than other fire corals.

Plate 100e
Large Star Coral
Montastrea cavernosa
This species forms very large coral heads in the form of mounds or domes. The polyps look like small blisters of variable hue when retracted. Like many coral species, the polyps are active at night and retracted by day. This species is found in a wide variety of reef habitats.

Plate 100f
Common Star Coral
(also called Boulder Star Coral)
Montastrea annularis
This species is common in a variety of reef environments. There are several distinct forms that some consider to be separate species. The most spectacular form, sometimes called mountainous star coral, has irregular pillars and bumps.

Plate 100g
Finger Coral
Porites porites
One of the most common coral species in the Keys, it occurs over a wide range of depths, from very shallow water to beyond that safe for diving. The colonies typically form smooth, stubby cylinders. When the polyps are extended, as they often are during the day, the projections have a fuzzy appearance. (colony size to 1.2 m, 4 ft)

Plate 100 **475**

a Staghorn Coral

b Elkhorn Coral

c Lettuce Coral

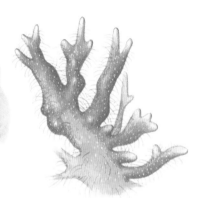

d Fire Coral

e Large Star Coral

f Common Star Coral

g Finger Coral

Plate 101a
Flower Coral
Eusmilia fastigiata
This beauty is another favorite of photographers. The coralites are often iridescent greenish-blue, with a lot of space between each. They form small round heads from which the polyps seem to emerge from a central core, somewhat like a hydrangea. The tentacles are extended only at night. This species is found in several reef environments but prefers protected areas.

Plate101b
Split-Pore Sea Rod
Plexaurella sp.
Named for the slit-like – as opposed to round or oval – openings that are evident when the polyps are retracted. The structure of the colony can often resemble organ-pipe cactus. This species is common in clear water environments, often in quite shallow areas. Shown with polyps retracted and extended.

Plate 101c
Corky Sea Finger
(a soft coral)
Briareum sp.
Colonies of this soft coral consist of several (or a single) cylindrical columns arising from a common base. When the polyps are retracted, the columns are reddish purple and smooth; when the polyps are extended, the rods look like they are covered with yellow-greenish or brownish hairs. This species prefers shallow and calm areas.

Plate 101d
Black Sea Rod
Plexaura sp.
This species forms bushy colonies that grow in one plane. The stalks are black, which contrasts with the yellowish-brown polyps. It prefers patch reefs in clear water.

Plate 101e
Common Sea Fan
(a soft coral gorgonian)
Gorgonia ventalina
This, and other closely related species of sea fans, are one of the more characteristic sights on a Floridean reef. The colonies form large, flat, fan-like structures that grow on a single plane. Upon close inspection, you will find an intricate vein-like network of branches, emerging from several large veins or branches. Usually a shade of purple, but sometimes yellow. This species prefers shallow reefs with clear water.

Plate 101f
Common Brain Coral
(also called Smooth or Symmetrical Brain Coral)
Diploria strigosa
A favorite subject for macro-photography because of the numerous wavy ridges that look something like the outside of a human brain. The effect is especially pronounced in the varieties that form rounded heads.

Plate 101 **477**

a Flower Coral

b Split-Pore Sea Rod

c Corky Sea Finger

d Black Sea Rod

e Common Sea Fan

f Common Brain Coral

Plate 102a
Christmas Tree Worm
Spirobranchus giganteus
These worms somewhat resemble the feather dusters but they belong to a separate family, the members of which construct calcareous tubes. The head appendages spiral around a single central core. Their color is variable but usually includes some red or orange with white highlights. They prefer to construct their tubes on living coral but they are not picky as to the type of coral or reef.

Plate 102b
Banded Shrimp
Stenopus hispidus
This attractive crustacean seems to be all appendages. Its skinny body and claws are covered with red and white bands. This is one of the cleaning shrimps, and it hangs out at the openings of sponges, waving its antennae to attract its fish clients. These shrimps are not particularly wary but will retreat into a protective recess when approached closely. However, they have been known to clean the hands of divers when extended slowly.

Plate 102c
Bearded Fire Worm
Hermodice sp.
This is a fairly active species that often forages in the open. It is covered with tufts of white bristles, interspersed with red gill filaments. Do not touch! The bristles contain a toxin that causes an unpleasant burning sensation, and sometimes a painful wound. When disturbed, the worm will display its bristles by way of warning. This species has branched and bushy appendages on the head that look somewhat beard-like. It can be found in a variety of habitats, including reefs, rubble, and grass beds.

Plate 102d
Spiny Lobster
Panulirus sp.
This lobster can reach impressive sizes in areas where it is not hunted. The carapace is brown to tan with two horn-like projections above the eye. The lobsters' very long antennae often project from their hiding places and they always seem to be moving. Being a favorite food item for humans, they are understandably wary and will retreat deeper into their refuges when approached, but will remain facing you. In protected areas they are quite common on the reef.

Plate 102e
Magnificent Feather Duster
Sebellastarte sp.
This marine worm is the largest of the feather dusters. Most of the worm is hidden from view; only the highly modified head region is visible, most notably the feather appendages that function both for capturing food and as gills for respiration. It will quickly retract when approached too closely. Once it retracts, remain motionless and it may slowly re-emerge. These worms inhabit a wide variety of environments, from patch reefs to pilings.

Plate 102f
Reef Squid
Sepioteuthis sepioidea
One of the most fascinating reef creatures, and the only squid that frequents the reefs. These are intelligent and curious creatures. If you remain almost motionless or swim toward them at an oblique angle, they will allow you to approach closely. Sometimes they will follow divers from a safe distance, observing you with those very large eyes. They will retreat if approached directly, and if they really feel threatened, they will turn on their jet propulsion and disappear in an eyeblink.

Plate 102 **479**

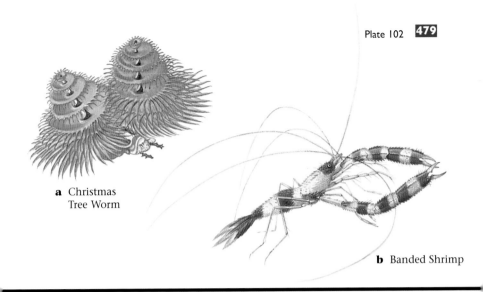

a Christmas
Tree Worm

b Banded Shrimp

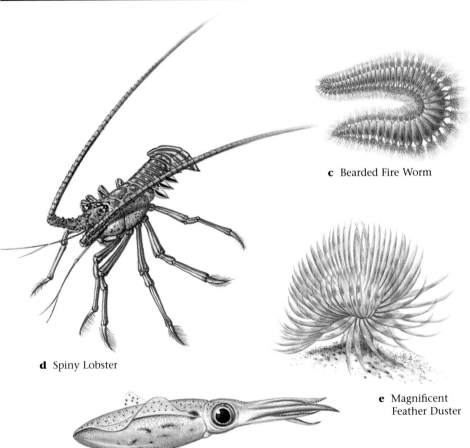

c Bearded Fire Worm

d Spiny Lobster

e Magnificent
Feather Duster

f Reef Squid

Plate 103a

Flame Helmet
Cassis flammea

This beautiful mollusk is coveted by shell collectors, and has become rare in many areas owing to their activities. It can be quite common where protected. The shell is ornamented with waves of reddish-brown color bands. Also look for the dark brown bands on the lip. This species feeds voraciously on sea urchins, whose spines do not in the least slow it down. (to 13 cm, 5 in)

Plate 103b

Flamingo Tongue
(also called Flamingo Tongue Cowrie)
Cyphoma gibbosum

At first glance this appears to be a nudibranch (sea slug) but the creamy white surface covered with orange spots is actually the snail's mantle covering a cowrie-shaped shell. The shell can be seen only when the snail retracts its mantle. Most often seen on the gorgonians, including sea fans, upon which they feed. Quite common and found in a variety of shallow water habitats.

Plate 103c

Florida Fighting Conch
Strombus alatus

This common mollusk can be observed feeding if you are patient. Active by day, it will retract into its shell when approached, but if you wait, it will extend its head and eye stalks in a relatively short time. Look for the short, thick spikes near the base of the shell whorls. It prefers grass beds and sandy areas. (to 9 cm, 3.5 in)

Plate 103d

Hawkwing Conch
Strombus raninus

Another common Florida conch, this species can be distinguished by its characteristic flared shell lip, and the two spikes on the last whorl. They inhabit sea grass beds and sand flats, and will resume feeding after initially retracting, if the diver remains still. (to 9 cm, 3.5 in)

Plate 103e

Netted Olive
Oliva reticularis

This mollusk can be found in sandy areas, usually in calm water. It often lies partially buried, and even forages under the sand. It is named for the elegant net-like brown lines that cover its exterior. (to 4 cm, 1.5 in)

Plate 103f

Queen Conch
Strombus gigas

This huge gastropod was once very common throughout the Caribbean; now its numbers are greatly reduced owing to overfishing, at least in shallow waters. The shells grow in a conical spiral with the outer lip flaring outward. The shell is various shades of orange but often obscured by algae and other encrustations. The snail itself is mottled gray. Its eyes are set at the ends of very long eye stalks. These conchs prefer sandy areas or grass beds between reef patches.

Plate 103g

Florida Horse Conch
Pleuroploca gigantea

Another common Florida conch, this species has an elongate spire with small knobby projections. Adults tend to be found in deeper water than the juveniles. (to 36 cm, 14 in)

Plate 103   **481**

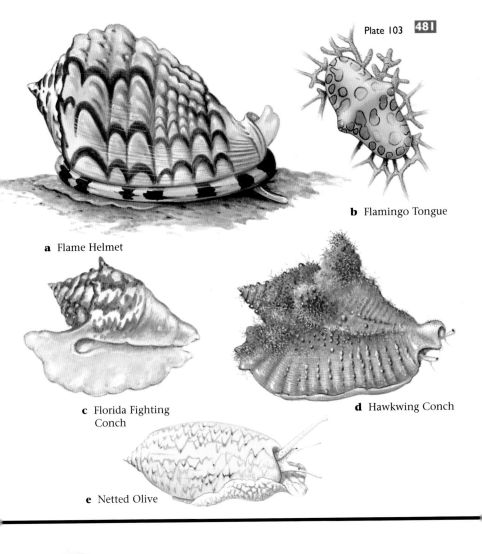

a Flame Helmet

b Flamingo Tongue

c Florida Fighting Conch

d Hawkwing Conch

e Netted Olive

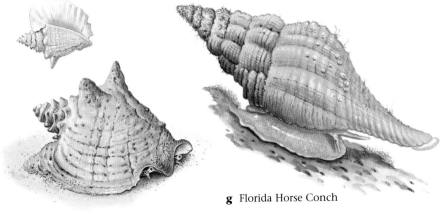

g Florida Horse Conch

f Queen Conch

Plate 104a
Variegated Sea Urchin
Lytechinus variegatus
Sea urchins are grazers. Their mouths are on the underside and the spines function to protect these otherwise vulnerable creatures. Urchins are a common cause of injury, because their spines, should they penetrate your skin, are difficult to remove. This beautiful species has short spines and well-defined grooves between plates. Coloration is variable, but usually white or some shade of green. Often camouflaged with sea grass or other debris. Look for them over grass beds or on reefs.

Plate 104b
Long-Spined Sea Urchin
Diadema antillarum
Formerly abundant throughout the Caribbean, but has experienced a dramatic die-back. This species is one of the main sources of injury for unwary bathers and snorkelers. The long spines easily puncture the skin, often causing infection. This species is typically black. It is found in all habitats.

Plate 104c
Slate-pencil Urchin
Eucidaris tribuloides
You are not likely to mistake this urchin for any other. It is named for its extremely thick spines, which are more like blunt rods. Most often found in sea grass beds and rubble, where it grazes for algae. (to 5 cm, 2 in)

Plate 104d
Red Heart Urchin
Meoma ventricosa
This common urchin resembles a sand dollar. Its extremely short spines form dense, almost furry mats. It prefers sandy areas between reef patches. It hides under ledges by day and forages at night. (to 15 cm, 6 in)

Plate 104e
Banded-arm Brittle Star
Ophioderma appressum
This common inhabitant of relatively shallow reefs typically exhibits distinct light and dark bands on its slender arms. Upon close inspection you can observe the numerous short spines that project from each arm. (to 3 cm, 1 in)

Plate 104f
Giant Basket Star
Astrophyton sp.
Basket stars are closely related to brittle stars; their five main arms branch many times giving the appearance of tentacles with a perm. During the day they curl up in a tight ball, usually on a gorgonian. At night, the arms unfurl and are directed toward the current, forming a sort of net by which they capture their planktonic prey. This species is a common reef inhabitant, generally colored orange to brown.

Plate 104g
Cushion Sea Star
Oreaster sp.
Sea stars are the most familiar echinoderms but they are not a particularly prominent component of the Caribbean reefs. This sea star has five short, thick arms. The color is usually some shade of orange to brown, with the dorsal spines forming a net-like pattern. They are common in sand flats and grass beds.

Plate 104 **483**

a Variegated Sea Urchin

b Long-spined Sea Urchin

c Slate-pencil Urchin

d Red Heart Urchin

e Banded-arm Brittle Star

f Giant Basket Star

g Cushion Sea Star

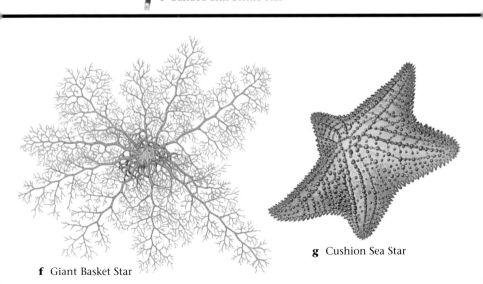

Plate 105

Plate 105a

Loggerhead Sponge
Spheciospongia sp.

This species is one of the barrel sponges, large squat creatures with a large central depression. It is often host to shrimps and others that dwell in the canals. Also check the depression for small fish.

Plate 105b

Bulb Tunicate
Clavelina sp.

Tunicates, or sea squirts, are among the most abundant marine creatures, and certainly among the least recognized. They are often mistaken for sponges, but they are more closely related to you and me. This is easiest to discern in the larval phase during which they look very much like tadpoles. Pelagic tunicates remain free-swimming for life, but most species settle out and metamorphose into the sponge-like creatures we observe attached to various substrates on the reef. This attractive species is one of the compound tunicates, in which a number of individuals are joined at the base and share a common excurrent siphon. Purplish-blue varieties, known as blue bells, are particularly attractive.

Plate 105c

Branching Vase Sponge
Agelas sp.

This attractive species is common on fairly shallow reefs. Typically there are clusters of up to 30 tubes, each with numerous conical projections. The color varies from lavender to gray. Search this sponge's surface for brittle stars.

Plate 105d

Leathery Barrel Sponge
Geodia neptuni

The most common barrel sponge in the Keys, this species comes in various shades of brown. It is often covered with sediment. (to 75 cm, 2.5 ft)

Plate 105e

Furry Sea Cucumber
Astichopus multifidus

This species has short knobby projections distributed over its entire body. Its color varies from deep brown to gray. Darker blotches are usually present in the lighter colored individuals. It prefers sandy areas between reef patches. (to 41 cm, 16 in)

Plate 105f

Giant Barrel Sponge
Xestospongia muta

These are some of the most spectacular creatures to be found anywhere on the reef. This species grows at depths that require SCUBA. They can grow to over 2 m (6 ft) in diameter and their central depression is large enough to contain a diver, but do not enter as these are fragile creatures that easily break. Large specimens may be over 100 years old!

Plate 105   485

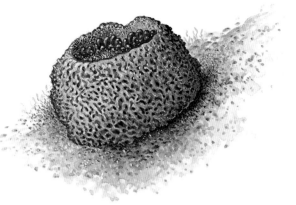

a Loggerhead Sponge

b Bulb Tunicate

c Branching Vase Sponge

d Leathery Barrel Sponge

e Furry Sea Cucumber

f Giant Barrel Sponge

Plate 106a
Giant Anemone
Condylactis gigantea
Anemones comprise another distinct group of cnidarians; they are very familiar to inhabitants of temperate regions. This species is the largest in the Caribbean and can be distinguished by the distinct swelling at the tip of each tentacle. The main body is usually hidden with only the tentacles visible. Several species of shrimp, including cleaner shrimp, frequently use this anemone for refuge, as do some blennies.

Plate 106b
Branching Hydroid
Sertularella speciosa
This common hydroid forms fern-like colonies. It is somewhat toxic, so avoid skin contact if possible. It occurs in a wide range of reef environments where there is water movement; also common on shipwrecks. (to 14 cm, 5.5 in)

Plate 106c
Turtle Grass
Thalassia testudinum
This shallow-water grass grows on sandy areas, forming beds that can cover large areas. This is a flowering plant, though its pale greenish-white flowers are not obvious. Individual blades are flat with rounded tips. Turtle grass beds are an important habitat for many small fishes and invertebrates, and well worth exploring.

Plate 106d
Upsidedown Jelly
Cassiopea sp.
This common inhabitant of lagoons and quiet sand flats has a flattened bell and typically orients with arms and tentacles facing upward, hence the name. These creatures have symbiotic single-celled algae from which they derive some of their nourishment. Sometimes they can be observed lying upside down on the bottom, which is thought to facilitate the algae's growth. The closely related Mangrove Upsidedown Jelly is often abundant, not surprisingly, among mangroves.

Plate 106e
Moon Jelly
Aurelia sp.
Jellies belong to a large group of animals known as cnidarians, which also includes coral, gorgonians, hydroids, and anemones, all of which possess a specialized structure, known as a nematocyst, which is a hook-like barb for injecting toxins. All cnidarians have a medusa stage in which the animal is free-swimming but only the jellies spend most of their lives in this mode. This is one of the more common species in the Caribbean; you are most likely to find them drifting near the surface over the reefs. The moon jelly is almost transparent; the four-leaf clover structure near the top is the reproductive organs.

Plate 106f
Yellow Tube Sponge
Aplysina sp.
This attractive sponge forms clusters of yellow tubes that are joined at the base. This is a soft sponge but don't squeeze it unless you don't mind a purple stain that will last for days. This sponge prefers open water reefs and reef walls. Look for gobies and other small fishes inside the tubes.

Plate 106 **487**

a Giant Anemone

b Branching Hydroid

c Turtle Grass

d Upsidedown Jelly

e Moon Jelly

f Yellow Tube Sponge

SPECIES INDEX

Note: Plate numbers refer to
    identification plates. Page
    numbers in *italics* refer to
    illustrations.

Abudefduf saxatilis Plate 86f
Acanthocephala femorata Plate 75h
Acanthurus bahianus Plate 79a
Acanthurus chirurgus Plate 79e
Acanthurus coeruleus Plate 79b
Accipiter cooperii 123, Plate 31a
Accipiter striatus 123, Plate 31b
Acer rubrum 17, 19, Plate D2
Acititis macularia 133, Plate 36a
Acoelorrhaphe wrightii 12, *240*, Plate B2
Acridotheres tristis 179, Plate 60d
Acris gryllus dorsalis 70, Plate 3a
Acropora cervicornis Plate 100a
Acropora palmata Plate 100b
Acrostichum danadifolium *244*
Actias luna Plate 71d
Aesculus pavia Plate H1
Aetobatus narinari Plate 99a
Agaricia agaricites Plate 100c
Agelaius phoeniceus 179, Plate 58b
Agelas sp. Plate 105c
Agkistrodon piscivorus 93, Plate 19c
Agraulis vanillae Plate 70c
Aimophila aestivalis 186, Plate 57a
Aix sponsa 117, Plate 28b
Ajaia ajaja 114, Plate 24f
Albula vulpes Plate 81a
Alligator
    American 45, 79–81, Plate 8b
Alligator mississippiensis Plate 8b
Alligatorweed 50
Aluterus scriptus Plate 96a
Amblycirrhitus pinos Plate 94d
Ambystoma opacum 67, Plate 5c
Ambystoma talpoideum 67, Plate 5a
Ambystoma tigrinum 67, Plate 5b
Amphiuma
    One-toed 67

    Two-toed 65, 67, Plate 7a
Amphiuma means 67, Plate 7a
Anas acuta 117, Plate 27a
Anas americana 117, Plate 28a
Anas clypeata 117, Plate 27b
Anas crecca 117, Plate 27c
Anas discors 117, Plate 27d
Anas fulvigula 117, Plate 26d
Anax junius Plate 73e
Anaxyrus quercicus 69, Plate 1b
Anaxyrus terrestris 69, Plate 1c
Andropogon virginicus 14
Anemone, Giant Plate 106a
Angelfish
    Blue 226, 227, Plate 78f
    French Plate 79c
    Gray Plate 79f
    Queen 227, Plate 78a
Anhinga 34, 38, 39, 40, 108, 109, 110,
    Plate 21d
Anhinga anhinga 110, Plate 21d
Ani, Smooth-billed 4, 42, 144, Plate 41f
Anisomorpha buprestoides Plate 72b
Anisotremus virginicus Plate 84a
Annona glabra *234*, Plate G4
Anole
    Brown 95, Plate 14b
    Green 94, 95, Plate 14d
Anolis carolinensis 95, Plate 14d
Anolis sagrei 95, Plate 14b
Anous stolidus 136, Plate 22d
Ant
    Fire 51, 52, Plate 76d
    Velvet Plate 76f
Antennarius multiocellatus Plate 94e
Antheraea polyphemus Plate 71f
Anthus rubescens 172, Plate 51f
Apalone ferox 86, Plate 12e
Aphelocoma coerulescens 161, Plate 48b
Aplysina sp. Plate 106f
Apogon binotatus Plate 91f
Apogon maculatus Plate 92c
Apple

Gopher 16
Pond *234*, Plate G4
Aralia spinosa 243
Aramus guarauna 129, Plate 24d
Archilochus colubris 150, Plate 43d
Archosargus probatocephalus Plate 82f
Ardea alba 114, Plate 23c
Ardea herodias 114, Plate 25d
Arenaria interpres 133, Plate 37f
Argiope, Silver Plate 77b
Argiope argentata Plate 77b
Argiope aurantia Plate 77d
Aristida purpurascens 14
Aristida stricta 14, 16
Armadillo, Nine-banded 195–7, Plate
  61b
Arrowfeather 14
Arrowhead 18
Arrowroot, Florida Plate F4
Ascia monuste Plate 69a
Ash 17
Asimina incarna 16
Aspidocelus sexlineatus 96, Plate 13c
Aster, Golden 16
Astichopus multifidus Plate 105e
Astrophyton sp. Plate 104f
Atala Plate 70a
Ateramnus lucidus 17
Athene cunicularia 146, Plate 42e
Atlantic Hawksbill Plate 9c
Atlantic Ridley 43, Plate 9a
Aulostomus maculatus Plate 94a
Aurelia sp. Plate 106e
Automeris io Plate 71c
Avicennia germinans 22, *241*
Avocet, American 130, 133, Plate 35e
Aythya affinis 117, Plate 28d
Aythya collaris 117, Plate 28c

Baccharis halimifolia 22
Baeolophus bicolor 163, Plate 49b
Balistes vetula Plate 95c
Barbfish Plate 94f
Barracuda, Great Plate 80b
Basket Star, Giant Plate 104f
Bass
  Black Sea Plate 88f
  Peacock 187
Bat
  Big Brown 198, 199, 200, 201, Plate
    67a
  Brazilian Free-tailed 197–201, Plate
    67b
  Eastern Yellow 200, 201, Plate 67c
  Evening 199, 200, 201, Plate 67d

Florida Mastiff 201
Gray 201
Indiana 201
Kitt's Hog-nosed 197
Northern Yellow 199, Plate 67c
Battus philenor Plate 69b
Bay 19
  Red 17
Baywing 178
Bear
  Black 4, 36, 201, 206–7, 222, 495,
    Plate 63a
  Grizzly *492*
Beaugregory Plate 85d
Beaver, American 216, *493*
Bee, Carpenter Plate 76g
Beech 17
Beetle
  Click Plate 74g
  Cucumber 200
  Ox Plate 74f
  Rhinoceros Plate 74f
  Tiger Plate 74d
Berry, Christmas Plate F2
Bigeye Plate 92b
Bignonia capreolata Plate H4
Bison, American 489, *491*
Bittern
  American 38, 110
  Least 114, Plate 24b
Blackbird 167
  Forbes' 179
  Red-winged 177, 178, 179, Plate 58b
  Yellow-shouldered 179
Blackfly, Asian Citrus 52
Blarina carolinensis Plate 65d
Blenny
  Redlip Plate 93b
  Wrasse Plate 93a
Blueberry 206
  Dwarf 14
Bluebird, Eastern 166, 167, 168, Plate
    50c
Boar
  European Wild 214
  Wild 214, Plate 63b
Bobcat 4, 36, 45, 209, 210, 211, Plate
    62b
Bobwhite, Northern 123, 125, Plate 33e
Bodianus pulchellus Plate 90c
Bodianus rufus Plate 90e
Bombycilla cedrorum 172, Plate 51c
Bonefish 227, Plate 81a
Bonnethead Plate 98c
Booby

Abbott's 110
Brown 110, Plate 22b
Masked 43, 110, Plate 22a
Borrichia sp. 21
Bothus lunatus Plate 94c
Bottlebrush, White Plate C4
Breadroot, Indian Plate F4
Briareum sp. Plate 101c
Brittle Star, Banded-arm Plate 104e
Bromeliad, Wild Pine *234*
Broomsedge 14
Brotogeris chiriri 142, Plate 41b
Brotogeris versicolorus 142, Plate 41c
Bubo virginianus 146, Plate 42d
Bubulcus ibis 114, Plate 23a
Buckeye
Common Plate 70e
Red Plate H1
Budgerigar 140, 187
Bug
Florida Leaf-footed Plate 75h
Milkweed Plate 75c
Palmetto Plate 74e
Bulbul, Red-whiskered 170–2, 187, Plate 60c
Bullfrog 70, 71, 72, Plate 4c
Bunting
Indigo 181, 182, Plate 56a
Painted 180, 181, 182, Plate 56b
Burrfish, Striped Plate 95f
Bursera simaruba 17, Plate B4
Buteo brachyurus 123, Plate 32a
Buteo jamaicensis 123, Plate 32c
Buteo lineatus 123, Plate 32d
Buteo platypterus 123, Plate 31c
Butorides virescens 114, Plate 24a
Butterflyfish
Banded Plate 78d
Longsnout Plate 78b
Reef Plate 78c
Spotfin Plate 78e
Buttonbush Plate F3
Buttonwood 22, 38

Cabbage
Saw Plate B2
Swamp Plate A2
Cacomistle 202
Caiman
Common 79, 81
Cuvier's Dwarf 79
Cairina moschata 117, Plate 26c
Calamus bajonado Plate 82e
Calidris alba 133, Plate 36b
Calidris alpina 133, Plate 37a

Calidris canutus 133, Plate 37d
Calidris mauri 133, Plate 36e
Calidris minutilla 133, Plate 36c
Calidris pusilla 133, Plate 36d
Calopteryx maculata Plate 73b
Calosoma sp. Plate 75d
Campsis radicans Plate I1
Canis latrans 205, Plate 62c
Canna, Golden Plate J3
Canna flacida Plate J3
Canthidermis sufflamen Plate 96f
Caprimulgus carolinensis 147, Plate 43a
Capybara 216
Caracara, Crested 35, 122, 123, Plate 32e
Caracara cheriway 123, Plate 32e
Caranx latus Plate 80c
Caranx ruber Plate 80f
Carcharhinus leucas Plate 98d
Cardinal, Northern 169, 180, 182, Plate 56d
Cardinalfish, Barred Plate 91f
Cardinalis cardinalis 182, Plate 56d
Carduelis tristis 186, Plate 59a
Caretta caretta 86, Plate 8d
Carp, Asiatic Grass 20
Carpinus caroliniana 17
Carpodacus mexicanus 186, Plate 59b
Carya glabra 17
Cassiopea sp. Plate 106d
Cassis flammea Plate 103a
Casurina equisetifolia Plate A1
Cat
Black-footed 209
Rusty-spotted 209
Catbird, Gray 169, Plate 51e
Caterpillar Hunter Plate 75d
Cathartes aura 123, Plate 29b
Catharus guttatus 168, Plate 50d
Catoptrophorus semipalmatus 133, Plate 35f
Cattail 18
Celithemis eponina Plate 73f
Celtis laevigata 17
Cenchrus incertus Plate K4
Centropomus undecimalis Plate 81b
Centropristis striata Plate 88f
Centruroides gracilis Plate 77f
Cephalanthus occidentalis Plate F3
Ceratiola ericoides 15, *243*, Plate G2
Cercis canadensis Plate D3
Cero Plate 80d
Ceryle alcyon 151, Plate 44a
Chaetodipterus faber Plate 84b
Chaetodon aculeatus Plate 78b

Chaetodon ocellatus Plate 78e
Chaetodon sedentarius Plate 78c
Chaetodon striatus Plate 78d
Chaetura pelagica 159, Plate 47b
Charadrius alexandrinus 133, Plate 34b
Charadrius semipalmatus 133, Plate 34d
Charadrius vociferus 133, Plate 34e
Charadrius wilsonia 133, Plate 34c
Chat, Yellow-breasted 176, Plate 55a
Chavnus marinus 69, Plate 1a
Chelonia mydas 86, Plate 9b
Chelydra serpentina 86, Plate 10a
Cherry, West Indies 17
Chickadee, Carolina 163, 188, Plate
   49a
Chigger Plate 76a
Chilomycterus schoepfi Plate 95f
Chinaberry Plate A3
Chipmunk, Eastern 218, 219
Cladium jamaicensis 18
Cladonia sp. 15
Chordeiles gundlachii 147, Plate 43c
Chordeiles minor 147, Plate 43b
Chromis
   Blue Plate 86c
   Brown Plate 86d
   Purple Plate 86e
   Yellow-edge Plate 86d
Chromis cyanea Plate 86c
Chromis multilineata Plate 86d
Chromis scotti Plate 86e
Chrysops sp. Plate 76e
Chub, Bermuda Plate 82d
Chuck-will's-widow 147, Plate 43a
Cicada Plate 74a
Cicindela scutellaris Plate 74d
Circus cyaneus 123, Plate 31d
Citrus sinensis Plate C3
Cladina evansii Plate N1
Cladium jamaicensis Plate L1
Clavelina sp. Plate 105b
Clepticus parrae Plate 90b
Cliftonia monophylla 19
Coati 202
Cobia Plate 82b
Coccoloba diversifolia 17
Coccoloba uvifera 22, Plate E3
Coccothrinax argentata 12, *243*
Coccyzus americanus 144, Plate 41d
Coccyzus minor 144, Plate 41e
Cockroach
   American Plate 74b
   Cuban Green Plate 74h
Cocos nucifera 12, Plate A4
Coffee, Wild 17

Colaptes auratus 154, Plate 45d
Colinus virginianus 125, Plate 33e
Collared-Dove, Eurasian 137, 139, 187,
   Plate 40b
Colocasia esculenta Plate M1
Coluber constrictor 89, Plate 16e
Columba leucocephala 139, Plate 40a
Columbina passerina 139, Plate 40e
Conch
   Florida Fighting Plate 103c
   Florida Horse Plate 103g
   Hawkwing Plate 103d
   Queen Plate 103f
Concocarpus erectus 22
Condor
   Andean 118
   California 118
Condylactis gigantea Plate 106a
Coney Plate 88c
Contopus virens 156, Plate 46a
Coontie Plate F4
Coot, American 127, 129, Plate 33d
Cooter
   Florida 83, 84, 86, Plate 11b
   Florida Red-bellied Plate 11a
Coragyps atratus 123, Plate 29a
Coral
   Boulder Star Plate 100f
   Common Brain Plate 101f
   Common Star Plate 100f
   Elkhorn Plate 100b
   Finger Plate 100g
   Fire Plate 100d
   Flower Plate 101a
   Ivory Tree 22
   Large Star Plate 100e
   Lettuce Plate 100c
   Smooth Brain Plate 101f
   Staghorn Plate 100a
   Symmetrical Brain Plate 101f
Cormorant
   Double-crested 34, 42, 109, 110, Plate
      21c
   Spectacled 110
Cornus florida 17, Plate B3
Corvus brachyrhynchos 161, Plate 48c
Corvus ossifragus 161, Plate 48d
Coryphopterus punctipectophorus Plate 93e
Cottonmouth 78, 86, 91, 92, 93, Plate
   19c
Cottontail, Eastern 219, 220, 221, Plate
   64d
Cougar Plate 62d
Cow Killer Plate 76f
Cowbird

Brown-headed 173, 175, 178, 179,
   Plate 60e
Giant 178
Screaming 178
Shiny 173
Cowfish, Scrawled Plate 95d
Cowrie, Flamingo Tongue Plate 103b
Coyote 201, 204, 205, Plate 62c
Crabwood 17
Crane
   Sandhill 8, 33, 35, 45, 126, 127, 128,
      Plate 25b
   Whooping 35, 45–6, 125, 128, Plate
      25c
Creeper, Trumpet Plate I1
Creeper, Virginia 17
Cricket, Mole Plate 73a
Crocodile
   American 79, 81, Plate 8a
   Indo-Pacific 79
Crocodylus acutus Plate 8a
Crotalus adamanteus 93, Plate 19d
Crotophaga ani 144, Plate 41f
Crow
   American 159, 160, 161, Plate 48c
   Fish 160, 161, Plate 48d
Cryptotis parva Plate 65e
Cubbyu Plate 97c
Cuckoo
   European 143
   Mangrove 4, 42, 144, Plate 41e
   Yellow-billed 143, 144, Plate 41d
Curlew, Eskimo 132
Custard Apple Plate G4
Cyanocitta cristata 161, Plate 48a
Cyphoma gibbosum Plate 103b
Cypress
   Bald 19, *236*, Plate B1
   Dwarf Pond 19, 38
   Hat-rack 19
   Pond 19
Cyrilla racemiflora 19

Daisy, Sea Ox-eye 21
Damselfish
   Bicolor Plate 85f
   Cocoa Plate 85b
   Dusky Plate 85c
   Longfin Plate 85a
   Threespot Plate 85e
   Yellowtail Plate 86b
Danaus plexippus Plate 71b
Dareen Plate M1
Darner, Common Green Plate 73e
Dasher, Blue Plate 73d

Dasyatis americana Plate 99b
Dasymutilla occidentalis Plate 76f
Dasypus novemcinctus 197, Plate 61b
Deer
   Key 214, 215
   White-tailed 42, 46, 192, 210, 214,
      215, 493, Plate 63c
Deerfly Plate 76e
Deirochelys reticularia 86, Plate 11c
Delphinius delphis 213, Plate 68b
Dendrocygna autumnalis 117, Plate 26b
Dendrocygna bicolor 117, Plate 26a
Dendroica coronata 176, Plate 53a
Dendroica discolor 176, Plate 53c
Dendroica dominica 176, Plate 54b
Dendroica palmarum 176, Plate 53e
Dendroica pinus 176, Plate 53d
Dermacentor sp. Plate 76b
Dermochelys coriacea 86, Plate 8c
Devil's Claw 17
Devil's Walking Stick *243*
Diadema antillarum Plate 104b
Didelphis virginiana 195, Plate 61a
Diodon hystrix Plate 95b
Diplectrum formosum Plate 89f
Diplodus holbrooki Plate 81e
Diploria strigosa Plate 101f
Distichlis spicata 21
Doctorfish Plate 79e
Dogwood 17
   Flowering Plate B3
   Jamaican 42
Dolphin
   Atlantic Bottle-nosed 32, 34, 212,
      213, Plate 68c
   Common 212, 213, Plate 68b
   Saddle-backed 212, Plate 68b
Dove
   Mourning 137, 138, 139, Plate 40c
   Rock 137, 138, 187
   White-winged 137, 139, 187, Plate
      40d
Dowitcher
   Long-billed 133, Plate 37c
   Short-billed 133, Plate 37b
Dropseed, Piney Woods 16
Drum, Spotted Plate 96e
Dryas iulia Plate 70f
Drymarchon couperi 89, Plate 16d
Dryocopus pileatus 154, Plate 45c
Duck
   Mottled 51, 117, Plate 26d
   Muscovy 114, 116, 117, 187, Plate
      26c
   Ring-necked 39, 117, Plate 28c

Ruddy 117, Plate 28e
Wood 39, 115, 117, Plate 28b
Dugong 212
Dumetella carolinensis 169, Plate 51e
Dunlin 130, 132, 133, Plate 37a
Durgeon, Black Plate 96b

Eacles imperialis Plate 71e
Eagle, Bald 4, 30, 31, 35, 46–7, 109,
    119, 122, 123, 125, 491–2, Plate
    29d
Ecpantheria scribonia Plate 72a
Eel
    Congo Plate 7a
    Sharptail Plate 97d
Egret
    Cattle 110, 112, 113, 114, Plate 23a
    Common 34
    Great 37, 111, 114, Plate 23c
    Reddish 34, 111, 114, Plate 23d
    Snowy 34, 37, 114, Plate 23b
Egretta caerulea 114, Plate 23f
Egretta rufescens 114, Plate 23d
Egretta thula 114, Plate 23b
Egretta tricolor 114, Plate 23e
Eichornia crassipes 20, Plate M2
Elanoides forficatus 123, Plate 30c
Elanus leucurus 123, Plate 30a
Elaphe guttata 89, Plate 16b
Elaphe obsoleta 89, Plate 16c
Elderberry Plate G1
Empidonax virescens 156, Plate 46b
Epidendrum conopseum Plate J4
Epinephelus cruentatus Plate 88d
Epinephelus fulvus Plate 88c
Epinephelus itajara Plate 87d
Epinephelus morio Plate 88a
Epinephelus striatus Plate 87f
Eptesicus fuscus 201, Plate 67a
Equetus acuminatus Plate 97a
Equetus lanceolatus Plate 97b
Equetus punctatus Plate 96e
Equetus umbrosus Plate 97c
Eragrostis sp. 14
Eretmochelys imbricata 86, Plate 9c
Eucidaris tribuloides Plate 104c
Eudocimus albus 114, Plate 25f
Eumaeus atala Plate 70a
Eumeces egregius 97, Plate 15e
Eumeces inexpectatus 97, Plate 15d
Eumeces laticeps 97, Plate 15b
Eumeces reynoldsi 96, Plate 15a
Eurycea auriculatus 67, Plate 6c
Eurycea longicauda 67, Plate 6a
Eurycea quadridigitata 67, Plate 6d

Eurycotis floridanus Plate 74e
Eurytides marcellus Plate 69d
Eusmilia fastigiata Plate 101a
Euyas planirostris 69, Plate 4a
Exothea paniculata 17

Fagus grandifolia 17
Falco sparverius 123, Plate 32b
Farancia abacura 89, Plate 17d
Feather Duster, Magnificent Plate 102e
Fern
    Bracken 16
    Giant Leather *244*
    Marsh Plate N4
    Shield Plate N4
Fetterbush 14, 15
Ficus aurea 17
Fiery Searcher Plate 75d
Fig, Strangler 17, 38, 42
Filefish, Scrawled Plate 96a
Finch, House 186, 187, Plate 59b
Fire Flag 18
Firefly Plate 74c
Flame Helmet Plate 103a
Flamefish Plate 92c
Flamingo Tongue Plate 103b
Flicker, Northern 152, 153, 154, Plate
    45d
Flounder, Peacock Plate 94c
Flycatcher
    Acadian 156, Plate 46b
    Great Crested 155, 156, Plate 46d
    Scissor-tailed 42, 155
    Variegated 43
    Vermilion 155
    Willow 493
Flying-Fox, Samoan 197
Forktail, Rambur's Plate 73c
Fox
    Fennec 204
    Gray 84, 204, 205, Plate 62a
    Red 51, 201, 204, 205
Fraxinus sp. 17
Fregata magnificens 110, Plate 20a
Frigatebird, Magnificent 8, 42, 43, 109,
    110, Plate 20a
Fritillary, Gulf Plate 70c
Frog
    Bronze 72, Plate 4e
    Florida Bog 72
    Florida Chorus 70
    Florida Cricket 69, 70, Plate 3a
    Gopher 71, 72, 84, Plate 4d
    Greenhouse 69, 187, Plate 4a
    Little Grass 70

Marsupial 69
Ornate Chorus 70, Plate 3d
Pig 70, 71, 72, Plate 4b
Southern Chorus 70, Plate 3b
Southern Leopard 71, 72, Plate 4f
Frogfish, Longlure Plate 94e
Fruit-Dove, Many-colored 137
Fulica americana 129, Plate 33d

Gallberry 15, 206
Gallinago gallinago 133, Plate 37e
Gallinula chloropus 129, Plate 33c
Gallinule, Purple 34, 40, 126, 127, 129,
    Plate 33a
Gannet, Northern 29
Gastrophrye carolinensis 69, Plate 1e
Gavia immer 106, Plate 20d
Gaylussacia dumosa 15
Gecko
    Caribbean Dwarf 94
    Florida Reef 93, 94
    Mediterranean 93, 94, Plate 13d
Gelsemium sempervirens Plate I2
Geodia neptuni Plate 105d
Geomys pinetis 217, Plate 66d
Geothlypis trichas 176, Plate 55b
Ginglymostoma cirratum Plate 98b
Glasswort 21
Glaucomys volans 219, Plate 64a
Globicephala macrorhynchus 213, Plate
    68d
Gnatcatcher, Blue-gray 165, 166, Plate
    50b
Goatfish
    Spotted Plate 96c
    Yellow Plate 96d
Gobiosoma horsti Plate 92e
Gobiosoma macrodon Plate 93d
Gobiosoma oceanops Plate 92d
Gobiosoma xanthoprora Plate 92f
Goby
    Neon 229, Plate 92d
    Rusty Plate 93c
    Sharknose Plate 93c
    Spotted Plate 93e
    Tiger Plate 93d
    Yellowline Plate 92e
    Yellowprow Plate 92f
Godwit, Marbled 133, Plate 35a
Golden-Plover, American 132
Goldeneye, Common 29
Goldfinch, American 183, 186, Plate
    59a
Gopher, Southeastern Pocket 217, Plate
    66d

Gopherus polyphemus 86, Plate 12c
Gorgonia ventalina Plate 101e
Grackle
    Boat-tailed 176, 178, 179, Plate 58c
    Common 177, 178, 179, Plate 58d
Grape, Muscadine 17
Graptemys barbouri 86, Plate 10d
Grass
    Love 14
    Salt 21
    Sand Cord 21, Plate N3
    Smooth Cord 21
    Turtle Plate 106c
Grasshopper, Southeastern Lubber Plate
    72d
Graysby Plate 88d
Grebe
    Atitlan 106
    Eared 104
    Horned 104, 105, 106, Plate 20c
    Pied-billed 104, 105, 106, Plate 20b
Grosbeak
    Blue 182, Plate 56c
    Rose-breasted 181
Ground-Dove, Common 137, 139, Plate
    40e
Grouper
    Black Plate 88b
    Nassau Plate 87f
    Red Plate 88a
    Yellowfin Plate 87e
Grunt
    Blue-striped Plate 83c
    French Plate 83a
    Spanish Plate 83d
    White Plate 83b
Grus americana 128, Plate 25c
Grus canadensis 128, Plate 25b
Gryllotalpa hexadactyla Plate 73a
Guiracea caerulea 182, Plate 56c
Gull
    Bonaparte's 42, 135, 136, Plate 38a
    Great Black-backed 136, Plate 38e
    Herring 134, 135, 136, Plate 38d
    Laughing 42, 109, 134, 136, Plate 38b
    Ring-billed 136, Plate 38c
Gum
    Black 19
    Sweet 17
Gumbo Limbo 17, 38, 42, Plate B4
Gymnothorax funebris Plate 97f
Gymnothorax moringa Plate 97e

Hackberry 17
Haematopus palliatus 133, Plate 34f

Haemulon album Plate 83f
Haemulon flavolineatum Plate 83a
Haemulon macrostomum Plate 83d
Haemulon parra Plate 83e
Haemulon plumieri Plate 83b
Haemulon sciurus Plate 83c
Haideotriton wallacei 67, Plate 6e
Haliaeetus leucocephalus 123, Plate 29d
Halichoeres bivittatus Plate 91e
Halichoeres garnoti Plate 91d
Halichoeres maculipinna Plate 90d
Hamlet
    Blue Plate 87a
    Butter Plate 87b
    Tan Plate 87c
Hammerhead, Smooth Plate 99c
Harrier, Northern 118, 119, 123, Plate
    31d
Hawk
    Broad-winged 30, 123, Plate 31c
    Cooper's 119, 123, Plate 31a
    Red-shouldered 34, 38, 119, 123,
        Plate 32d
    Red-tailed 90, 119, 123, Plate 32c
    Sharp-shinned 30, 123, Plate 31b
    Short-tailed 4, 119, 122, 123, Plate
        32a
Hawkfish, Red-spotted Plate 94d
Hawksbill 43, 82, 84, 85, 86, Plate 9c
Helianthus floridanus Plate J1
Heliconius charitonius Plate 70d
Hemidactylus turcicus 94, Plate 13d
Hemiemblemaria simulus Plate 93a
Heraclides cresphontes Plate 69c
Hermodice sp. Plate 102c
Heron
    Great Blue 34, 111, 114, Plate 25d
    Great White 42
    Green 38, 114, Plate 24a
    Little Blue 34, 111, 114, Plate 23f
    Tricolored 34, 114, Plate 23e
Heterodon platirhinos 89, Plate 16a
Hickory, Pignut 17
Highhat Plate 97a
Himantopus mexicanus 133, Plate 35b
Hirundo rustica 159, Plate 47e
Hog, Wild 214, Plate 63b
Hogfish Plate 90a
    Spanish Plate 90e
    Spotfin Plate 90c
Holacanthus bermudensis Plate 78f
Holacanthus ciliaris Plate 78a
Holacanthus tricolor Plate 79d
Holly 17
    Florida Plate F2

    Yaupon Plate H3
Holocentrus ascensionis Plate 91b
Hornbeam, Hop 17
Houndfish Plate 80a
Huckleberry 15
Hummingbird
    Giant 148
    Ruby-throated 149, 150, Plate 43d
Hydrilla 51, 52, 212
Hydrilla verticillata 20
Hydroid, Branching Plate 106b
Hyla cinerea 70, Plate 2d
Hyla femoralis 70, Plate 2e
Hyla gratiosa 70, Plate 2a
Hyla squirella 70, Plate 2b
Hylocichla mustelina 168, Plate 50e
Hypoplectrus sp. Plate 87c
Hypoplectrus gemma Plate 87a
Hypoplectrus unicolor Plate 87b

Ibis
    Glossy 34, 38, 114, Plate 25e
    White 34, 37, 38, 39, 42, 114, Plate 25f
Icteria virens 176, Plate 55a
Icterus galbula 179, Plate 59d
Icterus spurius 179, Plate 59c
Ictinia mississippiensis 123, Plate 30b
Iguana, Green 94
Ilex glabra 15
Ilex opaca 17
Ilex vomitoria Plate H3
Inkwood 17
Ipomoea sp. 21
Ironwood 17
    Black 17
Ischnura ramburii Plate 73c
Ixobrychus exilis 114, Plate 24b
Ixodes scapularis Plate 76c
Ivy, Poison 17, Plate K3

Jack
    Bar Plate 80f
    Bigeye Plate 80c
    Horse-eye Plate 80c
Jackknife Fish Plate 97b
Jackrabbit, Black-tailed 219
Jaguar 210
Jasmine, Carolina Plate I2
Jassamine, Yellow Plate I2
Jawfish, Yellowhead Plate 93f
Jay
    Blue 159, 160, 161, Plate 48a
    Florida Scrub 34, 35, 39
    Gray 160
Jelly

Moon Plate 106e
Upsidedown Plate 106d
Jewelwing, Ebony Plate Plate 73b
Jewfish Plate 87d
Julia, Orange Plate 70f
Junco, Dark-eyed 184
Juncus roemerianus 21
Junglefowl, Red 123
Junonia coenia Plate 70e

Katydid, Broad-winged Plate 72g
Kemp's Ridley 83, 84, 85, 86, Plate 9a
Kestrel, American 30, 118, 119, 120, 123, Plate 32b
Killdeer 129, 133, Plate 34e
Kingbird
 Eastern 155, 156, Plate 46f
 Gray 32, 42, 104, 155, 156, 169, 187, Plate 46e
 Loggerhead 43
Kingfisher, Belted 151, Plate 44a
Kinglet, Ruby-crowned 165, 166, Plate 50a
Kingsnake, Eastern 87, 89, Plate 18a
Kinkajou 202
Kinosternon baurii 86, Plate 12b
Kite
 Everglades 122
 Mississippi 123, Plate 30b
 Snail 4, 39, 119, 122, 123, 127, 187, Plate 30d
 Swallow-tailed 31, 34, 35, 38, 104, 119, 123, Plate 30c
 White-tailed 123, Plate 30a
Knot, Red 130, 133, Plate 37d
Kodkod 209
Krugiodendron ferreum 17
Kyphosus sectatrix Plate 82d

Lachnolaimus maximus Plate 90a
Lactophrys quadricornis Plate 95d
Lactophrys triqueter Plate 95e
Lagodon rhomboides Plate 81f
Laguncularia racemosa 22
Lampropeltis getula 89, Plate 18a
Lancewood 17
Lanius ludovicianus 172, Plate 51a
Lantana camara 51
Lantana depressa 51
Larus argentatus 136, Plate 38d
Larus atricilla 136, Plate 38b
Larus delawarensis 136, Plate 38c
Larus marinus 136, Plate 38e
Larus philadelphia 136, Plate 38a
Lasiurus intermedius 201, Plate 67c

Latrodectus mactans Plate 77a
Leatherback 35, 48, 82, 83, 85, 86, Plate 8c
Leopard 210
Lepidochelys kempii 86, Plate 9a
Lethocerus griseus Plate 75f
Licania michauxii 16
Lignum vitae 42
Liguus fasciatus 42
Lime, Ogeechee 19
Limnodromus griseus 133, Plate 37b
Limnodromus scolopaceus 133, Plate 37c
Limosa fedoa 133, Plate 35a
Limpkin 34, 38, 39, 126, 127, 129, 187, Plate 24d
Lion, Mountain Plate 62d
Lionia, Rusty 15
Liquidambar styraciflua 17, Plate F1
Lithobates capito 72, Plate 4d
Lithobates catesbeiana 72, Plate 4c
Lithobates clamitans 72, Plate 4e
Lithobates grylio 72, Plate 4b
Lithobates sphenocephala 72, Plate 4f
Lizard
 Eastern Fence 78, 94, 95, Plate 14c
 Eastern Glass 97, Plate 13a
 Florida Scrub 94, 95, Plate 14a
 Florida Worm 77, Plate 13b
 Mimic Glass 97
Lobster, Spiny Plate 102d
Loggerhead 29, 31, 34, 35, 36, 43, 48, 83, 84, 85, 86, Plate 8d
Longwing
 Orange Plate 70f
 Zebra Plate 70d
Lontra canadensis 209, Plate 61f
Lookdown Plate 80e
Loon
 Common 31, 104, 105, 106, Plate 20d
 Red-throated 104, 105
Lophodytes cucullatus 117, Plate 26e
Lotus, American *239*, Plate I3
Lotus-Lily Plate I3
Lovebug Plate 75e
Lutjanus analis Plate 84e
Lutjanus apodus Plate 84d
Lutjanus campechanus Plate 84f
Lutjanus synagris Plate 84c
Lycosa carolinensis Plate 77e
Lygaeus kalmii Plate 75c
Lynx 490–1, *492*
Lynx rufus 211, Plate 62b
Lyonia ferruginea 15
Lyonia fruticosa 14
Lyonia lucidia 14

Lysiloma latisiliqua 17
Lytechinus variegatus Plate 104a

Macroclemys temminckii 86, Plate 10b
Magnolia, Southern 17, *243*, Plate E4
Magnolia grandiflora 17, *243*, Plate E4
Mahogany 42
Maidencane 18
Malacanthus plumieri Plate 95a
Malaclemys terrapin 86, Plate 10c
Mallard 51, 116
Manatee
    Amazonian 212
    Caribbean Plate 68a
    Florida 36, 47, Plate 68a
    West African 212
    West Indian 4, 36, 47, 192, 212, 213,
       Plate 68a
Mangrove
    Black 22, *241*
    Red 22, *241*, Plate D1
    White 22
Mantid, Praying Plate 72f
Maple
    Red 17, 19, Plate D2
    Sugar *495*
Margate Plate 83f
Martin
    Purple 157, 158, 159, Plate 47a
    White-eyed River 159
Mastic 17, 42
Mastichodendron foetidissimum 17
Meadow Beauty Plate N2
Meadowlark, Eastern 179, Plate 58a
Megalops atlanticus Plate 82a
Megascops asio 146, Plate 42b
Melaleuca quinquenerva 52, Plate C4
Melanerpes carolinus 154, Plate 44d
Melanerpes erythrocephalus 154, Plate
    44c
Meleagris gallopavo 125, Plate 33f
Melia azederach Plate A3
Melichthys niger Plate 96b
Melospiza georgiana 186, Plate 57d
Melospiza melodia 186, Plate 57f
Meoma ventricosa Plate 104d
Mephitis mephitis 209, Plate 61d
Merganser
    Hooded 117, Plate 26e
    Red-breasted 117, Plate 26f
Mergus serrator 117, Plate 26f
Merlin 120
Microcentrum rhombifolium Plate 72g
Microspathodon chrysurus Plate 86b
Micrurus fulvius 90, Plate 19b

Milkwort Plate K1
Millepora alcicornis Plate 100d
Mimus polyglottos 169, Plate 51b
Mink 208, 209
Mniotilta varia 176, Plate 54a
Mockingbird
    Bahama 169
    Northern 168, 169, Plate 51b
Mole, Eastern 191, Plate 66c
Molothrus ater 179, Plate 60e
Monarch 30, Plate 71b
Monkey, Rhesus 51
Montastrea annularis Plate 100f
Montastrea cavernosa Plate 100e
Moorhen, Common 127, 129, Plate 33c
Moose *490*
Moray
    Green Plate 97f
    Spotted Plate 97e
Morus rubra 17
Moss
    Ball 19, Plate I4
    Deer Plate N1
    Spanish 13, 199, 216, Plate L3
Moth
    Cactus 50
    Giant Leopard Plate 72a
    Imperial Plate 71e
    Io Plate 71c
    Lunar Plate 71d
    Oleander Plate 72e
    Polyphemus Plate 71f
    Rattlebox Plate 72c
Mouse
    Beach 216, 217, Plate 65a
    Florida 84, 216, 217, Plate 65c
    Golden 191, 193, 216–17, Plate 65b
    Old Field Plate 65a
Mud Dauber Plate 75a
Mudpuppy 66
Mugil cephalus Plate 81d
Mugil curema Plate 81c
Mulberry, Red 17
Mullet
    Striped Plate 81d
    White Plate 81c
Mulloidichthys martinicus Plate 96d
Mycteria americana 114, Plate 25a
Mycteroperca bonaci Plate 88b
Mycteroperca phenax Plate 88e
Mycteroperca venenosa Plate 87e
Myiarchus crinitis 156, Plate 46d
Myiopsitta monachus 142, Plate 41a
Myna
    Common 51, 177, 178, 179, 187,

Plate 60d
Hill 177, 187
Myrica cerifera 15
Myrichthys breviceps Plate 97d
Myripristis jacobis Plate 91a
Myrtle, Wax 15

Nectandra coriacea 17
Needlerush, Black 21
Negaprion brevirostris Plate 98a
Nelumbo lutea 239, Plate I3
Nephila clavipes Plate 77c
Nerium oleander Plate G3
Nerodia fasciata 89, Plate 17c
Nerodia floridana 89, Plate 17a
Nerodia taxispilota 89, Plate 17e
Newt
    Peninsula 67, Plate 5e
    Sharp-ribbed 67
    Spiny 67
    Striped 66, 67, Plate 5d
Nighthawk
    Antillean 146, 147, Plate 43c
    Common 146, 147, Plate 43b
Night-Heron
    Black-crowned 34, 114, 188, Plate 24e
    Yellow-crowned 37, 112, 114, Plate 24c
Nightjar
    European 146
    Puerto Rican 147
    White-winged 147
Noddy, Brown 43, 135, 136, Plate 22d
Notophthalmus peristriatus 67, Plate 5d
Notophthalmus viridescens 67, Plate 5e
Nutcracker, Clark's 160
Nuthatch
    Brown-headed 163, Plate 49c
    White-breasted 162, 163
Nyctanassa violacea 114, Plate 24c
Nycticeius humeralis 201, Plate 67d
Nycticorax nycticorax 114, Plate 24e
Nymphaea odorata 17
Nyssa aquatica 19
Nyssa ogeche 19
Nyssa sylvatica 19

Oak
    Chapman's 15
    Live 17, 31, *243,* Plate C1
    Sand Live 15
    Scrub 15
    Turkey 16
    White 17
Ochrotomys nuttalli 217, Plate 65b

Oculina varicosa 22
Ocyurus chrysurus Plate 86a
Odocoileus virginianus 215, Plate 63c
Oleander Plate G3
Olingo 202
Oliva reticularis Plate 103e
Olive, Netted Plate 103e
Ophioblennius atlanticus Plate 93b
Ophioderma appressum Plate 104e
Ophisaurus ventralis 97, Plate 13a
Opisthognathus aurifrons Plate 93f
Oporornis formosus 176, Plate 55d
Opossum, Virginia 192, 193–5, Plate 61a
Opsanus beta Plate 94b
Orange Plate C3
Orchid
    Fringed Plate J2
    Greenfly Plate J4
Oreaster sp. Plate 104g
Oriole
    Baltimore 179, Plate 59d
    Martinique 179
    Montserrat 179
    Orchard 179, Plate 59c
    Spot-breasted 176, 187
Orthostethus infuscatus Plate 74g
Osprey 31, 32, 39, 118, 119, 120, 123, Plate 29c
Osteopilus septentrionalis 70, Plate 2c
Ostrya virginiana 17
Otter
    Eurasian River 209
    River 4, 31, 35, 36, 38, 192, 208, 209, Plate 61f
    Sea 207
Ovenbird 174, 176, Plate 55e
Owl
    Barn 146, Plate 42a
    Barred 38, 144, 146, Plate 42c
    Burrowing 35, 144, 146, Plate 42e
    Eastern Screech 146, Plate 42b
    Great Horned 145, 146, 188, 194, Plate 42d
    Short-eared 146
    Snowy 145
    Spotted 146, 492
    Tawny 145
Oxyura jamaicensis 117, Plate 28e
Oystercatcher, American 37, 130, 133, Plate 34f

Pachydiplax longipennis Plate 73d
Pagrus pagrus Plate 82c
Palm

Buccaneer 12
Cabbage 12, 17, 206, Plate A2
Coconut 12, Plate A4
Date 12
Everglades *240*, Plate B2
Florida Thatch 12
Key Thatch 12
Parautis 12, Plate B2
Petticoat 12
Royal 12, 38, Plate D4
Sabal 12
Silver 12, *243*
Washington 12
Palmetto
  Saw 12, 14, 15, 21, 206, *242*, Plate E2
  Scrub Plate E2
Panchlora nivea Plate 74h
Pandion haliaetus 123, Plate 29c
Panicum hemitomon 18
Panther, Florida 4, 37, 38, 46, 51, 191, 209–11, 221, Plate 62d
Panulirus sp. Plate 102d
Paper-bark 52, Plate C4
Papilio polyxenes Plate 69f
Parakeet
  Black-hooded 187
  Blue-crowned 187
  Carolina 142, 187
  Dusky-headed 187
  Mitred 187
  Monk 51, 141, 142, 187, Plate 41a
  Orange-chinned 141
  Red-masked 187
  White-winged 142, 187, Plate 41c
  Yellow-chevroned 142, 187, Plate 41b
Parrot
  Orange-winged 187
  Red-crowned 187
Parrotfish
  Blue Plate 89a
  Midnight Plate 89c
  Queen Plate 89b
  Redband Plate 89e
  Stoplight 228, Plate 90f
Parthenocissus quinquefolia 17
Parula, Northern 176, Plate 53b
Parula americana 176, Plate 53b
Passer domesticus 186, Plate 60b
Passerculus sandwichensis 186, Plate 57c
Passerina ciris 182, Plate 56b
Passerina cyanea 182, Plate 56a
Pawpaw 16
Pelecanus erythrorhynchos 110, Plate 21a
Pelecanus occidentalis 110, Plate 21b
Pelican

American White 32, 110, Plate 21a
  Brown 32, 107, 109, 110, Plate 21b
Pennant, Halloween Plate 73f
Pepper, Brazilian 50, 52, Plate F2
Perch, Sand Plate 89f
Peregrine Falcon 30, 118, 119, 120, 122
Periplaneta americana Plate 74b
Peromyscus polionotus 217, Plate 65a
Persea borbonia 17
Phaethon lepturus 110, Plate 22e
Phalacrocorax auritus 110, Plate 21c
Phoebe, Eastern 156, Plate 46c
Phoebis sennae Plate 70b
Phoenix dactylifera 12
Photinus pyralis Plate 74c
Phragmatopma lapidosa 22
Pickerel Weed 18, Plate K2
Picoides borealis 154, Plate 45a
Picoides pubescens 154, Plate 45b
Pig
  Feral 214, Plate 63b
  Wild 51, 214, 215, Plate 63b
Pigeon
  Passenger 138–9
  White-crowned 4, 42, 137, 139, 187, Plate 40a
Pine
  Australian Plate A1
  Loblolly 17
  Longleaf 15, 16, *242*, Plate C2
  Pond 15
  Ponderosa 492
  Sand 15, Plate E1
  Slash 15, *242*, *243*
Pinfish Plate 81f
  Spottail Plate 81e
Pintail, Northern 117, Plate 27a
Pinus clausa 15, Plate E1
Pinus elliotii 15, *242*, *243*
Pinus palustris 15, *242*, Plate C2
Pinus serotina 15
Pinus taeda 17
Pipilo erythrophthalmus 186, Plate 56e
Pipit
  American 169, 170–1, 172, Plate 51f
  Sprague's 172
Piranga rubra 182, Plate 55f
Pisonia aculeata 17
Pistia stratiotes Plate M3
Pituophis melanoleucus 89, Plate 18d
Pityopsis graminifolia 16
Platanthera ciliaris Plate J2
Plecia nearctica Plate 75e
Plegadis falcinellus 114, Plate 25e

Pleuroploca gigantea Plate 103g
Plethodon grobmani 67, Plate 6b
Plexaura sp. Plate 101d
Plexaurella sp. 101b
Plover
    Black-bellied 133, Plate 34a
    Semipalmated 133, Plate 34d
    Snowy 133, Plate 34b
    Wilson's 133, Plate 34c
Plum, Pigeon 17, 42
Pluvialis squatarola 133, Plate 34a
Podiceps auritus 106, Plate 20c
Podilymbus podiceps 106, Plate 20b
Podomys floridanus 217, Plate 65c
Poecile carolinensis 163, Plate 49a
Poisonwood 42
Polioptila caerulea 166, Plate 50b
Polistes sp. Plate 75g
Polygala nana Plate K1
Pomacanthus arcuatus Plate 79f
Pomacanthus paru Plate 79c
Pontederia cordata 18, Plate K2
Pontederia lanceolata 18
Poorwill, Common 147
Porcupinefish Plate 95b
Porgy
    Jolthead Plate 82e
    Red Plate 82c
Porites porites Plate 100g
Porkfish Plate 84a
Porphyrula martinica 129, Plate 33a
Prairie-Chicken, Greater 172
Priacanthus arenatus Plate 92b
Priacanthus cruentatus Plate 92a
Priolepis hipoliti Plate 93c
Procyon lotor 203, Plate 61e
Progne subis 159, Plate 47a
Protonotaria citrea 176, Plate 54e
Prunus myrtifolia 17
Pseudacris crucifer 70, Plate 3c
Pseudacris nigrita nigrita 70, Plate 3b
Pseudacris ornata 70, Plate 3d
Pseudemys nelsoni 86, Plate 11a
Pseudemys peninsularis floridana 86,
    Plate 11b
Pseudobranchus axanthus 67, Plate 7d
Pseudopeneus maculatus Plate 96c
Pseudophoenix sargentii 12
Psychotria nervosa 17
Pteridium aquilinium 16
Pterourus glaucus Plate 69e
Puma 201, 202, 205, 209–11, Plate 62d
Puma concolor 211, Plate 62d
Punk Plate C4
Pycnonotus jocosus 172, Plate 60c

Quercus alba 17
Quercus chapmanii 15
Quercus geminata 15
Quercus laevis 16
Quercus myrtifolia 15
Quercus virginiana 17, *243*, Plate C1
Quiscalus major 179, Plate 58c
Quiscalus quiscula 179, Plate 58d

Rabbit, Marsh 31, 219, 220, 221, Plate
    64e
Racer, Black 78, 87, 89, Plate 16e
Racerunner, Six-lined 95, 96, Plate 13c
Rachycentron canadium Plate 82b
Raccoon 31, 34, 42
    Common Plate 61e
    Northern 192, 202–3, Plate 61e
Rail, Clapper 126, 129, Plate 33b
Rallus longirostris 129, Plate 33b
Rat
    Black 216, 217, Plate 66a
    Brown Plate 66b
    House Plate 66a
    Lab Plate 66b
    Norway 216, 217, Plate 66b
    Roof Plate 66a
Rattlesnake
    Dusky Pigmy 91, 92, 93, Plate 19a
    Eastern Diamondback 84, 91–3, Plate
        19d
Rattus norvegicus 217, Plate 66b
Rattus rattus 217, Plate 66a
Raven, Common 159, 161
Ray, Spotted Eagle Plate 99a
Recurvirostra americana 133, Plate 35e
Redbud Plate D3
Redstart, American 174, 176, Plate 54d
Reeffish, Purple Plate 86e
Regina alleni 89, Plate 17b
Regulus calendula 166, Plate 50a
Rhexia virginica Plate N2
Rhineura floridana Plate 13b
Rhizophora mangle 22, *241*, Plate D1
Ringtail 202
Roach, Wood Plate 74e
Roadrunner, Greater 142
Robin 167
    American 166, 167, 168, Plate 50f
Rock Beauty Plate 79d
Romalea microptera Plate 72d
Rook 188
Rosemary, Florida 15–16, *243*, Plate G2
Rostrhamus sociabilis 123, Plate 30d
Roystonea elata 12, Plate D4
Ruff 131

Rynchops niger 136, Plate 38f

Sabal palmetto 12, 17, Plate A2
Sagittaria latifolia 18
Sailor's Choice Plate 83e
Salamander
  Cave Plate 6e
  Chinese Giant 65
  Dwarf 66, 67, Plate 6d
  Flatwoods 66
  Four-toed 67
  Georgia Blind 65, 66, 67, Plate 6e
  Many-lined 67
  Marbled 66, 67, Plate 5c
  Mexican Lungless 65
  Mole 66, 67, 496, Plate 5a
  Rusty Mud 66
  Seal 67
  Slimy 66, 67, Plate 6b
  Southern Dusky 67, Plate 6c
  Three-lined 67, Plate 6a
  Tiger 65, 66, 67, Plate 5b
Salicornia sp. 21
Saltbush 22
Sambucus canadensis Plate G1
Sanderling 130, 133, Plate 36b
Sandpiper
  Buff-breasted 132
  Least 133, Plate 36c
  Semipalmated 130, 133, Plate 36d
  Solitary 133, Plate 36f
  Spotted 39, 130, 131, 133, Plate 36a
  Western 133, Plate 36e
Sandspur Plate K4
Sapsucker, Yellow-bellied 152, 154,
    Plate 44b
Sarracenia flava 235
Sawgrass 18, 52, Plate L1
Sayornis phoebe 156, Plate 46c
Scaloporus aquaticus Plate 66c
Scamp Plate 88e
Scaphiopus holbrookii 69, Plate 1d
Scarus coelestinus Plate 89c
Scarus coeruleus Plate 89a
Scarus vetula Plate 89b
Scarus viride Plate 90f
Scaup, Lesser 117, Plate 28d
Sceliphron caementarium Plate 75a
Sceloporus undulatus 95, Plate 14c
Sceloporus woodi 95, Plate 14a
Schinus terebinthifolius Plate F2
Schoolmaster Plate 84d
Scincella lateralis 97, Plate 15c
Sciurus carolinensis 219, Plate 64b
Sciurus niger 219, Plate 64c

Scomberomorus regalis Plate 80d
Scorpaena brasiliensis Plate 94f
Scorpion Plate 77f
Scrub-Jay, Florida 160, 161, Plate 48b
Sea Cow Plate 68a
Sea Cucumber, Furry Plate 105e
Sea Fan, Common Plate 101e
Sea Finger, Corky Plate 101c
Sea Grape 22, Plate E3
Sea Oats 21, *238*, Plate L2
Sea Rod
  Black Plate 101d
  Split-Pore Plate 101b
Sea Star, Cushion Plate 104g
Sea Turtle 85, 86
  Green 35, 36, 43, 48, 82, Plate 9b
  Hawksbill 43, 82, 84, Plate 9c
  Kemp's Ridley 83, 84, Plate 9a
  Leatherback 35, 48, 82, 83, Plate 8c
  Loggerhead 29, 31, 34–6, 43, 48, 83,
    84, Plate 8d
Sea Urchin
  Long-spined Plate 104b
  Variegated Plate 104a
Sebellastarte sp. Plate 102e
Seiurus aurocapillus 176, Plate 55e
Selene vomer Plate 80e
Sepioteuthis sepioidea Plate 102f
Serenoa repens 12, 14, *242*, Plate E2
Sergeant Major 229, Plate 86f
Serranus tabacarius Plate 89d
Sertularella speciosa Plate 106b
Setophaga ruticilla 176, Plate 54d
Shark
  Bull Plate 98d
  Hammerhead Plate 99c
  Lemon Plate 98a
  Nurse Plate 98b
Sheep, Bighorn *490*
Sheepshead Plate 82f
Shoveler, Northern 117, Plate 27b
Shrew
  Least 191, Plate 65e
  Short-tailed 191, Plate 65d
Shrike, Loggerhead 169–72, Plate 51a
Shrimp, Banded Plate 102b
Shyrna tiburo Plate 98c
Sialia sialis 168, Plate 50c
Siren
  Dwarf 67, Plate 7d
  Greater 66, 67, Plate 7b
  Lesser 67, Plate 7c
Siren intermedia 67, Plate 7c
Siren lacertina 67, Plate 7b
Sistrurus miliarius barbouri 93, Plate

19a
Sitta pusilla 163, Plate 49c
Skimmer, Black 32, 134, 136, Plate 38f
Skink
  Blue-tailed Mole 96
  Broadheaded 95, 96, 97, Plate 15b
  Coal 95
  Eastern Five-lined 95
  Florida Sand 95, 96, Plate 15a
  Ground 95, 96, 97, Plate 15c
  Mole 95, 96, 97, Plate 15e
  Southeastern Five-lined 78, 95, 96,
    97, Plate 15d
Skipjack Plate 80f
Skipper, Long-tailed Plate 71a
Skunk
  Eastern Spotted 208, 209, Plate 61c
  Striped 208, 209, Plate 61d
  Western Spotted 209
Slider, Yellow-bellied 86, Plate 11d
Slippery Dick Plate 91e
Snail
  Apple 122, 127
  Giant African 52
Snake
  Atlantic Salt Marsh 89
  Banded Water 78, 87, 89, Plate 17c
  Big Pine Key Ringneck 89
  Brown Water 87, 89, Plate 17e
  Corn 89, Plate 16b
  Eastern Coral 86, 90, Plate 19b
  Eastern Garter 89, Plate 18b
  Eastern Hognose 87–8, 89, Plate 16a
  Eastern Indigo 84, 89
  Eastern Ribbon 89, Plate 18c
  Florida Brown 89
  Florida Green Water 78, 87, 88, 89,
    Plate 17a
  Florida Ribbon 89
  Indigo 87, 88, 89, Plate 16d
  Mud Plate 87, 88, 89, 17d
  Pine 87, 88, 89, Plate 18d
  Rimrock Crown 89
  Ringneck 88
  Rough Green 78, 87
  Scarlet 90
  Scarlet King 90
  Short-tailed 89
  Striped Crayfish 87, 88, 89, Plate 17b
  Yellow Rat 89, Plate 16c
  see also Kingsnake *and* Rattlesnake
Snapper
  Glasseye Plate 92a
  Lane Plate 84c
  Mutton Plate 84e

Red Plate 84f
  Yellowtail Plate 86a
Snipe, Common 133, Plate 37e
Snook, Common Plate 81b
Softshell, Florida 83, 86, Plate 12e
Soldierfish, Blackbar Plate 91a
Solenopsis invicta Plate 76d
Spadefish, Atlantic Plate 84b
Spadefoot, Eastern 68, 69, Plate 1d
Spanish Bayonet Plate M4
Spanish Dagger Plate M4
Sparisoma aurofrenatum Plate 89e
Sparkleberry 16
Sparrow
  Bachman's 183, 186, Plate 57a
  Chipping 186, Plate 57b
  Dusky Seaside 186
  Florida Grasshopper 186
  Grasshopper 184
  House 167, 183, 184–5, 185–6, 187,
    Plate 60b
  Rufous-collared 185
  Savannah 186, Plate 57c
  Seaside 186
  Song 184, 185, 186, Plate 57f
  Swamp 186, Plate 57d
  White-crowned 185
  White-throated 183, 186, Plate 57e
Spartina alterniflora 21
Spartina bakeri 21, Plate N3
Spartina patens 21
Spheciospongia sp. Plate 105a
Sphyraena barracuda Plate 80b
Sphyrapicus varius 154, Plate 44b
Sphyrna zygaena Plate 99c
Spider
  Black and Yellow Garden Plate 77d
  Black Widow Plate 77a
  Carolina Wolf Plate 77e
  Golden Silk Plate 77c
Spilogale putorius 209, Plate 61c
Spirobranchus giganteus Plate 102a
Spizella passerina 186, Plate 57b
Sponge
  Branching Vase Plate 105c
  Giant Barrel Plate 105f
  Leathery Barrel Plate 105d
  Loggerhead Plate 105a
  Yellow Tube Plate 106f
Spoonbill, Roseate 37, 38, 42, 111,
    113–14, 187, Plate 24f
Sporobolus junceus 16
Spring Peeper 70, Plate 3c
Squid, Reef Plate 102f
Squirrel

Big Cypress Fox 219
Eastern Fox 192, 218, 219, Plate 64c
Eastern Gray 192, 218, 219, Plate 64b
Sherman's Fox 219
Southern Flying 154, 218, 219, Plate 64a
Squirrelfish Plate 91b
Staggerbush 14, 15
Stagmomantis carolina Plate 72f
Starling, European 153, 167, 177, 178, 179, 187, Plate 60a
Stegastes diencaeus Plate 85a
Stegastes fuscus Plate 85c
Stegastes leucostictus Plate 85d
Stegastes partitus Plate 85f
Stegastes planifrons Plate 85e
Stegastes variabilis Plate 85b
Stelgidopteryx serripennis 159, Plate 47d
Stenopus hispidus Plate 102b
Sterna antillarum 136, Plate 39b
Sterna caspia 136, Plate 39e
Sterna dougallii 136, Plate 39a
Sterna forsteri 136, Plate 39c
Sterna fuscata 136, Plate 22c
Sterna maxima 136, Plate 39f
Sterna sandvicensis 136, Plate 39d
Sternotherus odoratus 86, Plate 12a
Stilt, Black-necked 37, 39, 129, 130, 133, Plate 35b
Stingray
    Southern Plate 99b
    Yellow Plate 99d
Stinkpot 83, 86, Plate 12a
Stork
    White 113
    Wood 34, 37, 38, 40, 111, 112, 114, Plate 25a
Strategus sp. Plate 74f
Streptopelia decaocto 139, Plate 40b
Strix varia 146, Plate 42c
Strombus alatus Plate 103c
Strombus gigas Plate 103f
Strombus raninus Plate 103d
Sturnella magna 179, Plate 58a
Sturnus vulgaris 179, Plate 60a
Sula dactylatra 110, Plate 22a
Sula leucogaster 110, Plate 22b
Sulphur, Cloudless Plate 70b
Sunflower, Florida Plate J1
Surgeonfish, Ocean Plate 79a
Sus scrofa 215, Plate 63b
Swallow
    Bank 158
    Barn 157, 158, 159, Plate 47e
    Cave 158

Cliff 157, 158, 159
Northern Rough-winged 158, 159, Plate 47d
Red Sea 159
Tree 157, 159, Plate 47c
Swallowtail
    American Plate 69f
    Black Plate 69f
    Eastern Tiger Plate 69e
    Giant Plate 69c
    Pipevine Plate 69b
    Zebra Plate 69d
Swamphen, Purple 187
Swan, Trumpeter 117
Sweetgum Plate F1
Swift, Chimney 157, 158, 159, Plate 47b
Sylvilagus floridanus 221, Plate 64d
Sylvilagus palustris 221, Plate 64e
Syntomeida epilais Plate 72e

Tachycineta bicolor 159, Plate 47c
Tadarida brasiliensis 201, Plate 67b
Tamarin, Wild 17
Tanager
    Paradise 180
    Scarlet 180, 182
    Summer 180, 181, 182, Plate 55f
Tang, Blue Plate 79b
Taro Plate M1
Tarpon 227, Plate 82a
Taxodium ascendens 19
Taxodium distichum 19, 236, Plate B1
Teal
    Blue-winged 39, 117, Plate 27d
    Green-winged 117, Plate 27c
    Ringed 187
Tern
    Arctic 133
    Caspian 31, 42, 136, Plate 39e
    Common 42
    Forster's 136, Plate 39c
    Least 42, 136, Plate 39b
    Roseate 43, 136, Plate 39a
    Royal 31, 42, 136, Plate 39f
    Sandwich 136, Plate 39d
    Sooty 43, 135, 136, Plate 22c
Terrapin, Diamondback 83, 86, Plate 10c
Terrepene carolina 86, Plate 12d
Thalassia testudinum Plate 106c
Thalassoma bifasciatum Plate 91c
Thalia geniculata 18
Thalypteris kunthii Plate N4
Thamnophis sauritus 89, Plate 18c

Thamnophis sirtalis 89, Plate 18b
Thrasher
    Brown 168, 169, Plate 51d
    Pearly-eyed 169
    White-breasted 169
Thrinax morrisii 12
Thrinax radiata 12
Thrush
    Bicknell's 167
    Hermit 168, Plate 50d
    Wood 167, 168, Plate 50e
Thryothorus ludovicianus 165, Plate 49d
Tibicen sp. Plate 74a
Tick
    Deer Plate 76c
    Dog Plate 76b
    Wood Plate 76b
Tiger, Siberian 209
Tilefish, Sand Plate 95a
Tillandsia recurvata 19, Plate I4
Tillandsia usneoides 13, Plate L3
Tillandsia utriculata 234
Titi 19
Titmouse, Tufted 163, 169, 188, Plate 49b
Toad
    Eastern Narrowmouth 68, 69, Plate 1e
    Giant 63, 68, 69, 187, Plate 1a
    Golden 73
    Oak 68, 69, Plate 1b
    Southern 68, 69, Plate 1c
Toadfish, Gulf Plate 94b
Tobaccofish Plate 89d
Tody-Tyrant, Kaempfer's 156
Tortoise
    Gopher 7, 32, 34, 39, 51, 71, 78, 82–6, 205, 208, 216, Plate 12c
    Radiated 85
Towhee, Eastern 183, 186, Plate 56e
Toxicodendron radicans 17, Plate K3
Toxostoma rufum 168, 169, Plate 51d
Trachemys scripta scripta 86, Plate 11d
Treefrog
    Barking 69, 70, Plate 2a
    Cuban 69, 70, Plate 2c
    Gray 69
    Green 69, 70, Plate 2d
    Pine Barrens 70
    Pine Woods 70, Plate 2e
    Squirrel 69, 70, Plate 2b
Trevally, Horse-eye Plate 80c
Trichechus manatus 213, Plate 68a
Triggerfish
    Ocean Plate 96f

Queen Plate 95c
Tringa flavipes 133, Plate 35d
Tringa melanoleuca 133, Plate 35c
Tringa solitaria 133, Plate 36f
Troglodytes aedon 165, Plate 49e
Trombicula sp. Plate 76a
Tropicbird, White-tailed 109, 110, Plate 22e
Trumpet Flower Plate H4
Trumpetfish Plate 94a
Trunkfish, Smooth Plate 95e
Tunicate, Bulb Plate 105b
Tupelo 19
    Swamp 206
Turdus migratorius 168, Plate 50f
Turkey
    Ocellated 124
    Wild 123–4, 125, Plate 33f
Turnstone, Ruddy 133, Plate 37f
Tursiops truncatus 213, Plate 68c
Turtle
    Alligator Snapping 83, 85, 86, Plate 10b
    Barbour's Map 83, 84, 86, Plate 10d
    Bog 496, *497*
    Box 7, 83, 85, 86, Plate 12d
    Chicken 83, 86, Plate 11c
    Common Musk Plate 12a
    Common Snapping 83, 86, Plate 10a
    Florida Redbelly 80, 83, 86, Plate 11a
    Green 35, 36, 43, 48, 82, 85, 86, Plate 9b
    Striped Mud 83, 86, Plate 12b
    see also Sea Turtle
Tylosurus crocodilus Plate 80a
Typha sp. 18
Tyrannulet, Restinga 156
Tyrannus dominicensis 156, Plate 46e
Tyrannus tyrannus 156, Plate 46f
Tyto alba 146, Plate 42a

Uniola paniculata 21, *238*, Plate L2
Urbanus proteus Plate 71a
Urchin
    Red Heart Plate 104d
    Slate-pencil Plate 104c
Urocyon cinereoargenteus 205, Plate 62a
Urolophus jamaicensis Plate 99d
Ursus americanus 207, Plate 63a
Utetheisa bella Plate 72c

Vaccinium arboreum 16
Vaccinium myrsinites 14
Vermivora celata 176, Plate 54c
Vespula maculifrons Plate 75b

Viburnum
  Small Leaf Plate H2
  Water Plate H2
Viburnum obovatum Plate H2
Vine
  Cross Plate H4
  Railroad 21
  Trumpet Plate I1
Vireo
  Bell's 173
  Black-capped 173
  Black-whiskered 4, 42, 172, 173, Plate 52c
  Blue-headed 172, 173, Plate 52e
  Red-eyed 172, 173, Plate 52b
  Thick-billed 43
  White-eyed 172, 173, Plate 52a
  Yellow-throated 173, Plate 52d
Vireo altiloquus 173, Plate 52c
Vireo flavifrons 173, Plate 52d
Vireo griseus 173, Plate 52a
Vireo olivaceus 173, Plate 52b
Vireo solitarius 173, Plate 52e
Vitis rotundifolia 17
Vulture
  Black 118, 120, 121, 123, Plate 29a
  King 119, 121
  Turkey 118, 119, 120, 121, 123, Plate 29b

Walking Stick 225, Plate 72b
Warbler
  Aldabra 166
  Bachmann's 175
  Black-and-white 174, 176, Plate 54a
  Blackpoll 175
  Golden-cheeked 175
  Hooded 176, Plate 55c
  Kentucky 176, Plate 55d
  Kirtland's 175
  Orange-crowned 176, Plate 54c
  Palm 169, 174, 176, Plate 53e
  Pine 176, Plate 53d
  Prairie 176, Plate 53c
  Prothonotary 176, Plate 54e
  Seychelles 166
  Yellow 42, 493
  Yellow-rumped 174, 176, Plate 53a
  Yellow-throated 176, Plate 54b
Washingtonia robusta 12
Wasp, Paper Plate 75g
Water Bonnets Plate M3
Water Chinquapin Plate I3
Water Hyacinth 20, 52, 212, Plate M2
Water Lettuce Plate M3

Water Lily 18
Water Moccasin 91
Waterbug, Giant Plate 75f
Water-orchid Plate M2
Waxwing, Cedar 169, 170, 171, 172, Plate 51c
Weasel
  Least 207
  Long-tailed 208
Whale, Short-finned Pilot 213, Plate 68d
Whistling-Duck
  Black-bellied 34, 114, 117, 187, Plate 26b
  Fulvous 34, 39, 117, Plate 26a
White, Great Southern Plate 69a
Wigeon, American 117, Plate 28a
Wild Batchelor's Button Plate K1
Wild Taro Plate M1
Willet 133, Plate 35f
Wilsonia citrina 176, Plate 55c
Wiregrass 14, 16
Wolf
  Gray 204, 493
  Red 201
  Timber *494*
Woodpecker
  Downy 153, 154, Plate 45b
  Hispaniolan 153
  Ivory-billed 34, 153
  Pileated 34, 153, 154, Plate 45c
  Red-bellied 153, 154, 169, Plate 44d
  Red-cockaded 29, 152, 154, Plate 45a
  Red-headed 152, 153, 154, Plate 44c
Wood-Pewee, Eastern 156, Plate 46a
Worm
  Bearded Fire Plate 102c
  Christmas Tree Plate 102a
Wrasse
  Bluehead 228, Plate 91c
  Clown Plate 90d
  Creole Plate 90b
  Yellowhead 228, Plate 91d
Wren
  Carolina 164, 165, Plate 49d
  Clarion 165
  Cozumel 164
  House 163, 164, 165, Plate 49e
  Marsh 164
  Socorro 165
  Winter 164

Xestospongia muta Plate 105f
Xylocopa sp. Plate 76g

Yellow Jacket, Eastern Plate 75b
Yellowlegs
    Greater 133, Plate 35c
    Lesser 133, Plate 35d
Yellowthroat, Common 176, Plate 55b
Yucca Plate M4

Yucca aloifolia Plate M4

Zamia pumila Plate F4
Zenaida asiatica 139, Plate 40d
Zenaida macroura 139, Plate 40c
Zonotrichia albicollis 186, Plate 57e

GENERAL INDEX

Note: Page numbers in *italics* refer to
    illustrations

accipiters 119
Accipitridae 118
acid rain 72
adult stage of insects 224
agriculture
    environmental impact 44–5
    pests 184, 200
Alcedinidae 150
alien species *see* exotic species
Alligator Alley 38, *244*
alligators 79–81, 202, 210, 214
    attacks on humans 80–1
    coexistence with 98–9
altricial young 59, 112, 155, 220
Ambystomatidae 65
amphibians
    family profiles 65–72
    general characteristics 62–4
    natural history 62–4
    population declines 72–4
    seeing 64–5
amphiumas 64, 65, 67
Amphiumidae 65
amplexus 68, 70, 71
anal gland fluid 208
Anastasia State Recreational Area *238*
Anatidae 114
anemones 23, 229
Anguidae 97
anhingas (darters; snakebirds) 106–10
Anhingidae 106
anis 142–4
anoles 94–5
anti-coagulant venom 92
antlers 214
ants 51, 52
    winged 199
Anura 62
Apalachicola National Forest 15, 154,
    207, *235*

Apalachicola River 20
aphids 224
Apodidae 157
Aramidae 126
arborial animals 58
Archie Carr National Wildlife Refuge 48
Ardeidae 110
armadillos 122, 192, 195–7, 205, 210
Arthur R. Marshall Loxahatchee
        National Wildlife Refuge *28*, 39
Artiodactyla 213
attacks on humans
    alligators 80–1
    snapping turtles 83
avocets 129, 130, 131

bachelor groups 215
badgers 207
Bahia Honda State Park *28*, *41*, 42
bamboo bats 198
barrier islands 34
barrow pits *see* roadside ditches
basilisks 94
basket stars 229
basking turtles 82, 83
bats 191, 192, 197–201
    activity patterns 198–9
    breeding 199–200
    echolocation 197–8
    feeding 197–8
    flight 197
    predation on insect pests 200
    roosting 198
beaches 8–9, 21, *238*
    sea turtle nesting 48, 85–6
bears 201, 205–7, 222
beetles 199, 202, 224
Big Cypress National Preserve 19, *28*,
        38, *41*, 207, 210, 211, 221
Big Cypress Swamp 188
Big Pine Key *243*
bills
        parrots 139

bioconcentration 122
biodiversity 1
biological control experiments 50
birds 100–2, 187–9
    classification 102–3
    family profiles 104–86
    fossils 6
    general characteristics 102–3
    natural history 102–3
    seeing 103–4
birds of prey *see* raptors
Biscayne Bay 25
Biscayne National Park *28*, 40, *41*
bites
    snakes 78–9, 86, 90, 92
bitterns 110, 111
black pumas 210
blackbirds 176–9
Blackwater River State Forest *28*, 29
blastocysts 209
Blue Springs State Park 27, *28*, 33, 47,
    236
bluebirds 166
boats
    encounters with manatees 212
    glass-bottom 4
bobcats 191, 202, 209–11, 214, 215,
    495
bobwhites 124, 125
Bombycillidae 169
boobies 106–10
boreal forests 173
box turtles 82, 83
branchers 145
breeding 59
    communal 143
    cooperative 160, 164
    explosive 68
    prolonged 68
brittle stars 230
broken-wing displays *see* distraction
    behavior
brood parasitism 143, 173, 175, 178–9
bufonid toads 63, 67–8
Bufonidae 67
bugs 224
bulbuls 169–72
buntings 180, 181, 182
butcher birds *see* shrikes
buteos 119
butterflies 224, 225, 495
butterflyfish 227, 229

caching behavior
    chickadees 162

corvids 160
    nuthatches 162
    owls 145
    shrikes 170
caciques 176, 177
caddisflies 199
caecilians 62
Caladesi Island State Park 21, *28*, 34
calls *see* sounds
camouflage
    sparrows 183
Canaveral National Seashore *28*, 35
Canidae 201, 204
canine teeth 201
canoeing 27
Caprimulgidae 146
car rental in Florida 25
carapace 76, 81
cardinal grosbeaks 180–2
cardinals 180, 181
carnassial teeth 201
carnivores 58, 201
    cats 209–10
    coyotes 204
    crocodilians 80
    foxes 204
    salamanders 66
    shrikes 170
    toads 68
    waterfowl 115
carrion 120, 214
catbirds 168
cats 201, 209–11
Caudata 62
cautions
    alligators 81, 98
    amphibians 65, 67
    venomous snakes 90
    see also hazards
caves 30
Cayo Costa Island *238*
Cayo Costa State Park 21
Cedar Key *241*
Central Florida (CFL) 24, *28*, 33–6
cere 137
Cetacea 212
cetaceans 212
CFL *see* Central Florida
Charadriidae 129
Charadriiformes 129
Chassahowitzka National Wildlife
    Refuge *28*, 36, *236*
Chassahowitzka River 192
cheek teeth 216
chelicerae 223

Chelonia 76
Cheloniidae 82
Chelydridae 82
chewing the cud 214
chickadees 161–3
chickenlike birds 123–5
chipmunks 217, 218
Chiroptera 197
chorus frogs 69
chorus-line hypothesis 132
chytrid infections of frogs 73
Ciconiidae 111
Ciconiiformes 110
CITES see Convention on
    International Trade in
    Endangered Species
citrus trees 7, 13, 216
clams 202
classification xi, 56
    birds 102–3
    mammals 191–2
clawed toads 68
clay licks 141
cleaners, fish 229
climate of Florida 11–12
coagulant venom 92
coastal ecosystems 21–3
cobras 89
cockroaches 224
Collier Seminole State Park 22, 28, 38
colonial nesting
    advantages of 188
    cormorants 109
    herons 112
color plate sections, information on
    60–1
coloration
    countershaded 104
    cryptic 93, 163
    quick changing 94
    see also camouflage
colubrid snakes 86–9
Colubridae 86
Columbidae 136
commensalism 55
    epiphytes 13
    human 161
communal breeding
    anis 143
communal courtship 124, 131
communal nesting
    parakeets 141
    snakes 88
communal roosting 121
    flying squirrels 218

communication see sounds
competition 54
    avoidance 127–8, 153
condors 118
'Congo eels' see amphiumas
conservation programs
    in Florida 45–9
    in North America 489–97
Convention on International Trade in
    Endangered Species (CITES)
    59–60
cooperative breeding
    corvids 160
    wrens 164
cooters 83
coots 126, 127
copperheads 91
coquina 10, 33
Coraciiformes 150
coral reefs 22–3, 226–7
    wildlife 227–30
coral snakes 92, 187
Corkscrew Swamp Sanctuary 19, 28,
    37–8
cormorants 106–10, 188
Corvidae 159
corvids 159–61
cosmopolitan species 58
cottonmouths 91
countershaded coloration 104
courtship, communal
    leks 124, 131
courtship displays
    cranes 127, 128
    frigatebirds 107
    gallinaceous birds 124
    grebes 105
    herons 112
    loons 105
    raptors 119
    ruffs 131
    shorebirds 130–1
    terns 134
courtship feeding
    corvids 160
    finches 185
    gulls 134
    tanagers 181
    waxwings 171
courtship flights
    flycatchers 155
    hummingbirds 149
    swifts 158
courtship rituals
    salamanders 66

coverable badges 165
coveys 124
cowbirds 172, 173, 175, 176, 177, 178–9
coyotes 204–5, 214, 215
crakes 126
cranes 125–9
crayfish 202, 208
crèches 116
crepuscular animals 58
  nighthawks 146
cricket frogs 69
crickets 198
crocodiles/crocodilians 76, 79–81, 187
Crocodylia 76
crop
  food storage in 138
  food regurgitation from 109
crossings, wildlife
  bridges and underpasses 221–2
  signs *244*
crows 109, 159–61
cryptic coloration 93, 163
Crystal River 27, 212, *236*
Crystal River National Wildlife Refuge *28*, 36, 47
cryptodirans 76
cuckoos 142–4
Cuculidae 142
curiosity of vireos 173
curlews 130
curly-tailed lizards 94
cursorial animals 58
  canids 204

dabbling ducks 115
damselfish 227, 229
darters *see* anhingas
DDT 46, 110, 122
death-feigning behavior 195
deer 213–15
deer flies 224
definitions 54–5
Dermochelyidae 82
dewlap
  lizards 77, 94
dialects, song 184
digging 195, 196, 207
dimorphism 182
'Ding' Darling National Wildlife Refuge 22, *28*, 37
disc-tongued toads 68
displays *see* courtship displays; territorial displays *and* threat displays

distemper 203
distraction behavior
  nightjars 147
  opossums 195
  pigeons 138
  shorebirds 131
distribution 56, *57*, 58
diurnal animals 58
diversity, species
  peninsular effect 188
diving birds 104–6
  ducks 115
dogs 201
dolphins 212–13
dominance hierarchies 185
doves 136–9
dragonflies 199, 224, 225
droppings 193
drumming 152
dry prairies 14
dry shrub communities *243*
Dry Tortugas National Park 8, 25, *28*, *41*, 43, 135, 136
ducks 114–17
dunes 21
dunlins 130

Eagle Harbor 29
eagles 46–7, 118, 119, 122, 495
echolocation 197–8
eclipse plumage 115
eco-history 6–8
ecology 54
ecosystems
  coastal 21–3
  freshwater 18–21
  upland 14–18
ecotourism 1–2
  guidelines 2–3
  history of in Florida 3–5
ectoparasitism 224
ectothermism
  frogs 63
  insects 223
  snakes 88–9
egg-laying, reptilian 76
  alligators 80
  anoles 94–5
  geckos 93–4
  glass lizards 97
  sea turtles 83–4
  skinks 96
  snakes 88, 90
  tortoises 84
  turtles 84

egg trading
fish 228
Eglin Air Force Base 207
egrets 110–14
eider down 117
eider ducks 115
El Niño 73
Elapidae 89
Emberizidae 182
Emydidae 82
endemic species 58
Florida mouse 216
rails 128
short-tailed snake 89
environmental threats 44–5
epiphytes 13
euphonias 179, 180, 181
eutherians 192
Everglades National Park 17, 18, 25, *28*, 39–40, *41*, 45, 49, 210, 211, *240*, *244*
exotic (alien; introduced; non-native) species 45, 50–3, 58
birds 167, 187–8
geckos 93
water plants 20
explosive breeding
toads 68
extinct species
Aldabra warbler 166
Bachman's warbler 175
Carolina parakeet 142, 187
dusky seaside sparrow 186
ivory-billed woodpecker 153–4
passenger pigeon 138–9
red wolf 201

facial structures
bats 198
Fakahatchee Strand State Park *28*, 38, *234*
Falconidae 118
falconry 121
falcons 118–23
false corals 23
family profiles, information on 55–60
feather trade 113
feathers, tertial 126
feeding
and colonial nesting 189
and flocking 162, 178, 185
by smell 120
by touch 112, 127
commensal 161
monophagous 122, 127–8

see also caching behavior; courtship feeding; fishing; foraging strategies *and* predation strategies
feet
cooling by defecation 118
totipalmate 106
Felidae 201, 209
fence lizards *see* spiny lizards
feral pigs 214
Fern Hammock Springs 32
finches 182–6
fire corals 22
fires, brush *14*, 15, 16
fish
parasite cleaning 229
sex changes 228
fishing
anhingas 108
cormorants 107
frigatebirds 108
grebes 105
loons 104–5
pelicans 107
skimmers 134
terns 133–4
fishing licenses 27
'flag marshes' 18
flatwoods 14–15, 61, *242*
flies 224
flight
backwards 148
bats 191, 197
birds 101, 102
hovering 148
hummingbirds 148
pipits 171
silent 144
speed 157
sudden take-off 125
sustained 156, 157
undulating 152
use of tails in 108
woodpeckers 152
see also courtship flights
flight formations
ducks 115
pelicans 107
flight maneuvers
shorebird flocks 130, 132
flocking
and feeding 162, 178, 185
and flight maneuvers 130, 132
and predation avoidance 121, 185
by wintering shorebirds 131
Florida Caverns State Park *28*, 30

Florida Forever Program 5, 48
Florida Keys 8, 17, 226
Florida Panther National Wildlife
   Refuge 211
Florida Reef Tract 22
flycatchers 154–6
flying fish 108
flying foxes 197
flying squirrels 193, 217, 218, 219
folivores 58
   deer 214
food caching see caching behavior
food preferences 58–9
   see also competition
foraging strategies
   gaping 177
   gleaning 172, 174
   hover-gleaning 162, 174
   probing 174
   rolling motion flocking 178
   sallying 174
   search imaging 162
   spinning 130
   tool-using 163
forest removal 44
Fort Matanzas National Monument *28*,
   32
fossils 6–7, 30
   birds 6
   marine animals 10
   sea turtles 81
   tortoises 85
fossorial animals 58
foxes 201, 202, 204–5, 208
fracture planes in lizard tails 97
Fregatidae 106
freshwater ecosystems 18–21, 61
frigatebirds (man-o-war birds) 106–10,
   188
Fringillidae 183
fringing reefs 23
frogs 62, 63, 202, 214, 222
   chorus 69
   cricket 69
   fungal infections 73
   leaf 69
   population declines 72–4
   toad-like 68
   treefrogs 69–70
   true 71–2
frogs' legs 71–2
frugivores 58, 181
   bulbuls 170
   doves 137
   parrots 140

pigeons 137
tanagers 180
waxwings 170
fruit bats 197

Galliformes 123
gallinaceous birds 123
gallinules 126, 127
gannets 107
gaping 177
Gaviidae 104
geckos 93–4, 187
geese 114
geography of Florida 8–9, 24
geology of Florida 10
gestation 59
getting around Florida 25–6
gizzards 137
glass lizards 97
gleaning 172, 174
global warming 73
gnatcatchers 165–6
goatsuckers see nightjars
gobies 229, 230
godwits 130, 133
gorgets 148
gorgonians 227
grackles 176, 177, 186
granivores 58
   blackbirds 177
   doves 137
   grackles 177
   pigeons 137
   sparrows 183
   starlings 177
grassbeds 227
grasshoppers 224
Great Florida Birding Trail 5, 26–7
grebes 104–6
grosbeaks 180, 181, 182
ground squirrels 217
groupers 228, 229
Gruiformes 125
grunts 229
Guana River State Park 21, *28*, 32
guano, bat 200
guard hairs 193, 206
guidebooks of Florida 25
Gulf Hammock area 21
gulls 133–6, 188
gulpers 181
Gymnophiona 62

habitat destruction and migrant birds
   175–6

habitat protection programs 5
habitat symbols 61
habitats
  beaches 21
  coral reefs 22–3
  dry prairies 14, 61
  dunes 21
  freshwater marshes 18, 61
  hardwood hammocks 16–18, 61
  high pine sandhills 16, 61
  lakes 20
  Longleaf pine-oak sandhills 16
  mangrove 22
  pine flatwoods 14–15, 61
  rivers 20–1
  saltmarshes 21, 61
  scrub 15–16, 61
  springs 20–1
  swamps 19
hacking 122
Haematopodidae 129
halcyon days 151
hamlets 228
hammocks 16–18, 61, *240*
hard corals 227
hardwood hammocks
  temperate 16–17, 61
  tropical 17–18, 61
hares 219–21
harriers 119
hawks 118, 119, 122
hazards
  alligator attacks 80–1
  gull colonies 135
  lightning strikes 78, 79
  mockingbird attacks 168
  snakebites 78–9, 86, 90, 92
  snapping turtle attacks 83
  see also cautions
hellbenders 64
hemipenes 88
hemotoxic venom 91, 92
herbivores 58
  deer 214
  hares 219
  manatees 212
  rabbits 219
  waterfowl 115
hermaphrodites 228
herons 110–14, 188
hibernation
  bears 206
  hummingbirds 149
  poorwills 147
high pine sandhills 16, 61

Highlands Hammock State Park 17, *28*, 34
Hillsborough River State Park *28*, 35
Hirundinidae 156
history
  eco-history 6–8
  ecotourism in Florida 3–5
home range 58, 160
Homosassa Springs State Wildlife Park 20, *28*, 36
honey production
  and bears 207
honeycreepers 179
horned lizards 94
host species 55, 143, 172, 178
hover-gleaning 162, 174
humidity 11
hummingbirds 147
  breeding 149
  defense of food resources 149
  feeding ecology 149
  flight 148
  metabolism 148–9
  pollination 149–50
hunted species
  alligators 98–9
  bobcats 210
  parrots 141
  shorebirds 132
  waterfowl 116
hurricanes 11–12, 40–1
hydrilla 20, 51, 52, 212
Hylidae 69

ibises 111, 112, 114, 188
Ichetucknee Springs State Park 20, *28*, 31
Ichetucknee River 19
Icteridae 176
iguanas 94
Iguanidae 94
implantation, delayed 196, 208, 209
incisor teeth 216
Indian River 47
information centers 121, 189
information on Florida *see* guidebooks; telephone hotlines *and* websites
insectivores 58
  bats 197–8
  chickadees 162
  cuckoos 142
  flycatchers 155
  geckos 93
  gnatcatchers 165
  kinglets 165

lizards 94, 97
nightjars 146
pipits 170–1
skinks 95
swallows 157
swifts 157
treefrogs 69
vireos 172
warblers 174
woodpeckers 152
wrens 163
insects
general characteristics 223–4
natural history 223–4
seeing 224–5
introduced species *see* exotic species
island nesting
feeding benefits 189

jaegers 133
jays 159–61
John Pennekamp Coral Reef State Park
23, *28*, 41–2
Jonathan Dickinson State Park *28*, 39
Joshua Dickson State Park 16
Juniper Creek 29, 32
Juniper Prairie Wilderness 14

katydids 198
Kennedy Space Centre 36
KEY *see* Keys and Islands
Key Largo 17
Keys and Islands (KEY) 24, *28*, 40–3
keystone species 84
kingfishers 150–1
kinglets 165–6
kingsnakes 87
kinkajous 202
Kinosternidae 82
Kissimmee River 14, 18, 45, 117
kites 118, 119, 122
kleptoparasitism 109, 134
knots 130, 132
kraits 90

La Chua Trail 33
lacewings 198
Lagomorpha 219
Lake Apopka 45
Lake Kissimmee 34
Lake Kissimmee State Park *28*, 35
Lake Okeechobee 14, 18, 20
Lake Rosalie 34
Lake Wales ridge *243*
lakes 20

land acquisition programs 48
Laniidae 169
Laridae 133
larval stage of insects 224
leaf frogs 69
leafhoppers 199
leeches 55
leks 124, 131
Leporidae 219
leprosy 196
licks, clay 141
lighting ordinances 85
lightning 11
and brush fires 15, 16
strikes 78, 79
Lignum Vitae Key 18
Lignumvitae Key State Botanical Area
28, 41, 42
limpkins 126, 127, 129
Little Talbot Island State Park 21, *28*,
31–2
lizards 76–7, 93–7, 210
Longleaf pine-oak sandhills 16
loons 104–6
Lower Matechumbe Key 18
Lower Suwannee National Wildlife
Refuge *28*, 31
Loxahatchee River 20, 39

macaws 140, 141
magpies 159, 160
Mahogany Hammock *240*
mallards 115
mambas 90
mammals 190–1
classification 191–2
family profiles 193–221
general characteristics 191
roadkills 221–2
seeing 192–3
manatees 21, 27, 29, 33, 34, 47, 187,
191, 212, *237*
maneuvers in flight
shorebird flocks 130, 132
mangroves 22, 227, *241*
forests 38
islands 34
man-o-war birds *see* frigatebirds
mantids 198
maps of Florida 24–5
geography *9*
parks and reserves *28*
southern tip *41*
marine fossils 10
marine mammals 212–13

Marjorie Harris Carr Cross Florida
    Greenway 222
marmots 217
marshes
    freshwater 18
    salt 21
marsupials 192, 193
martens 207
mashers 181
Matanzas River 32
mate-finding
    and colonial nesting 189
Matheson Tropical Hammock *240*
mating systems *see* monogamy;
    polyandry; polygamy *and*
    polygyny
matrilineal social groups 215
maxilla, prehensile 139
mayflies 199
meadowlarks 176, 177
Megachiroptera 197
Meleagrididae 123
mergansers 115
Merritt Island National Wildlife Refuge
    16, *28*, 36
metamorphosis
    amphibians 62, 63
    insects 224
mice 210, 216, 217
Microchiroptera 197
Microhylidae 68
migration
    and bird plumage 182
    warbler waves 175
mimicry
    mockingbirds 168–9
    snakes 88
Mimidae 168
mink 207
mistletoe 181
mites 223, 224
mockingbirds 168–9
moles 191
molting
    ducks 115
    insects 224
monogamy 59
    grebes 105
    long-legged waders 112
    loons 105
    owls 145
monomorphism 182
monophagous feeding 122, 127–8
monotremes 192
moray eels 229

morphology 55
Mosquito Lagoon 34
mosquitoes 39, 199, 201, 224
Motacillidae 169
moths 198, 224
mud turtles 82, 83
mudpuppies 64, 66
multiple nests 164
musk 208
musk turtles 82, 83
Mustelidae 201, 207
mutualism 55
Myakka River 20
Myakka River State Park 17, *28*, 34

nasolabial groove 65
National Key Deer Refuge *28*, *41*, 42, 215
natural history 54
natural succession 175
nectarivores 58
    hummingbirds 149
Neotropical migrants 176
nesting, colonial
    advantages of 188
    cormorants 109
    herons 112
nesting, communal
    parakeets 141
    snakes 88
nesting beaches, sea turtle 48, 85–6
nests, multiple 164
neurotoxic venom 90, 92
New World zones 56, *57*
newts 64, 65–6
NFL *see* North Florida
nighthawks 146
night-herons 112
nightjars (goatsuckers) 146–7
nocturnal animals 58
noddies 133
non-native species *see* exotic species
North Florida (NFL) 24, *28*, 31–3
no-see-ums 224
nostrils, perforate 126
nuisance behavior
    armadillos 196
    bats 199
    bears 207
    coyotes 204
    raccoons 203
nutcrackers 159
nuthatches 161–3
nymphal stage of insects 224

obligate mutualism 55

Ocala National Forest 14, 16, *28*, 32, 206, 207, 222, *242*
Ochotonidae 219
octocorals 22
octopi 229
Odontophoridae 123
Okefenokee Swamp 207
Oklawaha River 19, 20, 32
Old World zones 56, *57*
omnivores 59
    armadillos 196
    bears 206
    cranes 126
    crows 160
    jays 160
    opossums 194
    pigs 214
    raccoons 202
    skunks 208
    thrushes 161
opossums 84, 192, 193–5, 210
orchids 13
orioles 176, 177
oropendolas 176, 177
Osceola National Forest 15, 206, 207
ospreys 118, 119, 120
osteoderms 97
otters 207–9
oviparous reproduction 88
ovoviviparous reproduction 88, 92
owls 118, 144–46, 202
oystercatchers 129, 130, 133
ozone layer thinning 73

paedomorphism 66
pair bonding 105
palms 12
PAN *see* Panhandle
Panhandle (PAN) 21, 24, *28*, 29–30, 205
panther crossing signs *244*
parakeets 140, 141, 142
parasite cleaning of fish 229
parasitism 55
    see also brood parasitism;
        ectoparasitism *and*
        kleptoparasitism
Paridae 161
parks and reserves 24–43
parotid glands 63, 67
parrotfish 227, 228, 229
parrotlets 140
parrots 139–42, 187
parthenogenetic reproduction 224
Parulidae 173

Passeridae 183
passerines 103, 154
Paynes Prairie State Preserve 14, 18, *28*, 33, 222, *239*
peafowl 123
peccaries 214
Pelecanidae 106
Pelican Island National Wildlife Refuge *28*, 34
pelicans 106–10, 188
pellets, owl 144
Pelobatidae 68
peninsula effect 188
pepper-shrikes 172
perforate nostrils 126
pesticides 201
pests, agricultural 184, 200
pets, exotic
    releases 51
    trade 188
Phaethontidae 106
Phalacrocoracidae 106
phalaropes 130, 131
pheasants 123–4
Phocidae 201
photography, wildlife 37
Picidae 152
piculets 152
pigeons 136–9
pigeon's milk 138
pigs 213–15
pikas 219
pine flatwoods 14–15, 61
Pinhook 207
pipits 169–72
piscivores 59
    cormorants 107
    dolphins 213
    grebes 105
    kingfishers 150
    loons 105
    ospreys 119
    otters 208
    pelicans 107
    skimmers 134
    terns 133–4
pit-vipers 91, 195
pitcher plants 29, *235*
placental mammals 192
plankton 229
plant species, common 13–23
plastron 76, 81
playing behavior
    otters 208
Plethodontitae 65

pleurodirans 76
plovers 129, 131, 132, 133
plumage
 and migration 182
 eclipse 115
 subadult 118
 see also feathers
pocket gophers 217
Podicipedidae 104
poisons *see* toxins
pollination
 by bats 200
 by hummingbirds 149–50
polyandry 59
 sandpipers 131
polygamy 59
polygyny 59
 hummingbirds 149
 ruffs 131
 wrens 164
ponds, ephemeral 68–9
poorwills 147
populations
 declines (frogs) 72–4
 natural fluctuations 73
 surges (birds) 144
porpoises 212
prairie dogs 217
prairies *239*
 dry 14, 34, 61
 wet *14*
praying mantises 149
precocial young 59, 116, 124, 127, 131,
  220
predation 54
predation avoidance/escape strategies
 colonial nesting 188
 distraction behavior 131, 138, 147,
  195
 flight 101, 121, 198
 flocking 121, 185
 jumping 196
 musk-spraying 208
 startle-effect 125
 tail autotomy 93, 95, 96, 97
predation strategies
 echolocation 197–8
 flycatching 155
 leaping 204
 sit-and-wait 88, 91, 93, 112, 151
 stalk-and-ambush 201, 209
 washing 203
predators
 bats 197–8
 foxes 204

gulls 135
raccoons 203
raptors 119
snakes 87
see also prey
prehensile maxilla 139
prehensile tails 58, 202
prey
 eggs and nestlings 160
 hummingbirds 149
 insect pests 200
 opossums 198
 terns 135
 toads 87
 see also predators
prey caching *see* caching behavior
prey specialization 127–8, 153
probing 174
Procyonidae 201, 202
prolonged breeding
 toads 68
Proteidae 66
Psittacidae 139
'puff adders' 87
pumas 205, 209–11, 214, 215
pupal stage of insects 224
Pycnonotidae 169
pygmy mice 216

quails 123, 124

rabbits 210, 219–21
rabies 202
rabies-resistance 195
raccoons 193, 201, 202–3, 210
racerunners 96
rails 125–9
'rain crows' 143
Rallidae 126
Ranidae 71
raptors (birds of prey) 117–23
rats 210, 216, 217
Rattlesnake Island 32
rattlesnakes 86, 91–2
ravens 160, 161
Recurvirostridae 129
redpolls 183
reefs *see* coral reefs
re-introduced species
 whooping crane 45–6
reproductive strategies
 delayed implantation 196, 208, 209
 parthenogenesis 224
reptiles
 family profiles 79–97

general characteristics 75–7
natural history 75–7
seeing 78–9
reserves *see* parks and reserves
riparian vegetation 173
River Styx *236*
rivers 20–1
Riverside Island 16
roadbuilding 44
roadkills 201
  armadillos 196
  bears 206, 207
  opossums 193
  puma 211
  reduction of 221–2
  skunks 208
roadrunners 142
roadside ditches (barrow pits) *235*
rodents 215–19
rookeries 188
roosting
  bats 198
roosting, communal 121
  flying squirrels 218
ruffs 131
ruminants 214

safety
  and colonial nesting 188, 189
salamanders 62, 67, 214
  amphiumas 64, 65
  eel-like 65
  hellbenders 64
  lungless 63–4, 65
  mole 64, 65, 66
  mudpuppies 64, 66
  newts 64, 65–6
  sirens 64, 65, 66
  waterdogs 66
'salamanders' (pocket gophers) 217
Salamandridae 65
sallying 174
saltmarshes 21, 61
San Felasco Hammock State Preserve 17
sand dunes *238*
sand mounds 217
sanderlings 130
sandpipers 121, 129, 130, 131, 132
Sanibel-Captiva Conservation
    Foundation *28*, 37
Sanibel Island 21
scats 193
scaups 115
Scincidae 95
Sciuridae 217

Scolopacidae 129
scorpions 223, 224
scoters 115
scrapes 131
scrub 15–16, 61
scutes 81
sea fans 23, 227
sea grass 212
sea plumes 22, 227
sea rods 227
sea snakes 90
sea turtles 34, 76, 82–3
  egg-laying 83–4
  fossils 81
  nesting beaches 48, 85–6
  protection 48, 85
  threats 85
sea whips 22, 227
search images 162
seed dispersal
  by bats 200
  by tanagers 181
semiprecocial young 135
setae 93
sex changing in fish 228
SFL *see* South Florida
Shark Valley 40
shorebirds 129–33
shrews 191
shrike-vireos 172
shrikes (butcher birds) 169–72
shrimps 230
siblicide 113
Silver Springs 20
silverfish 224
Sirenia 212
Sirenidae 65
sirens 64, 65, 66
siskins 183
Sittidae 161
skimmers 133–6, 188
skinks 95–7
skuas 133
skunks 207–9
snails 122, 127, 202
snake skins, shed
  use in nests 155
snakebirds *see* anhingas
snakebites 78–9, 86, 90, 92
snakes 76, 77, 214, 222
  colubrid 86–9
  coral 92
  egg-laying 88
  kingsnakes 87
  mimicry 88

predation on toads 87
sea 90
skin shedding 91
threat displays 86, 87
venomous 89–93
water 87
snappers 227, 229
snapping turtles 82
attacks on humans 83
snipes 133
snorkeling 42, 43, 226
social groups
deer 215
soft corals 23
softshell turtles 82, 83
soldierfish 229
songbirds 103
sounds (calls; communication *and* vocalizations)
alligators 80
armadillos 196
bats 198
blue jays 159, 160
bobwhites 123
bulbuls 170
chickadees 162
cranes 126
crows 159
cuckoos 143
frogs 63, 64, 70
geckos 93
gulls 134
hummingbirds 148
kinglets 165
limpkins 126
loons 105
manatees 212–13
mockingbirds 168
nightjars 146, 147
owls 145
parrotfish 228
parrots 140
pipits 171
sparrows 183
swifts 157
towhees 183
vireos 172
warblers 174
woodpeckers 152
wrens 164
South Florida (SFL) 24, *28*, 37–40
spadefoot toads 68
Spanish moss 199
sparrows 137, 182–6
speculum 114

spermatophores 66
spiders 223
spinerets 224
spinning 130
spiny lizards (fence lizards; swifts) 94–5
sponges 227
spoonbills 111–14
springs 20–1
Squamata 76
squid 213
squirrelfish 229
squirrels 210, 217–19
St George Island State Park *28*, 29
St Johns River 18, 20, 47
St Joseph Peninsula State Park 21, *28*, 29–30
St Marks National Wildlife Refuge *28*, 30
St Marys River 20
St Vincent Island 16
staging areas 131
starlings 121, 176–9
startle effect 125
state emblems
mammal 210
tree 12
status 59
steppes 171
stilts 129, 131, 132
'stinkin-jims' 83
'stinkpots' 83
stony corals 23
stooping 119
storks 111–14, 118, 188
Strigidae 144
subadult plumage 118
subtropical coral reef species 226
sucker-footed bats 198
surgeonfish 227, 229
Surinam toads 68
Suwanee River 20
swallows 156–9
swamps 19, *234*
swans 114
swifts 157–9
see also spiny lizards
Sylviidae 165
symbiosis 55
syrinx 103

tadpoles 62, 63, 68
tails
autotomy 93, 95, 96, 97
cottontails 219

length 157
prehensile 58, 202
streamers 107
use in flight 108
talons 118
Tamiami Trail *234, 244*
Tampa Bay 27, 47, 188, 212
tanagers 179–82
tarsus, booted 166
Taylor Slough 40
teals 115
teeth
   canine 201
   carnassial 201
   cheek 216
   incisor 216
   parrotfish 228
Teiidae 95
telephone hotlines 26, 27
temperature
   and frogs 63
   and snakes 88–9
temperature regulation
   shorebirds 132
temperatures, daytime 11
Ten Thousand Islands 22, 40
terns 133–6, 188
terrestrial animals 58
   tortoises 82, 83
territorial displays
   raptors 119
   shorebirds 130–1
territories 58
   defence by lizards 77
tertial feathers 126
Testudinidae 82
thermals, soaring on 108, 118, 126
thrashers 168–9
Thraupidae 179
threat displays
   lizards 77
   snakes 86, 87
Threskiornithidae 111
thrushes 166–8
thunderstorms 11
ticks 55, 223, 224
Tiger Lake 34
times to visit Florida 11–12
titmice 161–3
toads
   bufonid 63, 67–8
   predation by snakes 87
tool-using birds 163
torpor 149, 197
tortoises 76

fossils 85
gopher 84–5
longevity and size 85
terrestrial 82, 83
Tosohatchee State Reserve 15
totipalmate feet 106
towhees 183
toxins
   salamanders 66, 67
   scorpion 224
   snakes 77, 90, 91, 92
   toads 63, 67, 68
tracks, animal 192–3
   bears 206
   coyotes 204
trails
   Great Florida Birding 5, 26–7
   La Chua 33
   Tamiami *234, 244*
tree islands *244*
tree squirrels 217
treefrogs 69–70
trees 12–13
Trionychidae 82
Trochilidae 147
Troglodytidae 163
tropicbirds 106–10
true frogs 71–2
true mammals 192
true seals 201
tubercules 68
tunicates 230
Turdidae 166
turkeys 123, 124, 125
turnstones 133
turtles 76, 81–6, 222, 495
   basking 82, 83
   box 82, 83
   mud 82, 83
   musk 82, 83
   side-necked 76
   snapping 82, 83
   softshell 82, 83
   see also sea turtles
Tyrannidae 154
Tytonidae 144

ultraviolet (UV) radiation 73
United States Endangered Species Act
   (USA ESA) 59, 60
upland ecosystems 14–18
urban areas, growth of 7–8
Ursidae 201
USA ESA *see* United States Endangered
   Species Act

UV *see* ultraviolet radiation

vegetation
  general characteristics 12–13
  see also habitats
venom *see* toxins
venomous snakes 93
  cobras 89
  copperheads 91
  cottonmouths 91
  kraits 90
  mambas 90
  pit-vipers 91
  rattlesnakes 91–2
  sea snakes 90
vents 66
viewing wildlife
  amphibians 64–5
  birds 103–4
  coral reef wildlife 226
  insects 224–5
  mammals 192–3
  reptiles 78–9
  see also parks and reserves
Viperidae 90
Vireonidae 172
vireos 172–3
vocalizations *see* sounds
vultures 118, 119, 120, 121

waders, long-legged 110–14
wagtails 169
Wakulla Springs State Park *28*, 30
walking catfish 187
warblers 173–6
washing behavior
  raccoons 203
Washington Oaks State Gardens 21, *28*,
    32–3
wasps 224
water snakes 87
waterdogs 66
waterfowl 114–17
waxwings 169, 170, 171, 172
WCS *see* Wildlife Conservation Society
weasels 201, 207
websites
  bald eagles 47
  Everglades 39
  Florida Park Service 25
  Great Florida Birding Trail 26, 27
  manatees 27, 47
  publisher xi
Wekiwa Springs State Park 16, 222

wet season 11
wetlands, drainage of 117
whales 191, 212
whiptails 95–7
whooping cranes 45–6
wigeons 115
wing-spreading 109
wings
  bats 197
wintering birds 176
wolves 205
wood warblers 173
woodpeckers 152–4, 493
worm lizards 77
wrasses 227, 228
wrens 163–5

yellowlegs 133

Habitat Symbols

= Dry Prairies (p. 14)

= Scrub (p. 15)

= Pine Flatwoods (p. 14)

= High Pine Sandhills (p. 16)

= Temperate Hardwood Hammocks (p. 16)

= Tropical Hardwood Hammocks (p. 17)

= Freshwater. For species typically found in or near lakes, streams, rivers, marshes, swamps.

= Saltwater. For species usually found in or near the ocean or ocean beaches.

REGIONS (see p. 9 and Map 2, p. 28):

PAN   Panhandle
NFL   North Florida
CFL   Central Florida
SFL   South Florida
KEY   Keys and Other Islands